ASIA, East by South

ASIA, East by South:
a cultural geography
SECOND EDITION

J. E. SPENCER
Professor of Geography
University of California
Los Angeles

WILLIAM L. THOMAS
Professor of Geography
California State College
Hayward

JOHN WILEY & SONS, INC.
New York   London   Sydney   Toronto

Library of Congress Catalog Card Number: 74–138920
ISBN 0–471–81545–4

Printed in the United States of America

10 9 8 7 6 5 4 3 2 1

for Kathryn and Loida

PREFACE

This volume is concerned with cultural geography in its widest interpretation. Most of the materials with which cultural geographers must deal are tangible and can be viewed in terms of regional distribution and analysis. These tangibles form the primary contexts of discussion throughout the book. Beyond them, however, there are important but less tangible characteristics of peoples and places that are important to an understanding of the ways of different men in separate sectors of the earth's landscapes. There can be no finite limit placed upon the variety of data with which regional geographers must deal in depicting human life in chosen regional landscapes. Regional cultural geography is the study of the outcome of culture groups living in, and doing things to, particular spatial units of the earth. In regions where many generations of people have lived, both living systems and their landscapes are cumulative developments so that it is incumbent upon regional geographers not only to describe present conditions but also to describe the processes by which these regions came to be what they are today.

The present book is a contribution to a more complete understanding of the Orient, a world culture realm possessing much obscured ground. In some countries there are better data than in others, and some countries have policies which prevent the outsider learning about conditions. Our personal contacts with the lands of Orient are uneven and less complete than they should be. This second edition has been brought up to date where possible, and it has been somewhat enlarged over the coverage of the first edition. Despite the fact that the first edition tried to do something not previously accomplished, it was organized in a rather conventional manner. Also, the quality of the cartography in the first edition was sacrificed to less costly pages of textual writing, and the photography which usually accompanies a regional textbook was omitted. In the present edition a reorganization has been effected, so that the order of the chapters in Part 1 is more appropriate to a cultural geography. The cartography has been brought to, hopefully, an adequate level, and slightly more than a token group of photographs has been added. The regional Chapters have been rationalized to accord with the regional political constructs of the Orient as they existed at the date of revision. The volume is still to be considered a study in cultural geography, and not a volume on the economic geography of Monsoon Asia. The original title has been retained, as descriptive of the culture realm of concern to the study, but this phrasing is in no sense an attempt to coin a name for a large sector of the earth.

There are hundreds more people to whom appreciation is due than when the first edition had been completed, and the lists are too long for recall. Students, colleagues, and friends all over the earth have contributed tations, and ideas, and our thanks are extended to them all.

Taipei, Taiwan   J. E. SPENCER
Laoag City, Philippines   W. L. THOMAS
July, 1970

CONTENTS

PART III: FOR USE IN REFERENCE

PHOTOGRAPH
CLUSTERS

MAPS AND CHARTS

INTRODUCTORY: ON THE GEOGRAPHY OF ASIA

In almost every discussion that involves Asia there turn out to be many definitions of Asia as a region. To the European mind, which conceived of the separation of the single landmass of Eurasia into the two continents of Europe and Asia, almost everything in Asia carries some connotation of "The East" but to a member of an eastern culture group much of the rest of Asia is for him "The West." In modern regional distinctions there is a northern part of Asia that is incorporated into the Soviet World, and there is a large southwestern sector which is part of the Moslem World and relates chiefly to the Middle East. The southern and eastern portions of Asia are often placed under the heading "The Orient." The theoretical bases for drawing broad regional zonings may be established on several different grounds according to the concepts of the discipline or the scholar drawing the boundaries. The geographer finds enough significant historical, cultural, agricultural, and climatic criteria to group together those Asian coastal lands from West Pakistan eastward to Indonesia and northward to Japan with those interior regions historically dominated by oriental cultures (Fig. Introductory 1). This great

zone may be designated Monsoon Asia working primarily from a climatic criterion, or Oriental Asia by working primarily from the concept of the cultural separateness of the related Chinese, Southeast Asian, and Indian culture realms. Using both of these criteria this volume deals with the peoples, cultures, and lands in the broad zone distinguished loosely as the Oriental Culture World. There are qualities of human living systems here that set the Oriental World apart from Soviet Asia and from Southwest Asia despite the elements of cultural convergence that characterize the various world-wide processes of modernization.

THE ORIENT AND THE OCCIDENT

In occidental literature there has been no common agreement regarding the usage of the several terms: East, Far East, Middle East, Orient, Malaysia, Indies, Southern Asia, Southeast Asia, Monsoon Asia, and others. The formerly regional term Malaysia is now the name of a political state, and Indonesia is also the name of a political state that does not quite encompass the whole of the old regional term East Indies. In some

I

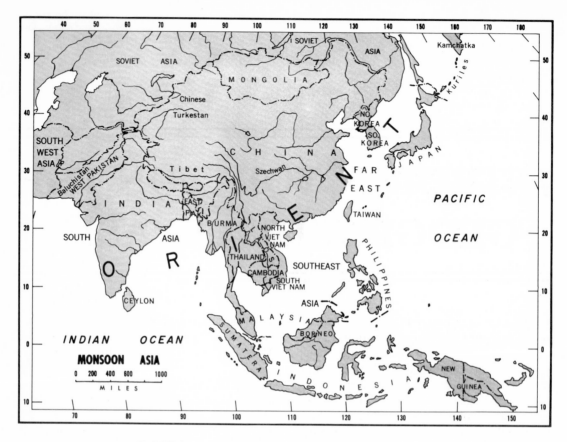

FIGURE I. The oriental culture world of Monsoon Asia.

literature the Orient begins at the Strait of Gibraltar if one faces the African shore. In other cases only those lands bordering on the Pacific Ocean are the Orient. India can be in the Middle East, the Far East, or Southern Asia. In this volume the two terms Monsoon Asia and Orient will be used as synonyms by which to refer to any portion of the entire realm from West Pakistan to New Guinea to Japan to Chinese Turkestan.

To further define terms clearly: Far East will apply to those lands fronting on the Pacific Ocean and the South China Sea; Southern Asia will refer to Pakistan, India, and Ceylon; Southeast Asia will refer both to the mainland countries of Burma, Thailand, Cambodia, Laos, and the two Vietnams, and also to Indonesia, Malaysia, and the

Philippines. The general term the East will be used only in poetic contrast to the West. The Indies will be used in broad poetic reference to the island world of Indonesia, New Guinea, and the Philippines. Occasional reference will be made, via the term Island Arcs, to the whole island world off the Asian mainland, from Sumatra east to New Guinea, thence north through Japan to the Kuriles. The term Peninsular India will be used in the historic and generic sense to refer to an India prior to modern political separation. The term Indochina will be similarly used in discussions of a generic sort having reference to the territories now politically separated into Laos, North Vietnam, South Vietnam, and Cambodia.

The contrast between the oriental and

occidental worlds is not as profound as implied in the usually quoted first line of Kipling's famous poem "The Ballad of the East and West," that: "The East is east and the West is west, and never the twain shall meet." Nevertheless, there is a very real difference in psychology, in outlook, in national aspirations, and in the judgment of group happiness between the several cultures of the Orient and those of the Occident. It is a commonplace to say that the West, particularly the Anglo-American West, rushes at life with a speed that is nowhere matched in the Orient. The slower tempo of the oriental, however, is projected into much more than his failure to rush from a committee meeting to a bridge luncheon to a cocktail party on a precise timing schedule. Fewer and simpler amusements and diversions are needed to fill a life, and there is no worry as to how to fill the random idle hour. The average expectancy of life is less, and the restless concern with the eternal will-o'-the-wisp progress is notably lacking. Tolerance, whether it be of transport, of his fellows' accomplishments, or of the tendencies to reform old institutions of society is characteristic of the Orient. It is customary for Westerners to think of the Orient as the unchanging land of mysticism, of strange customs, of queerly devious psychology which cannot possibly be fathomed by an outsider. Quite often this concept of the Orient is overdone.

It is necessary to point out that one cannot speak of the Orient as though it were an area of completely homogeneous culture in which every individual is like every other. Even as the Occident recognizes differences in temperament between Englishmen, Frenchmen, Germans, and Americans, so in the Orient one must recognize that the Indian, the Burman, the Japanese, and the Filipino occupy separate positions within the larger "oriental culture." One must also recognize that cultures change and that what may have been true of any oriental a century ago may well have been altered by the impact of time

and alien cultures. It is not all clear how great the change in group culture or group psychology is going to be in any single country within the next century, or just what the direction of change will be. Perhaps in one country there may be some rather fundamental changes coming about at present whereas in another the changes will be only superficial. Perhaps in a third country the acceptance of new customs, new tools, and new goods will expand the existing culture in very marked fashion without fundamentally altering the oriental psychology of the people. Whatever these changes may add up to, there is no section of the Orient that has not been affected by four and a half centuries of contact with the Occident, even as every section of the Occident has in some way been affected by that same contact with the Orient. Whatever comparison may be made of oriental and occidental, there can be no question that the Orient is undergoing some change with respect to what the several peoples expect of life. In some countries this is a relatively peaceful process, whereas in others it has been, and will continue to be, a militant and violent process that will continue until its goals are achieved. Unfortunately, in some countries there is no unanimity of opinion on just what the ends may be. It is not enough to describe the Orient as it was yesterday or is today. If we are at all concerned with our own future we must be concerned about where the Orient is going tomorrow.

THE QUESTION OF ISOLATION

It has been the occidental fashion in dealing with the eastern portion of the Eurasian landmass to make much of the point of isolation of those far corners in trying to explain why the mystic Orient is as it is. This seems only half an issue, for, if the orientals were so long isolated from the western end of the great continent, perhaps it is the West that was isolated overlong from the East. The fact is that for most of the early period of human history the two ends of the continent, comprising quite separate culture realms, knew almost nothing about each other. It does not follow that either end of the continent lived in isolation. It will be the burden of later chapters to indicate how much cross contact there actually was, and it must suffice at this point to state categorically that none of the countries and none of the cultures of the Orient evolved in isolation. Most of the several regions were not only in frequent contact with each other but also had contacts with the lands of central and western Asia and with the islands of the Pacific and Indian Oceans, outside the zone of the Orient itself.

The environmental setting of India may appear isolated from Scandinavia, just as Italy would seem to be in an isolated position with regard to China, or as Malaysia can be said to be isolated from Kamchatka. Certainly the Eurasian continent does consist of an enormous solid core around which are arranged a series of peninsulas, island arcs, and coastal seas. And it may well be that man has moved into certain of these peninsular portions from a centrally located Garden of Eden like traffic along a one-way street. This can be indicated for the western as well as the eastern peninsulas. But, as the increasing volume of prehistoric and historical records are continually read with more accuracy and understanding, there seems less and less possibility of proving the thesis of isolation for any selected peninsula or island arc.

It is not a negation of the above statement to admit that the whole of each regional environment did not participate equally in the mixing of man and his cultures. Certain negative zones in many of the countries served as lands of refuge to the oppressed, zones in which there was a degree of stagnation, of decadence, even of retrogression. And there were some islands at which not all wandering groups of visitors touched, so that some of them remained in the Stone Age until after the day of contact with the occidental. On the other hand, in certain positive zones the sheer volume of historical contact is so bewilderingly great that it is hard to get the story simplified sufficiently.

Beyond the simple matter of chance isolation or refuge in a negative and unattractive hill country there is the rather more complicated question of cultural hibernation. By this is meant the arbitrary decision on the part of a people that it wanted no contact with the outside world. The Occident has been both startled and annoyed to find that there were cultures that thought themselves sufficient, that felt that there could be no real worth in dealings with the West. In some cases the statement undoubtedly should read "no more dealings with the Occident after having witnessed some exhibitions of their customs," about which more will be said in a later chapter. Regardless of whether the Occident is itself partly responsible for the cases of hibernation, the very retreat from the world into a period of cultural hermitage produces a type of isolation. The repercussions from this kind of isolation were greater by far than the effects of simple distant environmental location.

ELEMENTS OF CULTURE SYSTEMS

There are more farmers in the Orient than in the rest of the world combined. Agriculture is the most widespread occupational activity of all human callings in the East. And the terraced ricefield with reflections flashing from its liquid surface is the most distinctive picture of the Orient. Among the most easily observed characteristics of southern and eastern Asia are its native agricultural systems. These patterns of agriculture have often been described under the general term hoe culture or garden culture. Fundamentally hoe culture is an agriculture of small fields, of much detailed hand labor on the part of the cultivator, of relatively few mechanical aids to cultivation, and of relatively small numbers of draft animals per farm unit. It was at one time primarily a subsistence, agriculture, concerned with food supply and only in minor proportions interested in a product for sale in a commercial market. Rice is its primary food crop, giving way to some other food plant only when water supply fails, soils will not allow rice cultivation, or local climatic factors other than precipitation make rice impossible. It is a crop of flooded fields, the world's only great crop so grown. This predominance of flooded fields and a concern for water management cause the rest of the agricultural pattern to be fitted rather closely to the landscape and the planting season in order to secure a harvest.

As a crop of small field units rice produces a distinctive landscape which varies considerably in appearance in the course of the year. Where rice, itself, is not the backbone of the crop series throughout the Orient one still finds the basic features of intensive garden culture, though in a few regions variations have been introduced in recent centuries. That hoe culture is at least partially independent of rice is clear from the fact that rice has not always been cultivated everywhere throughout the realm. Detailed hand labor, with the very simplest of tools, and close-knit social organization are more diagnostic of oriental agriculture than is any one crop. Small fields have long been effective in forestalling the evolution of mechanical aids to cultivation. And the very detail with which cultivation is carried on reaches out beyond agriculture into many other features of the several cultures to make its print upon oriental civilization.

Around the mainland margins of the Orient the contrast is very great between sedentary garden culture and the culture of the pastoral nomad. The location of the Tibetan Plateau limits the zone of contact between the pastoral nomad and the garden cultivator. Such a zone is best exemplified in Mongolia where the fixed Chinese dwelling, the cultivated field, the slow-moving cart or wheelbarrow, and the tall sorghum known as kaoliang push against the movable felt yurt home, the grass turf, the mobile horseman, and the flocks of animals. This contrast has long been expressed in conflict, with one or another of the two patterns of landscape use on the offensive against the other through the historic barbarian invasions of China or the ruthless push of the Chinese colonist into the grazing lands of Mongolia. The contrast again shows up in Baluchistan and parts of northwest Pakistan.

The contrast between hoe culture and the mechanized agriculture of the Occident as shown in the United States may be measured in many ways. The beautiful panorama of small terraced fields reflecting in their thin water cover the clouds piled up on the horizon is a world far removed from the American rolling prairie wheat field in which one can sight a harvester swath for miles across a single field. The grain elevator on the midwestern plains of North America past which thunders a freight train made up of refrigerator cars carrying green vegetables from California cannot be matched anywhere in the Orient. Nor can the Szechwanese professional porter, balancing two baskets of green vegetables or hand-winnowed grain from his shoulder pole, and shuffling five miles to the nearest village, be matched in our own realm.

This intense cultivation of the soil has long promoted a higher concentration of population than most other systems of agriculture. Once effectively organized, its very nature required a larger population to operate it well, which in turn made it more able to support a dense population. This circle of operation has had its checks and balances, just as it has had its extra stimulation from time to time. In simple comparisons, however, this region of hoe culture has become the most populous portion of the earth. But hoe culture has now about reached its maximum limits of support, and many regions no longer are securely able to feed themselves.

Both in the northwest of Peninsular India and in North China the rice landscape becomes altered into a wheat landscape and a more seasonal garden culture operating on "dry" landscapes dependent upon the vagaries of the rainy season or upon the development of irrigation systems. On these two margins animals have always played a somewhat larger role in the local economy than in the heart of the rice country.

Into the southern sectors of this landscape of small gardens and detailed agriculture the European brought the plantation system. Extensive plantings of such crops as tea, rubber, sugarcane, coconuts, and palm oil created broad mono-crop islands in the mixed landscapes, and established new routines of export trade in commodities designed for the world markets. Labor forces made up of local populations contributed their energies to this export agriculture while producing their own food supplies in traditional ways. As the colonial era drew to a close many of the plantations in particular countries were taken over from their former operators, to be turned into small holdings often operated in the traditional manner. In some areas, however, the plantation remains a feature of the landscape, now operated by unionized laborers, and a contributor to the gross output of the particular national economy.

Most recently, aspects of an agricultural revolution are coming to parts of the Orient. Hybridized varieties of rubber, coffee, rice, maize, wheat, and soy beans are greatly increasing the yields of farm landscapes, and new agricultural procedures are becoming diffuse. Variants of mechanization are changing the labor force requirements as electric power takes over the tasks of pumping water

through rice landscapes and as small-powered cultivating and harvesting equipment is being employed on more and more farms. Traditional agriculture is changing, but the forces of change have not yet reached everywhere into the rural countrysides.

Traditionally viewed, the Orient has been a land of mysticism and strangeness, in terms of its religious outlook, psychological viewpoint, and concept of the future life. Complex religious systems, heavily underlain with traditional folk custom and overlain with ritual and ceremonial have long seemed exotic to the European. Coupled with this has been the distinctive view of the relationship between mankind and the earth; oriental man lives in harmony with that earth and does not view it merely as something to be exploited for the improvement of material living. Such views led toward taboos on the killing of animals and yielded vegetarian dietary systems; there were restrictions on the exploiting of minerals, and emphasis on maintaining an "unspoiled" earth and simple handicraft manufacturing systems; landscapes became occupied by sacred groves and monumental structures affecting the harmonics of nature either by dispersing evil influences or promoting beneficial influences. These attitudes have struck the European as strange and mystically conditioned. But these aspects are changing as the East adopts from the Occident pragmatic attitudes toward material resources, systems of urban architecture, concepts of transportation, and secular concern for material welfare.

Following out of the rise of secular pragmatism in regard to the earth, much of the Orient today is engaged in a broad program of industrialization that aims to modify the agrarian tradition as fully as possible. There is variation in the approach to industrialization from wholehearted pursuit to reluctant venturing into selected aspects only, but the landscapes and the economies of every country in the Orient display the impact to greater or lesser degree. The process is relatively recent in many areas, and the patterns of landscape change are still immature almost everywhere.

Befitting populous agrarian societies, the traditional Orient has been a realm of tightly integrated social structures in which group living systems were highly developed. Whether formal social organization was highly convoluted, as in India with its caste system, or only loosely structured, as in Borneo among many ethnic groups, the solidarity of group living systems remained. Sometimes this integration put a high value on privacy, as in China, whereas at other times public hospitality knew almost no limits, as in the Philippines. Family linkage systems, whether by lineage, extended family, clan, or caste, have been strong and often presented a closed world to the non-member. Loyalties have often been personal or familial, rather than to the state. Under the impact of modern world contact this tight structuring is breaking down slowly, and social patterns are becoming looser and more open. But because several modern political states in the Orient are made up of diverse ethnic stocks separated by language barriers, there are strongly divergent trends within a number of countries. Such divergent trends create instabilities in political structuring for the modern political state. The divergent trends often are augmented by religious disparities, and political cohesion has been endangered by the persistence of primary loyalties to persons rather than to institutions.

Throughout the Orient ethnic variation has been historically characteristic of regions otherwise almost homogeneous. Only a few regions have been composed of ethnic stocks which within recent centuries could be said to be relatively uniform. Within the whole of the Orient a slow drift of human migrational patterns has been taking place for many centuries. Into northwest Peninsular India and northwest China there have been long-term trends of inward movement, accompanied by trends southward in both Peninsular India and in China. This has been matched by discontinuous drifts or temporary strong migrational trends into mainland Southeast Asia and spilling over into the island sectors. The result has been that every "country," and every modern political state, possesses distinctive variety in almost every manifestation of its own culture. There is no such thing as *the* Chinese point of view, *the* Indian outlook, or *the* Philippine opinion.

The Orient has been a troubled world for over a century during which time colonial controls and occidental influences have increasingly disturbed traditional patterns of living. As the era of colonial controls has come to an end, circumstances have promoted elements of drastic change. Both violently military and peacefully temporal changes have come about in every society. Minor crises have grown into major crises, and every political state in the Orient is engaged in a struggle to balance the pressures and the influences being exerted upon it. Temporal and secular influences have come into conflict with religious and moral traditions; social and economic pressures have created conflict with political pressures; both personalized group loyalties and narrowly ethnic regionalisms have opposed political nationalism and regional internationalism; particular political systems have been in broad conflict with other political systems; rural and traditional agrarian living systems have come into opposition to urban industrial and international trading systems as these have been evolving steadily; and over all other conflicts has hovered the basic problems of too many people, and of societies having too few and too small bodies of capital resources to cope with all urgent problems in the short-term run of time. The Orient today is a realm in the state of precipitous cultural flux, in which short-term programs aim at particular solutions, but in which the long-term resolution of cultural problems remains indeterminate.

Underneath the sometimes militant, but always dynamic, processes of cultural change taking place, there remains the rural farmer at work on his small unit of farm landscape, suffering through the local manifestation of militant change, coping with the vagaries of the seasonal monsoon while hoping that the rainy season is on time and adequate in volume, further manicuring his agricultural landscape to its utmost efficiency, seeking new crops and new crop varieties when he can, adopting new technologies when he can find a way of financing them, and eking out his annual living under tremendous pressures. And underneath it all, also, is the growing urban landscape, as natural population increase and steady in-migration make the cities of the Orient larger and more numerous. Here the complex conflicts are often more critically balanced as ex-rural peoples attempt to cope with the rapid shifts in the temporal, technologic world of industry, international trade, militantly unionized labor, conflicting political movements, loosened social structures, and plain economic poverty. The rural landscapes and living systems throughout much of the Orient retain something of their quiet and classical historic patterns; the main thoroughfares and better residential suburbs of the cities exhibit a somewhat gaudy jumble of both the old and the new, whereas the interior lanes and back alleys exhibit both a poignant and a pungent failure to bridge the gap from the traditional to the modern world.

THE SPECIFIC OBJECTIVE

The aim of this volume is to present a reasonable statement of the appearance of the several landscapes of the oriental realm, what goes on in them, how their peoples developed particular patterns of culture, and how these peoples happened to achieve their present positions in the world at large. This involves a composite geographical presentation, though primary emphasis is placed upon the cultural aspects.

In the organization of the volume there are two major subdivisions. The first section deals with certain topics systematically, covering the whole of the Orient in the sweep of each chapter. This section makes an effort to paint on a broad canvas the systematic framework of the oriental realm, including both its physical and cultural structural members. It lacks many pertinent details as presently written—because of limitations both of knowledge and of space.

The second section of the book is an attempt to deal with the evolution of group cultures according to the broad regional molds in which they have developed. In each of these units there is an attempt to evaluate the landscape for differing societies, to present the growth of culture in that landscape, to consider the factors making for progress or decadence, and to discuss the problems of modernization and the future world for each people. Along with this will be presented a survey of present-day agriculture, economy, resources, trade, and industry. Both in the first and in the second sections statistical material is held to a minimum in an effort to improve the presentation of the broad picture. In recognition of the real need for comparable date of measurement for all the Orient, a separate final section, an appendix, is devoted to the presenting of such statistical data as are available. It is hoped that putting all of this, concisely, into one single section will make it more usable, and will prevent the futile, random search through many a volume for facts that are never given twice in like manner and are seldom given completely.

PEOPLE

These Indian village women are drawing water for domestic purposes from a public standpipe, Haryana Province, northern India. (United Nations)

These central Java women and children have been harvesting rice. Many of the younger people wear western clothing today, in variably modified forms. (Asian Development Bank)

Burmese women regularly wear native dress, as do the men (at far right margin). In this picture Buddhist monks are being offered food. (Maung Maung Tin)

Most Thai women continue to wear native dress, as shown in this market scene at Sakol Nakorn, Thailand. (Asian Development Bank)

Chinese commuters at a railway station, Taiwan. Almost all younger people
have adopted western clothing styles. (J. E. Spencer)

Japanese pedestrians at an urban traffic crossing, Tokyo. Almost all younger
Japanese now wear western clothing. (J. E. Spencer)

PART I

SYSTEMATIC GEOGRAPHY

I

PEOPLES, LANGUAGES, AND POPULATIONS

WHERE IS THE GARDEN OF EDEN?

Regardless of just where in the Old World one located the Garden of Eden, it would probably provide access to some part of the Orient. It has become quite evident that from any such location early man wandered very widely indeed, and there probably are few, if any, sizable areas of land outside Antarctica through which early man did not pass many times. Sometimes these migrations left certain localities quite empty, whereas at other times groups of people remained to occupy a landscape for a period. The island group known as the Moluccas, for example, or the Malabar coast of Peninsular India, must have been discovered many times before the Portuguese and Spaniards started the modern search for the fabulous Spice Islands. Even though man went just about everywhere in his early wanderings, certain regions, at least, have been continuously occupied during most of the period of human existence. It appears that, despite some recurrent immigration from outside, modern east Asian man is a lineal descendant of earliest east Asian man (see pp. 9–11).

Whether or not the human races had a multiple origin, several regions have served as population incubators to spill out the human beings that have populated much of the earth since middle Paleolithic time. Apparently three major regions helped in populating the lands of the Orient. An east African locality seems the most probable source of the Negrito and other members of the Negroid family of races. Southwestern Asia contributed the strains lumped together under the heading of the Caucasoid family of races. Central eastern Asia served as the home region for the units making up the Mongoloid family of races. It seems reasonable that the Negroid and Caucasoid incubators were the earliest to start spreading their broods, and that the Mongoloid races diffused somewhat later.

Since 1600 certain regions have been producing large surpluses of people that probably exceed in number any incubator broods of the earlier past. The populating of Manchuria by millions of surplus Chinese from Chahar, Hopei, and Shantung since 1900 is a contemporary example of a racial incubator. Kwangtung has sent a smaller modern wave of Chinese into Vietnam, Cambodia, Thailand, Malaysia, Singapore, the Philippines, and Indonesia that may eventually have important results in terms of race mixture. Indian migration to Burma and

Malaysia is yet another example, less liable to race mixture owing to the labor-contract terms and restricted freedoms involved. The Dutch tried for years to start a Javanese exodus to the Outer Territories, without real success. The Japanese also failed in their efforts to colonize the Asian mainland.

RACE MIXTURE AND MOVEMENT

The suggestion of primary centers of human types does not preclude both later mixing and the evolution of special local strains as groups from the several centers have wandered widely, crossed paths, become swallowed up, produced new types, or stagnated in particular localities. This varied result must always have been the consequence of the peripatetic nature of human beings. Extreme mixing is the only explanation of the modern Japanese or the Indian, and wide wandering the only explanation to the Philippine Negrito and the Ainu of Japan.

As the early and late products of any one incubator certainly varied, the end product of race mixture also has varied. Such local variants as the Chinese Moslems of Kansu and the Anglo-Indian are expressions of the process. It is almost impossible to tell just how much of what racial elements have gone into the blend that is the contemporary Javanese. Most Javanese mixing occurred in the protohistoric era, and the rapid growth of population within the last 500 years has produced a hybrid strain that runs fairly true to type. The Chinese, Peninsular Indian, Arab, and Dutch additions to Java in the last five centuries are substantially small in proportionate volume and have not materially altered the Javanese subrace, though they have produced some radical local variants.

Stray columns of proto-Negroid and proto-Caucasoid peoples penetrated Southeast Asia and Australasia. The earliest mixtures of these strains must have occurred at a very early date (Fig. 1.1). Over most of Southeast

Asia went the Negrito, to be a factor in the makeup of almost every people south of Central China. Today there remain only remnants of Negrito on the Andaman Islands, in Cambodia, and in the Malay Peninsula, a few thousands in the Philippines, and an unknown number in New Guinea. A lowland-valley forest people by preference, Negritos often were unable to find the right kind of country into which to retreat when they were invaded; consequently, they have melted away over the centuries except in New Guinea to which fewer peoples came later. In New Guinea and nearby eastern islands, in the interiors, survival of mixed Negroid strains, such as the Papuans, is much greater than in the western islands of the Indies. The Philippines show little evidence of the earliest Caucasoid peoples, but considerably more of the Negrito.

On the mainland of Southeast Asia, it is difficult to recognize and label more than a small residual effect of the earliest Negroid, Negrito, or Caucasoid peoples, but unquestionably all three elements are present in the racial understructure of the region. Here proto-Mongoloid and Mongoloid stocks predominate.

It is difficult to suggest how and by what means race movement through today's island world occurred. It is not at all clear for how long the present distribution of land and sea has been fixed. The main oceanic deeps lie outside the Island Arcs, and most of the present coastal seas are very shallow. Man certainly was exploring the land world before the final close of the Glacial Epoch, and the diffusion and mixing of the earliest groups of contemporary men probably began before the contemporary landscape was cut up into islands by the rising and widening of the seascape to its present extent.

It seems fair to suggest that in Peninsular India the mixture of proto-Negroid and proto-Caucasoid was not at all uniform, yielding a northern variant with lighter

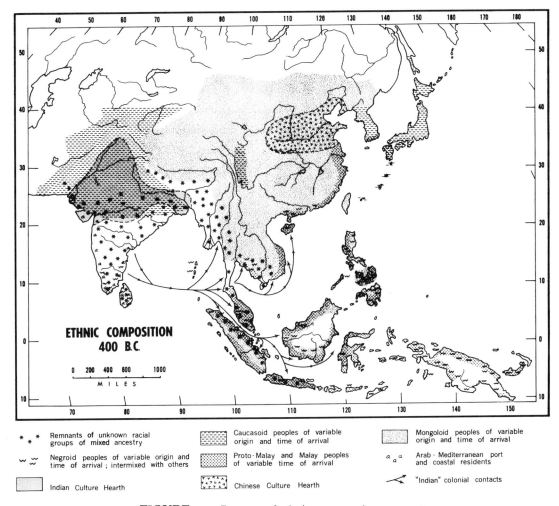

FIGURE 1.1. Patterns of ethnic contact, about 400 B.C.

colored skin and a southern one, more nearly black. The primary zones of Negroid and Caucasoid expansion lay not eastward into India but within Africa and Europe, respectively. Later Caucasoid additions to Peninsular India have been insufficient to lighten skin coloring and dominate the racial blend in eastern and southern India. Southeast Asia received directly only small numbers of later Caucasoid and later Negroid races. Instead hybrid peoples from different parts of Peninsular India moved eastward during the Christian era in sufficiently strong numbers to contribute significantly to the blood stream of the western Indies, and the southern portions of all of mainland Southeast Asia. A few centuries after the Christian era began, this Peninsular Indian movement slackened off markedly, to be resumed again at later dates. Within Peninsular India itself the prevailing trend of human movement has been southward and eastward ever since the last big Caucasoid immigration began in the third millennium B.C. This sometimes led to the deep penetration and isolating of certain racial groups as in the Nilgiri Hills of southern India, but in general it served to foster slow intermixture. There have been a few countermovements of peoples, the most notable of which is probably the emigration of the Gypsy strain from northwestern Peninsular India toward Europe about 1,000 years ago.

Out of the Mongoloid race incubator has come a succession of peoples as variable as those from the Negroid or Caucasoid hearths. The earliest waves probably spread in all directions, but found the easiest zone of movement in eastern mainland Asia. Into the Philippines, Southeast Asia, and the western Indies moved the early proto-mongoloid groups to share the region with representatives of the early Negroid and Caucasoid races. Some of these peoples spread out farther eastward into the South Pacific. The amount of true mixing may be questioned, but certainly there was some. The western Indies produced a countermovement of mixed peoples who are often termed proto-Malay. The line of this movement was locally into the Malay Peninsula, but also it trended northward along the coast and through the Island Arcs to southern Japan and touching most of the coast and all the islands between Sumatra and Honshu. Some areas received successive waves of these people; northern coastal embayments and islands were reached less often. The other directions of proto-Malay and Malay movement, eastward into the Pacific and westward to Madagascar, are of less interest in this study.

On the eastern Asian mainland the Mongoloid races were dominant and spread continuously southward in waves that carried them throughout mainland Southeast Asia, though not until modern times have they again moved into the Indies. Negroid, Caucasoid, and Malay blends of peoples have merged into the spreading Mongoloid races or remained as islands of isolation around the coastal fringe of southeastern Asia. Locally

this has noticeably altered the modern racial type, but nowhere did it stem the southward drift of Mongoloid peoples. In some cases only the barest of traces remain in the vague stories of myths and legends, and the random curly hair and facial features which point to some kind of Negroid people in the southernmost China at some early date.

The Mongols proper, occupying a home somewhere near the racial incubator location, may well be the youngest strain of the Mongoloid race. At an early date waves of proto-Mongoloid and Mongoloid peoples had gone into eastern Manchuria and Korea and had blended somewhat and probably mixed with some non-Mongoloids to become the source for the modern Koreans. Already beyond them were the Ainu, usually thought of as a mixture of proto-Mongoloid and proto-Caucasoid or Caucasoid-like people who had taken an unusual migration path to become lost in the enveloping Mongoloid realm and develop into a special physical type. The least that can be said is that the stocky, olive-skinned, curly-haired, brown- to hazel-eyed Ainu, growing heavy beards and much body hair, resemble no other Mongoloid people. At one time they seem to have ranged from the southern Ryukyu Islands to Hokkaido. They have entered strongly into the makeup of the modern Japanese and probably also the Koreans. There seem to be several racial elements intermixed but not synthesized in the modern Japanese, so that there are several kinds of "typical Japanese." In addition to Ainu there seem to be proto-Malay, early Mongoloid, and later Korean hybrids, but no satisfactory analysis of Japanese racial origins has yet been made. Northward spread a number of Mongoloid groups into Siberia and beyond, out of the scope of this volume.

Everywhere in the Orient there are marks indicating that the broad movements suggested above have not resulted in full racial synthesis and are still not completed (Fig.

1.2). That some Negritos exist in quite pure form in the Philippines is ample proof of the failure of synthesis, just as their impurity in the Malay Peninsula and also in the Philippines points to mixture. Throughout the Island Arcs there are numerous spots of refuge that housed some fairly pure racial strains and allowed them to escape some part of the blending process. On the mainland several rough hill land regions served both as homes of refuge and as lines of infiltration by which similar escape was possible. In particular the Chota Nagpur hill region of northeast Peninsular India and the Indian

and Chinese Tibetan borderlands have served the earlier races of men in the struggle to maintain themselves. On the Chinese side of Tibet there may well be remnants of Caucasoid migration groups. The invasions of barbarians into China throughout the Christian era and the coming of the Moslems to Peninsular India in the last 1,000 years are major items in the process. The coming of the Europeans since the discoveries, the drift of southern Chinese into mainland Southeast Asia, Malaysia, Indonesia, and the Philippines during the 18th-19th centuries, the mass migrations of Chinese during the Sino-

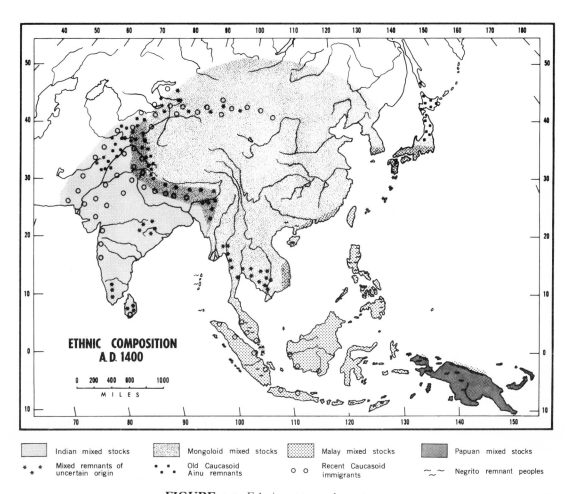

FIGURE 1.2. Ethnic patterns about A.D. 1400.

Japanese War, and the mass transfers of Moslem and Hindu Indians upon the division of Peninsular India are all important recent episodes in the further mixing of races in the Orient.

In regional summary one may describe the modern racial patterns of Eastern Asia in the following terms. No political state in the Orient is populated by a single race; every country contains a multiple mixture. Caucasoid stocks entered directly into this mixture in every country, early or late, Negroid stocks were early contributors everywhere except in Tibet and northern China-Manchuria. Since the end of World War II, there have been Negroid additions to the Korean and Japanese blood stocks that were derived from American military forces. This phenomenon is now showing up in Vietnam as well. Mongoloid stocks have contributed directly to every region except New Guinea, a portion of West Pakistan, and Peninsular India south of the Himalayan mountain wall.

Notwithstanding the extreme mixture of primary racial stocks, simple generalizations may be made. Pakistan is chiefly composed of Caucasoid stocks, both in east and west sectors. North India is largely Caucasoid, whereas southern India is very mixed in composition. Burma and Thailand are populated by early Mongoloid stocks over an early base of mixed peoples. Laos is inhabited chiefly by groups of ethnic stocks emigrating from China over a long run of centuries, but extending into the 19th century. Cambodia contains chiefly Khmer (Cambodian) peoples representing a mixed stock long resident in the core area of the old Khmer Empire, although there are also remnants of earlier substocks present. Lowland North Vietnam is populated by mixed ethnic stocks out of South China over a long period, but including relatively recent admixtures. South Vietnam shares the Chinese origin of its primary ethnic stock, but there are remnants of Malay mixed stocks and recent Chinese

additions. Peninsular Malaya contains chiefly Malay stocks and south China stocks of recent origin, both being mixed Mongoloid stocks, and there is a modern addition of peninsular Indians. The western Indies are mostly Malay, but eastward the Negroid element increases, and there enters a wide variety of mixture. The Philippines is populated by peoples mostly Malay in origin, but with considerable early Negroid and other mixed elements, and with a considerable addition of modern Chinese elements. China is chiefly Mongoloid, but this involves both very early and rather recent types. And in the south it includes some Negrito, and in the northwest some Caucasoid. Korea is a very diverse mixture of early Caucasoid and Mongoloid, with considerable late Mongoloid addition. Japan used to be considered predominantly Malay, but this now seems unlikely. More probable is a variety of early to middle Mongoloids drawn from different parts of the mainland, composing the larger source of the modern Japanese. Into this variety were absorbed the proto-Caucasoid Ainu, a proto-Malay element, and a steady increment from Korea, this latter itself a composite population. Obviously these simple generalizations are gross generalizations, but they are as valid as any one-or-two sentence answers can be to the question: "What are the peoples of the United States?" The two maps of ethnic patterns help to define regional patterns and to suggest changes in the period before the arrival of the occidental (see Figs. 1.1 and 1.2). These maps are more suggestive than factual, since little work has been done in historical biological anthropology in the Orient.

THE PATTERNS OF LANGUAGE

Language often may bear no relationship to race, a fact to which many third-generation Americans can bear strong witness. The language map of the Orient today is a complicated mosaic of nearly a thousand languages and their dialects (Fig. 1.3). To some degree this map exhibits facts in the movement and mixture of races, but there are borrowed languages among peoples who have lost their own original speech. Also there has been marked change in the structure and vocabulary of certain languages whose users have moved into new environments and rubbed shoulders with older, unrelated inhabitants. Certain language families or dialects appear dominant in usage and gain speakers by the spread of speech; others are recessive and gradually are replaced. The Indo-European languages of northern India are gaining ground against the Dravidian family of languages of southern India, and the northern dialect of Chinese is gaining ground against other Chinese dialects. Negrito remnants of southeastern Asia, except the Andamanese, have lost their own mother tongue and borrow the language of their neighbors.

Anthropologists and linguists often have tried to arrange the world's languages schematically into family groups by classifying them in various ways. For the Orient there has so far been no real agreement in these matters and the geographer or sociologist finds himself caught up in a quarrel over whether this or that tongue really belongs to one or another speech family. Admittedly it is a perplexing problem, one in which man's wanderings, cultural borrowings, linguistic shifts, and racial intermixture are involved. The problem of classification is not made simpler in that definitive studies have not yet been made of many of the recessive languages and even simple and accurate recordings are lacking for refugee groups who are hidden away in almost inaccessible regions. It will be decades before all the oriental languages are well enough recorded and compared to permit even a simple classification.

Despite these linguistic conflicts it is possible to map the distribution of language groups in very general terms and to tabulate their proportionate usage among the peoples of the Orient. Early wanderers into Asia spoke tongues that sometimes have been grouped into an Austro-Asiatic family of languages. These at one time covered much more territory than they do today, and they left their marks on several other language families. Today the group is represented on the mainland by scattered languages ranging from West Pakistan to Malaysia and possibly by a few languages in the Indies. Austronesian is the name often used to cover another series of languages that variably include several from mainland Southeast Asia along with all those reaching as far east as Polynesia.

The Dravidian languages of southern India form another large family with four main groupings. Race and speech have become disconnected in this case, with many borrowings and alterations. Certain subgroup languages have been used more frequently in recent centuries owing to population increase of their speakers whereas others are recessive in terms of region and number of speakers. From Persia through the Pamirs and eastward across northern India into Assam nearly forty major languages and four hundred dialects make up the three main branches of the Indo-European languages. In the northwestern mountain country there are many isolated groups that have lost their close relations to languages now spoken out on the North Indian Plain. In general these three language groups have been steadily pushing back the Dravidian and other remnant tongues of central and southern India, but they have suffered modification in the process. Numerous varied contributions into the major languages of the Indo-Aryan branch have increased their differences. Hindi, which with its dialects is the most common north Indian tongue, has maintained its own grammar, but its alphabet and script are Persian which belongs to another branch of the Indo-

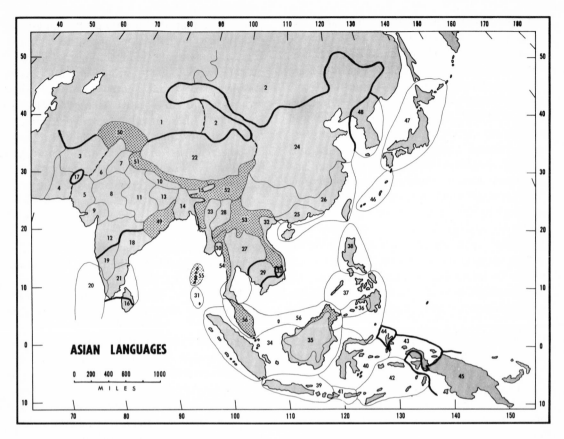

FIGURE 1.3. Modern Asian languages. See table at right for identification of numbers on the face of the map.

European languages. The modern vocabulary of Hindi is drawn from classical Sanskrit, several Dravidian languages, Persian, and Arabic. For the most part these effects were produced from within by Hindu Indians rather than by outsiders or conquerors.

At the latest count the Sino-Tibetan language family numbers over a hundred and fifty languages and some two hundred dialects distributed in a zone from southern Burma and Thailand through northern Manchuria, and from Japan and Taiwan into western Tibet. Within this great area there are many divergent linguistic elements, but there is not very much argument over the interrelation between and affiliation of tongues. Among the

modern Sino-Tibetan languages there are many striking instances of borrowing. Burmese and Thai alphabets and script were borrowed from India and quite recently fitted to the two tongues. Japanese, an unwritten polysyllabic speech, borrowed the Chinese script developed for a monosyllabic speech. More recently the Japanese evolved their *kana* "alphabet" in an effort to bridge this gap, the result being an extraordinarily complex linguistic system in which relatively few Japanese really are at home. Korean has gone through a similar evolution. Mongol and Manchu, on the other hand, are written vertically like Chinese but with Arabic script developed only after the thirteenth century.

A. Altaic family.
    I. Turkish branch.
        1. Turkish languages.
    II. Mongol branch.
        2. Mongol languages.

B. Indo-European family.
    I. Iranian branch.
        3. Pashto (Afghan).
        4. Baluchi.
    II. Indo-Aryan branch.
        5. Sindhi.
        6. Lahnda.
        7. Punjabi.
        8. Rajasthani.
        9. Gujarati.
        10. Nepalese (Gurkha).
        11. Hindustani (Hindi)
        12. Marathi.
        13. Bihari.
        14. Bengali.
        15. Assamese.
        16. Singhalese.
    III. Dardic branch, to which belong Persian and other languages spoken north and west of India.

C. Dravidian family.
    17. Brahui.
    18. Telegu.
    19. Kanarese.
    20. Malayalam.
    21. Tamil.

D. Sino-Tibetan family.
    I. Tibeto-Burman branch.
        22. Tibetan.
        23. Burmese.
    II. Sino-Siamese branch.
        24. "Peking" Chinese (Northern Mandarin).
        25. "Canton" Chinese (Cantonese).
        26. Mixed Chinese languages.
        27. Tai.
        28. Shan.

E. Austro-Asiatic family (relations very unclear).
    I. Mon-Khmer branch.
        29. Khmer (Cambodian, etc.).
        30. Mon.
        31. Nicobarese.
    II. 32. Vietnamese branch (relationship debatable).

III. Remnant languages.
    Several languages belong here, but they no longer dominate regions, and are not shown on map. Many are not yet adequately studied and classified.

F. Austronesian family.
    I. Indonesian branch (Malay).
        33. Cham.
        34. Sumatran Malay.
        35. Borneo "Dyak."
        36. Mindanao "Moro."
        37. Visayan.
        38. Tagalog, Ilocano, Bicol, and others.
        39. Javanese.
        40. Celebes.
        41. Soemba.
        42. Timor-Ceram.
        43. West New Guinea.

G. Papuan family (poorly studied; relations unclear).
        44. Halmahera.
        45. New Guinea.

H. Composite languages (mixed linguistic patterns).
        46. Ryukyu (composed of *B*, *D*, and *F*?).
        47. Japanese (composed of *B*, *D*, and *F*?).
        48. Korean (composed of *A*, *B*, *D*, *F*, and ?).

I. Regions of multiple languages.
        49. Munda-Oriya-Kurukh (*E*, *B*, and *C*).
        50. Turkish-Tibetan-Dardic (*A*, *B*, and *D*).
        51. Indo-European and Sino-Tibetan mixtures.
        52. Chinese - Tibetan - Tai - Mon - Khmer-tribal (*D*).
        53. Chinese-Vietnamese-Tai-Shan-Karen-Group *E*, III.
        54. Burmese-Karen-Mon-Tai.
        55. Andamanese - Burmese - Groups *B* and *C*.
        56. Malay-Chinese-"Indian."

Metropolitan city areas and other local areas of the Orient possess highly mixed language patterns in such small areas that they cannot be shown on a map.

Even Chinese itself has gone through many phonetic changes by virtue of borrowing and evolutionary change. The Mandarin dialect is rapidly dominating the spoken language picture; the continuity of the written language has given China a much closer bond of of unity than India or Europe.

THE GROWTH OF POPULATION

Enough has been said to indicate that many different regions have taken their turn at producing surplus human beings who irregularly wandered into far lands or who swarmed in mass migrations into neighboring regions. The process is an old one that in its early stages had more numerous checks and balances in it than are operative today. It is difficult to resurrect the population history by which the Orient has come to house over half the world's people, for the Orient always seems to disguise its numbers and to be disinclined to handle statistics with finite accuracy in the manner of the passionate modern occidental statistician.

A good environment coupled with a certain degree of inventiveness and curiosity and backed by favorable social organization stimulated successful operation of certain early societies, and gave them an advantage over much of the rest of the world. It seems likely that some parts of the Orient have been among the most heavily populated parts of the world throughout much of human existence. All the common factors that make for increase of population in any part of the world operate with equal effectiveness in India, China, or Java, and as the several cultural realms of Eurasia advanced in attainments and numbers, favored sections of the Orient probably kept ahead of the rest in population. India was in this favored list almost from the beginning, China entered it in the third or perhaps fourth millennium B.C., and Java and Japan worked their way into this position in the early centuries of the Christian era.

The first exploratory trade was launched and colonial feelers were put out by India whose peoples possessed a certain sophistication in social and political matters. Indian stimulus sponsored the formation, growth, and development of the cultural centers that arose in each of several distinctive regional environments of Southeast Asia. Southeast Asia had spawned numerous groups that lacked strong and cohesive cultures and so spread themselves all over the western Pacific Ocean. The strength of Hindu culture gave rise to a series of states that slowly concentrated population on Java and nearby islands to give Java a lead in numbers among the regions of Southeast Asia. Later, the more gradual drift of Mongoloid peoples to mainland regions gave the bases for real population increase, and the southeastern mainland entered the modern era with less than the normal oriental population density. Chinese cultural stimulus in Korea and Japan operated somewhat similarly to that of India in Java, with Manchuria and Inner Mongolia remaining relatively empty until the modern era.

The whole of the Orient shared in the increases that have affected the world during the post-Columbian era of environmental development and exploitation. Some regions, such as Peninsular India, Java, and China, were the first to jump ahead under the new stimulation. Next came Japan and Korea, a little late owing to their self-imposed hermitage. A few spots like Manchuria and the Philippines have attained large totals only during the present century. The increases of such regions as Thailand, Borneo, and New Guinea have been more gradual.

The rates of post-Columbian population increase are not so very different in the Orient from those elsewhere in the world but, because oriental populations were already large and productive, the sheer numbers that have piled up there are in excess of those anywhere else. Not only are the gross numbers greater but the net totals per square mile are higher, and the densities per square mile of food-producing land are far above those of the Occident. The accompanying simple map of population concentration suggests only a limited distribution of this state of crowding (Fig. 1.4).

The disturbing feature is that the West has helped remove many of the traditional checks and balances from population growth in the Orient without supplying the productive means to feed the increases. Preventive and curative medicine, and public health facilities, although inadequate, have still been effective in lowering infant mortality rates, preventing huge killing epidemics, and keeping child-

producing age groups alive. Flood and famine relief, the discouragement of infanticide, the relative peace, and the prevention of tribal and interregional wars all have been factors making for modern increase in population. The level of living steadily declined during the whole of the nineteenth century and during the first half of the current century. New keys to agricultural production need to be put into the hands of all oriental peoples, and new kinds of population check-systems need to be made available to all culture groups. India and China have long been among the more populous regions of the earth, modern China is the most heavily populated country on the earth today, and

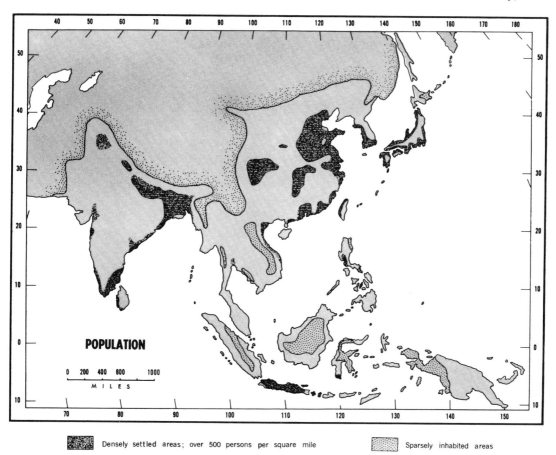

Densely settled areas; over 500 persons per square mile   Sparsely inhabited areas

FIGURE 1.4. The concentration of population.

India ranks second. Indonesia, Pakistan, and Japan, in population terms, are "large" countries today; only the Soviet Union and the United States rank above those three. Without modern checks to population growth the sheer numbers of Orientals may overwhelm the earth.

The population prospect is startling from any approach. Oriental economy, fed on the products of an intensive hoe culture, long led the world in achievement. It has been placed at a temporary disadvantage by the flowering and spreading of the technologically based civilization of the West. What will follow when the East masters western tools might be alarming or inspiring. Detailed regional consideration will be given to population growth and problems in Part II of this volume.

2

THE PATTERNS OF HISTORICAL CONTACT AND MODERNIZATION

THE PRE-COLUMBIAN OLD WORLD

In pre-Columbian times the two ends of the Old World lay a long way apart, with no clear connection between the two extremes. Chinese and Malays voyaged the seas south of China, Indians and the pre-Islamic Arabs operated early sea links in the Indian Ocean, varied Mongols and Turks opened and closed Central Asian caravan routes, and Rome and the Italian city states operated the Mediterranean link in the southwest. Perhaps the most knowledgeable people of all were the Arabic and Indian traders who ranged the sea routes between the Red Sea or Persian Gulf and the South China coast. They were not men who told their trade secrets or wrote serious travel books, but they did relate many a good yarn, as can be found in any collection of "Sinbad the Sailor" stories. From these wanderers both ends of the Old World learned a little, but all too little. When a blight fell over the West during the Middle Ages the Chinese still were expanding their geographical knowledge, but they never did expand their horizon to include western

Eurasia. A few curious Chinese always have wandered widely, but there never developed a widespread passion for geographical exploration, and the leaders of Chinese society never gave encouragement to travel and exploration beyond the margins of the Chinese known world. The Mongol "open door" administrative policy of the twelfth and thirteenth centuries allowed more travel in, and freer contact with eastern Asia. A little knowledge of the Orient reached the ears of men such as Marco Polo and inspired exploratory travel. At the dawn of the modern era, however, no one had been everywhere in the Old World, and no one could draw a reasonably good map of Eurasia. The accompanying sketch map is merely suggestive of this regional ignorance (Fig. 2.1).

As the European end of the Old World began to waken, it developed a curiosity about peoples and places and a passion for new products which never had existed anywhere as far as we know except for the curiosity of the early Japanese about Chinese culture. It was not, of course, merely pure curiosity that prompted the wakening of Europe to explore

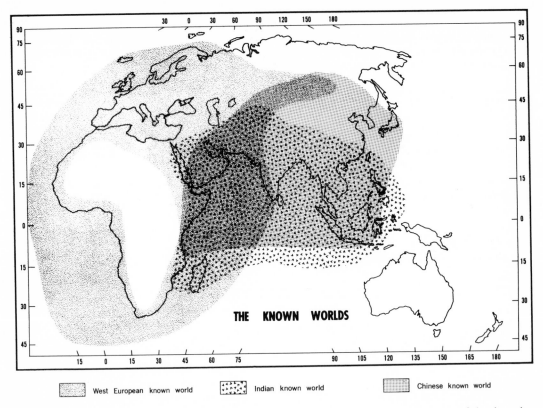

FIGURE 2.1. West European, Indian, and Chinese known worlds before the discovery of the Americas.

the edges of their known world. The European environment was not rich in useful products, nor was it favorably situated on the trade routes of the Old World. The blocking of those routes, or the levying of heavy taxes upon the products flowing along the routes, was of serious import to Europe. Out of this curiosity and self-interest flowered the government-supported great discoverers of early modern Europe, who finally did go everywhere in the Old World, and in the New World too.

In 1475 overland roads between West and East probably were in worse shape than they had been for centuries, and travel and transport were slow, costly, and full of risks. The Mongol empire had broken down, India was not a well-organized unit, and the Turkish peoples coming into ascendancy in western

Asia had too little appreciation of interregional trade to facilitate it. Products like pepper, sugar, and sandalwood sold in Europe for fabulous prices, but the fact was that small volumes did get through. Per tonmile costs were high, for goods making the whole trip from the Indies to England had to pass through the hands of many traders and transporters and to pay toll to many a regional overlord. The alternative sea routes were no cheaper, faster, or more capable of handling large volumes. European ships were small in size, poor in manageability, and inefficient in sailing power. Proper knowledge of the wind systems did not exist, there was no continuous sea route, and there were no charts that provided information on distances, ports of call, or sources of products.

In this situation both southern India and

western Malaysia were in a peculiarly favored position. Whereas the Mediterranean basin was the focus of many of the land routes of the Old World, the coasts of southern India and western Malaysia were the meeting ground of the chief sea lanes of the Old World. Here Malays, Indians, Chinese, and Arabs met in scores of ports. South Indian historical records are rich in accounts of busy ports with crowded foreign quarters in which many races were common and the economic products of the whole of the Old World were to be found. If the Malays inclined a little more to piracy, the Chinese had the biggest and fastest ships, and the Arabs may well have been the sharpest and most experienced traders.

THE COMING OF THE EUROPEAN

The sixteenth century sea route to India was a dangerous seaway strewn with death by wreck, starvation, thirst, and a host of malignant diseases. It was common for a fifth to a third of a crew and passengers to die on the way out, and for the story to be repeated on the homeward voyage. Not at all rare were cases in which so small a crew remained alive at the end of a voyage that a ship could not be properly worked. Although the West has made much of the leaders and commanders among the great discoverers, the lot of the common crewman was a hard one, and crews were hard to get. Although a few priests and men who were educated for their time went along, those of the crew remaining alive upon arrival in India or the Indies often were tough characters. Seldom could they be called the best representatives of European cultures. But, curiously enough, the European brought with him to the Orient two naive presumptions—superiority of white skin over brown, yellow, and black, and superiority of Christendom over the heathen and the infidel. The Arabs, the Indians, and the Chinese had their own standards and judgments of the superiority of culture, religion, and trading ability.

Europeans who visited the Orient often were entranced with what they saw and found, but it was the attraction of greed under heavy odds. These first European traders came into markets that were operated and frequented by races of men long skilled at sharp trading with each other. Prices of products were far lower than in Europe, and the potential profits were great, but the risks of an unsuccessful voyage home also were great. Then, too, the presence of interlopers in the Indian Ocean trade realm was widely resented, and the inexperience of the European in sharp trading often made him a loser.

The early European trader arriving in India found himself at a disadvantage, for European handicraft manufacture produced little that was of value to the high cultures of the East with whom first contacts were made. The industrial revolution had not yet begun to turn out its streams of products, and gold and silver soon were found to be about the only European products that interested oriental traders. In earlier days Roman Empire gold had found its way to India and China in payment for eastern trade products while Roman Empire porcelains and other goods were traded eastward. Pepper, sugar, and sandalwood did not long remain the only items which interested the European. Cotton and silk textiles in many forms, the full range of spices, many kinds of scented and beautiful woods, ivory, jewels, porcelain, all manner of carved and enameled art goods, and a wide range of tonics and materia medica were sought after.

Europeans did not get along any better with each other in their eastern contacts than they had back in Europe. Rivalry between Portuguese, Spanish, Dutch, English, and French, separately and in combination, was a standard part of the growth of eastern exploration and trade. This rivalry went so far as to justify piracy on each other's ships or to justify raiding a native port with one ship out of an expedition, only to have a second ship turn up later as rescuers who blamed some other nationality for the outlandish actions. On the other hand, the sea-empire of Madjapahit, centered in the western part of the Indies, had finally collapsed only shortly before the Europeans came on the scene. Moslem politicians-of-fortune, local regional chieftains, and varied port rulers had not yet completed their squabbling over the division of the spoils. Whereas the Islamic faith had spread rapidly in the Indies, so had the renewed art of piracy. A vital corner of the Old World was in turbulent flux.

The above factors gave rise to a variety of situations in the early meeting of East and West. Friendly contacts were not rare, but unfriendly ones generated stronger feelings. For the first time the two extremes of Eurasia were coming face to face. They met as traders with products and profits as the goals on each side. But contact involved more than the matching of skill and shrewdness at trade bargaining with simple profit or loss the total result. The European group of cultures was on the move, dynamic, eager, ambitious, and aggressive, but not completely unscrupulous by the standards of the day. The rate and the force with which Europe reached out into the several environments of the world to sample their products dictated the patterns of history and prompted the general trends in culture change the world over.

THE PROGRESS OF THE DISCOVERIES

The Portuguese went east, as the Spanish went west, toward the East. And to the Portuguese fell the job of first charting the new region. Their first sea visit to India, in 1498, disclosed the fact that India was a wholesaling center and not the producer of the spices that were the first order of business. Portuguese contacts, therefore, quickly touched Ceylon, Malaya, Sumatra, Java, and Borneo, groping eastward toward the primary sources. By 1525 they had probed their way to the Moluccas and had skirted the coasts of most of the mainland of southern Asia as far around as southern China. By 1542 they had reached Japan. Somewhat rowdy and lawless conduct caused some setbacks in a number of places, but the middle of the century saw the preliminary reconnaissance of the East completed.

Many Dutch crewmen were on the early Portuguese voyages of exploration, and eastern goods reached the Low Countries via Portuguese ports. In the political patterns of the Europe of the day, the Low Countries had been under Spanish rule, but they rebelled in the late sixteenth century. With the Spanish ruler also holding title in Portugal, Portuguese ports were closed to Low Countries ships. This stimulated ambitious Dutch traders to begin making their own ventures into the East. The spread of geographical knowledge and the independence of Holland from Iberian rule changed things, and it was not long before both Dutch and English began competing with the Portuguese. The Spanish reached the Philippines in 1521, with colonization beginning in 1565, but spread beyond only to a limited degree. The French were slow on the sea and were less active in the early period. On land the Russians were pushing eastward toward the Pacific, but their progress was slightly slower. Random explorers of several nationalities ventured to follow the old caravan routes eastward, returning to tell variations of Marco Polo's story.

By 1600 many islands were still unknown, and unexplored economic possibilities lay almost everywhere in the Orient. But by this date the Portuguese and Spanish monopolies had been broken, and competition began to lower prices and to heighten the tension between the European principals. During the seventeenth century Holland and England led the trade war in the Orient. Such countries as France, Denmark, and Sweden made a few ventures by sea. Throughout the century there was considerable shifting about from port to port and coast to coast by the numerous expeditions, with traders of one nationality trying a port or coast given up by others. At first this was trial-and-error sampling, but eventually the contest became one of strength, the strongest squadron of ships or the strongest nationality laying more or less permanent claim to trading rights at certain ports or along certain coasts believed to be profitable sources of eastern products. By 1700 the primary discoveries within the Orient were completed, an economic sampling had been made, and things settled down to a political and military contest among the leading countries of western Europe.

FROM TRADER TO RULER

In 1600 "The Governor and Company of Merchants of London Trading into the East Indies" was chartered as a corporation holding a monopoly on British trade with the East, which for this purpose was defined as the region lying between the Cape of Good Hope and the Strait of Magellan. Two years later the Dutch set up a similar company, and in 1616 the Danes launched a third. These companies set up trading stations known as "factories" in port cities thought to be points of vantage. Each company attempted to monopolize the trade of the local region. Conflicts soon arose over prices, quantity measures, the monopoly aspect, the rights of Chinese, Arab, and other traders, and sundry religious and social issues. The Europeans often found themselves unable to enforce what they callously termed their trade rights, and they gradually began to assume police power over the local port, its settlement, and the immediate hinterland. India was in a state of political readjustment during the seventeenth and eighteenth centuries, and such events were not good for trade. Similarly, the numerous petty states and autonomous ports throughout the Indies

made difficult the enlargement and extension of trade agreements. The Portuguese had first used this system, but the Dutch and the English soon followed suit.

Upon the heels of this self-assumed police power followed the trade treaty negotiated between the company "factor" or chief representative and a native governor or ruler. Treaty "violation" by the native brought reprisal by the European and the self-righteous extension of local police power. This slowly developed into regional political administration. The companies acquired armies, diplomatic staffs, and a kind of civil service corps having little to do with trade as such. Competition between Dutch, Portuguese, and English resulted in maneuvers on a constantly widening scale. The aims were economic spheres of influence in which each company's monopoly trade agreements would shut out traders of other companies and nationalities. Upon the sea naval squadrons and armed escorts were required to fend off resentful Arab shipping groups, unsympathetic rulers of native coastal states, and the ships of other European nations. In this struggle the Arab traders and many local Indian and Malay states stubbornly tried to maintain some independent privilege, but the Chinese rather rapidly disappeared from Indian Ocean waters and temporarily shifted out of the Indies sea trade. This increasing program ended with European political conquest in each case. The program consumed the whole of the seventeenth century and most of the eighteenth. Such was the unforeseen conclusion to the competitive philosophy of a Europe that had not reconciled its economic and political ideas with the great world its discoverers had found.

THE COLONIAL EMPIRES

The aim of each European country in the East was to corner the best sources of eastern trade products in order to control the European market. In the hands of trading corporations operating at a distance and somewhat out of touch with political issues at home, the end product of a vigorous trade policy inevitably was political and military control over extensive regions. In the latter part of the period it became openly a scramble for colonies with no apology of any kind. A brief statement of the geographical distribution of these colonial acquisitions is appropriate (Fig. 2.2).

Portugal's early influence was spread so widely and so thinly that before her local trading posts had grown into extensive regions England and Holland had seized many of the choice spots. Portugal gradually came

to hold only a few scattered ports more or less under sufferance by the British and Dutch. Today only the token control of Macao and Portuguese Timor demonstrate the former range of the Portuguese. The Dutch East India Company sent out many more ships than did the English concern in the early years of the seventeenth century, so that the Dutch were able to replace the Portuguese and to forcibly exclude the British from the regions nearest the Moluccas, the chief home of the spices.

Gradually the Indies became a Dutch preserve, though many islands were left entirely alone in the earlier period. The

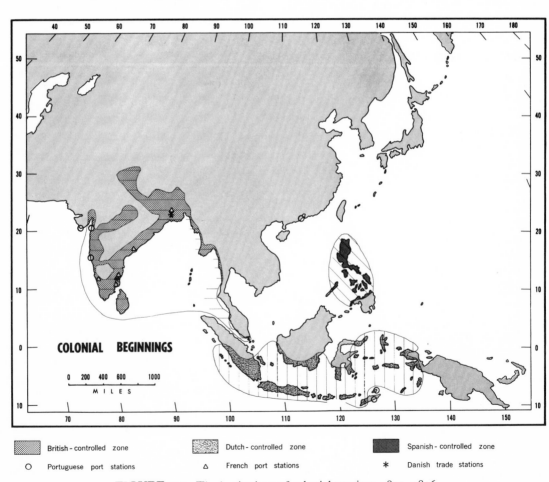

COLONIAL BEGINNINGS

0   200   400   600   1000
M I L E S

▨ British-controlled zone   ▨ Dutch-controlled zone   ▨ Spanish-controlled zone

O Portuguese port stations   △ French port stations   ✳ Danish trade stations

FIGURE 2.2. The beginnings of colonial empires, 1823–1826.

weaker British company concentrated on peninsular India and the trade bases along the northern shore of the Arabian Sea. As the British gathered strength they harried the Dutch, particularly, and gradually seized many ports and regions that the Dutch had taken from the Portuguese. In a last series of military adjustments between the two countries following the Napoleonic Wars in the early nineteenth century, Britain kept all Dutch holdings on the mainland of Asia and retired from the island world. This gave Britain full control of India, Burma, peninsular Malaya and Singapore. In the late nineteenth century a last British charter company picked a vacant space in the Dutch island world without being challenged, and planted a commercial colony that grew into British North Borneo.

France came late into the East not, by government policy, wanting an empire at an early date, only to be beaten off by the British in India, though a scattering of four small French port-territories remained until the 1950's as evidence. Anxious to have some part of a colonial empire, in the late nineteenth century the French moved on eastward to settle on Cochin-China, from which base they gradually worked north along the coast to gain control of what became French Indochina. French efforts also secured a number of islands out in the Pacific beyond the Indies. Denmark, Sweden, and the other countries that had trade interests in the East do not appear in the list of colonial powers because they never were in a position to acquire regional control over territory. The Danes lasted longest, finally selling out their last trading post to the British in the midnineteenth century.

Germany came very late upon the scene as a colony hunter. Little was left but an unoccupied section of New Guinea, and some of the islands marginal to the Indies, plus others in the open Pacific. These became the German share. During World War I they

were taken over by the Japanese and the Australians. Spain, having come early, concentrated upon the Philippines without serious challenge. Although her commercial effects were not great, her cultural effects upon the Philippines were marked. Last of all came the United States, perhaps accidentally, to acquire the only Spanish colonial holdings in the East, the Philippine Islands and a few small islands in the western Pacific. The two accompanying maps present the colonial picture at its beginning (see Fig. 2.2) and at its peak (Fig. 2.3).

By virtue of having few products that interested Europeans and by playing the Europeans off one against the other, Thailand was the only part of southern Asia able to escape the colonial net. China, Korea, and Japan were far enough away from the center of trade attraction to be less molested in the early developments. Each of these countries also was able, through a centralized government of some strength, to control European traders enough to prevent the accretion of European colonies within their boundaries. In South China the Portuguese were tolerated but restricted by being located on a small peninsula at a distance from the great port of Canton. The Portuguese were satisfied to remain there. The early Dutch, British, and Americans chafed at this sort of treatment but made little headway with the reluctant Chinese. The Dutch were similarly tolerated but restricted for a long period to southern Japan.

Only as the Chinese government weakened under a decaying Manchu dynasty did the occidental powers gain strength and succeed in securing concessions of territory and unequal trade privileges. These came in the shape of treaty ports and foreign concessions scattered along the China coast in the latter half of the nineteenth century. By then, however, every occidental country was wary of the other, though Japan was able to enter the picture and seize the Ryukyus, Formosa,

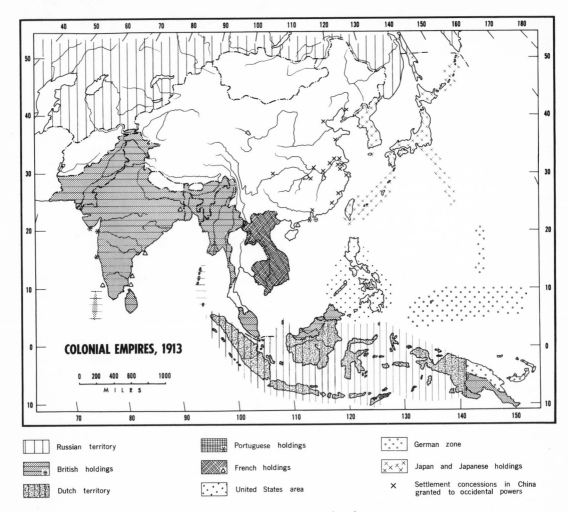

COLONIAL EMPIRES, 1913

0 200 400 600   1000
M I L E S

	Russian territory		Portuguese holdings		German zone
	British holdings		French holdings		Japan and Japanese holdings
	Dutch territory		United States area	×	Settlement concessions in China granted to occidental powers

FIGURE 2.3. Colonial empires in 1913.

and Korea, and then the Kuriles and southern Sakhalin. So-called spheres of influence were effective in limited degree, but the American Open Door Policy helped prevent further, final dismemberment of China. Germany, France, and Japan were at one time or another prevented from carving a political holding out of China proper.

It thus seemed for a time that the colonial dismemberment of the Orient had ended, only to be renewed by the Japanese in 1931 with the grab of Manchuria (Manchukuo), which expanded rapidly into the Japanese

bid to take over the whole of the Orient between 1937–1945. In the heat of the struggle with Japan the "secession" of Outer Mongolia from China and its "annexation" into the sphere of the Soviet Union was quietly achieved in such a way that it hardly resembled a colonial grab. Chinese Sinkiang Province has become a zone of trouble between the Soviet Union and China, as both states place new values on parts of Inner Asia which have never become fully integrated into a modern political state. Colonial acquisition today is of a different pattern than formerly. Alignment of regions and political entities with the Soviet Union may have all the force of colonial acquisition, yet it must be described in other political terms.

TECHNIQUES OF EXPLOITATION

The formation of colonial empires and spheres of influence was accompanied by the shift of political power from the hands of native groups to the hands of occidental governments. In India, Burma, the Indies, Malaya, and the Philippines the process was carried out in such a way that only the end products were noticeable. Indochina was a marginal case more obviously gobbled up. Formosa and Korea were special cases since they were the result of a purely oriental contest. In China, and to some extent in Thailand and Japan, the techniques were applied in piece-meal fashion at a rather late date by various occidental governments. A brief summary of these varied methods will help to explain several features in political geography.

The least political of the techniques was the conscious and systematic breaking of the natural trade monopolies. The regional control over sugar, spices, cotton and its textiles, tea, and silk are the most obvious of these though there were other lesser examples. Sugarcane spread very widely just at the opening of the world discoveries, and no Indian export trade in sugar ever had a chance to develop. Spices were introduced into many other tropical lands, and their natural production was so scattered that the monopoly of the Indies had disappeared long before contemporary synthetic spices had become important. Cotton growing was introduced into several new regions to break the Indian production leadership. Tea was spread to India and the Indies from China. Silk was widely produced in small quantities but many local conditions prevented the easy transfer of production leadership from China

to other regions. Its development in Japan came at a relatively late date.

The Opium War between England and China during 1839–1842 was a means of forcing trade upon China at a time when British economy still had not begun producing sufficient export products to pay for her own purchases in China. The development of the treaty-port system and extraterritoriality was the means of gaining legal entry into a resisting China without a deliberate military conquest. Consequent upon their limited victory in the Opium War, the British exacted the cession of the island of Hong Kong and special economic and political privileges in five Chinese ports in 1842. The United States and France promptly asked for the same privileges, and the treaty-port system had begun. From time to time other nations secured privileges, and more ports were opened at foreign demand. These are shown on the accompanying map (see Fig. 2.3). In such ports many nations held special territorial concessions, each in effect a colonial holding inside China. The system lasted for a century, and the ports involved became the centers of social, political, and economic change in modern China. The special privileges accruing to occidental corporations and individuals came to be used by unscrupulous Chinese to help undermine their own country's economy.

In neither Thailand nor Japan did the Occident succeed in setting up the sequence of events that operated so well in China. Thailand lost territory to the French, but in 1909 bought off the special British privileges with the cession to Britain of the four northern states of the present West Malaysia. Japan was successful in throwing off the early efforts at similar penetration in her own home territory and in Formosa and in Korea.

In countries which became colonial lands the European's ability to control taxes, levy export and import tariffs, rearrange the land systems, and manipulate the growth of the transport systems all operated clearly in the favor of the occidental exploiters. The early practice of giving natives only such schooling as was of value to occidental corporations and the lower ranks of colonial civil service was perpetuated for too long. Other developments in modernization were profitable mostly to the West and were a part of the whole colonial program. The granting of foreign loans, with quite ample interest provisions, to native rulers or to political states too often had exploitive economic concessions tacked on to them. Even in China the existence of treaty-port bases gave outside traders extremely favored positions. The Japanese abused these privileges as much as any occidental country did. The Chinese for a time lost control over their own import and export tariffs but never did lose control over their land system outside the treaty ports.

Another extension of colonial economic privilege was the growing occidental control over the carrying trade after the development of the steamship. Whereas all occidental lands have insisted upon the nationalization of their coastal trade by sea, occidental shipping interests exploited the trade of the Orient to the fullest. Only in Japan was there any real restraint upon this particular development. China's sudden ending of the freedom of her coastal waters and the closing to foreign shipping of most of her former open ports after World War II, made former shipping patterns impossible and aggravated her own economic recovery since she had no commercial fleet of her own.

THE INITIAL IMPRESS OF THE WEST

Has China been improved by her relations with the West and have the Javanese a pleasanter prospect for having had contact with the Dutch for 350 years? Many orientals today would interpret the contacts of the whole period as resulting in distinct retrogression for the Orient. Others would point out that the terms modernization and westernization are not synonymous. Many would assert that the Occident came off much the best in the interchange of culture. A liberal and tolerant observer would recognize that, since the Orient contains at least half the population of the globe, there can be no simple statement of the results of culture contact. Political colonialism and its aftermath throws an unduly large shadow over consideration of the interaction of East and West.

The first impressions created by the West were high-handed and lawless greed occasionally touched by an irrational, cruel sort of kindness which was governed by religious intolerance and backed by superior military strength. One must view these characteristics against the regional and group culture of the period.

In the sixteenth century the lower and middle classes of northern and western Europe still had not taken on a mellow cultural polish. Christendom was highly intolerant of other religions and, while curious about the mores of other peoples, was inclined to be suspicious of them. In southern India Vijayanagar was a wealthier, more highly developed, and more sophisticated state than any in Europe. The Ming emperors ruled a China whose cultural level surpassed anything in Europe for effete sophistication and maturity. But in the Philippines and the outer Indies people were still close to the Stone Age in their tools and equipment, cult magic, political structure, and social organization. Throughout China, mainland Southeast Asia, and India there were refugee elements unable to cope with the higher levels of either East or West. And in Korea and Japan were people becoming obsessed with the notion that the world could be shut out at will.

Repeatedly it has been pointed out that

race and culture contact produces varied results. Racial absorption may involve little culture change. Fusion of people and culture may occur. Race contact, without assimilation, may accompany side-by-side cultural evolution. Non-assimilative race contact may result in a large share of cultural synthesis by the simpler society. This cultural synthesis may include constructive and destructive elements alike. Generally speaking, in the Orient little of the racial extinction occurred that followed the white man about in the Americas. Trade and commerce of a high order were more important than colonization and settlement. Where the Dutch had tried a kind of limited assimilation in the Indies, the British set themselves up as a white super-Brahman caste in India. Cultural evolution side-by-side with effective interchange has taken place between the West and those eastern peoples of high native cultures. Cultural synthesis, partaking of both East and West, has occurred among simpler peoples. Some of the refugee tribesmen of the Chota Nagpur hill country in India have living relatives who have become urban residents and skilled workmen of Jamshedpur's great steel plant. If the West progressed more rapidly during the seventeenth through nineteenth centuries, the East now is rapidly gaining momentum and closing the gap.

THE OPENING WEDGES AND EASTERN REACTIONS

Several factors helped to start the process of change in varying parts of the Orient. Foremost was simple commercial trade, largely of an export nature, between the southern Orient and the Europe so anxious for spices, silks, cottons, and art goods. Those regions having the largest native trade and the most sought-after products received the greatest attention. Trading stations and permanent settlements became exhibitions of culture

and "county fairs" in many a port throughout the Orient. Early in the process the zealous Christian missionary appeared (Roman Catholic in the early period) and often interceded between the poor heathen and the avid trader. To put it bluntly, the economic advantages of becoming Christian soon became apparent to many orientals. The mission program, however, worked in ever-widening circles to originate an endless cultural chain reaction. The use of native personnel in police corps, clerical staffs, ships' crews, shops, and processing stations very early became a potent agent in teaching occidental techniques. The formation, by the European industrial revolution itself, of a whole new series of techniques, tools, equipment, and products produced reactions in many parts of the East.

Although no complete summary can be made, patterns of oriental reaction can be suggested. The widespread Arab trader class, with home ports around the Arabian Sea from the south Indian coast to Zanzibar on the African coast, usually made war on the interloping European traders. A period of sea fighting eliminated them as a serious threat to European commercial trade. The more general Indian coastal and Indies attitude was one of willingness to trade upon reasonable terms. Commerce was accompanied, however, by constant fighting over disagreements and unequal codes of conduct, by piracy and by looting on both sides. In the Indies the lack of unified political and social control by any group over the thousands of islands was conducive to a great variety of conditions. In the more developed areas trade interests largely controlled reactions; simpler societies reacted negatively and submissively as to a dominant force. Organized Indian states, themselves involved in a complicated game of power politics for the control of India, reacted variably. Sometimes they met the Occident openly and on even terms, but more frequently intrigue and counter-intrigue on all sides took the willing Europeans deeper and deeper into Indian political problems.

The Chinese met the Europeans with a tolerant disinterest, but with considerable control over events and the field of play. This resulted in a restriction of the exhibition and display of occidental culture to the Chinese, which made China slow to appreciate the dynamic power of the West. The very looseness of the bonds of Chinese culture lessened the impact of early western penetration so that it seemed that China did not change at all in the early periods of contact. In Japan conditions were almost opposite to those both in China and in India. A very tight set of cultural bonds was strongly reinforced by tightening political control. The first contacts with the West forcefully impressed a few very influential Japanese. On the decision of a few leaders Japan closed her doors to East and West alike. Somewhat similar was the reaction of Korea which was almost as effective in delaying the process of modernization.

All this variety of reaction established very different patterns of contact between East and West, and set up interactions operating at very different rates. In a number of instances the original reaction patterns were radically altered by later events to completely redirect the whole sequence of culture growth.

THE EXPANSION OF NATIVE ECONOMY

Between 1500 and 1800 the Occident stimulated the growth of a large volume of export trade in the special products of the East. Trade had flourished for centuries, but its volume was slight compared to that which began when the Europeans brought in new wealth and increasing numbers of ships. Every country except Korea and Japan was affected to some degree. As an added factor for China, by 1750 emigrants to the South Seas had again started a flow of cash remittances to South China.

Wealth from an increasing export trade reacted upon agriculture and the handicrafts since many of the products were agricultural in origin. Increases in agricultural productivity began to stimulate population growth. Such increases were quite uneven in different regions; areas suffering internal political strife, for example, failed to increase markedly until stability returned. Zones of lesser trade showed little early reaction. Perhaps the southeastern coast of India and the southeastern provinces of China were the first to show such increases.

A part of increasing agriculture involved new American crop plants which gave new range and depth to land use in almost every region. Some new plants became commercial products; others became basic foods of local regions. The sweet potato, maize, the peanut, white potato, pineapple, tobacco, and the tomato were among the earlier crops. The export demand for farm products has never slackened, though the crop and regional focus has repeatedly shifted. More recently other new plants have come into the Orient, or into new regions. Tea from China into India and the Indies, coffee, cacao, cinchona, several oil seeds, rubber, sisal, and the oil palm have all been added. New trade has arisen in old oriental crops such as tung oil, soybeans, abaca, jute, and ramie, along with a host of minor products. Current hybridizing programs continue the basic process.

Occidental industrial maturity, the completion of the Suez Canal in 1869, and the evolution of the steamship led to the introduction of other new products. In the realm of handicrafts the Orient had been dominant, but the power machine gave the advantage to the Occident. Gradually the Occident began to ship goods instead of cash to pay for its purchases in the East. Machine-made goods were attractive, and most of the Orient could afford to buy. During the late nineteenth century oriental imports grew by leaps and bounds.

Acquaintance with new products of all kinds brought a changing consumer demand to the Orient. This went hand in hand with learning to produce new crops. The stimulation of greater trade, agricultural production, changing consumer habits, and population growth were all instrumental in the modernization of both the Orient and the Occident.

THE CHRISTIAN MISSIONARY

To the Christian missionary there is almost no unknown land anywhere in the Orient. Both men and women missionaries have been almost everywhere. Their primary business has been to preach the Christian gospel, but no aspect of culture has remained outside their concern. Many missionary schools and hospitals were started to secure students and patients to whom to preach. Some of the results were generations of educated people and thousands of doctors, nurses, clinics, and improvements in public health. The missionary architect, often working with strange materials and unfamiliar craftsmen, has devised and created styles of building that have been copied far and wide. Hundreds of newspapers, journals, and local publishers stand in debt to the missionary evangelists who, in order to get their literature printed in odd languages, have done everything from devising new forms of writing to making type and teaching the craft of printing. Many a missionary has restored vanishing regional art motifs and handicraft skills through simple sewing guilds and workshops, and many a modern business family got its start on a loan from a missionary. The missionary often began by bringing from abroad seeds for his private garden and went on to motivate much of the work in improved plant breeding for the people of his region.

The Christian Church has made numerous assaults upon Asia, but the pre-Columbian programs of the Nestorians in North China and the "St. Thomas Christians" on the Malabar Coast of Peninsular India had only localized effects. With the early post-Columbian discoverers and traders went Catholic priests who had been restricted in program by the occidental culture of their period. The modern world-wide missionary movement began in the nineteenth century, and today it includes every form of Catholic and Protestant religion. In its modern program the Christian Church has confused many an oriental by its profusion of sects and contradiction of creeds, a condition made worse by the failure of occidental businessmen to follow a Christian code of life.

There can be no question that the modern mission program has succeeded in planting Christianity firmly in most of the Orient. There is almost no Christian program in Tibet-Nepal-Bhutan, some parts of Southeast Asia have not been touched, and Communist governments have restricted evangelical effort. Many individual mission stations seem only to hold their own in numbers of religious followers, while engaging in fruitful education and social welfare. Nevertheless, Christianity as such is growing. Since 1920 there has been rapid growth in native churches which indicates that the Christian religion is now partially self-perpetuating. Christendom continues to be an agent of cultural change.

It is worth noting that the Christian missionary program, on the whole, has succeeded better among animist groups than among those with well-developed religions. Few Moslems have been converted to Christianity. It often is said that orientals adopted Christianity when economic profit would be a result, but this is only a partial truth. Hindus of lower caste, socially underprivileged, have become Christians for more than economic profit motives. Obtaining an answer to why the Christian program has not succeeded as completely as the earlier spread of the Islamic religion would require an analysis of comparative cultural positions of the Orient at the advent of both religious systems and is beyond the scope of this volume.

THE GROWTH OF MODERN MECHANICS

Many an American has deplored the inability of an oriental peasant to use a wrench properly on a motor without pausing to reflect upon the situation. Many American youngsters grow up with tools and become familiar with the workability and fine tolerances of metals. Yet the American marvels at what the oriental can do with tools to which he is accustomed. There are orientals who are fully at home in engineering mechanics, but the number forms only a small fraction of the population. The automobile, for example, has been created wholly within the life span of men now living, and one cannot expect half the world's people to know just how to adjust a fuel pump when the total automobiles at their disposal at any one time number under 2,000,000 vehicles. In the United States there now are over 60,000,000 vehicles, and even Americans often do not dare to tamper with their own car engines.

Most of today's mechanical equipment is the creation of the Occident. Most of it is expensive, and only a modicum has reached the Orient, but the diversity of that equipment is great. Native mechanical skills are growing steadily. The changing equipment of transport, the world of print, and the technical manual are reaching into new regions. The growth of power facilities is slow still, but it is widely distributed. Industrialization is spreading in varied forms, and that India had the largest steel plant in the British Empire was no accident. Since the Orient started late it well may skip many of the early stages of industrialization which occidental countries went through.

The Orient for a long time lacked capital with which to launch needed enterprises. Slowly capital resources are accumulating, and the ending of occidental exploitation sped that accumulation. The slow growth of technical education remains one of the chief bars to the fuller modernization of the Orient. One cannot predict that peoples quite unfamiliar with modern mechanics will industrialize overnight. Nor can one predict that Chinese or Malays never will become mechanically adept.

THE WEAKENING OF TRADITIONAL CULTURE

When an oriental student learns English in school or becomes a Christian there is an irreparable damage committed to a native body of culture. Perhaps a greater good will result from the switch in language or religion, but the fact is that such shifts in culture traits throughout the Orient have seriously undermined a great many native cultures. There once came to the senior author's room in the inn of a little village in southwestern China an old man who alternately quoted Shakespeare and Li Po for a good share of an evening. He was a son of a landed family and by preference served as his native village schoolteacher despite a passably good education. He had turned his back upon the mechanical West but had retained some of its choicest flavor. Such admirable combinations of culture are not numerous. A language and its literature of oral folk tales or written classics is a significant share of a culture. The sloughing off of culture traits often follows rapidly upon loss of a religion by an individual, a village, or a region.

Throughout the Orient the advent of machine-made goods exacted a terrible toll from native handicrafts. In textiles, iron and steel, paper, inks and dyes particularly, machine-made goods have driven out traditional materials, techniques, forms, and patterns. The introduction of celluloid and plastics has played havoc with brass, copper, leather, and lacquer work. The toll among the handicrafts is twofold. Not only have machine-made goods mutilated the materials and forms of native products but they have destroyed the livelihood of the millions who produced them. Handicraft production often was only a part-time occupation, but its decline left the scattered rural population without adequate means of support.

Close upon machine-made goods the first factories came into the port cities. They came for the cheap labor which could be easily taught the skills of machine tending. Without thought for labor conditions, human welfare, or culture conflict, factories were operated under conditions that were worse than in any occidental industrial city. Only since 1920 has this begun to change for the better.

Almost everywhere in the Orient the village was the basic operating unit of society. Stimulated agriculture, new machine-made consumer's goods, the decline of handicrafts, the visiting missionary, governmental orders concerning schools, taxes, and labor contributions tended to undermine the control of the village over its culture. With the weakening of village authority went a decline of general civil authority, perhaps to be replaced by an alien police corps.

The growth of the factory, foreign trade, and new means of communication undermined many of the older upper classes and set up new ones. The rise of the Chinese compradore class, equivalent to the American commission broker, was an essential part of trade between Chinese and non-Chinese-speaking occidentals. Much of the wealth of this new class came from joining Europeans in the exploitation of China. The shifting emphasis in education replaced the time-honored scholars with people slightly learned in an alien culture and often quite ignorant of their own native culture. The established operators of government frequently were quite "at sea" when faced with new technical

requirements for administration. Over the course of a couple of centuries a considerable economic and social upheaval has occurred in almost every country.

This is but a partial survey of some of the disturbing changes that have accompanied modernization. The weakening of traditional culture is as much a part of modernization as the acceptance of brand new culture traits. It is consideration of some of these unfortunate results that has caused many orientals to question the ultimate values of the mechanical West.

ACCEPTANCE OF THE MODERN WORLD

The Indian Hindu often has been characterized as a negative, submissive mystic who clings persistently to his own creed and culture. If this is true, how do new traits ever spread among Hindu people? Cautious and careful experimentation with new traits, and zealous guarding of the old, is a universal attribute of human societies. But no human society has permanently refused acceptance of new culture traits when the advantages were clear. Too frequently the occidental has characterized the oriental as "unchanging." One cannot seriously hold the idea that the Orient has fundamentally rejected such a device as the railroad, for the individual objections have been little greater than those among our own parents. The occidental must understand that the Orient did object to accepting the railroad as a device for speeding his own transport at the unreasonable financial profit of the occidental stockholder, builder, and supplier of materiel. One must be sympathetic to the wish of the holders of an ancient culture to retain such of that culture as they choose. No occidental country is lacking in those who protest the passing of "the good old days." In effect, then, the Orient has objected less to new culture traits as such than to the terms of acceptance which they found forced upon them. No group, from the Andaman Island Negrito to the Chinese, has differed greatly in this regard.

Many people in the Orient have wished for, and worked for, too full and too rapid an acceptance of the modern world. The machinery of occidental international trade and industry is more difficult to operate than that of a confederation of self-sufficient village economies. The Occident has expected a greater fee for its cultural tutelage than the Orient has wanted to pay, and this expectation has resulted in complex struggles toward independence. Too many orientals have taken up the notion that when a small fraction of a population has learned to use an occidental language, give a political harangue, use a cigarette holder or a telephone, and wear occidental clothing styles their society readily can take its full position in the modern world.

Within each oriental country there have been slow-changing, conservative, and insurgent radical elements. Often their differences have concerned the degree of acceptance of some part of modern occidental culture. There are Chinese and Indians more pronounced in their exhibition of British culture than most Englishmen, Filipinos who out-do the American, and those who will have none of the foreign world. The great mass of the population in every society seeks for the retention of the most useful and precious elements in its own culture, to be combined with similar elements of occidental culture. No one who has been in any part of the Orient has failed to see both amusing and harmless, or sad and tragic, anomalies. There is a common search for that combination which will permit retention of the oriental spirit. Not every country has made equal progress in blending unlike cultures, and no two countries have reached a similar point in the integration process. Some of those which have moved most rapidly in the past now have much to do over.

HISTORICAL AND REGIONAL VARIATIONS

No two countries of the Orient have reacted alike in the face of occidental expansion (Fig. 2.4). Some of the earlier reactions to the coming of the European were mentioned above. The British introduced many features of modernization into Peninsular India well ahead of Indian request and made efforts to prune back some of the pernicious growths that had appeared in culture patterns. English has become the one common language among the mixed ethnic stocks, and many forms of the modern culture complex are fashioned upon British models.

The weight of culture history, however, has lain heavily upon the whole of the Indian subcontinent. Although the British had come closer to uniting the whole of the Indian Empire than had any other rulers in over two thousand years, they could not keep the region united as the varied pressures for independence became strong at the close of World War II. Repeated clashes between Hindus and Moslems in the north precipitated the partition of the mainland sector into the two states of Pakistan and the Union of India in 1947. In 1948 Ceylon achieved its independence without militant action. Since the basis of partition in the north lay in dominant territorial occupance by Hindus or Moslems, Pakistan became a divided state with units on both northern flanks of India, a thousand miles apart. Pakistan is an avowed Islamic political state whereas India is, in effect, a Hindu political state, although Moslems elected to remain in India and Hindus in Pakistan. Civil unrest, religiously motivated riots, and massacres followed independence, accompanied by massive migrations of people into the state of their choice, based largely on religious grounds. The northernmost sector, Kashmir, became a zone of militant contention on historic

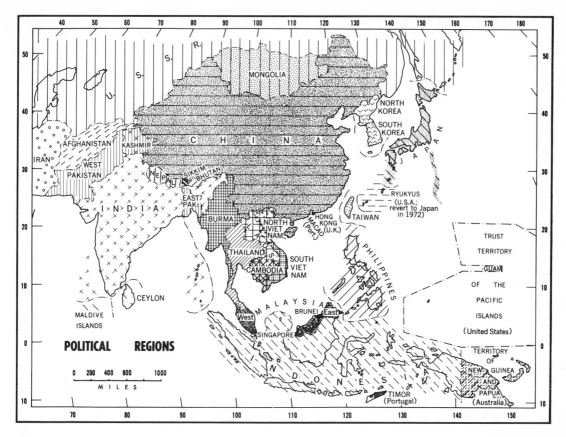

FIGURE 2.4. Political regions of the Orient, 1970. Each political unit is shown in a different symbol.

grounds, claimed by both India and Pakistan. The Kashmir dispute has not been resolved, each state controls a portion of the region, and each accuses the other of political treachery. In all three states, Pakistan, India, and Ceylon, religious, communal, ethnic, and linguistic factors continue to be sources of continued unrest. In the case of Pakistan the regional variance between two unlike portions provokes continued instability.

Burma was a relatively quiet colonial holding, showing slow growth of modernisms, until the explosive developments of World War II. Burma thus achieved colonial independence in 1948, far sooner than might have been expected. In Thailand the process of change never was conditioned by colonial status. This had its assets but also its drawbacks for, if an Asian country kept its political freedom, its technical training and long-range economic investment were not very great. Indochina suffered at the hands of chronic French maladministration, and in some respects was the least able of the lands of the southern Orient to manage its own affairs with satisfaction to all its varied peoples. Here most of the drawbacks of colonial status are to be found, with few of the long-range progressive advancements. The military contest between the French and the Communists was the result of this backward state of affairs. The subdivision of the former French colony of Indochina into the four states of Cambodia, Laos, North Vietnam, and South Vietnam reflects both political nationalism and processes of revolutionary change in political structuring. The current struggle between two political systems, Republican Democracy and Communism, is only a phase in the politico-economic restructuring of this portion of the Orient. The participation in the process by outside powers representing different political ideologies, the United States versus Soviet Union and China, complicates the issue but does not alter the basic problem. Malaysia, with a mixed ethnic structure and a history of resting political power in the hands of Malays, has yet to solve the basic problem of balancing political, economic, and social power within the framework of a single political state.

The Indies present one of the most complex problems. The steady development of Java stands in sharp relief against the retention of tribal culture and economy in New Guinea. In the island landscapes of the Indies processes of modernization can be found in every stage. The problems of structuring a modern political state, combined with the problems of developing a modern economic structure that is stable in nature in the face of such enormous cultural variations, remain to be worked out. The Philippines possesses an equal degree of contrast. The United States program to educate the Filipinos to political freedom in the shortest possible time differed from the Dutch program. There are many indications that Philippine political maturity was declared overly soon for some elements in the population, far ahead of the country's general economic and social maturity.

For a long time China was the prime example of the "unchanging East." Having barely escaped political colonialism in the full sense, she experienced the imposition of a system of unequal treaties that facilitated major economic exploitation by the outside world, including Japan. Restricted in form

and scope in the earlier period, the process of change has been in full swing in the last half century. The very size of China in population and territory and the strength of traditional culture have required time for the deep penetration of many cultural elements. The Chinese are a pragmatic people, given to full discussions of new proposals, and they will not be rushed. There is great occidental impatience at continued Chinese social and political instability. On the other hand, the Chinese will to accept most of the material equipment of the Occident is well beyond their own speed in learning to use the new machines and gadgets. The process of the modernization of China will take a long period still, but once completed it will be among the most successful of any oriental country. What seems to the non-Communist world a revolutionary shift in political systems is in reality less marked than it seems on the surface: but it remains clear that holders of power in China have not yet developed the political system, the administrative machinery, or the bureaucracy to alter the whole of the Chinese system at the rate required by the pressure-of-population demand. Within the pattern of historical tradition, China will yet spend a period in what has been called the "dynastic interregnum."

Korea has not had a fair chance at the modern world. Awakened out of a long hermitage, she was made the economic slave of Japan with every possible restriction upon the progress of her people. Material development of Korea, in Japanese hands, was remarkable, but it was entirely exploitive. Moving against this exploitation is the education and training of a significant number of Koreans outside their own country in the last generation. The arbitrary division of Korea into two parts at the end of World War II may be a short or a long tragedy.

Japan offers a quite different case history. Japan has been opened and closed at the will of a few leaders since the very first contacts were established with China in the second century A.D. She is unique in the tightness of the bonds held around her by her rulers. When a few Japanese decided to end the period of hermitage in the 1860's she had been affected less by the Occident than any other Asian country except possibly Korea. The concentration of energy applied to adopting the material equipment of the Occident could never have been achieved in any other oriental country. The speed of change and development in mechanical, industrial, and economic terms was greater than that of any other country. But also the controlled preservation of Japanese social and spiritual culture was greater. At the end of World War II, therefore, the sum total of Japanese cultural change had been less than it appeared on the surface. It remains an open question of how much true social and spiritual change can be induced. American success in the Philippines was not complete, but it was coupled with an atmosphere of hope and impatient expectancy which was not clouded by the ghost of crushing military defeat. Japan has done amazingly well with the revolution of industrial technology, but there remain the problems of social, political, and agricultural readjustment to the modern world.

It is impossible to generalize accurately, but what has been called the "equation of development" is rather interesting. In A.D. 1300, in respect to technical, economic, and social standing, the East and the West were roughly equal. In 1850, the East, in most respects, stood about where the West had stood in 1750, by then a full century behind. In 1935, the East, very roughly in many respects, had reached a point the West had reached about 1890, having recovered a half of the earlier separation.

It remains an open question what period will elapse before the East and the West are again equal. In 1970 it is almost impossible to express a single generalization about the position of the East, as against the West, for new kinds of problems have arisen in both hemispheres, but it may well be that there are overlapping levels of development, and areas of development in which each "world" leads or lags.

3

RELIGION, LAW, AND THE SOCIAL ORDERS

RELIGION AS A FORCE IN CULTURE

The occidental often feels that the Orient is motivated by deeply mystical religions that not only shape the culture of the several countries but emanate eerie vibrations that color the landscape and affect the very atmosphere. This "mystique" is, of course, the exact aim of the authors of fiction thrillers, the producers of oriental movie intrigues, and the promoters of so-called "oriental music." At the same time, however, the Occident does not often openly admit the strength of religion as an operating force in shaping its own cultures. Many of the great religions reflect an earlier common body of culture. Each religion has in it ideas, rituals, and symbols that are drawn from or motivated by the landscape of its home environment. In so far as these tangible attributes vary and seem strange to a foreigner, the whole religion appears alien. Each religion, in its own realm, is a force making for the perpetuation of a particular culture. There can be no question that certain religions exert greater influence upon a culture than others, and that in a particular region one creed will make headway at the expense of another with consequent changes in culture.

Throughout the whole of southern and eastern Asia one must reckon with primitive tribal animism as a reservoir of ritual, symbol, and practice which, over the centuries, has fed a great deal of material into the organized religions of every eastern country. In some cases this material today is reflected only in limited ways, having been thoroughly digested and transformed during its absorption, but in other cases the symbolism and ritual are little modified from the animistic prototype. Similarly, there are peoples that variably can be labeled tribal animists, pagans, or heathen, who have not taken up any of the organized religions. The animistic regions, and their peoples, have been decreasing steadily over the centuries, but they are not yet fully absorbed.

One must reckon also with the unaccountable missionary urge which is one of the very significant causes of cultural change. A missionary drive is not a part of every religion, nor is it a permanent characteristic. Other geographic aspects of religion are tied up with architecture, art, and sculpture. Significant to agriculture is the presence and variety of tabus against the use of particular foods, and rules related to cropping practices. The accompanying map presents a simple story of the distribution of religions in the Orient, in which there is emphasis upon daily practice rather than upon classification of theologies (Fig. 3.1).

THE RELIGIONS OF THE EAST

Hinduism

Of the major religions of the East, Hinduism is the oldest and, in many respects, the strongest of all. Its origins go back to a cultural memory housed outside India, and its earliest documentary texts related the invasions of northwest India and the settling down among a primitive people. Much of its added symbolism and ritual lies deep in the pool of primitive animism that belongs to the Dravidian peoples and their cultures. Hinduism always has been an amorphous religion, without finite creed or theology, tremendously absorptive in character, with unlimited numbers of deities and with infinite variety of permissible worship. Its absorptiveness has allowed the conversion of many alien peoples who have thereby been taken

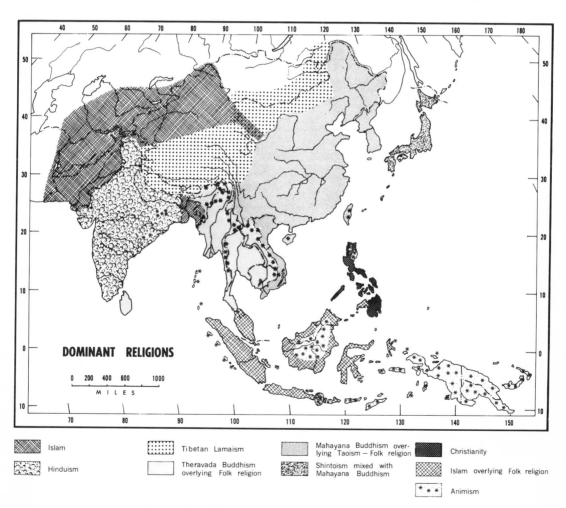

DOMINANT RELIGIONS

0 200 400 600   1000
M I L E S

Islam

Hinduism

Tibetan Lamaism

Theravada Buddhism overlying Folk religion

Mahayana Buddhism overlying Taoism – Folk religion

Shintoism mixed with Mahayana Buddhism

Christianity

Islam overlying Folk religion

Animism

FIGURE 3.1. Dominant religions.

completely into the Indian cultural realm. Hinduism is a hard religion against which to organize revolt; having no finite creed, it has time and again absorbed and enveloped its dissenters. In this way its textual body has increased through the centuries, until it has become more and more restrictive to the individual's freedom and society's flexibility.

The increasing bonds of the caste system of India are an emphatic example of the one-way road down which India has traveled for over 4,000 years, until the accumulated cultural weight of Hinduism in modern Indian life is almost more than society can bear. Similarly the evolution of the sacred status of the cow is a costly item to modern India. Earliest Hinduism had no such tabu on the use of meat, whereas the preservation of the 200,000,000 animals of modern India condemns millions of Indians to permanent malnutrition. The architecture of Hinduism is bewilderingly complex and varied, and a significant factor in almost any south Indian landscape. Both regional and historical changes have taken place in the form and decoration of Indian temples, shrines, and symbolic monuments to give them multiple variety in a crowded landscape.

In everyday terms Hinduism is a polytheistic religion which believes in the transmigration of souls throughout a universe immense both spatially and in time duration. The religion is a way of life, marked by passive and ascetic response to fate. Hinduism sanctions inherited social stratification and class structure, producing the caste system, and it accepts political and economic decision making by the higher classes. Every meal is a religious rite in which the higher the caste the more strictly vegetarian is the dietary. The prohibition upon the taking of any animal life increases from the lower to the higher castes. Pilgrimages, elaborate festivals, and complicated religious rites are characteristic. Although the modern urban Hindu neglects many of the injunctions of the religion, he may privately do penance for his public disregard.

Buddhism

Buddhism appeared in India in the sixth century B.C. as a protest against the accumulated evils of Hinduism, and it was the most successful of a series of early protests that were made over the centuries. Theologically it protested the growing materialism of Hindu creeds, and socially and economically it protested the shackles of caste and dominance by the Brahmans. But rather than take a course of positive action as a modern American might suggest, Buddhism chose the nonviolent route of ascetic withdrawal from the world into a realm of contemplation, prayer, and passiveness. Its emphasis upon peace, kindliness, and personal generosity gave it an appeal which spread it wide over India, and gave it favor which lifted it to the status of a state religion. A missionary drive then spread it over all southern and eastern Asia, though not without sectarian factionalisms. If its protest within India achieved no truly permanent good, Tibet, Mongolia, China, Korea, Japan, Ceylon, Burma, Laos, Thailand, and Cambodia owe a good share of their religious beliefs to Indian Buddhism. In most of the areas converted to Buddhism many of the original tabus, such as the taboo against taking animal life, have rested rather lightly and gradual growth of Buddhism in each country has produced special variations of the Buddhist faith. In the various countries architecture has taken as varied paths as theology, and in some the architectural heritage is today more noticeable than the social or philosophic one (see the first two photos, pp. 269-270, in the public buildings cluster).

Buddhism, historically, is divided into two primary sectarian divisions, Theravada and Mahayana, but there are today many overlapping sectarian groupings both in and outside the Orient, and many interpretations of

Buddhist theology. Theravada Buddhism, practiced in Ceylon, Burma, Thailand, Laos, and Cambodia, holds that each person must work out his own salvation, perform his own religious acts and, as a layman, go as far as he can on his own personal road to Nirvana, whereas Mahayana Buddhism, chiefly practiced in South Vietnam, North Vietnam, China, Korea, and Japan, holds that merit is available from superhuman sources and that followers may call for aid from any of the great Buddhas. In practice this has meant that many Theravadins spend short to long periods as monks and nuns, gaining personal understanding and merit, but then return to their normal callings, whereas Mahayanists do not don the robe but perform acts of contemplative worship while seeking merit from holy sources. Buddhism, of some sort, has spread widely over the earth in the last two centuries, is undergoing revival, and is today a worldwide religion.

Taoism

It is often said that the Chinese are not a religious people. Clearly they are a more pragmatic people than the Indians, but they have taken their religion no more lightly than the Americans, to whom their religions are quite similar in many ways. Confucius and his followers, in the sixth century B.C., were formulating a moral and ethical code, while Laotzu and his adherents were developing a spiritual philosophy known as Taoism, which promised immortality to those who accepted its complicated formula of "doing everything by doing nothing" and followed the mystic Tao or "Way." As Taoism evolved it borrowed heavily from Chinese Buddhism, and the two similar creeds satisfied many of those Chinese who had learnings toward spiritual and mystical things. A loose organization and a nonmilitant spirit kept Taoism within the bounds of China except as Korean and Japanese student visitors observed and reacted to it.

Certain features of Chinese life, such as ancestor worship and the moral code of the family system, were older and stronger than any one religious faith and became a common part of each Chinese religious pattern. A slow decline of both Buddhism and Taoism in the modern era left the Chinese without a strong native religion to help them face the modern world. But Chinese culture has not been weighted down with the accumulated burden of outworn religious institutions. In part this owes to the practical realism of the Chinese and in part to the vigilant and never-ending opposition of the Confucian bureaucracy to the too great expansion of any religious movement which might constitute a danger to the state. The visible architectural and sculptural expressions of Taoism are easy to confuse with those of Chinese Buddhism from which it borrowed physically as well as theologically. Under the force of modern social and political revolution in China, Taoism is not now an organized religion in any true sense. It long has depended upon personal faith and contributive action, in which the folk element has been strongly pervasive. Although the Chinese often have been labeled Taoist or Confucianist in religion, it seems more accurate to say that the Chinese have perpetuated a folk religion onto which they have placed various ritual practices taken from many formal creeds. Communist ideology in China today may root out the formal practice of any religious creed, but the folk religious beliefs will probably persist, as they have for so long.

Islam

The most militant of Southwest Asian religions has been Islam which came into India demanding alternatives of conquest, conversion, and taxation, or death by the sword. Without waiting for full assimilation of India, a missionary drive carried Islam on through Sumatra–Malaya and deep into the Indies, where it played out in Mindanao, Borneo, and Java. From Persia and Trans-Caspia it spread through central Asia into northwest China and has deeply infiltrated western China as far south as the Burma border. Such forced conversion often was superficial and resulted in the perpetuation of older folk religion. The only significant food tabus of the Islamic faith are bans on the use of pork and alcohol, both of which rest lightly upon much of Malaysia and Indonesia.

With Islam came the mosque and all of Arabic-Persian architecture which altered the urban landscape of northern India and changed monumental building in many parts of southeastern Asia (see the fourth and fifth photos, pp. 271–272, in the public buildings cluster).

Where the Buddhist faith sought its ends in quiet contemplation away from the world, the Islamic faith worked with political tools, with the strident emotional appeal in the marketplace, and with the sword. In time, therefore, the superficial acceptance of the Islamic faith often has become a full and ardent thing, with the result that wherever the Islamic faith is practiced today, latent political turbulence is found in which Moslems never have refrained from militant action when it seemed to promise results.

Christianity

Christianity and imperialism went hand in hand throughout the East. It probably was good fortune that imperialism was tempered by Christian contact for it certainly was not consciously arranged. Modern Christianity is a somewhat practical faith that never can let spiritual considerations blind all its advocates to the values of material improvement. Hence the evangelist preaching salvation has been accompanied by the medical missionary, the agricultural experimenter, the trade school man, and the teacher dealing in democracy, athletics, and the alphabet. If at times these things have boomeranged, the evolution of a new political system and an independent economy was implicit in the

whole process of contact of the Occident with the Orient. The oriental sometimes feels that the missionary was the only check upon an exploitation by occidental imperialism that would have led to complete prostration of oriental society.

There are almost as many kinds of Christians as Hindus, but normally the Christian native is an individual more literate and better prepared to face the modern world than the average non-Christian member of any oriental culture. In any event the Christian missionary has ranged more widely than the missionary of any other faith, and has touched every culture in every country of the Orient. There is some competition between Catholic and Protestant, and among Protestants themselves. Christian architecture is more difficult to isolate from occidental architecture at large, and religious building by the missionaries often has adopted older regional motifs. In India one can hardly hold up the stuffy Victorian style as the result of Christianity, though in China perhaps one can point to "modern Chinese" as at least partly owing its inspiration to the builders of schools and colleges who sought to fit their structures into the Chinese scene. One country in the Orient, the Philippines, is predominantly a Christian land, a result of the long and diligent, if strangling, efforts of the Catholic priesthood during over three hundred years of Spanish rule.

Sikhism

The Sikh religion arose on the turbulent fringes of an earlier era of Moslem-Hindu conflict. In the last century and a half it prospered greatly under conditions of peace and friendly tolerance guaranteed by British rule in India. With Buddhism, Sikhism stands as the second successful revolt against the Hindu religion. Socially a protest against the multiple corruptions of Hinduism, the theology of Sikhism has been at pains to distinguish itself from its older sources.

Many orthodox Hindus refuse to separate it from their own multiple faith, and there is mutual tolerance between Hindu and Sikh that is entirely missing between Sikh and Moslem.

More noticeable than its theology or its architecture has been the personal costume of those Sikhs who became members of a militant order developed to protect the faith against persecution in the open and mixed settlements of India's Punjab. The new order gave every male adherent the new, common surname Singh, a turban, long hair, a full beard, and other minor distinguishing features. The rest of the Sikh community cannot be distinguished from the lower ranks of the Hindu rural farming population from which most of the converts to Sikhism have come. From the knightly order of the Rajputs, however, has come a virile leadership that has kept Sikhism an active faith. It had its center in the Punjab, a region now split by the boundary between West Pakistan and India, but the Sikhs today are well spread over northern India. Since 1900 Sikhism has been the most rapidly expanding religious faith in India, surmounting even Christianity and losing very few adherents to the latter religion. Persecution during the continuing struggles over Indian separatism went hard with the Sikh community.

The Minor Creeds

Significant among the smaller religious orders of the East is the Zoroastrian faith of the Indian Parsees. Originally a Persian development, most of the adherents migrated to India in the early eighth century A.D. to escape persecution by Moslems. The Parsees settled along the west coast of India between Bombay and Surat, and became quiet farmers and herdsmen. With a hereditary priesthood and a number of distinctive beliefs, such as the "Towers of Silence" upon which the dead are exposed to the elements, the faith has been a clannish and closed group, seeking no converts from other faiths. Its total community today numbers about 125,000 people, scattered among the cities of India as a wealthy merchant class whose economic power in modern India far exceeds its religious impact upon the life of India. This position was achieved only with the rise of modern trade and the growth of Bombay and Surat as trade centers.

Jainism was a contemporary of Buddhism in protest against Hinduism, but its extreme asceticism long limited its growth. Without developing a missionary push, it formulated a simplified theology which had vitality and durability against the absorptiveness of Hinduism. It remained an Indian religion only, widely distributed over the country, but did not die out as did Buddhism. Today its 1,500,000 adherents are mainly located in northern Bombay and Rajputana. Many orthodox Hindus consider the Jains only a separate caste of the Hindu community today.

The Lingayats arose out of a twelfth-century protest against Hinduism in southern India, and, though they have maintained themselves as a separate group today numbering about 1,500,000 people, they are slowly becoming submerged again in the sea of Hinduism. In this they are but representative of other less successful protests which have already been fully reabsorbed into the parent faith, except for a current caste distinction.

Tibetan Lamaism is perhaps the most spectacular offshoot of the missionary drive of Buddhism. In the seventh century A.D. Buddhism was grafted onto a complex Tibetan shamanism having many highly developed cults whose operations bordered upon near magic. Several factional struggles have involved temporal as well as religious domination. The sects dominating for some centuries have been committed to priestly celibacy, unlike earlier sects, resulting in an almost universal Tibetan custom by which a family seeks to place at least one son in a monastery. This has operated to maintain a large parasitic class and undoubtedly to prevent population increases of spectacular proportions. In many parts of Tibet the only permanent settlements are lamaseries. By holding temporal power the leaders of Tibetan Lamaism have been able to restrain occidental missionary inroads into their fold more effectively than has any other oriental religion. Few alien visitors of any kind have been permitted in Tibet, but many followers of the faith succeed in making a pilgrimage to the religious capital, Lhasa, in southern Tibet. Chinese Communist control of Tibet, since 1952, has attempted reduction of the monastic system and religious rule, causing considerable social upheaval and political change.

The Shinto religion of Japan is the modern representative of early tribal animism heavily interwoven with ancestor and emperor worship from China and given theologic body by adoption of Chinese Buddhist doctrines. Shinto often is said not to be a religion at all, but a code of ethics and points of view as is Confucianism, but it contains more religious content than does Confucianism. During more recent centuries many of the native myths and items of nature worship have been eliminated, but Shintoism is still primarily a simple nature worship, with innumerable *kami* or "gods," surrounded by many fanatical concepts. Most such concepts promoted nationalism, in opposition to the long influence of external Chinese culture, and championed the divine status of the emperor. As such, Shintoism played into the hands of modern expansionist industrial and military clans seeking justification for their programs of aggressive nationalism.

Confucianism often is termed a religion whereas it more properly is a political-ethical state philosophy. It could better be compared with Democracy and Communism than with Christianity and Buddhism. Of course, all developed religions contain points of view regarding the state, and economic and social affairs, and such political cults as Confucianism, Democracy, and Communism contain patterns of ethics and an emotional aspect which borders on the theologic. The pragmatic Chinese often have been somewhat agnostic as regards strict theology, just as many Americans are sometimes termed nonreligious. Confucianism, therefore, took the place of religion in China among a share of the population. As it lost its hold in modern China a politically agnostic society first resulted, which currently has switched to Communism as a state cult.

CURRENT CHANGES IN RELIGIOUS AFFAIRS

In several countries today many religions are represented, some exhibiting closed-order tendencies and some openly aggressive and zealous in their appeal for new adherents. In a sense there is a competitive religious struggle going on in parts of the Orient as, for example, the Christian and Moslem vie for converts among the tribal animists of interior Sumatra. Among many of the cultures of the Orient, however, there is an awakening among many of the older religions that is carrying out reforms and enlivening the cultural scene generally. Often this aspect seems buried under the political and economic turmoil of the East, but it is a process definitely at work. In the same sense, in some countries the greatest growth of Christianity is not achieved by occidental missionaries but by the spontaneous growth of the native Christian churches. In China at least Christianity was slowly throwing off its missionary controls and launching forth on a program of its own when Communism took over. Although China was not yet a Christian nation, Christian leaders ranked high in political and economic circles. Despite the strong hold of Christianity in almost every country, it is doubtful if any one culture, except possibly that of the Philippines, will become as fully Christian as that of the United States within a long period to come.

After its ascendancy, Communism first declared for religious freedom, misleading both Chinese and occidentals. Gradually, however, the Chinese Communist Government restricted that freedom and then bent all religious bodies into machines to further Communism. These may be first and second steps in the abolishing of religious organizations which, in any respect whatsoever, could challenge the Communist Party in terms of group emotional mobilization. It is interesting to watch Chinese communists attempt to control Tibet, in which the Lamaist Church has performed so many of the functions of government. In Mongolia the power of the Church has largely been broken, though its earlier power in no part of Mongolia had been equivalent to that in Tibet.

SOCIAL STRATIFICATION

Everywhere in the Orient the value of a human life is far lower than in the Occident, and it is so much below the current American evaluation that it is hard for our average citizen to think realistically about the question. Interestingly enough, however, there are oriental cultures in which there is a tremendous separation between the top and the bottom of the social order. Among some cultures the upper ranks have become surrounded by privileges and rights that have given them vested positions of tremendous power in their society. To these relatively few the oriental cheapness of life does not apply. And at the other extreme are those hereditary classes who have no rights and privileges at all, but only the duty of performing the onerous and distasteful jobs which must be carried out in any society. To these numerous folk the phrase "value of a

human life" is but an empty mockery. No oriental society is completely free of these distinctions, though in some the degree of development is relatively slight. Perhaps in India and in Japan hereditary social stratification has become more fully developed than anywhere else in the oriental realm.

Back of all human social stratification is the simple classification of human beings by their occupations. In all societies the men who were the agents and exponents of religious cults and doctrines have held privileged positions. The warrior and soldier group inevitably occupied another niche in early and primitive social orders. The artisan and the cultivator frequently fell together in that often the same people concerned themselves with both kinds of work. All societies have maintained tabus the breaking of which lowered one's social position toward the bottom. These simple patterns hold in American society today just as they hold among the simple Papuan society formerly labeled "headhunter." Each oriental society has embroidered this simple classification with its own particular design in social matters, and just as some of the patterns seem fanciful to Americans, American patterns seem bizarre to oriental people. Burma possibly excepted, oriental society has recognized from the start that differences among men are fundamental, in stark contrast to the views of the framers of the American Declaration of Independence. Both religion and the force of law tend to support the maintenance of the native social order.

THE INDIAN CASTE SYSTEM

Outstanding in oriental social patterns is the extremely complex system of social castes that still prevails in modern India. The earliest Hindu annals record a simple system of three established castes and a fourth bottom layer: the Brahman priesthood, the Kshatriya military group, the Vaisya artisan cultivator, and the Sudra menial group made up of varied low-ranking elements. Slowly this simple grouping has become a host of over three thousand social strata today, eighteen hundred of them being Brahman subdivisions as the upper crust surrounded itself with more and more restrictions. The Lingayat religious faith mentioned above has, since the twelfth century, become subdivided into seventy-one separate castes.

The chief factors in caste distinctions are the rules of marriage, rules covering domestic food consumption, rules covering conduct of the individual, and rules concerning economic work habits. Individuals are born into their caste and cannot raise themselves. Every transgression that is not atoned for through elaborate ritual results in an individual sinking lower in the social order. Every revolt against Hindu society has ended in the enlargement of the caste pattern and in the formulation of yet more rules for human conduct. Migration, change of occupation, invention of new techniques in artisanry, all lead to lower caste levels. Particularly the last feature has tended to restrict and hamper the economic strength of Indian society.

And as time has gone on, multiple transgression of caste rules became more and more inevitable, and resulted in the accumulation at the sheer bottom of the Indian social order of some 60,000,000 "untouchables," outcastes to whom, and to whose descendants, there was no prospect other than the lowest of menial labor, the fewest prospects for betterment, and the barest of marginal existence. Such religions as Christianity, Sikhism, and Islam offer only a partial escape from the binding laws of caste. Modern occidental influence has been thrown against caste but sometimes it has worked to heighten the effects of caste rather than to lessen them. Although this complex social system is not a material piece of the physical landscape of India, it is of utmost significance in the cultural geography of the country. India now is moving toward abolition of the restrictive aspects of caste, but decades will pass before caste and its problems are banished.

THE DEMOCRACY OF CHINESE LIFE

Often it has been said that China was almost totally lacking in social stratification, and that it was nearest of all oriental societies to the concepts of American Jeffersonian Democracy. Perhaps the latter was true, but hardly the former. The literate Chinese ruling classes have been at some pains to maintain the notion that any individual could rise from the bottom to the top in one generation, and are fond of quoting the stories of famous men and women who did it, just as do Americans.

Detailed inquiry into Chinese history reveals that the minority who actually did rise to the top illustrate what is but an ideal principle in Chinese society. Confucius came not from the bottom but from a middling upper level, and the whole code of Confucianism was erected with a view to the maintenance of the established position of the cultured classes who were the proper managing agents of Chinese society. Confucian bureacracy operated with this thesis in mind and bitterly opposed the rise of too great strength in the religious orders, too great wealth among a trading class, and too great a growth of industry in the hands of a social class. In other words, the scholar bureaucrat was set up as the highest level in Chinese society. The military class was steadily played down, as a widely quoted Chinese proverb will attest: "Good iron is not made into nails, good men do not become soldiers." Into the Chinese bureaucracy of landed families sufficient numbers of new and poor scholars were always admitted in order to maintain the ranks in effective numbers and proficient ability.

At the bottom of the social order in China

have always been certain occupations and those who flaunted and disregarded Confucian standards of personal conduct and morality. Always there have been the marginal cultural groups who failed to practice the accepted social patterns. They have been termed "barbarians" in a variety of linguistic terminology and forced to put up with lesser social positions, economic privileges, and political freedoms. Communist ideology has remained faithful to old practices in this regard since membership in "the party" has been requisite for ranking status, and since those who oppose too vigorously end up in labor camps, deprived of privilege.

The foregoing is written not to criticize the standards of Chinese society but to clarify commonly misunderstood ideas. With some drawbacks the most populous society in the world did maintain more widespread personal dignity and individual freedom than have most other societies in oriental or occidental worlds, and this, in itself, was no mean achievement.

In the modern period the position of the scholar bureaucrat has weakened noticeably. The rise of new professional classes is based on many new culture traits. The modern bureaucracy is a more varied group than formerly, but tendencies toward perpetuation still are visible. Through the growth of modern trade and industry the trader, the engineer, and the banker have risen to levels never before attained in China. The military group has varied in favor according to whether they have been war-lord plunderers or defenders against aggression.

JAPANESE MODIFICATIONS OF CONFUCIAN DEMOCRACY

In Japanese society much of the Chinese Confucian pattern is visible, but at the same time important omissions, alterations, and additions have been made. The continued importance of clan organization in Japanese life has maintained vertical patterns which

have tended to prevent a strong horizontal alignment of social life. Certain hereditary groups occupy underprivileged positions at the bottom of the social order; there are the *eta*, about whom few Japanese will speak freely. The scholar bureaucrat never became a dominant figure in Japanese internal administration, but only an assistant, a tool for the imparting of lessons learned from China. Out of a long history of military expansion the *samurai* or professional soldier came to hold a more strategic position in Japan than in China, one which was duly exploited in the last century. The early *za* classes of artisans and merchants eventually grew into the *zaibatsu*, wealthy clans who held most of the land and the available wealth of Japan at the opening up of Japan in the 1860's, a position which allowed them to become industrial barons in modern Japan, socially and economically set apart from the balance of society.

Thus, the evolution of a social pattern in Japan has produced a less complex order than in India, but one with a number of sharply set-off groups, some of which have been able to achieve positions of privilege and strength not equaled elsewhere in the Orient. While this was achieved, a code of conduct evolved by which the mass of the population was urged to be obedient to the expressed will of the emperor, regardless of what special group had been successful in pushing through a particular decision. This has resulted in a quite different social pattern which is strikingly significant in the cultural geography of Japan.

THE OCCIDENTAL AND THE THE PROBLEM OF FACE

Within any oriental culture, and between oriental cultures, there is operative a somewhat elaborate social ritual which has come to be known, from the Chinese, as "saving face." "Face" is best defined as a combination of self-respect and personal dignity. In the elaborate social custom of every culture of the Orient the maintenance of self-respect and personal dignity while participating in the operation of a complex society is, in itself, a somewhat complicated business. The criticizing of personal actions without destroying "face" requires tact, patience, and a kindred feeling for the niceties and mores of a culture. When not at war with each other, oriental peoples have been at some pains to meet social and trade contacts half way. In no oriental culture was there ever much feeling of inferiority, but China held very positive feelings that its culture was superior.

When occidentals first arrive in the Orient, themselves suffering no inferiority complex but knowing little of oriental ways, they invariably run afoul of the problem of "face." The attitude of occidental superiority throughout the centuries of contact, implemented by military, political, and economic exploitation, usually has been rudely expressed, with no concessions of any kind to the "face" of the individual or group concerned. Some occidentals naturally handle their contacts well, just as there are blunt and abrupt orientals who can meet an American at least half way.

This problem of culture contact is alive today and will continue to mark oriental-occidental contacts in the future. The time has passed when an American can casually kick a Chinese ricksha puller out of the way or physically mistreat his servants. The same is true of every other occidental nationality also, for the colonial empires have crumbled and the future well being of international relations depends upon tactful cooperation.

THE GEOGRAPHY OF THE LAW

Space does not permit an adequate discussion of the role of law and the development of legal institutions in the cultural geography of the Orient. The following general discussion is intended only to introduce the topic and to suggest a few of its ramifications and implications. The basic developments of law in human society lie very far back, and it is difficult to determine clearly whether there are many really different systems of law. But there clearly are many different sets of legal institutions that have been developed among the many societies of our world. Within the Orient itself there are different kinds of legal institutions, so that law has been differently applied in the several regions. In many respects these institutions differ from the corresponding ones in the Occident, and their cultural results sometimes are strikingly different.

Many legal institutions seem to have grown up around the subject of religion and its organization, and around the issues of ownership and control over property and water. In that property in different environments varies tremendously, legal institutions reflect something of the environment. In that legal institutions are the means of enforcement of tribal tabus and the more formal religious sanctions, a system of legal institutions inevitably embodies these tabus and sanctions. A simple culture in an environment made up of similar regions may formulate a relatively simple group of institutions, whereas a highly complex culture occupying different kinds of landscapes and involving both rural agricultural and urban industrial occupations develops a complex and voluminous variety of institutions. A complex social order may include within its formal legal patterns many social controls which modify basic legal principles according to social level, or it may allow many social decisions to be made on an extralegal basis, often labeled "social custom."

Since a pattern of legal institutions goes with a culture complex, human migrations have moved institutional systems from given environments into totally dissimilar ones. The basic Islamic law of the Qur'ān with its desert concern over water rights, is a little out of place in the humid sectors of Indonesia, despite the importance of water control in the wet-field rice landscapes. Such contrasts eventually produce regional modifications in basic legal institutions. In the migration of cultures, groups of legal institutions come into opposition and conflict. Sometimes they exist side by side with continual strife, whereas at other times one system supplants another, as its native culture becomes regionally dominant. Out of the workings of each group comes political control and the operation of a political area by the leaders of the culture group. This may be only the tribal food-gathering range, or it may be the complex national state of modern times. Political regions seldom remain static, either expanding or contracting according to the relative level of culture strength in the regions round about.

The East shows a wide variety of legal institutions, from the primitive group of institutions governing the Sakai of West Malaysia to the complex patterns of Brahman Hindu India. Some of these institutions have been stable for centuries, whereas others have been expanding and increasing their territorial scope since 1880. In the case of small but distinct tribal groups variations in the institutions are few. The Indies, however, scattered over thousands of islands, has a great many local variations in its *adat* or customary law, and in the institutions developed to administer it. Most of the native cultural groups of the Orient possess their own customary law. Thus, under the modern political statutory law of Burma, Thailand, or Indonesia lies a distinct body of customary law stemming from growth patterns of earlier centuries.

In the history of the Orient three species of institutional pattern developed and spread out over south and eastern Asia in the course of centuries to overlie most of the tribal institutions of primitive societies. In some cases the new and incoming institutions achieved only a thin and patchy veneer over the older codes, but in others the new systems supplanted the older native codes. The new systems were the Hindu, Chinese, and Islamic systems in that chronological order. Each of these species has developed regionally centered subspecies that slowly have grown more and more distinctive, having less and less in common with each other. From the Chinese parent species have come the Korean, Japanese, and Vietnamese subspecies. Mongol tribal-pastoral legal patterns always remained separate from the systems of the sedentary Chinese and did not spread far out of the dry lands. From the Hindu species have developed the Tibetan, Burmese, Thai, and Cambodian systems. From both Hindu and Islamic root stocks has grown the Pakistan Moslem system. The Indian Islamic legal institutions spread into Malaya and the western Indies to cover about the same territory as had been covered earlier by the spread of Hindu institutions. The eastern half of the Indies and the northern Philippines never received an oriental overlay over their local tribal systems.

Hindu and Chinese legal institutions were quite deeply entrenched on the Asian mainland when Islamic patterns were carried into southeastern Asia. Rather quickly the Islamic system replaced Hindu institutions in Malaya and the western Indies and spread to the southern Philippines. This replacement took place at the top of the institutional standard, being the operative patterns of political overlords. Under a thin veneer of Moslem practices lay parts of the older Hindu system, and under both lay Indonesian tribal institutions. This Moslem veneer had not penetrated much of the whole body of customary law when the European discoverers appeared on the scene.

European legal institutions came to the East in two related species, the Roman pattern of continental Europe and the common law of England. Gradually these have been applied to almost the whole of the Orient in another thin veneer. Where a colony was staked out the veneer has finally become quite deep, but where no colonial overlordship was achieved the new European systems have not produced much change. An accompanying map attempts to present the distribution regionally (Fig. 3.2).

One can visualize the prospects for real dissension in a situation like this: Suppose a Chinese shopkeeper and his Malay customer become seriously involved with a Sikh moneylender in a small town in interior Malaysia. The law of the land is Islamic, but the Indian jurist (born in Malaysia but trained in English common law in England) thinks in British terms. Each of the three litigants emotionally reacts in the sense of what is right in his own culture and would argue by his own native legal system. Unless the judge were more conscientious than many civil servants he might well decide the case by English common law and enrage all three principals.

Riding high on dominant political status

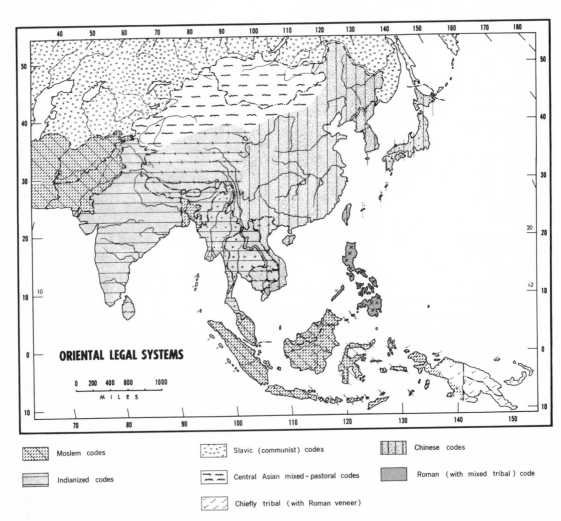

ORIENTAL LEGAL SYSTEMS

0   200 400 800   1000
M I L E S

Moslem codes	Slavic (communist) codes	Chinese codes
Indianized codes	Central Asian mixed–pastoral codes	Roman (with mixed tribal) code
Chiefly tribal (with Roman veneer)		

FIGURE 3.2. Systems of oriental legal institutions.

the occidental seldom has been subject to oriental legal concepts of justice in the past. In several countries the occidental long possessed what were termed extraterritorial rights and privileges, and several oriental countries were subject to what they termed unequal treaties. The Chinese treaty ports were a case in point, about which more will be said in a chapter on China. There have been injustices on both sides. The failure of China to recognize and honor the institutions of patents and copyrights has been almost as annoying to Americans as the United States privilege of extraterritoriality was to the Chinese. Out of such sources of conflict have come many of the "diplomatic incidents" of the past. During the Sino-Japanese War, 1937–1945, the United States took the lead in giving up her special rights and privileges in China, making Americans subject to Chinese civil and criminal justice and American firms subject to Chinese corporation and tax laws. The achievement of political independence in other parts of the Orient has replaced many other special privileges formerly used and abused by the Occident.

CONTROL OVER PROPERTY

Legal institutions express themselves in many directions in the framework of a regional culture. To the geographer one of the more interesting directions in which law operates is in respect to property and in matters of land tenure. In the Orient added to this is the very intricate aspect of water control in relation to wet-field rice culture.

Throughout the Orient native culture groups have long existed with a wide degree of complexity, some of them living almost side by side for long periods. Different social and administrative systems exist, each with its own institutions for control over property, land, and water. The many simple tribal cultures as a rule have not developed concepts of private property in land. Personal possessions may be privately owned, and tools, weapons, and houses are considered private, though in many such cultures there are age or group association houses that belong to all members of the tribe or village. Among such cultures the physical landscape usually is considered a common clan resource range, though hunting, gathering, or cropping use privileges may be assigned to units ranging from sub-clans to individuals. It is to such groups that one refers tribal or customary law.

Among higher cultures, rights of ownership of land and certain classes of property were claimed by the nobility or by regional rulers. Among these there was an extension of the concept of private property to more than personal possessions and homes, yet the concept fell short of the modern occidental concepts. Among such groups appeared a group of legal institutions pertaining to water rights, mineral rights, trade privileges, and customs collections. Early Hindu and Chinese institutions had approached this intermediate level well before the beginning of the Christian era, but few other culture groups at that time had progressed far in the growth of their institutional evolution. Out of the older Near Eastern kingly state cultures the full concepts of private land ownership spread to India and China before the beginning of the Christian era in company with the introduction of higher and more complex political systems. In India and China political-military nationalism appeared with the Mauryan and Han dynasties, and within the life span of both the institutional systems of both countries markedly matured.

After the appearance of the concept of private property in the Orient each of the more advanced cultures began to revise its institutions for control over land and property. No two systems developed along completely parallel lines or to equal extent. The appearance of Islamic elements in India and Central Asia-China, and gradually in southeastern Asia, brought an overlay of controls over land and property. The coming of the Europeans repeated the overlay in those regions in which Europeans developed control. Out of this long history has grown up the modern agrarian problem which besets almost every country in the Orient. Tenancy of farmers, landlessness of agricultural families, money taxes and land rental, and heavy debt burdens upon tenants whatever the local regional legal institutions, have become compounded into a tremendous problem for both the West and the East. It was largely because of this problem that Communism took over in China, and it is because of this same problem that Communism threatens in every country of the Orient today.

HOUSING

These two south Indian houses in Nilambur, Kerala, are built of locally quarried laterite blocks, and the front fence of the nearer house is also built of laterite. The house at the left is tile-roofed, whereas that beyond is thatched with rice straw. (J. E. Spencer)

Malay houses normally are set off the ground on pilings, and are built of wood which is usually left untouched to weather shades of brown. The house trim often shows considerable carbing. This contemporary house has a corrugated iron roof, a concrete foundation for the pilings, and has its lower section screened off by heavy wire. (J. E. Spencer)

The main rear portion of this Taiwan farmhouse is about one hundred years old, the forward wings enclosing the original threshing floor being later additions, and the wing at the right has recently been rebuilt. A new threshing floor occupies the foreground. The house now has electric lights, a television aerial stands at the left of the inner court, and a motorcycle ramp has been added at the right, but a pile of firewood is still kept to the right of the main doorway. (J. E. Spencer)

This Japanese farmhouse, on the west coast of Japan near Niigata, is built of wood and roofed in tile in the early 20th century style. A kitchen garden occupies space in front of the house, and ricefields surround it. (J. E. Spencer)

4

SETTLEMENTS AND THEIR ARCHITECTURES

Roughly half of the world's people live in the Orient. They range from small, shy refugee groups to large collections of sophisticated city dwellers. How do they arrange their living patterns to accommodate themselves to roughly one seventh of the world's inhabited area, and what kinds of houses and settlements do they occupy? These basic features of human living are supposedly commonplace elements of cultural geography, but the topic requires more space than can be allotted here. The present chapter is a suggestive approach to aspects of both subjects.

BASIC STYLES OF SETTLEMENT

Most orientals are village or town dwellers. Villages and small market towns accommodate perhaps three-fourths of the total population. The inhabited area is today so densely populated that many compact, closely spaced settlements are necessary. Most oriental villages, towns, and cities impress the American as being jammed tightly together without the usual "living spaces" which he associates with multiple human residence. Throughout the Orient there are no accepted definitions of what constitutes a village, a town, or a city, but on the basis of loose generalizations some totals may be estimated. There probably are close to 1,900,000 residential villages in the Orient, housing approximately 1.1 billion people. The many shapes, kinds, and sizes of residential villages range from two- or three-house clusters to villages of two thousand houses.

Towns are far less numerous but are of varied types and sizes. They range from small seaports and regional inland market towns to military garrison centers, resorts, mining towns, and political administrative centers. There are not more than about 10,000 such settlements, but they probably house in the vicinity of 200,000,000 people.

There is no easy definition of the city in the Orient but, thinking of compact settlements with complex functions, there are in the neighborhood of 5,000 cities of all kinds, grades, and sizes containing approximately 300,000,000 people. Perhaps 2,000 of these are quite small in population today, not having been affected by modern trends toward urbanism; most of these cities are old in date of founding, rich in historic function, and symbolic in the roles they have played. A few hundreds of these old cities today have declined into market towns, administrative centers only, or shadow cities occupying historic sites, to use modern criteria.

Perhaps 500 old cities have been caught up in the currents of modern urbanization and economic development, and are burgeoning entities. There are a few dozen cities that owe their foundings to the impacts of European programs of trade and industry. Well over fifty urban complexes (using restricted criteria rather than the most relaxed concept of the metropolitan unit) have exceeded the million mark. The generalization is that, for the whole of the Orient, urbanization comprises twenty-five to thirty percent of the total population, but that an era of rapid urbanization is approaching during which the urban percentages will grow markedly. Regionally, of course, the present percentages of urbanization vary widely from country to country, with Japan the most highly urbanized country, and New Guinea just barely commencing urban settlement (Table 1). Despite the fact that the percentage of urbanization for China still is relatively low, China is second only to the United States in the number of its "million" cities. In the sense of having large numbers of "cities" China, India, and Japan rank high among the countries of the world, whereas Burma, Thailand, Laos, and Cambodia rank low, and several other countries still have rather few.

Dispersed rural settlement is an old and widespread pattern in the Orient, but it is declining in frequency in modern time. In part this decline is a function of sheer increase in square-mile densities of rural population, in that many regions are so thickly settled that homesteads no longer can be considered dispersed. In part it derives from the sheer growth of housing clusters and hamlets into villages and towns. There still are over 100,000,000 people distributed in what, by convention, may be called rural dispersed settlement.

With hundreds of race and culture groups permanently living in situations that range from boats on rivers and on the sea to

TABLE 1
Urbanization in South and Eastern Asia

State	Number of cities over 1,000,000	Approximate percentage of urbanization*
Pakistan	2	15
Nepal	0	3
India	9	20
Ceylon	1	16
Burma	1	10
Thailand	1	11
Laos	0	4
Cambodia	0	13
North Vietnam	0	?
South Vietnam	1	?
Malaysia	0	30
Singapore	1	–
Indonesia	3	15
Philippines	1	30
Hong Kong	1	–
Taiwan	1	28
China	21	25
North Korea	1	25
South Korea	3	30
Japan	9	55
Total/Average	56	±25–30

*Estimated, as of 1970, as share of population resident in settlements of over 20,000.

isolated mountain-top homesteads and villages, there inevitably is wide variety in the methods of arranging both compact and dispersed settlement. In some large regions, inhabited by millions of people, the settlement forms and the housing patterns are basically similar. But in contrast to this are the zones of fragmentation of race and culture, wherein many different patterns of living can be found in small areas. Within the Orient culture complexes range from the Stone Age to the Atomic Age, from simple hunting and gathering economies to technologically advanced, industrial export economies. No simple generalizations, country by country, or large region by region, may be made for settlement and housing systems.

Dispersed Settlement

Although it is not the common manner of living, dispersed settlement is widespread, and it has been adopted by many kinds of people throughout the prehistoric and historic periods. It is found in many regions as a result of specific cultural stimuli though, at this date, not all the motivations can be diagnosed accurately. Some hunting-gathering or fishing peoples, remnants of earlier societies, still approximate dispersed settlement in parts of India, Pakistan, Southeast Asia, Indonesia, eastern New Guinea, and as far north as Taiwan. In some cases this is by single family units, and in others it is by the hunting band, the smallest and simplest social group. Residence often is semipermanent in good local environments, but also it is often seasonal, temporary, or shifting. Although people of this simple type of economy are widely scattered, they do not bulk large in total numbers. Some of the fishing peoples, in single or two-family units, may live seasonally or completely on their boats, often tied up at night in the same locality.

Some of the earlier agricultural peoples, like the present-day remnant groups or small communities never growing into populous or powerful societies, lived in dispersed patterns that still are in use today. These peoples now are thinly scattered throughout the hill country of India, Pakistan, mainland Southeast Asia, Indonesia, and the Philippines. Some live in single family homes, some in small clusters, and a few are seasonally dispersed throughout the cropped landscape during the intervals of the chief agricultural production cycles, living in villages during the off-seasons. The earlier societies normally practiced shifting cultivation, moving their farmstead locations from time to time under different rules and systems. Shifting cultivation tends to foster dispersion of the population rather than compact permanent centering of a society in villages and towns. The modern continuation of shifting cultivation may be limited eventually by the regional pressure of men upon the landscape, but it still is widely practiced today. It has been maintained as a complementary agricultural system by many peoples who have otherwise developed advanced cultures, thereby fostering rural dispersion of population in all parts of southeastern Asia. As far north as Korea and the highlands of eastern Manchuria a version of shifting cultivation, in Korea called "fire field" culture, still is used. This involves periodic shifting of location, the scattering of homes, and, essentially, dispersed settlement.

One large and significant region of dispersed settlement among a people of advanced culture is that of western China—the Szechwan Basin and near-by surrounding hill country. Here Chinese settlement took place in a landscape of irregular hill country, the Chinese settling down among, and displacing, an earlier population. Village and town settlement had been the earlier Chinese norm in the open landscape of North China. Towns as centers of culture and as defensive rallying points were used in the initial stage of Chinese occupation of Szechwan. As regional pacification occurred and as the earlier occupants withdrew southward to get away from Chinese control, the Chinese found compact villages less practical than dispersed dwelling in the hilly environment. Gradually they spread out over the landscape to better utilize the small and scattered bits of valley land. As population grew and terraces spread over the hills this pattern solidified, so that villages and towns now are service centers for the majority of the rural population rather than primary points of residence. The great majority of Chinese in this region live in single-family (including the extended family) farmsteads distributed throughout the hilly landscape.

In northern Honshu and Hokkaido, where larger farms are both more necessary and possible than in the southern part of Japan, some farmers also have spread out upon the land in homes that occasionally resemble the Russian Siberian or northern American style. This is a recent development, and it accounts for only a minority of the population. Throughout central and southern Honshu there is dispersed settlement in the upland regions. In the Philippines, during the American period of control, as highways improved, with consequent easier travel and transport, a rural scattering of homesteads along the roads dispersed significant numbers of families to reverse the Spanish policy of concentrating the population in compact settlements. Recent pioneer settlement patterns in the southern Philippines often show dispersal in continuation of the American influence.

India is chiefly a zone of village dwelling, but there are several areas that today are marked by dispersed settlement. Whereas the Malabar Coast of southwestern India once was settled chiefly in villages and towns, dispersed settlement is widespread today. The whole southern end of the Indian Peninsula shows considerable dispersed settlement. The Northern Circars region, north of Madras, has much of the population spread out upon the land. The eastern Bengal Delta region, perhaps because of the rise of jute as a commercial farm crop, is a region in which dispersed settlement is common today, although rural settlement here is so dense that it hardly constitutes dispersal. The hill country of the lower Himalayas, in almost its whole length, and the whole of the Vindhya Hills show widespread dissemination of single farmsteads, the Himalayan zone constituting the chief Indian region of dispersed settlement.

Among advanced societies that have developed complex living patterns, there always are a few families who prefer to live apart from their neighbors. Particular causal factors in local regions have promoted rural dispersion of residence. Commercial agriculture and the development of transport systems are important in this respect. In recent centuries, with heavier pressure upon farmland and living space, many local regions show rural dispersion of farm homesteads upon higher terraces, lands neglected until recently, along road and rail lines of easy access, in reclaimed areas, suburban fringes, and the like. Consequently, thin scatterings or small patches of dispersed settlement are to be found everywhere from Hokkaido and northern Manchuria to eastern New Guinea and to Baluchistan (Fig. 4.1, upper left).

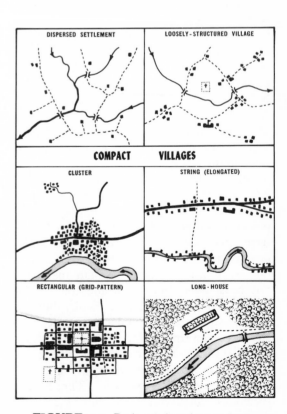

FIGURE 4.1. Basic rural settlement forms.

The Village

Of the many kinds of villages a variety of classifications are possible. One Indian classic on village and town planning recognized some forty different kinds of villages. Essentially the oriental village is a collection of farm homes, but the homes of fishermen, of miners, of transporters, and of other functional groups are normally clustered in compact villages. The sheer compactness of many oriental villages is striking, particularly in north China and northern India, and the American often is impressed by the total absence of space between houses, of the lack of gardens, streets, and other types of "living space." When the pressure of men upon the land is great these features are often given scant consideration by the oriental, or they are provided for outside the village itself, on river banks, shore lines, waste spaces, or other "common" areas.

One is tempted to assert that the historic need for common protection and defense by the villager may be the chief causal factor for this tightness of dwelling habit, but this may well be an after-generalization too sweeping in scope. Close-order dwelling may have become habitual among Chinese, Japanese, Indian, and other peoples as an integral aspect of their evolving, closely knit social systems. It is hard to separate the social system of some of the southeastern Asian groups from their habit of communal living in a single physical structure housing dozens of families. In many parts of the Orient walled villages still are the common mode, reflecting a protective need of earlier peoples, but the good policing provided by the European colonial administrations and some modern native governments has caused protective walls in other areas to disappear without markedly changing the basic compactness of the settlements.

But not all orientals live in tightly compacted villages. The Bengal, Travancore, Malay, or southern Japan village often is a loosely structured affair, with trees, clumps of shrubs, or patches of bamboo screening each house and providing shade for it. Garden patches may separate houses within a village. In many areas hamlets or clusters of houses constitute neither dispersed nor compact settlement, but administratively many of these groups or clusters constitute a village (see Fig. 4.1, upper right). This latter pattern is found in parts of Japan, the Philippines, in India, and in local areas in other countries.

Among many of the simpler social groups the village is built around a central feature, this varying from a shrine or a cleared threshing-ceremonial floor to a chief's house or a market place.

Ideally, the residential village does not contain stores, shops, fabricating plants, government service buildings, or other functional activities, but this cannot be taken as the sole characteristic of oriental villages. Probably a majority of villages show almost no secondary activities, but the Szechwan village today, in a region of dispersed settlement, has developed a particular tradition of social and economic service related to the market town, though it often is only a collection of thirty to fifty houses. The village through which a highway or rail line has been recently built may well have added a few secondary services without becoming a real town or city. Innumerable causal factors today make it impossible to define finitely what constitutes a village.

The pattern of livelihood, the social system, the presence of friction between local race and culture groups, the regional historic frequency of alien invasion, the habit of intergroup wars tied up with long preserved social patterns, the need for mass labor forces among peoples of simple power technology, all these are factors making for village dwelling of some sort as the normal thing in most parts of the Orient. It is likely that there are more villages of under fifty houses than any other size category, but it is equally likely that villages of 300–500 houses contain the largest numbers of village residents.

Villages in the Orient are arranged in many shapes and patterns. Some single patterns are common in large areas, or among particular race and culture groups. Conversely, many different shapes of villages exist in a given region wherein several causal factors have operated to determine the site and the space available for the building of a village.

Many factors have promoted the compact village of no definite shape or morphology, which is best labeled the cluster village (see Fig. 4.1, left center). It is to be found in all parts of the Orient, in all types of local site and situation. In regional terms a great many of the villages of north and northwest India are of this type, very closely built, with a maze of alley and access lines into the house units. Many North China Plain villages are of this type, though here they are less tightly built. Many South China villages are cluster-shaped, concentrated at a river fork, a bridge-head, or on the only bit of flat surface available, showing a hodgepodge arrangement. Many of the villages built by the simpler social and culture groups of India and southeastern Asia are really clusters of houses arranged in disorderly array. Some of these are circular clusters, or clusters grouped around a focal point. Tibetan villages frequently are elongated clusters in cramped sites in those lower elevations in which sedentary settlements are found.

Elongated or string villages are to be found everywhere in the Orient (see Fig. 4.1, right center). Often a site is chosen which promotes the string village. The seashore, a river bank, a natural levee or terrace, a highway, a dike line, or some other linear site form automatically arranges houses either in single file or double file over whatever distance is required to house the local population. Ten or twenty houses may be compactly grouped in a double row in less than 100 yards, or a thousand houses and their garden spaces may straggle out for several miles. The string village is an old form in the Orient, though it does not seem a natural one to the simpler societies. It is a culturally fixed form in many regions today in that a site for a new settlement may be chosen so that this form may be executed. The modern highway is a natural phenomenon upon which people may fix this type of village, and new dike lines are often chosen as practical sites for settlement.

The rectangular or grid-pattern village is a common form in many areas today (see Fig. 4.1, lower left). Though the grid-pattern settlement is a very old one, perhaps originating in northwestern India, its use in villages seems far less old than its use in town and city building. The form gradually spread over most of the Orient and was widely used among the more advanced culture groups well before the coming of the occidental. It is a traditional type in parts of southern Japan today, is old and widespread in China where plenty of space was available, and has been commonly used in many parts of India for a long period. Elsewhere it seems a more modern thing, perhaps promoted by the occidental in the recent period of developed transport.

Other forms of the village do not precisely fit into any of the three patterns mentioned above. The traditional Malay village is a straggly affair often built along the lower portion of a stream. But its scattered spacing of houses in garden patches, its lack of continuous road or trail connecting all the homes, and its orientation to water transport make it neither a string village nor a cluster village. The Javanese villages that cluster around the cultivable upper portions of a volcano's slopes fit none of these formal categories. The Borneo or Sulu Archipelago villages built on piles around accessible sea-water sites are more nearly cluster villages than anything else, but they are not type cases. The mountain-ridge or mountain-top villages built by many of the southeastern Asian peoples are often disorderly groupings of buildings that are hardly cluster villages. The villages of some of the peoples using the communal longhouse, wherein a whole population lives in one large, subdivided structure, can hardly be called either cluster villages or string villages (Fig. 4.1, lower right).

The residential village serves one primary purpose, the housing of a local population, its household animals, crops, and tools. It normally is characterized by simple architecture and cheap utilitarian construction that serves the basic needs of shelter, storage, and privacy. The oriental village seldom has amenities related to water supply, waste disposal, street cleaning, fly and insect controls, lighting, entertainment, and the like. In any of its common shapes and patterns the village reflects the culture level and variety of its inhabitants. House form and construction also reflect these regional culture patterns. Here and there, as among the Batak and Minangkabau of Sumatra, some of the Himalayan mountain peoples, or the Min Chia of Yunnan, architecture among village folk rises above strictly utilitarian patterns to create an artistic atmosphere not normally associated with village living.

Several kinds of differences can be noted in villages among the major culture realms of the Orient. Out of the strong Chinese demand for domestic privacy every village has an inn that provides shelter and meals, and travelers must patronize these services. In the Philippines, on the other hand, inns and hotels are never found in villages, and travelers always stay in private homes, for hospitableness is a highly cultivated national trait. Among some cultures a shrine is found in almost every village, but among others it is lacking. The Hindu Indian village always possesses zoning of residence, if inhabited by more than one social caste, with fairly strict

segregation of residence quarters for the several groups. The villages of most of the simpler cultures of southeastern Asia and Indonesia possess housing restricted to men, to women, or to other particular community social elements.

Considering the whole Orient, villages are located everywhere, on all kinds of sites, and no one generalization is possible as to where people choose to locate their villages. One can say that in floodplains where floods are frequent hazards villages most often are located on natural levees, dike lines, formally raised platforms, or mounded sites lifted gradually by rubbish discarded during a millennium of constant occupance. In Indonesia some of the native peoples always built on protected mountain sites, but the Dutch gradually required the building of villages near main roads and trails in more open lowland sites. Many of the earlier New Guinea villages were located in what once was forest but has now become grass country. Progressively village locations have shifted out of the grass country into the upland borders because of the lack of shade trees and construction materials. One can say that the Shan peoples of Yunnan and Burma prefer open, flatland sites for villages, but that the Palaung of northeast Burma and most of the other minority culture groups of upland southeastern Asia usually build on hill tops or ridge tops. In the hill country of southeastern Asia, from the flat lowland floodplain to the highest crest line one finds populations stratified at particular levels—a complex result of economy, military strength, cultural habit, and group aggressiveness. The Thai today are chiefly lowlanders, whereas the Lamet—a minority Kha people, descended from early Mon-Khmer stock—occupy ridge-top sites east of the Mekong River at about 3,000 to 3,200 feet altitude. These stratifications today are expressions of historic competition among many culture groups for living space and cannot be simple expressions of preferred choices, though they now often appear to be cultural patterns of some stability.

The Town

The town is a more complex settlement than the residential village, in that it accommodates several kinds of secondary activities. It normally is larger than the residential village, but this is not always true. Its most common activity is its marketing operations, and most of the towns of the Orient are market towns. Most of them, of course, also serve a primary function as residential communities to such primary producers as farmers, fishermen, miners, or transporters, and to that population devoting itself to secondary activities. In connection with this marketing function are warehousing, processing, wholesaling, and retail merchandising. At first glance these are ubiquitous human activities in which oriental towns differ only in specific terms from towns elsewhere in the world. The Chinese "cotton street" or "copper beaters' alley" each has a different appearance from those sections of American towns devoted to the same general operation, and the Indian "bazaar" carries a different atmosphere from the retail merchandising section of a midwestern American market town. The oriental town, far more than the American town, combines economic operation and residence in the same buildings, for shopkeepers live over, behind, or in their shops. Similarly, though there may be economic functional zoning, the well-to-do and the poor live in intermixed fashion, without class segregation. In these respects the oriental market town often is fascinating to the American tourist and offers both a cultural contrast and a lure to explore that is lacking in his own chain store market area (Fig. 4.2, upper left).

Beyond the ubiquitous facilities that provide for man all over the world, the oriental town does often seem to provide services in a way different from those provided by many occidental towns. "Coffin street" in many a Chinese market town permits the living person to shop for a container that will eventually house his remains in a manner quite different from that available to Americans. Chinese restaurants, particularly in market towns, normally display their foods and do their cooking next to the street, so that passers-by may make a choice seldom available to an occidental in his homeland. The Indian silversmith, to take a random example, doing much of his work in an open-front shop where his customer may supervise, provides a kind of service seldom found in the United States outside of a "while-u-wait" shoe repair shop. There are many ways in which the oriental market town does seem to differ from its occidental counterpart in the kind of service it provides its customers. One could easily overemphasize these differences, perhaps, for many of them are intricately bound up with the whole of regional culture patterns and are not simply differences in the market town as a functioning settlement pattern.

Functions other than marketing are performed by the oriental town, of course. There are transport terminals or way stations, for both land and water transport, fishing centers, mining settlements, garrison centers, political administrative centers, educational centers, monastery towns, religious pilgrimage centers, mountain resorts, fortified emergency refuge centers to be used in time of unrest, and other types of towns (Fig. 4.2, upper right, sample layout of the central section of an administrative town.) The small manufacturing town, often devoted to a particular commodity or category of manufacturing, such as pottery or weaving, is widely scattered over the Orient. In that it still uses simple sources of power and few complex machines, and often is organized on a pattern of community household industry, it has an appearance different from that of many occident manufacturing towns.

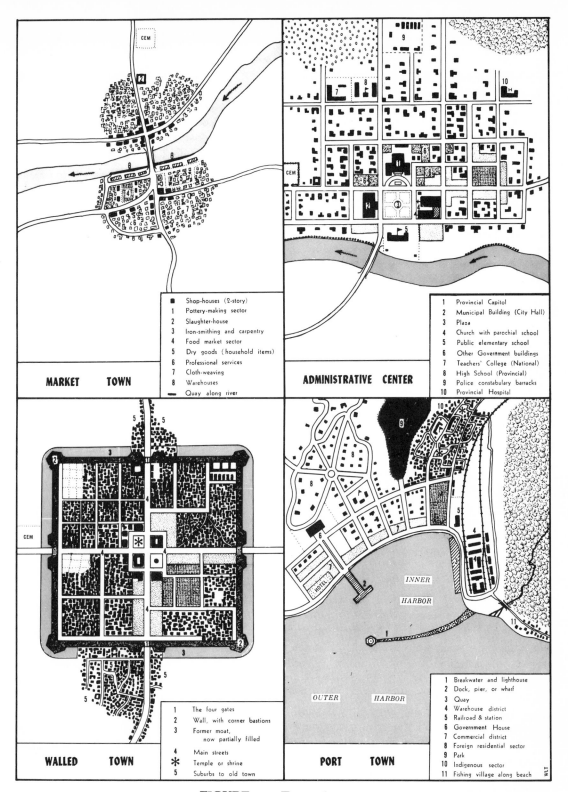

MARKET TOWN

■	Shop-houses (2-story)
1	Pottery-making sector
2	Slaughter-house
3	Iron-smithing and carpentry
4	Food market sector
5	Dry goods (household items)
6	Professional services
7	Cloth-weaving
8	Warehouses
▬	Quay along river

ADMINISTRATIVE CENTER

1	Provincial Capitol
2	Municipal Building (City Hall)
3	Plaza
4	Church with parochial school
5	Public elementary school
6	Other Government buildings
7	Teachers' College (National)
8	High School (Provincial)
9	Police constabulary barracks
10	Provincial Hospital

WALLED TOWN

1	The four gates
2	Wall, with corner bastions
3	Former moat, now partially filled
4	Main streets
✳	Temple or shrine
5	Suburbs to old town

PORT TOWN

1	Breakwater and lighthouse
2	Dock, pier, or wharf
3	Quay
4	Warehouse district
5	Railroad & station
6	Government House
7	Commercial district
8	Foreign residential sector
9	Park
10	Indigenous sector
11	Fishing village along beach

FIGURE 4.2. Types of towns.

73

Most oriental towns, being centers of multiple operations and functions, often show a considerable amount of functional zoning. Traditionally this has come about without formal controls and ordinances in most countries of the Orient. Grain shops cluster together, dealers in construction materials often occupy a particular quarter, transport operators and their equipment most often congregate on the outskirts, whereas textile, jewelry, food, and other retailers most frequently are to be found near the centers of towns. Many Chinese and Japanese towns have a fairly intricate pattern of zoning of this sort, all accomplished in the earlier day without formal controls. The Indian market town, on the other hand, traditionally has been administratively controlled by some kind of town council, and often has rigidly set limits and patterns.

Most oriental towns are laid out on some kind of grid pattern, a feature adopted by town builders in all parts of the Orient a long time ago. Its actual execution depended upon how clearly a particular people understood the whole concept of a formally planned and arranged settlement pattern. Indian towns, near to the center of origin of the grid plan, have used it longer than have Japanese towns, situated far from that center, but the grid plan is centuries old everywhere. In those towns built on spacious sites a quite rectangular settlement normally resulted, whereas on irregular sites town builders normally accommodated themselves to the site and modified their plan as necessary. Normally many lanes and alleys gave access from the chief streets to block interiors, which usually were solidly built upon (Fig. 4.2, lower left, the schematic layout of internal arrangements). A distinctive feature of many Chinese and Japanese towns lay in the failure to orient property lines to the grid plan, so that many Chinese towns today contain bewildering and irregular maze patterns within blocks. This is far less common in India, where the full implications of the grid plan were long ago appreciated. In parts of southeastern Asia in which culture levels and population long remained lower than in India or China, towns were necessarily fewer, simpler in layout, and normally less complete in the earlier period. In this region their growth in the period of occidental contact is a notable feature, but often the occidental had only slight control over the actual pattern of settlement as it appeared.

The protective wall was a common part of town building in most parts of the Orient, and most of the ancient towns possessed such a wall. Perhaps port towns possessed walls, whether on rivers or on the sea, least often. Gates, bastions, battlements, moats, and other features went with the wall as part of a complex. Wealthier communities first built in tamped earth or adobe brick, and later in kiln-burnt brick, or stone, though the use of burnt brick is far older in India than in China. The earliest towns in forested areas appear to have been surrounded by log palisades. In part of southeastern Asia the wood or bamboo palisade was more common until the coming of the occidental. Many old towns still possess their walls, though often the walls have been breached in the modern period to permit modern transport to enter. Many old towns have long had suburbs lying outside the walls. The small town often had but four gates, one in each cardinal direction. This normally caused some of the interior streets to end against the wall, funneled traffic in and out along limited lines, and concentrated suburbs in particular locations outside the wall (Fig. 4.2, lower left, a typically schematic arrangement). Few towns founded after the coming of the occidental have had walls built around them, but many of the first settlements built by Europeans were surrounded with walls. Most of these European settlements have grown into large cities since their founding and the walled towns now are small enclosures within the cities. Fort St.

George at Madras and the Intramuros at Manila are examples of this development.

Many market towns appear to have remained relatively stable in population for rather long periods of time. Some Chinese and Indian market towns now appear little larger than they were centuries ago, but there are many more to ns today, more closely spaced together, than were to be found in earlier periods. With limited facilities and sites, this suggests that the market town has an approximate maximum size and level of efficiency. No specific total population can be designated at this maximum level for the whole Orient, because different culture groups have developed different technologies and different cultural reactions to the functioning of the town.

Other kinds of towns, particularly administrative and religious, also have increased in number and closeness of spacing, as the total population of individual countries and particular regions has grown over the centuries. Many of the ancient port towns have disappeared, with silting up of river mouths and harbors, with changing political fortunes, and changing sea-trade patterns. Some of these port towns have remained small in size and restricted in regional functioning, particularly in the modern period in which the type and size of shipping has changed and grown, so that many ports formerly significant in international or interregional trade have become only local trade centers (Fig. 4.2, lower right, the schematic arrangement of a local port town.). A few of the modern, occidental-built towns grew up around the fishing villages or small trading shops of the native pattern, particularly the coastal port towns of India, the peninsular coast of southeastern Asia, and Indonesia. Numerous towns of an earlier period have, of course, grown and matured into modern cities of large size and complex function.

Modern developments in military government, civil government, transport, agricul-tural processing, and mineral exploitation have created new settlements that must be labeled towns. Military barracks, administrative facilities, milling activities, and mining camps gather around them subordinate service functions and small populations. This is particularly true of rail and road junctions, at which points servicing functions are numerous. Each of these modern elements often became located outside of, or near to, old compact cities and towns affording little internal space for new buildings and service yards. In China and India few of the modern highways penetrated the old walled cities, and rail stations normally were located close by, rather than inside, the old cities. In India and Pakistan the housing and administrative buildings of the "military lines," "civil lines," and "labor lines" were located at a distance from old cities and towns, creating either new suburbs or totally new town settlements.

The Older Oriental City

Some students of urbanism consider that the ancient city was a product of the maturing of the political state which, in process of development, formulated religious, economic, political, and social systems able to exploit resources in agriculture and animal husbandry, minerals, water, forests, and land. According to this view the city is a complex of people and human systems around which the political state crystalized. Another view is that the maturing of religious and sociopolitical structuring reached the level at which an aggressive leader could reshape the elements of control into a kingship combining charismatic personal hegemony in religious and political terms. In this view the city was the expression of the assumption of the role of God-King, a a physical expression of hegemony, in which the leader could manipulate the economic and social systems. According to this view the city was the result and not the cause. The initial establishment of a primary temple as the dominant religious site and symbol of religious authority went hand in hand with the initial establishment of a primary capital as the dominant political site and symbol of political authority. The combining of the two roles into one was the assertion of total personal hegemony over a region and a populace. The temple and capitol became the focal complex around which the following were established: storehouses, treasuries, working establishments for handicraft operations, points for gathering-in produced resources, subsidiary shrines necessary to the practical operation of the religio-political authority, garrison quarters for supportive forces, quarters for priests-bureaucrats, market sites necessary to the exchange of commodities among a sizable compact population, and residential housing required by that population. The earliest kingly states were not large, and perhaps were dominated by one such city, supported by outlying villages and rural scatterings of population. As states grew in area and in power, subordinate regional control points were established as secondary temple-capitols. As rival "states" were conquered, the former chief temple-capitol sites were downgraded into secondary settlements or were laid waste in the expression of the hegemony of the new ruler.

In this concept the state depended upon an agricultural base for its support, but its area was capable of sufficient handicraft manufacturing and regional trade to provide a broad variety of consumer goods and a multiple income pattern for much of its citizenry. The city specifically was both the point of organization and control and the center of manufacturing and commercial exchange. (In this context manufacturing is a handicraft-community workshop, dependent chiefly upon human and animal power and the high personal skill of the artisan, and commerce is akin to what today is internal or domestic commerce.) The city was the chief consumer of agricultural surpluses, the point of accumulation of wealth and tradition, and the chief developer of culture patterns—the center of civilization. It was the nerve center of the state, and the chief object of attack by an invader.

The above conceptual structuring does not fit the current concept of the rise of the city prevalent in the Occident, but clearly this kind of structuring fits the pattern of the oldest cities of the Orient, and it is exhibited in old cities throughout the whole of Monsoon Asia. Neither does the above construct fit the current concept of the pre-industrial city. The ancient cities of India, China, and Southeast Asia do not fit into the modern occidental concept of the rise of the city because they were different kinds of cultural mechanisms than both the oriental and occidental modern city of today.

It is not clear just when the city wall became an integral portion of the city construct, but in proto-historic and historic time the establishment of the wall and formal gates was part of the symbolization of kingly hegemony. In several cases at least, the laying out of the plan, the building of the wall, and the placement of temples and palaces, were the initial acts of founding a city and marked the firm establishment of a new kingly rule. Throughout much of Monsoon Asia the assumption of kingship was supposed to be accompanied by the formal establishment of a new city. Proper ritual and protocol were part of the formality. In time the wall became the more significant element of symbolism in several regions of the Orient, the wall and its gates became more and more imposing, so eventually the formal, gated wall distinguished the city from the town or village. In China, for example, though many settlements possessed simple walls around them, the common early word for city, *ch'eng*, was the word for wall. A city without a formal wall did not exist. Many of the Chinese words for villages and towns were related to the gathering of produce, its fabrication, its display, and the trade in commodities.

The ancient oriental city, in terms of physical structure, was dominated by walls and formal gates, by temples, palaces, and governmental buildings. Such construction showed tremendous application of labor and skill, and often these were the only types of construction that rose above the second story. There was great contrast between public or government buildings, and the homes and workshops of the artisan citizenry. In the matter of size of the settlement and in the presence of these large buildings lay the classical distinction between the city and the town or village. There is still an aura about Peiping, as the long-time center of the Chinese world, which is lacking in modern Shanghai, and it may well be that Communist removal of the political capital to Peiping was an effort to recapture this aura in order to surround the Communist regime with a little more sanctity. There also is an aura around Delhi, a long-term Indian capital, and the British sought to capture it by moving their capital from Calcutta to Delhi in 1911, and building a New Delhi.

All the early cities of the Orient were built on some interpretation of the grid plan. Perhaps their builders did not understand it completely or possessed too little political and cultural control over the populace to carry it out with high efficiency. The early core of many of the old cities today is hard to recognize and map, but the grid plan is at the bottom of every one of them. With varying political or cultural impact, different kinds of modifying influences were brought to bear on the old cities with the passage of time, and many of them today show but imperfect remainders of their origin and pattern.

On the mainland the chief early cities were cities of land and overland traffic. But throughout the Island Arcs and along some mainland shores the early city was often oriented to water routes, located on shore-line or river-mouth sites, and thus often of necessity cramped into less than the proper space. Such cities often required both special types of water-front building and modified zonal arrangement, and often shares of their populations lived on boats on the water. The early shore-line or river-mouth cities, therefore, frequently were at physical variance with the inland city. In that these sites often were subject to silting up, and the cities were organized by seafarers, the city oriented to the water was almost a transient thing, depending upon the fortunes of nature and sea power. These shore-line cities were often strange mixtures of people from many cultures, this in itself contributing to the transient nature of the cities when a harbor silted up or political power waned.

The city in southeastern Asia was a feature brought in by Indian or Chinese influences, depending upon the area. Prior to about 400 B.C. no development of the complex political state took place here, and it was only with Indian contact that the higher levels of culture and the more complex patterns of economy and political administration developed. Indian influence largely was felt around the coastal fringes, whereas early Chinese influence penetrated southeastern Asia overland, with the migration of peoples away from the expanding Chinese empire. In such an area as the Philippines no city existed prior to the coming of the Spanish, and in New Guinea even the occidental has not yet produced a true city. In mainland Southeast Asia and the Philippines cities are few today, and there is only one really populous cultural center in each of the countries. Java and Sumatra were exceptions in the Indies, each having several early cities, but these were expressive of regional states in separate sectors of the two islands, and the whole of the rest of the Indies has produced few real cities. In Central Asia Indian and Chinese influences, plus the natural motivation of settlement around sources of water, produced a small number of cities at an early date.

It must be pointed out that in several parts of southern and southeastern Asia early cities existed but that they have disappeared with the demise of the political states they controlled. Thus, Angkor in Cambodia, the capital of Sri Vijaya in Sumatra, several cities in Java, and several in Burma have all disappeared except for certain monumental architectural remains. In Central Asia the drying up of sources of water, plus the passing of political states, has caused the disappearance of a number of cities. In both China and India changing political patterns connected with the rise of empires out of kingly states and the changing fortunes of empires or attempted empires have caused the abandonment and gradual disappearance of a great many cities. In India and Ceylon historian-archaeologists are engaged in the identification and uncovering of many ancient cities, and the list is a long one which ranges from Mohenjo-daro and Harappa of the third millennium B.C. through Taxila and Anuradhapura to such cities as Kamatapura, the fifteenth-century capital of the Khyen kings of eastern India. The latter's size is demonstrated chiefly by a massive earth rampart over a 100 feet wide, 30 feet high, and some 15 miles in circumference. Kamatapura was laid waste by a Moslem conqueror in 1498 and has never been rebuilt or occupied since except by village dwellers.

In contrast to this decay and abandonment of some of the early cities, is the long life of others. Modern New Delhi is at least the eighth city that may be enumerated, in terms of buildings and streets, as having occupied a site in its locality, and Peiping became a city in the tenth century A.D. Canton now covers a larger area than ever before, but the general site has been occupied by a city for over 2,000 years. Many other oriental cities now stand on sites long serving as regional cultural centers, even though they have been torn down and rebuilt many times. Some of them have progressively changed both in morphology and architecture and in cultural pattern during their long histories.

One of the characteristics of the ancient city in most parts of the Old World, of course, was the tight packing of people into small area. In no sector has this feature been more pronounced than in the Orient, both in the earlier day and in the modern era. One of the factors discrediting the existence of large cities in the ancient world is the smallness of their physical proportions. However, in the modern Orient urban densities of over 100,000 people per square mile are not at all uncommon, and some sectors of old-style cities reach densities of over 400,000 people per square mile (close to 800 people per acre). Even villages are densely packed in many portions of the Orient, and many old villages have long had densities of a ratio of over 5,000 people per square mile without being considered crowded. Whereas single story buildings are common to villages, two story housing packed solid into row units fronting right on narrow lanes was a common feature of the old city. The sharing of common exterior walls, small room sizes, and the total lack of garden space have been other old-city characteristics. A final element in the high-density pattern has been the communal aspect of family life, in which large extended families have occupied very small square footage of housing.

Because the formalization of the ancient city lay in its religious and political monumentalism, it does not follow that populations were always small and that the cities were only ceremonial sites. The secular business of a city did not, in itself, call for the expenditure of large amounts of capital resources in buildings of permanent nature. When manufacturing technologies were simple, household or community workshop manufacturing systems were the rule, human labor was the chief power source, and finished products were neither large in size nor produced in tremendous volumes. The remains of kilns, furnaces, and working sites surrounding many ancient capitols, sometimes at distances of several miles, provide mute testimony to some of the kinds of manufacturing operations that went on around the capitols. Throughout much of Monsoon Asia the nature of secular and domestic architecture has always been notorious for its impermanence, its perishable materials, and for the slight marks left on the landscape after even short spaces of time in this humid tropical environment. The extraneous and inter-regional nature of many of the resources utilized is evidence of long-range transport of raw materials, and the sheer expression of man hours of labor with simple tools exhibited in the monumental architecture that does remain certifies to significant working forces, implying fairly large populations. The archeologic evidence of village settlements surrounding ancient capitols, in areas that have been searched so far also provides evidence of extensive regional populations. Throughout the Orient any useful materials remaining on an old site were often scavenged for the construction of new settlements. This tradition served to reduce evidence of earlier settlements.

The sacking and laying waste of the cities of downfallen rulers is another element of tradition throughout much of Monsoon Asia, epitomized in the old Chinese proverb: "The conquerors are kings, the beaten are bandits." The destruction of a conquered city became part of the symbolization of the establishment of a new hegemony, and this symbolization carried over into the monumental architecture of secondary settlements in that temples and other monumental constructs in such sites were allowed to fall into disarray and ruin, whereas new constructs characterized the strength of the new hegemony. In late historic time there was generally less such urban destruction in regions in which broad-based political controls continued within the same cultural context, so that remains of old cities, from the fifteenth century onward, often do exist in parts of Monsoon Asia.

Newer Oriental Cities

During the late 1960's there has been a growing tendency to differentiate the ancient and pre-industrial city from either the modern industrial-commercial city or, rather recently, from the so-called "colonial city" built by Europeans in their political colonies around the world. Another more recent tendency is to separate the urbanism of the developed world from that of the "third world," on the assumption that each is a supposedly peculiar kind of urbanism. There are some obvious characteristics on which this kind of differentiation can be based, but there also is some doubt about the validity of making such wholesale separations in urban patterns. There are tendencies of the tradiional in the creation of "civic centers" which express something more than secular efficiency for the modern industrial-commercial city—the attempt to "build in" a kind of "cultural soul" into the modern city which hints at the ideas of the spiritual and cultural mysticism embodied in the ceremonial center of the ancient city. The notion that "colonialism" is solely a product of the modern European expansion does not fully hold up against the critical evaluation of history. The concept that modern industry and trade are fundamentally different in kind and objective from earlier industry and trade makes perhaps too much of the differences in technological systems involved, and discredits the primary objectives of human action. There is no question that religious, political, social, economic, and technologic systems have altered their constructs and their emphases since urbanism first became a collective human habit. And there is no question but that cities are more numerous today than they were in the ancient world, and that large cities and metropolitan complexes hold larger numbers of people than ever before. But is it true that the city of today is fundamentally different from any city of the ancient world in the basic drives that lead human beings to come together in collective settlement habit?

One can suggest that those cities founded since the coming of the occidental and the development of modern economic and political systems differ considerably from the classical cities of the ancient Orient. Not only is there apparent a difference in architecture in the newer cities, but many of them are located on different sites, their organization appears different, and their very reasons for existence seem to be different. Singapore is one of the newer cities. Less than two centuries old, possessing more skyscrapers than many European cities, but lacking the monumental complex of religious and political buildings, Singapore is a gathering of people from many cultures and countries, held together only by the concern with world trade relations. Greater Shanghai, Hong Kong, Colombo, Manila, and Calcutta are similar to Singapore in their lack of concern for regional culture and their interest in world trade. Although these cities bear superficial resemblance to the ancient shore-line cities, they differ from them. The modern commercial port city often has grown out of an early local trade center, as did Shanghai, and Djakarta, but as often they may be on new sites as are Hong Kong, Kobe, and Calcutta. And seemingly very different are Jamshedpur, the new industrial city growing up in the Chota Nagpur hill country of eastern India, and Kuala Lumpur, the Malaysian city built on the trade in tin ores. For Jamshedpur, the reason for being is not trade with the world, but the modern industrial fabrication of metals on a huge scale; in Kuala Lumpur, colonial political administration, and then political nationalism

coupled with industrial planning have promoted economic growth. Yawata, in Japan, and Fushun in Manchuria, are such cities. In every country of the Orient cities of this type are now growing up, some of them into large industrial centers.

Another seeming modern factor in city development is the garrison or cantonment center built by occidental rulers in the cementing of their political colonial systems. Many of these have become sizable urban settlements. The appearance of modern transport, with its reorientation of regional traffic, has apparently produced a good many new cities that differ from the older ones by virtue of the changes in transportation. There are several other sources of motivation for some of the newer cities of the Orient.

In the building of these newer cities there are notable morphologic and technologic departures from older urban patterns. Most striking is the trend to tall buildings, with the skyscraper now a common feature of most of the newer cities, also invading the older ones. The bund, or improved harbor shore line, and docks and port equipment for large ships also are in contrast to the facilities of the older city, as are the deep waters that are a must to the modern port. The wide streets and mechanical, wheeled transport of the new city contrasts with the narrow lanes and irregular surfacing of many of the old cities, and this too is invading many of the older centers. The physical morphology of the newer cities usually is on a more spacious pattern than in the older city. The land-transport terminal, with its rail yards and truck depots, contrasts with the arrangement of transport handling in the old city. The large factory sites, and the large workers' residential quarters contrast with the arrangement, size, and distribution of these items in the cities of the preindustrial era. The garrison quarters for military and police units and the occidental residential quarter also form strong contrasts against earlier cities.

The very styles, patterns, and kinds of architecture in themselves form contrasts.

Often the newer city of the Orient seems to retain many of the poor features of cities native to both the East and the West. Too many attributes of the old remain, and the builders of the new have failed to build as well as they should have done. Some of the new suburbs and cities currently being built under native political control may fare better than those of the last four centuries.

The very term city is harder to define today than it was in the past. The senior author once resided in a settlement of over 100,000 people in eastern China which contained all the attributes of the occidental city except piped water and piped sewage disposal. To the Chinese of the region it was not a city, in proper terms, for it was new, without a wall, not a political administrative center, had few high skills of craftsmanship, and was not a settlement of very much culture. The juggling of minimal sizes and other criteria by statisticians lends no confidence to the variable definition now employed. Impressive totals of trade and manufacture, contributed to by large numbers of people packed into a small area and tabulated by a chamber of commerce do not clearly define a city. The very concept "city," in the Orient at least, has become as heterogeneous as the architecture and the things that go on there.

And is the modern city of the Orient so truly different from the ancient city of the Orient, after all, that it constitutes a truly new kind of settlement pattern? It seems possible to describe four basic kinds of settlement patterns: Rural dispersal, village settlement, town dwelling, and urban living, each differentiated from the other by definition in light of the kinds of living that characterize each. In this view the modern rural, dispersed homestead having the facilities of electric light and power equipment, automotive and airplane transportation, radio communication, and industrially manufactured consumer goods and food supplies does not constitute a different kind of pattern from the ancient Neolithic dispersed homestead fully dependent upon its occupants' own immediate resources and skills, for it is only the technologic systems that differentiate the two. Similarly, then, the view can be taken that the modern city differs from the ancient city only in horizontal and vertical morphology and in the multiplicity of technologic systems through which to arrange complementary patterns of living for large numbers of residents. It is possible to identify different motivational drives for the founding of ancient urban settlements, just as it is possible to identify different functional orientations among modern urban settlements. The secular viewpoint of much of the modern world plays down the importance of spiritual-mystical-cultural motivations in the analyses of cities. However, in the effort of the builders of the new Pakistan capital of Islamabad to develop something distinctively Pakistani and to create something more than a mere physical city, in the effort of the Chinese to retain something of the "aura" of classical Peking as expressive of "Chineseness," and in the attempt of the leadership of Malaysia to create something of a spiritual-cultural image around the burgeoning industrial city of Kuala Lumpur that evolves into "Malaysianism" there lies a bond that is common between the founders-builders of ancient cities and the planners-developers of modern cities. That New York and San Francisco embody something that Americans identify with "great cities," as opposed to the lack of that same thing in other cities, does not proceed from morphology, categorical divisions of the labor function, or differing elements of the sector hypothesis. This "something" proceeds from nonphysical elements of culture, as contrived by and perceived by Americans.

Although one cannot examine its morphology, economic indices, and sociopolitical arrangements, is it idle to suggest that the now almost mythical port of eastern India of the early world, Tamralipta, was concerned with inter-regional trade more than with other concerns, or that it was a collection of foreign and native merchants more concerned with pecuniary gain than with spiritual enlightenment? Is it idle to suggest that the Arabs, Indonesians, Indians, Chinese, and others who met as merchants in Canton during the ninth century A.D., were motivated so differently, and created urban structures so genetically different from the modern polyglot population currently assembling in Hong Kong? Is it idle to suggest that the colonial controls over the "native populations" of North China instituted by the invading Chou conquerors in the eleventh century B.C. were fundamentally different from the colonial controls instituted by the Europeans over "native populations" during their recent period of imperial control? The Chou capital was a double city, in one portion of which (laid out by new morphologic patterns) lived the imperial rulers, with the subjugated population resident in its own old settlement built on different lines. Although we are attracted to the elements of morphology that seem different, and though the elements of technology seem very different, there appears little that is really genetically different about the modern city, as opposed to the ancient city, and it can be suggested that, once urbanism became an element of settlement habit, it is the technical forms, the materials, and the technologic systems that have been altered through time. Each cultural system has interpreted these varied elements differently, to the end that Delhi (old and new), Bangkok, and Tokyo continue, in part, to be expressions of different systemic cultures, and that Singapore and Hong Kong continue to be products of the meeting of different cultures concerned with common aims.

Admittedly, populations have grown larger in the oriental city. Tokyo, Shanghai, and Calcutta today are larger than were any of the cities of the pre-Columbian Orient, though the pre-occidental Tokyo of 1800 was one of the largest cities in the world, it is possible that Peking in 1700 was the largest city in the world at that time, and the conventional rubric holds that Hangchou (the Quinsay of Marco Polo) on the central China coast was a city of over one million in the thirteenth century. Today there are many more huge metropolitan settlements than ever before, but these are less a product of the Orient itself than of world-wide developments. The larger settlements of today are functionally diverse, multiple creations of both the East and West, the old and the new. All of them are changing rapidly. The Batavia of 1941, with its half million people, hardly resembles the Djakarta of 1970, with its almost three million inhabitants, but in this case so far there has been only a change in size. The metropolitan Manila of the year A.D. 2000 will be far different from the Spanish Manila of 1650, or the American Manila of 1940. Probably the large cities of the Orient, in another half century, will trend more and more to a common pattern and tradition than they do today. The newer city, motivated by the occidental, differed greatly in certain respects from the classical city of the agricultural empires of the past. Perhaps, in the next half century, all cities of the Orient, both old and new, will come to resemble each other more closely, though, of course, the Japanese city will still possess an individuality different from that of a West Pakistan city. This is one of the elements of cultural convergence of our one world, in which urbanism everywhere is sharing characteristics, technologic systems, and common problems, as more and more people accumulate on our single earth and pile up in the settlements we euphemistically call cities.

Examination of the cartographic representations of some of the large metropolitan settlements of the Orient reveals interesting features (Figs. 4.3 through 4.10). The present patterns of Delhi, Osaka, and Peiping depict the modernization and enlargement of ancient centers; Tokyo and Bangkok present transitional cases; Calcutta, Singapore, and Hong Kong represent cities of the modern European era of imperialism.

Of these cities Delhi may have the oldest occupancy, for there are at least eight identified sites of settlement, of which six can be recognized under the rubric "city" (Fig. 4.3). Only four of

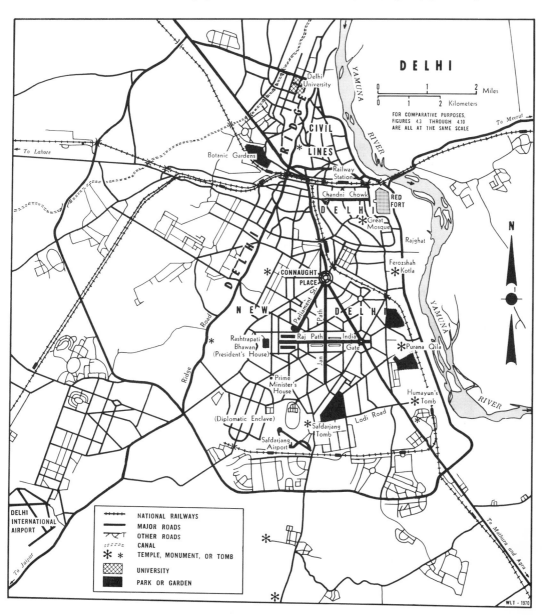

FIGURE 4.3. Metropolitan Delhi, India.

these cities lie within the contemporary urban zone, Ferozshah Kotla (site No. 5), Purana Qila (No. 6), Delhi (No. 7), and New Delhi (No. 8). The first site is not clearly known, and three other sites lie to the southwest beyond the new international airport, namely Raj Pithora (No. 2), the non-urban site around the Qutb Minar (No. 3), and Tughluqabad (No. 4). Only two of these are now considered as occupied urban sites, and these are conventionally known as Delhi and New Delhi, the seventh and eighth sites, respectively. Delhi, as the seventh city, began as the mid-seventeenth century Shahjahana-bad, a Mogul capital built in a classical Islamic motif. It is a tightly packed walled city of low buildings intensely crowded together, pierced by narrow lanes and alleys, with a high population density. On its eastern flank, fronting on the Yamuna River, is the ceremonial monumental complex of Shah Jahan, the Mogul Emperor, now normally known as the Red Fort. The lowering, terminal ridges of the Aravalli Mountains lie just west of the walled city, and scattered over these are the British administrative facilities of the decades prior to 1911, when Delhi was made the capital of India. Scattered out on the river flood plain and into the edges of some of the terminal ridges, south and west of the old walled city, lie other settlement sites, tombs, baths, remains of temple monuments, and other bits of monumental building marking the long period of occupancy of the area. Just south of the walled city is the spacious, low-density settlement of New Delhi, the modern political capital of India. A circular retail business center has wide streets radiating southward to the government buildings. Large residential sites filled with gardens and trees stand in striking contrast to the crowded pattern of the old walled city. Incorporated into New Delhi are the nearer of the old monuments, tombs, and mosques, now preserved as tourist attractions.

Recent expansion of the metropolitan region has spread streets in all directions on the west side of the Yamuna River, incorporating former suburban villages, distant establishments, many of the old tombs and monuments, rough hill lands, and some cropland areas. The former suburban airport, Safdarjang, as in other growing cities, now is restricted to small planes, and a new international terminal has been located farther out. The marks of ages of occupancy are everywhere to be seen, but out on the fringes are four of the early sites, still not incorporated into the modern city. The city chiefly functions as a national political capital, though light industrial establishments in the textile category are located at various points throughout the complex. Although the core of New Delhi was formally planned, the metropolitan community presents a peculiar jumble of monumental elements and urban sectors compounded over the centuries. An area of 573 square miles around Delhi has been made a federal political district, with a population of about 3,000,000.

The city of Osaka has been an urban settlement since about the fourth century A.D. (Fig. 4.4). Located at the eastern end of the Inland Sea on the bay shore of one of the larger alluvial lowlands of Japan, Osaka has been a commercial and trade city almost from the beginning. Its original core area was laid out in rectangular grid pattern, but the city long ago outgrew the core area. Numerous small streams entering the bay have been canalized, over time, and there are about 1,300 bridges over waterways. In the earlier era the shallow bay and canalized streams were adequate for the small ships that handled the huge domestic trade. By the eighth century Osaka was the port of entry for the Korea-China trade, and the harbor and canals were still adequate. As the chief port for the lowland, and the imperial capitals located inland, Osaka became the most important trade and handi-

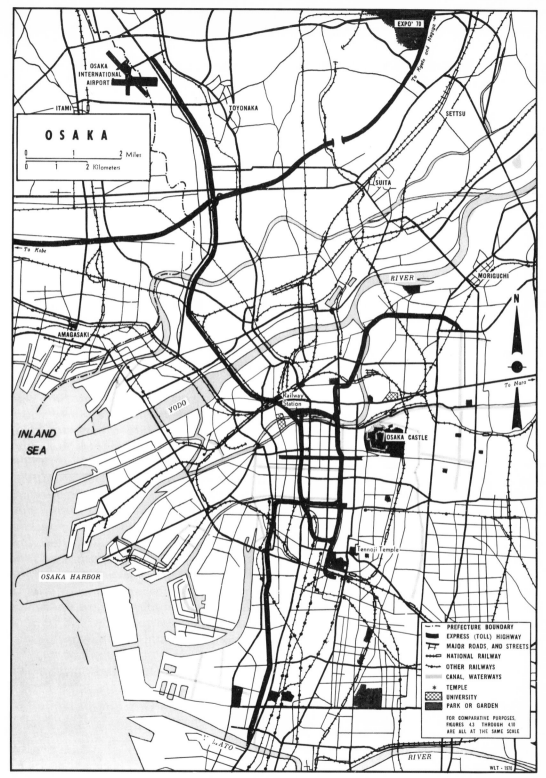

FIGURE 4.4. Metropolitan Osaka, Japan.

craft manufacturing city of Japan. Even as late as the early nineteenth century Osaka was the chief commercial-financial-trade center of Japan, its hinterland contained a large number of small manufacturing towns, and the basin of the Yodo River contained a large rural agricultural population. In the 1860's Osaka held about 275,000 people. The opening of Japan to foreign trade, in the 1860's, quickly showed that the canals of Osaka and the shore waters of Osaka Bay were too shallow for modern shipping, accounting for the rise of Kobe, located farther west along the bay at the point of deep water, but the two are not essentially different kinds of cities. In the late nineteenth century Osaka grew as a center for the cotton textile industries and for such heavy manufacturing as shipbuilding, heavy machinery, and the basic aspects of the chemical industries, to the end that Osaka became a grimy industrial city.

Although an old city with formal political status of long standing, Osaka's impressive feudal castle was built only in the late 16th century, located on a high diluvial terrace east of the city core. This higher ground, somewhat more free of urban smoke than the deltaic flats, has become the best residential district of the city. Osaka is not highly sectored off in functional districts, and manufacturing, residential areas, and commercial developments are somewhat mixed together in the modern city as the urban entity has spread out beyond the core. By the present era the grid-pattern core of the city is becoming filled with occidental style high-rise buildings despite the general subsidence of the deltaic flats. Urban developments have spread inland, particularly up the Yodo River basin, and the rural hinterlands are filling in, to the end that the Osaka metropolitan region is almost continuous, has almost enveloped a score of hinterland towns, and has absorbed many former agricultural villages. A web of short, private railways augments the national system to serve commuters from the south-and-east and the north-and-west suburban fringes. The newest railway connects the city center subway (not shown on the map) with the Expo '70 site (at the northern margin of the map). A new international airport has been located northwest of the main urban center, and is linked to the city by the extensive toll highway system. The metropolitan region now exceeds 3,000,000 population. An artificial harbor has been constructed and, through steady dredging, Osaka maintains a strong position as the port contact for a hinterland region totalling some ten million people. A significant element of its port function relates to the passenger traffic along the Inland Sea as a part of domestic vacation tourism.

Peiping has been a settlement site for over three thousand years, and conventional history refers to early "cities" located on or near the present site under a variety of names as the administrative headquarters for various small "states" (Fig. 4.5). One of these settlements undoubtedly was destroyed in the third century B.C., as the Ch'in dynasty turned China into a national political state; the site of the settlement is believed to have been located at about the northwest corner of the later Tartar city. Until after the third century A.D. a settlement thought to have been located near the southwest corner of the Tartar city functioned as a military frontier post. The region then was lost to Chinese control for several centuries, but it came under control of the T'ang dynasty and a frontier post again was located near the present city. Some settlement existed under variable regional controls during the ninth and early tenth centuries, and certainly true city status was achieved by the late tenth century when a town was rebuilt with a strong, formal wall and was made a Khitan Liao dynasty capital as the city of Yenching. The walled area was located just southwest of what be-

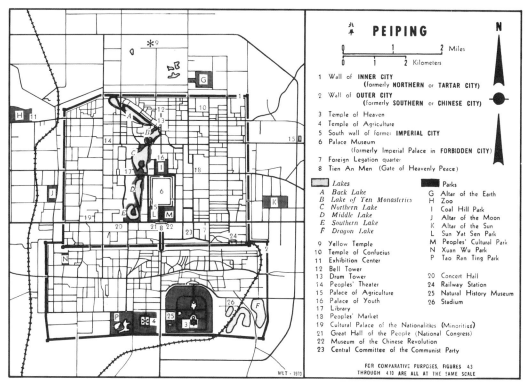

FIGURE 4.5. Metropolitan Peiping, China.

came the Tartar City, but no buildings remain of that city. From the twelfth century onward the city expanded under the hands of different ruling dynasties as an imperial capital. Enlargement or adjustment of the walls, the addition to, or removal of, walled units, and the expansion of the suburbs has been an alternating activity right down to the present.

In the formal sense it is possible to distinguish six divisions of the modern city as established at different times. The initial item is a thirteenth century redevelopment which set the primary morphology of the city's central section as it exists today, this being the building of the wall of the Tartar City, with its nine gates and a primary but skeleton grid plan. The Tartar City was the Canbaluc of Marco Polo. Within the walled settlement

there began the construction of elements which came to be the later Imperial City. The second feature is the fifteenth century wall which was built to enclose a then suburban sector on the southern margin. This became known as the Outer City, or the Chinese City, in the southern portion of which the Temple of Heaven and the Temple of Agriculture were built. The third division is the Imperial City, a palace sector surrounded by its own wall in the southern portion of the Tartar City, and the fourth is the Forbidden City located within the Imperial City as the residential palace area for the royal family. Both the third and the fourth divisions were formal completions of earlier beginnings, and date from the late fifteenth century. The fifth portion of the city comprised the suburbs around the Tartar and Chinese cities, all of which grew steadily under the Ch'ing, in the seventeenth-twentieth centuries. The sixth sector may be distinguished as the territory annexed to the old city in recent years, since the Communists have twice enlarged the political limits of the city. Peiping now includes an area of just over 6,500 square miles, and has a total population of over 7,300,000. The annexations have swallowed up five nearby counties and their county-seat cities, located at variable distances from the old main city, have also included large areas of agricultural land and their rural villages, and have incorporated into the greater city various suburban industrial towns of modern origin, along with several coal mining centers. The walls of the Imperial and Forbidden cities have been removed and the whole area turned into the Palace Museum of the present day.

At various times Emperors created artificial lakes, parks, preserves, summer houses, and palaces in the suburban region outside the walled city, and during Ch'ing times numerous reconstructions were carried out on the various walls. Originally of mud brick, the main walls were faced with fired brick during the fifteenth century, and relatively continuous improvements were made in walls and gates right through Ch'ing times. In the late nineteenth century the foreign Legation Quarter was established between the Imperial City and the south wall of the Tartar City, east of the main gate. Since the late nineteenth century additional "gate" openings have been cut through the Tartar City wall, and there now are twenty-one openings through the wall.

The modern growth of the urbanized area has surrounded the walled city and has sprawled out along the main lines of communication, with residential and commercial sectors chiefly spreading north and west from the Tartar wall, and industrial sectors spreading eastward from the walled margins toward the former county seat of Tungchou, which is now the eastern element of the enlarged city. During the 1920's and 1930's coal mines, steel mills, and other industrial establishments were located in surrounding towns or on new sites in the rural hinterland in all directions from the main city. The Communist enlargement of the city has included a great many of these within the new city boundaries. At the same time a tremendous amount of rebuilding, akin to urban renewal, has developed a new ceremonial-monumental pattern within the old walled city. Particularly in the southern section of the Tartar City has this rebuilding developed the great ceremonial-ritual area known as Tien An Men Square, in which the Communists hold their great mass meetings. The modern city of Peiping, therefore, bears the marks of a long line of imperial rulers who have proliferated monumental-ceremonial building of impressive nature. Peiping, today, is a polyglot phenomenon, a metropolitan governmental district extended to include all manner of suburban and hinterland settlements, rural agricultural sectors, and sites of mineral resource exploitation and industrial fabrication. Notably, the Communist program of current years has been rather careful to preserve almost all of the really fine monumental-ceremonial building of the past, to assist in the retention of the aura and the glory of the "Great Capital."

Tokyo has no recorded history of settlement prior to the twelfth century when a fishing village was known to have been located on its present site, though it is likely that some such small village had been there for at least a century (Fig. 4.6). The spot was chosen for a march-site fortress in the mid-fifteenth century, located on the old high alluvial terrace about where the Imperial Palace grounds are today. The population remained very small, however, until the end of the sixteenth century, when the Tokugawa came to power. During the whole of the sixteenth century Tokyo expanded rapidly, as regional feudal lords were required to

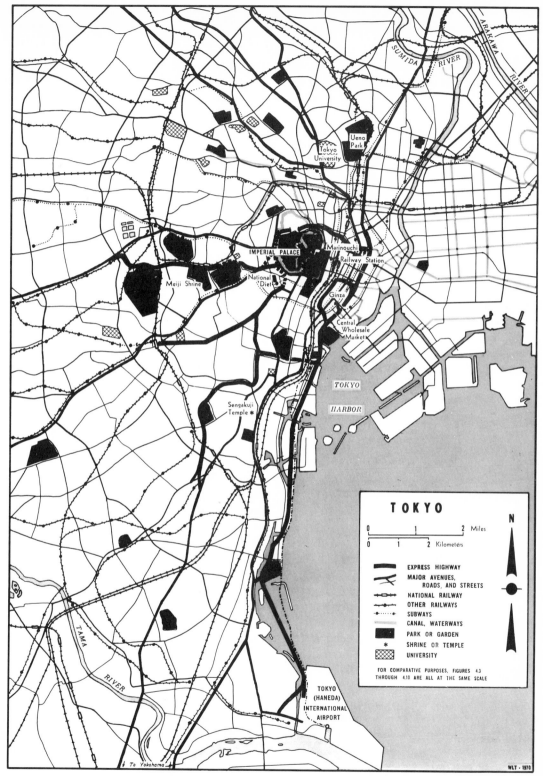

FIGURE 4.6. Metropolitan Tokyo, Japan.

build homes in the vicinity surrounding the castle and maintain portions of their families in the city, virtually as hostages. A great many temples and shrines were built during this same interval. Many of the *Daimyo* homes were fortified castles, surrounded by moats. At the end of the sixteenth century the settlement was a large city, still centered on the primary castle. Outside the moated area the supporting population of artisans, tradesmen, and others built its residences, primarily in wood, surrounding the fortified core. The street pattern at the start of the seventeenth century was a radial system, as spokes outward from the roughly circular core, and this remains the primary alignment of trunk roads today. Within the sectors between the main roads narrow lanes and alleys permitted passage.

Built chiefly in wood the city was subject to fires, as well as to earthquakes. During the seventeenth-nineteenth centuries large fires repeatedly burned off sections of the city, earthquakes caused repeated damage, and some portion of the city was under constant reconstruction. Late in the nineteenth century the *Daimyo* sold off much of their land to the east of the castle, the moats were filled, the castles torn down, and the modern, westernized central business district began to form (the Marinouchi district), with the street pattern realigned into a grid plan system. The central castle had already been rebuilt, in its moated park, into an Imperial Palace. In the outer ring of tradesmen-artisan quarters no realignment of streets took place, and the Ginza continued as the chief retail shopping street. The earthquake of 1923 and the bombing-fires of World War II permitted some widening of streets, but the narrow lanes and alleys remain typical of Tokyo, which has a relatively small percentage of its surface in roadways. North of the primary castle many of the *Daimyo* estates became the grounds of the numerous universities that have clustered in Tokyo. In the

mid-seventeenth century the Sumida River had been diverted to the east around the city, but waterways pierce the lowlands east of the castle site, and hundreds of bridges accrued as the city grew.

The waters of Tokyo Bay are shallow and silting is active. Tokyo did become a very important shipping port in the late sixteenth century, for smallboat domestic trade. The opening of Japan, in the 1860's, caused the development, to the south, of the deep-water port of Yokohama, and started Tokyo on a program of industrialization. An industrial region developed on the east of the city, but this gradually has expanded along the west bay-shore, now being almost continuous to Yokohama. As the city's modern growth began the high-level old terraces west of the castle became the chief residential section, but this gradually has expanded around the north of the city. Isolated retail shopping districts have developed in the western section of the city. Newer housing often is in housing estates developed in block units. Japan as a whole is becoming highly urbanized, but Tokyo remains the focus of urban growth. The modern expansion of the city has enveloped many old villages and satellite towns in the hinterland. Some 14,000,000 people live in the metropolitan region, but another 11,000,000 are found in a surrounding nearby zone, and Tokyo may become a gigantic urban complex in the near future. The political pattern has been readjusted through time, and Tokyo today functions governmentally on approximate prefecture status, over an area of 780 square miles, of which about 250 square miles lie within the urban metropolitan area.

Bangkok is a late illustration of the classical founding of a capital in oriental style (Fig. 4.7). An agricultural village had long occupied the location, twenty-odd miles above the mouth of the Menam Chao Phraya. In the late seventeenth century the village became a fortified post in defense of the capital

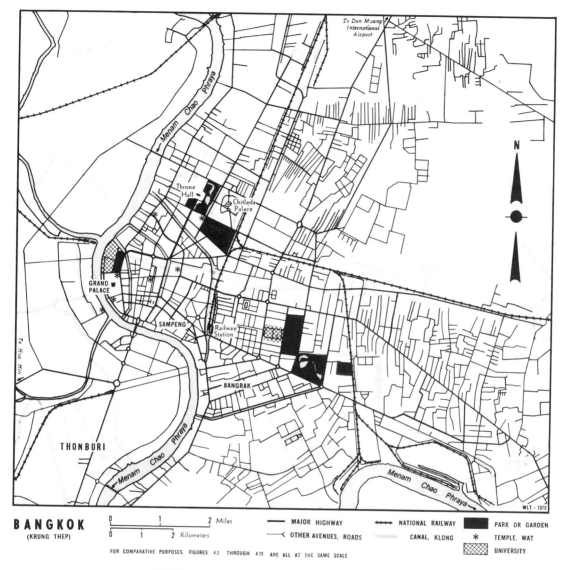

FIGURE 4.7. Metropolitan Bangkok, Thailand.

at Ayuthia. Following a Burmese invasion and the sacking of Ayuthia, in 1767, a resident Chinese leader rallied the Thai, assumed a kingly leadership, and began the reconquest of the country, establishing his capital in Thonburi, on the west bank of the Chao Phraya. To serve the new capital, Chinese traders soon established a market town, lo- cated across the river on the east bank, the present site of Bangkok. In 1782 the Chinese leader became insane, and a Thai general was proclaimed king and crowned Rama I. Rama's first act was to establish his own capitol, and he chose the site of the Chinese market town, which he commandeered. Rama began the building of a new capital on the east bank of the Chao Phraya, which here traced a wide loop to the west. A wall was built on the inland side across the lobe of land to protect its eastern flank. An imperial palace and numerous Buddhist temples were built on the former market site, developing the classical monumental-ceremonial complex. The displaced Chinese moved their market operations about a mile to the southeast, and the Sampeng sector continues to be the heart of the Chinese district of Bangkok. Gradually Thai moved into the general area, settling along the small waterways (*klongs*) flowing into the river, and locating their homes as pile-built houses overhanging the klongs, and additional Chinese came into the city to enlarge the Sampeng sector. The klongs were navigable for small craft much of the year in this wet lowland, and traders traveled the waterways peddling their wares. The Thonburi area remained chiefly rural agricultural land, providing the market produce and fruit for the new city, whereas the land on the Bangkok side of the river remained chiefly in wet-rice fields. This was the traditional beginning for a Southeast Asian state capital city.

Europeans had visited Ayuthia, in earlier periods, in search of trade. After a treaty opening Thailand to foreign trade, in 1855, European traders began to locate in Bangkok, and they gradually developed a new section of the settlement, Bangrak, locating their consulates, hotels, and warehouses along the river to the south of the Chinese market district of Sampeng. A modern-style roadway was opened in 1864 connecting the royal capitol complex to the Bangrak sector of the city, the first real road in a settlement that preferred the use of boats on the klongs and on the river. It was only after 1895, however, that other roads began to be built, leading away from the capitol complex, with cross roads forming connections. A first rail line was opened in 1893, connecting Bangkok to a port location at the mouth of the Chao

Phraya, with the Bangkok railway station being established just east of the Chinese district of Sampeng. By 1910 many Thai had shifted their residences from the klongs to the lands adjoining the roads, and immigrant urbanites began to fill in the residential sectors of the city. In the early twentieth century a European residential section began to form east of the railway station in a rural zone hitherto in rice fields, and hospitals, schools, a university, sports clubs, and parks were developed in the same area. The building of temples continued in the royal palace section, and additional royal establishments were located north of the original palace complex. The city grew steadily, but it has been growing at greatly increased rates since the end of World War II, expanding inland away from the river in all possible directions, leapfrogging sectors of vacant land, and pushing agriculture steadily farther back. Four bridges now connect Bangkok with Thonburi, and the truck gardens and fruit orchards are steadily being displaced away from the bridges as Thonburi increases in population as a dormitory community.

The city of Bangkok is changing rapidly at the present time, as steel-and-concrete buildings replace the older wood structures or become the new style. New streets are being opened continuously, some of which replace the older klongs, commercial strips are replacing housing along the roads, vacant lands are being filled in, and the city is altering character, without having developed a maturity. The city of Bangkok, in 1970, held a population close to 2,000,000, with another 600,000 resident in Thonburi. A large share of the population is Chinese, and Bangkok is a new city, but it is not a typical product of European impetus or influence.

Calcutta may commonly be attributed to British imperialism, but it was canny Scottish traders who located in the settlement that was to grow from the small agricultural village of Kalikata into one of the world's great urban problems (Fig. 4.8). European traders had been probing the Bengal Delta for trading post sites, and several other countries had secured such posts when the Scots finally secured permission to settle in a cluster of three villages on the left bank, outer bend of a Hooghly River meander in 1690, some eighty miles from the river mouth on the Bay of Bengal. A small fort was established, along with warehouses ("factories"), and a small and formless trading town emerged in a few years on the low natural levee between the Hooghly and a strip of wet-rice fields, beyond which lay a broad salt marsh to the east. In 1756 a Bengal native ruler seized the growing city, threw a large group of British into a small dungeon overnight, suffocating most of them, and leading to the disparaging

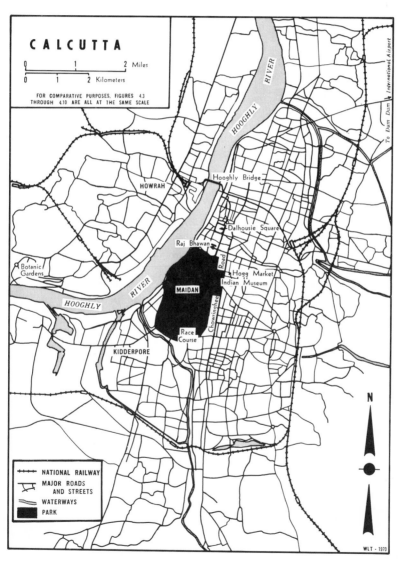

FIGURE 4.8. Metropolitan Calcutta, India.

phrase: "Black hole of Calcutta." The British retook the city in 1757, and a plan was slowly developed which improved the unhealthy local conditions and set the town on a course of economic growth. Over a few years a local marshy strip was turned into a two square mile open park, the Maidan, flanked on the south by a race course and a botanical garden, flanked on the north by government buildings around which slowly matured the commercial center of the city, and protected by a new Fort William set in the Maidan on the banks of the Hooghly. River quays and docks for shipping were developed below the Maidan at the deepest-water section of the meander bend in the suburban town of Kidderpore. By 1825 the main section of Calcutta had been provided with massive public buildings on models from Britain, statues of famous British were being erected on the Maidan, a line of European residences stretched along the east side of the Maidan, as the Chowringhee, and the British investment was paying dividends in a city of about 160,000 people. Other European posts to the north along the Hooghly prospered only mildly and gradually gave up the struggle, except for the French who held on at Chandernagore (twenty-two miles north of central Calcutta and on the opposite bank) until 1949, to the end that all these riverside settlements today are parts of the Calcutta metropolitan region.

Calcutta, in effect, had become the capital of British India in 1772, which status it retained until 1911, when the capital was moved to New Delhi. During the nineteenth century the public memorial and government buildings increased in numbers around and north of the Maidan, the statues increased in numbers on the Maidan, the northern sectors of the city became native residential quarters and centers for jute and cotton processing, factories and mills were located in what had been the rice field strip, the docks to the south increased in length and capacity, the

Chowringhee finally became a street of hotels, clubs, and shops, the city increased in population and developed some extremely high density sectors, marginal suburbs developed to the south, and the large suburban settlement of Howrah developed across the river on the right bank north of the Maidan as an industrial town at the terminals of the rail lines from the west. By the end of the nineteenth century Calcutta was beginning to have the problems that accrue to a city of a million people whose chief concerns were agricultural processing and foreign trade—inadequate city services, slum sections of too-great population density, and a death rate that almost approximated the birth rate in a city with more men than women and a constant inflow of predominantly male rural in-migrants.

During the twentieth century Calcutta's problems have increased in numbers and proportions. Urban development of the natural levees is fairly complete on both sides of the river for about thirty miles, Calcutta city has annexed many of the suburban towns and exceeds 3,000,000 in population, Howrah houses about 600,000, and the whole metropolitan region totals over 5,000,000 people in a situation providing great difficulties for a large city. Problems of garbage disposal, water supply, and sewage disposal are tremendous, the imbalance of population continues, in-migrants continue to arrive, central Calcutta is declining in population, but tremendous density rates plague the residential quarters with some of the world's poorest living conditions, the death rates now exceed the birth rates and, as the garbage piles in the streets grow higher, the phrase: "The black hole of Calcutta" threatens to take on new meaning as Indians struggle with the problems inherited from the founding of a British colonial city.

Singapore is a city-state located at a strategic point on the transport routes connecting the Pacific and Indian oceans (Fig. 4.9). The

FIGURE 4.9. Metropolitan Singapore.

present city is a creation of the modern concern for world transport strategy. Singapore Island has always been in this strategic position, however, and there have been long intervals when no active trading took place at this point. Strategic position, alone, is not enough. In the ninth-tenth and twelfth-thirteenth centuries there was active trading here, as there must have been at times in prior centuries. In the fifteenth century the local waters formed a pirate lair, but in the mid-sixteenth century there was an active port on the island. In the years 1800–1819, political conditions were disturbed in this whole region, Malacca and Penang were thought to be good trading points, and Singapore Island was occupied only by a few Malay fishermen and a few Chinese growers of gambier. British Stamford Raffles arrived at Singapore Island in January, 1819, to promise stable control, good management of local facilities, and freedom from piracy. Sea traders responded to the opportunity, and by 1825 the trade of Singapore was more than double that of Penang and Malacca combined. Port facilities, town administration, and tax administration were not really efficient at either Penang or Malacca, and Singapore got its modern start, therefore, from efficient and stable management of the conditions of trade. The city has prospered most when these conditions have been best since traders can then efficiently utilize transport strategy.

Raffles laid out the plan for the town fairly efficiently, placing Fort Canning on a hill near the anchorage, locating the Chinese along and west of Singapore River near the anchorage and the first elements of the port at what now is known as Keppel Harbour, on a rough grid pattern of streets, and allowing the Malays to cluster around the mouths of Rochor and Kallang rivers in an outlying situation to the east. Later expansion of the city built up a grid-plan section just west of Rochor River. Inland from this shore-fringe zone roads and streets have followed the topography, and early settlement was rather dispersed. More recently the density of settlement is increasing inland in all directions. The port development took place on the southeast shore of the island, with the business and residential town behind it. In time a British naval station was located, at a distance, on the northeast island shore, and a military air station at the east end, but the termination of the British occupancy of both of these may come in 1972. Much of the island was in extensive agriculture in early decades, but this has given way to intensive truck farming, and urban development is taking over more and more of the southern and eastern ends of the island. A large industrial zone is currently under development in the Jurong River section, off the map to the west, and residential development will follow. Early Singapore seldom showed more than two story development. Increasingly the high urban density is utilizing high-rise buildings for both commercial and residential purposes. Singapore never was noted for its architecture, in the early decades, but the high-rise residential developments of recent time are impressive in their bulk capacity, if not in their architectural grace.

As an entrepot, Singapore serves Southeast Asia. Traditionally over half its trade derived from, or went to, what is now West Malaysia. Rubber, tin, vegetable oil products, and timber have been its chief exports, and rice and other food commodities, manufactured goods, and petroleum have been its imports. The regional gathering for export, or distribution from import, have serviced other countries of Southeast Asia, but a significant share of its local revenues has derived from the dual servicing of ships coming from, and returning to, Europe in interregional trading voyages. Increasingly, Singapore's leadership is looking to independent political status in which world entrepot trade is bulwarked by local industry in service to the whole world, but that leadership realizes that future prosperity of the island's population depends upon the continuance of stable political and economic conditions, good port management, and the kinds of local conditions that permit the utilization of transport strategy by traders around the world. For a community of well over 1,700,000 in 1969, most of whom reside in the urban portion of the 209 square mile island, and most of whom are Chinese, simple strategic location is still not enough, and the fifth busiest world port will have to continue to provide efficient service, or lose its status as has happened in the past.

Hong Kong is an illustration of the case to be made in favor of the European founding of colonial cities (Fig. 4.10). Although there are Neolithic archaeologic sites in the area, and though there has been historic occupance by Chinese, only a few hundred fishermen

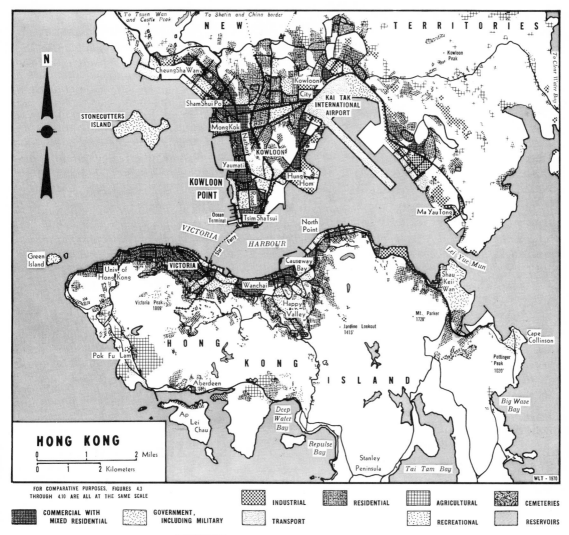

FIGURE 4.10. Metropolitan Hong Kong.

lived on the island and only local pirates used the harbor, in 1821, when British shipping bound for Canton began to use the excellent anchorage behind Hong Kong Island. The island had been stripped of its trees by woodcutters, and there were practically no resources. It was the need for politically safe anchorage for European shipping that led to development of one of the world's great ports. The harbor was used by British naval vessels during 1839–1841, and this led to the British demand for, and cession by China of, the 29 square mile island in 1841. Control of the opposite mainland shore was secured by the 1860 cession of 3.5 square miles of Kowloon Point, with a small Chinese fort and perhaps three thousand inhabitants, and the small Stonecutter's Island. The realization of the need for a watershed to provide a secure water supply led to the 99-year lease of the 365 square mile New Territories area behind Kowloon, then possessing perhaps 100,000 Chinese residents who were chiefly farmers and fishermen.

The small city of Victoria, opposite Kowloon Point, was the beginning development on the narrow lowland bay margin of the hilly island. A four layered pattern followed: The immediate shore line was devoted to shipping concerns; behind and above the shore was a single business street at either end of which Chinese residential sections were built up in typically compact, high-density manner; above the business street and scattered on the steep slope were the residences of Europeans; the crest of Victoria Peak first served as summer-resort housing for those who could afford it. With so restricted a site on the island, the development of Kowloon occurred steadily, with ferry services between the two shores. When conditions in China were turbulent Hong Kong grew extraordinarily; poor conditions of trade in Hong Kong produced an exodus of Chinese, who have made up almost the whole population from the beginning of British control. The holding is a Crown Colony, under an appointed governor and two councils, both of which include Chinese. From a population of 160,000, in 1881, the colony grew to 1,850,000, in 1949, only to swell to over 3,500,000 in 1969. Such growth has meant that, on the island, houses cling to every possible perch on the mountain sides, with access roads carved out of the mountain sides. High-rise business and apartment buildings are becoming the rule wherever they can be constructed. The normal high-density patterns of Chinese urban settlements are being exceeded in Hong Kong. Settlement is creeping round the margins of the island, and the urban pattern is spreading deeply back into the New Territories in two directions, flanking the mountain core behind Kowloon Point. Landfill on both sides of the harbor has added precious narrow strips

along the shores. Unlike many metropolitan settlements, Hong Kong's harbor and airport are in the center of the population cluster, Kai Tak airport being a filled-in strip in the shallow waters of the harbor just east of Kowloon Point.

Entrepot trade for a century kept Hong Kong flourishing, and that trade still is important but will not support the present population. Following a trade slump in the early 1950's, the colony turned to industrialization, and manufacturers now produce about half the income. There is little space for industry on the island, which has remained chiefly a residential and commercial area, but in Kowloon and in new satellite towns on Kowloon's flanks a wide variety of light manufacturing is expanding steadily, with cotton textiles and the apparel industries in the lead. Few of Hong Kong's manufactures go to China, but much of her import volume comes from China. Not only does Hong Kong continue to serve as an entrepot for world trade today, but she now is a manufacturing center dependent upon the world at large for her markets.

DOMESTIC ARCHITECTURES

There may well be a half dozen living traditions of house building in the Orient, and more than that number of methods of working out each tradition, so that there are many basic kinds of domestic housing. When one adds the impact of local cultural custom upon domestic architecture, one is confronted with a bewildering variety of products (see pp. 61–64).

Perhaps the most common building tradition is that of building in pounded earth or adobe blocks. This method relates to the very ancient Near and Middle East where it seems to have evolved when primitive cultures first began to abandon the pit house and build above ground. From the Middle East it spread both into India and through Central

Asia into China and Korea, replacing the pit house en route. Replacement of the pit house was very early in India where adobe blocks are preferred to pounded earth. China began using both pounded earth and adobe blocks perhaps prior to 1800 B.C., whereas in Korea above-ground building did not become common until the early centuries of the Christian era. The tradition first employed small-dimensioned floor plans, solid walls, few windows and doors, and the compound building of several house units together so that common walls often could serve more than one family. It used the flat mud roof supported on beams, and it lent itself to either one- or two-story construction. Stone as a building material was utilized when available in such shapes that it could be used without much working. Since its introduction into the dry margins of the Orient this tradition has spread throughout most of China, very widely in India, into parts of the Tibetan highlands and into parts of southeast Asia, well beyond what might seem the climatically dry and safe areas. In some of the more humid areas, such as central and southern China and Korea gabled sloping roofs were adapted for use on adobe housing and have gradually become common to most Chinese builders, and to all parts of Korea. In contrast the flat roof is often found along the central east coast of India in what is not really a dry climate.

A second basic tradition is that of the use of bamboo, reeds, and some of the grasses. The use of leaf and brushy materials may well be related to the bamboo tradition, but it seems older and more primitive, just as the pit house also was a tradition older than the pounded earth-adobe system of construction. Bamboo reed-grass housing had its regional development in some part of moist southeastern Asia. It produced a lightly constructed, airy house with numerous openings, that seldom is elaborately finished on the inside and often gives what an occidental terms a "barn-like"

appearance. Widely overhanging roofs and single-story construction appear normal, with room sizes ranging from small to large, as needed.

A third basic tradition employed wood in almost all construction, except possibly a stone foundation and sometimes lower parts of walls. Poles and crudely formed planks were the first construction materials, but the tradition gradually matured into an architecture which employed well-formed planks and boards, flooring, plank- or shingle-type roofing, and very elaborate carving of projecting timber ends. Multiple-story building on variable floor plan dimensions, many doors, windows, balconies, and numerous decorative features go with this tradition, though today not all wooden housing is equally elaborate. Well-developed domestic architecture in wood may possibly be younger than either of the foregoing systems, but its roots reach well back into the past. Regionally the developed tradition seems associated with the forested hill country of the Himalayas and the Chinese-Tibetan border zone, but some use of wood construction is found almost everywhere in the Orient as a development preceding the coming of the occidental.

A later, but prehistoric, tradition is that of the kiln-burnt brick, which is an improvement upon pounded earth or adobe blocks, in that it permitted of more variety and greater adaptability. This may also have come out of the Middle East into both India and China, but the two regions interpreted it quite differently. Since at least 2800 B.C. India has made excellent fully fired durable brick, red in color, in a wide variety of sizes. China shows a technique of only partial firing of the brick to produce a soft and short-lived gray brick in a range of sizes that was quite limited until rather recently. The Indian system of red brick firing spread eastward into Indonesia and is far more widespread than the Chinese interpretation of brick firing. In the Middle East, in northwest

India, in Central Asia, and in northwest China brick construction required no new roofing techniques beyond the old flat-roof system, but in the moist areas of southern China, eastern India, and southeastern Asia new roofing techniques were required. Straw thatching and sloping roofs were old features in southeastern Asia, and from moist India around to southern Japan, but such roofs did not fit burnt-brick wall construction. Here seem to lie the origins, for the Orient at least, of fired roofing tile and also the curved roof now often thought of as typically Chinese. The curved tile roof with its elaborate ridge-line decorations belonged to mainland southeastern Asia rather than to China proper.

Plaster construction, as a well-developed building technique, is a relatively late feature which may be related to Indian architecture, so far as the Orient is concerned. A simple mud plaster to cover pounded earth or adobe block architecture appears to be a very old feature, but this long preceded white burnt-lime plaster used as a primary construction material. If well-developed plastered construction matured in India, it eventually spread rather widely throughout southeastern Asia and into South China and involved different materials and systems of preparing the basic wall to which the plaster was applied. Plastering also is well developed in Japan and Korea. Plastered construction probably was always somewhat more costly than construction with simpler materials in many parts of southeastern Asia, so that it seldom became a dominant regional type. In the south, only in South India did it ever mature into a regional pattern of architecture.

The use of cut stone in building construction, in the Orient, is younger than the preceding systems. With minor local exceptions, it was slow to develop. Architectural working of stone in the Orient seems to have come out of the Near and Middle East several centuries before the beginning of the Christian Era and seems to be related to the upheavals of the Iranian and Greek culture worlds and to owe its technical skills and its motifs to that Iranian-Greek world. India received better teaching in the art of stoneworking than did China, not only in the first periods, but also later. In India, and in those parts of southeastern Asia to which Indians traveled, there gradually appeared a high tradition of building stone, whereas the Chinese stonework, except in bridges, often gives the impression of being thought out in wood and executed in stone. However, cut-stone building always was too costly to be common in domestic architecture, but it gradually became the medium of construction in religious and public building, in palaces, fortresses, and in monumental construction. It is these historical remnants of stone architecture, of course, that dot the Orient with interesting tourist vistas, be they the great temples of Cambodia, Java, and India, or the many bridges and memorial arches along the old-style roadways of China. In those parts of the Tibetan highlands where sedentary settlement is found above the tree line crude stone replaces wood in housing construction.

With the coming of the occidental new trends in domestic architecture appeared. At first these were mainly in the details of design and construction, but gradually some new basic elements are finally entering into the traditions of housing construction throughout the Orient, to modify the long-standing habits of all parts of the Orient.

From another viewpoint housing construction traditions may be worked out in several ways. The Chinese most commonly use a skeleton of wooden posts to hold up the roof, the walls being panel walls that fill in the space rather than support the roof. This is often done even when the building is in adobe or pounded earth, and sometimes even when the flat roof is employed. This principle may have descended from the tradition of late pit-house building, in which the roof frequently was raised above ground level on posts. But it could well derive from the bamboo building tradition in which a separate skeleton often is constructed and the walls covered with some kind of thatching. Normally the earlier Chinese preferred to build on a raised but solid platform, using earthen floors.

The skeleton of posts and panel walls are seldom found in India when wall construction is of materials strong enough to serve as bearing walls. But everywhere that well-developed plastered construction has become common, there is the use of the wooden skeleton to hold up the roof, the plastering normally covering some type of panel unit. The Japanese house followed the Chinese technique of using a wooden skeleton which supports the roof, the walls being commonly plastered panel walls, except for the south-facing walls—the front of the house when possible—which often are movable panels that can be removed to admit sun and air in warm weather. The Japanese house uses much more wood than is common in China, and floors of the main rooms normally are of wood. The Japanese housing patterns follow little of the pounded-earth or adobe-block techniques of Chinese architecture, but rather follow the tradition of the warmer parts of southern Asia in being light, airy, and open houses. Korean housing has gradually become a blend of Chinese pounded-earth and adobe-block construction, plastered over, and Japanese housing with its wooden floors, mats, and floor living habits.

Quite another thing is the pile-built house, standing off the ground 3 to 10 feet. The pile house may be built of wood, bamboo, or thatching materials, it may be a single or multiple dwelling, and it often is two story. The pile dwelling is today associated chiefly with the moist lowlands and aquatic fringes of southeastern Asia, but as a type it does not seem to be of great age in this region. Some students of oriental

culture history incline to the view that the pile dwelling originated on the mainland of southeastern Asia among peoples parent to those groups now termed Malay. The pile dwelling is used from Upper Burma and South China into the Philippines and central Indonesia. It used to be very common in South China but is less so today. The early pile house most commonly was floored with strips of split bamboo, so that dust, dirt, and unwanted scraps dropped through to the ground or water below and air circulated from beneath. The split bamboo floor gradually is being discarded today. Japanese housing in general seems to use a modification of the pile dwelling, after the southern tradition, most houses being set on short posts from 1 to 3 feet off the ground. The split bamboo floor is not employed in Japan.

The communal dwelling is one of the peculiar housetypes still found in southeastern Asia. It is a type used by simpler cultural groups possessing active clan organization, though there seems no universal simple criterion for determination of its use by any particular people. Today communal housing patterns are spread from Assam to Tonking, Palawan, and through Burmo-Malaya and the Indies to New Guinea, but gradually the communal house is being discarded in areas having contact with more advanced cultures. There are two types of communal housing, but their respective distribution is not well known. One of these is the multiple-family dwelling of no specialized shape in which several families live together without separate quarters for individual family units. This is a housing pattern intermediate between the single-family dwelling and the true communal house, and is widespread in the Orient. The true communal house, limited in distribution as suggested above, is a "long house" which on occasion may reach the extreme length of 400 yards. In such houses there normally is one long common hallway running the whole length of the structure, and dwelling compartments are located on either side of the hallway. In shorter structures entrances normally are located only at the ends, but in the longer houses many entrances are provided. In most cases there is but one single physical structure to a village. Most commonly such houses are constructed of bamboo, matting, and thatch.

The courtyard is a distinctive feature often associated with architecture in the Mediterranean and the Near and Middle East. But as a feature of housing it extends through Central Asia, is widespread in China, occurs in Tibet, and is occasionally used in India. It may well have descended from the threshing floor, which gradually became walled in for simple protection of stored crops or for more adequate protection from robbers. Nowhere in the Orient is it a dominant feature, but the Chinese, with their desire for family privacy, have often aspired to the closed courtyard both in rural and village or city building. The threshing floor, as such, is a feature associated with housing in every agricultural section of the Orient, but only where the courtyard has developed in rural housing does the threshing floor almost become a part of the floor plan of the house. Commonly the threshing floor may be the front or back yard for a home if settlement is dispersed in nature. Village settlements sometimes incorporate threshing floors within the physical plan of the village but more normally place them on the outskirts.

The summer home in the fields is a common housing feature which is very widespread throughout the Orient, but it is nowhere a regionally dominant type. The structure serving such needs may be a fully built house used for several months every year, it may be a very simple structure requiring almost a kind of camping-out living pattern, or it may be the very simple and small structure termed a crop-watching shelter, just large enough to protect one person from sun and rain, by day and by night, during the period between ripening and harvesting of crops.

The Loess Highlands of northwestern China possess one of the most peculiar developments of housing in the modern world. Here one might say that the ancient pit house went below ground rather than came out above it. The loess is soft, stands well in vertical columns, and can be left in arched but unreinforced overhead vaults. A great many Chinese families live in homes excavated horizontally into the face of a loess bank or bluff. Large cave rooms can be easily dug out, a door fitted into the opening with a frame of windows around and above it to admit light, and there is a reasonably weatherproof house. Where vertical cuts are not numerous enough or properly distributed, Chinese have dug large square pits to house depth, retained a ramp along one wall, and excavated caves horizontally behind all four walls. This provides a courtyard and several rooms, again weatherproof. Many thousands of families in the Loess Highlands live in such homes. Though they are relatively weatherproof, they are not earthquakeproof, and in recent centuries the occasional earthquakes that have been centered in the Tibetan foothill zone have killed thousands of people in the western portion of the loess country.

The flat mud roof supported by beams and covered with reeds, poles, and brush is common in dry northwestern India, throughout Central Asia, in much of Tibet, and in northwestern China, an importation from the Middle East. Throughout the rest of the Orient the earlier patterns of roofing have all employed the gabled roof and steeply slanted surfaces to shed water. Straw thatching long has been the great common material employed in surfacing roofs. In special local areas, such as the Tibetan border country or upland Japan and Korea, wood materials in the form of planks, shingles, or bark have been used. In parts of southeastern Asia bamboo has been split and used, and perhaps bamboo "tile" gave inspiration for the common oriental curved clay tile so widely used in Japan, China, Vietnam, Thailand, and Burma. Rural housing seldom has employed tile roofing, unless it be the occasional rich householder. Tile gradually supplanted thatch as the common roofing material of well-to-do city builders, owing to the inflammability of thatch, but the poorer sections of cities everywhere seldom were able to follow suit. In a few local areas slate roofing is found, but this depends clearly upon local availability. In parts of southeastern Asia, particularly in the Philippines and Indonesia, nipa palm thatching commonly replaced straw, and in local areas other types of leafy thatching has long been common. The outline and appearance of the roof has many variations. Peaked, curved, and variable gable roofs are widespread. Double roof units, one underset and projecting, are common, and in many areas very wide overhangs are normally used.

Examining floor plans and house sizes, one is impressed with the fact that most of the Orient has lived in homes with small square footage per person. Although there are few data on the subject, one- and two-room houses per family unit probably outnumber all others. Middle-class families tend to have three- to four-room houses, and only the wealthier families can afford what amounts to a room or more per person. This has led to certain kinds of use patterns not common in contemporary America, except among the crowded city tenements or among the inhabitants of single apartments. The simpler social groups seldom build houses with compartmenting of space by rooms; they normally place the cooking hearth in the center of the floor, either in a pit or on a surface of stones. Advanced culture groups

have tended to place the kitchen in an annex to the main house or even in a separate building to get rid of the smoke that normally goes with the oriental cooking stoves and wood, charcoal, or cowdung fires. Many oriental groups do not compartmentalize such living functions as dining, living, and sleeping. Furniture is often at a minimum and tables and stools or benches are all-purpose items. Sleeping areas often are used for other purposes during the day, so that sleeping on mats on the floor is common, the bedding being rolled up and placed to one side during the day. In both Japan and southeastern Asia this is the common rule, but throughout Asia wherever the one- or two-room home is found the sleeping area must serve other uses by day. On the other hand, there are some cases of meticulous compartmentalization of living space, as in some parts of Bengal, and the Catholic portions of the Philippines. Ceylon and parts of southern India have specific uses for particular rooms. When at all possible most Chinese reserve one room to be used as a dining room and a room where friends may visit.

Bathrooms and indoor toilets were rare in older oriental housing, as they were in the Occident. Public baths are an old institution in the towns and cities of the Orient, and toilets are commonly public also. The modern occidental, carefully coached in a convention of privacy, all too frequently finds himself embarrassed and nonplussed in those parts of the Orient where his own modern conventions have not taken hold. In the crowded Orient such matters are taken very casually and only in the larger cities is there a noticeable trend to change, except in a few local regions where modern public health programs have been vigorously carried out. In the Philippines programs of public health sanitation make the American feel less unhappy than in any other country in the whole Orient.

In much of the Orient the chief need is to cool or ventilate houses, but in the Tibetan Highland, North China, Manchuria, Korea, and northern Japan the winter heating problem is the more serious. Where the winter is cold the American finds the oriental home both cold and drafty; it is endured but not enjoyed by the local populace. Aside from the helpful but inadequate underfloor or underplatform heating device, sometimes used in North China, Manchuria, and Korea, no oriental heating techniques are effective or satisfactory.

Many of the oriental culture groups have developed particular twists to their housing patterns. In the Philippines and in parts of Indonesia a bathing veranda is common, also often used for washing and drying clothing. In much of South India a wide-roofed veranda is a common feature of house construction, and in Japan a narrow south-facing veranda is often found. In the Philippines a wide front porch is very common in older forms of housing, and much of daily life goes on there. The Chinese, with their strong demand for privacy, traditionally, never used the porch or veranda in private housing.

Related to the floor plan and house size is the matter of crop and tool storage, the maintenance of animals, and the presence or lack of auxiliary building. Where the pile-built house is found on land, the space beneath the house normally is used to pen chickens, goats, dogs, even cattle and horses, and it also often serves as a crop-storage area. Along the Tibetan border, where multiple-story building is common, the ground floor often serves in the same way, the family living in upper levels. In China and Korea it is common to use one room of the house as a crop-storage area. Everywhere roof overhangs, ceiling space, verandas, and other free spaces are used for crop storage by farming peoples. Many peoples throughout the Orient build special individual structures

for rice and crop storage, special pig pens, animal pens, tool houses, and the like. There is almost infinite variety in this matter, but one finds that culture groups tend to act alike, so that there is regional variation in the patterns by cultural regions. Nothing like the American elaboration of farm buildings is to be found anywhere in the Orient, even today.

In common with modern trends all over the world certain changes are appearing in housing patterns in the Orient. Where the use of paint, varnish, or lacquer on wood surfaces used to be a peculiarly local matter, a few houses in every country are beginning to be painted and decorated, inside and out. Galvanized-iron or sheet-aluminum roofing commonly is replacing the inflammable and short-lived thatch roof. Wooden floors are spreading. Functional division of the floor space is increasing, and occidental floor plans are appearing here and there. As piped water becomes available kitchen sinks, shower baths, bath tubs, and flush toilets are being installed. Cement for pilings and foundation blocks, for porches and kitchen floors are being used more and more often. Glass is replacing paper, skin, or shell in windows, and windows are becoming hinged rather than fixed or sliding. And though the shine on a new galvanized-iron roof in Bengal is like that on one in the Philippines, housing throughout the Orient is not yet trending into one common tradition. Regionality, individuality, and peculiarity remain in the homes of the Orient.

It is difficult to suggest how many regions of housing there are in the Orient, and it is almost impossible, as yet, to present a clear map of them. In the broad sense one can distinguish a few regional patterns, but discrepancies remain within each such region. Northwestern India, the Himalaya hill country, eastern India, the Deccan, and South India-Ceylon form recognizable divisions of India in which materials, form, and arrangement of housing vary one from the other. Throughout Burmo-Malaya the hill country everywhere is a region of many localized types, whereas in the several great lowland zones each lowland possesses its own regional pattern. Indonesia shows a mixture of house types, by islands and by culture groups, with Sumatra perhaps possessing the most striking individuality to be found anywhere in the Orient. The Philippines has zonal patterns within it but forms one regional major pattern. South China, the southwestern uplands, the Szechwan Basin, the Yangtze Valley, the North China Plain-Manchuria, the Loess Highlands, and northwestern China are perhaps possible regional divisions within such a large zone. Korea has a pattern of housing related to but distinct from that of China. Within Japan there is basic similarity again, but northern Honshu and Hokkaido can be distinguished from southern Japan in the way in which the house has been closed and made more weatherproof or in the way in which occidental housing patterns have been adapted. On a finer scale regional subdivisions are possible everywhere in the Orient.

COMMERCIAL BUILDING

In the older market towns and cities of the Orient one did not find much specialized building for stores, shops, manufacturing plants, warehouses, and the other buildings of commerce and trade. Characteristics of retail shops common to all parts of the Orient were the small street frontage, the open shop front, and shallowness in depth away from the street. And to a surprising degree these features remain common at present in the "native quarters" of cities today, and in the market towns, forming a contrast to similar buildings in the Occident and to the modernized sections of the larger and newer metropolitan settlements. In many areas the open air markets or "bazaars," and

the roofed, temporary stalls on fixed sites took the place of formal stores and shops. Within the common older tradition of the Orient most commercial building seldom rose to more than two stories, though offices and shops seldom were located on second levels, these being reserved as dwelling quarters. Dwelling areas of single-story commercial buildings normally lay behind the store units. Warehousing in the earlier Orient seldom required special construction. Any kind of building, otherwise unused, could serve as a warehouse for the small packages and cases handled by crews of manual laborers. In the handicraft manufacturing of the Orient any home, building, or open space could be adapted to the simple processes and machines normally used.

Apart from these common features the architecture of commercial buildings normally has reflected the general regional patterns of private building. An adobe-brick market town of North India has shops varying only in detail from the pattern of housing, and in the Philippines the shop has been housed in the same nipa-palm-leaf or wood patterns that house the residents. One of the easily noticed features is the fronts of shops and stores that may be closed at night, on holidays, or in times of civil strife. Store fronts that are fully open by day require more than simple doors as closing devices for the off-hours. The common older tradition involved some kind of movable panels, be they the solid wooden boards of China or the lighter thatch panels of the Philippines and Indonesia. Wherever Chinese influence in architecture has made itself strongly felt— Korea, Japan, Vietnam, Thailand—the practice is to use slotted ground and ceiling plates into which narrow vertical boards are fitted to fill most of the open space, with one or more door units, so as to present a solid front. Some variation of the movable panel is employed almost everywhere in commercial building. The sliding steel panel, commonly housed on an overhead roller, is now widely used in many oriental cities, to be pulled down over wood or glass storefronts as a secure safety device.

The earliest occidentals in the Orient rented, bought, or built native structures. Only gradually did they replace native construction with their own styles in the older cities and towns. In the newly founded settlements construction normally was that of the country from which the occidental came. British-built cities in India are full of ill-assorted old British buildings, Saigon came to resemble a French provincial town, and the Spanish in the Philippines built much as they did in southern Spain.

As more and more occidental business concerns came to operate in oriental markets, and as orientals returned from abroad, steady changes came about in commercial building of all sorts. Stores gradually became modeled on occidental designs, with changes in architecture resulting. Closed fronts and fixed doors appeared on retail stores along with newly styled false fronts and rearranged interiors. Warehouses gradually became specialized buildings, newly designed and built, and often located in particular sections of cities and towns. Factory buildings became specialized as power and machines came into general use, with formal layouts and occidental building materials and styles.

This pattern of change in commercial building began in those port cities to which the earliest occidental traders came. These cities, along with the new cities founded by the occidental, became the centers of architectural influence from which some of the styles, methods, and materials gradually infiltrated the broad hinterlands of the Orient. As native artisans and designers gradually gained familiarity with the new features they have adapted and adopted them more and more widely, and it is a rare city that does not now display something of at least pseudo-occidental commercial building. Some cities have become so transformed that, in their business, warehouse, or factory districts they are almost indistinguishable in architecture from occidental cities. This will be a continuing development, and gradually a blending in motifs and styling will increasingly spread a "modern oriental" architecture that revitalizes some of the old native elements in architecture to combine them with useful elements in occidental architectural design.

PUBLIC ARCHITECTURE

In the fields of religious, monumental, and administrative architecture there have been many separate traditions of building in the Orient, perhaps dominated by six main sets of influences: Babylonian, Greek, Chinese, Indian, Persian, and occidental (see pp. 269–272). Babylonian here is used with reference to the ancient tradition of the Middle East, the town and city building of the Tigris-Euphrates region. It is evident that this tradition strongly affected the architecture of fortifications, castles, and administrative buildings in North China from the first appearance of adobe-brick and pounded-earth walls around towns, cities, and states. It is difficult to distinguish clearly the continuing results of this tradition, amidst later developments and, as yet, to be sure of its relationships to religious and monumental building as such. Greek ideas in public architecture spread widely into Asia in the late centuries of the pre-Christian era, with other Greek ideas variably entering into regional complexes, and the resulting Hellenistic influences later and slowly spread almost completely throughout the Orient to some degree.

Chinese public architecture, as it finally matured, was a blend of local, Babylonian, and Hellenistic ideas, techniques, plans, and materials. Local is used here to include both the northern Chinese culture hearth and the southern regions sometimes called "barbarian." Developed Chinese influences affected Central Asia, Tibet, and the whole of the Far East, Korea, Japan, Vietnam, and Thailand, though the influences in Malaya, Indonesia, and the Philippines have been more recent and lesser in strength.

Earlier Indian architecture was also a blend of local, Babylonian, and Hellenistic components, but it developed profuse ornamentation in which native Hindu religious motivations came to dominate Babylonian and Hellenistic features and which led it to far different ends from those achieved in the plainer and more realistic Chinese architecture. Indian architecture spread its influences throughout mainland Southeast Asia, reaching deeply into Indonesia, and lightly touching the Philippines.

Persian influences were introduced late into the Orient, chiefly into India and beyond under the control of the Islamic immigrants. Gradually the older Indian construction in the northwest and north became replaced by a new kind of Islamic construction which eventually became dominant. This new pattern spread, to some degree, wherever the Moslems gained a foothold, but its effect beyond North India is light and incomplete. A Persian would hardly recognize an Islamic mosque, palace, or government building in the Moro country of the southern Philippines. Occidental influences in public architec-

ture have been the last in the long series to enter the field of public construction in the Orient. In the early centuries of occidental contact this set of influences, diverse in itself, produced some real monstrosities, designed by occidentals but executed by orientals who never quite grasped the full artistic implications of occidental design. Gradually some synthesis of East and West has here been achieved, with basic design, materials, and techniques from the occidental side, artistic motifs and execution from the native side, the whole revitalized into such creations as "modern Chinese" or "modern Japanese." Many of the newer Chinese university and administrative buildings are masterful combinations of occidental and oriental materials, design, and execution, and the best in modern Indian construction is an artful blend of Hellenistic, Indian, Persian, and occidental influences, erected in stone, steel, concrete, and brick. In the Philippines, Thailand, or Sumatra this artful synthesis has perhaps not yet come to full fruition in a regionally independent architecture. Every culture region of the Orient today is moving toward some such cultural blending of public architecture, interweaving the various traditional elements of design and materials with the modern elements.

5

THE GEOGRAPHY OF HEALTH AND DISEASE

China and India are often thought of as lands in which every edible object is covered with countless harmful germs. The whole Orient, like central Africa, often brings to mind the frightening names of serious epidemic diseases like cholera and typhus, or such disfiguring ailments as leprosy and the innumerable skin infections. With these exaggerated descriptions often goes the passing judgment that the occidentals are chiefly in danger, whereas the "natives" are immune to the trials of the environment. But statistical tabulations show that millions of "natives" die every year of preventible diseases and add to the belief that life is cheap in the Orient. Slowly and gradually the medical world is learning about both the threats to health in the Orient and the means of preserving and lengthening human life. It is occidental medicine, in the hands both of occidental and oriental doctors, that is achieving this result. Slowly it is appearing true that, in the Orient, all men are subject to the laws of health and disease when they lead the same kinds of lives. However, perhaps oriental and occidental peoples do differ in their resistances or susceptibilities to different ailments. It is much too early to try to record definitive information on this topic, but the general outline may be indicated.

THE ROLE OF CLIMATE

Since occidentals first arrived in the East the causes of ill health in the Orient have been laid at many doors. Decaying fish left by floods and high tides, foul air blowing off swamps, queer habits of human beings, disturbances of the harmonics of nature, despoiling of temples and shrines, and climate are but the commonest. Of all the causes that can be compiled, climate has been the most maligned. Everything in the way of human discomfort and ailment has been at one time or another laid at its door. Certainly there is discomfort in the moist heat of a long Yangtze Valley summer, or the year-long, unvarying heat of lowland Malaysia. Assuredly such climatic conditions favor the growth of bacteria, good and bad. However, it is not true that climate alone, any more than habits of eating, drinking, or clothing, cause all ailments. Nor does climate make it impossible for any one group, oriental or occidental, to live in the tropics or elsewhere in the Orient. There still are all too few data on life expectancy, the incidence of various diseases, and the causes of death to permit flat statements upon this whole subject.

Varying degrees of healthfulness, however, are associated with different landscapes of the Orient. For example, the heavy cloud cover that hangs over the Szechwan Basin of western China maintains winter-long temperatures between about 33 and 45° F. With a high relative humidity, and poor domestic heating arrangements, millions of Szechwanese inhabiting the Basin suffer a high incidence of winter-long chronic colds. Better economic ability and changed cultural practices could, of course, eliminate the seasonal epidemic of colds, but the climatic factor certainly is operative. Throughout the Orient the lower foothill margins seem the least healthful zone. South of about 35° N. latitude the vertical zone between some 2,000 feet and 5,000 to 6,000 feet seems, on the century-long experience of the hill stations and mountain resorts, to be the healthful one both for the oriental and the occidental. Man has been slow to learn of, and to utilize, this vertical zoning and, so far, only the well-to-do can take advantage of it. Assuredly there is a climatic factor tied up in this zonal inequality.

With respect to many of the communicable diseases, Japan, before 1937, was the healthiest part of the Orient whereas, in some respects, Tibet ranked ahead of all other oriental lands. Many false generalizations are circulated concerning these matters. The tendency, also, is to make generalizations about the virility of cultures in relation to the climatic factor, but in the long histories of the various oriental peoples proof can be found both for and against any specific generalization. Too many other factors have been operative to permit climate alone to be held responsible for the level of culture in the Orient.

THE ENVIRONMENT OF DISEASE

Many causes can be advanced for the rise and fall in epidemic waves of the various severe diseases that afflict the Orient. The causes of these outbreaks are not always

known, and many may lie in natural environmental conditions not yet understood by the medical world. To a considerable extent, however, the environment of disease in the Orient is a cultural one, vested in human traits, institutions, and customs. It long has been an accepted notion that the Chinese use of night soil as garden-plot fertilizer contaminates all produce grown thereon, though recently real doubt has been cast on the idea, and it certainly is an unproved theory. The Japanese habit of eating large amounts of raw fish induces a wide variety of intestinal ailments. The Philippine Catholic custom of juveniles kissing the hand of elders upon all occasions of meeting seems partly responsible for the rapid spread of tuberculosis. The Indian custom of periodic and massed religious pilgrimages induced recurrent epidemics of cholera until British medical services isolated endemic centers and instituted mass preventive inoculations. The very widespread oriental custom of family communal gathering, eating, and praying with and over a sick member often operates to spread the afflicting disease. Unsanitary habits of bathing and sleeping in many parts of the Orient account for many widespread skin diseases and ailments carried by lice and similar pests. Under normal conditions these and other localized customs may well be offset by others. Thus the very old Chinese custom of drinking hot tea and eating chiefly hot food fresh from the stove serve in normal times to prevent widespread sickness from diseases carried by germs on raw vegetables and fruits. However, in times of flood, famine, or civil and military unrest Chinese general living and food habits break down under pressure, so that epidemics of many kinds become widespread and take tremendous tolls.

In the oriental failure to understand, or the casual disregard for, the means of spreading diseases, the need for isolation of infectious diseases, the need for household cleanliness and for the clean handling of food products lies the explanation of much of the high incidence of disease in the Orient. In earlier centuries, when total populations were smaller, and crowded housing and close association in large cities was less than it is today, this misunderstanding produced fewer deaths from preventible causes. Preventive medicine has made great strides in many lines, but in others lack of understanding, excessive crowding in poor housing, and neglect have greatly expanded certain ailments. Affiliated with these contributory causes is the perpetuation of ancient medical beliefs. Though many of them have proved perfectly sound in the light of modern knowledge, many others are worthless as today practiced and only worsen the total health situation.

The oriental ricefield sometimes is held to be one of the chief breeding grounds for the malaria mosquito. Undoubtedly many malaria-carrying mosquitoes do breed in ricefields, but recent research makes it clear that there are a great many species of malaria-carrying mosquitoes, breeding under all kinds of conditions, and that in most cases ricefield mosquitoes are only innocent pests. Every oriental country has its own specific environment in which malaria flourishes, so that no one cure will operate for the whole region.

Increasing relative and downright poverty of the lower segment of society, coupled with the growing custom of using refined foods, in a number of countries today has induced many ailments of malnutrition, which in turn increase susceptibilities to other ailments. Difficult circumstances during the war years, 1937–1946, increased such conditions very greatly. The widespread and excessive use of opium in varied sectors of the Orient during the last four generations also has contributed to the serious problems of health.

The sheer abundance of flies, mosquitoes, fleas and lice particularly, plus the added presence of sand flies, mites, ticks, leeches, and many kinds of parasites in different localities, form a great problem. The simple housing of most of the Orient makes the exclusion of these pests very difficult. A large number of them are the primary or intermediary carriers for serious diseases; others, like the bedbug, are only haunting and distasteful pests. As in the Occident no agency, government or private, attempted their elimination in earlier centuries. The size of the job has been beyond the abilities of the small modern health services, particularly where public consciousness and cooperation is not yet fully aroused.

One rather interesting feature and distinct blessing, is that, although the mosquitoes that carry yellow fever in Africa are very widely distributed throughout the Orient, no yellow fever has so far been reported.

THE CHIEF DISEASES AND THEIR DISTRIBUTION

Certain of the diseases of the Orient are very general in their distribution. Others are more limited, being caused by particular local situations and customs, or being limited by organized medical services and natural environmental factors. The following discussion merely attempts to suggest the outline of conditions surrounding the more important of the oriental diseases. Figures 5.1, 5.2, and 5.3 present distributions for selected diseases only.

Widely Distributed Major Diseases

Considering the whole Orient it is probable that malaria is the most serious ailment. There are many specific types of malaria but our discussion will be general. Malaria is a disease in which cyclic paroxysms of chills and high fevers induce extended anemia and damage to the spleen, caused by the release in the blood stream of cyclic batches of the sporozoa *Plasmodium*. The anopheline mosquitoes are actually hosts (though often called vectors), and man is both the intermediate host and the victim of the ailment. It is one of the most widely distributed diseases, in the regional sense and, owing to the method by which it is spread, often has a higher incidence among the general population than does any other disease. In many regions practically the whole population suffers, and it is particularly hard on children. Statistics suggest that nearly 100,000,000 cases occur every year in India, almost 20,000,000 per year in the Indies, and at least that many in China. Its chief result is not death directly, but a lethargic and weakened population which falls prey to

secondary diseases. Nevertheless, incomplete medical statistics point to the probability that about 3,000,000 orientals die every year of malaria alone, in normal years. When widespread unsettled conditions obtain, this figure may be doubled. Figure 5.1 depicts the very general variation in seriousness of the disease.

Since there is no single species of vector, there is not just one set of breeding conditions or one method of eliminating malaria. In the southern Philippines and northern Borneo as the jungle is cut off and the lands are put into ricefields malaria recedes with the jungle, for here the vector is a jungle-

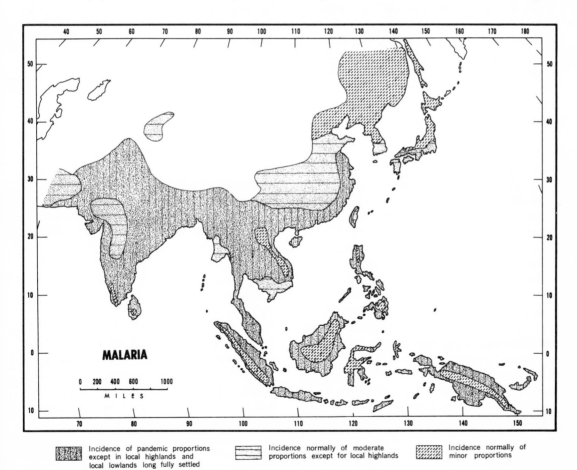

FIGURE 5.1. Distribution of Malaria.

breeding mosquito. In West Malaysia, however, cutting off the jungle only induces the invasion of a new malaria vector, breeding in fresh running waters under quite different conditions. In upper Bengal and Assam, after much land was cleared and cultivated, partial relief from malaria carried by mosquitoes breeding in sunny running streams was provided by planting shade trees along the streams.

Throughout the moist portions of the Orient today malaria is worst along the rough, lower foothill tracts that normally remain in jungle growth and forest. Below, on those flat plains that long ago became well cleared and populated, malaria seldom has strikingly high incidences today though mosquitoes are numerous and annoying. Above the foothills, at a regionally variable altitude of roughly 2,000–3,000 feet, mosquitoes disappear and malaria dies out. The foothill zones surrounding old settled plains remain constant and serious malaria threats. In the spread of population in southeastern Asia, the Philippines, and Indonesia the foothill jungle-forest fringes often threaten the success of settlement by causing extremely high incidences of several kinds of malaria, some of them having high mortality rates. This foothill health hazard may account for the failure of the Vietnamese to colonize the empty hill country behind the narrow and over-crowded eastern coastal plain of mainland Southeast Asia. The large amount of jungle and forest growth in southern China, the moist areas of India, and throughout moist southeastern Asia, both on the lowlands, and in the foothill zone just above the lowlands, make for almost permanently endemic zones of malarial diseases. Recurrent abandonment of once settled tracts through historic change sometimes renewed these conditions in areas once relatively free of such diseases. Thus, eastern and northern Ceylon, in the early 20th century, had a serious malaria problem in areas once healthy

and heavily populated. The spraying of mosquito insecticides in the late 1940's at least temporarily freed Ceylon of most of its malaria problem, resulting in a marked rate of population increase through the abrupt lowering of the death rate.

Despite modern medicine no truly adequate, cheap, and easily administered curative or preventive drug has become available to date for all the population of the Orient. Relatively efficient permanent reduction in malarial incidence may occur in selected localities, but complete success in the Orient still is questionable. Mosquitoes may become adapted to these drugs just as other insect life elsewhere has failed to become extinct under the application of modern scientific discoveries. The preventive problem has barely been tackled. There is reason to doubt that, in a region of very moist climates, of permanent forest and jungle, any full preventive procedure ever can be devised and adapted to the physical and cultural local environments now present. The mosquito net seems to be a permanent piece of housekeeping equipment among those peoples southward of central China who aspire to even relative freedom from malaria, but the failure to use mosquito nets is widespread. Unfortunately, it appears that malaria is going to be with the Orient a long time.

Tuberculosis is today an extremely serious disease almost everywhere in the Orient, and in some regions it is more serious than malaria. The causes for its rise are complex and not well understood. Very little is being done against its spread, except in a few selected regions and on a very small scale. Excessive crowding in cities and towns, malnutrition, and changed food and clothing habits are perhaps the more important reasons. Each of these will continue operative in the future. Whereas the well-to-do may secure treatment today, the huge poverty-stricken section of oriental society cannot afford the rest cure that is the best prescription the medical world can give at present. With a mortality rate from five to ten times as great as that of tuberculosis in the United States, and with perhaps 150,000,000 people afflicted to some degree, the problem is becoming steadily more serious.

The several types of dysentery, grouped together, form another serious threat to the health and life of the whole Orient. The several varieties are endemic almost everywhere, so that the disruption of normal living conditions generally results in an epidemic. Ordinarily the rainy seasons of the year increase the number of cases in some areas, though in regions with prolonged dry seasons and water shortages the dry season may be the worst period of the year. Usually the dysenteries are more serious in crowded urban regions than in rural areas. Lack of proper control over domestic water sources and over sewage disposal is a chief contributing cause, and proper control in these matters is very scattered and spotty throughout the Orient.

Typhus is a term for several diseases carried by fleas, lice, and a variety of mites. Too little notice of it was taken in much of the Orient until perhaps 1930, but the incidence is much greater than the sporadic records would indicate. Its vector in Manchuria, North China, Korea, and much of India is a louse, whereas in most of the rest of the mainland it is a flea. On the mainland borders of southeastern Asia and in those parts of the islands where heavy grass is important in the present vegetation cover, mite-borne typhus is found, although little was known of it until World War II. In the years of peace preceding 1937, typhus had been widely endemic but seldom epidemic. During the war years North China and Manchuria suffered severe epidemics, and outbreaks of "scrub typhus," the mite-borne variety, occurred among military forces and civilians throughout southeastern Asia. Under the best clinical conditions mortality

is not high, but under neglected wartime conditions it often ran above twenty percent.

Often associated with typhus in epidemic conditions is relapsing fever, also a louse-carried ailment widely distributed over the Asian mainland. In China relapsing fever is much more common in the south, where typhus is apt to be lighter. The kinds of conditions that promote epidemics of typhus also stimulate relapsing fever.

Cholera is one of those oriental diseases best known in the Occident. It is very widely endemic though medical control in most of the island regions has reduced it to an unimportant position. Cholera ordinarily is a late summer disease that flashes up from its endemic centers in rapidly and widely spreading epidemics when unsettled conditions prevail in a major region. Cholera is an acute diarrheal disease produced by bacteria ingested with food, resulting in rapid and extreme dehydration of the body. There seems something cyclic in the virility of epidemics of cholera, and in such years a high mortality results. Its treatment under organized conditions reduces the mortality greatly, and preventive measures applied regionally can reduce its threat. The unsettled conditions of many recent years in the Orient, and the inability of undermanned and ill-equipped bureaus dealing with large populations have rendered its complete control and eradication impossible. China and India have been the two worst regions; the island zone has been relatively free since 1930. Organized British measures reduced the impact of epidemics in India but never cleared up the endemic centers. Figure 5.2 displays the broad regional spread of cholera.

Plague is another oriental disease rather fatalistically accepted by many orientals but greatly feared by the modern Occident. Most of the Orient except western China, Tibet, and Central Asia are variably affected by plague. The south coast of China, central India, and a number of small areas in the

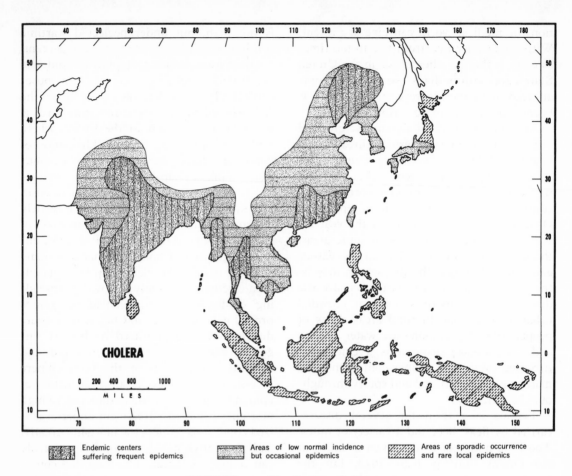

| | Endemic centers suffering frequent epidemics | | Areas of low normal incidence but occasional epidemics | | Areas of sporadic occurrence and rare local epidemics |

FIGURE 5.2. Distribution of cholera.

southeast Asian peninsula are endemic centers for plague and suffer almost annual attacks. Its regional distribution is shown on Figure 5.3. From South China, in the last century, it has spread north into Manchuria and now seems rather deeply intrenched in inland Fukien and in Manchuria. Annual epidemics, varying in intensity, have been rather common in local areas in many parts of the mainland Orient. Extensive efforts by organized medical services were making considerable headway when war stopped the work in 1937. Korea, Japan, and Taiwan, under Japanese efforts, have held control over the disease, and no epidemic situations

have developed in the last several decades. Similarly the Philippines and Malaysia have not suffered outbreaks since 1925. Indonesia houses a number of small endemic regions, but no serious outbreak has occurred in some decades.

Dengue fever and blackwater fever are two relatives of malaria that are widely spread but locally concentrated. Mosquitoes are the vectors in both cases. Mortality rates are not high, but both cause rather prolonged periods of ill health. The area from south China and central India through Indonesia is the chief zone of occurrence. Dengue fever is a disease which often afflicts occidentals newly

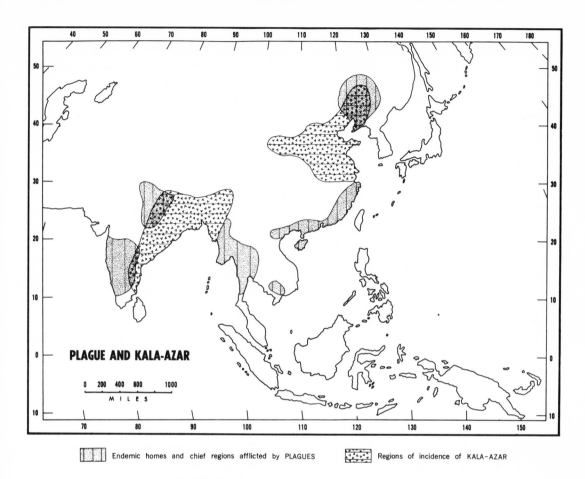

Endemic homes and chief regions afflicted by PLAGUES   Regions of incidence of KALA-AZAR

FIGURE 5.3. Centers of plague and kala-azar.

arrived in areas in which the disease is prevalent.

Under the general term filariasis are a number of types of worm infections for which some of the mosquitoes are the vectors. These diseases affect a rather narrow band of country from southern Korea and southern Japan westward to the Red Sea and south to the north coast of Australia. Occidentals, with ordinary care, seldom are affected, but sporadic epidemics and localized endemic situations occur very widely.

Yaws is a disease which affects the native peoples from the east coast of India and Hainan Island through New Guinea. The occidental seldom is bothered by the ailment. In considerable part a malnutritional ailment, it is also a disease prevalent in areas short of water supply. It is rather easily cleared up by medical treatment, though it will return unless the mode of living is improved. It has a rather low mortality, but it permits secondary infection and is uncomfortable and unsightly. It is not epidemic in the ordinary sense, though in some localized areas its incidence may run as high as ninety per cent of the population.

Widely Distributed Minor Diseases

A number of diseases prevalent in the Orient

are considered differently there from in the Occident. Typhoid fever, smallpox, measles, and similar diseases all are widespread, but not often do they reach large epidemic proportions. Mortality rates in local areas occasionally are high, but the over-all effect of each ailment is far less than for some of those already mentioned. For the occidental the oriental strains of some of these diseases often seem more virulent than those of his homeland, and precautions are mandatory.

Pneumonia and influenza are paid rather scant heed by the populace and the medical profession alike, but they occur in large numbers with rather serious results. Spring and autumn seasons, and the onset of the rainy season with its moist and cooler air, produce cyclic ups and downs in incidence.

Leprosy is a disease very casually accepted in the Orient, without segregation, except where occidental colonial control motivated it. The Philippines and British Malaya most completely put segregation into effect. Almost the whole of the Orient is affected, but South China and the central peninsular portion of India seem to be the chief centers. An estimated 2,500,000 individuals are afflicted in the whole of the Orient.

Serious eye ailments caused by trachoma, smallpox, and venereal diseases, afflict perhaps 40,000,000 orientals. Again China and India are the areas worst affected. Apathy and carelessness are the two worst cultural factors in the situation. The end result of complete blindness and physical incapacitation affects perhaps 5,000,000 people in the whole of the Orient.

Venereal diseases are very widespread everywhere in the Orient, with less concern over the final implications than in parts of the Occident today. Prostitution is more widely prevalent, and, among many societies and cultural groups, sexual promiscuity is rather common, promoting the scattering of all five types of venereal disease: syphilis, gonorrhea, chancroid, lymphogranuloma venereum, and granuloma inguinale. Very few statistics are available in this field.

Skin infections, such as impetigo, scabies, and the several tinea infections, also are extremely common in almost every part of the Orient. Normal peaceful conditions permit a population to exercise some control over many of these ailments, despite the warm and moist climate prevailing over much of the Orient. Unsettled conditions and extreme poverty rapidly increase skin infections. In many local areas a large share of the population seems to be affected. To the traveler parts of central and north China seem to have the highest incidence of skin ailments of any part of the Orient, but this may well not prove true when statistics become available.

Regionally Confined Diseases

A number of ailments are confined by environmental conditions to particular regions of the Orient. One of the most serious of them is kala-azar (Leishmaniasis), a group of chronic diseases causing fevers, anemia, liver deformation, and the malfunctioning of internal organs involved in protein metabolism. Its vector is a sand fly, and the pathogens are various protozoan parasites. Kala-azar occurs from the north side of the Yangtze Valley into Manchuria in China and from Madras into Assam in India. It is active during the summer, becoming locally epidemic. More active in rural than urban areas, it chiefly affects children and younger adults. Without proper medical care the disease has a rather high mortality. Its regional distribution is shown in Figure 5.3.

The central and lower Yangtze Valley is the chief home of a rather serious disease common among farming populations who frequent the many creeks and canals in fishing and farming operations. A snail living in the creeks and canals is the intermediary carrier for schistosomiasis (Bilharziasis), a group of diseases affecting the liver and intestinal tract, in which the microorganisms are flukes inhabiting the blood system of the afflicted person. The China coast southward toward Canton and some minor areas in interior South China also are affected.

Perhaps more properly listed under skin ailments is copra itch, common to the coconut-producing regions from Ceylon around to the Philippines.

Southern Korea and the main Japanese islands are peculiarly afflicted by a large series of parasites carried by fish. The custom of eating raw fish is largely responsible for this particular group of intestinal worms and other parasites.

Central western Yunnan, the Yunnan-Tibetan border, and northern Laos form a large region afflicted with goiter. This region consumes salt produced from local springs and wells, deficient in iodine, and is isolated from contact with the seacoast towns through which either sea salt or fish products can come in adequate quantities. Northern Borneo contains another small region in which goiter affliction is common. A few other minor regions are also affected.

A great many special regional diseases of significance affect particular territories of the Orient about which little is commonly known. Many missionary, private, and public health doctors have learned something of how to cope with them, but a large amount of exploratory and comparative medical work will be required to deal adequately with the mass of these diseases.

PROBLEMS OF MALNUTRITION AND FAMINE

Beri-beri is often thought of as a disease affecting occidentals on shipboard during the seventeenth to early nineteenth centuries. It is a disease of malnutrition caused by the lack of a well-rounded diet and the lack of fresh vitamin-rich foods. Several of these malnutritional diseases have affected various parts of the world in recent centuries.

It is not commonly known, however, that beri-beri and related diseases provoked by dietary deficiencies are extremely common throughout the Orient today. They have been increasing in seriousness within the last century and today are particularly common in the towns and cities of most parts of the Orient. There are a number of contributing causes, some of which are environmental but most of which are economic or cultural.

Not much is yet known concerning the comparative nutritional value of given foods grown on varying types of soils. It is common to assume a standard caloric value for rice, oranges, or carrots, for example, regardless of the variety or parent field. Vitamin and mineral content, as well as nutritional worth, are assumed as equivalent everywhere. Common consideration regards only quantity per acre as changing with different soils or cultural practices. Almost no oriental data of an objective sort are so far available in this field, but there can be little question that the overworked and the depleted soils of parts of India must not only produce low yields per acre but foods lower in quality than those young and rich soils of parts of Java or the culturally fortified soils of much of China. What may be the role of climate, soil, water, and other environmental factors in nutrition and general health is yet speculative, but certain it is that there are regional differences in this matter in an area as large and as variably used as the Orient. A considerable share of modern oriental malnutrition may derive from a misunderstood and overworked physical environment.

The economic factor of modern regional poverty of many oriental areas is a large factor contributing to widespread malnutrition. A majority of orientals today are simply too poor to be able to purchase foods adequate to maintain themselves in reasonable health. The prosperous, the rich, and the politically privileged can afford a sufficiently wide variety of diet to maintain a high level of health, but too many millions of people in all parts of the Orient must restrict their diets to what they can grow, purchase, or have rationed to them, and the variety of food types too often is very narrow and restricted to the cheaper, basic carbohydrates. Simple poverty often prohibits even an adequate volume of food consumption as well as an adequate range.

But it is on cultural practices that much of the blame must rest for modern malnutritional diseases. Just as the West shifted from whole-grain wheat breads to impoverished white-flour breads with the rise of industrial wheat milling, so much of the Orient shifted from whole rice to polished rice. In the Orient highly milled wheat is increasing in use, and gradually many other kinds of refined foods are coming into volume consumption. These practices first showed up in port cities frequented by occidental traders, missionaries, and orientals returned from abroad with new habits in diet. They have gradually spread to other cities, towns, and rural hinterlands and are part and parcel of the process of westernization commonly held as marking the progress of the Orient. And malnutrition has followed closely behind, so that beri-beri and similar diseases are an inevitable result. They affect chiefly the middle classes and the urban poor, who have accepted the milled rice, white flour, and refined foods but neither know as yet how to supplement diets nor can afford the expensive extracts made from rice milling.

Thus, the cities and towns of the Orient are the centers of extensive nutritional ailments that weaken and starve millions of people. And as these practices have spread into rural hinterlands they have affected whole populations of many regions of the Orient. Small-scale attacks on the problem, such as the fortification of milled rice, have made tremendous changes in the health and well being of regional populations, but much remains to be done to repair the impact of changed cultural practices of the last century and a half.

HOSPITALS, MEDICAL PERSONNEL, PUBLIC HEALTH SERVICES

Throughout the whole Orient medical services are scarce and completely inadequate to deal with the problems of the huge population. In selected cities the number of hospital beds, doctors, nurses, dentists, and technicians stands not far below the levels prevalent in the better-served parts of the Occident. In general, however, these per capita services for the rural countryside, the small towns, and the isolated hinterlands are almost hopelessly low compared to the needs.

It is true that in such old high cultures as those of India and China the development of curative medicine reached high levels at an early date, and that other culture groups developed local systems of curative medicine to variable degrees. However, rather general throughout the whole of the Orient, during the last three centuries, has been the decline in ancient skills, and the growth of taboos against surgery and experimental medicine. Accompanying this decline, in the face of growing populations, has been the continued absence of society-wide public health systems of real and effective value. During the 19th century occidental medicine was introduced into the Orient by evangelical missionary effort, supplemented by some colonial-government development of rudimentary public health education and preventive systems. These introductions resulted in the gradual diffusion of modern practices in materia medica, preventive medicine, surgery, and public health concepts. Today, native systems of medicine continue to operate in rural hinterlands, and to operate alongside occidental systems in cities, towns, and coastal regions. All governments today have operative public health systems of variable degree of country-wide reach and effectiveness. In no portion of the Orient, however, has the practice of medicine and the reach of the public health system caught up with the basic needs of the large populations involved. It is generally true that in the 1960's there were no great epidemics of the sort recorded during the last three centuries, but the per capita availability of medicines, doctors, dentists, nurses, out-patient clinics, hospitals, and clinical laboratories is still very low in many portions of the Orient. And there remains, unfortunately, a tremendous well of ignorance, indifference, acceptance of fate, and adherence to traditional practices (sometimes totally ineffective) that make for the continuance of endemic diseases to plague the populations.

In the modern era of marked urbanization and the accumulation of high rural population densities, the problems of safe domestic water are growing rapidly, and this has a bearing on the incidence of water-borne epidemic diseases. Despite the many efforts toward installation of modern reservoirs having integral purification mechanisms, and piped distributory systems, general pollution of all surface waters is becoming more common. Japan stands above all other sectors of the Orient in the efficiency of domestic water control and, so far, Hong Kong, the Philippines, and West Malaysia maintain good controls over the water pollution problem. Elsewhere, controls over domestic water supply are local and regionally inadequate, and threatening to reach the danger point at which public health controls could break down. This is not a problem unique to the Orient, of course, but the sheer regional densities of population make the future domestic water problem a most serious one for the whole of the Orient.

Perhaps the Philippines, West Malaysia, and Japan have the best relative medical services in the Orient today. India is making very concerted efforts in the medical field, and these are reaching out into the countrysides, but untouched hinterlands still are large. Pakistan, Taiwan, and Korea have developing programs. In China the self-directed return toward native medicine may, or may not, suffice to maintain sound public health conditions. Elsewhere, turbulent conditions, as in the two Vietnams and Laos, self-imposed isolation, as in Burma, or the lack of the means to provide strong programs, as in Indonesia, may endanger large populations at some point in the near or more distant future.

6

GEOMORPHOLOGY AND THE BARE LANDSCAPES

ASIA AS A LAND MASS

The continent of Asia is at once the largest, the most complicated, and the least thoroughly described of the land masses that make up our conventional list of continents. Any statement concerning the structure and surface of Asia must either leave many blanks or spread the brushwork of language, map, and diagram across great blocks of territory with some degree of error. And yet, for all the gaps in knowledge, a simple statement of the basic structure of the continent can be set down, and most of its surface can be described in fairly satisfactory terms (Figs. 6.1–6.3).

The western Arctic fringe of Asia is an extension of the great lowland of northern Europe. Southward and eastward from this Siberian Plain is a broad zone of ancient rocks that early in geologic time were folded, faulted, and intruded, not once, but several times. The worn roots of mountain ranges, plateaus, massifs, and other structural units today form a rugged and complicated area which serves as the headward zone for most of the Arctic-flowing rivers of Siberia. This zone occupies much of central and southern Siberia. Southward lie a number of major structural basins and truncated plateau surfaces covering hundreds of thousands of

square miles in the dry heart of Asia. The partially eroded roots of mountain ranges separate the several commonly recognized divisions, Russian Turkestan, the Tarim Basin, Dzungaria, and the Mongolian Plateaus. These basins are nuclear masses of the most ancient land units, surrounded and enveloped in the later mountain-building episodes. Some of the ranges still reach a considerable altitude, and some of the basins are deeply filled, though one of the world's lowest continental depressions below sea level occurs almost in the center of the continent. Most of the structural building and deformation took place a long time ago, with repeated but minor happenings occurring in more recent geologic time along the same general lines as previously. One more step southward brings one up onto the Roof of the World in the great Tibetan Plateaus, a structural product of more recent geologic time. This zone consists of a series of high, enclosed basins, set apart by mountain ranges that primarily trend east-west. The Tibetan area is a part of the long Alpine Chain that reaches from Spain across Eurasia. Tremendous folding, faulting, and overthrusting were involved here as in Europe, and the approximate record is just beginning to be understood. The northern sector of Tibet appears much older

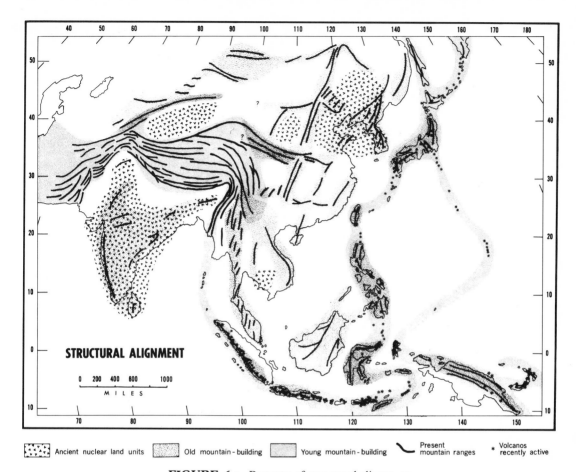

Ancient nuclear land units		Old mountain-building		Young mountain-building	

Present mountain ranges   * Volcanos recently active

FIGURE 6.1. Patterns of structural alignment.

in build and physical history than does the southern sector. Prior to the rise of the Himalayan chains of high mountains, northern Tibet lay more open to the sweep of the Indian monsoon, and exhibits a complex history of glaciation, subaerial denudation, lake development, and regional deposition of eroded detritus. The southern sector was apparently the active zone of late Tertiary orogeny, some of which continued throughout the Pleistocene. The southern sector has a very complex history, but in more recent geologic time the southern sector has been better drained by the great river systems, and has been the source of the materials that have

filled the trough now forming the North Indian Plain.

The eastern mainland of Asia is made up of a variety of units that range in age from Pre-Cambrian shields to Recent mountain arcs and recently foundered blocks. The several units cross and re-cross each other in a complex pattern in east Siberia, Manchuria, and China, and are in part eastward projections of elements previously described. The southern mainland of Asia consists of old blocks of deformed strata and Recent sedimentary basins lying next to or sandwiched into the Tertiary Alpine Chain which swings across Tibet and curves southward to form

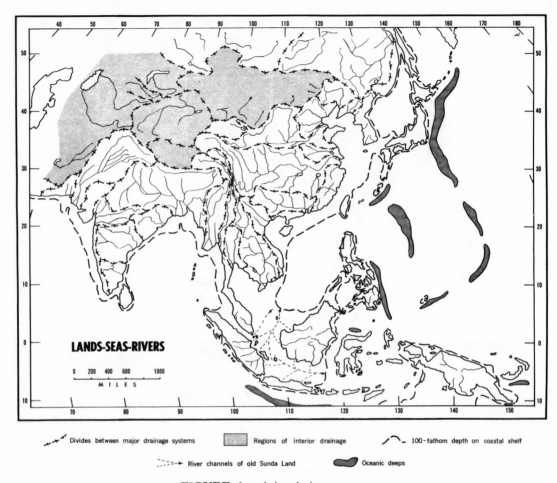

Divides between major drainage systems   Regions of interior drainage   100-fathom depth on coastal shelf

River channels of old Sunda Land   Oceanic deeps

FIGURE 6.2. Asian drainage patterns.

the backbone of mainland southeast Asia. Lastly, set off the mainland coast are several series of islands, from the Indies to the Kuriles, set on structural arcs of varying radius. Most of them are the products of Tertiary and Pleistocene geologic time in their present outlines, though most have older basement foundations. All the arcs are the result of the movement which has wrinkled up the edges of the several stable blocks of the earth's crust that join along the western margins of the Pacific Ocean. It is likely that certain mainland structural lines are related to the island arc lines in origin. Some of the

principal oceanic deeps lie alongside several of the island arcs, whereas but shallow continental shelf waters separate other arcs. These latter waters form a string of coastal seas which have been as significant to eastern Asia as the several seas separating the peninsulas of Europe.

GLACIATION AND RECENT MOUNTAIN BUILDING

In tracing the patterns of glacial action during the Ice Age most attention has been focused on the continental ice-sheets of North Amer-

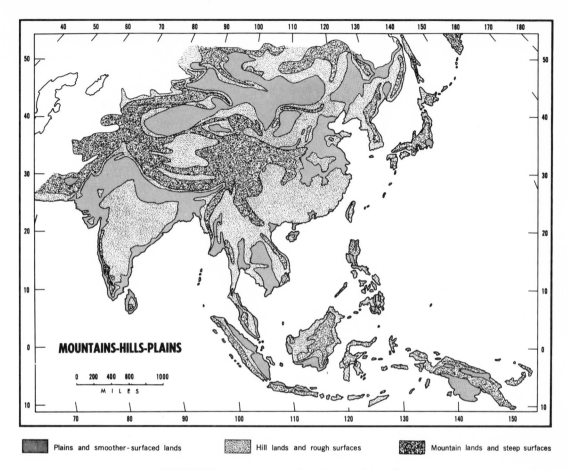

FIGURE 6.3. Patterns of surface configuration.

ica and northwestern Europe. Only slowly is it becoming accepted that fairly large portions of the Asian highlands were affected by one or more of the cool pluvial periods that caused the accumulation of ice sheets. A considerable amount of detailed study and even re-examination of certain regions are needed with this problem in mind. The main mass of the northern Tibetan Plateau may have been involved in the early glaciation, but only its higher sectors have been affected during more recent eras. The earliest glaciations may also have been widespread among the central Asian mountain systems, but later glaciation has affected only certain high mountain sec-

tions in somewhat smaller patterns. Southern Tibet, on the other hand, particularly the western portion, is the earth's largest area of Recent glaciation outside the two polar zones, and glaciers still feed the river systems of India. It is likely that glaciation was a significant factor in sculpturing the higher mountain zones of the Chinese Tibetan border and the higher mountain ranges of China, though much of the evidence has been mutilated subsequently. The higher mountainous cores of Japan, Taiwan, Borneo, and New Guinea, at least, show evidence of glaciation. More important than the erosion of hard rock surfaces by ice are the erosional and depositional effects of water and wind around the glaciated margins. Scattered throughout the Orient are a complicated series of terraces, benches, and shelves. Some are the normal erosional forms produced by running water or by marine planation in periods of high sea level. Karst landscapes of varying degrees of maturity are widely scattered but probably related to pluvial periods, and the zone from south China extending into West Malaysia is the world's largest area of karst landscapes, including some of the most spectacular surface forms. Other forms are depositional: shallow sea sediments or lake deposits now exposed; normal valley fill; glacial deposits of various kinds; and aeolian deposits ranging from fossil dunes to thick beds of loess. Loess, particularly, is now known far beyond its classical location in the highlands of northwest China. Until about 1940 these varied marks upon the landscape were being studied separately, but correlation of many of these minor landforms seems possible.   '

Important in this further study will have to be the events transpiring outside the range of glaciation but during the periods of ice advance. It is likely that the lands nearest the tropics had a relatively warm and moist climate even during pluvial periods of ice accumulation on the cool northern highlands. However, there must have been changes in climatic regimes for southern lands during the ice ages that had as much effect upon those landscapes as Himalayan glaciers had upon the landscape of northern India. And, in the expansion and contraction of the several climatic regimes during the ice ages, many minor landscape forms and soil types were produced that now are relict features under current conditions. Even plant and animal distributions are occasionally out of place as remnants or as invaders beyond their expected zones. It may even be that some of the curious and anomalous distributions of human beings are thus to be explained.

A significant item is the fluctuation in the shore line of eastern Asia. The depression of sea level during the last advance of the ice was on the order of 220–240 feet. This would empty the Gulf of Po Hai, much of the Yellow Sea, and expose much of the coastal shelf now separating the Indies from the mainland of southeastern Asia. During previous ice advances lowering of sea level as much as 330 feet occurred, further increasing the land area of eastern Asia. Apart from the issues of the eustatic shifts of sea level, there is some evidence that late Pleistocene and Recent effects of broad arching have been lifting the coastal margins of eastern Asia slightly.

A troublesome variable in this situation is the way in which whole mountain ranges have grown up during late Tertiary and Pleistocene time. Between the advance of the first and the last ice sheets in the western Himalaya the Pir Panjal range in the Lesser Himalaya, grew sufficiently so that it cut off rain-bearing winds and thus locally altered the effects of glaciation. The Indies, except for Borneo, might almost be called modern islands, in that they owe their primary build to Pleistocene structural arching accompanied by extrusive volcanism of ash, tuff, and flow-basalt, and owe their outlines to the rise of sea level in the postglacial period.

THE PATTERNS OF MONSOON ASIA

To shorten the focus from a view of all of Asia to an examination of the physical patterns of Monsoon Asia, one discovers that most of the variety of geomorphic structure that characterizes the larger physical framework is still present. For convenience a somewhat imaginative set of figures is sketched to indicate the general patterns into which fall the structure and landscapes of Monsoon Asia (Fig. 6.4). There is no more than a superficial resemblance between the continental margins and these imaginative shapes, but they will serve as the skeleton upon

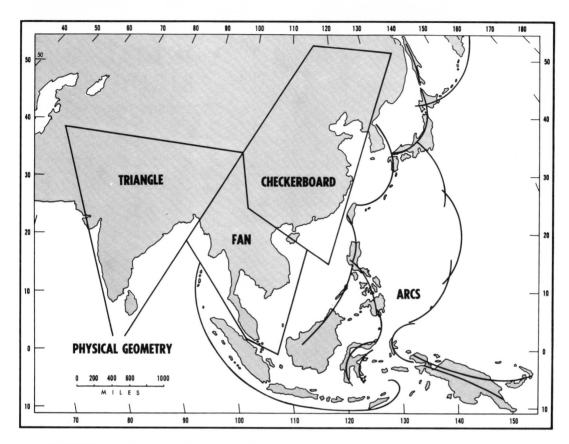

FIGURE 6.4. The physical geometry of the oriental world indicates four major physical units. For details, see Figs. 6.5–6.14.

which to build a detailed discussion of the geomorphology and surface landscapes of the several broad regions. There are four such sketch patterns. On the south is the Indian Triangle, including the territory from southern Tibet to the island of Ceylon (Figs. 6.5 and 6.6). On the southeast is the Burmo-Malayan Fan which takes in the mainland countries of Burma, Thailand, Laos, Cambodia, North Vietnam, and South Vietnam, and West Malaysia (Figs. 6.7 and 6.8). On the east is the Chinese Checkerboard ranging from south China to northern Manchuria, with its roots deeply buried in central Asia (Figs. 6.9 and 6.10). Off coast lie the southern and northern Island Arcs, reaching from

Sumatra and New Guinea on the south (Figs. 6.11 and 6.12), to the Kuriles and Sakhalin on the north (Figs. 6.13 and 6.14).

The Indian Triangle

If one could observe the whole of the Indian Triangle from the crest of Mount Everest, on top of the main Himalayan Range, it would be seen that it consists of four distinct parts (see Figs. 6.5 and 6.6). To the north lie range after range marking the high segments of the Tibetan Plateau. Alongside and underfoot are the tremendous curving ranges of the Himalaya. From its abrupt facing onto the low country to the south this crest zone is termed the Mountain Wall. Conforming

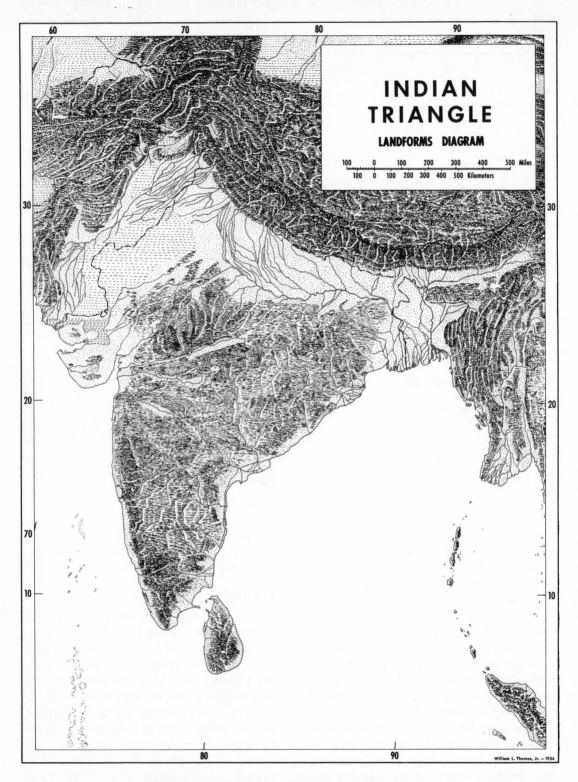

FIGURE 6.5. The Indian Triangle: landforms diagram.

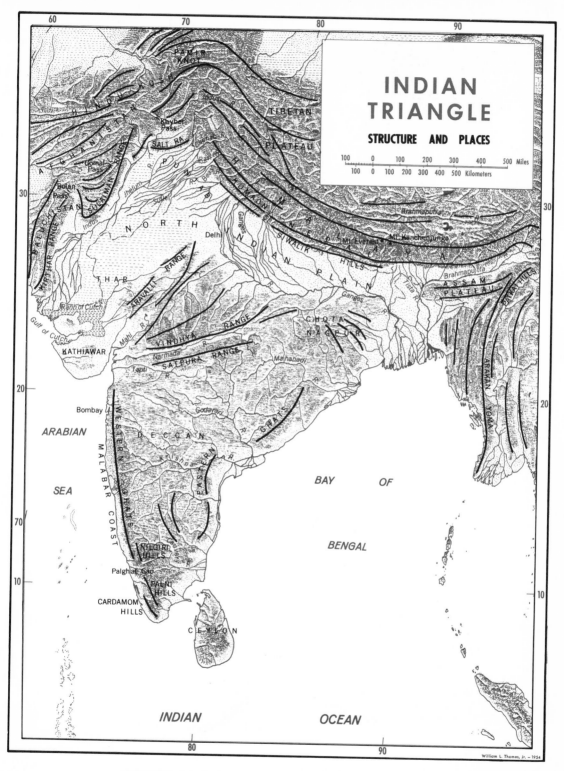

FIGURE 6.6. Structure and places in the Indian Triangle.

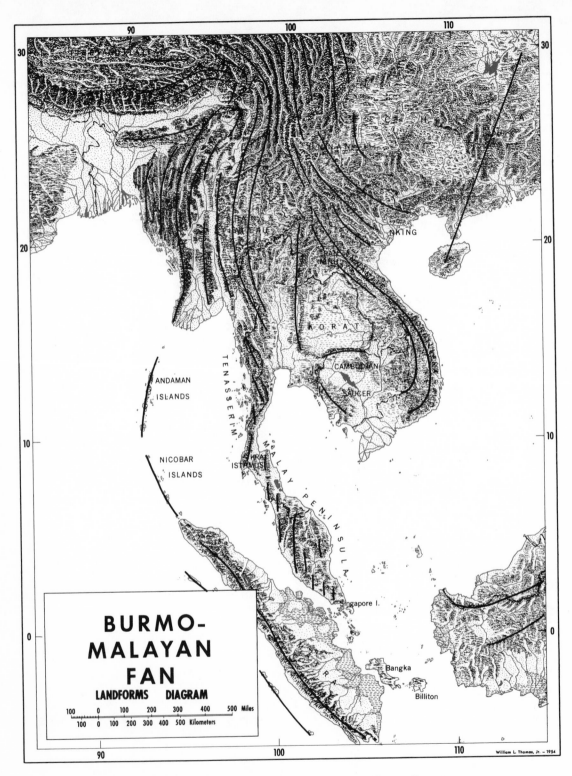

FIGURE 6.7. The Burmo-Malayan Fan: landforms diagram.

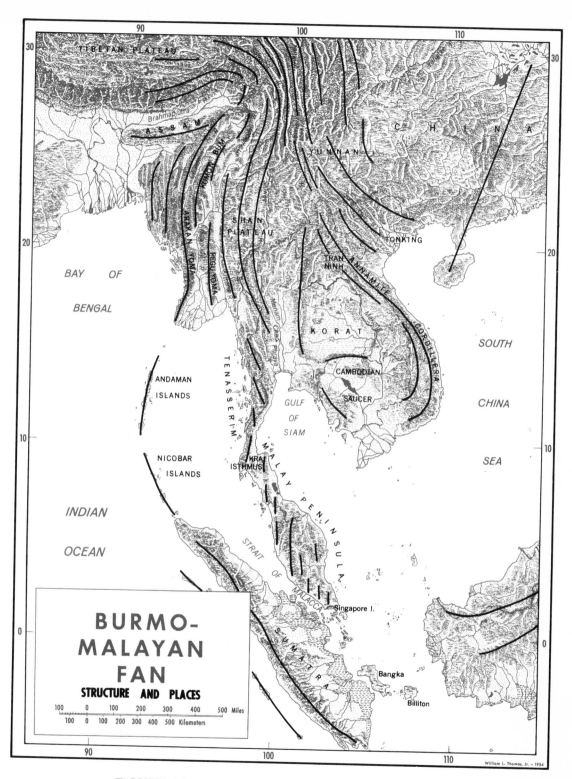

FIGURE 6.8. Structure and places in the Burmo-Malayan Fan.

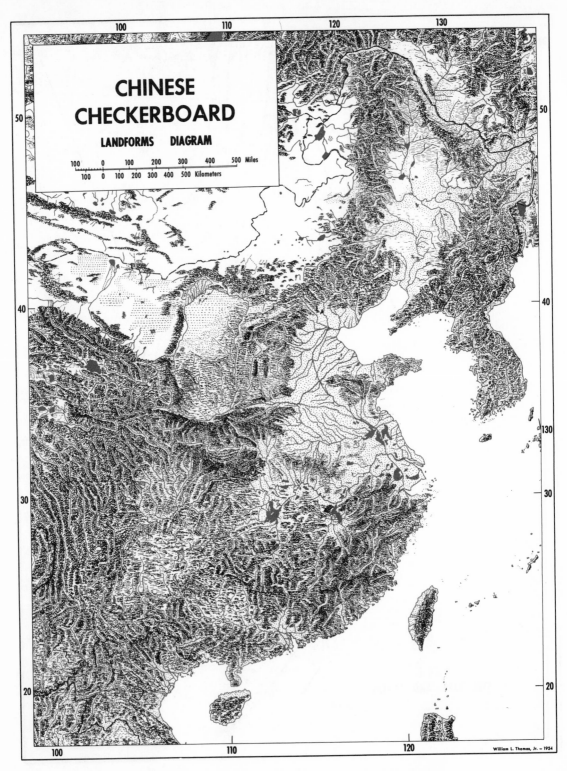

FIGURE 6.9. The Chinese Checkerboard: landforms diagram.

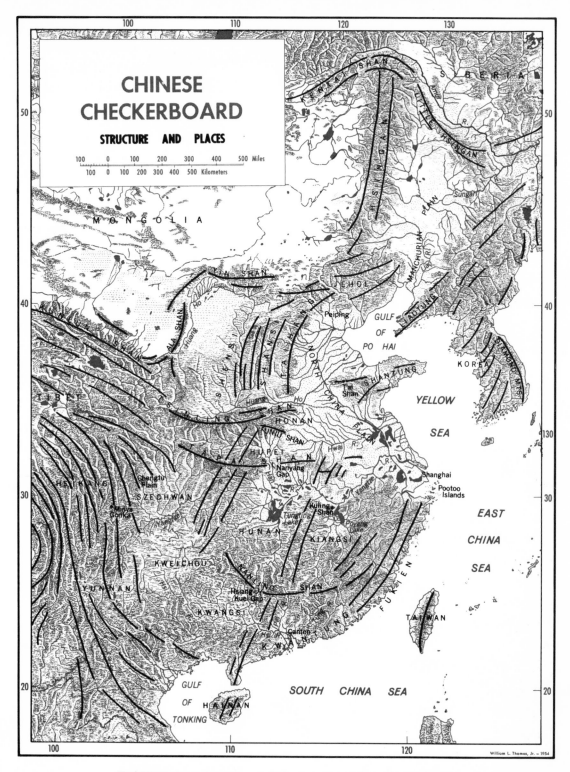

FIGURE 6.10. Structure and places in the Chinese Checkerboard.

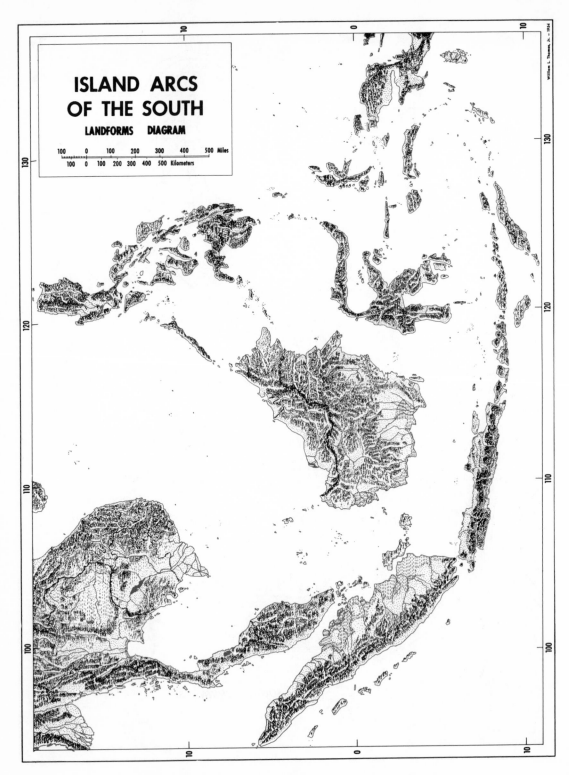

FIGURE 6.11. The Southern Island Arcs: landforms diagram.

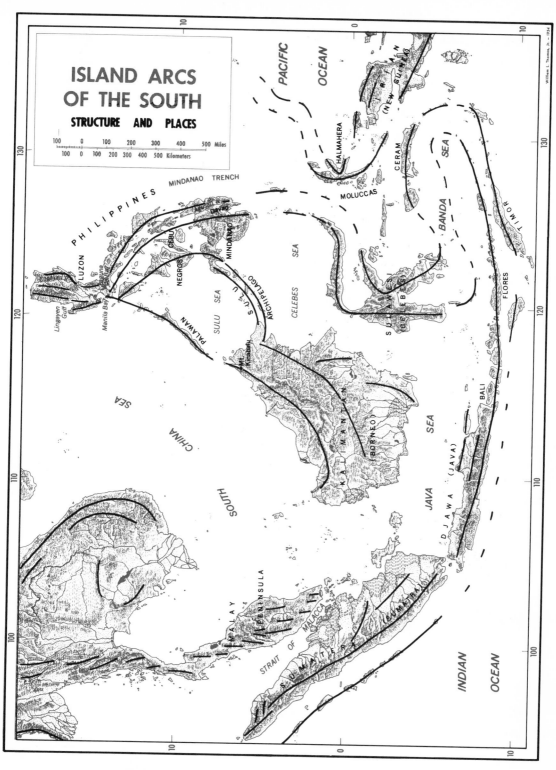

FIGURE 6.12. Structure and places in the Southern Island Arcs.

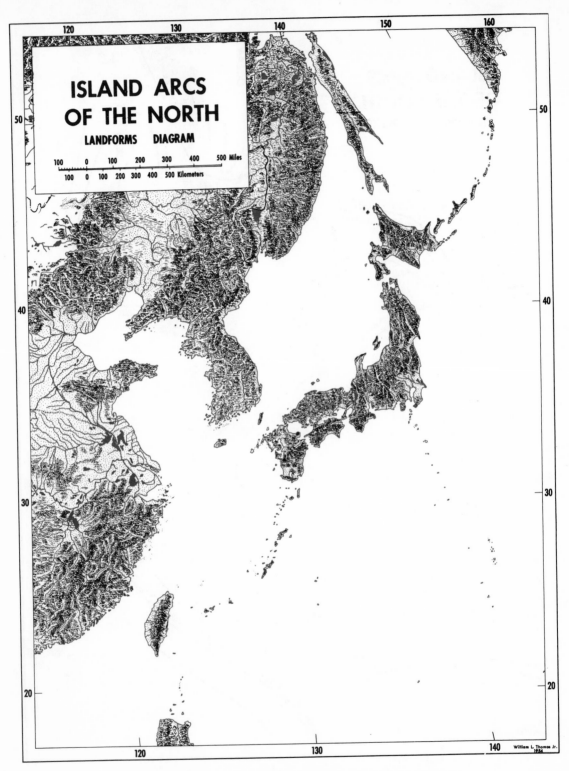

FIGURE 6.13. The Northern Island Arcs: landforms diagram.

134

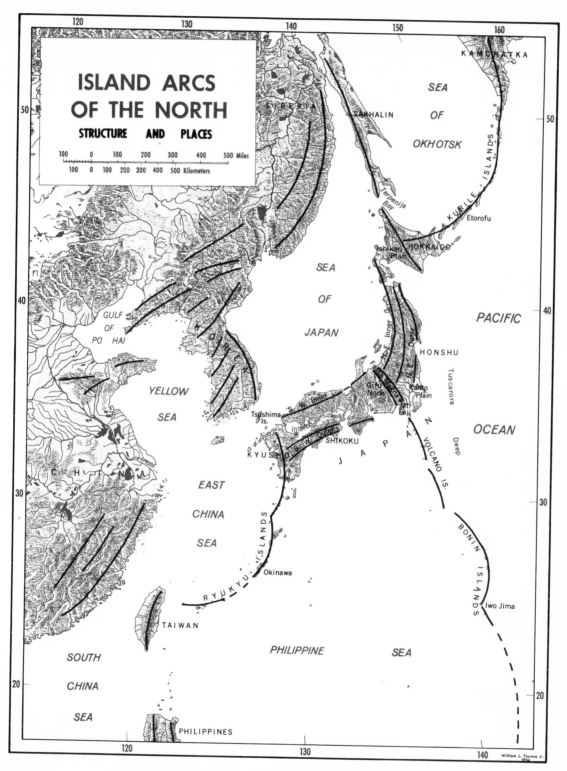

FIGURE 6.14. Structure and places in the Northern Island Arcs.

closely to the Himalayan line is the great sub-siding trough of the North Indian Plain, a 300,000-square-mile basin gradually being filled with the materials excavated from the Himalayan ranges and southern fringe of the Tibetan Plateau. Beyond the great plain rises gradually the fourth unit, the old and much worn surface of Peninsular India, about a million square miles of territory forming one of the world's great, ancient massifs.

THE TIBETAN PLATEAU

The body of the Plateau lies above 15,000 feet, fenced on the south by the Trans-Himalayan ranges and on the north by the Kunlun Shan, Altyn Tagh, and Nan Shan. Narrow and highest toward the western end, the great spiked ridges spread to the north and south as they trend eastward. There are many of these ranges, and they fill the whole plateau with ragged alpine topography carved in bold outlines. There are innumerable basins between the ranges, most of them longer east-west than north-south, and variably filled with rock debris from the near-by ranges. Many of the basins contain perma-nent lakes varying in size from small marsh-ponds to large bodies of water which fluctuate in size from time to time. There are many great alluvial piedmonts surrounding individual basins, and in parts of the plateau denudation and filling has broadened the passes into open saddles affording comparatively easy access from basin to basin. There are few real rivers in the heart of the plateau, though not all the basins are internal drainage units. Passes between basins often lie above 17,000 feet.

The section that best fits the above de-scription is known as the Chang Tang, which is the main body of the plateau. In area the region measures nearly 400,000 square miles, being about 1,500 miles long and having a maximum width of about 400 miles.

Set somewhat lower than the Chang Tang in the northeastern corner of Tibet is a large, irregular basin area partially divided by sub-ordinate branches off the Altyn Tagh and the Nan Shan ranges to the north. The Tsaidam is the largest single basin unit of Tibet, some 400 by 100 miles in rough measure.

South of the Tsaidam the east-west trend of the Tibetan ranges swings gradually south-ward, and the whole of eastern Tibet has been trenched by the headwaters of the great rivers of eastern Asia, the Huang, the Yangtze, the Mekong, and the Salween. Here there are fewer filled basins with open saddles, fewer lakes and internal drainage units, but en-trenched streams, greater relief, more ex-posure of the rock flanks of ranges, many marks of glaciation, and a steady deepening pattern of earth sculpture on a tremendous scale.

A portion of southern Tibet also is trenched by great rivers that have prevented the building of high, filled basins. Two major Indian rivers, the Brahmaputra and the In-dus, have circled the east and west ends of the Himalaya to drain a long and narrow strip of southern Tibet. The primary alignment of the drainage net is with the structural patterns of the plateau, with the deepest gorges placed where streams cut across ranges.

At the narrow western end of the plateau is the Pamir Knot. Here altitudes generally are somewhat lower than in the Chang Tang or Southern Tibet, but the ranges are closer together, the interrange basins are almost lacking, and stream dissection has deeply carved the outer edges of the highland. This is the spot at which the main Himalaya of the south, the enormous Karakorum of central western Tibet, the Tien Shan and Kunlun ranges from central Asia, and the Hindu Kush and Sulaiman ranges of Afghanistan intersect in a confused and complicated high-land knot.

THE MOUNTAIN WALL

For over 1,500 miles the Himalaya stand out above the alluvial plains of northern

India. In the west the several ranges of eastern Afghanistan and Baluchistan form a descending highland wall irregularly framing the North Indian Plain for nearly 800 miles. On the east the ancient rock mass of the Assam Plateau lies in front of a curving range system that projects southward along the Burma-India border country and, for nearly 500 miles, limits the North Indian Plain on the east.

In morphologic structure there is considerable variety in the many ranges that ring northern India. Some are simple folded mountain ranges formed during one portion of Tertiary time. Others are complex bodies of folded and overthrust rocks of varying ages, involving repeated mountain building operations throughout the Tertiary and Pleistocene epochs. All the ranges appear to be set on arcs of circles of varying radius, their convex faces toward the North Indian Plain. Most ranges have multiple structures with variable rates of curvature, and with bifurcations at points of curvature change. There appears to be some continuity clear around the Mountain Wall rather than mere orographic juxtaposition of three unrelated sets of mountain ranges. Mountain building has continued until very recent geologic time, and today an active earthquake zone blankets the inner side of the Mountain Wall.

The physiographic patterns of the Mountain Wall show great variety also. Though not exceptional in height the ranges of the northwestern and western border zone have been affected primarily by the dry-land processes of denudation. Seasonal streams, steepwalled canyons, precipitous gorges, alluvial fans, much bare rock exposure, and considerable aeolian erosion and deposition are elements in the formation of the present landscapes. In the Himalaya, on the other hand, there has been considerable glacial activity, and U-shaped valleys, hanging valleys, cirques, and the spectacular angular lines of ice work on hard rock are to be seen. At lower altitudes the depositional products of mountain glaciation are intermixed with voluminous amounts of landslide debris that periodically block stream channels, causing temporary lakes and subsequent serious flooding downstream. Most of the rivers of the Himalaya are youngish streams with precipitous upper courses and deep and often tremendous gorges where they cut across mountain ranges. Deep, flat-floored valleys alternate with narrow gorges until the streams finally come out upon the North Indian Plain to entirely change their behavior in the flat lands. In the border ranges of Burma glaciation is very evident in the northernmost sector. Farther south the humid-land processes operate much as in the Himalaya to produce a deeply dissected landscape.

The Himalaya Ranges. The Himalaya are sometimes divided into four units from east to west, the Assam, Nepal, Kumaon, and Punjab sectors, on the basis of the penetration across the main range by the headwaters of the Tista, Kali, and Sutlej rivers. These are not the only streams to penetrate the ranges, however, and it is somewhat more satisfactory to describe the Himalaya as three series of parallel mountain ranges with longitudinal valleys, set abruptly above the North Indian Plain. On an average the breadth of the zone is between 150 and 200 miles, somewhat wider in the west and narrower in the east. The highest elevations are in the central eastern sector. The western fourth of the zone is much less dissected than other parts and the water parting correlates closely with the main crest, whereas in the central and eastern sections headward stream cutting has pushed the water parting back of the main crest line some fifty miles and has cut many deep canyons into the frontal section of the ranges. A cross-sectional view of the Himalaya, south to north, shows the three following divisions.

OUTER HIMALAYA.   Set just above the

alluvial plains at altitudes of 2,500 to 4,000 feet is the Outer Himalaya, also known as the Siwalik Hills. This is a foothill zone, composed of Tertiary river-borne sediments similar to but older than those forming the North Indian Plain. In the west this foothill zone is perhaps 30 miles wide and well developed, gradually thinning out eastward until, in Assam, it is rather inconspicuous. Behind the foothills are open valleys running longitudinally and draining into the large streams that have cut deeply into the main range.

LESSER HIMALAYA. Above the foothill strip is an intricate system of ranges known as the Lesser Himalaya. Some fifty miles wide on the average it also narrows from west to east and gradually becomes less important. Altitudes seldom reach above 15,000 feet. It is composed of granites and other crystalline rocks, some ancient sedimentaries, and metamorphosed strata. Deeply dissected by many streams, it consists of bifurcations off the main Himalayan ranges which gradually shift in direction to become parallel ranges forming a continuous line. Both within and behind the Lesser Himalaya are more longitudinal valleys. These vary considerably in altitude, but are set a step above those of the Outer Himalaya, and sometimes contain small lakes.

GREAT HIMALAYA. Towering above the lesser ranges is the Great Himalaya, with a perpetual snow line and a great many peaks above 20,000 feet. The range system composed of granites and other resistant rocks contains bold and striking relief. There are numerous bifurcations north and south at points of curvature shift, and several outstanding peaks are set just south of the main line of the range system. Of the eighteen Asian peaks positively identified as standing above 26,000 feet, twelve are in the main Himalayan range, one in the west, and all the others in Nepal, where the Mount Everest

and Kanchenjunga clusters of peaks are situated. In the west the main crest sits far back from the North Indian Plain, but toward the east the lesser units of the Mountain Wall thin out and the high peaks stand close above the plains. There are hundreds of passes and avenues through the Himalaya, many of no current significance because they do not lead to any real objective. In the west the routes of travel must cross at true passes over the main Himalayan crest, but in the east most travel has always followed the shoulders of the many deep stream channels through the main range, seeking out the lowest water partings available behind the high peaks.

The Western Border Ranges. Apparently turning the corner in northwest India and swinging southward into Afghanistan is a part of the Himalayan structure pattern. Of concern here are only the easternmost limbs of the mountain systems, which spread as they extend south and west, their convex faces toward India. Nowhere is the Afghan or Baluch zone built to such a height as those in the Himalaya. The southward ranges fall off in height toward the Arabian Sea, from heights of some 13,000 feet in Afghanistan to around 7,000 in central Baluchistan, and extending to the Makran coast as rugged but low hill ranges. In the north, set just inside and across the elbow bend, lies the flat-topped Salt Range, rising sharply out of the plain but sloping back toward the elbow bend and cut by the Indus River. The Salt Range is a complex faulted region of old sediments.

West of the Salt Range the Sulaiman system rises above the Indus plain as relatively simple folded ranges composed of Tertiary rocks. Beyond it lie other similar ranges with alluvial valleys leading southwest to the Seistan Basin, but the drainage of much of the arid Sulaiman is southward and back to the Indus. After a 400-mile stretch the Sulaiman curves and merges into the next arc line to the west. The simple folded Tertiary Kirthar ranges continue toward the Arabian Sea, most of them curving westward along the coast. Drainage of the area is toward the sea by individual small stream basins that cut through the coastal hill ranges.

The western border mountain systems have served far less well than the northern systems to isolate India. The western border is passable at many points, through passes across the crest lines and by entrenched streams which cut behind the main ranges toward more westerly water partings. Many passes are located at altitudes which made animals or foot travel much more practicable in the past than the rough and arid landscape would seem to suggest to the modern traveler. Khyber Pass, in the north, is less than 4,000 feet, the Gomal Pass, behind the Sulaiman Range, is under 3,000 feet, and the Bolan Pass through the northern Kirthar is below 6,000 feet. Along the Makran coast travelers can remain close to sea level. Many other passes less well known in modern times at similar altitudes long have facilitated movement between India, Iran, and Russian Turkestan.

The Eastern Border Ranges.   Set out in front of the Burma border is the oblong mass of the Assam Plateau, reaching a highest altitude of 6,400 feet. This region really belongs to the ancient massif of Peninsular India, for it is composed of the same kind of rock and has the same structure. It is deeply dissected and is slowly being cut into three remnant portions. By its position the Brahmaputra cannot take the simple course to the sea followed by the Indus, but must traverse the long, narrow Assam Valley around the obstruction. The Assam Plateau also obscures the front of the long, sweeping arc of the several ranges of the Arakan Yoma-Lushai Hills-Patkai Hills that separate Burma from India and East Pakistan and become the island-strewn west coast of Burma fronting on the Bay of Bengal. The eastern border

ranges are placed convex to the North Indian Plain. They are composed of Tertiary rocks and, apparently, have a fairly simple general structure pattern. They are markedly parallel in alignment. This dissected and jungle-covered wilderness was one of the least studied portions of the Orient before the Burma campaigns of World War II.

Altitudes at the great bend of the Alpine Chain are somewhat higher in the northeast than in northwest India. The structural knot is not so tight or narrow, and the great rivers draining Eastern Tibet have dug very deep trenches. Consequently there are but few really passable avenues from the upper Brahmaputra across to China, and to mainland Southeast Asia. Movement into or out of India in this quarter faces far more difficult travel than in the northwest, and the barrier protection to the North Indian Plain here is almost as complete as along the Tibetan zone itself.

THE NORTH INDIAN PLAIN

When the Tertiary era of mountain building began, a shallow and retreating arm of the sea lay between the new and growing upland to the north and the old massif to the south. South of the trough the Assam Plateau was connected with the rest of Peninsular India so that the trough was very much elongated and open only at the western end. Into this region the streams draining the slowly growing Himalayan ranges piled their sediments. Later those first strata were folded into the Outer Himalayan foothill strip, as both heavy sedimentation and mountain-building pressures continued. At some period a 150-mile strip of the northern end of the massif foundered, opening a gap to the sea between the present Assam Plateau and the Rajmahal Hills. Coupled with major readjustments in surface drainage for all of southern Tibet, the opening of this gap gradually led to a reversal of direction for a considerable number of streams that now are part of the Ganges River system.

During and after the close of the glacial era the narrow central section, near modern Delhi, was built to a higher level, further separating the drainage of the Ganges and Indus river systems. Since Neolithic time a number of channels near this water parting have been abandoned or have continuously shifted their courses. Abandoned oxbows, natural levees, terrace levels, bluffs cut into older alluvium, silted-up distributaries, changes in regional centering of seasonal floods, widely braided and island-filled channels all attest the fact that local changes in surface are being produced everywhere in the North Indian Plain.

Today there is an enormous alluvial plain covering nearly 300,000 square miles. Its simple proportions are impressive. It is nearly 1,800 miles air-line distance from the Kirthar ranges on the west to the head of the Brahmaputra Valley in Assam, about 800 miles from the Himalayan front in northwest India to the Indus Delta margin. Generally the width of the plain is between 120 and 200 miles. The Indus Delta has a seafront width of 120 miles, the narrow Delhi Gap is but 85 miles, the Ganges Delta seafront is 300 miles wide. The valley of the Brahmaputra, however, is seldom over 50 miles wide throughout its 500-mile-long section behind the Assam Plateau. Most of the plain lies below 500 feet in height, and the Delhi Gap just tops 700 feet as the highest point between the Indus and Ganges drainage. Local relief is very slight and the open plains landscape is a monotonous one to a slow traveler. Its margins along the Mountain Wall are somewhat higher, and fairly smooth in alignment, with only minor irregularities. Most of the line of contact with Peninsular India, on the other hand, is marked by deep embayments of alluvium and protruding spurs of hard rock in the process of burial under the alluvial fill. In Rajputana this contact zone contains the

Thar Desert, a slowly expanding area of alternating sand and subdued bare-rock surfaces. Much of the western Rajputana rock basement has been almost base-leveled. South of the Thar lies the Great Rann of Cutch, in which the line of demarcation between plain and peninsula becomes even more difficult. A few bare-rock hills are the remnants of a period of marine planation of the corner of Peninsular India around which sedimentation from Rajputana and the Indus has taken place to raise the surface almost to sea level. In the winter the area is an enormous, dusty, salty, and desolate surface. During the summer the monsoon winds blow sea water into its lowest-lying sections and blow salt, sand, and silt off the higher portions back into the Thar Desert.

The Indus portion of the plain is served by one great river, the Indus itself, and five major tributaries that make up the Punjab's "five rivers," the Sutlej, Beas, Ravi, Chenab, and Jhelum, which carry more water than the Indus. The alluvial deposition of the Indus and its tributaries has built the upper Punjab to a higher level than other Himalayan piedmont margins of the plain. The water sources are primarily the Himalayan highland rains and snows, fed the year round but with a peak period of flood in April and May in normal years. Time was when the Indus could be navigated as far as the Salt Range gorge, but modern irrigation systems that feed millions of acres take too much water out of the rivers.

The Ganges system is a combination of nine or ten principal tributaries, most of which have their sources in the Himalayan front and, like the Indus system, are fed by seasonal snow melt and summer monsoon rain. With a rainier drainage basin the Ganges carries a larger volume of water than the Indus, but enormous irrigation canals seriously reduce the regular flow, and the river no longer carries significant shipping. The Ganges floodplain is flatter than that of the

Indus, with a greater amount of meandering and seasonal flooding.

The Brahmaputra with fewer large tributaries than the other two major streams drains a larger and rainier catchment basin, loses little water by irrigation, and has a much narrower floodplain for alluvial deposition. Its channel therefore carries more water, and it appears a much greater river, navigable for some 800 miles by river streamers, barges, and launches.

The three river systems bring to the two great deltas a total of not far from 3,000,000 tons of sediment per day. Both deltas are growing steadily, particularly the larger Ganges-Brahmaputra Delta, which has been changing rather markedly in recent centuries. The western and eastern distributaries have silted up, annual flooding has changed its patterns, the Ganges has shifted eastward, the Brahmaputra westward, and the tidal Sundarbans have grown outward considerably.

PENINSULAR INDIA

The foundations of Peninsular India consist of Pre-Cambrian igneous and metamorphic rocks. Over a little more than half of the peninsula this ancient basement lies directly below the surface. Extensions of the basic foundation reach northwestward under the shallow alluvial cover of the Thar Desert, and northeastward to the Assam Plateau, though a foundered block now carries a shallow alluvial fill over it in the upper Ganges-Brahmaputra Delta. Very early structural deformation created a number of linear patterns varying from northeast-southwest to north-south, which today show up in different physical features. A random scattering of Paleozoic and Cenozoic fresh-water sediments is distributed over the whole area, but there were only minor periods of small-scale marine deposition. Preceding and accompanying the earliest building of the Tertiary Alpine Chain was a long period in which

innumerable thin layers of basalt poured from fissures in the underlying basement rock. These beds variably total a few hundred to several thousand feet in thickness and mostly lie in horizontal position. They now total some 200,000 square miles in area, perhaps a third less than the maximum coverage once attained. On the northwest the basalt extends all the way to the coast, but the inland margins have been cut back until much of the previously covered basement structure is exposed again.

Considerably before Tertiary time the peninsular block was given its basic structural position, an elevation along its western edge with a tilt slightly north of east, a position never basically altered. Accompanying the building of the Alpine Chain were a variety of strains that have affected the northern margins of the peninsula. Later in the Tertiary minor fluctuations of the block occurred, with respect to sea level, for there are numerous evidences of changes in shore line on both east and west coasts.

The east-west water parting, in the peninsula, is amazingly near the west coast everywhere except in the northwestern sector, where three streams were able to excavate long, narrow trenches along fault or fracture lines to push the drainage divide eastward more than halfway across the peninsula. Otherwise, all the long streams flow toward the east, with the tilt of the block. Several of the east-coast streams have both falls and rapids in their headwater sections, with steep gradients and narrow valleys in this zone. Once out of the highland headwater zone, relief is rather subdued, though it may be considerable. Most streams are shallow and have graded courses, with well-developed floodplains, along their lower sections. Every stream has a delta, built proportionately to its basin area and flow. Numerous clumps of remnant hills and many inselbergs are distributed over much of the peninsula. The Eastern Ghats lie inland from the coast and are a discontinuous line of hills in the south, but increase both in bulk and altitude toward the north.

All the streams of the west coast, with the three northern exceptions, are short and precipitous in grade, with falls near their heads and rapids in their lower courses. Catchment basins are very small in all the streams, and the sediment load is small. Dependent upon the precipitation total, increasing southward, each stream can handle a much larger flow than the catchment area would indicate. None has very deeply notched the steep-fronted west coast, so that there are remarkably few gaps across the divide. From the sea the Western Ghats appear as a steep-fronted mountain range, with altitudes just above and below 5,000 feet for much of its length. Toward the southern end altitudes gradually rise and reach a maximum in the Cardamom Hills at 8,840 feet. Just north of the Cardamom Hills lies the Palghat Gap, a structural saddle pass only 800 feet in height, the only real pass anywhere in the Western Ghats. Though none of the west coast streams has cut the face of the Ghats very deeply, they do not form a smooth, high line. Their front is irregular throughout, with occasional remnant foothill patches and a number of deep embayments, which noticeably enlarge the narrow coastal strip.

Peninsular India does not easily divide into regional units, but the following notes on separate areas are helpful in attempting to describe the differing landscapes.

The Aravalli-Satpura Hill Ranges. In the northwest the worn-down edges of the ancient massif disappear under sand dunes and alluvium along an irregular and shifting line. Bare-rock exposures vary from almost flat and featureless surfaces to rugged hills of bold and craggy relief. Maximum altitudes approach or exceed 5,000 feet. Structure often is locally complex in the north, with a variety of ancient rocks exposed at the sur-

face; to the south the basalt flows mask the surface but have been carved into a varied relief. Marine planation gives the margins of the Kathiawar Peninsula a smoother, more worn-down surface but much of the central sector is covered by thin basalt sheets. The strike of the Aravalli Range is northeast-southwest, that of the Vindhya Range is east northeast-west southwest, whereas the Satpura Range is lined up almost east-west. None of the ranges is single, but each is a multiple expression of ancient deformation of the peninsular block. Draining this area are the three long streams flowing to the west coast, occupying structural breaks, the Mahi, the Narbada, and the Tapti. Drainage of the whole area is split between Arabian Sea, Indus, and Ganges systems.

The Deccan Plateaus. South of the Tapti River the main mass of the basalt forms a large tableland or low plateau from 1,000 to 2,000 feet in height, often known as the Bombay Deccan. On the west it reaches to the crest of the Ghats; its eastern margins are rather strongly dissected by the Godavari River system. The tableland itself bears only shallow stream valleys, and much more noticeable in the landscape are the terraced mesas and rolling plains formed by the many horizontal layers of basalt. Slopes connect many of these varying levels, rather than vertical cliffs as might be suggested by its basalt composition. To the south the altitude generally increases to above 2,000 feet as one passes out of the basalt region and into the red soil of the Deccan Plateau proper. The southern portion is above 3,000 feet. Here the Western Ghats form a high barrier margin, whereas on the east and south the plateau is quite deeply trenched by several stream systems.

The Nilgiri-Palni Plateaus. The high southern end of the peninsula is not all ragged mountain crest, for two small structural plateaus have been rather abruptly elevated above the surrounding lowlands. The steepness of the plateau margins and the height involved seem quite out of keeping with the description of Peninsular India as an old, worn-down plateau. The Nilgiri Hills cover some 700 square miles of area with open basins and highland swales at about 6,500 feet and rocky ridges and rounded domes rising above 8,000 feet. Across the Palghat Gap lies the Palni Hills spur, offset from the Cardamom Hills. The Palni Hills cover somewhat more than 500 square miles, with altitudes ranging from about 7,000 to 8,200 feet. The Cardamom Hills, farther south, have been so deeply dissected that no plateau surface remains. There are a number of peaks above 8,000 feet. This highland area presents a very different landscape from that of the lower lands of the south.

The West Coast. Below the steep front of the Western Ghats the lowland strip varies in width from 5 to 70 miles. Almost everywhere along the ocean shore the southwest summer monsoon has piled up a sand dune strip and keeps it annually agitated and changing in detail of pattern. In the north the monsoon is less effective than in the south, and here the rivers, aided by tidal sweep, keep their channels open to the sea. Southward along the coast the rivers are less and less able to maintain direct channels to the sea, until, in southern India along the Malabar coast, there is a permanent inland lagoon that extends for many miles behind the dunes and is broken only at intervals. Behind this dune zone is a flat lowland strip. In the north this is a wide bench of marine planation, with but slight alluvial cover, whereas to the south a larger amount of alluvium is frequently distributed over the lowland strip behind the lagoons. The long coast, therefore, changes gradually in appearance from the flat, dry, and barren north to the moist, tropical jungle-lagoon south. Good harbors are few in number along the coast, the natural harbor of Bombay being the only large one.

The East Coast. The east coast of India is in strong contrast to the west coast. Here, first of all, the Eastern Ghats form but a disconnected line of hills lying well back from the shore line. The delta lands are relatively large, and closely spaced, with distributaries usually reaching the sea. Between the deltas and the Ghats there is an emerged coastal plain of varying width. Rivers have deep embayments of valley lowland along them. Along part of the coast sand beaches, spits, and dune strips have created a marsh or lagoon strip behind them, but this usually is in the zone between stream deltas. The lowland is widest in the far south and narrowest between the Godavari and Mahanadi rivers, where the Eastern Ghats are nearest the coast and at their maximum in height and relief.

The Chota Nagpur Upland. In the northeast corner of the peninsular area is a ragged zone of hill country with several small inset plateaus. Much of the area is about 2,000 feet in height, with the marginal river channels below that and the occasional clumps of highland reaching up to 4,500 feet. The drainage is radially outward, mostly shared by the Mahanadi and the Ganges systems. Considerable deformation of this northern portion of the peninsula has occurred, and it is here that the coal and iron beds are located in structural depressions filled with sedimentary rocks. No easy route allows access through, across, or around this rugged upland.

Ceylon. The island of Ceylon is an offset unit of the peninsular mainland. The high point of the island is an 8,800-foot peak well toward the south, off center from a location that would give a symmetrical pattern to relief and surface. Around and north of this high point are set a number of small plateaus, shoulders, steps, and platforms. Below these features is a zone of rolling hill country, narrow around the south and extending well north along the island. Surrounding the whole is the coastal plain, narrower and with variable local relief in the south, broader and flat toward the north. The whole hilly and highland center is composed of ancient gneisses, whereas the coastal plain has an alluvial cover, replaced in the north by marine limestones. A shallow synclinal structure is aligned north-south along the main axis of the island. Drainage naturally is radial, in a series of streams that always are short, steeply pitched in their upper courses and smoothly graded in their lower sections. Much of the eastern coast is cliffed; parts of the west coast have a sand dune and lagoon fringe.

The Burmo-Malayan Fan

From a lesser peak than Everest in the southeastern corner of Tibet our observer now could look down to the south and see before him the whole of the Burmo-Malayan Fan (see Figs. 6.7 and 6.8, pp. 128–129). Its primary alignment is from north to south, and near his feet would be the base of the fan, with its ribs close together, high above the narrow veins. The ribs are the mountain ranges, the veins are the deep trenches of the master rivers of southeastern Asia. On the right a rib curves off to the west and south as the previously mentioned Arakan Yoma. Far to the south are the Andaman-Nicobar Islands in the line of the Arakan. The central ribs extend fairly straight, and the primary one stretches out for a long distance until, at the neck of the Malay Peninsula, its pieces are offset to the left as the Alpine Chain tightens its arc toward the Indies. The eastern ribs flare to the left, the largest one swinging in an S-curve around Laos and the two Vietnams.

As the ribs decrease in altitude southward and run into the sea the veins widen out and become broad valleys with deltas at their far ends. Set into the pattern of the fan are branching ribs and veins. Also inset are several old blocks of strata that partly upset the neat construction of the fan. These are ancient massifs which now occupy positions as low platforms or higher plateaus. Physically the whole zone is quite similar in structure pattern though it is variable in the age of its strata and in the date of mountain building. The two western ribs belong to the Tertiary Alpine Chain, and their uplift separated the old North Indian Trough from the Irrawaddy Trough. The Shan Plateau and all the fan to the east of it are the results of an older mountain-building era, though it is likely that all were somewhat affected by the events of the Tertiary period.

Historically this large area has come to be recognized as the political units of Burma, Thailand, Laos, Cambodia, North Vietnam, South Vietnam, and West Malaysia. Since there are no easily drawn regional subdivisions that facilitate discussion, most written accounts tend to follow political lines even when dealing with the natural landscape. The following pages attempt a systematic description by major physical features, regardless of prevailing political boundaries.

THE MOUNTAIN RANGES

At about 28° N. latitude the bend of the Alpine Chain structure is at its narrowest. Here, in an east-west air-line distance of some 30-odd miles, one can cross from the river trench of the Yangtze to that of the Irrawaddy. A total of 100 miles brings one to a tributary of the Brahmaputra. Within this latter distance are squeezed the folded structures that spread out southward to become many of the ranges of southeastern Asia. Here in the north the heights are just the dissected, knife-like interstream divides between the great trenches. Their altitudes reach nearly 18,000 feet at the elbow bend, and they carry a perpetual snow cover.

South of the tight bend the ranges spread out rapidly and send off branches. For a distance of 200 to 300 miles the mountains occupy much more space than the river canyons. Altitudes decrease rather rapidly both on the ranges and in the river trenches. This is the zone over which the famous "Hump" flights were made during World War II, from Assam to China. One jumbled range after another fills the whole landscape, with steep slopes leading down to V-shaped drainage channels. By about 24° N. latitude the spread of the ranges is very wide. They now are clearly differentiated, one from another, and must be individually considered.

The Burma side of the Arakan Yoma is a series of fairly simple Tertiary folded mountains containing numerous faults. Intricate relief and a highly developed drainage net make the country some of the most difficult in Asia to traverse. East of the Chindwin River lies a simpler edition of the border ranges, known as the Kumon Bum in the north and the Pegu Yoma in the south where they fade out to a range of hills in the alluvial lowland. East of the Irrawaddy a long narrow divide, in the north, shades into the Shan Plateau, to be discussed later. Between the Salween and the Menam Chao Phraya lies the peninsular spinal column. It is not one continuous ridge line but, as a series of elongated blocks placed *en echelon*, it maintains its place as the central water parting clear through the Malay Peninsula to Singapore. The core of all blocks is Cretaceous granite intruded into already folded and faulted flank formations of Paleozoic limestones and sandstones. Altitudes vary considerably, with individual sections rising to 8,800 feet on the Yunnan border, over 7,300 feet in Tenasserim, about 3,700 feet in the Kra Isthmus zone, and nearly 7,200 feet in central Malaysia. There are many passes and gaps through the ranges, located fairly high in the north but becoming low-level openings in Tenasserim and farther south.

East of the Mekong River, range structure ties into the alignment of the Sino-Tibetan border ranges, about which more will be said later. Southward from the great bend these ranges decrease quite rapidly in altitude, northern Laos reaching only somewhat over 9,000 feet and no point in the southern section reaching 8,000 feet. The main mass of highland sweeps southward in a double curve, S-shaped, known as the Annamite Cordillera. It is rather massive in build in the north, but thins out south of Laos to become quite asymmetrical in form. Its steep face is close to the South China Sea throughout most of its length, and its longer slope is toward the Mekong. In the north, inset between individual ranges, is the irregular plateau of Tran Ninh; to the south smaller plateau remnants are found in the upland zone. There are no good routes across the northern highland, but in the narrow, central section several passes lie below 1,300 feet, and a number of reasonably good routes lead across the southern uplands.

For some hundreds of miles the Annamite Cordillera parallels the Vietnam coast, falling abruptly away and leaving but a narrow fringe of lowland between the mountains and the sea. It is a rather irregular coast, with many open bays and anchorages, a few islands offshore, and many sections in which the shore is cliffed. Many small streams pitch down out of the highlands in short, independent courses that have built little delta patches and thin alluvial floodplains. A last, spreading rib of the fan is the short member north of the Song Hoi (Red River), running into the sea along the Chinese border of North Vietnam. It is much lower in height with a number of good gaps across it that facilitate movement between south China and the Tonking lowland. Both this and the Annamite Cordillera are composed of ancient crystalline rocks overlain with marine limestones, the whole considerably folded and faulted.

RIVER VALLEYS AND DELTAS

Like the ranges, most of the valleys of the great peninsula of mainland Southeast Asia trend from north to south. All of the present broad delta-mouthed valleys occupy subsiding troughs left over from a previous era of mountain building. The streams that feed the great valleys have their headwaters on the Tibetan Plateau. Unlike many other river systems elsewhere, the central, upper portions of their drainage basins are not extended catchment areas with many small tributaries feeding larger ones until the master stream is reached. Each river is individually framed with a double ring of mountains to isolate its valley from that of the adjacent rivers. No two river valleys are precisely alike but, the Salween excepted, all the great valleys are rather similar in their physical development.

In the west the Irrawaddy, Chindwin, and Sittang rivers jointly have filled the remaining section of the old trough. The Irrawaddy has moved its course considerably as Tertiary mountain building took place. The Irrawaddy system is shorter than either the Salween or the Mekong, but its lowlands are more extensive. Some 800 miles long, the lowland is divided into a number of sectors by rocky gorges. The Irrawaddy drains most of the Shan Plateau and the eastern units of the Arakan Yoma. Its delta is a rapidly growing one, 150 miles long by 120 miles broad at the seafront. A total lowland area of some 40,000 square miles is included in the Irrawaddy basin.

The Salween is so restricted that it has very few tributaries of any kind and has built no appreciable delta at its mouth. It flows in a long structural trench dug deeper by the river itself, flowing right through the tight base of the fan structure sketched above. Its water volume does not change so markedly from season to season as that of the other streams, for its lowland catchment basin is both small and sheltered from the rainy winds of both monsoons. There is almost no flat land along its channel, there are many gorges and sections of rapids, the river is not navigable, and its canyon leads to no objective. It is probably one of the least useful streams among the great rivers of the world.

The Menam Chao Phraya is the shortest of the great rivers of southeastern Asia, draining a rather compact basin. Its lowland area totals about 26,000 square miles, being some 300 miles long by 75 to 100 miles wide. It has been filling in the upper end of another old gulf of the sea, but has not yet finished its task so that its delta resembles an estuary fill.

The Mekong is the most irregular of the rivers of this area. Its course, at present, detours around several of the primary regional blocks of southeastern Asia. From northern Thailand to the sea it has a variably developed floodplain, with minor floodplains along a number of tributaries draining the Korat Plateau and the Cambodian Saucer. Tributaries with steeper gradients drain the west slope of the Annamite Cordillera. The Mekong is the largest river in southeastern Asia, with a tremendous flow of water. It has built an irregular delta some 75 by 100 miles in dimensions.

The smallest of the big rivers is the Song Hoi or the Red River. This stream drains a long narrow structural trench that is aligned very suggestively in an extension of the Yangtze River of China, which originally flowed out to the sea by this line. The lowland is little more than a subsiding embayment fitted into the structural framework of eastern Asia at a point of change in pattern. A true delta, some 60 by 100 miles in dimensions, has been built in this embayment.

THE INSET BLOCKS

Three large separate blocks of old strata today form significant exceptions to the description of the Burmo-Malayan Peninsula as a series of mountain ranges with intervening alluvial troughs. Each of these reacted to the enveloping mountain building in a slightly different way.

The Shan Plateau. The dimensions of the plateau are about 250 miles long by 75 miles wide, nearly 20,000 square miles of area. The Salween River's structural trench lies on one side of it, and a fault scarp zone fronts the Irrawaddy lowland on the west. At present its pattern is that of a folded and faulted block, uplifted as a unit. It is composed of sedimentary rocks containing deep intrusive masses of crystalline rock. It probably was elevated to about its present position early in the Tertiary as a part of the developments along the Alpine Chain. Today, though it still retains most of its highland features, it is fairly deeply dissected and is by no means a perfect definition of a plateau. In altitude it ranges between about 2,800 and 5,000 feet. As a rugged upland block it has little flat land for agriculture and presents few really favorable sites for concentrations of population.

The Korat Platform. The region frequently labeled the Korat Plateau is really a rather low platform set a few hundred feet above the floodplains of the Chao Phraya and Mekong rivers. Structurally the platform is composed of horizontal Triassic red sandstones which are slightly uptilted around the southern and western margins. This platform rim is a peculiar, narrow zone of strongly folded and faulted older strata much dissected into a rugged line of hills separating the platform from the Menam Chao Phraya Plain, and directing the surface drainage eastward to the Mekong. A stream net is lightly entrenched in the surface of the platform, which has a general altitude of about 500 feet in its central section, rising gradually to nearly 2,000 feet near the south and western rim of hills. Toward the margins of the platform are occasional mesas and

patches of hills standing a few hundred feet above the general level. The platform has an area of nearly 60,000 square miles, and its dimensions roughly approximate a square, nearly 250 miles on a side.

The Cambodian Saucer. Set below the level of the Korat Platform and just above sea level is the broad and shallow Cambodian Saucer. Fronting on the Gulf of Siam is a small patch of hill country almost connected to the rim of the Korat Platform. The oval-shaped saucer lies between these hills and the southern end of the Annamite Cordillera, with the Mekong flowing, now, across the eastern sector. The bottom of the saucer is occupied by a large fresh-water lake, Tonle Sap, whose dimensions vary with the precipitation cycle. Much of the surface of the saucer today is covered with alluvial sediments, but it appears to be another block of old strata that reacted independently to the last era of mountain building. There are a number of hard-rock hill patches standing above the lowland level. In total area the Cambodian Saucer approximates 45,000 square miles.

THE MALAY PENINSULA

The peninsula is here considered to be the whole elongated region from the head of the Gulf of Siam to Singapore, a section some 900 miles long. The Kra Isthmus, the narrowest zone, is about 40 miles wide, but shallow navigable estuaries and streams on either coast are less than 20 miles apart, with a drainage divide less than 500 feet in height in a number of places. Here the mountain ranges are in strictly linear pattern, with but a slight offset *en echelon*, though they do not form a continuous high crest. Farther south in West Malaysia more range blocks occur together in parallel formation over a wider span so that the peninsula spreads out to a maximum width of about 200 miles. The islands of Bangka and Billiton are the terminal pieces of the long system. Throughout the peninsular region occur limestones and quartzites, along with minor amounts of other sedimentary rocks into which the Cretaceous granites were intruded. The sedimentary rocks most often show up around the flanks of ranges as low foothills set above the alluvial plains. In some places, however, the limestones have developed into strong karst landscapes with spectacular relief resulting, as in northwestern West Malaysia. Normally the granite range cores stand boldly above the lesser relief pattern of the lowlands. Many peaks in West Malaysia are more than 5,000 feet, and a few are more than 7,000. In West Malaysia granites are exposed over about half of the surface area.

Short streams drain limited areas both to east and west. The peninsular divide generally is nearer to the west coast than to the east coast. Many of the streams flow northward or southward, taking their orientation from the alignment of the structural blocks. This is particularly noticeable in West Malaysia, where the drainage net is clearly developed on the *en echelon* framework. In West Malaysia streams are longer than in the isthmus region, but they still are shallow, have unequal catchment basins, and are without significant deltas. Much of the lowland is not flat but molded in subdued relief; it slopes gently toward the sea along both coasts. Marine terrace levels around the alluvial coast are the expression of changing ice-age sea level. The alluvial cover on the Malaysian west coast gradually deepens from the inland ranges toward the present shore line, where it locally exceeds 450 feet in thickness and extends downward below present-day sea level. Where hard, solid rock occurs numerous inselbergs rise above the lowland, or rocky islands lie in a strip offshore. The alluvial cover of the northern portion of the peninsula is restricted to isolated small patches or to stringy, narrow shore-line strips. It increases in thickness and breadth southward. The coastal plain

ranges from 20 to 40 miles in width along the Malaysian west coast, but on the east coast it rarely exceeds 20 miles. The alluvial cover is widely spread in much of the interior peninsula also, located at various levels. About one sixth of West Malaysia is surfaced by this alluvial cover. The foothills surrounding the mountain blocks grade off into the alluvial plains with no easy line of demarcation. Particularly in West Malaysia a considerable area of poorly drained flat lowland lies between the foothills and the coast. Though there are many islands along the central peninsular coast, there are few good harbors anywhere. The west coast of Malaysia tends to be a shallow, muddy coast. The whole east coast of the peninsula suffers from the wind and sea during the Northeast Monsoon: the surf is high then, sand bars are built across river mouths, and sand dune strips are piled up along the shore. At the other season a broad and hard beach strand frequently is exposed.

THE ANDAMAN-NICOBAR LINE

A distance of some 750 miles separates Burma and the northwestern corner of Sumatra. Scattered over about 600 miles are the 225 islands making up the Andaman and Nicobar Islands. The former group numbers over 200 bits of land and totals some 2,500 square miles. The latter totals about 20 islands and measures some 635 square miles in area. About a half dozen are sizeable islands, the rest being mere rocky islets. The line of the two groups forms an arc roughly parallel to the peninsular coast, smoothly indicating the extension of the Alpine Chain from Burma around to Sumatra. Most of the islets are, of course, only the rocky exposed tops of submerged mountains. The larger islands are irregular in shore line, steep sloped and rugged in surface, with minute patches of flattened lowland.

The Chinese Checkerboard

China consists of a large number of hilly,

plateau-like, or mountainous masses surrounding a variety of lowland units. Each section is placed at a different level, and no two accord with any one definition of basin, plain, plateau, hill, or mountain. The peculiar placement of units, the odd patterns of drainage systems, and the irregular blanketing of parts of the whole by wind-blown dust combine to defy any neat, simple, or concise description of the complex landscape of China. Unless recourse is taken to some systematic, and perhaps arbitrary, simplification, only a very considerable confusion can result in the mind of the reader. If only a mild confusion results from the following pages, therefore, the present attempt should be considered reasonably successful. This effort approaches the problem from the point of view of the structural skeleton of China rather than from that of a running account of its hills and basins (see Figs. 6.9 and 6.10, pp. 130–131).

The basic pattern of China, Korea, Manchuria, and eastern Mongolia is that of a lopsided and irregular checkerboard in which mountain systems are the separating lines, and subsiding blocks and basins are the squares inside the lines. Few of the lines are straight or perfectly parallel, and none of them meet at right angles, so that none of the blocks are rectangles.

The primary structural lines appear to be four massifs of hard rock running northeast-southwest as discontinuous lines. The most easterly forms the south China coast between Canton and Shanghai; the most westerly marks the line of the Huang Ho in west Shensi. Second, there appear to be four east-west tectonic lines, set several hundred miles apart. This set is a somewhat schematic matter, admittedly. The most southerly is a vague line today, expressed as the Nanling Shan of South China; the most northerly is the Kentai Shan just south of the Siberian border. A third set of lines is a series of north-south ranges that form the borderlands of Chinese Tibet and carry on their eastern flanks the plateaus of southwest China. Placed irregularly between the three systems of lines are the subsiding basins that today show up as lowlands and sections of the coastal seas.

On this framework the physical history of China has been built in repeated and successive geologic eras. Some of these lines go back into the Pre-Cambrian, but were quiescent elements part of the time. Others have been the scene of significant happenings in every major tectonic period. At intersections of lines subordinate branchings and oblique forms have developed to complicate the description and understanding of the present landscape. Very generally speaking, eastern China is lowest, and each line to the westward is set at a higher level until one comes out on the Plateau of Mongolia or rises into the highlands of Chinese Tibet.

THE TIBETAN BORDER RANGES

South of the Kunlun-Tsinling line there is a wide zone of the Tibetan borderland that has not been fully canvassed as to its physical relations to the Tibetan highland patterns. From east to west this strip is perhaps 300 miles wide, and it is 450–500 miles long. On the south these border ranges tie into the range alignments at the base of the Burmo-Malayan Fan. On the north, against the Tsinling, the ranges bend westward to fit into the general Tibetan alignment. A few peaks atop the higher borderland ranges rival the second-rank mountains of the main Himalayan range. Minya Gonka is the only one whose altitude is fixed with even tentative accuracy, at 24,891 feet, but there are a number of others close to 20,000 feet, and snow-covered crests extend for hundreds of miles. This is a zone of deep river canyons and gorges excavated along structural lines. Primary alignment is very old and is basically north-south. In late Jurassic or very early Tertiary, prior to the main Alpine Chain orogeny, western Kueichou, Yunnan, westernmost Szechwan and Hsikang were folded and faulted in a two-dimensional field whose primary orogenic lines ran north-south, but across which ran several important east-west lines such as that framing the southern flank of the Szechwan Basin. In this primary north-south trend lies the connection with the main ranges of the Burmo-Malayan Fan.

Mid-Tertiary orogeny of this border zone involved much differential uplift and probable overthrusting of a large order as the Himalayan ranges were elevated to the west. The eastern part of this old structural field is the Yunnan Plateau and its associated Kueichou Plateau; the western part forms the massive Tibetan foreland. Tectonic movements and adjustments have continued into Recent geologic time, and the western section still is an active earthquake belt. Late glacial stream erosion has markedly deepened the upper courses of the major rivers. A number of isolated ranges, high but open basins, and minor inset plateaus occur as products of differential uplift and faulting. Glaciation has had a considerable share in shaping the present landscape, and there are U-shaped valleys and a wide variety of glacial and alluvial deposits on terraces, platforms, and shoulders. There is little flat land, however, and much bare-rock surface.

THE ANCIENT MASSIFS

Primary structural control over the physical geography of China is exerted by the ancient massifs aligned northeast-southwest that are spaced between the east coast and the highlands of central Asia. Three of these properly can be described as massifs, but the fourth and most westerly, the Ala Shan Line, is really only the roots of a folded mountain system. Along the other three members the ancient bedrock of eastern Asia shows up. In all three there are Pre-Cambrian igneous and metamorphic rocks, with later granitic intrusions. Each zone is from 50 to 125 miles in width. All three have been variably affected

by faulting, fracturing, and folding, most of which is developed lengthwise along the zones. All now are discontinuous strips, owing to the foundering of sections of each massif at a late geologic date. The three zones are separated by synclinal troughs. This pattern is one that goes back into early geologic time and has frequently been recurrent. The alignment is also somewhat similar to that of mainland southeastern Asia and may have shared with it some of the earlier mountain-building history.

The Fukien Massif.   The easternmost line of the northeast-southwest series, forming a sea border to the Chinese mainland, extends from the Canton lowland to the Pootoo Islands in one sweep. Internal structural lines run northeast-southwest through the massif, though there are minor cross faults. The seaward side now is an irregular coast, with numerous islands, bays, inlets, estuaries, and cliffed coastal sections. Present-day topography is developed across the structural grain, with a water parting toward the western margin of the old massif. Most of the streams have cut separate and independent channels to the coast, with their tributaries set into structural weaknesses longitudinally to form trellis stream nets. Stream gradients are rather steep, and gorged and open sections alternate along the main streams. None of the streams is very large, their sediment loads are light, alluvial floodplains are small and narrow, and there is but little alluvial filling of the estuary which is the normal stream mouth. Each end of the massif has a stream entrenched along the structural line, and some of the highest, western portions beyond the water parting drain northward into the Poyang Lake division of the Yangtze Basin. Altitudes along the crest zone average 3,500–4,500 feet, with a few strips over 5,000 feet. The whole massif is a rugged zone of hard rock and fairly strong relief, turning its back on mainland China and oriented to the sea-coast along its separate valleys.

The Shantung-Liaotung Massif. The second positive segment of the northeast-southwest set of lines extends from south China through the Shantung and Liaotung peninsulas. A shallow reverse curve then carries the massif into the highlands of eastern Manchuria. There are many fault and fracture zones which both run the length of the segment and cut across it at various angles. This causes the margins of the several pieces to be lower and to be set with blocks of old strata enclosing younger sediments. The northern end is more massive and less distorted, but also less well studied. In Shantung and Liaotung rounded and domed granite landscapes are cut in bold outlines and fairly strong relief. Heights vary considerably from north to south, and just exceed 5,000 feet in Kiangsi where Kuling Shan stands abruptly above the lowland plain. West Shantung also just exceeds 5,000 feet in China's most sacred mountain, T'ai Shan, but east Shantung is considerably lower. West Shantung has many embayments of alluvium around its ragged margin as part of the North China Plain, but in eastern Shantung these become cliff-lined bays, harbors, and inlets of the Yellow Sea. The Liaotung Peninsula, on its seaward side, is very like the corresponding section of Shantung. Northward in the Manchurian Highlands the zone grows broader, altitudes are greater, and various segments become separate mountain ranges. Along the Korean border altitudes reach a maximum of 9,000 feet where the ancient rocks are capped with much later extrusive igneous rock.

South of Kuling Shan, toward southern China, the massif runs underground and continues only as the somewhat uplifted water parting between Kiangsi and Hunan provinces to the intersection with the Nan-ling Shan. Around the junction of the two

structural lines severe denudational processes have left only rugged hill country. South of the Hsi River valley lie low ranges of sub-dued hills, in continuation of the Shantung-Liaotung Massif, which run into the peninsula pointing toward Hainan Island. The latter stands right on the line of the massif, but too little is known to make this affiliation more than a suggestion. Hainan appears to have a central highland core and a roughly radial drainage pattern. The central highland reaches about 5,000 feet, but is deeply dissected, and there is an irregular belt of spurs and river plains between the highland core and the coast. Parts of the coast now are very subdued in relief, and there are a number of wide alluvial coastal plains. If Hainan is a piece of the old massif, its island position has permitted denudation to sculpture its surface deeply to produce a landscape somewhat different from that found in the northern sectors.

The Taihang-Hsingan Massif. This third line suggests itself as one of the master lines of eastern Asia. It would appear to extend from northern Laos north to the Siberian border in a multiple curve as the third ancient massif. It has a monoclinal structure, with an eastern tilt, that sets the country to the west some 3,000 to 6,000 feet above the basins to the east. The southern half is fairly well buried under the marine lime-stones of the Kueichou and Yunnan plateaus, but the structural expression correlates with the physiographic one. The typical granite topography does not appear until north of the Huang Ho where the Taihang Shan fronts the North China Plain. From this point northward the third segment is continuous. In Shansi the Taihang is only one of the ranges that make up the massif segment, for faults, fractures, and overthrust zones have split it up considerably and separated its pieces. The roots of the separate ranges are similar in composition, but there are many sections of younger sediments distributed over the province that yield different topography.

As the ranges of Shansi trend northward their orographic expression is confused, in southern Jehol, by the intersection of one of the east-west lines, to be mentioned later. In northern Jehol northeast-southwest hill ranges fill much of the area between the main massif and the Gulf of Po Hai. These gradually subside northward, merging into the denudational surface of the Manchurian Plain. To the west the Hsingan ranges carry the monoclinal massif pattern northward toward the Siberian border, where the Amur River skirts its tapering ridges on the north.

Everywhere strong relief and rugged topography are common. From the eastern basins the massif often appears a high and rugged mountain front with but few good passes through it. From the west, however, it is much less formidable, since the plateaus are set well above the basins. Crest altitudes range between 8,000 and 9,000 feet in the Taihang, and between 4,000 and 5,500 feet in the north and in the south. General altitudes in the mountain country are less than these figures, and there are some deep river canyons and structural breaks in the massif line.

The Ala Shan Line. Approximately parallel to and some 250 miles west of the Taihang-Hsingan Massif, and just west of the Huang Ho, runs the short line of the Ala Shan, a series of ranges marking the westernmost northeast-southwest structural line. The mountains are the upfolded and fractured edges of sedimentary strata and the faulted and intruded igneous core. Little field work has been done in this region, but the Ala Shan appears to be the highest of the northeast-southwest members. Rather than a broad massif the ancient core here is but a narrow mountain upland. At its junctions

with the Tsinling and the Yin Shan are curving offset ranges. These are much more pronounced in the north, against the Yin Shan, where the curving lines give the mountains a semblance of continuity. Since the physical displacement involved is not great, the Ala Shan is not a high mountain range standing above the plateau level. Rather it is a rough, ragged, and dissected series of desert hill and mountain ranges. Its crests reach heights of over 8,000 feet, but stand out above the surrounding plateaus no more than 3,000 feet at most. South of the Tsinling the line of the Ala Shan is replaced by the much greater ranges of Chinese Tibet. North of the Yin Shan in Mongolia there appears to be no surface continuation of the line.

THE EAST-WEST TECTONIC LINES

Opposed to the alignment of the ancient massif segments are four east-west tectonic zones that help cut China into separate blocks. These appear possibly younger than the massifs and are somewhat narrower in their physical proportions. All except the southernmost have their roots deep in central Asia. Three of the four do not present, today, great mountain ranges along their lines since they have not been active in recent geologic time, their last products being somewhat worn down at present. The fourth zone, however, has been a line of considerable Tertiary and Pleistocene activity and is one of the most significant physical lines in all China. Wherever an east-west tectonic line crosses or intersects a northeast-southwest massif line, curved or offset units result as the extension of the tectonic line, and there is structural complication and orographic confusion. Several different kinds of pressure have been exerted on the earth's crust which, particularly at intersections, has produced variable branchings, cross connections, and oblique mountain ranges. Much denudation and, in some cases, further tectonic distortion have made the complete analysis of the resulting pattern very difficult. Eastern Asia has not yet been adequately studied to allow the unraveling of all component threads of crustal development.

The Kentai Shan. Near the northern border of Outer Mongolia runs the Kentai Shan in a trend that is largely east-west though there are major deflections in the line. To the east, as it approaches the Hsingan member of the Taihang-Hsingan Massif, its ranges appear to swing northward. East of the Hsingan is a southward curving group of ranges known as the Little Hsingan, that terminates against the next massif to the east. These two sets of ranges are complementary parts of an east-west tectonic line whose clean trend is affected by the mass of the older massif. This portion of Asia is too little studied to allow more than a suggestive comment. However, the mountain ranges of this line do form a margin to the Chinese checkerboard on the north, setting a northern limit alike to the Mongolian Plateaus and the Manchurian Plain.

The Yin Shan. On the southern side of the Mongolian Plateaus the line known as the Yin Shan has a trend very similar to that of the Kentai Shan farther north. Across northern Shensi, just north of the Huang Ho, its ranges trend roughly east-west. But as its members come up against the Taihang-Hsingan Massif they bend northward very much as do the ranges of the northern line. East of the massif there is a suggestion of a similar southward curving orographic trend, comparable to that of the Little Hsingan, but it shortly terminates northwest of the Gulf of Po Hai. The intersection of the two zones appears to be a rather complicated one, with various curving offsets not yet fully mapped. Throughout the whole line of the Yin Shan there is folding and simple faulting of strata. In addition a considerable amount of overthrust faulting has produced some sharp contrasts in local landscapes.

In the west the lines of the Yin Shan system run out into the dry open spaces of the southern Gobi country and seem more structural roots than upstanding highlands. Orographically the Ala Shan and the Yin Shan show some continuity. Eastward across Shensi and Shansi the ranges begin to gather bulk, greater height, and stronger relief. Near and on both sides of the Taihang-Hsingan Massif dissection has so effectively jumbled the present topography that is is difficult to pick out predominant lines. The intersection makes passage outward from the North China Plain difficult, both into Manchuria and into Inner Mongolia. It is significant that the best passes occur close to the intersection. Though this is not a rainy landscape today, an intricate stream net has been cut into the rugged mountain country, giving a maximum percentage of steep slopes and a minimum total of flat or open lands.

The Tsinling System. A very different mountain complex is the Tsinling Shan. Northeastern Tibet is not well known, but it would appear that the Tsinling is an extension of the Kunlun system of northern Tibet. It has been a zone of major tectonic activity as late as mid-Pleistocene, has a very complicated structure, and stands up as tall and precipitous ranges along its western sector. Leaving Tibet it consists of two slightly divergent segments, the Tsinling Shan proper on the north and the Tapa Shan on the south. The two segments extend as far as the intersection with the Taihang-Hsingan Massif, but beyond this only a single contorted line continues. In the west strong Tertiary and Pleistocene earth movements complement similar movements in the north-south border ranges of Chinese Tibet. Simple faults and complicated overthrusts of considerable proportions are part of this development.

The Tsinling emerges from Tibet with altitudes of over 16,000 feet and a north face that is among the world's great fault scarp zones. Altitudes taper gradually toward the intersection with the Taihang-Hsingan Massif. The southern segment, the Tapa Shan, is less rugged and high than the Tsinling proper, and its southern flanks have been deeply laid open by Yangtze River tributaries. The Han River, draining the zone between the two segments, has cut upland valleys both north and south. Although the natural orientation of the Han Valley is eastward, there are enough passes at practical elevations to enable movement across the Tsinling even in its highest sector.

In the intersection of the Tsinling with the Taihang-Hsingan Massif there are some branchings in Honan, known as the Funiu Shan. Southward contortions of the main line of the Tsinling close off the eastward extension of the Tapa Shan and turn the Han River southward toward the Yangtze. East of the intersection just mentioned the Tsinling displays little evidence of recent tectonic activity. Consequently relief and altitudes decrease so that the general level is between 2,000 and 3,000 feet. Though there are no great or sheer scarp zones, relief is very rugged and dissection seems nearly complete, so that travel across the line is almost as difficult as in the western zone unless the pass routes are followed. Near the Taihang-Hsingan intersection occurs the lowest gap across the whole of the Tsinling, a level route under 1,500 feet, known as the Nanyang Gap. To the east there are a number of low passes none of which, however, is so easy to traverse as the Nanyang Gap. Southeastward the Tsinling line continues under several names as a tapering range of rugged hills. About where it again should have intersected a massif segment the trend of the hills shifts northward, and it dies out as low and tapering spurs and inselbergs in the edges of the North China Plain.

The Nanling Shan. The most southerly of the east-west lines is hard to trace structurally and ill preserved physically. It is a line of older activity than that which built the border ranges of Chinese Tibet and elevated the Yunnan Plateau. The Nanling shows no correspondence with the western segment of the Tsinling, but only with its central and eastern end. In the west the Nanling line is buried under the Yunnan Plateau and to the east is a recurved line which swings northward along the southern flank of the Fukien-Korean Massif. The south China water parting between the Yangtze River system and the rivers of Kwangtung and Kwangsi provinces lies just north of 25° N. latitude. Dissection has proceeded very far in the west, where only the remnants of karst landscapes exist, producing spectacular scenic effects and a low-level, canalized route through the hills, known as the Hsiang-Kuei Gap. Eastward karst features decrease as the country rock changes from limestone to older, less soluble sediments. General altitudes increase eastward also until the oblique curves of the Nanling join the Fukien Massif, where altitudes above 5,000 feet are common. Passes through the hills are frequent and practical for land travel along the whole length of the Nanling, those to the east being true passes and not low-level gaps as in the west. This is a hilly country with almost a maximum of dissection outside the karst landscapes, an intricate drainage net, and very little flat land in the hill lands themselves.

THE SYNCLINAL BASINS

On either side of each massif segment is an elongated synclinal trough, divided into sections. The several troughs did not react alike, any more than did sections of any one trough. The Yellow Sea now does cover parts of both, massif and trough, and the East China Sea covers the synclinal area between the Fukien Massif and the nearest junction of Island Arcs in Taiwan. Some of the trough sections, however, did not founder completely but remain as subsiding basins of varying amounts of movement. In some basins alluvial sedimentation has kept their bottoms above sea level, just as it has elevated a few foundered sections above sea level as deltas. Several sectors show synclinal structure but only very shallow physical basins, whereas in one or two sectors not even synclinal structure developed in the appropriate location. Thus there are no two checkerboard squares exactly alike.

The Manchurian Plain. The amount of recent subsidence of the northern section of the central trough is only moderate and has not been continuous. The present surface of the Manchurian Plain is the result of denudation rather than deposition, and is divided between the two river systems, the Sungari on the north and the Liao on the south. The water parting between the two systems is a gradual one, not noticeable in the landscape so that the basin retains its unity. The margins of the plain, both east and west, are irregular, as there are embayments along tributary streams draining the massifs on either side. Much of the plain ranges in altitude from 400 to 700 feet, and the surface is a gently rolling one, with stream channels rather lightly entrenched in most places. In the north the intersection of the Little Hsingan with the Shantung-Liaotung Massif is not a tight one, and the Sungari River has developed a wide gap through to the Amur River. This is the only real gap in the whole northern rim of the basin. In the south the breadth of the lowland is restricted by the eastward projection of the Yin Shan line and the thickening of the uplands around its intersection with the Taihang-Hsingan Massif.

The North China Plain. The North China Plain is the filled area of both trough and massif segments between the Yin Shan and Tsinling lines east of the Taihang-Hsingan Massif. The Huang Ho was principally responsible for the large northern

sector, the Yangtze River for a small southern sector, with the smaller Hwai River giving assistance in the central southern area. Early in the sedimentation process Shantung was an island in the Yellow Sea, but such was the volume of materials available that the whole of the narrow trough was filled, the island half surrounded, and over one third of the original water area filled in. Innumerable shifts of the Huang Ho north and south of the former island have kept both sections progressing seaward approximately alike at a present rate of about a mile a century. Many small streams come into the present plain but, like even the larger Hwai River, their sedimentation effects are minor and obscure compared to the effects of the Huang. These subordinate streams cause many floods, however, for they cannot maintain their channels to the sea against the Huang, and their waters become ponded behind the natural levees, alluvial fills, and torrential flood deposits of the larger stream. There is a surface uniformity about the North China Plain that gives it a considerable monotony as a landscape. There are minor differences in relief and surface forms, but almost more important than these are the differences in soils and water supply conditions. The plain slopes gradually eastward to the sea from an altitude of almost 500 feet against the Taihang and Funiu ranges. The Huang flows above the plain most of the distance to the sea, on a mud ridge built of its own sediments, and the task of keeping the river on the ridge is a difficult and a recurrent one. Throughout parts of the southern plain inselbergs stand out as bare rock, and long low swells of hard rock at the surface indicate marine planation before the filling of the the sector above sea level.

Poyang Lake Plain. South of the Yangtze River and between the Fukien and the Shantung massifs is a portion of the eastern trough that forms a separate synclinal basin with a lake in its bottom. This is one of the smaller basin units occupying a square on the checkerboard. Poyang Lake varies with river and flood level, between 20 by 65 miles in winter low water and 30 by 90 miles in summer flood periods. Into it drain a series of streams, the largest of which flow from the south. The southern lake margins have been filled above average summer level, and the streams themselves have developed floodplains. The lake has become steadily smaller during historic time but the rate of filling is much less than in the North China Plain. Subsidence may be continuing, slowly, to maintain the permanent water body, for the floor of the lake is just below sea level. The margins of the basin are quite irregular, being full of lowland embayments and protruding hill spurs consequent upon a long-continued active denudation.

Tungting Lake Plain.   This is the next basin west, beyond the Shantung-Liaotung Massif. The synclinal basin covers northern Hunan and south central Hupei across the channel of the Yangtze River. Historically the Chinese name for Hunan and Hupei was "liang hu," meaning "the two lake provinces," and within historic time alluvial sedimentation has considerably reduced the area of permanent water surface. The northern section has been more completely filled than the southern, which now contains the only large body of water, Tungting Lake. The big lake varies from 20 by 60 miles in winter to 50 by 80 miles in summer, but there are numerous small lakes in the central and northern part of the basin. Tungting Lake itself is being filled by summer flood waters of the Yangtze River which escape the normal channel through overflow cutoffs, in peak periods of upper river floods, into the northwestern margins of the lake area.

Large rivers enter the plain both from north and south, and river floodplains reach far back along several streams. The central portion of the basin in summer is a watery marsh maze, with small lakes, old river channels, canalized channels, natural levees, and major and minor dike lines forming an almost indecipherable pattern. Because more sediment is available in this western basin than around Poyang Lake, more filling has been done and the land level is higher than that of the eastern basin. The basin margins are as irregular as those of the Poyang Basin but the chief embayments are deeper.

The Szechwan Basin.   Set a step above the two main trough lines is a western trough which contains only one obvious synclinal basin. Central Szechwan was a Cretaceous-Tertiary lake basin partially filled with buff, red, and purple sandstones and shales. The Szechwan Basin consists of the lowland heart of Szechwan Province and is ringed by hills and mountains belonging to the positive elements in the checkerboard. The basin now is drained by the upper Yangtze River system which has cut a mighty series of gorges into the surrounding mountain landscapes on all sides to maintain the drainage of central China. Inside the basin the Yangtze and its tributaries have lightly etched the floor of the basin with an intricate stream network. The intensity of elaboration of this stream pattern is difficult to visualize, but there probably are few spots on the globe that surpass it. It is this region which contributes the color and the largest share of the sediment volume to the Yangtze River with which the lake basins and the delta to the east now are being filled. The floor of the basin is less than 900 feet in altitude, but its outer margins reach 1,500 to 1,800 feet. A number of minor late Tertiary structural ridges run northeast-southwest across the basin to give it local subdivisions. One of these, in the northwest corner of the basin, fences off the only flat territory in all Szechwan. The Chengtu Plain is an enormous, flat alluvial piedmont built behind a protective ridge, and is a local area of real contrast to the etched and irregularly hilly main portion of the Szechwan Basin.

Minor Synclinal Basins. Of a number of remaining squares on the checkerboard none is a synclinal basin in the obvious physical sense, but brief comments about some of them will help fill out the description of China.

THE SHENSI BASIN. Between the Tsinling and Yin Shan lines and between the Taihang-Hsingan and Ala Shan massifs is the structural basin of Shensi. During later geologic time this has not been a subsiding basin, so that its classification is geologic. Having been also an arid region for much of recent time no stream system has turned it into a denudational lowland as in the case of the Manchurian Plain. On the contrary, during part of Recent time it has been an area of accumulation of loess in the southern section, and of dune sand in the northern section. Even more recently tributaries of the Wei and Huang rivers have been rapidly eating into the loess cover and have turned much of eastern Shensi into a desiccated badland of strong relief.

THE EAST MONGOLIAN BASIN. Between the Yin Shan and the Kentai Shan, west of the Taihang-Hsingan Massif, the open plateau surfaces of eastern Mongolia show several gentle, local synclinal units. Being also an arid region no water volume ever accumulated sufficient to cut across one of the bounding limits to drain the area. Much of the Mongolian Plateaus to the west seem to consist of alternate swells and hollows of structural nature.

THE YANGTZE ESTUARY. At the southern end of the North China Plain is a small subsiding zone just inside the Fukien Massif line. This is now the filled estuary mouth of the Yangtze River, aided by other small streams. Not all the zone has been filled in so far, as Hangchou Bay is a part of the subsident zone.

It is not entirely clear what the relation of this part of the trough is to the larger portion listed as the Poyang Basin.

THE CANTON LOWLAND. The little submerged unit at the collective mouth of the three river systems of Kwangtung is also a minor synclinal unit along the eastern trough line, for it clearly is not a true delta in the usual definition. South of the Nanling Shan and southwest of the Fukien Massif, it would occupy a square of the checkerboard that runs out to sea. The three rivers have filled a considerable area of lowland that still has karstic inselbergs sticking up through the plain. Offshore lie numerous islands that still are beyond reach of the fill.

THE KWANGSI PLATFORM. Central western Kwangsi is another checkerboard square in which no obvious synclinal structure can be noted, though geologic field work is by no means complete. The Kwangsi Platform lies below the uplifted Yunnan Plateau, just as the Manchurian Plain lies below the uplifted Mongolian Plateau. Here, however, the positive lines on east and south are only weak ones which fail to provide a positive physiographic framework. The country rock in this portion of China is largely soluble limestone, and this is the northern end of the great zone of southeastern Asian karst development. The northern and eastern portions are in the very late stages, so that only spectacular remnants stand above a basal riverine, alluvial lowland. Westward landforms increasingly range from mature to early stages of karst formation, into the edges of the Kueichou and Yunnan uplands. From southernmost Hunan, in the mature-to-highly developed sectors of karst landscapes, come many of the motivations for the more spectacular of Chinese landscape painting. The Hsi River has developed a drainage net that includes the southern slopes of the Nanling Shan and the edges of the Kueichou and Yunnan plateaus. The landscape of the platform is shallow and open, with wide floodplains and deep waterways which have not yet developed many meanders.

The Southwestern Plateaus

Previously it was suggested that, except for the Szechwan Basin, the territory west of the Taihang-Hsingan Massif is an elevated plateau region. Where the north-south ranges of Chinese Tibet approach and impinge upon the massif in southwest China the normal upland was lifted even higher. Here were produced two distinctive landscapes, the Yunnan Plateau on the west and the lower Kueichou Plateau on the northeast.

The Yunnan Plateau. The plateau consists of alternating basins, mountain ranges, and broad rolling highlands. The general altitude is above 6,000 feet, with mountain ranges standing above the broad highlands. Most of the ranges are oriented north-south, but there are some transverse elements, as suggested on an earlier page. In the south they reach about 9,000 feet, increasing toward the north to altitudes approximating 16,000 feet. The Yunnan Plateau then shades north and west into the ranges of Chinese Tibet with still higher altitudes. The basins vary in size from units of a few square miles to districts over 1,000 square miles in area. Normally the basins are bounded on at least one side by a fault scarp, and usually they possess a permanent lake. Many of the isolated ranges, some of the basins, and most of the lakes are the products of very late Tertiary and Pleistocene mountain building, and today the western section is still an earthquake zone. Glacial features show up in the west, and toward the east incipient karst features appear, with numerous small basins. This karst landscape increases in degree of maturity in an eastward descent onto the Kwangsi Platform.

The plateau is deeply trenched by streams on all margins. The Yangtze cuts a long and tremendous gorge in making its way eastward across the northern end. On the west the Mekong and Salween trenches bound the plateau, with minor Mekong tributary gorges on the west and southwest. On the south the Song Hoi (Red River) has deeply cut into the body of the plateau; on the east the Hsi River and its tributaries have cut some enormous canyons and trenches. Much of this deep erosion is thought to be early Pleistocene interglacial in age.

The Kueichou Plateau. The southern ramparts of the Szechwan Basin and the western uplands above the southern Tungting Lake Basin form the Kueichou Plateau. Except for its western margins, joining the Yunnan Plateau, it is a poor example of the physiographic species: plateau. It consists of strongly folded and faulted marine limestones for the most part, so that much of its surface is divided into separate structural basin units. Its primary structural alignment is northeast-southwest, but there are many local variant lines. Its southern and southeastern margins are strongly affected by karst developments so that many ragged and streamless basins with spectacular highland rims dominate the landscape. To the north and east streams have cut gorges and canyons deep into its front. It is difficult country through which to travel by any means of transport. Extensive deforestation and soil erosion have added to its rough and barren appearance. A rugged, rocky landscape of strong local relief and irregular local landscapes, it is one of the poorest sections of China.

The Drainage Pattern

The somewhat confusing patterns of the checkerboard resolve into a rather simple set of drainage divisions or stream systems (see Figs. 6.2, and 6.9–6.10, pp. 122 and 130–131). Those squares lying in the Mongolian Plateaus obviously are internal drainage units of their own, by patterns not well mapped. The

Manchurian Plain is the only basin unit with two independent drainage systems. All the squares of the checkerboard between the Yin Shan and the Tsinling Shan proper belong to the Huang River system. The rather curious course of the main stream itself derives from the fact that as the separate steps between the sea and the Tibetan Plateau were elevated steadily higher in the building of Tibet the river adapted itself to changing conditions. Every major change in the course of the stream after leaving Tibet is now dictated by some part of either massif members or tectonic lines.

The Yangtze River system now drains all the region between the Tsinling and the Nanling lines, divided into several separate divisions corresponding to the synclinal basin patterns. The stream originates in eastern Tibet, swings southward along the ranges of Chinese Tibet and formerly flowed into the Gulf of Tonking. Tectonic earth movements promoted stream capture of the Tibetan stream by a headwater tributary of the Yangtze.

Between the divergent Funiu Shan and Hwaiyang-Shan section of the eastern Tsinling system there was room for a small river drainage basin, and here the Hwai Ho elaborated a normal basin. As the Huang built up its own delta, however, it appropriated the Hwai Basin upon occasion, a performance repeated several times within the historic period. Eventually the Hwai Ho has been boxed off from the sea by the depositional action of the Huang and the Yangtze.

Fukien, as suggested previously, drains to the coast in its own separate pattern of short streams, forming a whole series of separate, small drainage basins.

South of the Nanling Shan there are three rivers that join in the Canton Lowlands, the Tung, the Pei, and the Hsi, the East, North, and West rivers. The Tung and the Pei drain the southern end of the Fukien Massif and the southern slopes of the Nanling Shan. The Hsi drains the main territory south of the Nanling Shan, the Kwangsi Platform, and the edges of the Kueichou and Yunnan plateaus. It has sunk a shallow but distinct basin so that a line of low hills separates it from the seaward slope of the littoral.

LOESS AND THE LOESS UPLANDS

The structural patterns of China have been partially disguised by the blanket of yellow dust blown out of inner Asia during winter windstorms. This fine yellow dust is known as loess, and there are a number of unsolved problems around its origin and movement. Whatever the final answers may be, it does cover much of north China today, and is an important factor in the landscape. Settling as a layer of variable thickness over most of north China it covered much of the landscape produced by denudation during late Tertiary and early Pleistocene time. The higher and steeper surfaces either never received or quickly lost their dust blanket to keep protruding through the soft and smooth new landscape as inselbergs and remnant mountains. Also some of the more important Huang Ho tributaries kept their own basins nearly free of the dust blanket and today are relatively deeply set into the loess landscape as elongated strips of quite different nature. In the central area of western Shansi, northwestern Honan, and southern Shensi the dust blanket became several hundred feet thick in the deeper hollows and protected spots. All around the margins the blanket gradually thins out. Depositional dust storms heavy enough to darken the sky were part of the late Pleistocene seasonal weather pattern almost everywhere in China north of the Tsinling Shan. Very little dust is being added to north China today, though considerable local redistribution does take place by means of winter windstorms. A large amount of resorting by stream action has occurred almost everywhere in northern China. In any one local area the loess is uniformly fine in texture, shows only slight differences from bottom to top, stands in vertical columns or walls when cut or eroded, absorbs water like a sponge and returns it to the surface in the same way, is easily cultivated, and is everlastingly rich as a farm soil without the addition of fertilizer. The addition of a loess cover to almost any landscape in the world would improve it, from the standpoint of its agricultural resource. To the hard and ancient rocks of the Taihang-Hsingan Massif loess soils prove a tremendous contrast.

On the other hand, the cessation of loess deposition has allowed free action to denudation over all of north China. The very softness of loess has made it very easily eroded by the work of water and wind. With a given expression of energy the forces of denudation can produce a rougher landscape with a higher relief component in loess than in almost any other landscape material. Consequently much of the loess landscape has changed greatly within the historic period and now parts of it are a rough and dissected badland region difficult to cultivate or to travel through. The material removed by water has largely been redeposited in some portion of the North China Plain, an incidental factor in building an extremely rich delta landscape.

In blanketing the underlying landscape and in providing a new surface of variable thickness and distribution, loess deposition has given the geographer an added problem. The pattern of deposition did not fit the regional patterns of the older landscape. One may question whether the surficial unity of the loess uplands is greater and more significant than the underlying structural pattern and remnant features of the older landscape, particularly when they show through as clearly as in north China. There can be no easy answer to this question, and there is no agreement among geographers.

THE KOREAN PENINSULA

Off on the northeast corner of the checker-

board the east Asian coast is close to a junction with the long loops of the Island Arcs, and here crustal blocks did not perform quite as they did elsewhere. Most of Korea is sometimes considered to have been part of an ancient north China massif, whereas south Korea has been considered an extension of the Fukien Massif. The Korean Peninsula, though showing definite relation to the northeast-southwest massif alignment, does not today exhibit the clearly alternate massif and synclinal pattern that marks China. There are no evidences of the east-west lines. On the other hand, along the southeast coast appear features that belong to the Island Arcs. In the simplest analysis Korea can be divided into three separate structural units, each involving several subdivisions of an order too detailed for individual consideration here.

Northern Korea. Closely aligned with the northern sector of the Shantung-Liaotung Massif northern Korea has an underlying ancient rock complex that is faulted and tilted to present a steep eastern scarp zone and a gentler slope westward to the Gulf of Po Hai. Along the northern border early Pleistocene extrusions of basalt built inland sections to altitudes averaging above 6,000 feet, culminating in higher volcanic peaks. Consequent dissection, with further faulting, has created a rugged landscape of high relief, confused local patterns, and very small patches of land level enough to permit easy cropping. Along the northeast coast there is a narrow dissected coastal bench set above sea level and between fault scarps. It is a strip of hardrock outcrops standing in bluffed headlands along the coast, with intervening bits of alluvial lowland built by steep, short streams. On the west, in contrast, there is a wide belt of country which tapers from the high interior to the Yellow Sea in a descending scale of relief. Much of this was once a synclinal trough but later was strongly compressed in folded and faulted structures on a northeast-southwest trend. The present landscape is cut into the folded and faulted surface. Toward the volcanic highland relief is strong and streams are deeply entrenched. Nearer the coast relief becomes subdued and the landscape open, with wide floodplain strips along rivers. The littoral is a zone of alluvium and low spurs protruding seaward, with an outer strip of shallow water sediments and marine-planed flats alternately washed by high tide waters and exposed as muddy flats at low water. Tide ranges reach nearly 40 feet at maximum in some of the inner embayments.

Southern Korea. A large portion of southern Korea is a block nearly 300 miles long, bounded on the north and east by major fault scarps and tilted southwestward during Tertiary time. Though a massif during much of geologic time, the block was broken by internal fault and fold zones, so that parts of the region reacted somewhat independently. The primary alignments are northeast-southwest, both structurally and orographically. Since there are different rock strata involved the whole massif is not uniformly dissected and landscaped. The Diamond Mountains are perhaps the most spectacularly sculptured. The backbone is close to the east coast, and reaches heights well above 6,000 feet. Off this main ridge line numerous spurs run southwestward, gradually decreasing in altitude until, as peninsulas, they dip into the sea with island peaks in line beyond them. On the northern west coast there are fewer of these protruding spurs and the littoral resembles that of northern Korea, but along the southwest and south this indented and cliffed coast is highly developed.

The drainage of the southern block is less simply arranged than that of the northern, and the pattern of stream dissection has added to the complexity of the physiography by cutting across the structure. Three primary streams have cut valley systems into the block, drain most of the territory, and have floodplains along their lower courses.

These streams drain to different corners, northwest, southwest, and southeast, leaving a central highland zone which effectively separates the lowland units of southern Korea.

The Eastern Coast. Below the high scarps of the backbone of southern Korea lies a very narrow, curved bench that is the east coast of Korea. It reaches from the northern end of the block to the south end of the Korean Peninsula, widening out somewhat in the last 100 miles. The coastal bench is a narrow section between major faults which are the northern ends of one of the lines of the Island Arcs. Therefore, this is a junction between continental and Pacific Margin structural elements. This rocky bench has short, steep streams spaced along it, each with a minuscule alluvial formation at the coast. There are few good passes along the central reach of the coast to connect this narrow land with the main bulk of the peninsula.

The Island Arcs

Three of the primary crustal segments of the earth meet in south and eastern Asia. Separating each of the three run the lines of Tertiary-Pleistocene orogeny in a variety of folding, faulting, overthrusting, uplift, volcanism, and earthquake spasms. These major lines are rather old geologically and have repeatedly been the scene of continued action. On the mainland this mountain building is expressed as the high, curving Alpine Chain. Beyond the mainland these same curving arcs are expressed as chains of islands. There are nearly a dozen separate arcs with varying lengths and rates of curvature (see Figs. 6.11 through 6.14, pp. 132–135). Some have but a single main axis and no branches, but others show multiple lines and a variety of branching spurs. Almost all the Asian arcs are convex toward the Pacific Basin. A few are pitched rather high above present sea level; others are set lower and expose only their mountain tops as small islands. Many contain much more mass than shows above the sea. Along several are the deepest of the world's marine trenches, and the physical separation of mountain peak and trough bottom is greater in a number of cases than that along the main Himalayan range.

Some of the island arcs are Tertiary in origin, but most of the large ones are much older, for some of the same pressures were applied in earlier geologic times. It is likely that some pattern of land has long been a part of the contact zone between the Pacific, Indian, and Asian crustal segments. Whether these were the whole continents sometimes inferred as the source of present continental sediments or whether some of them were but island chains is difficult to answer. Almost every present island chain shows a volume of simple or metamorphosed sedimentary rock. In addition some of the chains show considerable old intrusive granitic rocks. Some of these old cores have very complex structures. Late Tertiary and Pleistocene mountain building appeared to express itself in arcs set along two master lines, an Asian and a Pacific line. Both master lines are double lines. The first is an extension of the Alpine Chain of western Burma around through Sumatra, Java, and Timor. Then commences a series of sharp curves which carry the line north and west through Ceram, north again through Sulawesi (Celebes) and into the Philippines. Passing on to Taiwan the line then loops back through the Ryukyu chain into Japan. From northern Japan divergent arcs approach the mainland of northeastern Asia. The second master line is one out of the south Pacific into and through New Guinea. Its northern projection is more speculative as a continuous line. Swinging northward at the Moluccas it loops back through Palau, the Marianas, and the Bonins to join the other master line in central Japan. The near contact of the two lines in

the Indies is at the common junction of all three crustal segments, and is more complex than the line marking the meeting of any two of the segments.

Volcano building is the only form of vulcanism that has been active in the Pleistocene and Recent periods. In the Asian master arc only the inner line shows volcanos from Sumatra to the Philippines; elsewhere volcanos are more scattered. There are hundreds of old craters, but the active volcanos number in the vicinity of two hundred, over half of which are to be found in Indonesia.

Along the Asian master arc there are a number of individual arcs. The ends of some of them seem to intersect or cross, and at each point of crossing is found a rather massive island buttress. Taiwan, Kyushu, and Hokkaido are certainly such intersections, and several small arcs meet in Honshu. Luzon and Mindanao are less clear cases of such arc meeting. North of Mindanao the largest islands are the buttress points of the arcs.

In southeastern Asia the present arrangement of land and sea, and the number and configuration of individual islands, is a matter of Pleistocene geologic time. During the periodically lowered sea-stands of the Pleistocene, Sumatra, Java, Borneo, and Malaya were at times connected in one great land mass called Sunda Land. Present island streams are but the headwaters of much larger rivers. In reverse, the present single island of Mindanao was at one time (pre-Pleistocene) separated by shallow waters into about five islands. Throughout the whole of the Island Arcs this kind of fluctuation of land and sea has gone on ever since early Tertiary time.

An added complication is the Tertiary, Pleistocene, and Recent coral reef building. Like the whole south Pacific a great many of the islands south of Okinawa are fringed by active coral reefs. Some of the smaller islands are really thin layers of accumulated sediment resting on coral reef foundations. Coral reefs are found along many coastal sections of large islands, and here they are but a small part of the structural basement. Throughout the Indies there are many raised coral reefs, some now resting as high as 5,000 feet above sea level. Coral does not seem to be present along many of the volcanic coasts, owing to the steady outwash of sediments. Recent submergences of a small order characterize at least the Sunda Shelf region, and aggradation marks most coral reef islands. Along the main Island Arcs here discussed coral reefs are but a minor aspect of the physical history of the larger islands, are important parts of many of the smaller islands, but atoll clusters are less frequent than in the open Pacific Ocean.

THE SOUTHERN ISLAND ARCS

Most of the hundreds of islands that compose the groups known collectively as the East Indies are set along both master arc lines (see Figs. 6.11 and 6.12, pp. 132–133). In the Indies at least both master arcs are double lines, so that there are either two rows of islands or two structural axes. In the open parts of the arcs island contours are relatively simple, but in the sharply curved junction zones there have resulted some peculiarly shaped mountain ranges. In the Indies also, structure of a part of the continental shelf makes chain arrangement less obvious than in such groups as the Kuriles or the Ryukyus. Borneo and certain lesser islands were not actually a part of the most recent mountain building. Some of the islands are large and complex blocks; others are just the tops of volcanos built above present sea level. Among the hundreds of islands and islets there is a great and real variety of landscapes, varying from the smooth lowland marsh fringes to the high mountain scarps and boiling volcanic caldrons.

Sumatera (Sumatra). Third largest in size, 163,000 square miles, Sumatera is set on the western lobe of the inner arc with a northwest-southeast trend, almost bisected by the equator. Its west coast is steep and cliffed most of the way, with a very narrow lowland fringe, since the axis of the volcanic line lies close to the Indian Ocean coast. On the east side of the line folded and faulted spurs branch off toward the coast, tapering gradually until they run under the wide alluvial zone which, itself, ends in a broad strip of tidal marsh and mangrove swamp. The volcanos are perched atop the sedimentary core of the highland and reach heights of 11,000 and 12,000 feet.

Djawa (Java). Djawa is only the fifth largest of the islands of the Indies, with a total of about 48,000 square miles. It is set on the same inner arc line as Sumatera, with a similar structural pattern. The main highland axis is nearest the south coast, and there are offset spurs, branches, and minor fold axes running along the north side of the island. Its south coast along the Indian Ocean is a narrow fringe only, cliffed and rugged. The north side of the island is variable in relief, from hill patches to alluvial plains. An alluvial plain stretches along much of the Java Sea littoral, backed by a rolling to hilly zone. Through the central highland runs the volcanic zone, with craters at many different altitudes, the highest being above 11,000 feet. Few good harbors on the south coast, in contrast to a number on the north coast, help orient the island northward.

Sulawesi (Celebes). With an area of 73,000 square miles Sulawesi is a group of peninsulas representing the folded and volcanic tops of the two main axes of the Asian master arc at one of the points of tightest curvature. It is mostly hilly to mountainous upland, with heights above 5,000 feet along the spine of every peninsular unit of the island. Narrow lowland strips and little lowland embayments cut by short streams surround the island, along with narrow marine terraces.

New Guinea. The largest island of the Indies totals about 304,000 square miles and is the main land mass on the Pacific master arc line. It shows a double axis pattern, one mountain fold line running parallel with the north coast and close to it, the other forming the inland mountain core. The northern range of hills has but few spots above 5,000 feet, but the central range has several peaks above 16,000 feet and is one of the world's great mountain ranges, extending through the island for a distance of over 1,000 miles. South of the central range a broad, subsiding lowland slopes gradually off to the shallow sea north of Australia. Peninsular extensions project east and west at both ends of the island, along the main axis. Until World War II this was one of the least known parts of the world, and there still remain sections in which simple exploration still must be done.

Kalimantan (Borneo). Kalimantan is the second largest island of the Indies, with an area of approximately 287,000 square miles. Lying on the Asian crustal segment, Kalimantan is inside the Asian master arc. There seem to be at least two Tertiary structural lines that trend northeast-southwest and intersect the Asian master arc in the Philippines. Orographically, a central spinal column extends from the northwest corner of the island, where the granite mass of Mount Kinabalu stands over 13,000 feet in height, south through the center of the island. Spurs branch off both southeast and southwest, and there are many peaks scattered over the island above 7,000 feet in height. A radial drainage pattern has developed, with numerous streams. Some are short and steep, but others have cut deep lowland embayments with subdued hill lands and wide floodplains.

A coastal plain extends along most of the shore line, though several spurs branching off the highland run into the sea as hilly uplands. This is another of the world's unexplored remainders, for little is known about the highland core.

Minor Islands. There are hundreds of small islands and islets scattered along the arc lines and lying on the crustal shelf. Some of these islands are in clusters; others are single islands in a close-order chain. Many of the large islands have a scattering of small islets around their shores. Off Sumatra's west coast the Asian outer arc line parallels the inner and is marked by several clusters totaling about 60 islands. In eastern Indonesia one of the most important of the small island groups is the Moluccas, some 40 islands totaling about 30,000 square miles. This is a group on the Pacific arc line at its sharpest turn, where Halmahera repeats the peculiar pattern found in Celebes. On the Asian coastal shelf, between the Asian master arc and the mainland, are many small islands, worn down mountains, hills, and irregular remnants, now separated from each other by shallow water. A small shift of the crustal segment or of sea level would tremendously enlarge the land area here and tie the region together again. Repeated shifts of this sort must have happened since the Pleistocene period began.

PHILIPPINES

Over 7,000 separate pieces of land above sea level make up the Philippine Islands, with a total coastline of over 14,000 miles. Only 11 are more than 1,000 square miles in area, and only about 460 are larger than 1 square mile each. The largest is Luzon, almost 41,000 square miles in area; the only other large island is Mindanao, covering some 37,000 square miles. Thus, except for these two, the islands are just the crests of a series of mountain ranges or coral-capped flats. Except for the Sulu Sea most of the waters separating islands are shallow, and a relatively small downward shift of sea level would nearly triple the total land area.

The structural ranges forming the skeleton of the island system are numerous but fairly simple in their arrangement. The oldest lines are those proceeding northward from east Borneo, through the Sulu Archipelago into western Mindanao, Negros, and Cebu, and from west Borneo through Palawan into Luzon. Around the ends of these sweep the later lines of the Asiatic master arc in a multiple series of ridges. Most of the structural lines have variable kinks in them which denudation has deepened, so that now the ridge crests describe a quite variable series of paths. Most of the islands have a simple north-south alignment, being longer in this dimension than in the east-west. Mindanao is almost an exception, being a series of north-south units tied together above sea level by volcanism. Most of the islands also consist of but a single mountain range and its foothill spurs. Both Mindanao and Luzon differ in this respect. Beyond Luzon the arc tapers off toward Taiwan, with only a few small mountain tops to mark it.

Many of the mountain cores are composed of igneous rocks, both intrusive and extrusive. Around their foothill belts frequently occur Tertiary sediments capped by Recent stream deposited alluvium. These Tertiary beds often are warped by Recent uplift and cut into considerable relief by radial stream patterns. Many spurs of hills project clear to the coasts and end in cliffed fronts on narrow beach strips. Between them small streams have cut valleys which sometimes disregard structure. Around most islands there are bits, patches, and larger tracts of alluvial land in estuaries, delta fills, and sea-front alluvial plains. Many islands from Cebu southward contain patches or long reefs of coral limestone uplifted above sea level.

The highest altitudes in the islands are volcanic peaks, a number of which exceed 7,000 feet. There are at present more than a dozen active volcanos, but there are several dozen dead craters with truncated tops, indicating that explosive volcanism has been active since the close of the Tertiary period. There are few sheet flows of lava, most igneous materials being basaltic ash, pumice, tuff, and similar debris. These cones are mostly set along critical fault or fracture zones, some above highlands and others on the flat lowlands. There are numerous active fault lines running longitudinally through the islands. Associated with these active lines is the long Mindanao Trench, which has a recorded depth of over 35,000 feet just east of the northern point of Mindanao Island.

Mindanao. This southern island is a series of peninsulas topped by mountain ranges, joined together by plateaus and lowland strips. There are four north-south range systems spaced across the island, with one east-west volcanic cross line. Extinct volcanos are scattered along the range systems, and ash, tuff, and some sheet basalt have built up the Lanao and Bukidnon sectors as rolling plateaus, capped by high volcanic peaks. Every range has several peaks of more than 5,000 feet, and a few of more than 8,000 feet. The slightly truncated crater of Mount Apo, 9,610 feet in height, in the southeastern part of the island, is the highest point in the Philippines. Bays and gulfs reach into the lowlands between the peninsular range systems. There are three extensive alluvial lowlands, the Agusan, Davao, and Cotabato valleys. The first two are set between the two eastern range systems, opening northward and southward, whereas the Cotabato Valley opens westward in the southern part of the island. Both the Agusan and Cotabato valleys are only slightly above sea level and contain extensive marshlands. Elsewhere there are but narrow and discontinuous fringing lowlands along the coast.

Luzon.   Toward the northern end of the Philippines Luzon consists of an elongated and joined set of peninsulas set *en echelon* and on a somewhat variable alignment. Numerous bays and gulfs occupy the sections between the ranges, and a very slight subsidence would turn Luzon into a number of islands. Several of the southern peninsulas are only rough to hilly areas with tall volcanos perched upon them, so that there is a significant amount of sedimentary and alluvial lowland of but slight relief. The central section is a lowland floored by volcanic tuff and shallow alluvial fill, all very close to sea level except for scattered volcanic cones. Manila Bay and the large lake, Laguna de Bay, are the remains of the shallow Tertiary sea which covered most of central Luzon. North of Manila Bay a broad lowland stretches northward, ending in another embayment, Lingayen Gulf. This lowland drains both to north and to south, and is the most important plain in the Philippines, placed between mountainous east and west coasts. In northern Luzon the highlands are more massive. Particularly in the northwest relief is strong, general levels are above 5,000 feet with peaks above 8,000 feet, and topography is rough and deeply dissected. A lower, narrower range of mountains parallels the east coast rather closely. Between the two highlands lies the long Cagayan Valley, with its river meandering northward over a wide floodplain.

TAIWAN AND THE RYUKYU CHAIN

Taiwan is the buttress upon which the Philippine arc is suspended in the north. Similarly it is the southern anchor island for the Ryukyu chain which stretches northward some 900 miles to Japan. Taiwan itself may well not be an integral part of either island arc, whose lines hinge on the east coast, as

though they ended against the steep eastern scarp of the island. It is a rugged and high-backed island, longer north-south than east-west, with its axial line closer to the east coast than the west. Its maximum altitudes are over 14,000 feet, and Pleistocene glaciation has marked the crests. It presents a steep, faulted eastern face above a cliffed and narrow coast. The west coast is a wide foothill zone of subdued relief. Small stream basins and a series of gravel-covered terraces are set behind foothill strips reaching to the west coast. Floodplains broaden out along the lower courses of these streams, and the western littoral itself is a wide and flat coastal belt of alternating tidal marsh, low rocky projections, and moving sand deposits.

The Ryukyu chain consists of some 55 islets, totaling just under 1,000 square miles. There are several clusters of islands; the Japanese recognize three groups. Only the northern islands show Recent evidence of volcanism. The others are rocky masses of Paleozoic to Tertiary sediments, metamorphosed rocks, and intrusives. Most of the islands have rather a strong relief, with rocky shores and only minute bits of arable land. A few are relatively flat, low islands of simple relief pattern.

The Ryukyu arc line appears to project beyond its northern buttress in Kyushu along the east coast of southern Korea. The two small islands of Tsushima, lying between southern Japan and the Korean coast, appear suggestively related to this arc line.*

THE JAPANESE ARCS

From a quick glance at a large map the

---

*Most customary in the interpretation of the structure pattern is the suggestion that southern Korea is part of a shorter, tighter arc connecting Korea and southwestern Honshu, sharply convex toward the Pacific. The present interpretation sees no conflict in the existence of such a minor arc. It would be strange if the intersections of some of the arcs did not involve some of the same offset shear forms that accompany the intersections of the northeast-southwest massifs and east-west tectonic zones in China.

Japanese islands seem just another wide-swinging arc on the Asian master line. From southwest Kyushu to northern Hokkaido it is some 1,100 miles along the curve. It would be better, however, to think of the Japanese islands as an arc system, recognizing that it is composed of elements of several shorter arcs and minor curved forms (see Figs. 6.13 and 6.14, pp. 134–135). There is a double structural line through Japan, customarily known as the Inner and Outer zones. The Gifu Node and the Fossa Magna of central southern Honshu are, respectively, the complex junction of minor arcs of the Japanese system and the junction of the Pacific master line with the Asian master line. This double zone of structural and orographic confusion separates the Inner and Outer zones into northern and southern sectors. Four primary morphologic zones are recognized in Japan, namely, the Southwest Inner Zone, the Southwest Outer Zone, the Northwest Inner Zone, and the Northwest Outer Zone. Kyushu, the southern buttress-node, lies in both Inner and Outer zones, as does Hokkaido, the northern buttress of the Japanese arc system.

The amount of mountain building involved in this arc system is tremendous, for the depth of near-by Tuscarora Deep almost equals the Mindanao Trench off the Philippine arc, and the tops of the Japanese Alps exceed 10,000 feet. This activity must have been initiated prior to the Tertiary, but a great deal of uplift took place during the late Tertiary and the early Pleistocene. At many relatively high points in the islands are the fairly clear marks of old denudational surfaces, indicating earlier subdued relief, glaciation, and possibly planation. The Japanese islands have undoubtedly suffered the greatest amount of faulting of any of the Island Arcs, and that this intense fracturing process is not yet completed is seen in the 1,500 earthquakes per year that affect Japan today and in the many raised and drowned shore lines. Accompanying the block faulting has been the process of volcanism, by which some 500 volcanic cones have been built in the islands. Though cones and craters are found widely distributed over Japan, concentrations occur in several sectors. The northern and southern buttress islands, Kyushu and Hokkaido, have many cones along the line of contact with the Ryukyu and Kurile arcs. Similarly the junction of the Pacific arc, along the Fossa Magna, is marked by a series of cones, including Mount Fuji, the highest point in Japan (12,461 feet) and the most revered Japanese mountain. Not including the volcanos in the Ryukyus, Kuriles, and Bonins, over 40 craters in Japan have been active within historic time.

In the composition of its rocks there is represented in Japan material from every geologic era and almost every lithic variety, with igneous intrusive and extrusive rocks making up something over a third of the total surface. So completely cut into separate and differently placed blocks is the land mass that there is little regional continuity of rock type. Many local and acute changes in type and hardness of country rock are normal.

The combination of rather complex structure, a voluminous block faulting, a rapid and strong mountain building, and an extremely varied lithic composition have promoted an intensely complicated pattern of denudational processes that, since the Pleistocene, have produced an intricate physical landscape. This island landscape is dominated by high altitudes, central highland blocks, strong relief, steep slopes, fault scarp cliffs, volcanic peaks, and strongly dissected uplands. Almost completely excluded are large unit areas of low relief, extensive coastal plains, valley floodplains, sizeable deltas, and the like. The stream network is a highly developed one, notwithstanding the fact that the two longest rivers are only some 225 miles long, and each drains basins of about 5,000 square miles only. On many heights the preservation of subdued and truncated ancient surfaces and the rounded knob forms of granites contrast strongly with the highly dissected uplands. In the latter angular forms, both of faulting and of normal but rapid denudation, predominate, so that the landscape is usually made up of steep slopes and sharp lines. Even the alluvial lowlands have suffered recent uplift and are dissected. Most such lowlands are divided between an older, upper remnant surface and a lower, flatter zone separated by angular bluffs and steep slopes.

The detail of this landscape makes generalized description difficult. The 146,000 square miles of Japan proper, a little less than the State of California, have been divided into 196 physiographic districts with the accompanying remark that the list was "... merely a broad outline, incomplete in many respects, which will serve as a guide for more detailed study in the geomorphology and general geography of the Island Empire."[*] The Kanto Plain, Japan's largest alluvial lowland, contains only about 5,000 square miles and, itself, contains several subdivisions of different characteristics and utility. In all Japan there are nearly 3,000 separate islands, though perhaps only about 450 of them are more than isolated rocks. The coastline is even longer and more intricate than that of the Philippines. The central and northwest coast is relatively smooth and in agreement with basic structure. Elsewhere the coast is extremely irregular. Southern Japan generally, and southwest Japan in particular, have undergone a tremendously varied physical history that is rather plainly exhibited along its varied and island-studded coast.

The Morphologic Regions. Since there are differences in the Japanese area that do

[*] R. B. Hall and A. Watanabe, "Landforms of Japan," *Papers of the Mich. Acad. of Sci., Arts and Letters*, vol. 18, 1932, p. 207.

not accord with the occurrence of land areas in islands, brief comment is needed upon the morphologic units of the Japanese arc system.

THE OUTER SOUTHWEST ZONE (The Shikoku Arc). One of the cleanest lines in Japan is the long fault scarp zone, placed concave to the Pacific in contrast to most arc lines, that overlooks the Inland Sea and cuts through the islands of Kyushu, Shikoku, and southeast Honshu. This whole sector is fairly uniform in its structural and geologic patterns. Except at the Ryukyu arc intersection there are no volcanos, and there is but little early intrusive granite exposed at the surface. In Shikoku Island there are two parallel fault scarp zones, with a line of fault valleys between. Local downwarping of portions of the zone has submerged three sections, giving two broad gaps into the Inland Sea and one deep embayment into the Honshu coast. Altitudes gradually decrease toward the southwest. There are numerous marine terraces expressive of recent local uplift. Also indicating recent uplift, most of the rivers are entrenched in meander patterns in their valleys and show very little floodplain area at present. Flat-topped remnants of earlier subdued landscape forms are few in this part of Japan. Normal erosion has been strongly operative and has produced a landscape that is nearly mature, strongly dissected, and consists of steep slopes and rather high local relief.

THE INNER SOUTHWEST ZONE (Tsushima Arc). Southwest Honshu and northern Kyushu is the region of Japan in which block faulting has been most highly developed. There are many kinds of block units, but uplifted horst blocks and down-dropped graben blocks are most common. Fault scarps extend in several directions, but there is a maximum trend that would suggest a probable arc line convex to the Pacific, opposing the Shikoku Arc, and related to or offset from the larger Ryukyu Arc. This is a zone in which intrusive granites are very common and, to the Japanese geomorphologists, granite and block faulting go together. There is a general decrease in heights westward from the Fossa Magna into Kyushu, where the volcanic peaks stand well above the older landscape. Many crest areas preserve remnants of an older subdued landscape surface, and granites produce rounded and knobby outcrops. The many fault valleys and down-dropped blocks have been partly filled to produce basins, lowlands, or surfaces of low relief. The Inland Sea is an irregular submerged section between the two opposing arcs. The Kyushu end of this zone was lowered less than the northern end and, by virtue of its volcanic cover, closes off the Inland Sea. The submerged shore line is the most common shore form in this sector. There are few plains areas of any extent, but numerous small patches are found at varying elevations. Mostly a rugged and hilly landscape, the region has been strongly dissected and consists mostly of steep slopes.

THE OUTER NORTHEAST ZONE (Eastern Honshu Arc). The Tsushima Arc ends just south of Fossa Magna in a confused highland mass known as the Gifu Node. The Fossa Magna itself is a downfaulted trough partly filled with volcanic material which marks the junction of the Pacific and Asian master arcs. It forms a barricade across the island of Honshu for, to the north, is another bunched highland mass almost as high and as formidable as the Gifu Node to the south. Farther to the north this highland separates out into linear mountain ranges with intervening valleys. These are set on a single broad arc pattern known as the Honshu Arc. The distinctions between outer and inner sectors are less clear than south of the Fossa Magna.

The Outer Zone of the Northeast includes the easternmost mountain ranges of Honshu and the central north-south ranges of Hok-

kaido. There are four mountain units involved. These have cores of old metamorphosed sediments and intrusive granites, are uplifted as separate block units, with both folded and faulted marginal basin elements. The highland crests show remnants of old erosional surfaces, somewhat deformed and warped during uplift. In general this is a region of rugged terrain, of hard rocks and steep slopes. Within the mountain block units themselves there is but little flat land, though lowland sediments have been built across the marginal roots of the ranges from the structural valleys west of the ranges. In Hokkaido east of the central range line, the junction of the Kurile Arc has built a line of volcanic cones with marginal alluvial-ash slopes which replaces the erosional landscape found elsewhere. Whether this is one complex arc or whether it is the orographic grouping of several arc units is still a matter of conjecture.

THE INNER NORTHEAST ZONE (Northwestern Honshu Arc). This sector is made up of two roughly parallel range systems and the three related basin strips. The central mountain system of northern Honshu, the eastern of the two ranges here considered, is the drainage divide for the island. It is a high massive folded range system, with intrusive granite roots, a Tertiary sedimentary cover capped by a number of volcanic craters and some lava flows, particularly in its southern half. The western range system is less formidable and continuous, having been breached and cut away in a number of places by streams. It is also structurally a folded range system. The Inner Zone of the Northeast has a minimum of faulting in rather parallel linear patterns which do not break up the country into the many separate blocks found farther south.

The two inland basin strips are structural basins set on linear pattern. The eastern strip has been filled so that its parts slope directly toward the sea, around or past the mountains of the east coast. The central series of basins now drains out to the westward, each through a stream that cuts across the western range system. There are nine such basins, set off from each other by transverse ridges connecting the two mountain systems. The western lowland fringe along the Sea of Japan is a narrow one, with embayments along the streams that cut across the western range system. The whole zone is an area of strong relief contrasts, of steep slopes, of angular patterns, of little flat land, but of beautiful scenery.

The Primary Units. In addition to the above, brief comments on individual islands and the Inland Sea are needed to form a picture of the island empire of Japan.

KYUSHU. This southern island of less than 14,000 square miles forms the buttress of the Ryukyu Arc and the Japanese arc system. It is made up of three kinds of landscapes, rather jumbled together. The southern half of the island belongs to the massive faulted Shikoku Arc; the northern half is related to the block-faulted landscape of the Tsushima Arc. Widely distributed over the island are the volcanic surfaces, volcanos, craters, and hot springs that mark the junction of the separate arcs. The more massive uplands are blocks of old hard rock, strongly dissected and steep sloped. A number of short streams penetrate the central highlands rather deeply, and little patches of lowland are scattered around the coast. Northwest Kyushu is a varied assortment of small block peninsulas, downfaulted lowlands and gulfs, volcanic uplands, and a very irregular shore line.

SHIKOKU. The smallest of the main group of islands, Shikoku totals slightly less than 7,000 square miles in area. Its main mass forms the highest section of the upfaulted Shikoku Arc. Overlooking the Inland Sea is a long highland ending in a fault scarp zone. Below this is an irregular sector that is part of the Inland Sea structurally but that remained above present sea level as part of the island. At the western end the primary fault scarp stands high above the Inland Sea directly. Behind this major fault zone minor faults have been opened into linear fault valleys. The southern peninsulas are lined with a succession of marine terraces ending in wave-cut cliffs at the present sea margin. The main block of the island tilts southward, so that the two peninsulas taper off into the sea. The whole island is a rugged upland region with very little flat lands or true lowlands.

HONSHU. This is the chief island of Japan, measuring about 88,000 square miles. Within its relatively small area it combines a tremendous variety of landscapes. Elongated north-south, it is some 825 by 160 miles in major dimensions. Its northern and southern extremities are quite dissimilar, though many of these differences are related to climate and vegetation, rather than to inherent differences in the landforms themselves. Southwestern Honshu is a region of small fault blocks, a submerged coast on the Inland Sea side, and a fringe of minor islands, small bays, and inlets. It is markedly oriented to the Inland Sea. Small patches of lowland are scattered here and there, at the heads of bays and in fault valleys. Northward toward the Fossa Magna altitudes increase, the island thickens in width and becomes more massive in its proportions. The Fossa Magna itself makes a strong mark across the island, with its faulted lowland and tall volcanic peaks. Just north and east of this transverse barricade lies the Kanto Plain, the largest alluvial lowland in Japan. Northward the island is a series of linear mountain ranges and intervening river basins, having no common orientation except outward from the central highland line toward the sea. This rugged northern landscape the Japanese have found difficult to utilize in their preferred manner.

HOKKAIDO. The odd-shaped island of Hokkaido measures about 260 miles from north to south and a little more on the east-west axis, to total about 30,000 square miles. Its shape derives from the fact that it is the buttress junction of three arcs. Its southwestern fish-tailed peninsula is related to the structural pattern of the inner side of the Honshu Arc. The main backbone of the island is a north-south linear range system connected with the Sakhalin Arc, producing the northern and southern peninsulas. The eastern peninsula is formed by a line of volcanic peaks at the end of the Kurile Arc. Thus, each arc is related to a highland sector. The three do not meet at a common center, however, and the marginal sections are occupied by structural lowlands and alluvial-ash piedmonts. The higher parts of these sloping margins are rather strongly dissected today, whereas the bottoms are low-lying marshy tracts. Around the island are many gravel-surfaced marine terraces, set at a number of different levels. Only a small proportion of Hokkaido is amenable to agricultural use, comprising a landscape of a kind the Japanese do not thoroughly appreciate. That one of the largest alluvial lowlands in all Japan is located in Hokkaido is an unfortunate circumstance. This is the Ishikari Plain, of southwest Hokkaido, totaling about 850 square miles.

THE INLAND SEA. Nearly 250 miles long and varying in width from about 5 to 50 miles, the Inland Sea of Japan occupies the lower portions of a number of down-faulted blocks, which lie along the margins of the Tsushima Arc. The upper parts of the several blocks are represented by the hundreds of islets and small peninsulas of the three large islands that surround the sea. Rather than a negative unit of the island empire, and merely the space between the large islands, the Inland Sea is a very vital region and is one of the more significant parts of Japan. Though its distinctive character is partly derived from its climate, the Inland Sea shores and islands might be termed the "typical Japanese landscape." There are five sections of relatively open water, representing the blocks now most deeply submerged. Depths everywhere are quite shallow, and a lowering of sea level by more than 150 feet would again expose almost the whole of the severely dissected zone now covered by water. The many islets are arranged in roughly parallel structural lines. Many of them are but steep rocky peaks; others are of larger size and are of irregular shape and surface. Some have miniature deltas and alluvial fills situated at protected spots, with exposed headlands surrounded by marine benches and cliffs. Strong tidal currents move through the Inland Sea, sweeping out channels and locally forming a serious navigational hazard.

THE SAKHALIN ARC

Offset eastward 100 miles from the Honshu Arc of northern Japan lies the Sakhalin Arc, extending from the south coast of Hokkaido through the northern end of Sakhalin Island. Some 900 miles long, this arc swings close to the Asian mainland before terminating in the Sea of Okhotsk. It describes a shallower curve than do most of the other arcs along the Asian master line. Two large islands make up the arc, the southern buttress island of Hokkaido and Sakhalin itself.

Sakhalin. The island is some 600 miles long by perhaps 50 miles wide throughout most of its extent. It consists of two folded and faulted mountain systems with an intervening structural lowland. The eastern member is composed of Paleozoic sedimentary and metamorphic rocks, rugged in outline but of locally subdued relief. It is at its highest in central Sakhalin, where altitudes exceed 6,000 feet. A disconnected segment of this member forms a small peninsula at the southeastern corner of the island. The western member is a late Tertiary structural unit running the whole length of the island, broadening out toward the northern end and decreasing in altitude. Maximum altitudes are less high in the western ranges than in the eastern system, but relief is locally stronger and the degree of dissection in many places is greater, since the country rock is younger and somewhat softer. The structural depression extends from the upper east coast southward between the two range systems to Terpenija Bay. It now is covered with an alluvial fill from both highland areas. The structural depression is continued at the southern end of the island, a lowland lying across the small peninsular section of the eastern range system. Elsewhere flat lowlands are but thin strips of alluvial material piled up along the coast.

THE KURILE ARC

The last northern island arc on the Asian system stretches for some 750 miles between mainland Kamchatka and the buttress island of Hokkaido. The Kamchatka Peninsula itself appears to be set on this same Asian arc line but as an arc set concave to the Pacific, its northern end being in alignment with the structural trend of northeastern Siberia. Kamchatka at its broadest appears to be the junction zone of the two arcs which, being reversed in curvature, give the peninsula a wide spread in its central region.

The 32 islands in the Kurile group total somewhat over 6,000 square miles. The largest island is Etorofu, toward the southern end of the chain, with an area of about 1,000 square miles. Primarily the rugged and steep-sloped tops of mountains, the chain contains a number of active volcanos, the tallest of which exceeds 7,000 feet. No significant areas of flat land or of lowland occur on any of the islands, steep shore lines often dropping directly into the sea. On some of the larger southern islands there are minute patches of alluvial fill at stream mouths, and a few wave-cut benches. The Kuriles are the least populated and least significant of the island arcs, but their position gives them a value in the military strategy of the northern Pacific Ocean.

7

CLIMATOLOGY AND SENSIBLE CLIMATE

The "monsoon" of Monsoon Asia was perhaps the first intricate aspect of regional climatology to bother man mentally, well over 2,000 years ago. Between the mouth of the Red Sea and the Solomon Islands the northern and southern hemispheres are not even faintly symmetrical in the distribution of land and sea, and atmospheric phenomena do not behave as elsewhere around the globe. There still is a serious shortage of data, and its summarization is very uneven. The region has often been studied piecemeal rather than as a whole. And in this large climatic realm there are very real differences between the climates of the Malabar Coast of India, the north coast of Java, the Szechwan Basin of China, and the island of Hokkaido in north Japan. That there is a common rainy period and seasonal agreement in air movements does not make these diverse climates amenable to inclusion in one simple classification. The following pages discuss the topic from the subjective viewpoint of sensible climate rather than from that of impersonal objectivity.

TEMPERATURE PATTERNS

Maps of actual temperatures for the respective seasons indicate several important features. It is notable that much of the total lowland area has no really cold weather, though every country has some cool territory. The southern lands all possess highlands, mountain ranges, or peaks that project above the hot lowlands. In the southern zone temperature variations are vertical rather than horizontal. On the other hand, in spite of the fact that the northernmost lands are really part and parcel of the Orient by cultural inclusion, they really have long and severe winters with short growing seasons (Fig. 7.1). And in the northern zone horizontal temperature gradients are marked, both regionally and seasonally. Japan's temperature map reveals that only a small portion of the island empire has the subtropical weather that supports the bamboo groves and paper houses of the popular picture of Japan. The thermal contrast between the southward-facing portion of Japan and the northern regions is sharp and strong, with consequent variation in the length of the growing season.

Although the eastern Yangtze Valley country has real winter weather, Szechwan then is a subtropical enclave comparable to southern Asia. In summer the whole of the Yangtze Basin is extremely hot and sticky, with but few breaks in the monotonous heat. Yunnan and Kueichou form a transitional zone

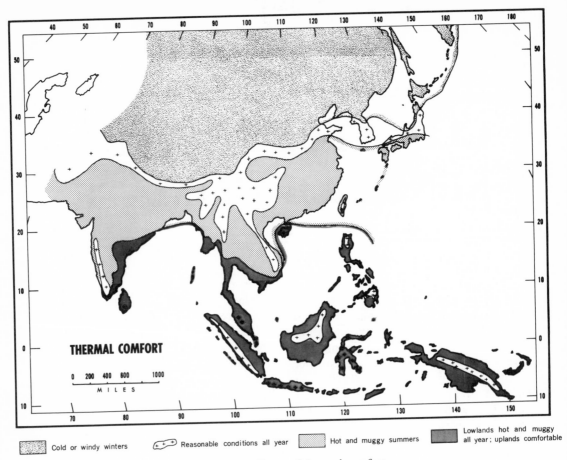

THERMAL COMFORT

0   200   400   800   1000
MILES

Cold or windy winters | Reasonable conditions all year | Hot and muggy summers | Lowlands hot and muggy all year; uplands comfortable

FIGURE 7.1. Zones of thermal comfort.

rather comparable to tropical highlands in their mild but even-tempered conditions. China's thermal contrast in summer, from north to south, is relatively slight, but in east China it is notably strong in winter, central and south China having the coolest winters for their latitudes of any part of the world. This is related to the strong outblowing winter monsoon winds. The difference in the length of the growing seasons from Hainan Island to northern Manchuria is great.

India and mainland Southeast Asia are notable for a peculiar seasonal division of the year into three periods rather than two or four as is customary in so much of the world. This is produced by the cooling effect of the onset of the summer monsoon period, and by the peculiarities of monsoonal air movement. It is significant that northwestern India has a hot zone quite separate from the central Asian high-temperature center. This seems to serve as a local attraction to the Indian sector of the summer monsoon air drift. Across northern India and Burma there is an all-year sharp temperature gradient, lying roughly along the Himalayan mountain wall.

Generalized maps cannot possibly show the vertical thermal gradations of the island arc zone, in which many mountain-crest

CLIMATOLOGY AND SENSIBLE CLIMATE

localities have relatively cool weather the year around. Southern India and southern Burmo-Malaya share with Indonesia and the Philippines this characteristic to a considerable degree. The great river trenches of northern Burmo-Malaya show some extreme contrasts from range divides to canyon bottoms.

THE MONSOON AS A CLIMATIC AGENT

The old Arabic word *mausin* applied to a season of the year, and hence to the wind that prevailed during the period. Modern English usage has also applied it to the precipitation regime. The prevailing pattern of air movement at the earth's surface for south and eastern Asia is most simply described as "double," with reversal of directions between winter and summer periods: Outward drifts of air from the Asian heartland during the winter, and inward drifts from the oceans during the summer. Formerly it was thought that the cooling and heating of the great central land mass of Asia was the causal mechanism for both the seasonal shift and the directional components. Although an element of this simplistic concept remains operative, since Asia is the only zone having a true monsoon, the surface seasonal flow of air now is recognized as being controlled by several complex mechanisms broadly related to the world-wide adjustment of the seasonal heat budget between the northern and southern hemispheres. The Asian monsoon, as a double seasonal pattern of air movement, is variably affected by the movement of, and perturbations within, the Intertropical Trough, the primary actions and shifts of the Jet Stream, periodic surges within the Trade Wind systems, the variable impact of earth-surface orographic systems, and the variable regional and seasonal development of thermal convection systems.

There still are quite variable patterns of thought regarding the interworkings of these several mechanisms on a world-wide basis, and particular interpretations condition the explanation of the precise functioning of the Asian Monsoon. However, it is clear that there is not just one Asian Monsoon, but that there are three large regional components to be considered as variably affecting south and eastern Asia. These are the Indian Monsoon, the Malayan Monsoon, and the Japanese Monsoon. In most years the Indian Monsoon controls air movements over Pakistan, India, Ceylon, and the west coast of Burma; the Malayan Monsoon is operative over Indonesia, the Philippines, most of mainland Southeast Asia, and most of China; the Japanese Monsoon affects Korea, parts of northern China, most of Manchuria, and Japan. Although each of these regional components obeys the same broad controls, the precise causal mechanisms do not always operate equally or at the same time for all three, and no one physical explanation accounts for weather phenomena in any one year for all three. It is beyond the scope of this chapter to deal substantively with the Asian Monsoon, but certain broad generalizations may be made, and some regional variations can be stated as applicable. In the precise development of weather phenomena in any one year variations in the strength of any regional component may be quite marked, yielding quite irregular results on the surface of the regional sector of this portion of Asia.

During the northern winter generally southward and eastward air movements occur, with local directional divergences according to location and with variable length of the season (Fig. 7.2). In the north these winds fortify the prevailing westerlies; in the south they complement the northeast trades. In Indonesia, the monsoonal effect is obscured by the patterns of the northeast trades and by local land and sea breezes. The

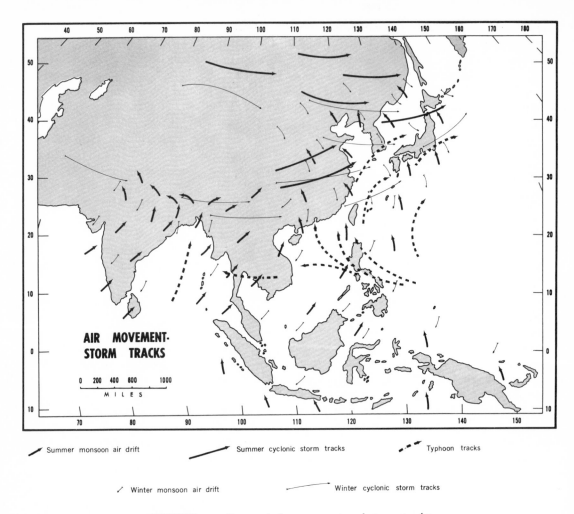

FIGURE 7.2. Seasonal air movement and storm tracks.

winter monsoon starts as a dry wind, but in various sectors it absorbs considerable water vapor as it crosses coastal seas to become a rain provider to several coastal and island regions. In the north velocities are much greater than in the south where the movement is but a gentle drift. In the north, also, the winter monsoon is a cold wind; in the south its coolness is but relative. Lastly, the northern winter monsoon often begins with a sudden cold windstorm, an unheard-of happening in the south. In the northern Philippines, across the northern portion of mainland Southeast Asia, and across northern India

the matter of winter cold is purely relative and, though temperatures may not seem very low, an unusually strong burst of the cold air drift may carry chilling weather into such areas, often referred to in the local press as a "cold wave."

During the northern summer, on the other hand, the prevailing air drift is from some southerly direction, its precise compass reading and period of duration again depending upon location, varying from southwest in southern India to almost east in northern Japan. In this season the southern regions experience stronger winds than the northern, which may have but fitful and gentle breezes. The summer monsoon "bursts" upon India, but comes gradually to China, and in Japan it may seem but a summer variant of normal cyclonic weather. The summer air drift is relatively a warm wind and, until it reaches inland localities, is a moist wind, but local orographic conditions may, periodically, turn the summer monsoon into a drying wind. Sumatra and West Malaysia do not show a well-developed summer monsoon drift, and in central and eastern Indonesia local variations in air movements are marked. The Philippines are affected by the major air mass movements drifting toward China and northern Asia.

Both seasonal movements are comparatively shallow, surface layers of air, not often extending above 10,000 feet. Two exceptions to this are the Indian sector of the summer southwest monsoon and Japanese sector of the winter northwest monsoon, both of which appear to be somewhat thicker. Particularly the northern end of the summer monsoon drift and the southern end of the winter monsoon drift appear to be shallow layers. Neither monsoon drift is a steady current, but each possesses somewhat variable pulsation tendencies. In the south the field of motion is across the equator; in the east it appears to lie between the northern continental and central Pacific Ocean pressure structures. The dates of cessation and reversal in direction of the two air drifts are not equally timed in all sectors; they vary considerably from region to region.

Both air drifts possess irregularities of a large order in timing, in distribution, and in volume of moisture carried. The seasonal air drifts themselves possess no inherent mechanisms for precipitation production or other weather manifestations, but the changes that take place in the inward or outward sweeping air masses determine the weather and precipitation of the Orient. As suggested below there are a number of different storm mechanisms and control factors that operate

variably throughout the Orient to produce its variable weather.

The Tibetan highland, with its southeastern projection, appears to separate the mainland Orient into two primary sectors, there being some intermixture along the coastal fringe and in the Island Arcs. The southern sector primarily exhibits tropical weather and climate, with only a minimum of extratropical phenomena during the winters or at high altitudes. The northern sector exhibits rather emphatic extratropical phenomena during much of the year, though some of the basins and blocks of the Chinese checkerboard show rather anomalous winter conditions and southernmost China is almost tropical the year around. The Island Arcs from the Philippines southward belong to the southern sector.

If both monsoon air drifts are considered as regional displacement of air masses, the Japan sector receives large amounts of Polar Siberian (Ps) air during the period of the winter monsoon to carry cold winter weather across all of Korea and Japan and as far south as the Fukien hill country in eastern China. Protected by the Tsinling Shan and the Tibetan Plateau, western China and the whole of the southern sector are not normally and directly affected by cold Polar air masses. Some cool Polar air does penetrate Thailand, Indochina, and the Philippines occasionally. The southern sector during the winter receives returning Tropical air masses (Tropical Indian and Pacific, Ti and Tp) which have become cooler, drier, and, in the eastern sector certainly, mixed with some Polar air in the seasonal interchange. In summer the first northward advance of the monsoon involves warm and moist Tropical air from the Indian Ocean and the South Pacific (Ti and Tp), and it is likely that this is followed by Equatorial Marine (Em) air masses during the main period of the summer monsoon. Southwest China appears, along with all of northern Burmo-Malaya, to receive considerable Tropical Indian air, and it is likely that south China's summer weather is produced by a seasonally variable mixture of Tropical Indian, South Pacific, and Equatorial Marine air. For the Indies the situation is complicated by a position across the equator, by highly complex local conditions of land and sea, and by southern-hemisphere air movement over Australia. Since the whole region is out of reach of purely Polar air masses from either side, only mixtures of Equatorial, Tropical, and Polar air are involved. The multiplicity of islands of varying sizes and shapes interjects the land and sea breeze into weather and climate in a very positive way. There appear to be many situations in which the land or sea breeze may cancel the normally prevailing monsoon air drift, to make local air movement the dominant factor in local weather and climate, even though the two-way monsoon drift does provide a major, seasonal exchange of air masses from one side of the equator to the other.

The action of the monsoons in response to primary pressure gradients, therefore, seems to be that of very generally circulating the surface atmosphere on a broad scale, thereby seasonally providing alternating winds and volumes of moisture over the whole of the Orient which storm mechanisms fashion into a variety of local weather patterns. For centuries traders from Arabia to Japan have sailed by the monsoon's alternating drifts, and farmers have prayed for its regularity of arrival and dependability of precipitation.

MECHANICS OF WEATHER CHANGE

Most simply stated there are five different mechanisms that produce weather changes and precipitation throughout the Orient. The extratropical cyclonic storm is the most widespread of the five, the others being the convectional thundershower, the typhoon, what may be termed the "orographic squeeze," and the perturbations that result

from convergence phenomena within the Intertropical Trough. Each has its area of maximum significance, though in many localities all either may combine or remain completely inactive.

The extratropical storm moving eastward frequents a series of paths from northern India in the winter to the all-year Siberian route (see Fig. 7.2). In these zones it is a significant factor in fluctuating weather, naturally being more effective in the more northerly sectors. East China and the Yellow Sea receive about 85 storms per year, spring being the most active period. Storm diameters are smaller than those of United States storms, and the action usually is somewhat less vigorous.

The southernmost of the cyclonic paths extends across the North Indian Plain and into southwest China, south of Tibet, during the winter, regeneration sometimes taking place by the time the storm reaches China. Storms crossing north India often are not casually noticeable in daily weather, owing to the absence of the strong intervening cold wave of Polar air, but in mountainous northern Burma heavy falls of snow may result, the source of summer flood runoff in the Irrawaddy, Salween, and Mekong rivers.

Other winter cyclonic storms reach the Far East after crossing Siberia, swinging south into northern China or Manchuria and out across Japan and Korea. They produce little more than windstorms over China, but over Korea and particularly Japan they cause rain and snow. Intervening anticyclones bring cold waves and accompanying dust storms to northern China but not often do they fully succeed in crossing the Tsinling system to harshly freeze central and south China.

During the winter and spring periods cyclonic storms seem to appear over central China that, then, pursue a normal track northeastward over Japan. Normally such storms do not affect the Szechwan Basin or Kueichou, but do bring weather changes to central China. These may be derived from lee-position eddies (east of the Tibetan Plateau) produced by pulsations in the Jet Stream as it shifts position from south of the Tibetan Plateau to north of the highland mass, but the surface effects of this shift, and its timing, are not yet well known.

The summer convectional thundershower is rather common almost everywhere in the Orient. It often precedes the dramatic summer rainy season in India and Burmo-Malaya, in Indonesia appearing the year around, and in China being associated with the monotonous and sticky heat of the summer. Japan has amazingly few thundershowers, whereas Taiwan, the Gulf of Tonking, and Bengal are centers of this type of storm. Data are inadequate, but it would appear that those Indonesian islands nearest the equator receive the largest number of thundershowers, with Java recording well over 300 per year. As a source of precipitation the thundershower is almost as important as the cyclonic storm. In many sections thundershowers both precede and follow the main monsoon rainy season. Although the meteorological records often do not enumerate separate thundershowers during the main rainy seasons, they certainly occur. Personal experience suggests that Chungking averages more than 16 thundershowers per year, and the contrast between official records for Chungking and western Java must lie partly in unequal criteria for tabulation. Not all thundershowers are convectional in origin, for convergence of major or local regional air masses and the passage of cyclonic fronts sometimes provoke them.

The typhoon, known in American literature as the hurricane, and in India as the cyclone, has two zones of occurrence, the Indian Ocean and the western Pacific Ocean from the southern Philippines northward to Japan. In both regions the storms are destructive to shipping, to agriculture, and to shore installations. Some of the Bay of Bengal storms do not reach full hurricane intensity but climatically serve the same purpose. Late summer is the peak period of occurrence, but in the western Pacific the season is rather a long one, extending from May to January. Aside from its locally destructive aspect, the typhoon is important as a precipitation producer for many miles on either side of its path. Eastern India, northern mainland Southeast Asia, most of the Philippines, the southeastern coast of China, and southern Japan are the regions receiving significant amounts of moisture from this source. The typhoon thus is an important late summer and early autumn weather agent. Pacific Ocean storms move westward and Indian Ocean storms move mainly northward, both sets recurring to the north and east into the patterns of movement normal to the extratropical cyclones. A good many Pacific Ocean typhoons fail to curve northward along the China coast, sweeping somewhat southward and across Vietnam. Some of these continue intact into the Bay of Bengal, where they regenerate and swing northward and eastward into eastern India and north Burma. Storms that pass along the China coast provoke rainfall as far inland as 500 miles. In Japan typhoons passing close to the south coast attract masses of cold northern air, upon occasion, to cool much of Japan unduly, and to contribute to autumn rainfall. The Philippines also receive cool spells and some autumn rainfall from October to December from this same source.

The term "orographic squeeze" involves more than the simple matter of air blowing over a mountain. Often there appears to be horizontal convergence of air masses, along oblique obstructions or in funnel-like lowland embayments, which may be more important than the vertical lift over the obstruction. Such is certainly the case in Assam; against both the Himalaya and the Assam Plateau the Indian Monsoon piles huge volumes of moist air in converging patterns.

In many instances horizontal and vertical elements are intermixed and rather complicated. Under this heading, for lack of clear interpretation, may be included some of the results of the weak tropical lows. The "squeeze" mechanism is very widely operative in the southern sector, and is significant, though less important, in the northern sector also. The west coast of India, the eastern Himalayan front, the Burma coast, the Vietnam coast, and many localities in the Indies and Philippines have steep mountain fronts obstructing with spectacular results the movement of relatively strong monsoon winds. Horizontal convergence is a significant factor in producing rainfall over northern India during the peak summer period. There is a tremendous and continued thrust of air into the Bengal Delta, against the Himalayan front, forcing major air currents to wheel leftward up the Ganges Valley and rightward up the valley of the Brahmaputra. On the west coast of northern Japan the squeeze play on cold winter air produces extremely heavy falls of snow.

The last of the mechanisms providing weather change in the Orient is the generally rather weak "storm" that results from some perturbation within the Intertropical Trough. This type of weather mechanism usually is thought of as primarily affecting the tropical sectors of the Orient, but it often ranges as far north as central-northern China during the summer when the Intertropical Front shifts far northward. The perturbation within the Intertropical Trough often has been labeled a cyclonic storm or disturbance, but such storms are nonfrontal and are not related to the extratropical storms of the same name that circulate within the belt of the Westerlies. High-level eddies, pressure-ridges, low pressure pockets, and other fluctuations in upper-air conditions take place during much of the year in the tropical zones, within the Intertropical Trough, causing weak surface disturbances that be-

come moving rainstorms often resembling conventional thundershowers. Such patterns normally affect Malaysia, Indonesia, the Philippines, and the southern western Pacific Ocean all during the year.

It is likely that hemispheric balancing of the heat budget produces repeated fluctuations in the Jet Stream flow of air at high levels to serve as the primary causal factor behind the surface disturbance operating as a tropical weather mechanism. In particular areas in which pulsations in the monsoon drift of one of the three regional monsoons combines with the upper air disturbance an intense local rainstorm may occur on the surface. In areas in which orographic squeeze and normal convectional heating may also be involved, very heavy falls of rain may occur. As the Intertropical Trough shifts northward during the northern summer, some variable combination of mechanisms may produce several days of torrential rainfall over central China, bringing serious conditions of flooding. The irregularity of the several elements, involving the chance failure of any element to produce precipitation for a period of days to weeks may be followed by the chance combination of several elements to yield very heavy totals of precipitation within a short interval. The senior author experienced both of these conditions in the summer of 1935 in west-central China during which a long dry spell of clear weather at rice-planting time was followed by unceasing rainfall which produced about thirty-five inches of water in thirty-six hours; a serious drought was followed by a serious flood.

MOISTURE AND ITS DISTRIBUTION

In spite of the fact that the Orient is a humid landscape with perennial lowland floods, and with a large amount of water visible in the landscape much of the year, a number of regions with serious rainfall shortages belie such a description (Figs. 7.3–7.6). The first factor in this regional shortage is the rain-shadow position of many of the lowland basins and river valleys (see Figs. 7.2 and 6.5–6.14). The several lowland veins of the Burmo-Malayan fan are in rain-shadow position during both summer and winter wind drifts. Of these central Burma is most seriously affected. The central peninsula of India is in rain-shadow position during the summer monsoon and out of position to receive either monsoon or cyclonic rains in winter. Both northwest China and north-west India are out of position for the summer monsoon rainfall and in rain-shadow position for winter cyclonic moisture. The Island Arcs all have their local rain shadows and

peculiar characteristics in one or another season of air drift. Only in northwest India and central Asia is this rain-shadow effect strong enough to produce true desert. Else-where the moisture shortage is a relative situation.

The second important factor contributing to regional shortage of moisture is the enormous variability of the monsoon air drift and the irregular operation of the several storm mechanisms. This variability is both in timing and in annual total. Though native folk calendars and almanacs through-out the Orient long have had set dates for the commencement of their respective rainy seasons, vagaries in actual commencement are common. Delays often are times of elaborate prayer and penance rituals. Flood

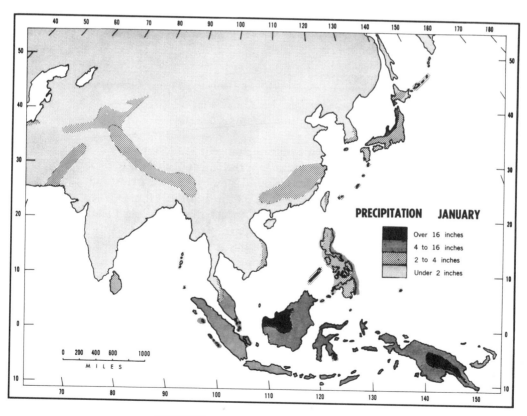

FIGURE 7.3. Precipitation in January.

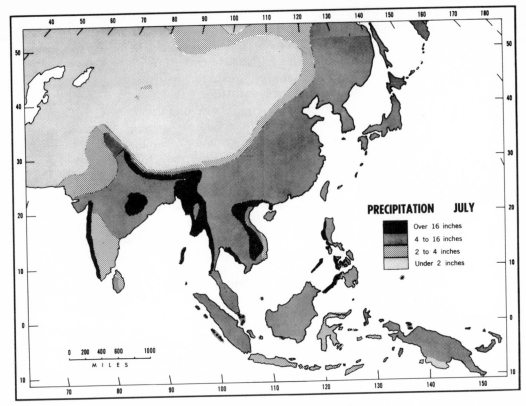

FIGURE 7.4. Precipitation in July.

and drought in the same summer are not un-heard of. Variation in total often exceeds 100 per cent, though in the humid sectors this usually goes unnoticed. Average variability becomes critical on the dry margins particularly, in Peninsular India, in central Burma, in northwestern India and the border country, and in north and north-west China. Some of the islands of the Indies east of Java receive too little moisture. Elsewhere shortage of moisture through variability is less frequent, though in in-dividual years it may cause serious economic and social repercussions (Figs. 7.5 and 7.6).

And as there are zones with too little moisture, so are there areas with possibly too much rainfall. There are several mountain walls lying directly in the path of one of the monsoon drifts over which several storm mechanisms combine to raise the total precip-itation to spectacular figures. Cherrapunji at an altitude of 4,300 feet in the Assam Plateau of northeastern India, directly in the path of the summer monsoon sweep, holds the precipitation record, with 431 inches per year, 905 inches being the maximum for any one year. This is over 35 feet for the average and just over 75 feet for the record annual fall, and the majority of this flood descends during the 6 months of the summer mon-soon. The southwest coast of India, the eastern Himalayan front, the Arakan Yoma-Assam Plateau line, the coast of lower Burma, and the central Vietnam coast are the out-standing regions of excess rainfall.

It has been mentioned that the Orient

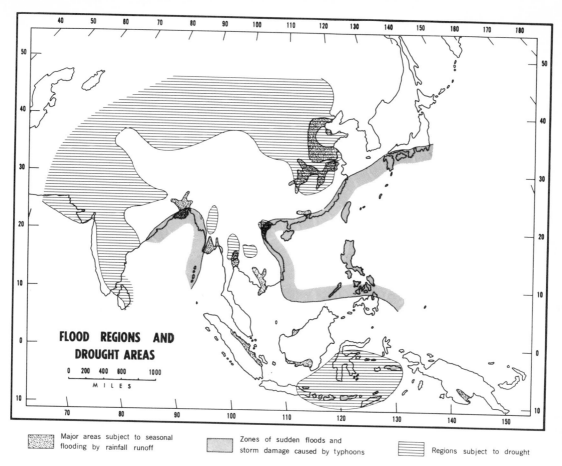

FLOOD REGIONS AND DROUGHT AREAS

0   200   400   800   1000
M I L E S

Major areas subject to seasonal flooding by rainfall runoff

Zones of sudden floods and storm damage caused by typhoons

Regions subject to drought

FIGURE 7.5. Regions subject to floods and droughts.

primarily receives its moisture during the summer growing season, this being a factor in its productive agriculture. Most of this summer rainfall comes as heavy downpours. The onset of the rains often finds the earth dry and parched, but after the first few days the balance is excess moisture even in a rice-growing land and runs off the soaked mountains and ponded slopes to pile up torrential floods in the lowland valleys. Comparison of the two seasonal precipitation maps indicates that some areas receive a considerable part of their total moisture as winter rain or snow (see Figs. 7.3 and 7.4). In northern lowland India and the upland mountain wall,

and from central China northward, winter moisture primarily is cyclonic in origin, is apt to come in smaller volumes per time period and is less destructive than the summer rain torrents. In the upper Himalayas or in northern situations there are considerable falls of snow, which in northwestern Japan often exceed six feet in depth.

In those areas near the equator there is, of course, no winter or summer distinction of wind or rainfall seasons in the ordinary sense. In the Indies particularly the two seasonal sets of winds affect different local areas of small dimensions, resulting in a mosaic of differently timed and patterned

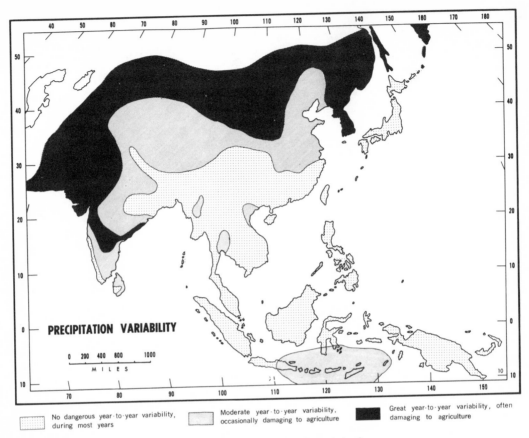

FIGURE 7.6. Variability of precipitation.

rainfall regimes. Except for western parts of the Philippines and for eastern Java and near-by islands, the island areas do not experience long dry seasons or moisture shortages.

Since the monsoon air drift is comparatively shallow the altitude of maximum rainfall is not very great. In India at least this level is not far from 4,000 feet, and above 5,000 feet rainfall totals decrease steadily, so that the highest mountain ranges do not receive abnormally heavy precipitation totals. Where cyclonic effects are added proportionately larger amounts of moisture are received at altitudes higher than 5,000 feet.

An aspect of moisture of great subjective importance is the humidity pattern. It is the moist heat of the Orient, particularly, which makes it uncomfortable and unhealthy for the white man, and for the native too, though there has been less said about this phase of the problem. Examination of data for Rangoon and Tokyo, cities chosen at random, makes clear the seasonal discomfort of the climate (Tables 2 and 3). The table for Rangoon uses mean monthly data. Hourly humidity data for Tokyo are more suggestive of one phase of the problem.

These two tables indicate that the summer humidities do build up to a rather high point. In Rangoon during the summer it rains heavily almost every day and, although temperatures are somewhat lower, this is

TABLE 2
Selected Climatic Data for Rangoon, Burma

Period	Mean Temp.	Mean Maxima	Mean Minima	Relative Humidity, %	Precip., in.	Rainy Days	Cloud Cover
January	77	89	65	70	0.21	0.3	1.1
March	84	96	71	68	0.32	0.6	1.2
May	84	92	77	83	11.98	14.0	5.9
July	81	85	76	93	21.42	25.0	8.7
September	81	86	76	92	15.27	20.0	7.2
November	80	88	73	83	2.79	0.3	2.9
Annual	81	89	73	82	99.03	122.0	4.5

offset by the increased humidity. Examination of the Tokyo data shows that the night hours have the highest humidities at all seasons. The inability to sleep soundly at night is a critical item in climatic discomfort.

TABLE 3
Hourly Climatic Data for Tokyo, Japan

For the Month of January

Period	Relative Humidity, %	Mean Temp.	Mean Cloudiness	Precipitation
1 AM	71	33.8	3.8	0.09
6 AM	73	31.5	4.3	0.10
2 PM	50	45.2	4.5	0.09
9 PM	68	36.3	3.7	0.13
Monthly mean	64	37.4	4.2	Total 2.42

For the Month of July

Period	Relative Humidity, %	Mean Temp.	Mean Cloudiness	Precipitation
1 AM	92	72.1	6.8	0.26
6 AM	92	75.7	8.3	0.28
2 PM	69	81.9	7.4	0.04
9 PM	87	74.3	6.3	0.28
Monthly mean	82	76.0	7.5	Total 5.01

"I would not mind the days so much, if I could just sleep at night" is a wail that is uttered by both white man and native, undoubtedly related to the daily curve of humidity, as well as to the daily temperature curve.

VARIETIES OF WEATHER

Selecting a residence in terms of weather alone, we would pick New Delhi, north India, from early November to late March, spend April and May in Kashmir in northwest India, stay in western Kueichou or Yunnan in southwest China from June until mid-September, and pass the remaining weeks on an island in the Inland Sea of Japan. This would provide steady sunshine with warm days, cool nights, comfortably low humidities, and a few interesting thundershowers. Other people may have different climatic preferences. Since few people can arrange life so neatly there is abundant climatic discomfort for both native and white man during much of the year everywhere in the Orient (see Fig. 7.1).

CLIMATIC REGIONS

Most climatic classifications now in use are formulated upon simply devised vegetative or uncritical weather-seasonal criteria. Such schemes, variably adjusted to fit conditions in Europe or the Americas, do not lend themselves to adequate climatic differentiation of the several monsoon regions of eastern Asia. Vegetative reaction to climatic elements is rather complex and is involved with a variety of geologic soil, and cultural effects. Ordinary annual weather patterns shaping human comfort are produced by seasonal air mass movements and storm mechanisms. Climatology has not yet produced a satis-

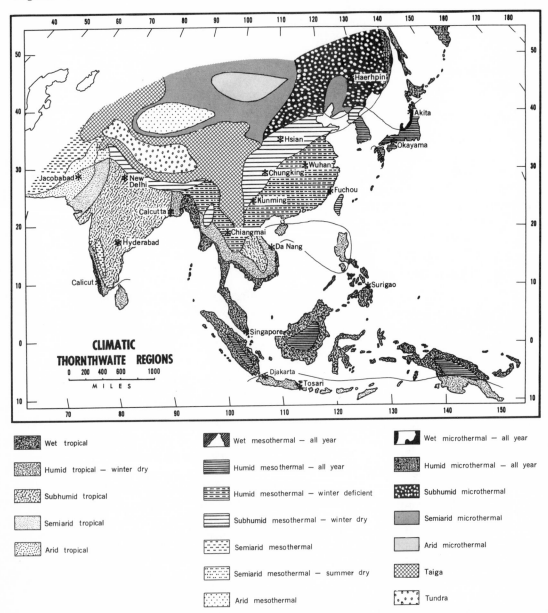

FIGURE 7.7. Climatic regions (Thornthwaite classification).

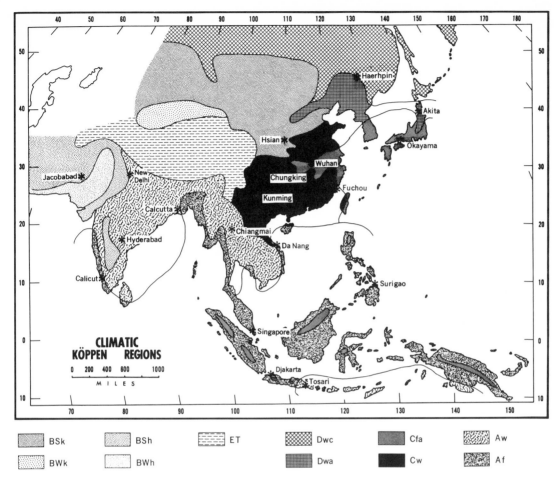

FIGURE 7.8. Climatic regions (modified Köppen classification).

factory empirical set of formulae applying equally well to all parts of the world. Climatologists in Japan, China, and India have studied their home areas with little attention to the over-all application of their regional systems. For any large region, such as China, it is fairly easy to describe subjectively five or six different kinds of climatic regions as these are perceived by human subjective judgment. It is difficult, however, to arrange a simple classification for such a large region that is objectively accurate, that will permit the drawing of effective boundary lines, and that groups regional climates in those ways sug-

gested by human reactions. Presented for comparison are maps of the whole of Monsoon Asia drawn according to the modified Thornthwaite and the Köppen systems (Figs. 7.7 and 7.8). Despite the broad similarities there are obvious differences in interpretation between the two, and neither yields the effective differentiation perceived by human beings on hot summer nights in New Delhi or frosty winter mornings in Wuhan, and neither makes clear the human reaction to Chungking's drab and raw, cloudy winter or its sticky hot summer. In these terms we offer no full attempt to differentiate climatic regions in the full sense, but the map of thermal comfort placed in the early portion of this chapter is a simple attempt to differentiate seasonal weather patterns as human reactions perceive them (see Fig. 7.1).

The assemblage of climatic charts presents data for representative stations in many parts of the Orient, and the summary notations below each chart suggest the variety of weather to be expected at each point, in subjective terms (Figs. 7.9 through 7.27). Each chart presents monthly and annual data on several different aspects of the annual march of weather.

General note for all charts:
The solid-line curve presents average monthly temperatures in Fahrenheit degrees.
The dashed-line curve indicates average monthly humidities in percent.
The vertical columns represent average monthly precipitation in inches.
The location of each station is represented by the name on the maps of climatic regions (see Figs. 7.7 and 7.8).

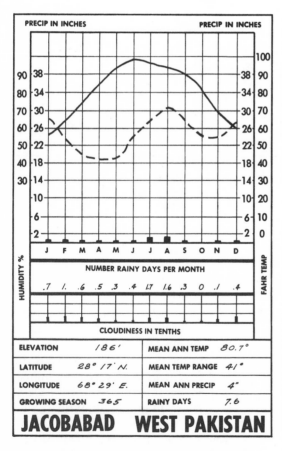

FIGURE 7.9. Climatic chart: Jacobabad, West Pakistan.

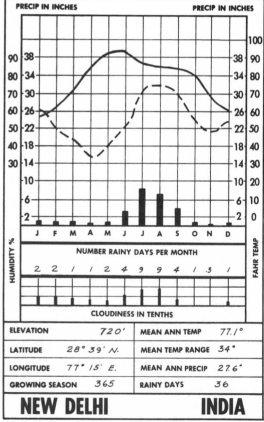

FIGURE 7.10. Climatic chart: New Delhi, India.

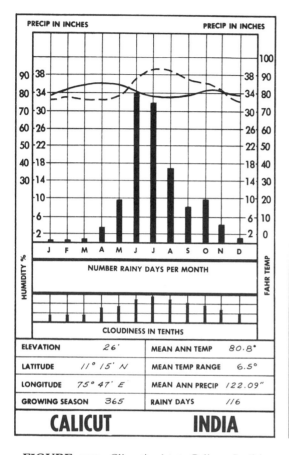

FIGURE 7.11. Climatic chart: Calicut, India.

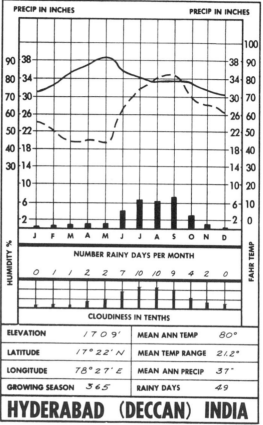

FIGURE 7.12. Climatic chart: Hyderabad (Deccan), India.

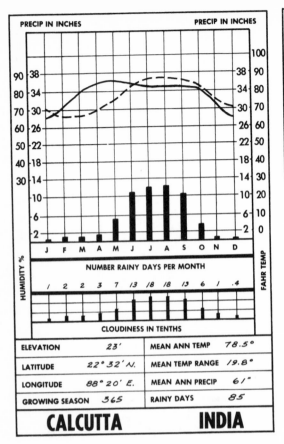

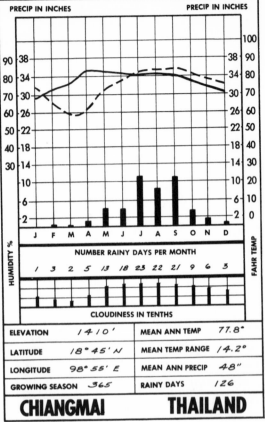

FIGURE 7.13. Climatic chart: Calcutta, India.

FIGURE 7.14. Climatic chart: Chiangmai, Thailand.

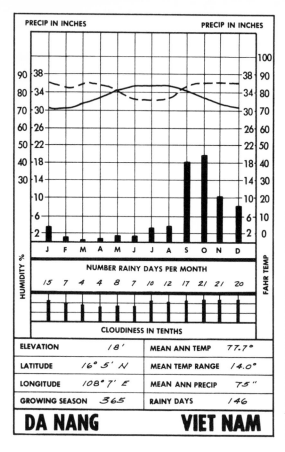

FIGURE 7.15. Climatic chart: Da Nang, Vietnam.

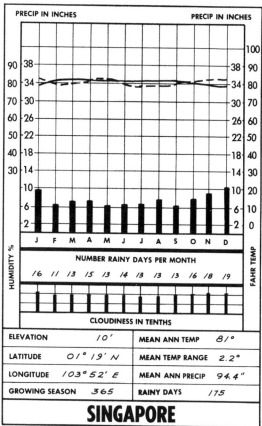

FIGURE 7.16. Climatic chart: Singapore.

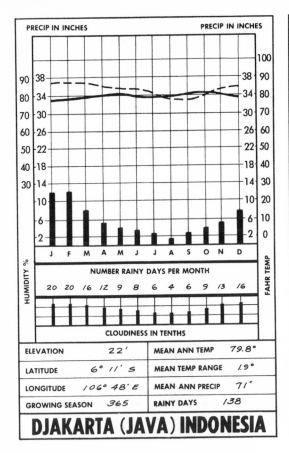

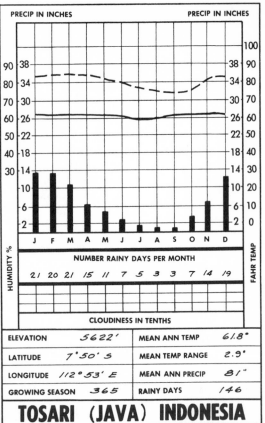

FIGURE 7.17. Climatic chart: Djakarta (Java), Indonesia.

FIGURE 7.18. Climatic chart: Tosari (Java), Indonesia.

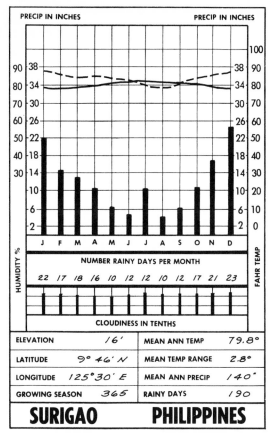

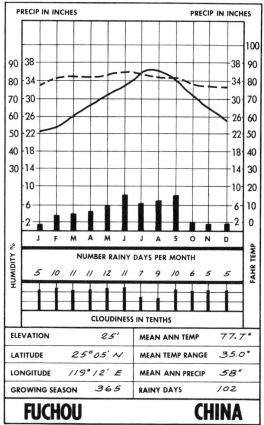

FIGURE 7.19. Climatic chart: Surigao, Philippines.

FIGURE 7.20. Climatic chart: Fuchou, China.

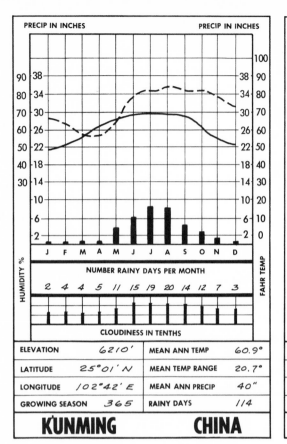

FIGURE 7.21. Climatic chart:
K'unming, China.

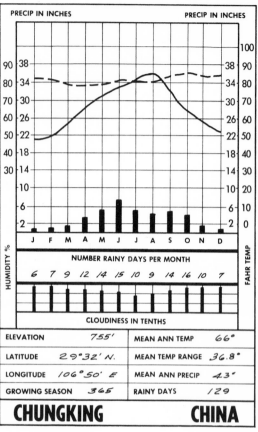

FIGURE 7.22. Climatic chart:
Chungking, China.

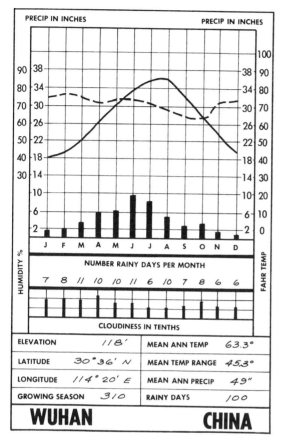

FIGURE 7.23. Climatic chart: Wuhan, China.

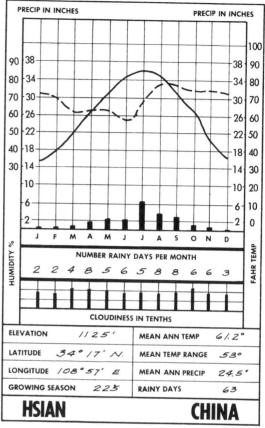

FIGURE 7.24. Climatic chart: Hsian, China.

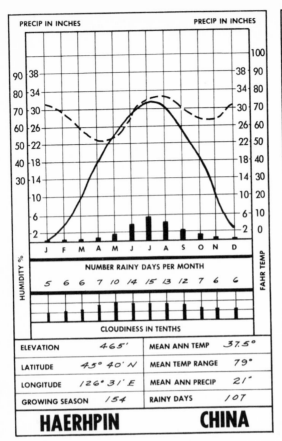

FIGURE 7.25. Climatic chart:
Haerhpin, China.

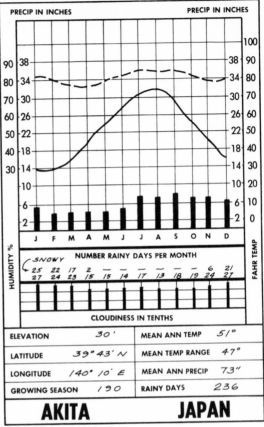

FIGURE 7.26. Climatic chart: Akita, Japan.

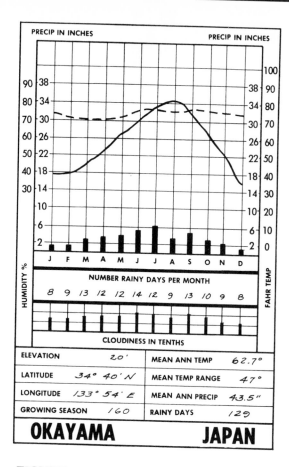

FIGURE 7.27. Climatic chart: Okayama, Japan.

8

GEOGRAPHY OF MINERALS AND PATTERNS OF USE

THE BEGINNING OF MINERAL USE

The accepted origins of mineral technology can be traced to ancient Southwest Asia, the classical Near East. The fabrication of metals is held to have first taken place in that same zone, and diffusion of techniques to other regions must, then, involve later dates for use in distant regions. The archaeologic record of copper and bronze fabrication by Indus Valley cultures clearly relates to the third millennium B.C., the North China record is clear for at least as early as the start of the second millennium B.C., and both areas show high skills in both copper and bronze. The Chinese developed very high skills in bronze casting very early during the second millennium. Elsewhere in the Orient the dating is still unclear, and problems of dating make firm statements difficult. It is clear that New Guinea remained in the stone age until modern time, but for the rest of Southeast Asia there are uncertainties. There is recent suggestive evidence pointing to the possibility that fabrication of bronze, a mixture of copper and tin, began in mainland Southeast Asia, rather than in the western sector of Asia, diffusing westward through India and, a bit later, into North China. The conclusion seems sound, however, that working of some metals had spread almost everywhere throughout Monsoon Asia by at least the start of the first millennium B.C.

India was not the original center of iron technology, but its manganese-alloy iron ores allowed a very early production of superior steel long before the use of alloys was consciously developed. India was probably an early source of what became known to the West as "Damascus steel." The use of iron and ability to produce it must have been carried into southeastern Asia by Indian trader colonists. It is known that iron did not become at all common in China until a few centuries B.C. The Chinese soon became expert at iron casting but never developed a really high proficiency at working steel. On the other hand, the Chinese early and thoroughly mastered the handling of bronze and with it created a variety of utilitarian products that in the modern era rank among the world's finest art goods. It is not certain how bronze penetrated the Island Arcs, but it preceded iron by some centuries in most areas.

Since nothing similar to a modern geological survey was ever carried out, the sources of common minerals only gradually became widely known. A number of sources of copper were widely scattered, and some trade developed in the raw metal and its products. Iron ores are scattered so widely that probably nothing more than local trade ever developed in iron ores and their simple products. Steel, on the other hand, was a very different commodity, and Indian steel circulated over much of the ancient world in small amounts. Tin was a trade specialty of the Malay Peninsula as a whole, though gradually tin ores were mined from Bangka to Yunnan.

Mercury, cinnabar, salt, sulphur, and saltpeter were also minerals enjoying a certain trade movement. Their use in China and India was a very early development, and the use of salt and sulphur was extremely widespread and appeared almost as early as any kind of trade. Jewel stones of various kinds were quarried, traded, and used from early Stone Age time in every populated region, though gradually certain areas became famous for particular stones. The precious metals and stones of the Orient naturally attracted more spectacular attention than tin, copper, or salt, and were the subject of many stories and tales that grew into fabulous legends. Gold, gathered widely in the earlier eras, is another mineral of very early interest. The earliest gold was alluvial, picked up in some of the rivers of most countries. Slowly it became a mine product in a number of areas.

The collecting of alluvial gold, collecting of jewel and semiprecious stones, and gradually the quarrying of each of these probably were a spontaneous activity at an early time widely over the Orient. Mining as a developed kind of quarrying seems to have had its origin somewhere west of the true Orient. It would seem that real mining was an activity learned by most Orientals after they had already become interested in gold and decorative stones. Copper, iron, lead, zinc, silver, tin, and perhaps some other minerals had

their first conscious use in some part of Southwest Asia. The knowledge of use, ore mining, and metal smelting spread eastward toward India, through Central Asia into China, and gradually beyond these two regions. Some of the mixtures of ores and metals may have developed in some part of the Orient, as has been suggested as possible for bronze, but others appear introduced at a rather late date. Brass, for example, a mixture of copper and zinc, appears old in use in India but rather recent in use in China, although bronze is old in both areas. Coal was first used consciously in north China, and mica may well be an Indian introduction, but the large-scale mining of both is relatively late in appearance.

DISTRIBUTION OF MINERALS

Considered in terms of simple unit area the Orient would appear almost to have its share of the world's economic minerals. In proportion to population, however, the Orient has less than its share; in addition there is an uneven distribution of the separate minerals among the countries of the realm. Adequacy of supply is a variable situation, dependent upon the use to which a given society may put its minerals. In the earlier judgment of an agrarian society, whose primary agriculture was complemented by handicraft industry, China or Thailand might be said to have been adequately supplied with iron ore, and in the past the supply generally was sufficient to the need. However, in terms of modern industrial requirements, the earlier judgment was that the whole of Monsoon Asia was deficient in mineral resources except for the Chinese resources in coal. The Japanese shortages began to be evident only when Japan launched upon her campaign of modern industrialization of her economy. Surveys still are everywhere incomplete, except possibly in Japan, and many new minerals and larger reserves may be widely present but still unknown. At least Japan owned her own minerals, and their exploitation was of her own choosing. But in every country of the Orient, in the past and even now to some extent, production has been controlled and profits extracted by some distant exploiting corporation or country. The petroleum of Indonesia or the iron ores of Korea were of little value to the population of either country. In the coming era these conditions will change to whatever degree local industrialization takes place. The following Table 4 is but an estimate of this situation of resources at the start of the 1970's, couched in terms of peaceful circumstance and peace economy, assuming that trade in surpluses and deficiencies may continue. Each regional chapter will deal variably with the matter of mineral resources, mineral production, and industrialization.

SOURCES OF POWER

China and India, as the two largest units of the Orient, possess the largest potential volumes of industrial power. China stands fourth among the countries of the world in coal resources. Coal resources are well scattered and varied in quality, though the best reserves are concentrated in Shansi and Shensi. Coal is mined in every province of China proper, and the annual total rarely exceeded 30,000,000 tons until the late 1930's when wartime acceleration began to stimulate production. Since the 1950's Communist effort has greatly increased yields, and it is clear that China can produce as much coal as required by industrial needs, the volume being dependent only on internal political stability. Modernization of mining techniques appears comparable to that anywhere in the world at present.

India's coal reserves are small compared to those of China, but sufficient for a reasonable period, unless production increases tremendously in the near future. The coal is not of the best quality and is not well dis-

tributed, the Chota Nagpur hill country having most of the reserves. Production is currently controlled by patterns of economic investment. Pakistan owns only small coal reserves, though survey is still incomplete. Japan was the leading oriental producer of coal in the early half of this century, her annual figure having exceeded 45,000,000 tons after about 1930. Coal is widely distributed throughout Japan, but it is low in quality for industrial use and reserves are comparatively small for a country with industrial ambition. Korea has fair reserves of coal that, mined for her own use only, will answer most needs for a long period. During the years 1910–1945 Japan mined Korean coal for the good of Japan only. North Vietnam has considerable hard coal, but not much good soft coal. The other countries of the Orient have only very small amounts of fair to poor coal. It is mined in every country in small amounts, but only in Indonesia is it a significant addition to available power.

Indonesia stands high among world petroleum producers, but only modest now-proven reserves are known, though much surveying remains unfinished, and current prospecting promises to develop large resources. Sumatra, Borneo, and Java are the leading productive islands, but New Guinea will one day appear in the list. A wide range of oils is included in the annual production average. Occidental corporations produce, control, and export oil from Indonesia, this being the Orient's current major trade source of petroleum products. Burma is the only other significant source of petroleum, from fields northwest of Rangoon in the folded mountain country. Natural seeps have been producing oil under very crude native methods for centuries. Political isolationism, during the 1960's, stopped the production and shut off the export of petroleum from Burma.

Both China proper and India now produce significant amounts of petroleum, but the prospects for the future in neither country can be considered extremely bright, measured against prospective needs, although Chinese Central Asia and the margins of the North Indian Plain cannot now be ruled out as potential sources. Pakistan began her separate political career with a small petroleum production, has increased that considerably, and may possess significant resources around the hilly margins of the North Indian Plain. Northern Japan is a very small petroleum producer, without prospect of larger yields. Sakhalin's modest petroleum production has been returned to Russian control after a period of Japanese exploitation. No other country appears certain to possess petroleum resources, although Philippine expectations may materialize. A fair volume of oil shale and very soft coal gives China a source of petroleum products once the industrial procedures are mastered and in operation. Japan, Korea, India, and Thailand have small amounts of oil shale, but these do not merit optimism as regards adequate petroleum.

The Orient as a whole possesses a hydroelectric potential estimated as well above that of North America or Europe. Of the total India and Pakistan hold nearly forty per cent, China just over twenty, Indonesia nearly fifteen, Japan about seven, and the Laos-Cambodia-Vietnam region six per cent. Each other country has a significant though smaller power potential based on water. Much of the 103,000,000 horsepower estimated as available ninety-five per cent of the time in the Orient will be rather costly to develop, requiring both money and engineering. It will be a long time before much of the potential is actually available in many countries. In the present developed volume of water power innumerable simple water wheels are operating in every country, which are used for the grinding of grain and similar operations. In terms of developed hydroelectric power available for industrial use, Japan with her seven per cent of the total

potential has already developed most of her resources, and is looking toward atomic power as serving future needs. Elsewhere only relatively small beginnings have been made toward development of potentials. India, Pakistan, and China have major programs under way, and the Lower Mekong River Basin multi-nation project is beginning a serious start.

Monazite, a thorium-producing mineral, has become more than a minor product with the growth of atomic energy research. For many years the southwest coast of Peninsular India and the west coast of Ceylon have produced monazite and related minerals. Used in the normal pre-atomic industrial processes, a small tonnage satisfied the world's needs. No other part of the Orient is yet known to produce more than sample amounts of any atomic energy mineral although it must be presumed that China has found sufficient resources to support her small nuclear program.

INDUSTRIAL METALS

For the metals group China, North Korea, India, and North Vietnam are the best off, according to modern industrial needs. Each has a wide variety of metals in respectable quantities. China, formerly thought to be short in copper and iron ore, now appears to have quite adequate resources in each mineral. Taiwan copper has moved away from China since the Japanese began its production. China still appears short in some of the ferroalloys but possesses exportable surpluses of others. More complete geological surveys may yet turn up deposits of needed metals to widen more fully the present respectable basis for an industrial program. Korea's metal minerals are now fairly well known through Japanese survey and exploitation and exist in adequate proportion to her needs in rather a wide range, although North Korea is better off than South Korea in this

TABLE 4

Occurrence of Mineral Resources

	Japan	South Korea	North Korea	China	Taiwan	Philippines	Eastern New Guinea	Indonesia	Brunei	Malaysia	Cambodia	South Vietnam	North Vietnam	Laos	Thailand	Burma	Ceylon	India	Pakistan
POWER SOURCES																			
Hard Coal	v	+	+	+				v					+					+	v
Coking Coal	v	+	+	+	v			+					+					+	v
Low-grade Coal	v	v	+	+	+			+		+			+	v	+	+		+	v
Petroleum	v		v	v	v	v		+	+						v	+		v	v
Oil Shale	v		+	+				+	+						+	+		+	v
Water Power	+	+	+	+	+	+		+				+	+	+	+	+	v	+	+
Monazite								+						+	v		+	+	
INDUSTRIAL METALS																			
Iron Ore	v	v	+	+	+	+		+		+	+	+	+	+	+	+		+	+
Manganese	v	v		+		+		+		+	+				+	+		+	v
Tungsten		+	+	+						+					+	+		+	
Chromium	+					+				+			+		+			v	+
Nickel	v	v	v	v		v		+							+	+			
Vanadium	v							+							+				
Molybdenum	v		v	+		v									+				
Antimony	v	v		+			+				v				+				
Lead	v	+	+	+		+		+				v	+			+		v	v
Zinc	v	v	v	+							v	v	+			+		v	v
Aluminum Ores		+	+	+	+	+		+		+		+			+	+		+	+
Copper	+	v	+	v	v	+	+	+		+					+	+		v	v
Tin	v			+	+	+		+		+			+	+	+	+			

TABLE 4 (*Continued*)

	Pakistan	India	Ceylon	Burma	Thailand	Laos	North Vietnam	South Vietnam	Cambodia	Malaysia	Brunei	Indonesia	Eastern New Guinea	Philippines	Taiwan	China	North Korea	South Korea	Japan
PRECIOUS METALS AND GEM STONES																			
Gold	v	+								+		+	+	+	+	+	+	+	+
Silver	v	v		v	v							v	+	+		v	v	v	v
Platinum		+		v															v
Diamonds		+										+							
Jades				+	+				v							v			
Rubies		v		+	+				v										
NON-METALS																			
Phosphates	v	v					+		+	+		+				v			v
Nitrates	v	+						v						v		+			v
Potashes		v												v		+			v
Sulphur	+	+												v	+	+			+
Salt	++	++		+	+					v		+	+	+	++	+	+	+	+
Gypsum	+	+			+							+		+	+	+			v
Mercury																+			+
Graphite		++			v			+							+	+	+	++	v
Mica		+++														v	v	v	v
Magnesite		+														v			v
Asbestos					v											+		+	+

Tabular estimate in terms of peaceful conditions and the normal flow of trade.

+++ Outstanding resource,
++ Surplus beyond domestic need of modest industrial program,
+ Adequate for present and modest future use,
v Present but insufficient for modest use,
blank No commercial resource known in 1969.

respect. North Vietnam, a considerable mineral storehouse, has not had the opportunity of economic development.

Japan possesses a wide range of the metals in quantities adequate for a modest, peacetime industrial program producing for home markets. Even so a shortage of iron ore would still exist. The upsurge of her modern industrial growth revealed that Japan is short in the large volumes and basic reserves of many metals so needed by an aggressive industrial export economy. India was in moderately good position under rule as a single country with shortages in lead, zinc, and some of the ferroalloys. Under a divided pattern of government the shortages of Pakistan are rather great, whereas those of India are not so marked, although current survey is turning up significant resources in both countries.

The other countries of the Orient are but imperfectly known geologically, and the story changes with each decade. Present-known metals distribution is irregular, and quantities vary widely. Malaysia has one of the smaller ranges of minerals of any region, yet one of the most active mining programs, centered on tin, manganese, bauxite, and iron ore, so far chiefly utilized for export purposes. In comparative terms Thailand perhaps was long thought to be the least mineralized area in Monsoon Asia, but current surveys are turning up significant resources of several metals. In the famous Bawdwin mines Burma possessed a rich mineralized area that had been worked by the Chinese for centuries before the British began exploitation. World War II inflicted serious damage upon the mines, and Burma has not engaged in serious redevelopment of her mineral resources so far. In the Philippines surveys have found rich deposits of iron, manganese, and chromite ores, to add to the copper resources. It is possible that other industrial metals will also be located to make the islands relatively well supplied with the metals of the modern world. Additional geologic surveys throughout the Orient undoubtedly will change the scoreboard of resources available in the future.

NON-METALLIC MINERALS

In this group India, Pakistan, China, and North Korea are in the best relative positions, with Japan again short a number of critical items. Southeast Asia has an irregular distribution of these items, more significant for its absences and shortages than for its valued resources. Perhaps most serious is the shortage of adequate fertilizer minerals. Though it is true that the nitrates and phosphates can be synthetically produced, this can be done only in industrial countries with a large hydro-electric supply, and the countries which most need the fertilizer are in no position to produce their own synthetically. North Vietnam, Cambodia, Malaysia, and Indonesia possess the only known phosphate rock resources. Large deposits of such minerals as graphite and mica provide India and South Korea with export surpluses.

PRECIOUS METALS AND STONES

The varying value placed upon the several precious stones is a distinguishing feature between oriental culture groups. Rubies, sapphires, diamonds, and pearls long have been the most prized precious stones in India, and this pattern is variably shared by those parts of southeastern Asia, and the Island Arcs that were culturally affected by India. The Chinese realm, on the other hand, has always put the highest value on the jades. Pearls, diamonds, sapphires, turquoise, beryl, amber, crystal quartz, and other stones are esteemed but none rank with jade. The precious stones, among different peoples, carry a religious significance, a more noticeable feature of the Indian realm than the Chinese.

Over the centuries there have been various sources of pearls scattered around the coast of India, along the southern coast of China, the Sulu Archipelago, and in parts of Japan. Diamonds have long come from Borneo and Peninsular India. Rubies and sapphires are products both of Burma's Shan Plateau and of Ceylon. Lesser stones are very widely scattered. There are many kinds of jade, ranging in color from cream to brilliant green, and fashions have changed repeatedly. The sources of jade are as scattered as its variety. The Tsinling Mountains, in southern Shensi, are one of the most accessible sources, currently providing one of the modern green jades. Regions as distant as Lake Baikal in southern Siberia, the highlands of Russian Turkestan, the border ranges of northern Tibet, and the hill country of northern Burma have been tapped again and again for varying grades and color shades of nephrite, jadeite, and related stones that pass as jade or its counterfeits.

Gold occurs rather widely throughout the Orient in varying amounts. Peninsular India, Sumatra, and Borneo have been the historically fabulous sources, but it is possible that the best deposits have been worked out, for a lessened production over recent centuries has not lived up to the fabulous legends. South Korea and the Philippines are significant modern additions to the list of producing regions. Both North and South Vietnam, western China, Taiwan, and Japan are small producers. Silver occurs less widely than gold, and often is a by-product of other mining. Burma, Indonesia, South Korea, and the Philippines are the notable contemporary sources. India and China, the world's primary long-time buyers of silver, produce almost none. A little platinum is produced in Indonesia, in Burma, and in Japan as a by-product of gold and silver mining.

Everywhere throughout the Orient are active and abandoned quarries and mine workings from which precious stones and metals have long been taken. Some of the sources were already mythical when the Portuguese first tried to trace the home of oriental riches. Others have been worked out in recent centuries; some continue to yield their precious wares today at a steady rate.

SUMMARY NOTATIONS

The positions of the countries of Monsoon Asia are distinctly open to change in the future regarding both the mineral industries and the national patterns of use. Prior to the eighteenth century local populations carried on varying amounts of mining of usable resources for domestic handicraft use, as in iron, copper, zinc, gold, or jades, and sought out those resources of gold and precious stones useful in barter trade with other peoples elsewhere. The Europeans, in their world-wide contacts, stimulated the exploration for the precious items in the first instance and, as the steamship came into general use, began the search for and exploitation of coal resources for ship fuels, as a second kind of operation. The development of the colonial system then stimulated the search for particular minerals of utility to the particular imperial power. The growth of world trade, during the nineteenth century, stimulated mining in a wider range of resources, chiefly for export to the Occident. European businessmen organized local mining concerns in many regions, carried out the first modern surveys, and brought in new mining practices. Minerals were exported as raw materials, and the Occident shipped into the various countries all kinds of metal manufactures. Japan excepted, this pattern continued until after 1945, with local domestic mining development struggling along in a slowly growing pattern without much support of government. Geological survey organizations were only slowly established, and seldom were strongly effective. The judgment of total mineral resources varied considerably, but usually was on the side of underestimation.

In the post-colonial era, national political organization of geological surveys, the adoption of national industrial programs, and the restriction of mining concessions held by foreign interests has taken place in almost every country, Japan again excepted (since Japan never was a colonial subordinate and since she managed her own modern development program). Many of these programs now suffer from inadequate financial and technical support, but changes are in progress. Both the judgment of national resources and programs of exploitation of those resources will change almost yearly in the near future. Local people are becoming skilled as survey geologists, miners, fabricators, and industrial engineers. Industrial programs are taking on sophistication and comprehensive completeness at varying rates in the several countries of Monsoon Asia. The use by local populations of mineral products in manufactured form is increasing steadily. The "bamboo world" is passing and, for the average inhabitant, the "metal world" is coming into existence. In some countries the per capita usage of metals will not become large for some time to come, but both cultures and economies are changing everywhere. Dependent upon the variable focusing of capital resources, individual countries will make extremely rapid strides, or more slowly-paced strides, into the world of industrialization. The mineral resources picture, therefore, both in terms of reserves and in production-usage, will continue to alter.

9

MARINE LIFE AND ANIMALS IN ORIENTAL ECONOMY

Both marine and animal life have significantly entered into the total economy and culture of the oriental world, despite the frequent characterization of the Orient as having a vegetable economy. Marine life is here meant to include both fresh- and salt-water fish, mollusks, crustaceans, corals, and other aquatic life forms. Animal life includes both the higher animals, the rodents, the fowls, and the reptiles, domesticated and wild, large and small. In many areas fish forms the second most important source of food, and at least one of the animals is a significant food source in every part of the Orient. None of these forms of life has been adequately studied throughout the Orient in terms of its economic significance, and at this stage of our knowledge a completely effective presentation still cannot be made. This chapter must serve only as a preliminary statement of the subject.

ANIMAL GEOGRAPHY

The area discussed in this volume falls into three of the five major faunal zones of the earth, the Holarctic, the Oriental, and the Australian. The eastern Asian portion of the Holarctic zone usually is termed the Pale-arctic. Between the Oriental and the Pale-arctic zones no definitive boundary can be drawn, owing to the long-continued land continuity along the eastern fringe of Asia. This continuity, coupled with major Pleistocene shifts in environmental conditions, has led to a great amount of intermixing of animal forms between the north and south of Asia. The most appropriate line of division separates Japan and the Ryukyu Islands, crossing inland and along the Tsinling Mountains to the higher Tibetan foothill country. It then sweeps southward, zigzagging into the deep valleys and outward around the higher ranges until it turns westward along the Himalayan front. The lesser Himalayan front range forms the boundary westward into Kashmir.

On the west the Oriental zone intergrades into the Ethiopian life zone of Africa, for a number of African fauna have penetrated northwestern India. On the other corner rather clear boundaries between life zones exist in the Indies, separating the Oriental from the Australian zone. This sector often is known as Wallacea, after the great nineteenth-century naturalist Alfred Wallace. Wallace's Line first was drawn north-south across Indonesia between Bali and

207

Lombok, Borneo and Celebes, Mindanao and Celebes. Various modifications have been suggested, such as shifting its northern end westward to run between Palawan and Mindoro, and between Taiwan and the Batanes Islands. Another line has been drawn between Australia and Timor, between Tanimbar and Aru, between New Guinea and Ceram, between New Guinea and Halmahera. This is known as Weber's Line, after Max Weber, another great naturalist.

Wallace's Line is usually taken as limiting primary eastward penetration of the large complex of Oriental life forms, and Weber's Line as the limit of primary westward penetration of the Australian life complex. The several groups of islands lying between Wallace's Line and Weber's Line now are often termed Wallacea, for they form a transition zone in which some of the Oriental and Australian life forms intergrade. Even so, the division between zones is far more discernible than that between the Oriental and the Palearctic zones (Fig. 9.1).

A few Palearctic forms have not naturally occupied the Oriental region within Recent time, such as the horse, the moose, or the yak. Conversely, some Oriental forms have not occupied any portion of the Palearctic within Recent time, such as the rhinoceros, the tapir, the apes, and the slow lorises. In contrast, the great majority of animal forms are widely distributed throughout both zones, though this is not commonly recognized. The cats, tigers, lynxes, wolves, foxes, bears, dogs, weasels, otters, martens, badgers, pigs, shrews, rats, mice, hares, rabbits, squirrels, antelopes, deer, goats, sheep, and cattle, all are to be found in both zones. Species differentation has occurred, certainly, and today it is true that there are northern and southern species of each of the above animals, which now are acclimated to particular local environments. For example, the polar bear (*Thalassarctos maritimus*) never ranges south of the Amur River, and the Malayan bear (*Helarctos malayanos*) never ranges far north of upper Burma; the Siberian roe deer (*Capreolus capreolus pygargus*) never runs south of the Tsinling Mountains, and the Indian muntjak (*Muntiacus muntjak vaginalis*) never runs north of central Yunnan; our common cattle (*Bos taurus*) of their own accord remain in the north and the Zebu (*Bos indicus*) keep to the south.

In earlier times, late Pleistocene and early Recent, through the land continuity of eastern Asia and the variation in climatic-floristic environments, the intergrading of fauna was of even greater degree than at present. Over sixty animal groups transgress the limits of Palearctic and Oriental life zones as these are presently delimited, representing remnants of earlier patterns of zoning. A large number of animals ranged from Burma and South China into southern Siberia along the mainland, and others may have spread along the Island Arcs nearest the mainland, from Malaysia to Japan. Thus, the tiger (*Panthera tigris*) is considered a northern form which earlier was at home in southern Siberia and North China. Slowly the tiger migrated southward through China, into Burmo-Malaya, and finally into India. Its present range is from Manchuria to southern India to Java in a series of discontinuous local environments. In Manchuria the tiger still depends upon wild pigs for food to a considerable extent, and shows a distribution similar to that of the Holarctic pig (*Sus scrofa*). Elsewhere, its own subsistence patterns have varied somewhat and, as more forest and jungle have been turned into settled farmland, the tiger often has had to raid man's domestic animals or to prey upon man himself, thus becoming a dangerous pest. The civets are another northern group now widely spread throughout the Holarctic and Oriental zones.

On the west a number of Ethiopian life forms have relatively recently invaded India.

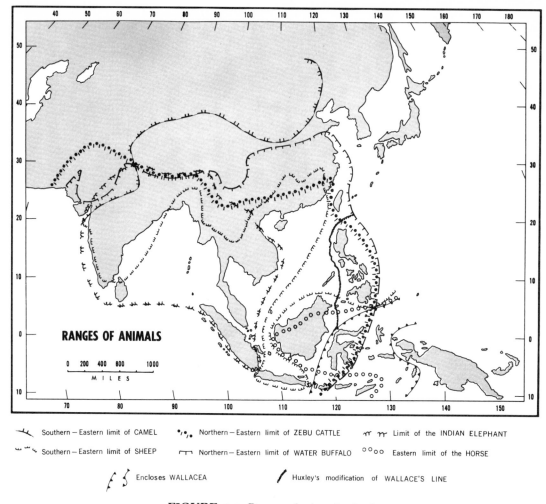

FIGURE 9.1. Ranges of oriental animals.

The lion *(Panthera leo)*, which penetrated India as far as the western Ganges River valley, is a late arrival from Africa. Some of the antelopes of African origin are restricted to northwest India.

Within the Oriental zone certain animal groups seem to have become regionally acclimated at an early date in India and the mainland portion of southeastern Asia and were early migrants into what today forms the western portion of Indonesia. Thus the macaque monkeys, squirrels, palm civets, deer, buffaloes, pigs, and others, as early

migrants, are more widely spread in the islands of western Indonesia than are some of the later animal groups of the Oriental region. Some of the early migrants even crossed Wallace's Line and perhaps acted to prevent the northward and westward migration of the Australian animals. Thus Weber's Line is a better single line demarcation than is Wallace's Line. Other major groups, such as the apes, leaf monkeys, cats, weasels, bears, Zebu cattle, rhinoceroses, and elephants were later migrants toward the southeast and did not become established in the far corners of the old mainland before the last major changes in sea level. These later migrants are not therefore well represented in the island fringe of the western Indies, none of them of their own accord crossed Wallace's Line, and many did not even reach Java and Borneo. Among the reptiles the Asian poisonous snakes all stop short of New Guinea, and the New Guinea group do not occur west of Weber's Line. New Guinea has many lizards, large and small, not found to the west. The marine turtles are at home in western Indonesia and along coastal edges of the mainland of southeastern Asia, as far north as Hong Kong but were not limited by the patterns of land and sea.

Within the Oriental region itself, therefore, there exist a number of regional concentrations of animal groups which serve to allow delineation of several subdivisions of the Oriental zone. It would be possible to draw regional boundaries of animal distributions between the drier and more moist parts of India, between the Himalayan mountain country and the lowland, between Burma and India, between Burmo-Malaya and western Indonesia, between Burmo-Malaya and southern China. Similar subdivisions could be delineated within the Palearctic zone, separating Tibet, the dry interior of Asia, North China and Manchuria, southern Siberia, and the northern ends of the Island Arcs. A factor in regional distribution lies in the fact that the heavier, canopied forests carry smaller animal populations than jungles, secondary forests, and grassland margins.

Within the Australian life zone there live seven groups and roughly four hundred species of mammals. Some, such as the bats, seals, and sea cows, are not unique to Australia or the eastern Indies, since their powers of mobility made it possible for them to cross barriers insurmountable to other forms. The dogs were introduced by man. Two special Australian forms are the monotremes:

The aquatic duckbilled Platypus *(Ornithorhynchus animatus)* restricted to Australia, and the Echidna or Spiny Anteater *(Tachyglossus aculeatus)*, a nocturnal land animal found from Tasmania into New Guinea. The Australian rodents are all members of the Muridae or rat family, and not all of them are truly unique to Australia. Many of these animal groups are found only in parts of the life zone; others are scattered throughout, westward to Weber's Line. The Australian life zone possesses many marsupials such as the kangaroos and koalas. Some of these are found in New Guinea, such as the arboreal brushtailed possum *(Trichosurus vulpecula)* and the tree kangaroo *(Dendrolagus lumholzi)*. Of the marsupials, some of the smaller species of wallaby are found throughout New Guinea and related islands, as well as in Australia itself. The rat bandicoots, living on insects, worms, and beetles, are widely spread from New Guinea south and east. The koala is restricted to ranges supplying eucalyptus plant foods and, therefore, is seldom found in New Guinea. It is obvious, therefore, that here, too, one can draw regional subdivisions of significance. New Guinea and its related islands form a subregion of importance to this study.

In very real degree there is also a regional concentration of bird life in various parts of Asia. Many species are distributed on the broad zonal outlines suggested above, though others are not limited by such regional bounds and are found in many other parts of the world in identical or related species. Some birds are only seasonal in any one country, like many of the ducks which winter in India or Vietnam and summer in Soviet Siberia. Along the Island Arcs some seasonal bird occupations also occur with summer ranges both northward to Hokkaido and southward to New Zealand, winter ranges lying in Indonesia and the Philippines. On the other hand, many species present in lowland India, Burma, or Thailand during the winter merely shift northward and upward into the near-by mountain country for the summers. A few species, like some of the pheasants and jungle fowls, are permanent residents of restricted jungle and forest environments of southeastern Asia. Others prefer rocky coastal sites from western peninsular India to Celebes, like those chosen by the sea-swiftlet *(Collocalia fuciphaga)* and related species, which produce the edible gelatinous nest-lining termed "birds' nests" so prized by the Chinese. Several of the multicolored birds of New Guinea have been economically significant for their feathers, and the cassowary bird has been important as a source of food, sinew, bone, and feathers. All the New Guinea birds have restricted territorial ranges.

ANIMAL DOMESTICATION

Our concepts concerning wild animals useful or dangerous to man, and the relations between them and man that led to domestication need much more examination before we can account for the phenomena of domestication and properly orient its regional development. It has been a commonplace to think of the dog as the first domesticated animal, but neither the reasoning accounting for its early domestication nor regional relationships have been well marshaled. Next in line has been the commonplace notion of the domestication of the Holarctic *Bos taurus* as the first economically useful animal. The evidence for this as the first of our useful animals, similarly, has not been well pieced together. We cannot pretend, therefore, to present a completely articulated story of animal domestication, but it seems very doubtful if *Bos taurus* was the first useful animal on the list. We need to know much more of the problems of taming animals, of the significance of pets in early cultures, of the habits of many wild animals such as the scavengers, herbivores, and the cats, and of

the development of religious sacredness attaching to various animals before we can explain the whole phenomenon of domestication.

Many peoples have long tamed various of the deer, and yet the reindeer seems to be the only deer domesticated, a late accomplishment. Simple taming does not seem the chief tool in domestication. Among many of the simpler cultures, and the pastoral cultures, it is not uncommon for women able to nurse their own offspring to suckle the young of small animals such as the dogs, pigs, goats, and sheep. Was this an important element in taming and domestication? An ancient sacredness of the pig has been all but obliterated under the late spread of the tabu upon the pig as an unclean animal. Our modern love for the dog as a pet has colored our thinking about his usefulness as a source of food to early man, and our reaction to that use among some of the less complex human groups today is one of abhorrence. Americans now suffer under the partial tabu upon horsemeat. Could pets be eaten if they first were made sacred and used as items of sacrifice?

There is evidence that both the dog and the pig, as small jungle scavengers around campsites, were tamed and domesticated very early in southeastern Asia, but the technique of domestication is not at all clear. There is some evidence that these two animals, as pets, useful, or sacred animals, spread out of southeastern Asia in all directions both with early movements of man, and as animals were passed from group to group. The tabus upon the eating of both do not generally relate to early times in southeastern Asia, but were later developed elsewhere by peoples of different cultures. It seems possible that southeastern Asian techniques in taming and domestication of both of these animals started the process, and that techniques perhaps elsewhere already partly applied to local animals finally succeeded in domesticating other animals as the techniques matured.

Within the oriental life zone domestication seems to have succeeded with a significant number of life forms. In addition to the dog and pig, cattle of the Zebu strain, (*Bos indicus*), the water buffalo (*Bubalus bubalis*), and the elephant were domesticated, though there is some argument about the degree of domestication of the latter animal. These latter events are assigned to a slightly later time in India-Burma. The domestication of the water buffalo is complicated by variant forms, which may have been later domestications of related forms of the buffalo. The Zebu seems related to the open and drier plant ranges of central to northwest India, the water buffalo to the wet lowland littoral, and the elephant to the grass-jungle-forest ranges of the moist lowlands. The mithan now seems accepted as a domesticated form (*Bos frontalis*), but there remain wild bovines in southern and southeastern Asia, and variable amounts of breeding between wild and domesticated forms produces various hybrids, so that the discussion often becomes confused. As yet we know little of how the fowls were brought into the picture, but there were a number of them disciplined to handling by man in the oriental zone. The duck, the goose, the peacock, the pheasant, and the chicken, all were domesticated in this large region. Taming of certain other animals, perhaps constituting a first step in domestication, also is found here, but there is an uncertain line between the taming of individuals and domestication of a species line. The performing Himalayan bears, the monkeys, the apes, the mongooses, and questionably the handling of even the dangerous cobra come within this framework.

In the process of hunting animals for food, for leather, for sinew, or for ivory and bone, many animals must have been restricted to much smaller ranges than they occupied in their wild state within Recent time. The elephant once ranged in central China, but has not lived there wild within historic time. The true wild water buffalo is thought by some authorities to be totally extinct, though many have gone wild again, and related animals are still found in scattered remnant locations. We cannot at this time specify how significant taming and domestication of certain animals was to some people, as opposed to rejection of taming and domestication of the same animals by other people. It is likely that the variable interest of culture groups in certain animals significantly enters the question of distribution today. Though the elephant motif and the use of ivory in Chinese art is strong, the Chinese do not seem to care for the live animal. And the elephant in Borneo seems a matter of rather recent cultural introduction to the northwestern portion of the island.

Outside the Oriental region a number of significant domestications must be placed. There is evidence that the goat and the sheep came first out of the rougher hill country, the goat seemingly related to western central Asia and the sheep possibly to Afghanistan or near-by areas. Through a combination of domestication of, and the interbreeding by various wild sheep, a number of different types finally appeared. Such are the hairy highland sheep, the open-range soft-wool sheep, the fat-tailed sheep, and the fat-buttocked sheep, and necessarily a wide range of local environments must have been finally involved. The yak of modern Tibet seems to have originated in southern Siberia as a domesticated animal among northern peoples, with its restriction in Tibet coming fairly late. Our modern cattle *Bos taurus* is a late form, domestication having begun perhaps with *Bos namadicus* and *Bos brachycepheros* among Indo-European and proto-Tibetan peoples somewhere on open grassland ranges of central Asia. The domestication of early cattle may well have had much to do with the onset of the Neolithic phase of culture in that its overlay upon early crop growing brought the rapid rise of levels of culture in southwestern central Asia. The whole question of milking is involved here, along with the dairying complex. Young children often drink directly from goats and sheep among people keeping them, and the use of milk possibly began with the first goat and sheep peoples. Its later extension is both varied and complex, full of tabu and acceptance.

The origins of horse culture lie north of the great mountain ranges of central Asia. This involved several kinds of horses, several Turkish peoples, and portions of western and central Asia. The camel involves at least the two forms, single- and double-humped camels, a variety of peoples, and territory ranging from central to southwestern Asia. The donkey seems to relate to this same range of territory but is mixed up with the early history of half domestication of the onager in Southwest Asia or North Africa.

All of these Holarctic animals came slowly and in succession into the area of concern to this volume. Two approaches are involved: through the mountain wall of northwestern India and through the Kansu Corridor into North China. Each form has penetrated to the limit of its physiological ability, but none has been able to compete with the domestications of the Oriental zone in utility to man except on the drier and cooler margins.

All the Holarctic animals mentioned may have lived over such distributional ranges that they could have entered the Oriental zone in their wild states, had they chosen to do so. For all except the hardiest of the sheep and goats, and also the yak, this would have meant crossing the northwest mountain wall of India or approaching eastern Asia through the Gobi Desert. The three animals just mentioned are probably the only ones which naturally could have crossed the Tibetan highlands into the Oriental zone. There is evidence that some of the goats and sheep

did intergrade the Oriental region through northwest India and northwest China-Manchuria. It is unlikely that any other of the now-domesticated animals from the Holarctic zone did willingly migrate into the Oriental zone in their wild states. Each of them has been taken by man throughout the zone, but not one of the Holarctic forms is truly at home deep in the Oriental zone. Except on the drier, cooler margins, all downbreed rapidly, losing size, stamina, and utility. Thus the horse in Yunnan often is but half as large as the central Asian pony, and the sheep of the lower Indian peninsula are poor animals, both for meat and for wool. Of all the Holarctic domestications perhaps the goat is the best able to survive, in what today must be a selected strain which no longer could survive in its original homeland.

Conversely two of the Oriental zone domestications do not live easily far outside their own types of environments. The water buffalo does not do well either in cold climates or in totally dry ones. Away from the wet littoral he must be provided with bathing pools in which to cool himself frequently. The Zebu cattle do better than the water buffalo but they do not adapt well to regions with really cold winters. The current distributional limits for selected animals native to the Holarctic and Oriental life realms are cultural limits, in part, set by man rather than by the animals concerned (see Fig. 9.1).

ANIMAL ECONOMIES

In south and eastern Asia both domesticated and wild animals play significant roles in regional economy. Except where religious tabus against the taking of life have historically become effective, all levels of culture indulge in hunting wild animals, both for sport and for economic gain. This has ranged from the earlier, organized, great autumn hunts of the Mongols and Manchus, which combined military field maneuvers with sport and the securing of food, to the daily food hunting of primitive groups. The very abundance of wild animal and bird life in most parts of the realm is astonishing. Wild duck, partridge, or other game birds are often obtainable in markets almost all over China, and venison often is a preferred food in many areas. By the winter's end many a village in the lower Indus Valley possesses a large pile of duck feathers—testimony to the frequency of migrant wild duck in the seasonal food economy of the local villagers.

Different culture levels, of course, have their own techniques of hunting, vary in the animals or birds which are their objective, and also vary in their utilization of the proceeds of hunting. Many of the simpler peoples, using simple techniques, hunt small game and birds, eat animals that higher cultures no longer value, or use the products in ways long since discarded by higher cultures. The spear, blowgun, bow and arrow, the snare, pitfall, antique firearm, and modern rifle plus many other hunting techniques are used by one people or another. The proceeds of hunting among many groups form important additions to their material economy.

Except upon the inner Asian margins of the Orient pastoralism in the normal sense is missing from the Orient. In earlier times in northwest India and north China-Manchuria it was practiced by peoples who, as pastoralists, invaded these two margins of the Orient. Invaders successful in gaining a foothold in either margin always concluded by slowly giving up their pastoral economy for the more sedentary calling of agriculture, though they seldom completely gave up their attachment to animal economy. This carry-over of animal economy in northwest India and north China-Manchuria introduced the Holarctic domestications into the edges of the Orient. With the animals as such came significant additions to the cultures and economies of the Orient. The horse, camel, and donkey changed transport and supplied draft power in agriculture. They entered into military tactics, art motifs, and the field of clothing. Since many of the later invaders were not just simple pastoralists but were also crop cultivators, they were instrumental in introducing the plow and other agricultural tools. Perhaps in this way dairying was introduced to India, but the Chinese rejected dairying, for some reason not easily explained.

It is not yet clear just how far transport and draft agricultural application had been developed within the ancient Orient, using the Zebu and the water buffalo. The peculiar usage to which elephants can be put seem entirely native to the Orient, but they are not closely related to the economic usage of the other animals.

Gradually the Holarctic domestications became spread very widely throughout the Orient, within their physiologic limits, and today Holarctic cattle, Zebu cattle, the water buffalo, and the horse make up the population of large animals of such an area as Java or the Philippines. Slowly a distinct division of labor has come to be assigned to the several animals in many areas. In the Philippines today, for example, horses pull passenger carts, are ridden, and perform at race courses; both Zebu and Holarctic male cattle pull sleds and two-wheeled cargo carts, and cows serve a small dairy purpose; water buffalo chiefly are used to cultivate ricefields, but occasionally they pull sleds or carts, and sometimes stamp out grain on the threshing floors.

All the domesticated animals of both life zones are important sources of food supply to the many culture groups of the Orient. In early times there were no tabus against the use of any animal as food. The dog and the pig were eaten by many groups, but common use of the dog as food has been kept only by some of the simpler peoples who do not yet use the large animals as food sources. The use of the dog for food by the Chinese was common until recent centuries. Animals were bred particularly for food and fed on special diets, in which grain foods predominated. Beyond the food problem, almost every people in the Orient makes use of leather in clothing or equipment. A considerable amount of bone is utilized in the making of tools, charms, and curios. There are few tabus against the use of leather, sinew, bone, feathers, or shells. There are almost no tabus against the use of sheep wool, goat hair, yak wool, or camel hair. Both in the unprocessed forms of leather garments with the wool or hair still attached and in the finished forms of woven textiles, the products are widely used around the cooler edges of the Orient and penetrate considerable distances. There are, of course, regional patterns of significance in this use of animals.

In Manchuria and Korea neither the Zebu cattle nor the water buffalo do well, owing to the cold winter conditions and, therefore, are not significantly represented in the animal population. The pig, a more adaptable animal, is common in both areas. The Holarctic animals, cattle, sheep, goats, and horses, are relatively numerous in Manchuria and, both as meat and commercial products, play a significant role in regional economy. Cattle and horses perform most of the Manchurian local transport and draft labor in a somewhat interchangeable role. Cattle and pigs are the only numerous animals in Korea, cattle having to serve as all-purpose animals. Though cattle never have been present in adequate numbers in the modern era, the Koreans take good care of them and strongly appreciate their value. Japan perhaps makes less use of animals than any other portion of the Orient. The landforms of Japan do not favor animal husbandry, and the natural browse is poor. Cold winter climates keep out the animals from the Oriental life region, and the hot summers of central to southern Japan do not favor those of the Holarctic zone. Holarctic cattle and horses are the only numerous large animals. The Japanese never have learned how best to use any domestic animal. Fish has taken the place of meat, and the Chinese were not the people to teach the Japanese dairying. Cattle and horses today are fairly common for transport and draft purposes, but less than half the farm families of Japan have one of either animal. Pigs are only slowly becoming more common; chickens are widely scattered in small numbers. Since World War II the Japanese have been expanding both the dairying and beef-producing aspects of animal husbandry and, in the late 1960's, the use of milk and beef in the Japanese dietary began to expand rather markedly.

The Chinese everywhere eat all the animals that they can raise. In the north this means almost the whole range of domesticated animals, excepting the Zebu cattle, the water buffalo, and the elephant. In the northwest Chinese who have accepted Islam do not favor eating the pig. In Szechwan and western China generally the goat is more numerous, in relative terms, and supplies a considerable meat volume, plus a volume of skins. In South China the Holarctic cattle, goats, and sheep disappear, Zebu, water buffalo, and the pig becoming dominant. Although cattle, camels, horses, and water buffalo are used in transport and for draft purposes, there are not enough animals for those purposes. Chickens and ducks all over China are depended upon for food to a considerable extent. Statistically, the animal population per capita is relatively low and, therefore, the per capita consumption of meat is low. Were the pressures upon land for food crop growing less severe, however, the Chinese would use larger amounts of animal foods.

In India-Pakistan today it is only the Islamic and the pagan groups that make use of animal foods. This is a historical matter, however, for very early India had no tabus against any animal. The tabus against the killing of animal life have grown steadily and slowly, starting with the cow and the pig, until today strict Hindus will not kill domestic animals or even the dangerous wild forms of life, such as the tiger, the cobra, or other lesser pests. This has meant, among Hindus and in predominantly Hindu areas, that the hunting of wild game has died out and that animal economy has become modified. Although the very highest Hindu castes will not eat fish, the middle and lower levels of Hindu castes do not accept the tabu on fishery products. Tabus upon the use of milk products and upon eggs have not developed among Hindus, so that chickens are numerous almost everywhere, and the use of milk and butter (particularly in the melted form, as ghee) is common to all caste levels. There is a thriving dairying industry in India, but Indian use of milk products does not extend to the wide range of cheeses common to dairying elsewhere. Among Moslems there is only the tabu on the pig, with no other strictures operative today, so that in predominantly Islamic regions animal economy is well developed and comprehensive.

Neither have there developed tabus against the use of animals as power sources in India. Therefore, all possible animals are used in transport and as draft animals, to turn grinding mills, pump water, cultivate the fields, and do other miscellaneous chores. Whereas the tabus rest very strongly upon the upper castes of Hindus, and to an extent control animal economy for the whole Hindu population, the lower castes and outcastes are much less bound by these strictures. Lower-caste Hindus often seem to have no scruples about the raising of animals and fowls or about selling them to Moslems who perform the slaughtering and processing of meat products, hides and skins, and other by-products.

As the Indian tabus against killing developed, modification resulted in the animal population, both domestic and wild. There is an abundance of wild life in most parts of the country, the species varying with local environments, so that parts of India today remain paradises for the hunter and collector. India today is one of the chief exporters of wild animals, snakes, and birds. Monkeys, elephants, tigers, and a variety of birds are most in demand, the monkey export amounting to thousands of animals per year. As the pig lost favor as a food source, his lack of utility in other ways caused him to become unimportant in numbers, particularly since in more recent centuries he could not be sold to the Moslem. Sheep today are common everywhere except on the peninsular west coast and from Bengal eastward; goats are common almost all over India. The camel has a limited climatic range in India and is chiefly confined to the northwest. The few horses, mules, and donkeys are chiefly for riding or cart pulling in the northwest and in the central northern peninsula. Holarctic cattle, as separate breeds, are not now common but undoubtedly have historically interbred with the Zebu varieties fairly deeply into India. This mixed cattle population, with the rise of the tabu on killing cattle, has steadily increased until today in India-Pakistan the cattle population stands close to 200,000,000. The water buffalo no longer is restricted to moist areas only, but is to be found everywhere except in the most arid parts of the Indian subcontinent, and today reaches a total of about 50,000,000 animals.

With the rise of tabus on the killing of animals, control over domestic livestock has lessened in respect to their personal freedom and their breeding. Therefore, most of the domestic animal population today is relatively low grade. Certain local regions have used care in breeding cattle or water buffalo to give regional inequality to the value of the stock. Gujarat, the Indian section of the

Punjab, and Mysore have good breeds of cattle, both for draft and for milking purposes. Today there are perhaps fifty regional varieties of cattle, some of which are of high quality for draft purposes, food purposes, or dairy use. Around some of the large urban centers modern breeding of water buffalo for dairy stock has reached a fairly high plane. In the modern dairy industry water buffalo form the best dairy stock, producing more milk and higher ratios of butterfat than do zebu cattle, but yields remain low in comparison to those of occidental dairying, averaging 400-500 pounds of milk products per animal per year. The per capita consumption cannot be effectively expressed for either meat or dairy products, because of regional and religious differences, but the Indian use of milk cannot be over six ounces per person per day. Meat consumption is very low, and, although the milk products consumption total also is low as compared with the United States, the total is higher than that of any other oriental country.

Southern Asian animal economy is more restricted than that of north China or northeast India. Many of the Holarctic animals are not adaptable to the region climatically, nor do they do well upon the browse available. Horses, sheep, and goats are present only in small numbers and are relatively modern in origin. On the drier Lesser Sunda Islands horses do fairly well, and Flores is a local horse-breeding center. Zebu cattle are found in considerable numbers, but even they are not numerous east of Celebes, the scarcity being largely a historical matter of non-introduction and non-familiarity on the part of local populations. The water buffalo becomes the most important animal in local economy in the southeastern mainland countries and in the western Indies and Philippines, but it becomes very scarce in the middle Indies and is rare in New Guinea and related islands. This again is a historical matter rather than an environmental one.

The pig comes back into its own in these lands and in many areas is the only useful domestic animal familiar to many of the simpler population. The Islamic tabu on the pig is operative to some degree in Malaysia and western Indonesia but is less effective than it is in India or the Near East. The Buddhist religious practices in southeastern Asia continue to retain in nominal form the India-derived tabu against the killing of animals, but nowhere in Southeast Asia is the tabu as strong as in India. In regions such as the Philippines where the Spanish and Americans have tried to increase the population and range of domestic animals, most of the common ones are to be found. This is true of Sumatra and Java also, but not of the eastern Indies. The chicken, however, and the duck, to a lesser extent, are widely distributed and steadily depended upon. Until man establishes the proper living conditions and sources of animal foods, the domestic animal population of southeastern Asia and the island zone will remain relatively low, the role in economy will be small, and the material economy will be restricted as compared to that in most other parts of the world. Only the water buffalo, the pig, and the chicken seem well able to inhabit this area in large numbers, but since it is their home environment they do well in the matter of survival.

In summary it must be pointed out that, whereas the use of domestic animals for draft and transport purposes is fairly well developed in most parts of the Orient, the use of both domestic and wild animals in food economy adds far less to the dietary of most oriental peoples than is true in the Occident. The average consumption of meat in China probably does not exceed 30 pounds per person per year from all sources, excluding fish products, against the figure of close to 160 pounds in the United States. The figure for Pakistan is probably comparable among the Moslems, but well below that total among all the peoples of India. Probably the Filipinos eat as much meat as any other oriental people, but even here the figure is little over 30 pounds per person per year. The use of eggs from several types of fowls is fairly high in parts of China and in the Philippines, but elsewhere it probably is below that of much of the Occident today.

The use of dairy products is most highly developed among the Hindu peoples of India, and the annual total of dairy products compares with that of the United States. The per capita consumption, however, is considerably lower than that of the United States by virtue of greater division among a far larger number of consumers. Elsewhere in the Orient the per capita consumption of dairy products is very low indeed. Neither the meat consumption nor the use of eggs and dairy products will be raised very high in the near future, owing to the widespread tabus and the already existent severe pressure of men upon the land. A general exception to these remarks, of course, is involved with respect to the pastoral peoples of the inner Asian frontiers of the Orient.

THE GEOGRAPHY OF AQUATIC LIFE

The salt and fresh water fringing the southern and eastern Asian coasts, both at sea and on land contain a tremendous variety of aquatic life. The water territory probably possesses the richest fishery resource in the world, both as to species and to economically useful volume. The value of the salt waters of northeastern Asia is now recognized, since modern Japanese fishery yields are so heavy, but the resource of southern Asia is still questioned because a neat body of statistics to demonstrate it is lacking. It has been standard practice to speak of small fish populations in tropical waters, but in the Orient, at least, we believe this to be a fictional conclusion unsupported by fact.

Over half the world's marine fish are shore fish, and these are the important food fish. Their distribution and numbers depend partly upon the volume of food available to them and partly upon their preference for certain aquatic environments. The food volume depends upon the nutritive value of the waters, the light available, and the temperature conditions of the waters. Although water temperatures that are too high operate to decrease the water storage of food supply, shallow waters are more productive of food than are deep waters, and the light factor in low latitudes is more productive of food than in high latitudes. The aquatic environments of southeastern Asia include a great deal of shallow, brackish to fresh-water swamp and marsh lands that form an inviting and productive home to many kinds of fish. The shallow, warm shore waters of southeastern Asia present one set of conditions making for large fish populations; the shallow, cool waters of northeastern Asia present another set of conditions also making for large fish populations of different species. In southern waters there are over 2,000 species of fish, against over 1,000 species in the waters off Japan. Other forms of aquatic life are far more numerous in southern than northern waters. Statistically we cannot produce figures from southern waters as to numbers of fish, but we believe the populations to be large, to be important in past economies, and to be potentially significant to future economies.

A general uniformity in aquatic life of fresh waters, coastal, and near-coastal waters, from the Arabian Sea around to the South China Sea, suggests a single major tropical zone of aquatic life, usually termed the Indo-West Pacific region. The salt-water margins of this great region taper off to the Hawaiian Islands. This Indo-Pacific area contains more families and genera of fish, crustaceans, and mollusks than are found elsewhere. In part this wealth of forms relates to the common history of drainage of the old Sundaland shelf, long a part of the continent of Asia.

Northern salt waters, such as the Sea of Japan and the Sea of Okhotsk, possess a uniformity of their own, to suggest a second zone, which often includes the whole North Pacific region. The waters of the eastern Indies and Australia show a fair degree of uniformity that separates them into a third regional unit, the Australian region. Factors in this unit are the scarcity of fresh-water aquatic forms to be found east of Wallace's Line and the localization of many life forms in and around the eastern Indies.

Over and above these regional patterns of aquatic life, of course, are some features common to all tropical salt waters of the earth. Coral growth is common everywhere in southern Asia, under the right conditions, and extends as far north as Taiwan and the southern Ryukyu Islands. With corals go certain fish, crabs, and other minor life forms. Related species of many forms, such as the herrings, the oysters, and the mackerels, seem to inhabit all three zones. Other forms, such as the giant crabs of far northern waters, or the giant mollusks of Indian Ocean waters, seem to inhabit a single zone only. Environmental conditions control localized distributions within any one zone. Although oysters live in all three zones, they are not to be found everywhere, owing to locally unsuitable environments, and pearl oysters are to be found only in a few scattered environments of particularly suitable nature. Some forms, such as the tunas, some of the sharks, and some of the sardines, are pelagic, migratory rovers, and their distributions and ecologies are dependent upon oceanic conditions rather than upon conditions of the coastal shelves. The catfishes are a very old group with southern origins and areal relations. The fresh-water carps and carp-like fishes are younger and, in origin, are related to China. Although the carps now are distributed to the edges of Africa and into

western Indonesia, they do not reach Australia, and few of the catfishes are to be found in Australia.

In respect both to marine and fresh-water life forms this triple zoning results from basic differences in geographic environments. Northern waters are cool to cold and produce and store large amounts of food materials for all forms of aquatic life. Here are stimulated distinctive rhythms of reproduction, long life cycles, long-range migration patterns, and particular ecologic conditions that affect the aquatic populations. Japanese waters, particularly, undergo variations in temperature from year to year as the major Asian warm and cold currents fluctuate in volume and in relative location. Many species of fish are extremely sensitive to temperature ranges and, in some years, simply do not appear in Japanese waters.

Southern waters also possess environmental continuity, but of a different sort. The close connections of the western Indies with the mainland of southern and southeastern Asia, and the continuity of coastal waters throughout this large region, contribute to a common history of aquatic life. Here life cycles are often shorter, and reproductive patterns are often related to estuarine conditions. Different but even more voluminous patterns of food production support more aquatic life than can be supported by northern waters. Migration habits seem of shorter range, and quite different sets of ecologic relations exist among far more species. When rivers flood the flat lowlands, inland penetration of many kinds of aquatic life takes place. Spawning often occurs away from stream channels, and the natural planting of fish covers wide areas, which contain ample food supplies. Many of the fish species native to this region possess auxiliary breathing equipment that enables them to live under poor water conditions. Some species can even estivate in mud at the bottom of shallow ponds and drying flood surfaces.

The separation of the eastern Indies and Australia is a matter of geologic history, and voluminous biologic and botanical research testifies to the relative completeness of the separation. East and south of this zone of separation occurs another set of coastal marine and fresh-water environments, with their own patterns of reproduction, migration, life rhythms, and regional ecologies.

Shifts of sea level consequent upon glaciation, deglaciation, and mountain building have markedly altered the areas of land and of coastal seas during the Pleistocene geologic time. These changes have rearranged the fresh-water river systems, coastal seas, and ocean currents of most parts of southern and eastern Asia. Changes in marine climate and physical changes in aquatic environments have altered species distributions and ecologic conditions within local regions. The paleontologic and archaeologic record clearly indicates that early Asian man in any one area had available slightly different life forms from those that are present in the same waters today.

Such changes produced in fresh-water and marine environments caused shifts, from time to time, in the dividing lines between life regions, but it seems likely that the triple division is one of long standing. Wallace's Line was first thought to be a definite boundary, whereas today the separation between Asian and Australian life regions is recognized to be transitional. This separation is, of course, far more noticeable in fresh-water life forms than it is in those of salt water. No such demarcation can be placed upon the map to distinguish between the northern and southern regions, either fresh or marine. At sea Taiwan lies close to a possible zone of division, and in fresh water the dividing zone seems to lie close to the drainage divide that separates China from Vietnam. Naturally, within the major regions a number of secondary regional distinctions doubtless

exist, but our knowledge does not permit a full elaboration of these detailed patterns.

THE PRACTICE OF FISHING

Everywhere around these coasts man has long used marine products, both for food and for other purposes. Early man probably considered fish merely as aquatic animals requiring only a specific application of general hunting techniques. His methods of exploiting marine products, and his yields, have increased in variety with the passage of time. As the most recent deglaciation progressed, raising sea level and flooding large areas of lowlands throughout the world, the numbers of close-in shore fish increased markedly in waters accessible to man. This permitted an increase in fishing as an economic activity, and it is in this relatively recent period that fishing tools and techniques, and dependence upon aquatic food, became really important. No part of the world was more benefited in this respect than southeastern Asia, and no people developed further the practice of fishing than did those peoples around the littoral of the present southeastern Asia. Fresh water has long been well utilized everywhere in the Orient. Fishing of shore waters is old and often is well developed, though today yields could be greatly increased by improved equipment and a better knowledge of marine resources. Pelagic fishing seldom has been highly developed in oriental waters, and only the Japanese have efficiently exploited this zone of marine resources. Elsewhere fishermen have many ingenious pelagic fishing methods which enable them to catch large fish, but their simple resources do not permit a highly productive fishery yield. Deep-sea fishing has been but scantily practiced in the Orient, and again only the Japanese do much of it. Even Japanese pelagic and deep-sea fishing is quite recent in appearance.

Perhaps earliest and easiest of fishing methods was the beachcomber technique of the strand line, most productive on those rocky shores marked by a distinct tidal range. Here shellfish, crustaceans, seaweeds, and small fish can be acquired for food, and various other usable products can be picked up. This can be a simple system of gathering, and, since it can be repeated with every tidal cycle, it has a permanent aspect that does not require great mobility. At an early date it may even have inhibited progress by being too amply productive of food supplies— simple food problems here were too easily solved.

Gradually man has supplemented the natural productiveness of the strand line, however, by walling off small catchment ponds or corrals and by building a variety of fish traps. The shores of many parts of the Orient are lined by these devices, particularly those flat shores containing no natural barricades and those lacking marked tidal ranges. Today in Japan, particularly, one can see the coastal folk follow each ebb tide, gathering in the harvest in what must be an age-old technique. And southeastern Asia, particularly Malaysia, the Philippines, and western Indonesia, shows a high density of coastal fish traps of many sorts. They often are ingeniously built, artistically patterned, and possess considerable regional specialization in design. These marine traps also include small hand-set underwater traps of a number of types. Traps in general are used for many kinds of fish, and also for crabs, lobsters, prawns, and other crustaceans.

A second major group of procedures employed by coastal fishermen involves spears, hooks, and nets. From the water's edge these tools have but limited application, however, and some device for getting man out beyond wading depth was a necessary early complement. This need led to a great variety of floats, rafts, and boats. Each of these separate subgroups of fishing tools has considerable variety, for each involves an ancient technique, long practiced and well developed in many areas.

Spearing of fish is an old and primitive technique that still is widely used in the Orient, from the Laccadive Islands to New Guinea to Japan. It is chiefly a remnant technique today, used for subsistence fishing mostly, but also indulged in as a recreational activity. Variants of it involve torches and night fishing, goggles and underwater work, floats, harpoons and, on the southern west coast of India, even the blowgun. Hook-and-line fishing is employed in a wide variety of ways, but today it is chiefly significant for boat fishing in shore and pelagic waters. One sees rod-and-line fishermen in almost all parts of the Orient, working with equipment so simple as to horrify an expert American dry-fly caster.

Small circular hand-casting nets are used in every part of the Orient, with regional specialization in materials, form, and method of use, depending on water depth, the product sought, and the skill of the populace. Fish, shrimp, prawns, and lobsters are obtained by means of nets. Most parts of the Orient have developed large and more complex types of nets, used with boats, catamarans, or rafts. Today many kinds of nets are used, requiring from one to a dozen boats and crews of from two to thirty men. Specialization in the use of a given type of net and concentration upon particular kinds of fish are frequent, and varied systems of division of labor, sharing of the catch, and marketing have developed. In detail these often depend on local fishing conditions, but they are also related to social systems and to factors in the over-all economy of a local region.

Not all peoples are equally good net fishermen. The southern west coast of India, the Bengal delta lands, West Malaysia, the north coast of Java, the Philippines, the northern Kwangtung-Fukien coast of China, the Shantung Peninsula of China, the southwestern coast of Korea, and the Inland Sea coasts of Japan are sections in which fishing skills and equipment are notable today and the annual catch of fish is large.

Trawling, a modern, advanced system of net-and-line fishing, today is found in all parts of the Orient, but the Japanese are the only fishermen to make effective use of it so far, though in the Philippines trawling is beginning to be significant, and there are small starts elsewhere. Since 1900 the Japanese have progressively spread their range of power-boat fishing from their own waters northward into the North Pacific, southward through the South China Sea, and out into the open South Pacific. Out of almost every major port elsewhere in the Orient move a few modern power boats to fish near-by shore waters, but no country in the Orient other than Japan has really developed modern scientific and powered fishing methods.

It is in estuarine and fresh-water zones that some of the most distinctive fishing methods appear. The Orient undoubtedly presents the richest complex of estuarine and fresh-water fishing methods of any part of the world. The lowland river valleys of southeastern Asia present unusual conditions, both as to physical environment and as to types of fish. Part of this peculiarity pertains to the variety of plant life that surrounds these lowlands. Early man, working with a wealth of plants, searching for textile fibers and edible products, long ago discovered that many plants contain strong poisons. In these procedures he discovered that these poisons temporarily stupefied fish and caused them to float to the water surface where they were easily caught. The process works less well in salt water than in brackish or fresh water. It gradually became a common method of fishing among peoples in river valleys who could not apply the beachcomber techniques of the tidal strand line. Moist southern India to Borneo and Sumatra probably were the original center of this technique in the Old World, but it spread west to the Red Sea and north to Japan. It still is common in the more moist parts of southeastern Asia where the poisons are available, but it is decreasing in favor of better methods developed at later dates. A related modern technique is the use of explosives, but this is discouraged as a destructive process that kills fish of all ages, many of whom are too small for use.

Bengal perhaps is the center around which are clustered more varieties of catching fish with traps than in any other part of the world. The Bengali has devised a trap for every possible type of fish and every circumstance of water from the shallowest of ricefield covers to the deep waters of the Ganges estuary. From India out into Indonesia runs this multiple pattern of fresh-water fish traps, slowly decreasing in number. The Bengali is serious about his fishing as an aid to his material economy, but he also loves to fish for the fun of fishing, perhaps more so than any other oriental people. His lines, hooks, and rods may be ever so simple, but it is in finesse of the multiple compounds used as bait that he discloses his true relationship to Izaak Walton.

Throughout southern Asia, when the water in tanks, ponds, and isolated channels becomes low it is common to hold fish drives. Women and children gather about a spot where the drive is to end, while a crew of men goes into the shallow water at a distance, wading and thrashing about, but gradually working toward the selected spot. Small nets, turbans, sarongs, baskets, and other implements come into play when a volume of fish have been cornered, everyone getting into the water in a scramble to scoop up the fish before they can disperse.

When the tanks, ponds, and old river channels sometimes dry out so that there is only mud in the bottom, it is common to dig fish out of the mud with spades and similar tools. Many of the species of the Oriental life region, as mentioned previously, estivate in the mud at the bottoms of ponds, where they can survive a considerable dry spell.

China shows less multiplicity of tools and techniques for the catching of fresh-water fish than does Bengal, though the devices are both numerous and ingenious. One of the most common and widespread methods is the counterbalanced dip net, rigged on bamboo poles and mounted either on a medium-sized fishing boat or on a river bank.

Allied to the nets, lines, and traps that catch fish are the boats, catamarans, and floats that often assist in the operation either in fresh or salt water. It cannot be stated flatly that the evolution of boats is tied to fishing, and yet a great many of the regional styles of boats, building methods, and sailing techniques certainly have long related to the practice of fishing. There appear to be at least five separate boat-building complexes in the orient, all amenable to influence by the fishermen. The west coast of India, with coasts of Arabia, seem to share one tradition, and the end of Peninsular India and Ceylon share another. There is the inland-waterway, dug-out canoe tradition, originating in the lowlands of southeastern Asia, but now distributed from south India to the Philippines and into Oceania. Fourth is the complex tradition of the outrigger canoe, for sea-going purposes, now scattered from Madagascar to Hawaii, touching Ceylon, Malaysia, the Philippines, and Indonesia. Indonesia now is the center of the outrigger techniques, but this is a secondary development. It is not certain whether the Indonesian boat-building tradition is a separate one, or one derived from India. In eastern waters there is the separate North China junk tradition with its fresh- and salt-water variants. This Chinese tradition may have derived in part from Korean boat builders, but it spread to Japan and southward along the coast, recently af-

fecting local boat styles as far south as Singapore. The inland water boats of China show more variety in design than do those of any other part of the world.

Behind all these, possibly, are the still older reed, raft-like boats often termed balsas from the Spanish-American name. There are suggestions of carryover of this ancient tradition into later ones, as in the boat of the Tenasserim sea gypsy, which possesses a wooden keel and reed-built sides. There well may be other and still older boating complexes in the pre-history of the Orient that enabled man to learn marine fishing and helped to execute early island hopping in intervals of high sea levels which divided southeastern Asia.

Behind the individual boat-building techniques also is the catamaran, still used in south Indian waters. This involves several shaped logs lashed together into a wet, boat-like sea-going raft. It is used by many groups for several purposes in shore waters, and certainly was very widely dispersed in earlier time. Today the catamaran usually is worked in pairs of two, lashed together and equipped with a lateen sail.

More directly related to fishing practices are the various kinds of floats used by fishermen. These begin with the simple block of wood used by the lower Ganges River fisherman who, equipped with a small net and a creel, floats downstream with the current, scooping up fish as he goes. He may carry his block back upstream to repeat his operation. They include the large pottery jars upon which the Indus River fishermen squat while handling a net, and the raft-like assemblage of pottery jars used in large Bengal tanks and ponds. They also include the large wooden tubs used by the canal and pond fishermen of China and other ingenious devices used in several local areas.

In any one area undoubtedly a succession of fishing methods has been applied by successive generations, but there is little comparative data on the subject. In the Philippines, for example, it is thought that the spear, bow and arrow, and poisons are among the oldest of fishing methods. Fish corrals or stone dams across beach embayments and tidal inlets were a later method, in turn followed by various types of traps. Last to come into use were the variety of hand nets and the larger nets involving the use of boats in the pre-Spanish period. Pond culture is also pre-Spanish. Recent techniques are trawling and dynamiting. The efficiency of fishing practice varies with the diversity of methods in use in any one region.

Fishing practice in the Orient has one other aspect, that of pisciculture. By this is meant the planting of spawn or fingerlings in controlled waters and the later harvesting of fish and other aquatic products. The raising of carp and carp-like fishes began in South China possibly before 1000 B.C., and variants of old Chinese practices have spread throughout the Orient. In most of the areas that grow wet rice, fish are introduced into ricefields. For the most part Chinese fish-farming practices today are those of hundreds of years ago, and the best methods now used are relatively recent developments in newer areas, though South China productive yields per acre still are the highest in the world.

In China small controlled lakes, canals, and ponds all are used for raising fish. Several kinds of fish are often raised in the same waters, their different diets and feeding habits making for greater efficiency. An estimated 400,000 acres in central and south China are devoted to such farming. In addition to half a dozen kinds of fish, a variety of mollusks and crustaceans are produced in these same waters.

Javanese fish farming has reached a rather mature status. Permanent ponds are laid out, regular feedings and controls over water movement, breeding, and marketing turn this kind of fishing into a developed type of land use. As coastal ponds gradually become desalted they are turned into ricefields, and new fish ponds are built on the seaward margin. For these coastal fish farms spawn of the bandeng, *Chanos chanos*, are taken in shallow coastal waters and placed in controlled ponds. The bandeng, a vegetarian fish well adapted to pond culture, weighs from 3 to 10 pounds when marketed. In the interior hill country fish farms the gurami is grown, an Osphromenidae, which is native to the area from Burma to Borneo. This fish is an air breather, having an air chamber just above the gill cavity, so that large numbers of gurami can be grown in restricted waters. Elsewhere in Indonesia fish farming is not so well developed as in Java but today is spreading gradually along many coastal strips, and the acreage of fish farms is well over 300,000 acres for Indonesia. Thailand and Vietnam have expanding patterns of fish farming, and West Malaysia is just beginning the practice though in none of the three is there a large development as yet. The Philippines in 1968 had 340,000 acres in salt-water fish ponds, with steady annual additions to the area and a potential of about 1,200,000 acres suitable for fish farming. The chief fish raised is the same salt-water fish used in Java, *Chanos chanos,* here called bangos.

The Koreans have done a certain amount of fish farming, though not so much as the landscape of the west coast would permit. Japan has a small but significant variety of water farming, producing the widest range of products of any oriental country. Pond raising of carp began only about 1800, and planting of fish in ricefields began to be extensive only about 1850. Currently about 30,000 acres of ponds and reservoirs are used for raising fish of several types. A variety of seaweeds are grown in coastal ponds, and a significant pearl industry along the central east coast of Honshu depends upon culture methods that amount to farming.

Fishing, in the larger sense, also seeks such other aquatic products as shells, pearls, coral, seaweed, whales, turtle eggs, shark fins, and a variety of minor products. India is probably the area with the largest interest in shell, though the southern waters of the Philippine Archipelago produce a significant shell volume. From Kathiawar around to Madras a shallow-water mollusk, *Turbinella pyrum Linn,* is gathered at low tide for a variety of uses. Large specimens of the shell termed conch are sacred religious items in Hindu India, but the shell has a variety of secular uses also in the field of jewelry and personal adornment. This fishery, begun long before the Christian era, is gradually losing its importance today. Various types of mollusks have shells that have long interested man; they range from marine green snails and those producing mother of pearl to that used for windowpane making in the Philippines and the wide variety of cowry shells used for decoration and as a medium of exchange in earlier periods. Pearl diving is an old fishing pattern in the Indian Ocean, which well could be the region in which the pearl became more important than the oyster in fishery work. The Gulf of Mannar, between Ceylon and India, is one of the oldest pearl fishing banks. Local shifts in area and annual irregularity of production are marked in these waters, and may be typical of most pearl oyster banks in the Orient. Along the west coast of India-Pakistan good pearling banks are found only near Karachi in the northwest. The Tenasserim coast of Burma, south of Mergui, is a minor source of pearls. Some pearls come from the Sulu Archipelago, which has a very old record of production. Some of the shore waters of Borneo yielded seed pearls to the Japanese in the 1930's. Japan also has old pearling waters. The modern Japanese production of cultured pearls is the first well-known effort to increase the yield of this natural fishery. Elsewhere in the Orient in modern times it has been tried in a small but never successful manner.

Never an important phase of fisheries has been the gathering of, and diving for, coral around a number of islands in the southwestern Pacific. Black coral comes out of the Sulu Archipelago, and other types of coral are sought in other areas. Similarly seaweed is sought in a minor way in many parts of the Orient. Japan is the only region in which seaweed harvesting has become at all significant, supplementing the total Japanese food supply, though in many parts of the Orient a few people go after selected seaweeds. Whaling, as a purposeful part of fisheries, seems to have been practiced only in the northern Orient, where the aboriginal Ainu of the Japanese islands did some whale hunting with poisoned harpoons. The Japanese long have been whalers, having learned from the Ainu, and the attention paid to this form of fishery has increased during modern times, as the Japanese have developed and copied some of the more efficient whaling methods.

Turtle egg harvesting, an applied hunting-fishing pattern, is widely practiced in western Indonesia, with Borneo as a center. Shark fishing, earlier for fins and a few choice bits, is an old fishery wherever peoples have been in touch with the Chinese, and today the demand for fish liver oil has enlarged shark fishing. Edible bird's nests, the mucin-like product of the sea swiftlet collected around several rocky coasts of southeastern Asia, are not fishery products as such, but primarily are gathered by fishermen as a side-line activity. Various minor phases of the fishery industries are locally practiced in several parts of the Orient.

ORIENTAL FISHING ECONOMIES

The approximately 3,500,000 full-time fishermen in the Orient use in the vicinity of 1,000,000 boats, plus an uncounted volume of fishing equipment, and produce in the vicinity of 10,000,000 tons of edible aquatic products per year. Many millions more are part-time fishermen, but their catch cannot be tabulated. The total product ranges from fish little larger than minnows to huge fish eight feet long, from little shrimp to big whales, from turtle eggs to edible mollusks and edible seaweeds. This volume of products forms a most important secondary food pattern in the dietary of the Orient. Since the consumption of meat and other proteins is extremely low in many parts of the realm, the per capita consumption of fish products is relatively more important than in many other parts of the world.

The Japanese probably eat more aquatic products than any other oriental people, with an annual figure of over 100 pounds per person, against a figure of about 8 pounds for the United States. Probably second stand the Filipinos, who consume about 40 pounds per person per year, including the fish imported from abroad. West Malaysian consumption of fish per year is just under 40 pounds per capita. Effective data for other oriental countries are not available, but some suggestions may be made. Korean fish consumption perhaps is close to 12 pounds per capita per year, Chinese use about 8 pounds per person per year, and Vietnam uses perhaps 15 pounds per person per year. The figure for Thailand is somewhat higher, perhaps 25 pounds per person per year, the annual per capita figure for Indonesia may stand at about 12 pounds, the Burmese figure is not more than 7 pounds, and India stands at the bottom with an annual per capita figure of about 4 pounds per year.

These simple averages, of course, do not adequately express the role of aquatic products in the whole economy or in the dietary customs of the several countries. Almost all coastal people today have fish products available to them, but the peoples in the interior portions of many countries have no such opportunity, owing to the absence of fresh-water aquatic products and to inade-

quate transport facilities for marine products. All parts of Japan can procure adequate volumes of fish products in one form or another, whereas in far western China fish products in any form are rare and so high priced that only a few well-to-do people may consume them often. Even between the coasts of the larger Philippine Islands and the island interiors fish consumption drops from perhaps 125 pounds of fresh sea food per capita per year to 15 pounds of cured or tinned fish per year. In both western China and the Philippine Islands interiors this modern scarcity of local aquatic products is in part a matter of exhaustion of local resources almost to extinction, in part a lack of conditions in the natural environment for replenishment of aquatic resources, and in part a lack of transport and trade facilities.

In contrast to this scarcity of aquatic products in western China or interior Mindanao is the situation of Thailand, lowland Laos, southern South Vietnam, and central China, in which great rivers with open courses provide easy access far inland for many forms of aquatic life. The fresh-water fisheries of the upper Mekong River are of economic significance to local Thai and Vietnam populations, and the fisheries of Hupei and Hunan play a considerable role in the food economies of those two Chinese provinces. The fisheries of the Tonle Sap of Cambodia produce a huge and widely consumed volume of produce. The widespread distribution of overflow river channels, reservoirs, and ponds throughout the more moist parts of India is a factor in the widespread local distribution of aquatic products to a large number of people, even though the total supply of fish products in interior India today is not great enough to permit a large per capita consumption.

The coastlines and large river banks of the whole of the Orient total a tremendous mileage, in the vicinity of 60,000 miles, serving to place a large share of the population fairly close to some water body productive of useful aquatic life. The concept "useful" has a far wider application throughout most of the Orient than in the United States, owing to the severe pressure of man upon the environment. Around coasts, along river banks, in areas of seasonal and permanent water bodies, and even throughout the rice landscape of the more moist parts of the Orient live millions of people of many culture levels, primarily employed with agriculture or other callings who augment their food supplies when they can by using some of the hundreds of tools for obtaining aquatic products. No statistical data indicate accurately either this total population or the value of their product.

In the northern portion of the Orient the problems of handling aquatic products are relatively simple much of the year, as temperature conditions are not such as to make them spoil rapidly. In Japan, of course, where conditions are relatively good, the best facilities have been developed for long-term handling of fish products, namely the canning industries. Elsewhere throughout the Orient it is only in purely local situations or in the big cities that much of the aquatic products can be delivered to the consumer in the fresh state. In local situations in which the fisherman or his neighbors often are the chief consumers most fish products can be used fresh, since a time interval of only a few hours normally elapses between the catching and the consuming. Around the big city fish markets served by power boats, and with refrigeration available, a large volume of fish is delivered to urban consumers as fresh products. In southern waters producing a number of fish with auxiliary breathing apparatus the problem of keeping fish alive is not difficult, and so here, also, fresh fish delivery is actually fairly extensive at considerable distances from sources of the catch. It would take elaborate refrigeration and transport equipment to provide fresh fish products to a large share of consumers of the Orient.

A large share of the fish consumed in the whole southern half of the Orient must be preserved in some manner. Salting and sun drying are the commonest techniques, with local variations, and smoking is often practiced in many areas. The smaller fish may be strung on reeds and sticks, as on the Tenasserim coast of Burma, or most fish may be salted and packed in baskets as in West Malaysia. Many of the fish caught off the coasts of China do not can well and are normally salt-cured. Different kinds of aquatic products are handled in different ways. The sea slugs known as bêche-de-mer, produced along the west coast of Borneo, and the shark fins widely produced, are usually sun-dried but not salted for export to southern China. The native peoples of Burma and Thailand usually mix small fish, shrimp, and prawns together and prepare them as fish paste, whereas the Chinese fishermen in these waters boil the shrimp and prawns and then dry them for export sale. Indian fishermen normally dry and salt the surplus that cannot be disposed of as fresh fish, and the Indians do not use much fish paste. From Burma and Ceylon around to the Philippines and well out into Indonesia, on the other hand, partly fermented and spiced fish paste, made from many different aquatic products, is an extremely common method of preservation for the surplus catch. Particularly the Burmese, Thai, Vietnamese, Javanese, and the Cambodians are partial to the somewhat odorous fish paste as a part of their daily menu.

Trade in fish products within the various portions of eastern and southern Asia is fairly considerable. Java no longer provides her own supply and imports fish pastes and cured fish from Vietnam, Thailand, and various islands of the outer Indies. Borneo is an exporter of several types of aquatic products, ranging from salt-cured fish, pearl shell, and agar-agar to bêche-de-mer, shark fins, turtle eggs, and edible bird nests, many of the exports going to China. Indian fishing ports export local specialty products to West Malaysia to be consumed by Indian plantation labor. A large volume of fish passing through Singapore moves in many directions within the oriental trade realm. Practically every country lists a variety of aquatic products both in its imports and exports, though for Indonesia, the Philippines, and China the imports greatly outweigh the exports. Korea, throughout the period of Japanese control, contributed a large volume of sea produce to Japan, and aquatic products have been one of the large Japanese exports for decades.

In most parts of the Orient fishing is properly termed subsistence fishing. Much of this is carried on by full-time fishermen who barter small surpluses for their other economic needs, but much of it is spare-time or slack-season endeavor by family members not otherwise employed. Around the major cities and seaports in all parts of the Orient the fishery industry has become something of a commercial activity. In southeastern Asia and western Indonesia there is considerable small-scale commercial fishing, in which the Chinese are important, either as fishermen directly, as processors of surplus, or as wholesalers and traders. Prior to World War II Japanese commercial fishermen, with power boats, improved equipment, and even small canneries had spread throughout much of southeastern Asia. Undoubtedly such fish canning could be made to pay its own way as an economic development in most areas.

In some areas shell gathering and related phases of the fishery industry are full-time occupations, but many of these also are auxiliary occupations. The pearl diving of the Gulf of Mannar off southern India is a short-season auxiliary activity that brings participants from a rather wide area. Rice-field fishing is strictly seasonal, as are many of the special kinds of fishing, such as drives, mud digging, and pool fishing that go on during the dry seasons. The fishermen of the east coast of West Malaysia do almost no fishing from November to March, during the height of the winter monsoon storm conditions along this rough coast; the fishermen of the central west coast of India do no boat fishing in shore waters between June and late September. In Ceylon professional fishermen shift from the south and west coasts during the summer monsoon to the north and east coasts, shifting back again during the winter monsoon. In the far north Japanese and Russian salmon operations are confined to the short season when the fish migrate to spawning grounds.

In contrast to the seasonality of many direct fisheries is the regularity of some of the coastal fishing by large marine traps on quiet shores and that of controlled-pond fish culture where it has become maturely developed. Many of the estuarine and fresh-water fisheries, and those of protected coastal bays, also continue the year around. Power-boat fishing around urban centers has developed a year-round pattern to accommodate its modern commercial pattern. Pond culture in China, Thailand, Java, and the Philippines now supplies an appreciable share of local markets. That of the Philippines, for example, produced in 1963 about 146,000,000 pounds of fish, approximately fourteen per cent of the total island production. South China pond culture locally produces up to 4,000 pounds of fish per acre on a regular cycle of annual harvesting.

The occupation of fishing, for the full-time professional fishermen of the Orient, with their simple equipment, basic techniques, and limited markets does not produce a high level of living. The failure of fish to appear in regular waters, the occasional bad weather, the loss of boats, nets, traps, or other equipment during storms or accidents, the occasional glut of fish that overwhelms a market pattern unprepared to cope with large surpluses, and the other random difficulties that beset the small fisherman without capital funds, all make for fairly small returns and many financial hazards during the year. Financial returns range from $50 to $300 per fisherman per year for a large number of the full-time fishermen. A part-time fisherman may merely add fish for a few meals during the year.

One remaining item of significance is the acceptance of edible aquatic products as food by the peoples of the Orient. Religious scruples of the higher sects of Buddhists and Hindus prohibit any but a vegetarian diet, thus ruling out all fish and related aquatic foods. A fair generalization may be that over eighty per cent of all Indians may freely consume fish and related food products. In Ceylon fish curing has probably been the second most important economic activity for centuries and practically all classes of native Singhalese and more recent immigrants consume fish. Though Burmese priests technically decry fishing, all ranks of Burmese eat fishery products. The limits upon fish consumption, therefore, are less those of religious scruples than availability of supply. This points toward the fact that improvement of fishery techniques in all parts of the Orient is an acceptable method of improving the dietary and food economy. Much can be done in almost all parts of the Orient to improve the yield of fishery products.

THE RICE LANDSCAPE

In hill country terraced rice fields are laid out on the contours of physical relief, as shown in this view along a stream valley in western Java, Indonesia. Most of these fields have been plowed, leveled, covered with water, and are about ready for the transplanting of seedlings. (S. Bunnag, FAO, United Nations)

The terraced rice fields on this mountain highland in the upper Beas River, Kulu Valley, Himachal Pradesh, northwest India are also fitted to the contours of the physical surface. Fields surround the village at the left, in all stages of crop development, and a planted fir forest covers the mountains in the background. (Government of India)

On the low-gradient valley floor of the Min River, western Szechwan, China, rice fields need only water-holding bunds, and the fields often are more regular in shape and size than are those in the hill country. This is a region of dispersed settlement, with scattered farmsteads. (J. E. Spencer)

On the flat lake plain of the Laguna de Bay, south of Manila, Philippines, the fields are also somewhat regular and larger in size. Here the wet-field harrowing operation employs a simple vertical harrow and a water buffalo, working the wet soil level and into shape for transplanting. (J. E. Spencer)

A Ceylon rice grower sows his seedbed in rows, although elsewhere broadcast seeding is employed for the seedbeds. The seedlings will be ready for transplanting in five to six weeks. (United Nations)

Farmers in the Cauvery River Valley, southern India, still utilize an ancient device for lifting water from a main ditch to a field distributory channel. There are several human-powered devices still widely employed in lifting water, but in Japan and Taiwan electric motors now are performing much of this labor. (United Nations)

These Sinhalese women, in Ceylon, are pulling rice seedlings from the seedbed in groups, and tying them into bundles, for transport to the fields for transplanting. (United Nations)

A transplanting crew is at work on the Laguna de Bay lake plain, south of Manila, Philippines. The transplanting of rice is a labor-intensive operation, and farmers often utilize cooperative labor at transplanting time. On the field bund at the right is a guitar player who often goes with the crew, in central Philippine practice. (J. E. Spencer)

A harvesting crew is at work in southern Panay Island, Philippines, in a field of lodged rice—the stalks have been beaten down by the wind. Harvesting is also a labor-intensive operation at best, using the small hand-knife in cutting stalks, but in a field in which the rice has lodged the chore is particularly tedious. (Philippine Tourist & Travel Association)

On the Laguna de Bay lake plain, south of Manila, Philippines, the traditional harvesting-threshing operation often employs cooperative labor exchanged among neighbors. A field becomes a threshing floor on which large piles of cut grain, straw, and rice-in-the-husk accumulate from the fields round about. (J. E. Spencer)

In some areas, as in this scene from southern Taiwan, modernized procedures are speeding up the harvest operation. This portable threshing bin can be skidded around the fields, a threshing wheel powered by a small gasoline motor speeds up the work, and the rice is sacked in the field by a small harvest crew, to be dried later on a threshing floor. (J. E. Spencer)

10

SOILS, PLANTS, AND AGRICULTURAL SYSTEMS

Not enough is yet known about soils, plants, cropping systems, and agricultural technologies in many parts of the Orient that we may set down a comprehensive account of the practice of oriental agriculture. Discussion of the separate aspects of the subject-complex, in scientific terms, is not the objective of this chapter. Rather, we approach the subject from the position of the interested observer looking at agriculture and farmers.

Landform attributes, climatic regimes, soils complexes, and water supplies form primary elements of the environmental face of a three-part interacting ecologic complex pertaining to the nature, quality, and productivity of those land surfaces utilized in crop growing and animal husbandry. Plants, bird-animal populations, and insect-microbial populations form the primary elements of the active-agents face of this same ecologic complex. Man, himself (although he also is an active agent), operates in the role of the manipulator of both sets of elements, and he thereby affects the processes of interaction within the ecologic complex. By unwitting over-action in some manipulatory performance man may not only disturb the ecologic balance in some locale, but he may cause lowered quality and decreased productivity, ending in the alteration of the fundamental nature of the regional ecologic complex. On the other hand, by unconscious or knowledgeable constructive performance, man may improve upon the fundamental nature of the regional ecologic complex. Historically it seems true that throughout the Orient the cumulative sum of human manipulation has involved both destructive and constructive performances. In any one region elements of the environmental face may be both unfavorable and favorable to human use, and the same is true of the elements of the active-agents face of the ecologic complex. That is, landforms may be such as to make crop growing extremely difficult, or they may make agricultural usage quite easy; soils may be intrinsically poor or hard to till in one locale of a region, but rich and easily tilled in another locale; surface materials may be anaerobic in one spot but aerated and containing good mixes of microbial populations that generate useful volumes of soluble plant nutrients in a nearby location; plant covers may abound in noxious plants that are difficult to cope with while yielding few items of value, or they may be useful covers that aid in the production of organic materials useful to crop plants and that yield volumes of useful items; man himself may cause severe deterioration of soils, or he may follow practices that build up productivity in the soils.

No large part of the Orient, outside the high mountain margins inhibitory to any plant and animal life, is uniformly high in quality with respect to all elements of the ecologic complex, and no large part is totally useless, given the proper human understanding and the application of effective technologies. An agricultural system plays the active agents against the environmental elements in some particular manipulation of the ecologic complex. Simple systems utilize very rudimentary technologies to unsophisticated ends, and highly advanced systems employ complex technologies to accomplish highly sophisticated objectives.

These abstractions are broad generalizations about the human use of the surface of the earth in the whole of the Orient. There are culture groups barely beginning the practice of crop growing in local regions of high agricultural quality, and there are culture groups carrying on some form of scientific agriculture with consummate skills in regions lacking high environmental quality. Most of the population of the Orient falls between these extremes, and the regions they inhabit also fall between the extremes of quality. The large culture realm of the Orient ranges through almost all the levels of ecologic complex and human manipulative ability to be found anywhere on the earth, and no brief discussion can cover all the characteristics. Too little is known, still, concerning many of the elements composing the environmental face, the active agents, and the effective manipulatory actions in many parts of the Orient; that is, we still do not fully understand the nature and proper manipulation of tropical soils, the usage and control of grasslands, or the applications of tillage and fertilizers under all the given conditions. This chapter, then, is but a tentative survey of selected phases of the three-part ecologic complex.

SOILS CHARACTERISTICS

The soil resources of the Orient have been surveyed and assessed on very unequal bases by many different systems, but comparable knowledge of characteristics and qualities is lacking in many regions. No effective map can yet be constructed for the whole of the Orient on the basis of the newest system employed in the United States (the 7th Approximation), and the maps presented here retain older points of view (Figs. 10.1, 10.2, and Table 5). The major groups have been divided into two standard American categories, the pedocals or calcium-bearing soils, and the pedalfers or aluminum- and iron-bearing soils, the letters "cal," "al," "fe" standing for the three distinctive elements. In simple terms this division separates the basic soils from the acid soils. These maps do point to some very general broad differences between the humid tropical-subtropical regions and the more arid and non-tropical regions. From the Yangtze Valley southward, excluding northwest India-Pakistan, most soils fall into some category of the yellow to red leached soils formerly described as lateritic yellow and red earths, now more frequently described as latosols (ultisols and oxisols). Exceptions to this are the soils composed of materials resulting from volcanism, in which the leaching processes have not been carried to great lengths.

In earlier studies it was assumed that two fundamental soil-forming processes operate in the humid zones of the earth, podzolization in the cool wet regions and laterization in the hot wet regions. Too simply stated, the first was thought to remove the soluble salts, iron, and aluminum compounds from the surface horizons, leaving a gray silica residue. The second was believed to begin by remov-

Soils Groups and their Distribution

A. Pedocals	Zone of Occurrence
1. Chernozem group	NW China, Inner Mongolia, Manchuria.
2. Tropical black earths	Central India, Central Burma, lowland patches in middle eastern Indies
3. Chestnut earths	NW China, Inner Mongolia, Manchuria
4. Lakeland soils group	North China Plain, Upper Ganges Valley

5. Alluvial soils group
  a. Younger flood plain soils
  b. Older bench and terrace soils
	Both subgroups scattered in North China, Manchuria, central Asian Outer Zone, N and NW India

6. Loessial soils group	NW China, SW Manchuria, southern Inner Mongolia, NW India

7. Non-saline arid land soils group
  a. Brown soils
  b. Sandy light-colored soils
	NW China and central Asian Outer Zone; NW India; patches in middle eastern Indies; Central Burma
	Widely scattered; North China and NW India have significant areas

8. Saline soils group
  a. Desert saline soils
  b. Coastal saline soils
	NW China and central Asian Outer Zone; NW India and NW Frontier

9. Skeletal desert soils group
  a. Sand-dune types
  b. Piedmont sands and gravels
  c. Upland rocky soils
	NW China and central Asian Outer Zone; NW India and NW Frontier

10. Podzolic soils group	Lowlands of N. Japan, Korea, N and E Manchuria

B. Pedalfers	Zone of Occurrence
11. Slightly podzolic brown soils group	S Manchuria, N China; hill country of S China; highlands of Indochina; NW India; highland patches of tropics not shown on map West and SW China
12. Slightly podzolic purple-red soils group	

13. Podzolized red earths
  a. Older red earths
  b. Younger yellow earths
  c. Rice-paddy soils
	From central China southward on lowlands into India and Indies in particular localities
	
	Found in lowland valleys and terraces where rice has been long cultivated

14. Podzolized skeletal mountain soils group
  a. Northern colder
  b. Tropical version
	Widely scattered from S Japan and central China southward on uplands at increasing elevations into tropics

15. Lateritic red earths
  a. Immature red earths
  b. Mature laterite
	Widely scattered in southern zone on lowlands; fossil red earths on lower uplands
	Scattered areas of peninsular India, Thailand, Indochina, and the Indies

16. Alluvial soils group
  a. Lateritic older bench alluvium
  b. Floodplain soils
  c. Fresh delta soils
	N Japan and Central China southward through southeastern Asia and Indies, and around to India, Deccan and N and NW India being exempted

17. Peat, muck, and marsh group
  a. Midlatitude peat and moor
  b. Tropical marsh swamp
	Scattered patches in Philippines, Indies, Malaya, and Indian peninsular coast

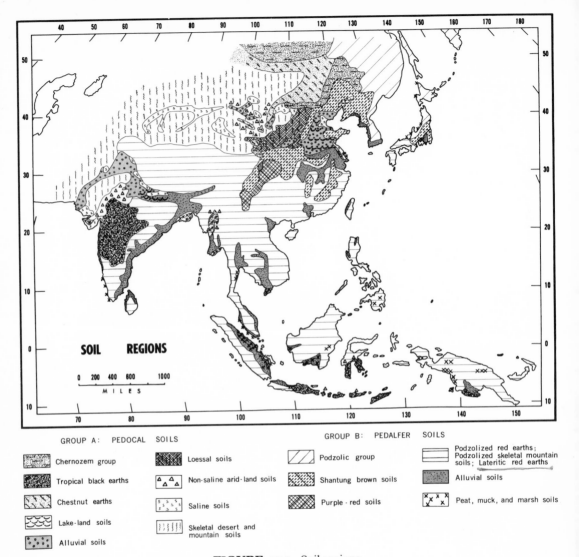

GROUP A: PEDOCAL   SOILS

Chernozem group	Loessal soils
Tropical black earths	Non-saline arid-land soils
Chestnut earths	Saline soils
Lake-land soils	Skeletal desert and mountain soils
Alluvial soils	

GROUP B: PEDALFER   SOILS

Podzolic group	Podzolized red earths; Podzolized skeletal mountain soils; Lateritic red earths
Shantung brown soils	Alluvial soils
Purple-red soils	Peat, muck, and marsh soils

FIGURE 10.1. Soil regions.

ing the soluble salts, and transferring the iron and aluminum compounds to the subsoil, but to conclude by removal of silicates and the restoration of iron and aluminum compounds near the surface horizons with the clays accumulating just under them, producing red to mottled red and gray soils.

More recently podzolization has been found active well into the tropics, and advanced laterization is admitted as restricted to certain situations wherein alternate wetting and drying regularly take place. Very porous surface soils in the tropics frequently seem to become podzolized, but some rice-field soils are also similarly affected. Where black soils once were thought to be confined to midlatitude grassland dry margins, and their formation understood, they now are recognized within the tropics without, as yet, a satisfactory explanation of their origin and development. Better understanding of the upward and downward seasonal movement of ground water and the position of the water table appears essential to further progress in understanding tropical soils. Better knowledge of Tertiary and Pleistocene climatic variations is needed to fathom the history of soil formation.

Perhaps the two most common misjudgments that the Occident has made about soils of the tropics concern their fabulous richness and their complete lack of organic matter. Many tropical and subtropical soils are very deep, but not often are lowland tropical soils really rich soils with a long productive life.

Tropical soils supporting a real plant cover do have organic materials in their surface horizons. The speed of decomposition never permits a deep layer of unrotted humus to collect on the surface. As long as a heavy plant cover remains undisturbed the plant association, working with solar energy and moisture, is able to feed into the soil dead organic material to maintain a balance in the supply of soluble elements and to support soil bacteria, both of fundamental value in the growth process.

A long period is required for the plant cover to build itself up to heavy forest even where precipitation is adequate. But, when

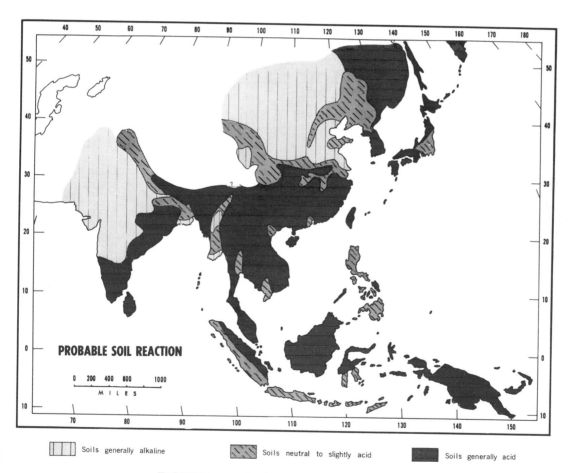

FIGURE 10.2. Regions of probable soil reaction.

the plant cover is removed, the slim reserve of soluble plant foods is removed from tropical soils far more rapidly than is true in midlatitude soils. Within a few years a soil that supported a 200-foot multilayered tropical rainforest may be so exhausted that it will support only the poorest of scrubby plants. The tropics are dotted with the marks of nature's and man's removal actions and nature's slow recovery program.

On some of the islands of the Indies and the southern Philippines, volcanism periodically provides a new layer of unweathered soil material. Where basic rather than acidic volcanic extrusives are provided, young and immature soils are extremely productive. Here the very speed of weathering and the rate of soil formation are counter to all midlatitude experience. Such volcanism provides a reshuffling of soil horizons and a renewal of fertility of extreme importance.

Most tropical soils are some shade of red or black. The oxidation of iron compounds provides a color stain that frequently is dominant over other coloring elements. The origin of the black coloring is not well understood. However, under situations in which relations of ground water, precipitation, vegetation, denudation, aggradation, and weathering processes are altered locally, a wide variety of colors may exist, from black to buff, brown, and light gray. Redness of color does not always denote lateritic soils. Many red and yellow soils of the tropics and subtropics are soils in some immature or arrested stage of development. Considerable attention has been given to laterite and the term often has been misused. In lowland situations of long stability of major causal factors, with a relatively high water table, seasonal wetting and drying, the lateritic process has sometimes proceeded to maturity, producing crusted layers properly termed. Mature laterite is scattered widely throughout the southern Orient, but does not bulk very large in square-mile total. Such

mature products are often worthless as agricultural soils and usually support only a scant native plant cover. Laterite varies considerably in chemical formula and physical characteristics. Sometimes it has provided building stone by simple quarrying; at other times its high iron content has permitted its use as iron ore. Bauxite ores at or near the surface appear related to the formation of mature laterite.

Outside the tropical regions, and including arid northwest India-Pakistan, soils tend to be neutral to only slightly acidic or to range far over into alkaline condition, reflecting the slower action of leaching processes under lower temperatures or the total lack of leaching processes. The addition of variable amounts of wind blown loess in northwest India-Pakistan and in northern China adds a higher qualitative element to these regional soils patterns. Where this is a heavy blanket, as in the Loess Highlands of northwest China, soil quality is normally high and cultivation is relatively easy. Although Japan possesses many areas surfaced by volcanic products most of these are acidic in nature and soils tend to be lower in quality and not comparable to the recent volcanic soils of Indonesia.

Occidentals often have closely related soil quality to workability. European agriculture in higher latitudes has been accustomed to use considerable cultivation in its cropping practice and, therefore, to regard easy workability as a good soil characteristic. The soil chemist suggests that under cold to warm temperatures stirring the soil is a useful act. Cultivation on the dry margins, to save moisture, has furthered the soil-stirring idea. Heavy clay soils usually have not been regarded as good soils, owing to low workability and the low content of soluble salts. In the tropics under permanently high temperatures too great stirring of the soil promotes too rapid chemical and bacterial reaction, resulting in loss of plant foods.

Heavy clays in the tropics give surprising yields when properly handled.

The alluvial soils, to the farming populations of the Orient, are the most important groups of soils (see Fig. 10.1 and also Fig. 6.3). Where alluvial flood plains receive active additions of nutrient material through annual inundation, soil quality tends to remain high and workability remains easy. However, many of the larger flood plains contain margins, strips, and islands of older, higher alluvium no longer reached by current seasonal flood waters, in which leaching aspects of soil forming processes have degraded much of the surface soil into some variation of the yellow to red earths approximating the latosols.

Much of the surface of the Orient is in rough to steep surfaces on which only skeletal soils are found. Many such areas have soil materials of a quality sufficient to support short-term cropping only, and need periodic regeneration under wild vegetation. Many such areas have been cropped by traditional shifting cultivation, in which the cyclic use does provide that periodic regeneration of small volumes of plant nutrients.

Apart from the issue of the intrinsic characteristics of the soils themselves, is the matter of the handling of the soils by generations of farmers who have used them. Shifting cultivators throughout the Orient have cyclic patterns of use, under which natural regenerative processes are operative. There is wide variation, however, in the handling practices of sedentary farming populations permanently cropping soils over periods of hundreds to thousands of years. It has been a broad generalization that many oriental peasant farmers have not employed practices restoring plant nutrients to the soils they farm. Particularly, this generalization is often applied to India-Pakistan, though there are many local regions in which this is not true. In some parts of India, however, centuries of overuse have lowered the quality and pro-

ductivity of soils without changing the soil type in any essential manner. Parts of Pakistan, Burma, Thailand, Cambodia, Vietnam, Indonesia, and the Philippines suffer in this same way. Where Chinese practice has obtained for any period soils are usually productive regardless of their intrinsic soil type. Korea, Japan, northern North Vietnam, and those areas of southeast Asia in which Chinese farmers today are active, have followed Chinese practice. The continuous use of human wastes, garbage, and green manures maintains a relatively high ratio of organic matter and supplies of nitrogens, potashes, phosphates, and other needed soluble elements to compare with the best in occidental fertilization practice. The limits in these techniques have been the supplies of available materials.

Rather closely related to the human factor is the action of termites in many parts of the tropics. The building of mounds of subsoil above the water table where aeration can oxidize chemical elements and speed up soil formation is significant in a number of countries. Termites appear to operate everywhere from southern Japan and the southern Yangtze Valley southward in the lowlands. The use of old termite mounds for garden planting is frequent in several parts of the Orient. The long-range effect of termites on soil formation is little understood at the present time.

The individual oriental farmer judges his own land as better or poorer than that of a neighbor in the next village. From the farmer's point of view almost every region possesses rich and poor soils. The student of regions concludes that every country has a share of naturally richer and poorer soils. In the Orient, at least, the soils of no one country condemn it to poverty or guarantee it most of the wealth. Man's manipulation of soils, by groups, types, or individual fields, can and does supplement or nullify this particular natural resource in his landscape, and certainly management of some soil groups is easier and cheaper than that of others.

The division into acid and basic soils is sound agriculturally. The degree of soil acidity is subject to marked changes within short distances, for many factors enter into promoting this characteristic, and no simple map of this sort can be completely accurate (see Fig. 10.2, and Table 5). Some crops prefer soils that are definitely basic, among them being wheat, some of the sorghums and millets, most of the oil seeds, cotton, and numerous vegetable crops. Others prefer definitely acid soils, among these being rice, tea, and the oil palm. Maize, some of the millets, tobacco, the coconut palm, coffee, many of the tree fruits, and many vegetables prefer neutral to slightly acid soils. Many domesticated plants have a rather wide range of tolerance and can be grown on many different types of soils without the strong penalty of reduced yields.

In every region with an old and well-established agriculture the farmer long since has worked out the soil preferences and tolerances of the common crops. Many plant varieties have developed to allow the farmer to take advantage of soil and moisture conditions of a particular sort. In this way there have come to be over ten thousand varieties of rice, many of which are grown only on particular soils and in certain water depths. Where new crops have come into a region there often must be an experimental period before the regional and locational preferences and tolerances of a plant can be discovered.

The effect, in terms of soil forming process, of the wet field of much of the Orient is not taken into proper account in many discussions of soils. Soils on old lake-land areas tend to be heavy, sticky, and difficult to work. The best wet-rice field lands are also heavy soils that will hold their water cover. Yet the impact of constant cultivation, the turning-in of weed growth and stubble, and the centuries-old shallow water cover in many areas in which rice has long

been grown, is not fully understood in respect to soil forming processes. Many old rice field lands show podzolization in areas otherwise composed of latosols affected by the laterization process. Such soils often are of rather low quality, judged by their productivity under crops other than rice, yet they go on producing acceptable returns under rice cropping.

A last element altering the natural soil forming processes in many portions of the Orient has been the creation of the terraced field, in which case the mantle of regolith often is fully disturbed. Subsoils are dug out on the upslope margin, filled in on the downslope margin, and new layers of surface soil are spread over the terrace flat. Terracing is very old in some regions, quite new in others, with a fairly steady progression of action, in the historic sense, to increase the amount of agricultural land that is under terracing. Terraced landscapes amount to culturally controlled soil surfaces, in which creation, maintenance, and handling under cropping practice may be more important than the original intrinsic characteristic of the soil involved.

In many of the long settled portions of the Orient, in which the soil has been cropped by hundreds of generations of farmers, the conclusion is almost inescapable that in the long run the handling of the soil is more important than its innate physical characteristic, chemical content, and color. In particular, soil color is noticeable to the traveler and helps distinguish one regional landscape from another, but it often seems to mean little as to productivity. Where nature developed and maintained a heavy forest man can do the same or can maintain productive crop plantings. Poor soils can be built up to high productivity in a very few decades by careful handling and feeding. Few soil bodies cannot be quickly impoverished by one-way exploitive use within a short span of years. Particularly are these conclusions applicable within the regions of the Orient we commonly call tropical, in which the chemical and microbial processes are active. The modern introduction of commercial fertilizers promises relief from the steady continuation of exploitive cropping in areas in which good management procedures have not been traditionally followed, but this introduction also poses some problems in the maintenance of proper ecologic balance, about which we know too little at present.

THE VEGETATIVE ASSEMBLAGE

In a large share of the Orient today there is no such thing as natural vegetation. In many regions man has been cutting and replanting landscapes for more than 3,000 years. Elsewhere the practice of shifting cultivation has been going on since man first domesticated plants. Almost everywhere the lowlands are pockmarked with the effects of burning and girdling the forest to permit cropping for a year or two. Within recent centuries this type of cropping has been carried clear to the tops of mountains, and has reworked the most favored sites repeatedly. A simple conception of very early patterns of plant cover is presented without any attempt to designate regional genera or species dominance (Fig. 10.3).

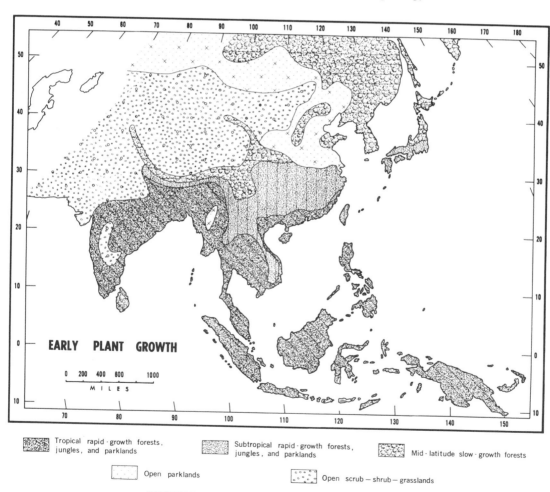

EARLY PLANT GROWTH

0 200 400 800 1000
M I L E S

Tropical rapid-growth forests, jungles, and parklands

Subtropical rapid-growth forests, jungles, and parklands

Mid-latitude slow-growth forests

Open parklands

Open scrub – shrub – grasslands

FIGURE 10.3. Probable early natural vegetation.

Nature's replacement of a break in the vegetative formation takes time and some kind of plant succession. In warm, moist regions plants rapidly fill in any "vacuum" created by a clearing. If these first entrants are helpful "nurse-plants," a succession may proceed rapidly, with an early replenishment of soil fertility. If they are monopolistic, they may inhibit a succession and retard restoration of soils. Retrogressive succession in vegetation and soils often occurs where man too frequently destructively uses fire and other forces. It is difficult to know how many species earlier made up the native flora of China or Java, but a well-based estimate suggests reduction by over half. In the Philippines, about fifty percent of which is forested, casual observation might suggest little serious cultural tampering with plant life or the soil. However, there is little old or mature forest left, and many species of useful plants are almost extinct, though human pressure on the Philippines has been less than in many other parts of the Orient. Where man has used a large part of the landscape only those plants maintain themselves that are tolerant in respect to semicultural treatment, fire, soil fertility, conditions of light, "nurse-plant" assistance, and later surroundings.

In some parts of the Orient cultural influence has increased the coverage of tall grasses, particularly where such influence has been accompanied by fire and shifting cultivation. In other areas bamboo jungle replaces grass on such disturbed surfaces. Eventually succession replaces the grasses and bamboos with other plant associations, provided man does not continue burning. The replacement program is slow, and much land is rendered nonproductive in the early stages of the sequence.

Man fosters many trees and shrubs selected out of the early plant formations which ordinarily are not termed domesticated plants. Most of the forests, jungles, parklands, scrublands, and open grasslands of the Orient today are secondary growths. In many areas these plant ranges have been managed well and in others very poorly indeed. About 1520 Krsnadeva Raya, the Emperor of the south Indian state of Vijayanagar and an active political theorist, said in connection with peace preservation: "Increase the forests that are near your frontier fortress and destroy all those that are in the middle of your territory. Then alone will you not have trouble from robbers."[*]

Altitude, affecting temperatures, and moisture are the chief environmental factors determining plant life in the tropics and subtropics. The so-called frost line, a function of altitude, is important. It is found at varying heights in different areas, of course, but above it grow mountain associations, below it those of the lowlands. About 2,500 feet is commonly a significant altitude equatorward of south China and Luzon, with the critical temperature somewhere between 60 and 70° F. Of importance also are exposure, geology, and soils. An annual rainfall, in monsoonal distribution, of about 40 inches ordinarily separates the thorny scrublands of southern Asia from the monsoon forests, and 80 inches ordinarily divides the monsoon forest and the evergreen rainforest, but this is not always true. There are good rainforests supported in favored sites on 60 inches of moisture, poor monsoon forests on poor, rocky soils receiving well over 100 inches, and poor scrub covering very moist but highly laterized soils.

Distribution of Wild Vegetation

May we accept the judgment that wild vegetation (in place of natural vegetation) is any plant growth not arranged formally by field patterns and not seasonally cultivated? The

[*]T. V. Mahalingam, *Administrative and Social Life under Vijayanagar*, Madras, 1940, pp. 155–56.

regional patterns of plant life, in the modern Orient, are those largely dominated by man (Fig. 10.4). Only the broader patterns can be indicated on a map of this scale, and innumerable patches of fields, forests, or grasslands are omitted. Areas predominantly forested are indicated as such whether "natural" or cultural. Cultivated landscapes include many much-used, noncultivated plants. These range from the wild fruits

gathered from jungle growth around village clearings and marketed in the cities to the firewood twigs and branches annually stripped from trees growing on ricefield margins, and the tool wood, firewood, and general-use poor lumber cut from the field margin thickets of many areas of dry field crop areas.

Students have worked on different principles and varying scales in every country of the Orient in describing plant associations.

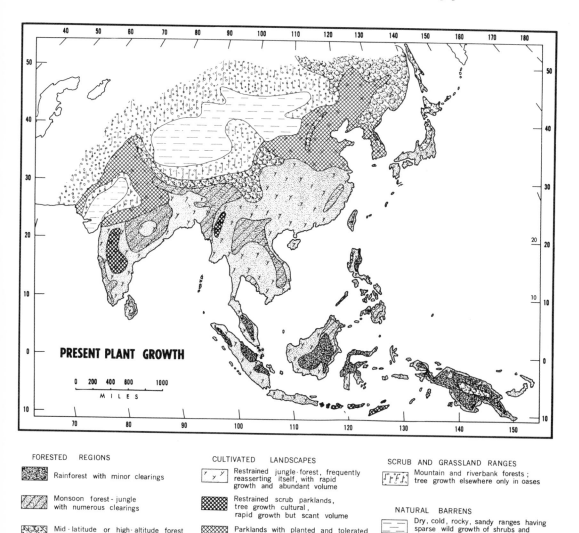

PRESENT PLANT GROWTH

0   200   400   800   1000
M I L E S

FORESTED   REGIONS

Rainforest with minor clearings

Monsoon forest - jungle with numerous clearings

Mid - latitude or high - altitude forest with numerous clearings

CULTIVATED   LANDSCAPES

Restrained jungle - forest, frequently reasserting itself, with rapid growth and abundant volume

Restrained scrub parklands, tree growth cultural, rapid growth but scant volume

Parklands with planted and tolerated trees of slow growth and sparse volume

SCRUB AND GRASSLAND RANGES

Mountain and riverbank forests ; tree growth elsewhere only in oases

NATURAL   BARRENS

Dry, cold, rocky, sandy ranges having sparse wild growth of shrubs and grasses ; tree growth only in oases or at higher altitudes

FIGURE 10.4. Present varieties of plant growth.

This has immensely increased the broad descriptive task and has motivated the present simplified approach. Easiest to block out are the naturally barren areas. Lowland sectors of central Asia and Mongolia, including some parts of northwest China, much of the Tibetan highland, and some of lowland northwest India-Pakistan fall in this category. Causal factors are extreme drought, strong denudation leaving but bare-rock expanses, sand-dune accumulation, and sheer alpine cold. Locally unusual water supply, protected situations, and other favorable agencies promote vigorous plant oases. Some form of plant life, however limited, is to be found almost everywhere, but there is little that can support life for man or the higher animals.

Next it is possible to block out those arid-land margins and high, cold localities that only occasionally permit tree growth. Parts of central Asia, Mongolia, non-mountainous north China and southern Manchuria, the lower fringes of the Tibetan highlands, some surfaces of the Yunnan Plateau in southwest China, limited parts of northwest India-Pakistan, and a few localities of central Indonesia belong in this group. In this zone gallery forests naturally occur along streams and in deep clefts in the highlands. Favored situations promote scrub and thorn forest. The normal open-country plant cover is grasses and a variety of shrubs. In the arid lands where man has used his ability to lend protection and provide extra water, trees, shrubs, and flowering plants create cultural oases. These are subject to historic shifts of location and to periodic growth and abandonment with the fortunes of sedentary settlement in a landscape that normally requires mobility on the part of man. Plant species are limited, and seldom does the added planting amount to more than rows, clumps, or clusters around settlements. However, where large-scale irrigation projects are developed, as in the Indian Punjab, the added vegetation

often is sufficient to alter the appearance of the arid landscape.

In well-populated areas seldom is wild plant growth allowed to interfere with economic and cultural activities of farming, grazing, cutting cheap timber, or exploiting particular plants. These predominantly cultural landscapes range from the dry margins to the wettest of the equatorial rainforests. They naturally exhibit a wide range of trees, shrubs, grasses, flowering plants, epiphytes, and parasites. What the farmer calls weeds are today a constant problem. In some areas the plant cover reclaims its own if man's diligence and group ability declines, as indicated in the forest cover of Cambodia, when, in 1859, a French naturalist first stumbled upon the ruins of the twelfth-century Khmer capital of Angkor. There are many possibilities of subdividing such regions (see Fig. 10.4). This culturally dominant zone varies in relative size in each country. In India it is today a large share, in Indonesia outside of Java a small one. In some countries it is sandwiched in between hill and dale, mountain and swamp, with the result that wild growth may appear dominant. In others, with great expanses of flat and open country wild growth is scant and restricted to odd corners or to such chosen spots as temple gardens.

Scanning what remains, the country dominantly forested, one finds it in bits and pieces that do not fit easily into any simple causal pattern. There are sound historical reasons for many forested spots, good climatic reasons, reasons of physiography, and reasons of physical isolation to account for the remaining forests of the Orient. In some regions that remainder is fast disappearing, and in others the area under managed permanent forest is increasing in total, though with changes taking place in location. The Indian plan to return some 50,000,000 acres of culturally bruised land to permanent wild growth will change the landscape of parts of

India, as in the southern Western Ghats, where large young teak forests now are growing under tight controls. In the forested zone, too, the variety of species is great in the sweep from the arid margins to the equatorial rainforest.

Economically valuable timber trees, wild fruits, and oil- and gum-producing plants vary from region to region. With a number of unknowns and inequalities in the mapping of forest distributions, the accompanying map does not attempt detailed representation of forest regions.

Floras and Plant Domestications

Plant explorers and botanists have long prowled through parts of the Orient, hunting for useful crop and decorative plants and filling out the taxonomic record, though this is far from complete on both counts. Far too little attention has been given to the economic plants in the systematic study of floras, and we know comparatively little about the whole range of economic plants. Many of them are extremely old in use, there have been many transfers from one region to another, and there are hundreds of varieties of many of them, some quite localized and others very widely distributed.

Although too little is known of precise regional patterns of the several floras of the Orient, it is possible to make some useful crude generalizations. In the northeastern part of the Orient there is a northern coniferous-broadleaf forest flora that resembles that of eastern Anglo-America in species, autumn coloration, and distribution. This covers Manchuria, northern Japan, Korea, and the upland parts of northern China. It has a high economic utility to modern man in its good timber and wood pulp resources, but it provided not many sources of plant foods to early man. In northwest China and Mongolia is a grassland-shrub flora of relatively few species. Much of North China, the region of loess deposition, may

never have been heavily covered with plant growth, the lowlands sharing the floral characteristics of inner Asia, and the uplands sharing the northern forest flora. Central China possesses a numerous flora of wide variety and species. The Tibetan high country possesses a distinctive flora of its own, sparse in species, in variety, and in utility. The mountain and valley country of southwestern China, the Tibetan border, northern Burma, Thailand, and Vietnam is one of the most varied of all, and one of the richest, for it combines elements of other regional floras with a large number of endemic species. An India-Burma flora belonging to the moist lowlands is a significant member of the floral picture, one with a wide range of species and a high degree of value both in early times and to modern man. A Malaysian flora related to the old Sundaland shelf zone, existent prior to the last major shift of sea levels, has contributed many thousands of species, probably more than any other zone. A Papualand flora, related to that of the Sahul shelf zone, evolved with a center on New Guinea, and spread predominantly southeastward.

Although there have been no sharp boundaries successfully drawn around each of the suggested floral centers, owing to their large amount of intergrading, earlier practice, using Wallace's Line, sharply divided the Asian floras from those of Australasia. This now proves to be an inadequate boundary in respect to plants, though it is useful in relation to animals. Rather than to draw sharp zones of demarcation between source regions, it is better to recognize that there are horizontal and altitudinal climatic zones throughout the Orient and that floras of different derivation and climatic preference overlap each other at different altitudes or occur in disjunct distributions in satisfactory climatic regions, provided there has existed an avenue of plant migration. Thus, southern bamboos and flowering subtropicals live in lowland, southern Japan, and a northern coniferous-broadleaf association occupies upland and northern Japan. Himalayan temperate mountain and alpine plants are at home in upland Sumatra, and Central Asian species are at home in northwestern Pakistan and northwestern China. The wealth of plant species found in the region from central China south and west to the middle Himalayas is a result of the mixing together of several regional floras, combining both endemic and immigrant species from many different sources.

Multiplicity of species alone does not signify a flora highly useful to man in the most general sense, in view of all the levels of human culture. The 5,000 species of orchids at home in Indonesia or the 3,000 species of timber trees of the Philippines were far less important to early man than smaller numbers of plants that provided varieties of products that he could use. There obviously were regional differences in the usability of plants in the whole of the Old World in the past, and man slowly came to recognize these differences. Certain regions can be picked out as centers of economically useful plants, and it is around these that the history of domestication of crop plants in this part of the world hinges.

It is a curious thing that, with so much movement within the Orient, so many items should have remained restricted to certain regions. Examination suggests that the natural distribution of wild plants sometimes did include distant areas, but unrelated human cultures did not make the same choices. Perhaps the outstanding example of this is tea, the wild shrub scattered from north India into central China. People in south China did, and the Indians did not, domesticate the plant and learn to drink tea, a trait all Chinese eventually acquired. In breaking the Chinese monopoly on tea in the midnineteenth century the British brought Chinese tea plants to India, later to find the wild relatives growing in the very area to which they took the importations.

Within the Orient there perhaps are four centers of significance in the domestication of plants. These are north central China, south China-Tonking, the moist lowlands of southeastern Asia including all of Indonesia-New Guinea (one kind of region but in several pieces today), and eastern India-Burma. Related plant centers are southwestern Asia (actually overlapping into northwest Pakistan) and Ethiopia, lying just outside the Orient but in close contact with it.

From these several centers both India and China eventually drew almost all the commonly used Old World plants. Some transfers took place so early that the plants appear native to far areas. Rarely has a century gone by, since the historic era began, without the coming of some new plant to China. Almost all the economically significant crop plants of the Philippines are cultural importations during the long period of human occupation. Localities such as southern Thailand, which lies far from the plant centers outside the Orient and which possesses a limited range of climate and soils, never accumulated the great wealth of domesticated plant life that is possessed by China or India. Thai agriculture remains that basically developed with the plants from the southern oriental domestication centers. In those countries with a wide range of climate, soils, and opportunity, agriculture has become a very complex matter, shifting somewhat over the centuries as new plants come to compete with the older ones. Modern plant breeders and agricultural missionaries have done much to broaden the economic botany of most regions in a short period.

To mention the basic items briefly, wheat, some of the pulses, a range of vegetables, grapes, melons, some of the stone fruits, and a variety of other fruits and nuts, all came from southwestern Asia into India and China. Except for some of the vegetables none of these products has successfully been utilized throughout the whole of the Orient. On the other side, the coconut and a number of other palms, the yams, the taros, sugar cane, and a host of tropical fruits such as the jackfruit, breadfruit, mangosteen, and durian were domesticated somewhere in the mainland-island fringe of southeastern Asia. Many of the tropical fruits still grow wild also. From the original centers many of these plants spread outward in all directions, some going far outside the Orient even in the pre-Columbian period. Within the Orient various of them spread to the approximate climatic margins of growth, or to the cultural limits of acceptance, in India, China, or Japan (Fig. 10.5). South China-Tonking contributed most of the citrus fruits, most of the

bananas, tea, such fruits as the lichee and longan, many of the Chinese cabbages, most of the Asian rices, some soybeans, and the mulberries. The northcentral China center contributed the persimmon, some of the pears, the apricot, some of the peaches, some of the millets, soybeans, and a variety of vegetables and lesser fruits. The eastern Indian areas provided some rices, some sorghums, some of the millets, and some of the subtropical fruits such as the mango and some bananas. Cotton came to India from northeast Africa so early as to seem at home there. *Acacia arabica* also seems a very early introduction into northwest India as a wood-

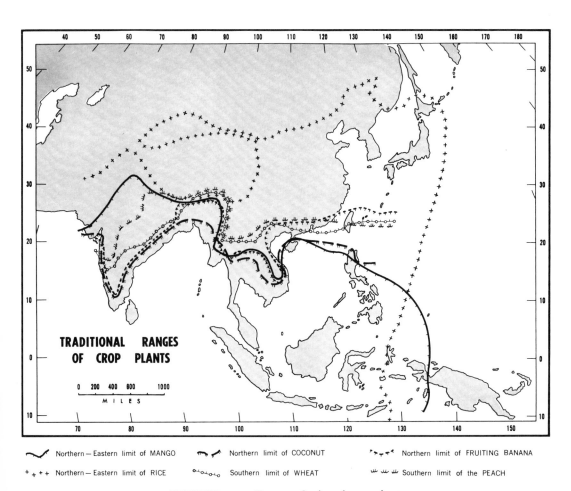

Northern—Eastern limit of MANGO	Northern limit of COCONUT	Northern limit of FRUITING BANANA
Northern—Eastern limit of RICE	Southern limit of WHEAT	Southern limit of the PEACH

FIGURE 10.5. Ranges of oriental crop plants.

supplying tree. Coffee, on the other hand, came surprisingly late.

Plant transfers took place steadily, though there were peak and slack periods in the exchange. Periods of importance in Indian agriculture were the second millennium B.C., the several centuries preceding the onset of the Christian era, and the sixteenth and seventeenth centuries. In China very significant periods were the four centuries from 200 B.C. to A.D. 200, the eighth and ninth, the thirteenth, and the sixteenth and seventeenth centuries. To almost every country of the Orient, except Korea and Japan, the sixteenth and seventeenth centuries were important in this respect. Not mentioned above is the period from the midnineteenth century to the present day, during which scientific plant introduction and plant breeding has been a lesser or major part of the economy of every country in the world. Many new strains of older plants have been moved about, overlooked items have been developed, old breeds improved. The whole of the Orient has been combed by the plant explorers, searching for useful and decorative plants. In this process many economic plants of value to the Orient and Occident alike have been turned up. The task is far from complete, and the effects will continue to be felt for a considerable period.

THE PRACTICE OF AGRICULTURE

One thesis holds that plant domestication and crop growing began in the moist tropical lands which abound in species of plants directly of use to early man. This thesis suggests that fishing peoples, perhaps well provided with a food supply, began the first specific working with plants and plant products in net and trap making, and that they discovered the many gums, poisons, and spices that are so frequent in the tropics. Tubers, roots, and rhizomes, gathered both for food, for body paints and other dyes, and

for use in ritual magic activity, came within their working patterns and gradually came to be the first specific crop items in a simple small-patch garden system that depended upon vegetative reproduction of live plant material. Seed cropping and other cropping practices, in this thesis, are held to be later developments. It follows that digging-stick subsistence crop growing as a camp-site form of shifting cultivation took shape and should constitute possibly the oldest crop-growing system, that more complex systems of subsistence cultivation would be later in evolution, and that systems of agriculture concerned with surpluses, trade, and commercial practices would evolve last of all.

Much uncertainty still exists concerning the whole complicated matter of plant domestication, centers of domestication, Old World-New World transfers, and the evolution of agricultural systems. But it is clear that a digging-stick shifting cultivation, originally concerned primarily with roots, tubers, and rhizomes lies at the bottom of agriculture in the Orient. This still shows up among the simpler cultures in many parts of the moist tropical regions, but it is today at its peak in the eastern Indies where the taros, yams, and other root and tuber crops have provided the staple bases of food economy. In India and south China these cropping elements are now minimal, except among some of the Naga peoples of northeast India, and elsewhere in mainland southeastern Asia many elements have died out in the last few centuries as rice has expanded its spatial range as a primary crop. This early primitive digging-stick culture gradually increased in crop variety and practice, evolving into formalized shifting cultivation (Fig. 10.6).

Shifting cultivation now has a number of regional oriental names, *caingin* in the Philippines, *ladang* in Indonesia, *tam rai* in Thailand, *taung ya* in Burma, *jhum* in northern India, and *chena* in Ceylon. Also, in English

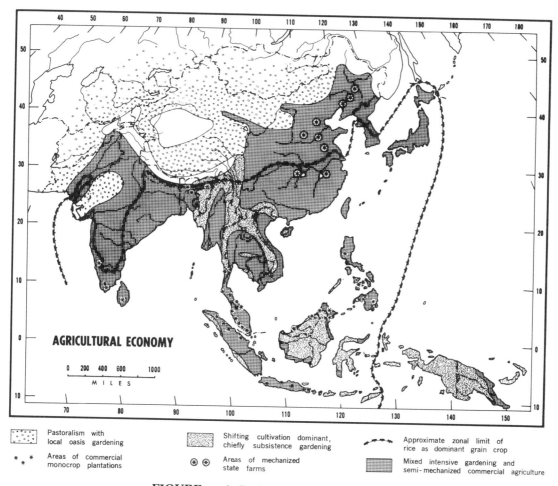

AGRICULTURAL ECONOMY

0   200   400   600   1000

M I L E S

Pastoralism with local oasis gardening	Shifting cultivation dominant, chiefly subsistence gardening	Approximate zonal limit of rice as dominant grain crop
Areas of commercial monocrop plantations	Areas of mechanized state farms	Mixed intensive gardening and semi-mechanized commercial agriculture

FIGURE 10.6. Regions of agricultural economy.

there are many near synonyms. The commonest of these are: migratory agriculture, digging-stick agriculture, transient agriculture, slash-and-burn cultivation, and fire-field agriculture. Today there are a number of typological variants of shifting cultivation utilized in different parts of the Orient by peoples at different culture levels in unlike ecological environments. Essentially, any form of shifting cultivation involves making a clearing by girdling, felling, or topping the forest canopy, slashing the lower layers and burning as much as possible to let light down to the ground, give free space, and fertilize

the soil. With no formal cultivation seeds, roots, and tubers are placed in holes made by simple digging sticks or hoes. Among many peoples the plantings are fenced and precautions are taken against wild pigs and other animal pests. The rankest weeds are kept out and the plots are watched against theft and damage until the harvest can be gathered. Seldom is a given plot cropped more than three times in some successive sequence of crops, when the process is repeated on a new site located nearby or at some distance, for the weeds become too rank, soil productivity decreases, and yields decrease. There are many different field-shift systems employed, but some form of cyclic re-use of plots is common, after plant growth has regenerated. Upland rice today is the crop most frequently grown on such fields west of Celebes and south of China, though yams, taros, bananas, and various vegetables are also important. Rice appears not to have been important in the earliest patterns, but to have increasingly become dominant as the primary crop grown in India, mainland southeastern Asia, and western Indonesia. Outside the tropics a related shifting cultivation was, in the past, often used in China, Manchuria, and Korea on steep mountain slopes, where a variety of crops adapted to upland culture were planted.

It is wrong to consider a cropping system of this kind as only an elementary one forced upon peoples by the difficulties of their tropical environment, but always abandoned by a society that has become advanced, stabilized, and sedentary. Such cultivation, when not under pressure, is really a long-range soil and crop rotation system, the wild plant growth of jungle and forest alternating with planted crops. When not under pressure such cultivation seldom ruins soils or permanently destroys the plant association. For a light population able to shift widely over jungle and forest ranges such a system could be permanently productive. Shifting cultivation has been used by culture groups living by rural dispersal, with dwelling sites moved every year, by groups that periodically moved their residence sites, and by peoples inhabiting permanently sited villages. The cropping system formed an integral element of the whole way of life, for other elements of a given culture complex were built around the cropping system or closely related to it. As such it was long practiced over a large share of the Orient. However, where a large population built up, or where aggression restricted territory, the frequency of "rotation" increased, and the extractive drain upon the

reproducing jungle or forest became great; a landscape under heavy pressure could not bear up permanently. Suggestions have been made that the Khmers of Cambodia and some early south Indian and Ceylon peoples used shifting cultivation until they so overworked the available landscapes as to induce soil exhaustion and diminishing agricultural returns, producing decaying societies ripe for the militant raids of expanding neighbors.

The facts are that under pressure of sheer need for land in many parts of the Orient contemporary farmers have pushed shifting cultivation, both in and outside the tropics, clear to the tops of mountain ranges in a desperate effort to maintain an existence. Modern governments discourage such cropping systems because they make census and taxation difficult, destroy timber, interfere with lowland water supplies, and induce violent soil erosion when carried out on too steep slopes or slopes that are cleared too thoroughly and too frequently. Under population increases and the growth of foreign trade economy, pressures and stresses are accumulating all over the Orient today. Despite government discouragement shifting cultivation will continue to persist in many parts of the Orient among varied elements in the whole population. In the modern era a good many American crop plants have entered into cropping systems utilized in shifting cultivation. Outside the moist tropical regions shifting cultivation spread over much of the Old World, as crop production replaced the appropriation of wild plant resources, and there developed ecologic variants in the different regional environments.

In central and northwest India, and in north and northwest China, another early and rather simple system of crop growing gradually matured. This gradually became a hoe culture working on permanent fields to till the soil periodically to permit the planting of seed crops. Both in India and China the chief elements of this hoe culture began with small village societies, closely knit in their social structuring, and productive of co-operative labor. In both regions the system may have been autochtonous or it may have been a product of diffusion from south-western Asia, but each apparently was a seed-planting cropping system. The earliest seed crops are not certainly known but the millets, sorghums, legumes, oil seeds which could also be grown as green vegetables, and some minor crops were utilized. Eventually wheat and some other grains entered this pattern, and so did a number of the shrubs and trees producing fruits and nuts. Many of these crop plants originated outside the Orient but they became adapted to the cooler and drier margins long before the historic period began. In both China and India this sedentary hoe culture was really a form of intensive gardening based on human labor inputs and rather simple tools. Small plots of ground were used for these primary gardens, but it well may be that some shifting cultivation was carried on at distances from the villages, and that some appropriation of wild resources continued. Through time these simple systems improved their cropping technologies, but the Indian and Chinese systems began to grow in different directions. In China the good management practices of using human wastes and other types of organic matter as garden-plot fertilizers entered the operation. The pig, the dog, the chicken, the duck, and possibly other birds became integral elements of the Chinese system, but the larger animals did not. Eventually, a few centuries prior to the start of the Christian Era, the Chinese learned the use of the plow, and began to make some use of the large draft animals; they never became integral elements in the operational system, but the Chinese continued to eat meat animals of all sorts, though they evolved a tabu on the use of milk products as being barbarian customs. By that point there already had crystallized a detailed gardening

system which was rapidly expanding its spatial patterns over all of North China and spreading southward. This detailed and intensive garden culture, requiring large inputs of human labor, has remained the mainstay of the Chinese agricultural system down into the present century. Such new crops and new techniques as were adopted were integrated into the system rather than altering its fundamental procedures.

In India the Aryan invasions were strong enough to re-orient the early agricultural system of northern India in that cattle were integrated into the system as sources of labor power, both on the land and in transport. At that early point the tabu on killing animals was a tabu on the killing of the cow only, and the bullocks were not then so spared. Nor had the Indian dietary yet developed its vegetarian trend, but there was the acceptance of milk products as part of the regional dietary. However, the tabu on killing the cow gradually increased its range to become a tabu on the killing of all animal life, and an Indian version of a sedentary agricultural system shaped up in which there was much less intensive gardening, much less human labor, and a growing trend toward vegetarianism. The Indian system was, however, also based on small villages, tightly knit in social structures, cropping sedentary permanent fields near the villages and carrying on shifting cultivation in outer lands away from the villages. As the population grew the spatial patterns widened more significantly than did general Chinese practice, developing the well and the tank as important adjuncts of the agricultural system and the landscape in an environment requiring artificial water supplies for successful dry season cropping.

We can, at this point, only speculatively sketch the spread of Indian and Chinese practices into southeastern Asia and western Indonesia, to start the replacement of shifting cultivation in several lowland regions. It is clear that this sort of spread did take place, at a point in time just before or after the start of the Christian Era, and that in the Irrawaddy, Chao Phraya, Mekong, and Song Hoi valleys agricultural systems developed in which permanent-field cropping systems supported villages in a broadly spread lowland pattern. Such systems also developed in such other local areas as the coast of Vietnam, and on Java, at the very least. From north China the Chinese agricultural system spread only into southernmost Manchuria in the early periods, but it was adopted in northern Korea and, with local variations, developed into the basic Korean agricultural system. Aspects of the system also spread into Japan, including the good soil management features, to underlie the development of the Japanese agricultural system. The question of when and how rice entered the cropping combinations and came to dominate the agricultural systems of the various local subtropical and tropical regions is involved with the development of permanent-field agricultural systems everywhere in the Orient.

The origin of wet-field rice culture, today the mainstay of much of the Orient, is somewhat puzzling. It may have begun as a dry-field crop, or it may have commenced as a simple swamp and marsh culture somewhere on the subtropical margins of the Orient. Wild rices are widely scattered in the Orient, though their taxonomy and use history are poorly known. But eventually rice did enter into the patterns of shifting cultivation on the one hand, and became the central crop of a sedentary and permanent-field, wet-field culture on the other. Whatever the origin, wet-rice cultivation evolved into a specific system through the development of terrace building, field leveling, plant selection, water control, seed bed starting of young seedlings and transplanting of seedlings into wet fields, puddling of soils by wading men and animals, and plowing, harrowing, and other techniques of soil preparation. Such items as the plow seem to have come into the Orient from the area of western Asia, but the water buffalo obviously is a product of southeastern Asia in the most general sense. In the wet-field agricultural system a variety of tool modifications took place in time, such as the shift from a horizontal, multi-toothed dry-field harrow to the vertical-framed wet-field harrow having but a single row of teeth across the bottom.

Although the origins of the separate items of the complex of wet-field rice culture cannot be pinned down, the complex is a product of moist southeastern Asia. Within the Orient it is obvious that rice culture, and the auxiliary crops that go with it, has been a spreading and expanding pattern of agriculture throughout much of historic time. Even as late as the arrival of the European, rice was not the dominant food crop on Java, and rice has not spread throughout the whole of the island zone even today. Some mainland culture groups do not yet grow rice, though their environment would permit it. Modern statistics suggest that rice culture has spread very greatly in the last century, so that one can even describe the agriculture of Thailand, Burma, Vietnam, and western Indonesia today as dominated by rice. The expansion of rice growing has faced not only cultural inertia among some peoples but also climatic limits. North China never can make rice the chief crop, since the supply of water has been limited and upland rice does less well than several other crops available to the Chinese. Northern Korea is too cold and too rough to grow rice well. In India in the past irrigation facilities could not provide sufficient water for rice in parts of the Deccan and in northwest India, and this also held true for West Pakistan. Recent development of large-dam irrigation resources in both India and Pakistan are facilitating the expansion of rice acreage. The same kind of expansion could, of course, take place in the Huang Ho basin of north China.

Although wet-field rice culture differs in some respects from the dry-field cultivation of the drier margins of the Orient, they are both part of the intensive agriculture of the Orient that is almost a garden culture. Small fields, a large volume of hand labor, simple tools, and the minimum use of draft animals and animal-powered tools go with it. High production per acre is found in many areas where farmers have been efficient, but the productivity of much oriental agriculture is lower than is often assumed. And its man-hour total of labor per acre is extremely high for many crops and in many regions. The sheer pressure of men upon the land in regions where 3,000 people are supported per square mile of cultivated land has forced an intensification uncommon in other parts of the earth. The growth of modernized and mechanized cultivation systems in all parts of the Orient is beginning to change the labor input factor, wherever field areas are such that large-field units can be established for cropping. The many areas of terracing on surfaces of marked relief will not permit whole-sale mechanization of cropping systems.

Space is lacking in which to illustrate the sheer variety of precise field patterns that is present in the many different physical landscapes, agricultural regions, and local ecological environments of the Orient, but the one general characteristic of small field sizes shows up in almost every one of the varied territories in which crop growing is the dominant aspect of the agricultural system (Fig. 10.7 and see photos in the landscape cluster, pages 231-236). In the fully-settled, relatively level, and fairly uniform lowlands, field patterns form a mosaic of small bits and pieces. The upper half of Figure 10.7 is the 1957 field map of a rice-growing section of the alluvial flood plain of the Mekong River in eastern Cambodia, in which the population density is over 500 people per square mile, and the generalized landholding averages between 2.5 and 5.0 acres per family, with

considerable fragmentation of parcels within family holdings. The size of individual parcels in such a situation reflects such local matters as minor landforms, the directional gradient of water flow, variations in soils, system of settlement, economic history of land inheritance and subsequent division among heirs, cropping combinations employed, and the sheer density of population in some complex and interlinked fashion. In such situations there often is marked fragmentation of holdings among the farm-operator families.

In more recently settled lowland situations the mosaic element has not become so complex, since land exchange, division through inheritance, and other localized factors have not been operative long enough to have reduced the size of parcels, or the fragmentation, to the very small patterns often found in areas of long occupation. The left lower section of Figure 10.7 is the 1957 field map of a rice-growing section on the immediate river-margin flood plain of the Mekong River in eastern Cambodia, with the same population density and landholding average as the upper half of the same figure. On the immediate river bank situation, in the left lower section of Figure 10.7, on either side of the string village, is illustrated the frequent tendency to divide holdings into linear strips at right angles to the river bank, in order to provide each family with a plot of fresh alluvial soils annually rejuvenated by flood deposition. The local situation for this village is one of a semi-aquatic environment in which many plots are naturally water-covered during the whole year.

In the hill country the agricultural landscape often takes on the appearance of irregular and elongated fields molded to the contours of the physical surface (see the first two photos in the landscape cluster, pp. 231-232). The narrow width and long length of the fields directly expresses the gradient of local relief, in which terraces are separated

FIGURE 10.7. Patterns of farm fields. Parts A and B are from Jean Delvert, *Le Paysan Cambodgien*, Mouton, Paris, 1961, and C is from F. H. Wernstedt and J. E. Spencer, *Philippine Island World*, University of California Press, Berkeley and Los Angeles, 1967.

by vertical risers of varying dimensions. This is notably the case for the wet-field rice landscape in which the size and shape of the fields is determined by the gradient of relief and the dimensions of the surface that can be made sufficiently level to hold a shallow layer of water over the whole of each field (see Fig. 10.7, lower right section, the 1966 field pattern near Banaue, in northern Luzon, Philippines). In such situations the bottom portion of the zone of drainage flow may permit field plots of what broader dimensions than can be constructed along the margins of the valley or ravine. In areas of low relief terraces will be separated by mud embankments in which the height of the riser will be slight, but in areas of marked relief the riser wall between terraces may range up to twenty feet, sometimes being even greater than the horizontal width of the terraced field. In broad flood plains, on the other hand, the mud embankment separator between water-holding units may be only a water-holding bund, for the general relief gradient is so slight that the field itself may absorb the difference in level. In terraced landscapes family land-holdings often conform to the units of terracing that are practical under conditions of relief and provision for water supplies. Fragmentation may occur here too, and land inheritance systems may cause sharing of fields that cannot readily be separated by water-controlling bunds within already terraced units. Above and around the terraced units of the agricultural landscape in hilly country there are often sloping field units that form part of the crop landscape. Sometimes these fields may be contoured into terraces on which the field surfaces have considerable gradient toward the fronts of the terraces.

Outside the zone of rice cropping field patterns are similar to those of the rice zone, in areas long settled and carrying a heavy population, though the landscape often does not show the field boundaries so clearly since fields lack the quite-visible water-holding bund system. Terracing in dry-field zones often is somewhat more crudely done, since the precise level and the water-holding bund are not needed. There are variations in the detail of the mosaic in different countries and regions, reflecting the efficiency of the farming system and the care given the fields by their operators. Portions of India show irregularities and a certain disorderliness, as compared to the often beautifully tailored and highly efficient Japanese landscapes. Areas of relatively recent settlement often show larger field patterns than those illustrated here, frequently reflecting lighter population densities and the lack of subdivisional happenings that mark the older, long-settled landscapes. Areas in which shifting cultivation still is practiced regularly show marked patchiness of wild plant cover, owing to the sequential patterns of clearing and regeneration of the wild plant cover. Waste land not used for cropping purposes often is irregular in contour and in dimensions, often contributing to the mosaic pattern of the croplands.

Dooryard plantings of fruit trees of many kinds are common throughout the Orient, particularly in southeastern Asia. There commonly is little order to these plantings, from the European viewpoint, but in fact there often is an excellent ecologic balance among the plantings, which require little steady maintenance effort. Many such plantings are almost wild plantings today, but they constitute a significant share of native agricultural production. Only in a few parts of the Orient are the fruits grown in regular single-crop orchards, and most of these are relatively recent in origin.

In many parts of the Orient today a varied shifting cultivation, intensive wet-field rice culture, vegetable and fruit culture are carried on side by side, sometimes even by subunits of the same culture group. But there are few large regions in which agriculture is as productive as it needs to be to support the resident populations. Many areas no longer provide their own food supplies, and, expressed in political units, only Burma, Thailand, and South Vietnam are potentially able to produce the surpluses of food supplies that have been the main object of oriental agriculture in the past.

The stimulus of the newly-bred and so-called "miracle rice" varieties, adding notably to crop yields on the best lands in several countries, lends at least a temporary prospect of averting possible famine and other serious consequences in the food-deficit regions of the Orient. The complementary breeding of improved varieties of wheat, maize, and some other grains adds to the prospect. However, the long-run impact of such crop-breeding advances is still uncertain for three reasons. First, the new varieties demand improved cultivation practices, the ample use of fertilizers (which traditional varieties did not require) and, for rice, careful provision and control of water. It does not seem likely that the new crop varieties can be quickly spread to all kinds of lands operated by all levels of crop growers, since the rather demanding conditions probably cannot be met everywhere. Second, the long-run impact of the new varieties is still uncertain, both on the lands that grow them, and on the internal economic systems of the several countries. Third, unless population-growth patterns can be brought under control the food demand may approximate the production increases, to the end that the day of accounting is merely postponed a few years.

Although commercial production of selected agricultural commodities is very old in the different parts of the Orient, such commercial production in the past always was a minor factor in regional agriculture. The modern period has brought change to agriculture in most parts of the Orient, owing to the influence of the occidental and his interest in cheap crop commodities for sale in markets outside the Orient. This com-

mercialization has introduced a new element into traditional small-farmer agriculture, and also has introduced a new system of agriculture, the plantation. The new element has been the cash crop production of a wide range of commodities in volumes far beyond the needs of the producing locality. First were the spices of the Indies, followed by silk and tea in China. Gradually a number of crops have been added to the list, some traditional in the Orient, such as sugar, soybeans, jute, abaca, and coconut, and some are new crops introduced from abroad or moved to new regions, such as rubber, tea, maize, coffee, and palm oil in India and Ceylon. The introduction of the plantation (estate) system into southeastern Asia was a profitable thing for the occidental, for it utilized abundant cheap labor producing its own food supply and yielded commercial agricultural products having a ready market outside the Orient. There are eighteenth century forerunners, but the commercial expansion of the plantation properly began in the 1830's, reaching its heyday in the 1930's. This grafting of commercial export agriculture onto traditional agriculture helped to upset the economy of every region and every country in southern and southeastern Asia. It resulted in the Orient's becoming a source of cheap commodities competing for world markets and taking space from subsistence production to the extent that few regions now feed themselves under the patterns of marked population growth that have characterized the last half century.

In those commodity patterns in which new crops were introduced to the various regions, native populations only slowly took to growing the crops on small holdings, and native-owned plantations were slow to develop, so that the plantation was an exploitational form of foreign economic development. After World War II plantation production trended downhill, as newly independent governments confiscated foreign-held lands, did not renew concessions, or invoked requirements for native capital controls. There has been large recent expansion of native smallholder plantings in such crops as rubber, coffee, abaca, and maize, as well as in some of the older commercial crops, and plantation production of the exports crops no longer is so dominating. The economic growth of a strictly cash-crop agriculture has now blurred the former contrasts of native-subsistence and foreign-plantation patterns of production (see Fig. 10.6). Diversification of agriculture in every country in the Orient has made marked strides since the 1930's and today only Thailand could be said to retain the small range cropping systems that characterized much of the Orient in the early nineteenth century.

Forest cropping, through reforestation programs, has not yet developed into a specific form of agricultural practice in the Orient. Forest management, of a sort, is very old in several countries but, on a modern commercial basis, is just beginning to develop. The area and opportunity for profitable forest economy are ample, and indications are that it is on the way. In some areas this can be through private initiative; in others it will involve long-range government programs. There are large areas of land in some countries that should be returned to managed forest cover as both land conservation and economic production, and for those countries that have depended significantly upon the export of forest products, such

programs are vital. Forestry programs, in total land use terms, are most vital in India, Thailand, and the Philippines, but almost everywhere else the future shortages of wood products will require major forestation developments.

In any country, or region, in the Orient the overall land use pattern today is some complex of the features, systems, and production patterns described above. Upon many areas the pressure of man, foreign trade, and dollar profits rests but lightly. In some areas it is easy to provide the things that local society has desired in the past for every person, and the landscape reflects this lightness of pressure. New Guinea is such a region for, in eastern New Guinea, the Iron Age only now is replacing the Stone Age, and Cambodia has been such in the last century or so. However, the natures of local cultures are changing, the desires are increasing, and the demands placed upon the land are greater than they were in earlier periods. And in North China, the Indian Punjab, and in the Philippine island of Cebu the pressures have been heavy and the landscapes show them clearly. Unequal landscapes, however, do not react in the same way to human pressures. The fresh and fertile island of Java, about 49,000 square miles in area, bears the impact of over 60,000,000 Javanese more easily than does the hard rock "island" of upland Shantung, about 28,000 square miles in area, bear the pressures of perhaps 20,000,000 Chinese.

TRANSPORTATION

As shown here at the Elephant Pass, northern Ceylon, solar-evaporation salt pans, a great deal of transport throughout the Orient is still performed by human labor. (United Nations)

This scene from Hyderabad, Deccan, southern India, demonstrates the wide use made of the bicycle and bicycle-pedaled "tri-shaw" for both passenger and commodity transport. In some large cities the "tri-shaws" have been banned as powered equipment replaces that operated by human labor. (Government of India)

In Taipei, Taiwan, as in some other metropolitan urban areas, the slow motor-powered "tri-shaw" is about to be banned from the central business district, but the device is widely used in the Orient to haul larger and heavier loads than can be handled by a pedaled cart. (J. E. Spencer)

Outside the village of Hangala Pura, Mysore, southern India, cart bullocks
are being taken to water at the end of a working day, as the carts are left by
the roadside. (Eric Schwab, WHO)

On the Malabar Coast lagoons of Kerala, southern India, as in many other aquatic environments throughout the southern Orient, the dugout canoe still provides a significant means of local transportation. (P. N. Sharma, WHO)

Of the thirty-one vehicles in this portion of a Taipei, Taiwan, traffic circle on a normal morning rush hour, only the two motorcycles and the Volkswagen in the center are privately owned, since private cars are not yet numerous in the Orient. Visible in this photo, also, are two pickups, one truck, eleven taxis, and fourteen buses. (J. E. Spencer)

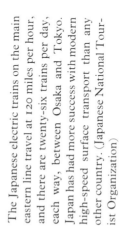

The Japanese electric trains on the main eastern line travel at 120 miles per hour, and there are twenty-six trains per day, each way, between Osaka and Tokyo. Japan has had more success with modern high-speed surface transport than any other country. (Japanese National Tourist Organization)

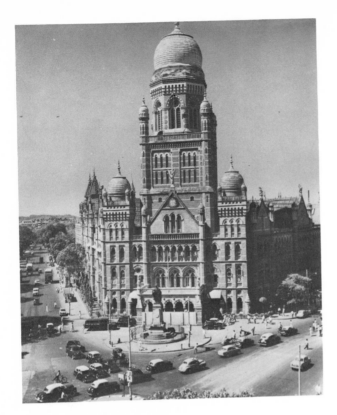

The structure housing the Bombay Municipal Corporation, Bombay, western India, was built in the 19th Century to combine Islamic and European motifs. (Government of India)

These buildings of Victoria, Hong Kong, display the architectural styles of the early and middle 20th century, but they also display the advertising signs so common throughout much of the Orient today. At night many cities in the Orient show brilliant patterns of neon lighting. (J. E. Spencer)

II

REGIONS: PHYSICAL, CULTURAL, AND GEOGRAPHIC

It is customary among scholars dealing with large portions of human affairs to seek units of division of their material, so that specific discussions may bring out details, contrasts, likenesses, uniqueness, or ubiquity. Many scholars use regional or territorial patterns of divisions and apply to them the word "geographic." Geographers naturally use these territorial patterns of distribution of the phenomena with which they deal. Among some geographers a cult of regionalism developed which attempts so to refine the divisional units that by the use of a map and a key there can be expressed the essential core of the message to be told. In those parts of the world where data are precisely gathered upon all manner of subjects, the geographer, by the use of statistics and cartography, can produce all manner of mapped distributional phenomena and translate combinations of these into regionalisms. But in those parts of the world where data are scant upon many subjects the undue pursuit of this tendency can produce only imaginative, artificial, or partial results. The Orient is such a region.

In a crude way it would be possible to delimit a bewildering number of different kinds of regions for the Orient. On the many maps of this volume there are sketched many distributional matters, but it does not seem possible to combine all these things into a composite, and have it produce a meaningful result. The incomplete map of languages has little relation to the map of crop regions, and neither of these concurs with the maps of religion or of climatic areas, incompletely as these areas are understood. On a more restricted scale, the map of zoogeographic regions of Thailand would have only broad resemblance to any maps of climate that could be drawn from the scant data available. For the whole Orient the map of customary beverages has never been drawn, but one cannot expect that it would be closely related to the crop map, the language map, or the map of religions. The map of native costume has not been drawn either, and to what other map it would closely correspond there is no way of knowing at present. There is a complex map of domestic housetypes to be drawn, for which there are but fragmentary portions filled in so far. Yet these three latter subjects would seem to be important items in the fuller delimitation of meaningful human regionalisms.

Too often the geographer has presented a concept of geographic regions that bears close relation to the maps of landforms, climates, and dominant crops. This is an obvious kind of related regionalism, and its application in the Orient produces maps of some real utility; maps of both geographic regions and of agricultural regions will be found in the regional chapters. Such a map, however, has no overwhelming relation to many of the details of the daily life of many of the peoples of the Orient. If this volume fails to present a complete and satisfactory summation pattern of geographic regions for the Orient, it is because this seems impossible to accomplish in view of the limited knowledge of those things that are significant to the issues of geographic regionalism in the Orient. In the Chinese proverb "The North is salt, the South is sweet, the East is sour, and the West is hot," there is expressed a significant factor of regionalism. That this corresponds to the dominant use of salt, sugar, vinegar, and pepper, respectively, in the daily diet of millions of people makes it important, but it is extremely difficult both to draw lines between the separate dietary regions and to fit this into a larger framework of Chinese regionalism.

The geographic region, if there be such a thing, should be a regional territory in which the whole complex assemblage of factors, affecting nature, area, man, and his culture, expresses itself in collective terms, since geography is concerned with all of these. Since culture is a changing thing, since man himself changes location constantly, since man alters his landscape, and since both plants and animals also possess mobility, it is likely that *the* geographic region never can be identified as a fixed territory for a long period of time. The interrelations of man, culture, and environment not only are com-

plex but also are subject to constant change. It requires maintained censuses of data of very great variety to identify the status of separate elements of this complex at any one time, and to map the alterations. In the Orient too much of the pertinent census data is lacking to make possible the identification of the complex geographic region.

As man increasingly has adopted more complex political systems, and as political nationalism has emerged as a force in regionalism, the political region has emerged into a position of steadily greater importance. That man has not correlated this region with other kinds of regions often is extremely evident. The division of India into the two political states India and Pakistan, in 1947, is perhaps a most obvious illustration. Behind the separation of North and South Vietnam at the 17th parallel in 1954, there lies a significant cultural boundary, though the elements forming the boundary are not often recognized and are not so finite as a political line. The administrative utility of the political region has grown with the passage of time, regardless of its obvious clash with the simple environmental regionalisms based upon landform and climate. But the political region in an old and stable culture often tends to become, in itself, a synthesis of the factors of regionalism. In China proper the political province often seems as effective a regional division as any other that the geographer can conjure up based upon a few selected criteria only. The evolution of the Chinese political boundaries has been slow, as the Chinese, themselves, recognized and utilized the features which make it possible to draw regional boundaries. Both the tangible and the intangible seem well expressed in the Chinese proverb "In Kueichou there are no three steps on the same level, no three days without rain, and no man has three coppers in his pocket to jingle." Obviously the new and still unstable political subregions of Thailand or Burma are susceptible neither to the formation of regional proverbs nor to the use of political areas as significant regional entities.

This volume falls in the fields of cultural and regional geography, and in it there have been utilized many kinds of regional criteria. In the early chapters of Part I there have been presented some matters of regionalism, though many of them are incomplete or inconclusive. In each regional chapter in the latter section of the volume there is concern for the matter of regionalisms but, again, they are incomplete and sometimes intangible. At no time are these precisely delimited matters prescribed by sharp lines. There is an obvious political regionalism to the regional chapters upon separate coun-

tries. In the Philippines political regionalism has been growing rapidly on a national scale, and it has worked to the end of separating from the Indies a new kind of region despite the landform regionalism that places the Indies and the Philippines in one large physical division. Ceylon is going in a different direction from India in many matters, because of political regionalism, entirely contrary to environmental regionalism and many of the elements of cultural regionalism.

Many regionalisms are the slow workings of cultural change and are unconscious matters of peaceful operation. The changes in cropping patterns of the Indus Valley or of Szechwan, in which rice and the sweet

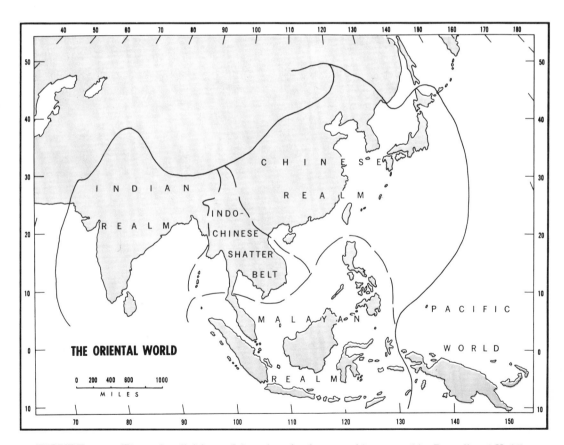

FIGURE 11.1. The major divisions of the oriental culture world, as zoned by Russell and Kniffen, based upon a composite set of criteria.

potato, respectively, have altered agriculture and food supply, amount to these kinds of changing regionalisms. Other changes are militant matters accompanied by the force of arms and the wilful action of a population. The northern expansion of the Japanese into the territory of the Ainu for several centuries altered the regionalism of Japan. The separation of India and Pakistan was less a matter of aggressive militant procedure as such than of the political inflaming of religious and cultural prejudices that had been long ago implanted upon the soil of Mother India. The spread of the Vietnamese throughout the lowlands of Indochina, or of the Tai throughout Thailand has been a militant matter at some times and a peaceful one at others, but both operations have altered the regionalisms of this part of southeastern Asia.

In some manner or other we have tried to take these and other developments into account in this volume. But the easy diagraming of the issues of regionalism remains largely undone. The Orient as a whole is a cultural realm rather than a physical one, though it has as a supporting base a broad regional matter of physical climate throughout much of its area. Its primary divisions now are political ones, with an increasingly important role to play in the lives of all orientals. Two large bodies of culture, those of China and India, traditionally have given to the Orient much

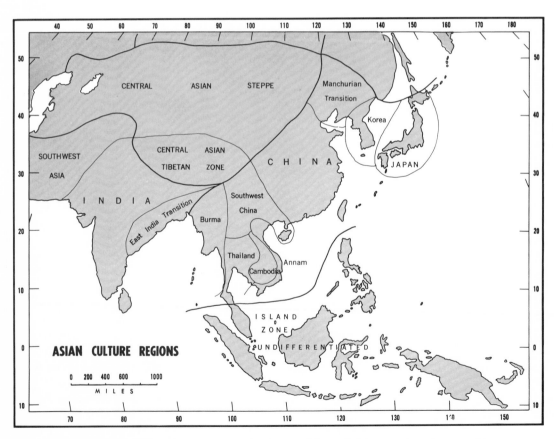

FIGURE 11.2. Asian culture regions, after Bacon. These divisions are based upon arbitrary anthropologic criteria considered somewhat debatable in some terms.

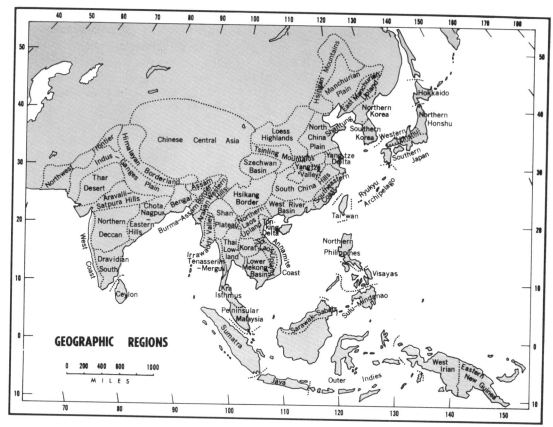

FIGURE 11.3. Boundaries of geographic regions, after Cressey. Fifty-nine regions are outlined here, based upon an assemblage of criteria, chiefly those of the physical environment.

of its peculiar cultural character, that of India and that of China. Southeastern Asia and the southern Island Arcs find these two bodies of culture overlapping and competing with each other in some respect (Fig. 11.1, and see also Fig. 16.1). The cultural forces of the Occident have so broadly entered into the life of the Orient, however, that they threaten to obscure much that is environmental and much that is native. And more recently a Communist cultural complex has invaded the Orient, to threaten new patterns of culture and new patterns of regionalism. The entrance of state trading agreements into the economic operations of the Orient is threatening to establish a totally new kind of economic

regionalism, equaled only by the regionalism that arose out of Yen-bloc, Dollar-bloc, and Sterling-bloc developments. The latent nature of a super-political regionalism based upon the affiliation of countries of southeastern Asia into regional economic and political combines similar to those of the European world is still another of the new items of regionalism that may well have a long-run effect.

There are, then, many bases for regionalism in the Orient. Some, geographers have dealt with, but many remain unstudied and unmapped. In this volume a considerable amount of this material is presented, but much of the highly pertinent material is lacking. Failing the data on which to outline adequately based geographic regions, there still remains the problem of how to break down large areas into units sufficiently distinct to permit comparison and detailed study. For such purposes, therefore, we have presented in the maps that follow regionalisms based upon selected criteria (Figs. 11.2-11.3). They are presented for convenience and, collectively, are best described as maps of regions of convenience.

PUBLIC BUILDINGS

The Angkor Wat, near modern Siem Reap, Cambodia, was the crowning religious monument of the Khmer kings. The temple was built in the 12th century, suffered neglect after 1432, and recently has been undergoing restoration. (United Nations)

275

The Hanuman Doka, a Lamaist temple on the Palace Square, Katmandu, Nepal, is often used as a marketplace on ordinary days. (Eric Schwab, WHO) (See opposite page.)

The Phra Pathom Chedi, at Nakhon Pathom, Thailand, is the oldest Buddhist Stupa in Thailand, marking the place of introduction of Buddhism to Thailand. The stupa is characteristic of one of the main architectural forms of Theravada Buddhism. (Tourist Organization of Thailand)

The Islamic Bodhshahi Mosque, in Lahore, West Pakistan, was built by
Emperor Aurangzeb, and was completed in 1764. (United Nations)

PART II

THE REGIONAL EXPRESSION OF CULTURES

12

MOTHER INDIA: IN THE BEGINNING

THE EARLY ENVIRONMENTS

As the last pulsation of the Ice Age relaxed and the contemporary Indian environment began to take shape the greatest significant change lay in climate. The yearly temperature cycle lifted a few degrees, and now no part of lowland India suffers seriously cold winter weather. The moisture cycle receded somewhat and probably increased its variability. Cloudiness and humidities probably decreased a little. Subjective comfort of the body has been increased, but so has mental anguish over whether the rains will come on time and in adequate amounts. Most of these changes were complete well before the historic period began, but not before man began trying out the utility of various parts of the Indian landscape.

Much of southern India is a warm, moist, and muggy environment of lowlands and low hill country in which plant growth is rapid, and one in which early man probably found it difficult to cope with the plant world about him. As long as he was content to gather its products, however, the plant world was a productive one. There were some good spots in the south of India, but none of them were very large, and their complex of conditions was less useful than that of some other regions. The highlands of northern India, on the other hand, were a difficult landscape to

use for two reasons. The handicap of strong relief was great, and a wet, heavy forest cover contained fewer items of value than did the plant cover of the lowlands and the hill country. Parts of the North Indian Plain and certain portions of the central peninsula seem to contain a combination of elements that facilitated the gathering culture of earliest man and also permitted the exercise of the curiosity and initiative that resulted in agriculture. In early postglacial times these lowland and hill country zones were better than they are today in that slow desiccation had not then caused rainfall variability to become as serious as it is today. The zones of greater than average utility were widely scattered and covered a considerable total area. They are not contiguous regions, nor are they all alike in their local conditions. The upper Ganges and central Indus valleys, the Narbada and other similar valleys of Rajputana, a few of the peninsular river valleys, some of the deltas of the east coast, and the southeastern portion of Ceylon were among the more useful spots of early India. These regions constituted a number of similar ample environments that facilitated the parallel growth of several culture patterns. The cultures had certain things in common but also possessed numerous unlike features.

It is in the nature of the plant and animal

resources that these local environments notably differed. Northwest India lay not far from the southwest Asian plant and animal nursery and shared most of its products from a very early date. Apparently the horse was one of the few animals not used in India before the Caucasoid invasions. The Ganges Valley and peninsular Indian sites, on the other hand, shared a great many of the plants and animals that were at home in some part of southeastern Asia. The yams, taros, and other root crops were basic food plants. It still is a moot question where, and how early, rice came into the food grouping. If India is not within its original home region the origin is close by, and rice became one of the early plants cultivated in eastern and southern India. Sugarcane is a plant that seems to have been brought into India at a very early date, becoming an important food item. Both northwest India and Peninsular India had available a wide range of plants and animals, usable at different stages of economic organization. It is difficult to suggest which environment had the greatest potential value, but it does seem probable that no local area in either environment stood out very far above the others.

THE EARLIEST SOCIETIES

The beginnings of Indian cultures cannot be even approximately dated or adequately described. From archeologic sampling it is clear that India was populated during the Paleolithic by peoples who used the Stone Age culture of western Asia-Africa and was at least affected by Far Eastern peoples of a rather different Stone Age culture. The western realm reached into northwest India and throughout the peninsula, whereas the eastern zone reached into eastern India, and probably into the Ganges Valley and into the northern part of Peninsular India. The samplings make clear that almost all parts of India were inhabited sometime during the

Paleolithic. There is a marked gap between the Paleolithic and Neolithic in India. Knowledge of the Neolithic still is very spotty and inconclusive, and it is likely that many peoples moved into or through southern India then. The early cultures of the Iranian highland certainly included parts of the Indus Valley. Data for what now is termed Indus Valley culture indicate a tremendous advance in many ways, but the regional extent and affiliations are not yet certain (Fig. 12.1). Evidence of southern India culture, contemporary with Indus Valley culture, is even more vague. Another gap exists between the Indus Valley culture and the Caucasoid invasions. From this point on the story reads fairly continuously, though confusedly, since the Indian peoples never have possessed the historical passion that documented Chinese or Roman culture history.

The tentative picture of the Indus Valley is one of a rather sophisticated urban culture, well-planned cities of flat-roofed, multi-storied buildings occupying the alluvial lowlands along the Indus River. Fired brick were expertly handled in building homes, baths, drainage systems, and wells. Many a modern Indian town compares unfavorably, item for item. Fortifications were massive and well developed, but it is uncertain if they surrounded the whole of the city. There clearly are remains of ritual sites and ceremonial buildings, and there was at least one storehouse serving as a state granary. Craftsmen's skill in gold and silver work, in seal and bead making, and in pottery manufacture was first class. Irrigation agriculture grew most of the crops common to southwestern Asia, plus cotton at least and very likely a number of others domesticated in India. The Indus Valley of that day possessed more easily available fuel than it does today, much of which was cut off to fire the bricks used in building construction. More big game animals also were available then than are present today. In pottery, art motifs, trinkets,

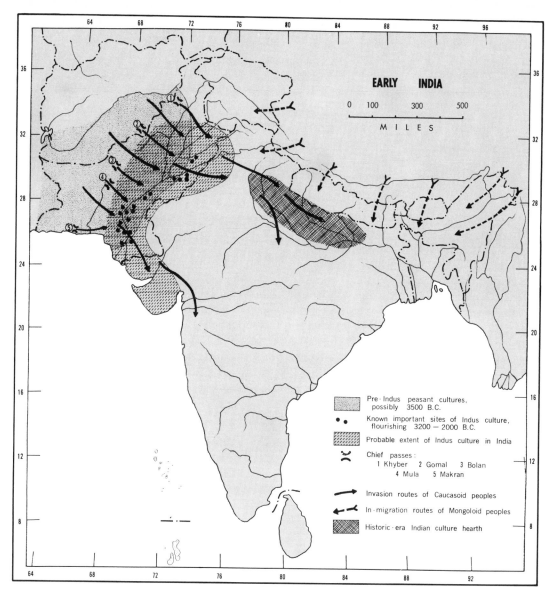

FIGURE 12.1. Early India.

brick types, and other relevant features the Indus Valley clearly shows an active relationship to other lowland cultures of the Near East. The duplication is not complete and there are a number of items that show real individuality. Undoubtedly there was a flourishing trade with the Near East.

It is thought that Indus Valley culture reached from the western hill country throughout the Indus Valley, eastward toward the divide between the Indus and the Ganges, and southward to the Kathiawar Peninsula. It seems possible to suggest that Indus culture was properly a northwest

Indian culture using items from each major realm appropriate to its local environment. In a somewhat drier environment than possessed by much of the rest of India this would suggest that the main trade relations, racial contacts, historical ties, and social motivations lay with southwestern Asia. The beginnings of this culture unfortunately lie below the present valley water table, buried by recent alluvial deposition of the Indus. The ravages of severe floods and changing river channels may be read in the local landscape today, suggestive of causes of abandonment of Mohenjo-daro, at least, the best-known city. In the time sequence Indus Valley culture appears contemporary with that of the Mesopotamian lowland.

No such clear presentation of typical south Indian culture can be made. Later less formal and less well-executed building in smaller settlements indicate a lower level than that achieved in the Indus Valley. They also suggest competition among peoples for possession of a landscape. More religious architectural remains of a varied sort indicate more concern with the mystical side of nature and life. Suggestions are toward greater contact with southeastern Asia than northern India, though whether by purposeful trade movement or by accidental folk migration is not yet clear. A subtropical cropping system which shared many things with southeastern Asia possessed a few unique items and shared some with the Indus Valley.

Nothing positive can be said at this point on racial affiliation and linguistic relations between the Indus Valley and the rest of India. It would seem that the south possessed more diverse peoples than the north. At the close of the Neolithic, as the modern period began, it seems almost as though Indus culture and southern culture held less in common than each held with its outer marginal realm. That is, in southwestern Asia and northwest India were the several parts of an early common culture realm, whereas southern India and southeastern Asia were the variant parts of another and separate realm. If this is true it may indicate a reversal of the regional relations that appear to have held true during the Paleolithic when southern India's connections lay mostly with Europe and Africa and North India was connected to the Far East. The argument in such matters often becomes partisan and in the face of insufficient evidence, it is too early to make more than a suggestion to this end.

THE CAUSCASOID INVASIONS

The dating of the earliest expansion of peoples from the Caucasoid racial incubator is impossible to predict. Around 2000 B.C., however, the peoples of southwestern Asia again were in flux, competitively pushing about their home territory. For a little more than a thousand years this process went on, constituting an important chapter in the race history of Eurasia. Early during this period groups of people began moving eastward through Persia and Trans-Caspia, as they also moved westward toward southern Europe. Finding the numerous gaps in the western Mountain Wall, they began to filter through Afghanistan and Baluchistan and to scatter out on the lowlands of the Indus Valley. The Mountain Wall proved no more an isolating barrier than than it had during the stone ages. In fact the physical situation may have stimulated some movement into India. Passes through the high country were low and short enough so that crossing was practical at all seasons of the year. Wood, water, and pasturage undoubtedly were better than today, after centuries of overuse. The Mountain Wall was often a sufficient physical barrier to divert elsewhere the attentions of predatory tribes seeking territory in Persia and Trans-Caspia. The old culture connections were sufficient to make known the existence of a land beyond the mountains. Across them lay relative safety in the turbulent period of Caucasoid expansion (see Fig. 12.1).

The peoples who came into India at this time were not all of one physical mold, nor did they possess the same culture. They are variously named Aryan, Indo-Aryan, Caucasoid, and Indo-European. They were crude crop growers who also grazed animals. They brought some of their own breeds, including the horse for the first time. They were not pastoral nomads in the full sense, nor were they builders of a high order of cities. They were a belligerent folk who had fought for their living space previously and who fought for a place on the North Indian Plain. They were less sophisticated than had been the city folk of Mohenjo-daro and Harappa. It is not clear whether the newcomers drove out, or wiped out, the remaining city culture, or whether flood, famine, and pestilence earlier had achieved much the same result unaided. From the earliest folk sagas of the newcomers it is evident that the North Indian Plain was inhabited by people who impressed the "Aryans" as dark skinned and of an inferior culture. Successive waves of immigrants pushed the line of settlement out across the Indus. Semipermanent villages became scattered over the dry country of northwest India, and the newcomers employed an economy that still combined their own crude crop growing with open-range animal breeding. This economy was like that of their previous home, but it involved some new Indian crops and irrigation of a higher order than they had employed previously. There still must have been ample wood for human use and range fodder for more animals than were present.

In the course of the thousand or more years during which the Caucasoid invasions took place the line of infiltration and settlement spread steadily outward from the Mountain Wall. The spread always was a militant one, and it always involved the kind of race mixture that results from conquest, with men often slain and women and children taken as slaves. The color line caused some trouble socially, and feeling about it undoubtedly aided the other basic causes in the slow evolution of the caste system. There always remained the change in skin color from northwest to south and east, and with it went a difference in culture, in language, in social organization, and in political sense. Gradually these Caucasoid invaders grew less Caucasoid and became definitely a part of the North Indian landscape as the Indian bonds tightened at the expense of the Near Eastern ones. Little was clearly defined about their culture as yet. It was a village culture, concerned with a generalized arid-margin agriculture, but possessing considerable mobility in animal care. There were many groups in varying stages of this cultural shift.

THE FORMATIVE ERA

At the close of the Caucasoid invasions India was an amorphous collection of many peoples and many simple cultures, all scattered over a physical landscape whose natural and human divisions were seldom finite in character, boundaries, or qualities. Everywhere social stratification still was simple, though slowly growing. Religion was slowly combining Aryan priestly philosophy with Dravidian cult magic. Livestock, wild fowl, and wild animals still were items of commonplace consideration, eaten, worked, hunted, and used in many ways. Little was being done in the way of roads or irrigation works, but a progressive deforestation was stripping the growth from the lightly covered arid and dry margins as population and settlement increased. The good spots in the Indian realm were productive enough for population to grow, villages to increase in number, and a few towns to evolve at favored points. Much of humid India still was jungle, rainforest or scrub parkland, occupied by an abundant wild life, among which the scattered cultural landscapes were a very minor share of the total area of India. Even in the heavily forested regions, however, shifting cultivation and selective usage had its effects upon both the plant and animal resources, and probably by this period no truly virgin landscape existed. In this situation there were few human controls over progressive cultural change. No one region was held by a people whose cultural mores were a standard, or whose strength dominated a wide area.

The several centuries between 1000 and 500 B.C. were a formative era in which an unmistakably Indian stamp became clearly visible in all parts of the realm. It was a turbulent period in which tribal priests matured into religious philosophers, tribal chiefs became regional rajahs, soldiers acquired formal social position, and strong groups pushed weak ones toward refuge zones. Artisan craftsmanship multiplied its skills and its products, and trade began to grow again, connecting all of India's subregions and reaching out to the Near East and to southeastern Asia. The domination of the Brahmans clearly set the tone for all higher societies as the priests spread throughout all parts of India with the steady growth of Hinduism. The simple social framework of Caucasoid society hardened into the patterns of caste stratification. Many protests over Brahman usurpation and corruption of the old simple cultures set in motion waves of culture change which spread throughout India.

Despite primitive transport facilities India became surprisingly mobile. Pilgrims, missionaries, traders, artisans, soldiers of fortune, migratory clans, emigrating tribes, political opportunists, and many others surged north, south, east, and west throughout India. Some true blood mixture occurred in all this movement, working toward a composite Indian type, but far less resulted than should have been the case. Such things as Hinduism, Buddhism, and Jainism became

known everywhere, caste and customs of dress spread very widely, and local crops and practices spread to the simple limits of climatic tolerance. These common features were not enough to unite India. The written languages of Brahman and Buddhist priests never replaced local languages. Though innumerable common customs spread over the country they did not tie India into one unit. There is a curious contrast in the period, of trends toward unity of culture but the failure of regional cohesion. This same conflict appears again and again in Indian culture history. Many efforts to ascribe it to specific causes have been made, but perhaps there is no one answer to the query of why human cultures achieve the results they do.

Out of clan and tribal politics and village settlement came the institution of the *sabha* or village council government. Essentially a democratic political institution, it operated by elected representatives who formed a permanent managing body that handled every aspect of village economy and local culture. Gradually the democratic process became selective, representation in some villages being restricted to Brahmans; but a large percentage of the villages were non-Brahman, so that the village council became one of the most significant of Indian institutions. Out of this primary control came important features of land ownership and systems of taxation. Joint village tenancy, all-private ownership, and varied mixed land systems gradually developed, often depending upon caste composition of a village or geographic factors of local economy. In the hands of the *sabha* lay the power of taxation and the use of funds in the maintenance of such public features as temples, market places, the assembly hall, streets, and monuments. This village development, throughout the breadth of India, most often skipped the mobile, simpler tribes of peoples practicing a hunting-gathering economy. To them the open jungle and forest ranges were ample, and they chose retreat into the back country rather than accept a lower position in a society involving irksome changes in their mode of life. Such a village development also, unaccountably, skipped other peoples and limited areas within the Indian realm. This evolution of an autonomous village system preceded the appearance of more formal and large-order political systems. The village system persisted into the modern era as one unifying feature which resisted the encroachment of all superimposed political authority. The durability of the system is responsible for the settlement patterns of modern India.

And out of tribal politics and priestly domination of social and religious rules came the domination of the Brahmans and the formulation of the essential laws of Hinduism which, ever since, have motivated the largest segment of Indian life. The Sacred Law became what the priestly class made it over the centuries. Political states headed by despotic rulers, administered by Brahman priestly ministers who surmounted a graded bureaucracy, composed the central theme around which political theory, Hinduism, caste, and the ordinary rules of society were grouped. Rulers were as subject to the laws as were other human beings. Militant competition among the kingdoms that appeared in the Indian realm was conceived as the normal circumstance. Out of this competition came the earliest regional dominance of the Indian realm by a part of the North Indian Plain.

THE FLOWERING OF EARLY INDIA

Sometime in the sixth century B.C. the growing turbulence of Indian culture began to produce results. Evolutionary achievements surpassed anything in the past but changed the direction of Indian culture growth not at all. The Caucasoid peoples

from beyond the Mountain Wall had grafted themselves tightly onto basic Indian culture. Landscape, plant and animal resources, and man were about to achieve a synthesis in the first Indian empire. This was the century into which Gautama Buddha and Mahabir were born, the founders of Buddhism and Jainism, respectively. Both were born into good places in society, in the central Ganges Valley, but both became dissatisfied with the increasing Brahman domination of Indian society. They and their movements were expressive of one side of the yeasty stirrings in Indian life of this period. On another side were the growing concept of the political state and the gradual enlargement of the petty kingdoms that had been growing out of tribal domains during the past centuries. Indian history does not record the long struggle that must have gone on among the new ruling class, their military aides, the soldier caste, and the priestly lawyers that both operated Hinduism and formed the new and growing bureaucracy.

If one examines the regional focus of the center of this cultural emergence, it appears to center in the middle Ganges Valley (see Fig. 12.1). There are sound reasons why this should be so. Although the primary Caucasoid invasions had tapered off some centuries previously, northwest India still was subject to invasion from Persia. This was the era of the great Persian rulers from Cyrus to Xerxes, and the Indus Valley section of the North Indian Plain was either an outlying sector of the Persian empire or a marginal zone constantly subject to predatory raids. So unprotected was northwest India by the Mountain Wall that the Indus sector was not the wealthy and prosperous part of northern India. Far to the east the very wet lower Ganges valley and delta were yet too hard to use, were but lightly populated, and also were marginal parts of northern India. The best conditions were found in the central and upper Ganges basin. Here was a landscape that was easy to use, was well equipped with those natural resources most useful to the age, and was at a distance from troublesome invasion and raid. This was the region into which the early Caucasoid invaders had pushed, out of the way of later invaders. Here there combined native peoples and cultures with Caucasoid peoples and cultures. The higher political sense of the Caucasoids perhaps made the difference in promoting the effective political state before it was conceived by any native group or earlier mixture in any south Indian region. The critical element seems less the environment than the superior mixture of race and culture achieved in this particular region. Earlier in Indian history the dominant culture had lain in the Indus Valley, until militant invasion had made the zone untenable. Later Indian history was to see the center of gravity shift to another region, under a variety of causes.

A declining Persian empire was terminated by Alexander and his Greeks, who also pushed across the Mountain Wall into the Indian lowland, only to be lured eastward by stories of wealth and prosperity of the Ganges Valley kingdoms. The inability of Alexander to permanently bridge the distance between Greece and India gave India its chance for expression of its cultural maturity. This came in the Mauryan Empire set up by Chandragupta somewhat before 300 B.C. Its capital was Pataliputra, on the site of what today is Patna, in the central lower Ganges Valley. This had been the base of the small kingdom seized by Chandragupta, from which his conquest of North India began. Under several able successors this minor kingdom grew to include the territory from Bengal to the Hindu Kush and from the Himalayas perhaps into modern Mysore (Fig. 12.2). The greatest Mauryan ruler, Asoka, became a Buddhist convert and turned his energies from political and military conquest to running his realm peacefully, morally, and

happily. The Mauryan Empire lasted, as an entity, until about 185 B.C., when it split into a number of pieces.

The Mauryan era was a mature expression of Indian culture of the time. Buddhism and Jainism were then most successful in their attempted reform of Hinduism. The Buddhist missionary push outside India was sent off by Asoka himself. Within the North Indian Plain, at least, man had learned to operate his environment to the maximum extent of his cultural concept, developing cropping systems and irrigation systems well suited to environmental ecologic regionalisms, and developing base-village plus satellite expansion-village systems designed to spread close social structures over increasing territory. A productive agriculture based on rice and tropical tree products had been developed for the moist lands of the east, and a wheat-millet-sorghum agriculture had spread with increasing efficiency over additional territory on the dry margins. Cotton, sugarcane, and many minor grains now were widely distributed, but the general expansion of acreage was the most significant item as the jungle and forest were steadily cut back. Range-animal culture had begun to decline in relative importance, and there began the evolution of the sacredness of the cow. This notion spread first to oxen and gradually to other animals and birds, under the urging of both Hindus and Buddhists.

Roads and a transport service linked the far parts of the empire. Pataliputra was connected with the Arabian Sea ports of Karakala, Broach, and Musiris, with Taxila in the upper Punjab, and with Tamralipti and Tosali on the Bay of Bengal. The practical application of new political theory of the empire evolved many of the basic concepts of government administration that were used later in history. Despite this mature political growth economic structure remained simple. A repetitive, self-sufficient village

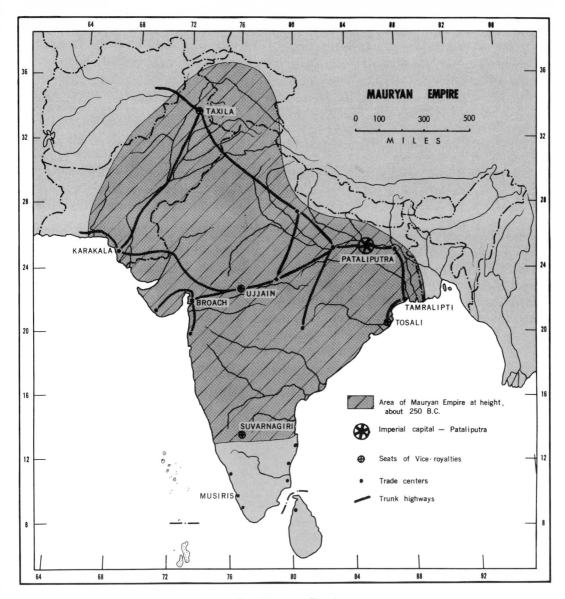

FIGURE 12.2. The Mauryan Empire, about 250 B.C.

economy permitted little real growth in internal trade, as we understand it. A fairly considerable export trade did grow in better-ruled and well-placed regions, but this did not free India from the restrictions of its village economy. It is notable that early during the Mauryan era architects had begun again to build with the fired bricks that had characterized Indus Valley culture but which had not been commonly used in the interval of the Caucasoid invasions. Mauryan architects used stone as though it were wood.

PATTERNS OF INDIAN HISTORY

There are three primary elements that compose the fabric of Indian history and that have been variably interwoven into its complex patterns. They are: invasion, the rise of a region to dominance, the collapse of political power and the failure of regional unity. These elements must be described briefly.

Invasion

The early Caucasoid invasions have been mentioned. In the period between perhaps 1000 B.C. and A.D. 900 there were no more major invasions of India by large groups of peoples looking for living space. Almost continuously, however, the northwest of India was subject to predatory raids and invasions of political conquest through the Mountain Wall, and much of the Indus Valley was in alien hands. Also to a minor extent in this period there were similar invasions in the northeast corner of India as various of the Mongoloids crossed the great river trenches and touched the margins of India. In the northwest, seriously beginning in the tenth century, the spreading wave of Moslem religious and political conquest broke over the Mountain Wall and poured through the passes into the North Indian Plain. Once this contact was established by land, the sea lanes between Arabia and the Malabar coast again became well traveled. For over 700 years in intermittent surges the invasions of Afghans and Turks continued, whereas in the last two centuries the pressure has lightened to become merely a border problem involving mobile and predatory tribes of hillmen. The Islamic invasions rather closely followed the pattern of the Caucasoid invasions, surging across the Punjab and down the Ganges Valley to wear themselves out in Bengal and Assam. These invasions never penetrated deeply into the Himalayas, but they did infiltrate the peninsula in variable fashion, bypassing some of the strongest of the Hindu Rajput kingdoms in the Aravalli-Vindhya hill country to establish a foothold in the Deccan, and to carry raids to the very south of India (Fig. 12.3). The use of mercenary Islamic soldiery by southern rulers and the gradual enlargement of the Mogul Empire in the sixteenth and seventeenth centuries carried varied mixtures of Moslems rather deeply into the peninsula. Many of these latter folk, however, were north Indian converts to Islam rather than fresh newcomers to India.

By sea since the dawn of the historic period had come innumerable traders to India, but never had a lasting invasion struck until the Europeans appeared upon Indian shores. Out of the Indonesian island realm came one short and troublesome attack, but it produced no lasting racial or cultural effects. From the Arakan coast of Burma pirates for centuries harried the east coast of India, and from the Persian Gulf coast they intermittently had disturbed the west coast. The Europeans, however, were a new element with a new power and new techniques. Gradually their invasion of India spread almost all over the country, but the British, like the Islamic Turks and Afghans before them, and like the still earlier Caucasoids, never succeeded in penetrating all the physical pieces that make up the mosaic of India. No people, since at least the Paleolithic so far as one yet can tell, ever has swept completely over India, planting their stock and their culture in every region of that great land.

Regional Dominance

It has been suggested that during the protohistoric period the Indus Valley probably was the home of the dominant culture, and that during the formative era the Ganges Valley became the hearth of modern Indian

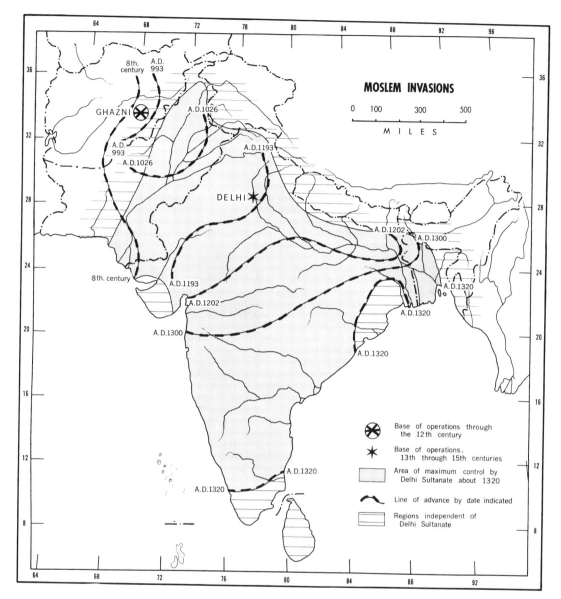

FIGURE 12.3. The Islamic invasions of India, eighth to fourteenth centuries.

culture and the seat of the earliest political empire. Certainly environment had something to do with this, in that the landscape of each area was amenable to development of extensive social institutions. But certainly too, it was people that made of each environment a definite cultural landscape. Each used selected resources to specific ends, and each altered that landscape by cutting back its plant cover, changing its water distribution through irrigation, running trails and roads across it, and building settlements upon it.

With the variety of landscapes in India possessing inherently useful characters, it is hard to suggest one outstanding region. Throughout Indian culture history, however, one area has stood out above the others in cultural attainment during each period.

This regional superiority or dominance may be a partial illusion, the historiography of India being sufficiently intangible so that a flat statement cannot be documented satisfactorily. After the Mauryan era there stands out the Punjab under the Kushan, in the first century A.D., with the Gandharan schools of art a significant development in Indian culture. The Guptas again brought the Ganges Valley to the fore in the fourth century. The Pallavas made the country between the Godavari and the Kistna outstanding from the fifth to the seventh centuries, and the western Deccan under the Chalyuka rivaled the later Pallavas. The Colas developed the southern east coast as the outstanding region of India between the eighth and twelfth centuries. Several groups holding the Delhi Gap in the thirteenth and fourteenth centuries fought most of the rest of India, and came to exercise control over most of India. The central Deccan under the Bahmani was an important region during the fourteenth and fifteenth centuries, only to lose out to the southern peninsular combine of Vijayanagar for the next century. The sixteenth century was shared by Vijayanagar and the Moguls before the latter dominated the scene from their home base in the upper Ganges Valley and the Delhi Gap. This regional dominance is more than political or military strength alone, for it involves the integration of agriculture, handicraft industry, interregional and international trade, manpower, social organization, and Hindu or Islamic religious unity. These were mobilized behind an aggressive leadership of a family, a clan, or a racial minority either newly come to India or long kept from race mixture and diffusion by the restrictive caste system. These eras of regional dominance seemed to come about when a group could unite and mobilize the resources of landscape and of society for a period of creative effort.

Failure of Regional Unity

If the history of India reads with a bewildering change of pace and locality, it in part is owing to the lack of regional definition in the landscape of India and in part to the fact that new competitors were so often surging through the Mountain Wall to engage in the struggle for control of some part of India. Often the Punjab, the Ganges Valley, or the Deccan was the scene of a mad scramble during a whole century, producing a regional anarchy and a struggle for paramountcy which failed to produce a positive result. Sometimes in widely separated parts of India two regions stood out above the remainder at the same time. If this happened side by side there ensued a bitter struggle, often resulting in the final dominance of one contestant. On the other hand, the contest sometimes ran for centuries, as that between the Colas and the Pallavas, with one side and then the other having the upper hand. Significantly, too, there are negative spots of rough hill country, desert, or overwet mountain fringe that never have been the seat of a leading culture or group.

The struggle for regional dominance, as a natural part of things, is a segment of Hindu political philosophy. As an undercurrent in Indian life it has been present as far back as any record can be read. In the competitive struggle of the parts of the subcontinent of India there seems to be something akin to the struggles of another Eurasian subcontinent: Europe. Always before one group could bring the whole of India together and cement the unity into a fixed pattern, its energy or its resources ran out or some new invasion came to overwhelm the waning leaders. The Mauryan rulers failed to achieve complete hegemony over the Indian realm, though they codified the administrative and political principles that were to be used in every later empire. Innumerable Turkish tribes possessing only the common bond of Islam never could dominate Hindu India. The British, coming with new tools and new political concepts, gave up the task in 1947. In 1940 Islamic leaders raised the cry of Pakistan around the cultural concept of Islam. The prompt division of the realm into Pakistan and India when the British removed their restraining hand is completely in keeping with the long-range failure of regional unity of the Indian subcontinent. It is impractical to try to determine whether this is an inherent characteristic of the Indian landscape or whether it is primarily a product of a migratory and argumentative human race that cannot rise above the personality and psychology of some of India's first inhabitants.

THE ERA OF THE COMPANY

The coming of the Portuguese in 1498 heralded a new era in Indian life, but it took a century for the preliminary skirmishes of Portuguese, British, Dutch, French, Arabs, and Indians to establish the pattern of development. The end of the skirmishing came with the formation of the British and Dutch East India companies and the reduction of Portuguese strength. Since the Dutch effort focused mainly on Ceylon and Java, the British settled upon the Indian coast, slowly working inland. A concerted French attempt to gain control of India was thwarted. This British geographical spread was accompanied by economic and political penetration along the lines suggested in an earlier chapter. The European came at a time when the Mogul rulers were building their own empire and making one more attempt to unite India. The Mogul rulers brought little that was really new to Indian culture to bear on their problem. Occi-

dental culture, on the other hand, was virile, expanding, and ingenious in its maneuvers, if crude in its techniques and social approach. In the face of the traditional stumbling block of Indian regional disunity, and badgered by increasing swarms of disruptive Europeans, Mogul power faltered and faded slowly away. A mosaic of political regions scrambling for autonomy, hegemony, or loot fell prey both to British offers of friendship and to accumulated animosity (Fig. 12.4).

Not only was India the chief entrepôt of pre-Columbian trade in the southern Orient, but she was the chief source of manufactured goods. Iron and steel products and many types of cotton textiles led the list of Indian handicraft products that found their way to the markets of all Southeast Asia. Indian ports were the meeting ground of Chinese, Arab, Indonesian, and Indian traders. Slowly the British came to comprehend the nature of this going economic operation, and gradually they excluded the other participants. Relegated to the role of petty traders, native shipping interests often took to piracy to make a living, in itself no new occupation in the East. The growth of British India is shown in Figure 12.5.

The charter of the East India Company periodically was subject to review in the British House of Commons, and the more ruthless exploitation of India repeatedly was checked. Nevertheless India was made to carry the whole of the expenditures of Company operations, while tremendous profits flowed away to England to stockholders and private employees, and almost no permanent investments in the future of India were made. Though the Company kept the peace, developed certain port cities, and trained such clerks as they needed to carry on their trading operations, India benefited only secondarily. However, the fact is that it did benefit during the eighteenth century. The increasing assumption by the Company of effective police

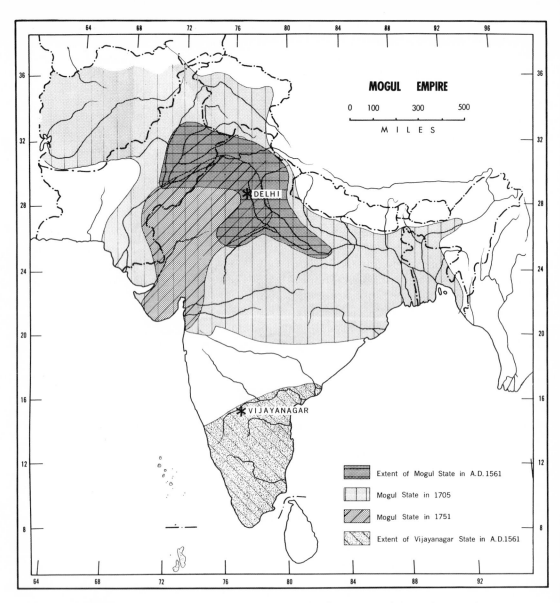

FIGURE 12.4. Rise and decline of the Moguls, sixteenth to eighteenth centuries.

power and the functions of supervisory government left an Indian local community with a share of village autonomy not greatly different from that held throughout most periods of Islamic or Hindu imperial rule. The well-organized trading efforts of the Company increased the market for Indian products abroad during the eighteenth century.

However, stresses began to develop within India, and within the Company, early in the nineteenth century. Commercial operations had become hopelessly entangled in governmental and peace-preservation machinery.

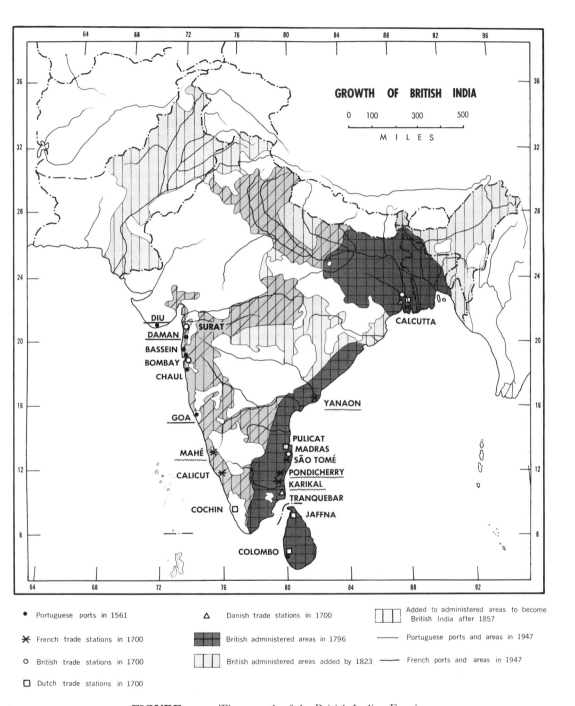

GROWTH OF BRITISH INDIA

0   100   300   500

M I L E S

DIU
DAMAN
BASSEIN
BOMBAY
CHAUL

SURAT

CALCUTTA

GOA

YANAON

MAHÉ

CALICUT

PULICAT
MADRAS
SÃO TOMÉ
PONDICHERRY
KARIKAL
TRANQUEBAR

COCHIN

JAFFNA

COLOMBO

● Portuguese ports in 1561

✳ French trade stations in 1700

○ British trade stations in 1700

□ Dutch trade stations in 1700

△ Danish trade stations in 1700

▦ British administered areas in 1796

▥ British administered areas added by 1823

▦ Added to administered areas to become British India after 1857

— Portuguese ports and areas in 1947

〰 French ports and areas in 1947

FIGURE 12.5. The growth of the British Indian Empire.

The increasing cost of maintaining the Company's huge staff produced constantly heavier tax levies upon the regions under control. Attempts were made to enter the field of production and thus increase the earning span. Elements of trade were initiated that provoked great trouble, such as the insistence upon shipment of opium to China to pay for tea purchases. Within India unrest developed owing to the failure of the Company to develop transport, to attend to education, to supervise religion, to concern itself with Indian political and social institutions. Earlier Indian governments, however regional, had made efforts in all these directions. That none of these things were the recognized business of a trading corporation in the nineteenth century only increased the anomalous situation in which the British found their East India Company.

The British government began taking a hand in matters early in the nineteenth century, as the strains began to show more clearly. Concern over affairs in India, upon renewal of the Company charter in 1833, abolished most of its monopoly features. It slowed down, but did not fully stop, the tendency of the Company to increase its political control, leaving in the hands of Indian princes and rajahs a large area of India, most peculiarly distributed over the country. Actually, the Company had been making efforts in education for some years, aimed mainly at preservation of the traditional learning. In 1835 Lord Macaulay, newly arrived as a legal member of the Company's Council, keynoted a new policy, to educate as Englishmen a selected group of Indians who then were to become interpreters of occidental culture to the rest of India. This was a decision which was slow to bear fruit, but whose final results have had profound effects upon both modern India and Pakistan. The increasing stresses finally led to rebellion in the 1850's, known in British circles as the Mutiny of 1857. In the next year the East India Company was abolished. The administration of India became the duty of a newly created British cabinet post, the Secretary of State for India. Thus, India frankly became a British colony, most of which Britain ran directly, but in part of which she recognized the selective independence of native rulers. Unconsciously, therefore, the British perpetuated regional disunity, an old feature in Indian life.

THE MATURING INDIAN LANDSCAPE

India possesses a distinctive landscape in which cultural features today are fully as significant as the natural elements of landforms and vegetation. Many of these cultural elements are of great age, completely Indian in origin, whose distinctive stylistic lines belong to the whole span of Indian culture history. A few native Indian features belong to a particular period, and go with a religious or art movement. Others have been introduced from outside India at different times, eventually to become blended into or to remain isolated in the Indian landscape. Some rather distinctive cultural items are simply the result of the dense packing together of 500,000,000 Indians.

India is a land of villages and small towns. Examining the pattern in 1941, prior to the separation of India and Pakistan, the census tabulated some 658,000 settlements in India, excluding Ceylon. Of these about 450,000 were villages of under 500 people; in each of 124,000 villages resided between 500 and 1,000 people. About 325,000,000 people lived in settlements under 5,000 in size. Some 4,000 towns and cities housed about 65,000,000 people. Of the latter group there were but 57 cities having over 100,000 people each. A simple average statement indicates that the average village had not far from a hundred houses, and that many small towns had from one to two thousand houses.

Smaller settlements normally are cluster villages in shape and form, with only occasionally an elongated shoe-string village or other shape definitely related to some local landscape stimulus. This is an old feature which goes far back into early Indian settlement history. Within the village narrow and irregular lanes, often ending in blind alleys, are the rule. In the often invaded northwest the cluster is tight and presents a protective solid outer wall, though newer villages established in the last two centuries often are more open. In moist parts of India villages often are less tightly clustered together than elsewhere. Normally, villages in other parts of India and Pakistan are not walled, but they have around them strips or patches of uncropped common land on which animals are tethered, crop threshing is done, tools are stored, and manure heaps are piled for fuel storage. Around the village in fairly close order are grouped the fields and gardens. Field patterns are irregular and have been developed in accord with various local criteria. Often the Indian field system impresses the Chinese and the occidental as being somewhat inefficiently laid out, with considerable waste space and a certain amount of sheer disorder. This latter aspect is noticeably missing from those parts of Assam, south India, and Ceylon where plantation crops like tea, coffee, and rubber are grown today under occidental planning.

Larger than the small residential village is the small town, often fortified, that has matured out of the original market village and tribal political center. These today are merchandising and administrative centers as well as the homes of the landlords and upper classes. Such settlements almost always have been laid out on grid plans. The smaller towns may have but a single pair of streets, laid out to form a simple cross, and permitting a fourward political organization. There usually are narrow lanes penetrating the blocks of houses which are densely packed together.

Primary streets are of fair width, permitting two-way wheeled traffic, and along them are arranged the retail shops and professional offices that go with a service town. Near the gates or the edge of town are the grain shops, lumber yards, and those handicrafts requiring more space than can be afforded along the central main streets. Around the town margins are cleared spaces where crowds may gather, the wandering entertainment group may hold forth, animals and carts may be parked, the fair-day stalls may be erected, and barter may take place. Sometimes outside the town, but as often inside it, are the Hindu temples or the Islamic mosques. Often high-ranking castes reside exclusively in one section of town, while low castes and outcaste menials have huts in a suburb outside. Historic and religious monuments often are numerous and scattered about the town and its environs. Ruins of historic buildings and shrines sometimes occur, but durable building materials usually are gradually removed and incorporated into new buildings, so that the marks of ancient occupation are fewer than might be expected. Many a modern small town has a ragged fringe of suburbs strung out along the roads approaching the settlement.

Whatever may have been the history of house types in early India, there is a simple general zoning to these matters today. In the north and northwestern lowlands the adobe brick structure is most common, sometimes with a mud-over-matting roof and sometimes with a simple gable and a variety of roofing material. In much of the moist and warmer parts of India housing is flimsy as regards the walls, crude matting and even brush often being used by the rural peasantry today. In such housing the well-thatched roof with an overhang is more important than the walls. Such houses often have separate crop storehouses, built to a better standard. In the Deccan flimsy farmsteads often are surrounded by thorn fences. Everywhere in the villages the usual house consists of two rooms or less, mud floors are almost universal, windows are small or absent, and decorative features are few in number. In some sections whitewash is fairly common, whatever the building material. The small town possesses some better architecture. Two-story buildings are common, often with fired brick and plastered walls, whitewashed or color-surfaced. Balconies are frequent features of Indian town housing, as are good tile roofs and decorative tile floors in the better houses. Deep verandas and terraces also are common features. The flat roof is a persistent feature of public and private building in towns and cities almost all over India and has led to characteristic use of rain spouts and drains, and the low, simple balustrade around the tops of the walls. Flat sandstone slabs on timber beams, with cement-caulked cracks, or cement over rubble stone in massive arched-roof building form the commonest roofs on better buildings. There has been considerable historical variation and repetition in building materials. In the Himalayan mountain zone wood is the primary building material, with considerable carving, gabled roofs, and interesting decorative features. In northeastern India, the Himalayan foothills, along the Malabar coast, and in parts of Ceylon the gabled roof is normal, these being the rainiest parts of South Asia.

Early in the historic period villages were few in number, set in small clearings scattered throughout the parkland, jungle, or forest. The small fortified town was slow to develop, despite the era of city building that had marked the Indus Valley. The Bactrian Greeks, Sakas, and Parthians brought into northwest India various Hellenistic features of architecture and decorative motifs that were woven into standard Indian concepts. The field areas and commonly used grazing lands were but a minor share of the total area in the early period. Gradually, with the native expansion of population and with steady immigration, the settlement clearings expanded against the native plant cover and, in populated areas, became fairly continuous. With this steady expansion the variety of the cultural landscape increased. The rice, palm, banana, and green tree-strewn landscape of Bengal, Assam, south India, Ceylon, and the Malabar coast has steadily grown more complex as more fields, new crops, and more settlements spread against the jungle and the forest. Whenever man has stopped for a time the jungle has reclaimed its own, and trace is soon lost of the earlier cultural works. In the drier parts of India the wheat, millet, small-grain, and parkland pattern also has grown more complex with more dense settlement. Irrigation canals and tanks have multiplied, and today there are shallow wells being operated by hand or by animals throughout the drier parts of the North Indian Plain. Steadily over the centuries this cultural landscape has been extended until today only about twelve percent of India and Pakistan remains in forest, largely in rough and permanently uncultivable parts of India. A considerable amount of cultivable waste and useless waste land is scattered throughout the cultural landscape.

Over the centuries there slowly matured several distinctive patterns of Hindu public architecture. Referring to a period in the fourth and fifth centuries A.D. one writer quoted the remark: "The architecture of the country is divided into three broad styles and ten types, corresponding to the geographical divisions and the political entities."[*] These three styles were a northern one involving mostly quadrangular shapes, a southern style using hexagonal and octagonal shapes, and an eastern style using rounded shapes. The introduction of Islamic architecture in Arabic, Persian, and Turkish styles since the ninth century has added significantly to the

---

[*]P. K. Acharya, *Indian Architecture according to Manasara Slipasastra*, Allahabad, 1927, p. 181.

cultural landscape of India, both in style and in building materials. Stone and cement became much more frequently used. In the Punjab Islamic building is mostly Persian in its stylistic relations; in the Deccan and, particularly, in the city of Ahmadabad this Persian style has been Hinduized somewhat. East of the Punjab on the North Indian Plain Turkish or Mogul styling is most noticeable, but again it has been Hinduized to varying degree. South India possesses a great many historic temples and public buildings that are completely Hindu in their architecture, yet even here there are varieties that sometimes are regional and sometimes are sectarian in their relations.

The coming of the European introduced a new series of elements onto the cultural landscape of India. Often ugly interpretations of Elizabethan and Victorian styles of public buildings are to be found, somehow rendered unreal by Indian workmen and the Indian surroundings. In some of the earliest European settlements, Dutch, Portuguese, French, and British building styles were transplanted into the subtropical Indian landscape directly out of cool northwestern Europe. These styles have inoculated Indian builders sufficiently to produce some curious blends of products, found in and around some of the older urban centers, and in Ceylon. On the other hand the spacious layout, beautiful gardens, wide streets, and flat-roofed, tile-floored multiunit and detached houses of modern Indian urban suburbs derive part of their charm from the blend of Hindu, Islamic and European styles.

In many new cities a combination of architectural styles has produced a variety not known before. Many of these new towns and cities are railroad towns or military cantonments built near the old and densely packed Indian centers. Most of the big port cities are new towns created within the span of occidental contact and are cosmopolitan settlements. In the very spread of the railroad, the road, the factory, commercial agriculture, and the plantation, both complexity and maturity have been added to the Indian landscape. The present scene is one of rapid change rather than stability and permanence. Many of the changes more recently introduced have entered only selected parts of the Indian landscape, or have not become Indianized as yet. In this next century both the spread and the Indianizing of these and other features will go on, to further intensify an already crowded cultural landscape.

RESULTS OF BRITISH RULE

Political conquest and economic domination are obvious results of British control of India. Many other effects of four hundred years of Indian contact with European culture are less obvious. If Britain did bring a kind of peace and stability to Indian life in the various regions as she took them over, one may almost question their worth. That very stability initiated economic programs which have saddled the Indian peasantry with a debt often estimated at thirty times their annual income. In the earlier eras, political change had been sufficiently frequent to permit periodically erasing the slate clean of accumulated debts, though, of course, this produced other handicaps. British efforts to simplify the land ownership and tax patterns of this complicated Indian landscape did indeed produce simplification in many regions. Often, however, the British raised the tax collector to a dominant position and slowly undermined the strength and vitality of the village *sabha*, thus destroying the small amount of freedom the rural peasantry retained. In the tax simplification procedures often the final result was to solidify the vested position of the *zemindar* class of tax farmer-collectors into a parasitic middle and upper class group.

Under foreign encouragement Indian foreign trade continued to expand above the level it held in pre-Columbian times. Gradually, however, there came about a change in the nature of this trade. India once a manufacturer and an entrepôt became a producer and exporter of raw materials and an importer of manufactured goods. Once the trade monopoly of the East India Company was removed, British interests in India changed in nature and the flow of manufactured goods began. The decline of handicrafts and the growth of exploitative competition with other parts of the world in agricultural exports slowly lowered the level of living for the middle sectors of the peasantry. A decreasing level of living is difficult to describe fully and document clearly, but, despite the science of the Occident and constructive British efforts, it does seem true that many a Pakistani or Indian peasant is relatively worse off today than when the European first came to India.

Occidental contact with India has produced many significant benefits which clearly can be pointed out. Transportation and communication facilities compare favorably with those in many other parts of the world, and millions of acres now are cultivated through irrigation canals engineered by the British. The establishment of industrial plants, the development of Indian universities, and the spread of occidental medicine are concrete aspects of modern Indian life. British struggles against the burning live of female widows and the system of child marriage have been valiant efforts against strangling social customs. Reform measures against the caste system had some effect, though not all British opinion was strong for reform. The lowered death rate and the increase in total population are positive proofs of the benefits of British rule. And yet these things do not seem fully to compensate for the serious inroads upon Indian life, for the decreasing level exists in spite of multiple benefits.

It perhaps is pertinent to ask whether the present state of Indian-Pakistani affairs can be laid on the doorstep of the British. It has been popular in some circles to do so. Certainly the British have been to blame for many evils in 400 years of contact of East and West. But Indian culture is not free from blame. In the post-Columbian changing world Indian culture has lacked the flexibility that characterized it during the formative period and the Mauryan era. The modern Indian people are the inheritors of one of the most restrictive and complex bodies of culture in the world today. This fact, itself, is partly responsible for the plight of the Indian-Pakistani peasant populations. Recently change is increasing its tempo, but change still has far to go.

One of the distinctive results of British control over India was the curious patchwork composing the political pattern. When the East India Company charter was canceled the extension of police power and political administration had not yet taken over all of India. Still outstanding were about 700,000 square miles of area in very irregular distribution. Upon taking direct control over British India the Crown honored the existing treaties of the Company with the older independent Indian states. The difficulties that led to the decline of Mogul rule freed from Mogul supervision numerous minor kings, regional governors, petty princes, and ambitious feudal wardens. These then shared the same independence and treaty relationships to the Crown as did the larger Indian states.

In the late nineteenth century over 600 separate regions claimed sovereign status. These ranged from little plots like Bilbari, 15 acres, to Hyderabad, 82,313 square miles. The Kathiawar Peninsula was the area of most numerous divisions. Slowly the number was reduced slightly, at the outbreak of World War II totalling 562 states, with a total area of 715,964 square miles and a population of 93,189,000. To an American, with a passion for orderly arrangement of the obvious parts of government, the British arrangement in India seemed most haphazard and inefficient. Obvious order has never been a primary component of British colonial administration, and so the British kept the system, making it work, and taking occasional advantage of a chance to increase administrative unity. Some of the native states had kept pace with developments in British India; others were striking examples of feudalism carried into the modern world. The alteration of these features fell to the reconstitution of governmental structures in the three new countries of Pakistan, India, and Ceylon.

13

MODERN INDIA AND ITS STRUGGLE FOR VIABILITY

As a result of the withdrawal of British political controls in 1947 there now are seven independent political regimes and one region in dispute in the subcontinent termed India in the preceding chapter. The Union of India (officially known as Bharat) inherited the largest area (1,269,640 square miles), encompassing the predominantly Hindu regions; the Republic of Pakistan (365,529 square miles) consists of two separated but chiefly Islamic regions; Kashmir (82,258 square miles) is a mixed Hindu-Islamic region in the northwest still in dispute between India and Pakistan; Nepal (54,362 square miles) is a Himalayan mountain kingdom of mixed Buddhists-Hindus-Lamaists north of India; Bhutan (officially known as Druk-Yul, and comprising 19,305 square miles) is a second Himalayan mountain kingdom toward the northeast of India (with political ties to India), chiefly Lamaist in religion; Sikkim (2,744 square miles) is a Himalayan princely state between Nepal and Bhutan, a protectorate under India, offically Lamaist in religion but with a largely Hindu population; the Maldives (115 square miles in 2,000 coral islands and banks, 220 inhabited), off the southwest coast of India, became independent in 1965 and an Islamic republic in 1968; in the far south off the tip of India is island Ceylon (officially known as Sri Lanka, in area 25,532 square miles), chiefly Buddhist in religion but including a militant Hindu minority.

The several states now are separated politically and statistically, and in the future they will develop separate cultural trends. However, they have all shared the same broad patterns of culture history, they are tied together by simple locational situations, they will continue to be interdependent in economies and regional relationships, and they will have to "live together" in the future. Current animus resulting from the events surrounding their separations from British influence, and from the first expressions of political nationalism, may wear off in time. The continuing difficulties of the settlement of the Kashmir problem, and the detailed aspects of the final demarcation of the boundary between Pakistan and India, will make headlines in the world press, and will precipitate intercountry headaches, for many years. The positions of Nepal, Bhutan, and Sikkim in the mountain boundary zone between two great states, India and China, now engaging in competitive maneuvers along the boundary zone may, at some point, raise the issue of continuance of any one of them or all three, as separate political states.

This chapter will deal with India and its northern dependent appendages. Two separate chapters will deal individually with Pakistan and Ceylon in necessary terms, but relevant data for the whole subcontinent will be found on the maps in the present chapter.

THE AGRICULTURAL ECONOMY

Problems in Agriculture

India is a region in which two different agricultural complexes overlap and compete for space in the landscape. These are the wet-rice and tropical crop complex of eastern India-southeastern Asia, and the dry field grains and mid-latitude crop complex of southwestern Asia. The two complexes involve separate sets of plants and animals domesticated under particular combinations of climate, soil, and human sponsorship. The zone of meeting and the amount of competition between the two have been steadily changing through the centuries. Significant in this meeting are the plants native to India which have been a variable part of each basic pattern. Important also is the variable use of irrigation during different historic periods. Vital to agriculture are the post-Columbian crop additions which have widened the range of Indian products. Of regional significance is the nineteenth-century introduction of the plantation and of commercial export agriculture.

A fundamental fact of modern Indian agriculture is the low per-acre yield of crops. This variably has been ascribed to poor soils, the inroads of soil erosion during 5,000

years, small use of fertilizer, poor tools and poor cultivation techniques, a peasantry ignorant of beneficial practices and sometimes inefficient in the use of good practices, the increasing fragmentation of family holdings, voluminous pests, the irregular monsoon climate, and British imperialism. Here and there in India there are illustrations of great agricultural skill among a people or regional group, producing impressive local landscapes, but these are unusual rather than normal situations.

Throughout much of the northern Deccan and the North Indian Plain west of Bihar the modern scarcity of wood for fuel has produced the standard practice of burning dung from such animals as cattle, water buffalo, horses, and camels as cooking and heating fuel. Nearly half the total animal manures are burned as fuel. Though this may be a very old custom its mass application is fairly recent. Its practice in any one village means that the lands of that village are permanently deprived of their major source of fertilizer. Where the fuel shortage is sufficiently severe to have promoted the practice, stubble and plant wastes also must be used as fuel, so that the land seldom receives any energy replacement. In many parts of India, however, all animal manures and plant wastes are stored and used on the fields. Almost every village is ringed by a zone of better, more productive soils whose fertility is maintained by the natural disposal of human wastes, and by courtyard sweepings and miscellaneous humus-creating wastes. The current fertilizer needs exceed the total supply of animal manures about four times, so that the replacement of fuel is but one aspect of the fertilizer problem. The fertilizer value of animal manures from the poorly fed Indian cattle is relatively low. The Indian peasant is too poor and debt ridden to buy commercial fertilizer.

In many parts of India today soil quality and workability are low. Though the peculiar black soils of the Deccan retain their fertility without much human aid, the more widespread red earths are relatively infertile. And today soil quality is poor on much of the higher-lying, older alluvium of the North Indian Plain and the larger valleys of the peninsula. Over the centuries native practices maintained long-range productive capacity which now is being lost as extreme pressure upon the land forces agriculture toward short-range goals without provision for the future. Though the acreages under crop have been increasing it is discouragingly true that per-acre yields have declined in some crops, with smaller net yields than were formerly secured. Much of the rest of the world has adopted the use of commercial fertilizer to secure increased yields, India having been left behind in the race for crop production. The problem perhaps can be handled, but now it calls for major improvement operations to be carried out by the government of India, since the problem has exceeded the stage at which haphazard individual initiative will suffice.

Indian agriculture already uses a larger share of the landscape than is common in many countries, and more reserve land is being brought under cultivation regularly. When this reserve volume is fully put to use slightly over half the area of India will be in cultivated fields. Somewhat less than one seventh of the fields are double-cropped, but about one sixth of the cultivated land is annually fallowed, some fields being left idle for several years in a row. Irrigation, in addition to the use of water on rice land, is employed on nearly one fifth of the fields, a proportion which has increased markedly within the last century as British engineering skill developed massive irrigation systems copied the world around. In northwest India over half of the cultivated land is irrigated, in the upper and central Ganges Valley about one fourth of the land is irrigated, and throughout Madras Province the figure is

nearly one third. Despite the growth of industrialization in India, the percentage of the population related to agriculture has not markedly decreased, and about eighty percent of the 1961 working force remained tied to the land.

India has the largest total of domesticated animals of any large country. There are about 175,000,000 cattle, 50,000,000 water buffalo, about 60,000,000 goats and sheep, and perhaps 4,000,000 horses, donkeys, camels, and elephants. Even so, draft energy is insufficient, the dairy products volume is far short of the need and there is but a small surplus of low-grade wool and mohair. Many agricultural areas must share work oxen. Although some urban dairy yields are relatively high, the country-wide average is far below that of other world dairy figures. Mother India traditionally paid scant attention to animal food crops, and today most livestock is downgraded, malnourished, and unproductive. Since 1930 fodder acreage has risen at a time when India can ill afford to feed such unproductive animals. Overgrazing in many parts, but particularly in the northwest, is causing increased soil and range destruction and a spread of the desert landscape. That meat is not used by Hindus or Buddhists is a matter of tradition. Religious prejudice also stands in the way of improving conditions by decreasing the animal population, and breed improvement can make little headway at present.

Food producing agriculture is strikingly concentrated upon three grain crops, rice, wheat, and millet, which alone accounts for over two thirds of the food-growing lands. Since 1930 increases in sugarcane, vegetables, and the legumes have improved the balance slightly, but this has been partly at the expense of the cotton acreage, which cannot really be afforded. Tea, coffee, and rubber have been cultivated on lands taken from the cultivable waste volume rather than that devoted to crops. Increased production of a few other commercial crops has cut into food-growing acreage. Between five and ten percent of many crops, since 1930, have been improved by the introduction of better plant varieties, but productive increase in this line barely manages to keep up with the increase in population. The very recent introductions of the "miracle" breeds of rice and wheat may well change this picture, and great claims were being made in 1969 in this matter. The introduction of more productive, but thereby more demanding, plants could boomerang in a short period unless some fundamental improvement is made in soil fertility. In simple arithmetic, for each Indian there now is about three-fifths of an acre of crop land from which to provide food and clothing, produce his exports, finance most of his imports, and attempt to raise his level of living in the modern world!

The Regional Crop Pattern

The complementary position of the three primary grains, rice, wheat, and millet, is rather interesting (Figs. 13.1-13.4). Conforming fairly closely to the regional pattern of rice are such subtropical crops as coconut, palmyra, and areca palms, of domestic importance in the production of food and oil, sugar and toddy, and betel nut, respectively. In coastal southern India coconut production has been commercially important within the present century. A number of spices, the mango, the banana, citrus, and other subtropical fruit once well matched this same pattern, but some have been taken outside it today. Wheat, grown in a different region of India, competes with rice in a limited zone only. Durum wheats are grown in the peninsula and bread wheats in the north and northwest. Barley competes with rice a little more than wheat but has been a diminishing crop for some decades; it often is sown in mixed plantings with gram, a legume similar to the chickpea. The stone fruits, apricots, peaches, cherries, and plums, and such products as

apples, pears, grapes, melons, and walnuts belong on the side of wheat and are found in the northwest and in the Mountain Wall uplands. There are vegetables that go with both zones too. Camels, horses, and donkeys fit the wheat zone fairly well, but cattle have spread all over India as draft-energy and milk-products producers. The water buffalo, superior as a dairy producer to the average poor Indian cow, has spread outside the rice-growing zone as an urban dairy animal.

Millet, cotton, and several legumes, which go under the term "pulse," occupy a middle ground, being most at home in the Deccan and the edges of northwest India. Here often is mixed planting of two and even three grains in one field. Well-timed, plentiful summer rains stimulate the millet into producing the major grain yield, but light rains retard the millet and then sorghum forms the chief harvest. Long-range yields thus are better than from fields planted singly, particularly where a legume is interplanted. Various crops have been taken into both the rice and the wheat zones and fitted into agricultural patterns according to local advantage. Sugarcane may be grown almost anywhere on the Indian lowland, but since 1910 has centered in the Ganges Valley. The oil seeds are spread all over India, different crops preferring particular regions. Some are native field plants, others are tree crops, and a number are introduced plants.

Some native crops such as jute are very clearly regional monopolies, belonging to Bengal. Such post-Columbian introductions as the peanut, tobacco, pineapple, maize, cacao, coffee, tea, and rubber were first tried in different parts of India, then slowly have settled into particular regions or preferred types of environments. About 800,000 acres of tea, and 150,000 acres of rubber mainly are British-owned. About 225,000 acres of coffee are grown in South India on numerous small holdings. Jute, primarily an East Pakistan delta crop, has only about a

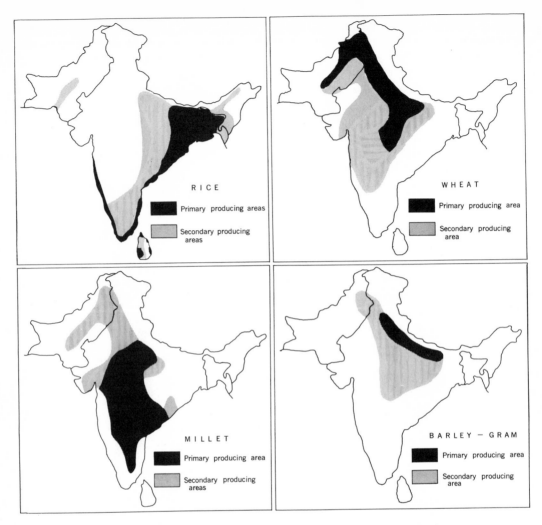

FIGURE 13.1. The main food crops of India, Pakistan, and Ceylon.

1,500,000 acreage sector in the Indian part of Bengal.

Increasingly restricted in scope is the typical economy of earlier, simpler societies of India. Along the Mountain Wall, along the Burma border to the Bay of Bengal, and in lessening areas in central and southern India variations of hunting, collecting, and shifting cultivation still are practiced today by some millions of people, chiefly members of simpler culture groups. Such irregular economy neither contributes much to the welfare of India nor makes many demands, though it has played a widely significant part in altering the ecological balance of local environmental conditions in the past.

Forest Utilization

Forest trees are more typical of the remaining Indian vegetation than are grasses, a factor in itself important to animal culture. A large share of the Indian landscape once was forested, under liberal use of the term. Today not more than thirteen percent of the total area is in forest and scrub cover of some sort, though it has become stripped and down-graded; for future self-sufficiency of wood products in general India should maintain nearly twenty percent of her total area in forest growth of some kind. Firewood is a major item in this consideration, not requiring timber forests. Of wood for lumber the Indian forests today show little reserve, not more than five percent of the total area. Over the centuries considerable cutting and reforestation has been practiced in varied parts of India. Between 1850 and 1910 an increasing amount of timber was cut without any reforestation program. From 1910 onward forest management has improved steadily, and many good timber-producing trees now are growing in new forests. With continued good management, sufficient rough lands unavailable for cropping can be returned to forest producing to provide for most domestic needs.

Forest woods of economic significance vary by vegetation zones. In the lower Pun-

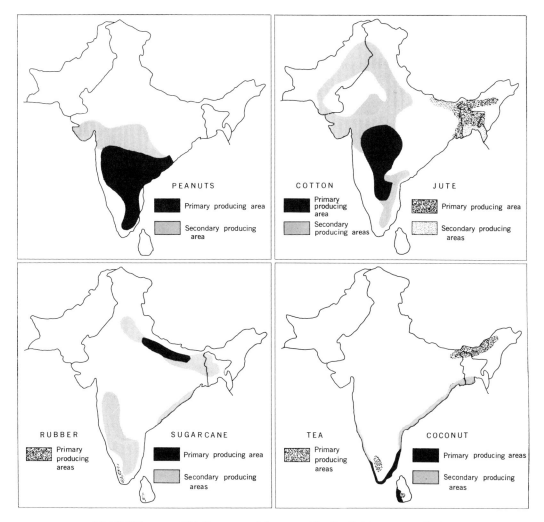

FIGURE 13.2. Chief commercial crops of India, Pakistan, and Ceylon.

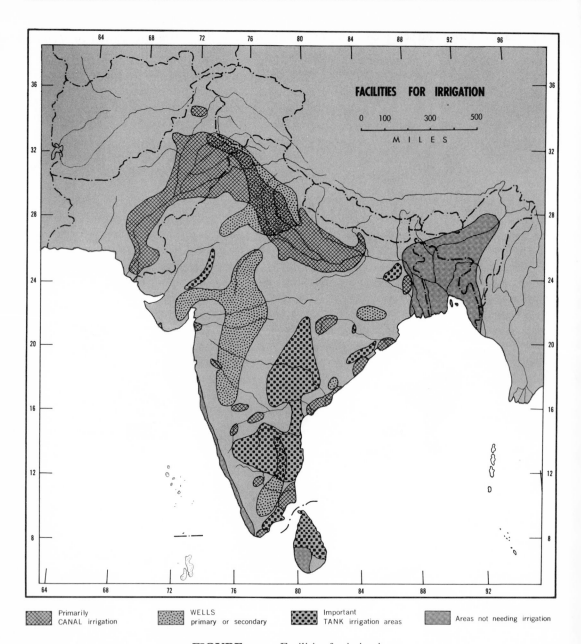

FIGURE 13.3. Facilities for irrigation.

jab and driest parts of northwest India today a thorny, shrubby tree (*Prosopis spicigera*) often is the only wood locally available for firewood and miscellaneous use. In better areas the long-ago introduced babul (*Acacia arabica*) provides lumber and tool and general-use wood. In and along the Himalayas a variety of woods are used. In the western zone deodar cedar (*Cedrus deodara*), chir pine (*Pinus longifolia*), blue pine (*Pinus *excelsa*), silver fir (*Abies pindrow*), and Himalayan spruce (*Picea marinda*) are the most useful woods and today are marketed widely in the lowlands of the Punjab and the upper Ganges Valley. Farther east in the Himalayan foothills, in the Chota Nagpur upland, and in preserved lowland tracts sal (*Shorea*

robusta) and related species, teak (*Tectona grandis*), sissoo or shisham (*Dalbergia sissoo*), and toon (*Cedrela toona*) are the most common forest timber woods, but bamboo and numerous minor woods are used for special purposes. Sal is a better wood than teak for many uses, grows in pure stands, and ranges

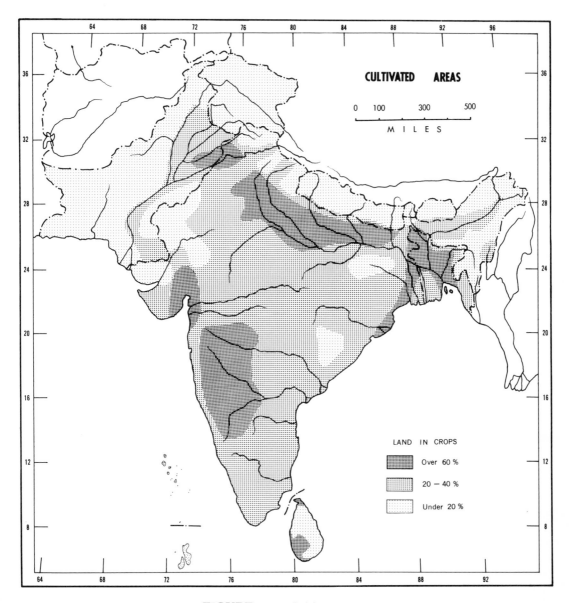

FIGURE 13.4. Cultivated areas.

from the Punjab to Assam and from the Deccan into the Himalayan foothills. From Kathiawar to Chota Nagpur and from the Deccan to the North Indian Plain grows the mahua (*Bassis latifolia*). In early spring it yields very edible blossoms and in summer seeds rich in oil that are used as a butter substitute. It produces a good wood, but so prized are its other products that today it is cut for timber only when most necessary. In eastern Bengal, Assam, and the Burma border hill country there are many woods that are commonly used. Teak, mesua or ironwood (*Mesua ferrea*), pyinkado in Burma or irul in India (*Xylia dolabriformis*), and padauk or rosewood (*Pterocarpus* spp.), are the species common to both areas, along with bamboos, canes, and rattans. Kokko (*Albizzia* spp.), is a much used wood common to the eastern Himalayan foothill. Sandalwood (*Santalum album*), is a South Indian wood much used for carving toys, figurines, other curios and utensils, and for its scented oil. Though cultivated for its nuts, the coconut tree is almost the most useful of all trees grown in southern India, since its wood, leaves, fiber, and shells have myriad uses. Over much of lowland central and eastern India mango wood (*Mangifera indica*), is a commonly used, cheap wood in many villages and small towns. Usually it is only available in small quantities because the mango today is an important cultivated fruit tree rather than a forest tree.

MINERALS

The people of the Indus Valley culture already were skilled in the use of most of the common metals of history. Indian bronze never equaled that of ancient China, and perhaps its gold work was excelled by that of some other region, but after iron reached India, Indian iron work compared favorably with that of any part of the world. Indian iron ores often contain small amounts of ferro-alloys in natural combination. In late pre-Columbian times Indian iron and steel circulated from the Near East to the Indies. Only slowly has modern industry replaced Indian handicraft skill in the metals. The village silversmith still thrives, and the modern urban Indian silver and gold craftsman is one of the world's finest. Primitive iron furnaces and forges still are scattered throughout the peninsula, but the village and small town blacksmith today prefers to work with ready-made rods or strap rather than native pig iron.

British industrial investment in India largely skipped metals production. The ores became significant as raw materials for expanding factories only in the West. The British early developed a bureau of geologic survey, but the actual survey was never completed. In more recent years careful examination has done much better, and today the country has been fairly well canvassed and its resources fairly well tabulated, in terms of minerals survey knowledge. The current assessment of mineral resources suggests that India does not have either the volume or the variety adequate to the long range developed industrial needs of a populous subcontinent. Compared with an equally populous part of Europe, India's resources are both smaller and poorly situated, though this picture may change in the near future (Fig. 13.5).

Coal is the chief source of industrial power. India ranks eighth among the countries of the world, with an estimated reserve of not over 60 billion tons. Neither quality nor variety is very high, and the volume is concentrated in the Chota Nagpur upland, with minor deposits in Assam, and in southern India. An annual production of nearly 65,000,000 tons is used mostly in rail transport and in industry. Petroleum primarily is an import product. Small-producing fields lie in the Punjab and in Assam, and others perhaps may be found elsewhere around the folded fringes of the North Indian Plain.

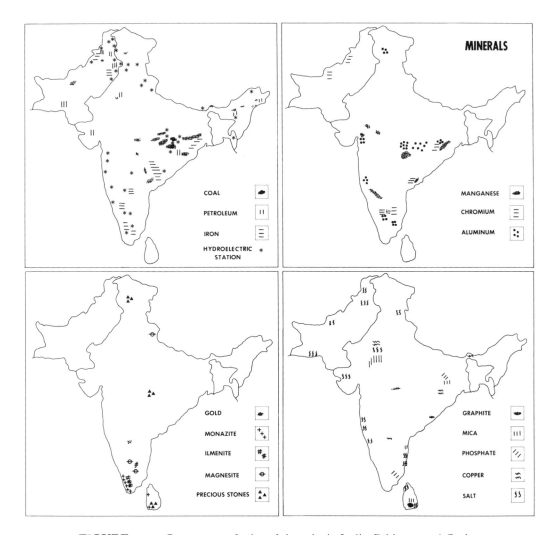

FIGURE 13.5. Occurrence of mineral deposits in India, Pakistan, and Ceylon.

Hydroelectric power promises a rather high potential to India, though the seasonal drainage of monsoon moisture is a severe handicap. Before this source can be utilized, rather costly dam and conservation projects must be undertaken such as that in the Damodar Valley west of Calcutta.

Widely distributed iron ores helped the traditional handicraft production, but they prove less helpful to modern industry, owing to the difficult nature of many of the ores and to the concentration of coal deposits. Good ores are found accessible to coal, limestone, manganese, and chromium in the Chota Nagpur upland, in huge volume, capable of meeting domestic needs for a long period. Newly located sites in the southern peninsula possess good iron ore in large volume. Manganese ore is widely scattered over the peninsula, and chromium occurs in amounts sufficient for Indian needs for some time. Manganese and mica have been export products, but their relatively low value lessens their cash contribution to Indian economy. Copper, bauxite, refractories, and mined rock salt are produced in small quantities. Most Indian salt is a product of evaporation of sea water, of domestic rather than industrial use. Gold still is the second most valuable mineral product, though its production is declining. Indian gold was one of the fabulous attractions of the East, but the chief producing region, the Kolar fields of Mysore, appear to be nearing exhaustion. Lead, zinc, tungsten, tin, and silver are not produced within India, though the former inclusion of Burma within Indian statistical summaries suggested such production. Saltpeter once was an important export, but the volume has declined since the 1860's. Thorium-producing ilmenite sands from Travancore were a minor export used in making gas mantles until atomic energy projects advanced the importance of thorium, but the simple economic worth of the mineral product to India will not be high within the near future.

Several precious and semiprecious stones have been Indian products, among them pearls, rubies, beryls, topazes, and diamonds from the peninsula, and sapphires from Kashmir. Chank shells from the Gulf of Mannar have been in steady production over the centuries, the whole shell used in religious ceremonies and shells being cut into bracelets and armlets as one of the old Bengal handicrafts. It is likely that a steady export of these items reached wide limits within the pre-Columbian Old World, but modern production of none is particularly significant.

INDUSTRIALIZATION

Traditionally, India held a position for many centuries as one of the most important handicraft manufacturing centers of the premodern world. Its iron-steel products were of very high quality and widely distributed, its gold, silver, brass, and enamel wares were famous afar, its worked-wood products were fine art goods, and its cotton textiles were the world's finest. The rise of European industrialization, and the colonial economic linkage of India to Britain brought an end to much of this, though in the hinterland towns and rural villages the handicraft skills and arts lingered on, struggling to hold a declining market. The lessening of princely court patronage, and the urban consumer shift toward western manufactured commodities proved severe handicaps against the maintenance of high-quality handicraft manufacture. Some types of handicraft production continued, but it was chiefly in lines and commodities not of interest to modern industry or in products peculiar to the consumer habits of the lower class Indian market. In recent years, however, handicraft manufacturing has been making a comeback in several different lines, exploiting particular types of consumer interest or catering to international markets for commodities of peculiarly Indian cultural motifs. Government assistance has provided support for the continuance of handicraft manufacturing in traditional commodities, primarily in particular types of consumer goods.

The first steps in modern industrialization are over a century old, but they were developed within the economic linkage to Britain's world markets, by British capital and initiative, utilizing the cheap labor of India. Gradually, this picture has changed during the present century. World War I provided considerable incentive for the beginnings of several lines of manufacture, and World War II strongly stimulated the growth of Indian industrialization. The primary patterns of progress have come since independence, in a series of five-year plans, in which government investment has strongly stepped up the initiation of manufacturing in many different lines aided by investment of capital from abroad. India, in 1970, is a ranking industrial power, in world terms, and the rates of growth in almost all categories of manufacturing are strong ones. India finally has reached the take-off point, at which her future development of both the range and quantity of manufacturing can carry the country into the mature state of industrialization, provided political stability can continue to that point. Both the regional aspects of industrialization and the commodity patterns of manufacturing suffered from the separation of India and Pakistan, but these are features which can be readjusted in time through developmental programs. For India the effects of separation have been less severe than for Pakistan.

At present Indian industry shows a four-zone regional concentration, a result of historic development, with major industrial manufacturing regions located in northeastern India, on the peninsular west coast, and in the far south (Fig. 13.6).

The Calcutta-Jamshedpur region is the primary manufacturing region of India, having both a longer historical background and a wider range of operations. Calcutta continues to be one of the primary ports for India, both in the import and export trades. It is in this region that the best concentration of basic mineral resources is to be found, in the Chota Nagpur hill country west of Calcutta. Jamshedpur is the oldest and largest of the basic iron and steel manufacturing centers, but new centers are developing at Bokara, Durgapur, and Rourkela. Calcutta, along with its suburban and nearby towns, has become the general manufacturing center, greatly expanding its range from the earlier concentration on jute milling. Light manufacturing plants are locating throughout the region in former small towns and agricultural processing centers, the use of by-products in secondary manufacturing lines is growing, and the region is beginning to develop mature characteristics. Large investments in basic heavy industries, such as iron and steel, and the heavy chemicals, now are supporting the development of the electrical manufactures, metals manufactures, railway rolling stock, rubber manufactures, automotive manufactures, machine tools, paper products, glass manufactures, plastics, fertilizers, and pharmaceuticals. Cotton textiles now complement the jute milling industry. The manufacture of a wide range of consumer goods now has, within the region, a large urban consumer population.

The Bombay-Poona region is the second ranking manufacturing region of India, having its early start in cotton textiles, and as a center for the colonial export trade. Agricultural processing and the food manufactures probably rank second to the cotton textile industries, but Bombay has gradually developed a wide range of operations, in which there are important engineering industries, automotive manufactures, both petro-chemical and organic chemical industries, paper and printing industries, and ranges of light manufacturing. Originally centered in the city of Bombay, manufacturing has spread into the hinterland towns along and across the crest of the Western Ghats, closer to the sources of hydroelectric and atomic-electric power for the whole region.

The Ahmadabad-Baroda region, though it had an early start in the cotton textiles field, is a more recent development as a manufacturing region in the broad sense. The area long has been important in Indian regional economics, for Broach and Surat were ancient port cities and trade terminals. Cotton textiles still form key manufactures for the four cities of Ahmadabad, Baroda, Broach, and Surat, but the light dye chemicals, ceramic manufactures, agricultural processing, food industries, and light manufacturing activities related to consumer goods industries now are spread throughout the region, and numerous small manufacturing towns are growing into production centers. Petroleum refining, and the associated petro-chemical industries and plastics manufactures are among the newer

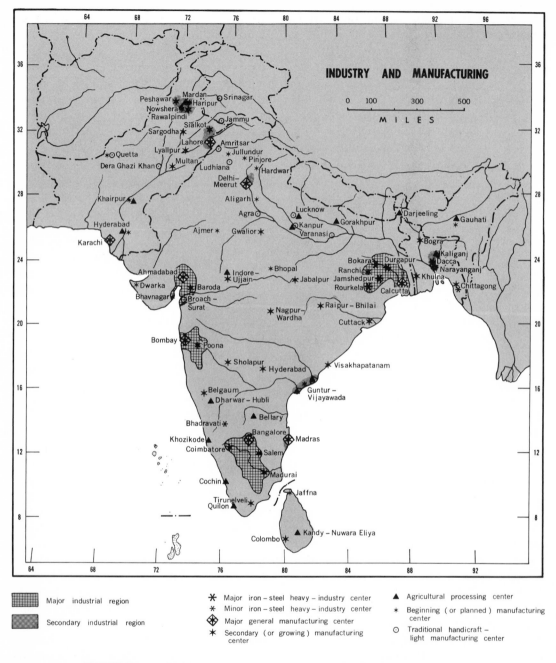

FIGURE 13.6. Industry and manufacturing in India, Pakistan, and Ceylon.

developments, located near Baroda. This region is also a center of some of the very high grade handicraft manufacturing lines producing fine clothing textiles.

The Bangalore-Coimbatore-Madurai region in southern Peninsular India is the fourth regional concentration of manufacturing activities in India. Cotton textiles here, too, were the basic beginnings of modern manufacturing, but modern development has taken wide ranges of activities. Aircraft manufacture, chemicals industries, engineering industries, light manufacturing, and food processing industries all are to be found in and around Bangalore. Machine tools, electrical manufactures, and precise engineering developments are being located around Coimbatore, but also such products as cement are now important products of Coimbatore. Many of the new research institutes developed in India are located within the larger region. This zone is not yet a mature industrial region, and it lacks a concentration of heavy, basic manufactures, but it is a region in which new development presently is being located, and it will continue to grow rather rapidly.

Although the four main regions display a concentration of manufacturing and processing activities, the industrialization of India is not to be described in these terms alone. Madras has long been an important cotton textile center, and in the present era the urban area of Madras is an important center of modern industry. Automotive manufacture, engineering industries, and general manufacture also characterize the urban entity, and the small towns around the city are becoming increasingly important, so that another regional manufacturing district is maturing. The same generalization can be made for the area encompassing Delhi-Meerut, in which woolen textiles, cotton goods, pharmaceuticals, food products, and light manufacturing is creating a significant manufacturing district. The old port of Visagapatam is now the modern industrial city of Visakhapatanam, the chief ship-building center for India, around which considerable agricultural processing has developed, and to which an increasing number of secondary manufacturing plants are being drawn. The Guntur-Vijayawada secondary manufacturing region has in the past rested primarily on agricultural processing, but

food manufactures and light general manufacturing are growing steadily. Most plants in this locality still are small and the technical level of manufacturing is not yet very high, but there is steady growth and development. The woolen industries are largely located in north Indian cities, and many Punjab and Ganges Valley cities, heretofore chiefly centers of handicrafts of localized specialties, are beginning to turn to more modern applications of manufacturing.

The impact of government planning, through the several five-year plans, clearly shows as one examines the broader patterns of distribution of modern development in industrialization (see Fig. 13.6). Consequent upon mineral surveys, hydroelectric power developments, and formally planned capital investments new manufacturing centers for particular kinds of products or wholly new and comprehensive manufacturing centers are being developed in all parts of India. For example, four heavy machine-tool factories are arbitrarily being placed at four separate locations, one each at Bangalore and Hyderabad, and the other two in northern India, as part of a government project. Petroleum refineries are formally being located in well-distributed locations around the peninsular coast, along with petro-chemical and plastics manufacturing plants in such a way as to provide minimum transport hauls to regional markets. Many of the cities labeled as secondary or growing manufacturing centers on Figure 13.6 will shortly deserve upgrading into general manufacturing centers.

Much of the industrial effort presently being expended in India derives from government planning and financial investment, but private entrepreneurs also are active in the Indian scene, and large corporate undertakings today have nation-wide ramification in terms of plant locations and range of manufacturing enterprise. India is making a tremendous effort at industrialization, an effort that shows in almost every regional landscape. The various five-year plans have separately aimed at particular sectors of activity, but the long-term implications are comprehensive. As could be anticipated in such a wholesale surge of industrialization the productive efficiency of many levels of manufacturing is not yet very high. Indian labor has not yet developed either the skills for, or the attitudes toward, modern manufacturing which make for high productivity and strongly efficient operation of the total industrial plant. Much of the managerial talent still retains older attitudes and cultural habits, and modern technological skills are in short supply at present. In cultural terms, one can see, here, the lack of maturity and the reluctance to wholly accept modern industrialization. There still is imbalance between the physical industrial plant and the human component that is needed to make the plant operate to full capacity and efficiency, but this is characteristic of any new program of industrialization anywhere in the world. If the sociopolitical problems of India can be held in check until the industrialization of India can reach a somewhat more mature level, then the payoff for the whole program may be successful.

TRANSPORTATION AND COMMUNICATION

As the British spread the modern network of roads and highways over Mother India they followed many an ancient route, sometimes utilizing the actual road embankment. Highways were developed with an eye to military movement and effective control of India. More recent improvements were made to provide transport for the population. The network in 1947 approximated 300,000 miles, of which about two thirds could be termed all-weather roads (Fig. 13.7). The road mileage in 1968 stood at about 420,000 miles, about three-fourths of which could be termed all-weather roads. Current expansion of the road network aims to bring wheeled trans-

port to every village, but it will be some years before this is achieved. A serious shortage of paving materials in the North Indian Plain puts the best roads in the southern peninsula. Some secondary roads are graded but still are narrow and poorly bridged. In addition to the above mileage are thousands of miles of cart tracks, bicycle and pack trails, not maintained, unbridged, and subject to flood and the Indian farmer. The automotive equipment in 1970 totals almost one million vehicles, but most Indians still must utilize less efficient means of transport (see photos in the transport cluster, pp. 263-268). This would provide fine motoring conditions were it not for the thousands of darting bicycles in urban areas and what seem like millions of plodding oxcarts on the urban fringes and in the rural market towns. Bus transport is an important phase of motor transport, about 140,000 buses linking many towns not connected by rail. These services, overcrowded and badly equipped, are usually privately owned and often are irregular in performance.

The railway system started out to parallel the road system, unprofitably. The railways use the European small-tonnage freight cars, compartment-type passenger cars, light engines, light rails, and a variety of gauges. Accumulated mileage for India totals about 36,000 miles (Fig. 13.8). The railways now are government owned, with operation divided between government and private companies. Trains carry a large passenger traffic (over two billion passengers per year), mainly on short trips at rather cheap fares, since most people travel third class in crowded, wooden-seated cars. Programs of electrification and converting engines to diesel power have increased the carrying capacity by reducing the coal-for-engine-fuel need. Some construction has compensated for the separation of India and Pakistan on border region line connections. Programs improving signalling and traffic control are going forward, and

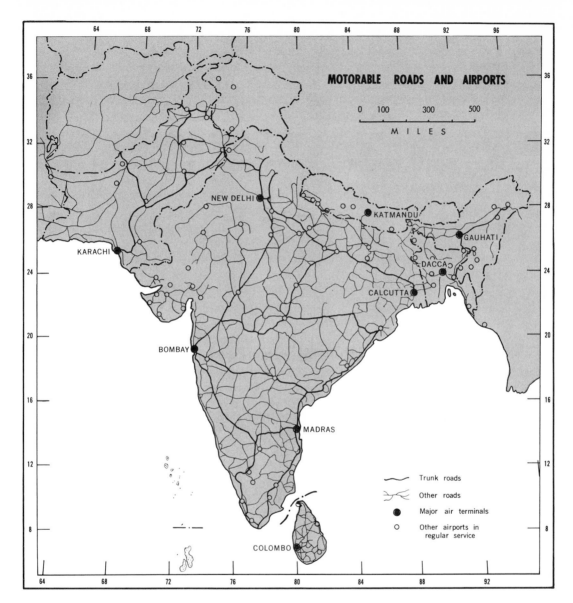

FIGURE 13.7. Roads and civil airports.

considerable double track has been installed. Although the multigauge, patchwork pattern of lines fairly well covers the country, about half the mileage is in the Ganges Valley. Many of the older and the narrow gauge lines, built for noneconomic reasons, do not serve real needs at present, but political pres-

sures so far prevent real modernization of the Indian rail network. India now manufactures her own railway equipment.

Both highways and rail lines focus on key points scattered over India. Delhi, Bombay, Madras, and Calcutta are major road and rail terminals. Secondary points are Allahabad,

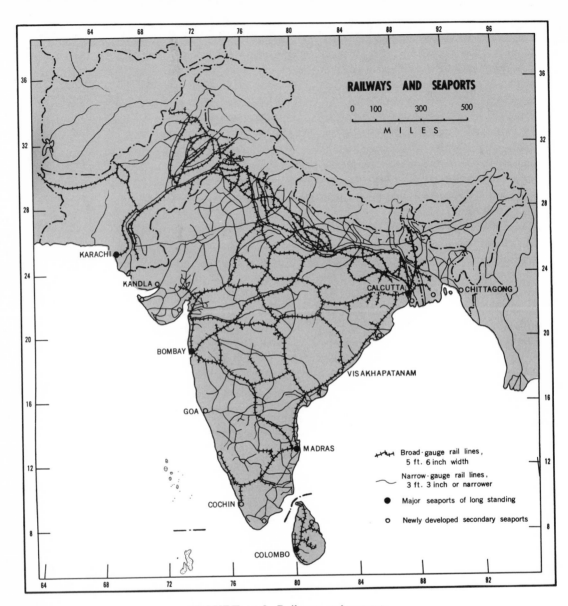

FIGURE 13.8. Railways and seaports.

Ahmadabad, Jabalpur, Nagpur, Vijayawada, Hyderabad, Bangalore, and Madurai. Both transport systems have more than their proportionate length in what was British India, whereas large districts that were in native states totally lack rail lines.

The telegraph and telephone systems, like the road and rail systems, are hybrid combinations of old and new, though modernizing programs are improving communications. Commercial radio had made little advance before World War II, but broadcast radio had quite a following, and today the listening audience is numbered in the millions. Air transport, as internal transportation, was uncommon before World War II, though India was fairly well tied into world airways. A government airlines system now operates several thousand miles of routes, and India is well linked by air services (see Fig. 13.7).

The chief ports during the past century are hard to locate now. Shifting sands, moving deltaic distributaries, naval conflict, and changing political fortunes have obliterated dozens of them. Such an ancient port as Tamralipti, just west of the Bengal Delta, is not used today, and the ancient port town of Broach today is a manufacturing city but not a port at all. Few of the chief ports of earliest sixteenth-century European contact are now used in foreign trade. The leading modern ports are those developed by late British East India Company activity. Bombay, Madras, and Calcutta are the primary large ports, given added facilities between 1920 and 1947 as British developments. At the present time Bombay and Calcutta dominate all other ports in traffic volume. Recent development has focussed on Kandla (in 1970 converted to a free-trade port), Visakhapatanam, Goa (Marmagao), Madras, and Cochin (see Fig. 13.8). Future development of additional ports, under five year planning, is subject to change, but apparently Port Okha (on the Gulf of Kutch in Kathiawar), Bhaunagar (on the Gulf of Cambay in Kathiawar), Mangalore (on the lower west peninsular coast), Tuticorin (near the southeast tip of Peninsular India), Paradip (on the upper east peninsular coast near Cuttack), and Haldia (below Calcutta as a deep-water river port) are now to be developed into major ports (see Fig. 13.8, on which each of the above is shown as an unnamed circle). Besides these are over 200 small ports and landings used by coastal traffic, handling large numbers of passengers and small-package cargo. India is currently expanding her shipping fleet, and now builds her own ships. In 1968 Indian bottoms handled only about fifteen percent of the foreign trade, whereas the long-run program aims at the carrying of about half the total.

THE TRADE OF INDIA

It is unlikely that much produce has ever moved overland out of India. It has been suggested that Mother India was the chief entrepôt of oriental trade and that the main warehouses in this movement were the cities of the peninsular coast. The impact of the Europeans was emphatic. First they scattered their trade among the many ports but attempted to drive all competitors away. Next they concentrated on picked ports, leaving others to die off. The British finally began to deal in India's best export commodity on ever larger terms, selling cotton textiles everywhere. As the modern era approached and the British East India Company faltered, the export trade slackened, whereas the import trade grew steadily under new appetites for material goods. Within the last century the export trade has recovered, but on different grounds.

Prior to World War II the export trade listed agricultural and raw and processed mineral products. Jute products, raw and manufactured cotton, tea, and oil seeds were the big items, followed by hides and skins, raw minerals, rubber, lac, and a series of minor, processed crop and forest products. Almost all were competitive products ranged against the same or related products of other lands. Even a monopoly like jute competes against sisal and hemp. No export was of high value, and in some cases the Indian share has been mainly cheap labor, final profits going to British corporation investors.

The import trade listed fine cotton and its finished products far above other imports. Next came chemical products and machinery, both increasing since 1930. A third group was made up of petroleum, unfabricated iron and steel, tools and instruments, and motor transport equipment. These larger groups were followed by a long list of other manufactured products in smaller volumes. Notable for its minor position was sugar, a declining import under a protective tariff and increasing home production. Statistically new after the separation of Burma from India in 1937 was rice, which was imported at a rate of about 1,500,000 tons per year.

Since World War II the items of trade have been changing steadily. Large volumes of raw materials still are exported, and specialty manufactures still are imported. However, India has been increasing her exports of manufactured goods of all kinds in recent years, and is beginning to import volumes of specialized raw materials. Varying amounts of food have been continuing on the import list, as the agricultural modernization of India lagged and the population increase continued. Such tropical fruits as bananas are now being exported to Japan, still in small volumes, but indicative of a future trend. The new items on the export list from Indian industry are iron and steel products, engineering goods, electrical manufactures, and varied metal fabrications.

The main volume of trade formerly was with four countries. Of the chief products tea, oil seeds, hides, and skins went in largest volume to Britain, raw cotton to Japan, and jute to the United States. Germany long was the fourth ranking united Indian customer, taking smaller volumes of a variety of products. In supplying Indian imports the order of rank was Britain, Japan, Germany, and the United States. Cotton textile imports were split between Britain and Japan before World War II, but Britain led in almost all other categories. Canada, Australia, Argentina, France, Italy, and Belgium were other countries with whom trade exchanges were significant. Rice and petroleum from Burma were the chief oriental imports, whereas distinctly Indian products went to those lands containing an Indian population. In

general India has exported a larger value of goods than she has imported. This flow was to some extent equalized by the import of silver, gold, and services and by the drain of industrial and trade profits homeward to England. The total volume of Indian foreign trade was rather small, and so long as India, Pakistan, and Ceylon offered for sale only cheap agricultural products they could afford only a modest purchase abroad. Many Indians now look forward to a tremendous expansion in foreign trade, and plan for a continued trade exchange which will facilitate internal industrialization and gradual elevation of the level of living.

In more recent years the patterns of trade have altered, and Great Britain's share of Indian trade has tended to decline, though she still is India's best market and source of imports. The USSR and eastern European countries have grown larger in trade exchanges with India, though balancing of the trade quota has caused some trouble in each case. Japan has been more important in Indian trade than formerly, and the United States has maintained a fairly stable role as a strong customer and import source for India.

With the growth of modern transport India has developed a very important internal trade. What technically is foreign trade, between India and Ceylon, and between India and Pakistan, is only so by a quirk of history, similar to that which, until 1937, tabulated foreign trade between Burma and India as domestic trade. The separation of the three states India, Pakistan, and Ceylon, has reordered the long-term trade statistics, many former domestic trade items now becoming foreign trade commodities. The flow of actual trade has not been greatly affected by the statistical changes. In quantity terms coal and coke greatly exceed other items. Rice, oil seeds, jute, cotton, salt, wheat, sugar, and the fruits are the chief items. The fruit trade is growing, as shipping techniques improve. There is little trade in vegetables, but a fairly considerable one in wood and fiber products. The northwest frontier, the hinterlands around Calcutta, Bombay, Madras, and the island of Ceylon are the chief food deficit areas. Calcutta and Bombay both import wheat flour and rice, the wheat going to the upper classes. Ceylon consumes much Indian rice, shipping to the mainland betel nut and spices. The rise of the industrial centers of India is altering the flow of minerals, other raw materials, and the flows of manufactured goods. Whereas these formerly moved away from ports in earlier years they now flow out to hinterlands from domestic manufacturing centers. The transfer of semi-manufactured goods within India to fabrication and assembly centers is promoting new patterns of internal trade.

MODERNIZATION AND POPULATION GROWTH

Lord Macaulay's cultural interpreters, as visualized in 1835 under British East India Company policy, have been slow in producing positive results, but they have deployed themselves upon many cultural fronts. The impact of their programs upon Indian life is rather irregular. The urban architecture of Bombay compares favorably with that of many an older city in the Occident. An Indian businessman may be as intelligent in international economics as his English opposite number. The Sikh congressman is as skillful as any United States representative engaged in a congressional filibuster. Change among some of the Indian tribal peoples is less than that among the refugees on reservations in southwestern United States. And India still restricts its lower castes and keeps its "untouchables" out of some walks of life. Legislation since 1948 has abolished the status of the untouchable, but it will linger long. Statements of legality are not enough

in the Occident or in India to effect rapid social change.

In the long period of cross-contact many elements have entered into modernization. The establishment of British enterprise in varied forms was necessary for modernization, though exploitation went too far. A decline of handicrafts was perhaps inevitable. The Parsee factor in Indian industrialization finds no clear parallel elsewhere. The distinctive locations of industrial materials and agricultural surpluses produce in India a peculiar scattering of initial modern enterprise, which planned industrialization is both altering and regularizing. The operation of the Christian missionary movement has been far reaching, affecting secular and Christian education, medicine, agriculture, and modern artisanry. The leadership of modern India has come mainly from students who have returned from England. A village-minded people still cling to traditional culture in spite of the debt that they have accumulated. An inclusive Hinduism that eventually has swallowed every effort at reform from within and a conservative Islam certainly are factors in this modernization.

Since 1940 much of the will to change has become galvanized into action. With British goading, India became an important productive element during World War II; with Indian prodding, Britain afterward let go the restrictive control that she had held over India. If the prospect is bright on the one hand, and if change has been great, problems are arising on the other hand, and the need for further change is tremendous.

It is difficult to estimate the population at the time the European first came, but the Indian subcontinent, along with China, perhaps constituted the most populous units on earth. Entering the modern world with a large population, India has grown rapidly. She possessed a fairly high level of living when the European came, and modern population increase has taken place despite a gradually declining level of living. Several occidental countries have increased greatly in population in the past century and a half, during an unequaled opportunity in world history, and some occidental rates of increase actually exceed oriental rates. Oriental increase has been in spite of a disadvantage. For example, the present Union of India's share of the 1941 population was 320,000,000, and in 1969 the total was probably close to 515,000,000 (Fig. 13.9). Projections for the future can be staggering. This increase in population is one of the most significant aspects of modernization. Much earlier British energy went into famine prevention made necessary by flood and drought. The growth of a transport network has alleviated

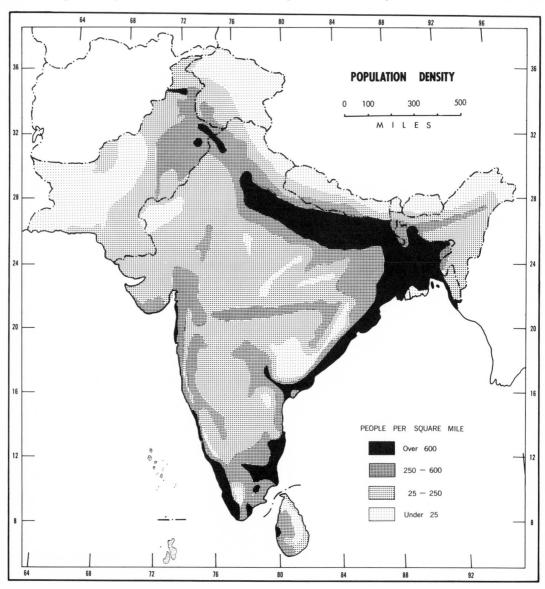

FIGURE 13.9. Population density in South Asia.

the old form of the famine problem, since it permits large volume transport of food supplies to deficit localities. Since 1920 more has been accomplished by preventive medicine and since 1947 the malaria prevention campaign has borne strong results. The single disease, malaria, annually had claimed well over 1,000,000 lives per year. Preventive measures have retarded the expansion of loss with population increase. Research identified cholera epidemics with religious pilgrimage, and preventive inoculations of endemic regions have reduced this danger. Prevention of childhood and infant ailments has been extending life expectancy for India, which in about 1947 stood in the vicinity of 31 years, and which, by 1968, had increased to 52 years.

Medical study, however, has detected the fact that increasing numbers of Indians are permanently malnourished and close to the starvation margin, so that even small diet changes threaten disastrous results. Very recent foreign purchases of large volumes of famine-alleviative basic foods have been necessary, restricting the volume of capital investment in productive development. So far the increasing productivity of modern India apparently has not greatly exceeded the increase in population. An increasing level of living and a deeper cushion of group resistance to minor economic fluctuations would be present if productivity really had exceeded consumption. Just how close to a balance and a ceiling India now is cannot be stated. As industrialization proceeds, and as the reserve land of India is put under crop, the slowly lifting level of balance may allow an ever larger total population. It is certain, however, that, unless some fundamental lifting of the ceiling can be accomplished, or some major voluntary reduction produced in the birth rate, neither the relative standard of living nor the level of living can be lifted for the country as a whole. This is not a pleasant prospect for the discerning Indian citizen, but there is open question as to how many Indians understand the critical issues of the problem.

The frequently stated elements of progress are impressive, but do their effects reach far enough into the rural hinterlands in affecting conditions of daily life for rural villagers? The record of progress is clear in sample production figures comparing 1950–1951 against 1967–1968: Food grains were 51,000,000 tons against 95,000,000, petroleum was 200,000 against 14,400,000 tons, bicycles manufactured went from 99,000 to 1,707,000, children in school were 23,500,000 against 71,800,000, electrical generating capacity was 2,500,000 k.w. against 13,100,000, and villages electrified went from 4,000 to 62,200. However, population increased by about 140,000,000 in the same interval, and about 500,000 villages still were without electricity! There is such imbalance in socioeconomic conditions of Indian life that millions of children are born into abject poverty, and there is such imbalance in the patterns of exercising political control as to result in great privilege for a relative few and no privilege at all for millions of people.

Historically, the city as a form of settlement comes close to being as old in India as anywhere else on earth, yet urbanization has been slow to develop in the modern period. However, urbanization is beginning to take place in the modern sense in India, and the results are startling. Some of the highest per-acre densities, and some of the poorest urban conditions, to be found anywhere are showing up in Indian cities today. Dependent upon the definition accepted, present Indian urbanism may be stated as about ten percent of the total population living in cities of over 100,000, about fourteen percent of the population living in cities of over 20,000, or about twenty percent of the total population living in settlements of over 10,000. By the latter traditional definition, India has over 2,000 urban places. There now are 8 cities of over a million: Bombay, Calcutta, Delhi, Madras, Hyderabad, Bangalore, Ahmadabad, and Kanpur, though some of these include units technically separable. Poona, Nagpur, Lucknow, Howrah, and Agra are over 500,000, though Poona can be grouped in a "Greater Bombay" as Howrah can be grouped in a "Greater Calcutta." In all, there are 250 cities of over 50,000 population in present-day India. If India does go through a strong phase of urbanization, there will be need to develop strong, new urban planning systems if urbanism is not to turn into some expression of how the human race ought not live.

Social, economic, and political modernization have not kept up with population increase, despite the improvements that have taken place. Increases in population have produced millions of persons for whom the prospects of livelihood are grim, both in the rural scene and in the towns and cities. Urbanism is growing, but urban institutions are ill-prepared to cope with the problems in the Indian scene in which growing numbers neither can find economic opportunity, social betterment, nor a place to sleep at night. Currently industrialization is the great hope, but whether conservative-minded sociopolitical management can prepare the Indian population for effective participation in a maturing industrial society is a very large question. It is clear that India needs more than an industrial revolution, alone, to cope with her own future and, though passive acceptance has been a hallmark of Hindu outlook, some violent breaks with cultural tradition appear almost inevitable. It is quite unclear as to the directions such change may take.

SEPARATISM IN MODERN INDIA

There are two phases of cultural development in which Mother India has not risen above her past. These are the issues of internal division within the now independent state of India, and the matter of separatism of the subcontinent as a whole.

To take the internal issue first, language, religion, landforms, settlement system, domestic cropping economy, housing systems, climatic regionalism, variations in soils, transport regionalisms, regional social structurings, and historic political factionalisms are among the criteria that must be faced in deciding what the internal administrative political structure of the Indian state should be. Geographers have long constructed systems of geographic regions that theoretically rose above individual characteristics, but seldom have these become operable patterns. Modern India began with some very complex historic patterns, attempting to integrate these into a workable system. The language issue, however, came to the fore, with a demand by some groups for their own political state within the Indian Union. This could be like opening Pandora's Box, and there are many latent problems to be solved by India in the realm of regionalizing her many factors of separatism and sectionalism that, historically, have pulled and pushed against the formation and maintenance of a truly national state.

Mother India followed historic precedent and broke apart again in 1947. Aided by modern transport in the last generation, Britain had come closer than any previous Indian overlord to operating India as one political and economic unit. Politically, Britain had to manage it in pieces, but all economic planning had envisaged one India. The Indian subcontinent is a sound regional unitary realm from the environmental viewpoint, and it is human customs and viewpoints that have repeatedly divided the large region, lacking easy physical, sectional criteria, into various pieces where boundaries have not been easy to demarcate. The urge to separatism was raised to fever heat in the decade 1937–1947 by the efforts of the Moslem League, using the religious call of Islam. Nationalism and a will to independence had been growing in India over a period of some twenty years. No common, single formula for the political operation of an independent united India could be agreed upon by native leaders in the spring of 1947. All kinds of Indians were too united in a "hate Britain" and "quit India" campaign to hold back. Britain's postwar home plight forced her hand, and she reluctantly granted independence to the whole, divided into six political entities: Pakistan, India, Nepal, Bhutan, Sikkim, and Ceylon. The release of Nepal, Bhutan, and Sikkim was, in effect, the removal of a protectorate (Fig. 13.10).

In the divergent currents of internal opinion within India there were many in 1947 who would not have chosen independence from Britain because they were against division of India. This group was composed of the rulers of Indian states, the Sikh community, many Moslems, industrialists, traders, the "untouchables," and many Hindu and Christian leaders. The reasons behind their agreement were many and varied. Rulers of most Indian states had considerable to lose. Sikhs feared a renewal of their old struggle with the Moslems. Many Moslems were Indian nationalists first and Moslems second, as were Christians. Since the tide of events could not be stayed, many Hindus, Sikhs, and Christians went forward reluctantly, if hopefully, foreseeing problems in the future. They rejected the name Hindustan on the ground that it did not fit a political state composed of Sikhs, Christians, and Hindus, and chose the name Bharat, from the Hindu literary reference to the subcontinent. In world practice the name became India. Moslems jubilantly but blindly surged into a future filled with problems that few had thought seriously about, hailing their Pakistan. Some Indian rulers promptly joined one side or the other, others slowly gave in, and some held out hopefully. Practically no long-range planning had preceded the division, since the major currents of thought and planning had been toward a united India.

The lines along which a division occurred are both old and new. The dry lands of northwest India are the core of Pakistan. Today a majority of the population is Moslem, whereas in the sixteenth century no more than fifteen percent of northwest India followed Islam. Various distributional criteria may be suggested to fortify the notion of Pakistan's validity. The distribution of the camel, the 20-inch rainfall line, the old line dividing the wheat and rice crops, the zone of the historic invasions, the spread of the Islamic faith, these and more have been used many times by Pakistanis. No group of lines thus drawn proves very sound, however, for the actions of men in North India over the centuries have altered some natural distributions to suit their passing judgments. The inclusion of an isolated territory in the wet heart of the Bengal Delta, even though it was predominantly Islamic, violates every "dry land" criterion. The division of the Indian realm into the six states is a willful political separation of Mother India by articulate minorities who cried the unity of Islam, the unity of Hinduism, or the historic tradition. Although considerable mass migration occurred, and most Sikhs and Hindus left West Pakistan, the Moslems had to leave behind a considerable minority, both in the west and in the east, and many Hindus remained in East Pakistan.

The separatism of Nepal and Bhutan is modern, even though the region is not completely Indian in blood and culture. A strong Mongolic element always has been present. Traditionally the area always was tributary to strong Indian states, becoming autonomous in periods of lowland weakness or strife. Modern separatism originated in Indian Rajput elements seeking refuge from Moslem domination during the fifteenth to eighteenth centuries. "Gurkha" consolidation of Nepal in the eighteenth century led to an isolationism against British encroachment which has remained a guiding principle ever since. Gurkha enlistment in the British

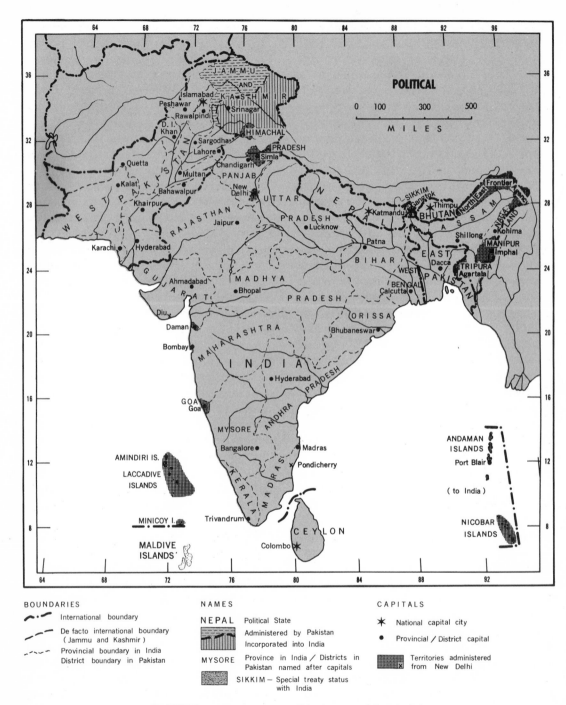

FIGURE 13.10. Present political states of South Asia.

Indian Army was an economic opportunity compensating for the regional isolation. Political pressure being exerted by modern China may alter the Nepalese view of the value of isolation. The case of Bhutan is as much one of physical geography and location as anything else. Chiefly inhabited by simpler cultural groups, it presented little interest to the British. Sikkim, on the other had, was accessible, and it appealed to the British interest as a summer hill station resort at which to escape the muggy heat of the lowlands, so that it early became a protected principality.

REGIONALISM ON THE SUBCONTINENT

Mother India is an interesting if puzzling study in regionalism. Among the varied kinds of distributions within the subcontinent there are not many that show sharp, clean boundaries. The crest line of the Western Ghats and an upper line along part of the Mountain Wall are significant for many natural distributions. Man, however, has paid little attention to either line. Around the eastern two thirds of the Mountain Wall an important cultural line exists that is not matched in physical terms. Elsewhere man has carried plants, animals, working techniques, and human institutions across, and himself has gone across, the transition zones and definitive lines of the landscape until today it is almost impossible to suggest rational division of the subcontinent along sharp lines. Any such division is certain to disregard important criteria. Criteria then become selective, and the selection becomes variably subjective.

A certain number of divisions of the country have been recognized as valid from many points of view. These divisions mean something to Indians. They are useful in setting down a simple description of the landscapes of the subcontinent. To mention the major units only: the Northwest Frontier, Punjab, the Himalayas, Ganges Valley, Bengal, Assam, Chota Nagpur, Rajputana, Deccan, Malabar Coast, Mysore, Madras, Madura, and Ceylon. To an educated Indian each of these carries connotations as to landscape, crops, people, and culture, but no one of them can be sharply defined except Ceylon, the island. Within certain limits they follow both natural and cultural criteria. For example, every educated north Indian distinguishes between the Punjab and the upper Ganges Valley, between "the Hills" and Assam. And he separates a Bengali from a Punjabi, a Tibetan from a Gurkha, a Sikh from a Baluch. But a Punjabi and a Sikh both come from the Punjab, which now is divided between Pakistan and India, just as Bengal is so divided. And the Tibetan and the Gurkha both come from "the Hills," the upper Ganges Valley has no one clear human type, and Assam has nearly a dozen. Everywhere in the subcontinent simple divisions are compounded and regrouped to fit the occasion and the need.

At the one extreme the subcontinent may be divided into three pieces, the Northwest, the Northeast, and the South. This has its uses but tends to generalize too greatly. Detailed criteria may be assembled to show many kinds of regionalisms (Figs. 13.11 and 13.12).

Nepal, Bhutan, and Sikkim

By virtue of their marginal positions within the Himalayan highland several upland sectors escaped much of the turmoil that affected the Indus and Ganges valleys during the Islamic invasions and the spread of British influence. Although what is today Nepal is the partial consolidation of four separate historic princedoms, Bhutan is a rugged mountain zone never really claimed by any political state in concrete terms, and Sikkim is a historic principality, the political pattern for the three became consolidated

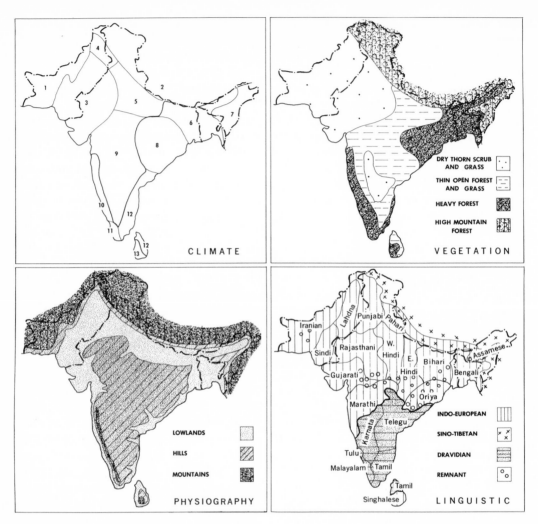

FIGURE 13.11. South Asian regionalisms: climatic regions, vegetation, physiographic, and linguistic.

only during the nineteenth century for Nepal and Sikkim, and early in the twentieth century for Bhutan (see Fig. 13.10). The central-western Himalayan high valleys were the refuge zone for numerous groups of peoples from the lowlands over many centuries, and these lands became sacred both to the Buddhists and the Hindus of earlier India. Religious pilgrimages, over the centuries, brought both peoples and cultures to the highlands. The whole upland lies within the traditional range of the Lamaist Tibetans,

to the end that there has been a mixing of ethnic stocks, culture patterns, and religious creeds. In the thirteenth and fourteenth centuries, under Islamic pressures, there was much refugeeing into the mountains, and small territorial principalities based on the traditional "capital city" were the result of local war, intrigue, and competitive struggle. By the end of the eighteenth century Nepal had taken shape under a single control, but its expansion was checked by the British in the early nineteenth century, and the state continued as a marginal entity on the highland fringe of British India. Sikkim, as a principality, was split off Nepal, under British pressure, in 1815. Bhutan is a more rugged zone lacking the east-west lateral valleys and the clear presence of a foothill sector characteristic of Nepal, and the region received fewer refugees from the lowlands, thereby retaining its lighter population of Tibetans and tribal migrants from the east. Bhutan was long a turbulent zone under Tibetan competitive controls, but in the early twentieth century the region came under somewhat unified control and the nominal overlordship of Great Britain, to the end that it has been a relatively peaceful if marginal element.

All three units are agricultural with strong contrasts within short distances. Terraced wet-rice fields in the valleys, bare mountains above them, scattered patches of upland cropping on shoulders and less rugged slopes, and tracts of forest or jungle are to be found in all portions. Relatively dense popu-

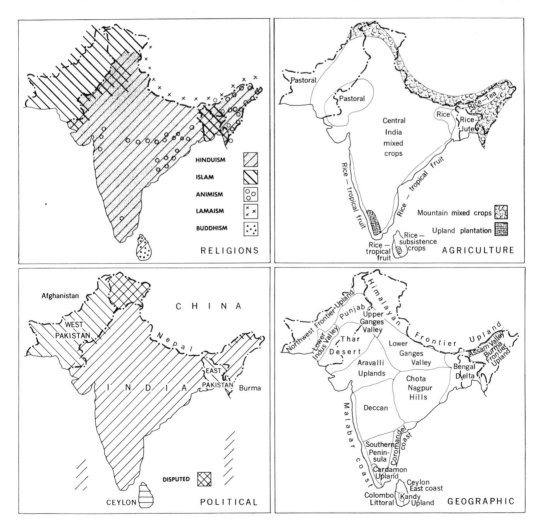

FIGURE 13.12. South Asian regionalisms: religious, crop, political, and geographic.

lations have accumulated in the better localities, with close-set hamlets, villages, and small towns, connected both to Tibet and to the lowlands by traditional trails. In Nepal the valleys are broader and more open than in Bhutan, and both population and agricultural development are greater. Katmandu has grown into a large city in modern time. The British interest in a hill station at which to escape the summer heat of the lowlands led to the development of Darjeeling, secured from Sikkim in 1833 and now part of India; the heights now form a summer resort town, and the more open valley fringes have been put into tea plantations.

In the present century change has been coming to the hill country, as roads replaced trails and contacts expanded. Nepal, aside from supplying the British armed forces with the famous Gurkha regiments, has made moves toward modernization in several different respects. Currently its capital, Katmandu, is at the end of a branch airline, and Nepal has become the fashionable tourist trek for many from all over the world, who come to enjoy the mountain scenery and the strange blend of religiously dominated culture.

This marginal mountain zone lies on the bounding elements of India and China and, in recent years, has felt the impacts of competitive political strategy as Communist China expanded its controls over Tibet. In that historic claims and counterclaims are hard to place in the rugged mountain landscapes the northern border zone will continue to be a zone of friction so long as the aggressive approach is taken by one side or the other. The continued independence of these three margin mountain kingdoms, therefore, lies somewhat at the mercy of modern big-power political strategy.

Kashmir: The Disputed Region

This is not the place to argue the merits of the Kashmir problem, and no such argument will follow. The upland region is of critical importance to both Pakistan and India in terms of the water supply that flows into the lowlands. The highland region, with its cooler climate, wonderful scenery, upland valleys, and alluvial valley floors set with streams and lakes, has long been a matter of emotional regard to the inhabitants of northern lowland India-Pakistan. The failure of the effective separation of British-controlled India into two parts, cleanly, owes in no small part to this long emotional attachment. A population that was in the majority Islamic by religion was ruled by an orthodox Hindu princely family, at the date of the separation of Pakistan and India. Within Pakistan the ruling family had no future, and within a Hindu India the majority population of Moslems felt it had no future.

Traditionally a land of highland pastoralism, valley agriculture, handicraft manufacturing of silks, wools, and metals-woodwork, the beauties of Kashmir have been in the literatures of Moslems and Hindus alike, and pilgrimages and vacations in the Vale of Kashmir have been the object of many a northerner. Kashmir has long had a population that was ethnically mixed, and culture patterns that are ethnically mixed, beyond the matters of religious preference.

It is a matter of record that the Pakistan army was not strong enough to occupy Kashmir as the issue rose to serious proportions, following the failure of peaceful partition. It is a matter of record that neutralist India did use its army to gain control over an area of strong emotional attachment for Prime Minister Nehru. The failure of peaceful control resulted in open war, with the present line a cease-fire truce-line set by the United Nations. In this demarcation the larger share of Kashmir fell to India, including a sector of territory inhabited by Moslems.

Each political state is doing what it can to integrate its sector of Kashmir into its own political state, and there seems every likelihood that a permanent division has been made on grounds other than those that originally separated Pakistan from India. Transport connections are being steadily improved by each state, and patterns of economic development are under way. In that neither side will agree to peaceful discussion of the problem, that both sides indulge in exaggerated propaganda, and that the United Nations can get nowhere with any proposal, it appears that the realities of human political control of the landscape will dominate over the elements of natural and regional ecology, to the end that Kashmir will take on a permanent political division.

14

PAKISTAN: THE GEOGRAPHY OF A BIFURCATED STATE

Pakistan began its modern existence under an anomalous set of conditions. The new political state had an initial *raison d'etre* of sorts in Islam, and it had some eloquent and able leaders, but it had the handicap of being in two unequal parts separated by a thousand miles, between which parts only religion and animosity toward the British and the Hindus served as the binding element. Many did not expect it to survive, but it has held together for over twenty years. Although there still can be put forward questions as to ultimate survival as a single state, we should probably accept the possibility that it can survive as one state. Separated out from an on-going political and economic construct, in 1947, Pakistan began its separate life as fractional elements of a working whole.

Pakistan took with it about one fifth of the area and the highways of the previous united India, about one sixth of the population and the rail lines, about one seventh of the cultivated land, a tenth of the army, a segment of reactionary large landholders, a minority of the educated middle class, very few of the shopkeepers, tradesmen, pro-fessional classes, and artisans, only a few thousand industrial workers, almost none of the known minerals, a fraction of the industrial equipment, no mills for three fourths of the jute crop, a few small mills for one third of the cotton crop, one major port, Karachi, and one minor port, Chittagong. The agricultural surpluses, jute, cotton, wheat, and hides, were cut off from their normal internal and external markets. A Hindu middle class operated most of the economic machinery for united India, and, upon division, a very large share of the Hindus moved out of northwest India, along with most of the Sikhs, taking much of the liquid wealth and the technical skills. The Islamic population had been the most conservative group in former India, with the highest group illiteracy. Well over eighty percent of the Pakistan population was peasant farmer or pastoral herdsman in occupational orientation, and the total remaining industrial, managerial, or administrative skill was rather slight.

Aided by foreign loans and United Nations aid Pakistan forged ahead. Karachi has been turned from a regional port into an industrial city and has multiplied its population several times, the buildings and facilities being added after the increases of population. A new political capital is still under development in northern West Pakistan, at Islamabad Concerted efforts have built new towns, new power plants, new schools, and new factories. Irrigation systems and leveling of desert lands in West Pakistan parallel drainage development and improved diking in East Pakistan. Productivity is increasing and slowly a little more balance will appear in the economy. This is still an artificial country, not yet smoothly operating and rounded in its activities, but certainly it is changing with great rapidity and shaking off much of the conservatism that has marked the Islamic regions in the past.

The two sectors of Pakistan involved West Pakistan, the dry alluvial lowland-mountain sector of the west, 310,403 square miles in area, with a 1941 population of just over 28,000,000, and East Pakistan, the hot, humid deltaic lowland sector of the east, 55,126 square miles, with a 1941 population of just under 42,000,000 (see Fig. 13.10). In 1961 the regional-unit populations had grown to almost 43,000,000 for West Pakistan, and almost 51,000,000 for East Pakistan, and the total 1969 population was estimated at close to 110,000,000 (see Fig. 13.9).

In one sense Pakistan is a country without a historic culture, since its past has been part and parcel of the historic culture of Mother India. But in the sense that West Pakistan was the zone of occupance by the early Indus culture, that the Aryan invasions came through the northwest, and that the Islamic invasions came first into this sector, Pakistani patriots have been able to graft these elements onto their culture tree in such terms as to provide a long pattern of continuity for West Pakistan, projecting this for the whole of the national state (see Figs. 12.1–12.5 and

13.11–13.12). For East Pakistan the patterns of distinctly Islamic culture complexes involve a much shorter time span with less cohesive integration into the national culture tree.

THE PRIMARY ECONOMY

Most of the problems itemized for Indian agriculture in the previous chapter exist in much the same way for Pakistan. Arid West Pakistan has land available to which it has been impossible to deliver water for any kind of cropping pattern, and in the humid Bengal Delta the problems have been to control summer floods and to deliver water to fields, during the winter dry season, that could grow the third crop of wet-field rice. Waterlogging and increasing salinity have become increasing problems in West Pakistan, owing to relatively inefficient canal-delivered flood irrigation systems that have provided too much water to certain crop lands. Soil erosion, historically, has rendered many portions of West Pakistan costly to restore to the agricultural landscape. Recent and current major water control projects in both sectors of the country are increasing the agricultural potential, in the total sense, but there is some question as to whether the long-term gains will continue to be greater than the increases in demand for agricultural lands on the part of the rapidly growing population. The introduction of new high-yield grains and the expansion of crop lands through new irrigation facilities are now giving agricultural production a strong upward trend. In 1970 West Pakistan appeared self-sufficient in the basic wheat staple.

In simplest terms East Pakistan is a mono-crop region specializing in wet-field rice production, complemented by the cash crops jute, tea, sugarcane, tobacco, and coconut, whereas West Pakistan is a region of mixed cropping of grains dominated by wheat and complemented by maize, millet, sorghum, gram, sugarcane, and minor grains and oil seeds as dry-field crops, and by some wet-field rice, with cotton the most important of the cash crops (see Figs. 13.1–13.4). The rice growing pattern of East Pakistan can involve three crops per year on such lands as can be supplied with water the year around, but in the past the largest sector has been able to grow only two crops per year. The current water control projects in the east aim significantly at complementing water supplies for the second crop and at making possible large areas of third crop planting. The heart of the jute growing area is the central-upper delta where annual alluvial accretion by flood waters maintains soil productivity for a demanding plant which is the leading export commodity for Pakistan. Commercial tea plantings are restricted to the higher and well drained lands in the northern and eastern section of East Pakistan. Sugarcane is chiefly grown in the western section of East Pakistan, whereas coconut production comes from the lower delta fringes. Tobacco is more important in the eastern sector but is rather widely scattered.

In West Pakistan the shape of the major agricultural region resembles that of the river systems (see Figs. 6.5 and 6.6). In the north the zone spreads from east to west across the foothill and higher alluvial plains areas, similar to the spread of the rivers that emerge from the Himalayan front. These streams coalesce southward as tributaries join the Indus, and there is a long tapering belt of crop lands down the Indus Valley. By agreement reached in 1961, the waters of the Punjab are apportioned for irrigation purposes: India uses the three easterly streams, Sutlej, Beas, and Ravi, and Pakistan the three westerly streams, Chenab, Jhelum, and Indus. In West Pakistan, canals connect the river systems, redistributing water southeastward across the Pakistan Punjab (see Fig. 13.3). Smaller sectors of cultivated land

lie along smaller alluvial-plain streams in the northwest and western portions of the country, but these are more in the nature of scattered oases. West Pakistan agriculture is essentially irrigation cultivation, and cropland expansion is tied to the development of irrigation systems. Wheat is primarily a spring crop, chiefly grown in the northern sector, and wet-field rice is largely restricted to lands close to rivers and canals. The other crops are integrated into the cropping systems according to their need for water, their seasonal patterns and economic values; for example, minor acreages of barley replace wheat on poor soils, upland localities, and drier fringes.

The Pakistan agricultural economy has two other sectors needing comment, although the statistical data do not permit effective exposition of the importance of either. Fruits and vegetables on the one hand, and an animal economy on the other, are locally significant aspects of rural economy. Fruit and vegetable growing are items of homestead gardens, chiefly, in both East and West Pakistan, with only a moderate commercial element to date, though some small orchards in West Pakistan support a growing canning industry. The fruits of East Pakistan are essentially those of the humid subtropics, such as mangoes, papaya, guava, bananas, and the citrus, whereas those of West Pakistan chiefly are the mid-latitude cold-winter fruits such as peaches, pears, plums, apples, and grapes. The hill country of Baluchistan, the northwest frontier sector, and parts of Kashmir have long produced small volumes of good fruit. In neither region is fruit and vegetable production as well managed, properly developed, or as significant economically as it could be.

The animal economy of East Pakistan is quite minor, and significant only as urban dairying, although there is an export of cattle, buffalo, and goat hides, whereas that of West Pakistan is relatively more significant in the drier, rougher, and more mountainous areas, although it is not well developed as an element in modern agricultural economy. Sheep and goat populations are large in the western and northern hill country, producing an annual export volume of hides and carpet wool, and urban dairying is a significant part of the animal economy.

Fisheries are not a highly significant element in Pakistan economy. In West Pakistan, until very recently, only on the coastal fringe was fishing important, but the development of pond-fishing is under way, and there could be a useful development of fresh-water fisheries along with irrigation projects. East Pakistan, on the other hand, has an old and widely distributed habit of engaging in fresh water fishing, for food and for sport, and fish are an important element in the dietary. Pond-raising of fish has been an indifferent element in rural economy, but this aspect is currently under expansion. East Pakistan provides a surplus volume of fishery products, most of which are exported into the urban markets of India's West Bengal.

Although there are some millions of acres in fairly good forests in the more humid hilly sectors of West Pakistan and in the rougher East Pakistan fringes, the country possesses too little good forest land and has suffered excessively from past exploitation. Afforestation programs are developing under modern management and may restore a productive element to the economy. At present, however, wood products are relatively scarce, of low quality, and this sector of the economy is very poorly developed.

INDUSTRY AND TRADE

The regions now forming Pakistan were primarily marginal sectors of united India, prior to 1941, in which almost no industrial development had taken place. There was the normal regional pattern of handicraft manufacturing, with some specializations, but the area primarily formed sources of raw commodity exports, such as the jute, tea, and hides of East Pakistan, and the wool, hides, and cotton of West Pakistan. The loss of Hindu educated and technical personnel left Pakistan with very little technical skill. There was little in the way of developed power facilities, and the transportation network, which had depended largely on coal from an inner portion of united India, was severely handicapped at the outset. Of the roughly 13,000 factories of united India, with a work force of about 3,000,000, Pakistan inherited about 1,400 of the smaller factories and a labor force of about 200,000. Nearly half the Pakistan factories were in food manufactures or agricultural processing, and none were in the basic heavy industrial lines. The development of modern industry in Pakistan, then, must be viewed in terms of the initial beginnings of industrialization. In these terms Pakistan has made a very respectable beginning, but it is too early to be able to assess the balance and mature productivity of the industrial sector of the economy.

Obviously, there has been a continuation of, and expansion in, the older handicraft manufacturing elements in Pakistan, primarily in regard to consumer goods utilized by the rural sectors of the population. The old, colonial-era fine cotton textiles of eastern Bengal have not returned to strength, but the wool cloth, clothing, and rug manufacturing of West Pakistan continues. There has been a large expansion in handicraft manufacturing in cotton textiles and cotton clothing in both East and West Pakistan, and there was the initial beginning of jute manufacturing at the handicraft level in the east, although this will probably not continue once an adequate assemblage of modern machine factories has developed. Silk weaving in East Pakistan, leather and pottery manufactures in West Pakistan, and embroideries, silver and gold ware, and wood products from local centers in both East and West Pakistan add to the total volume of production.

Large scale industry has faced the problems of sources of raw materials, supplies of initial machinery, basic fabricating skills, and the dearth of capital resources. Significant accomplishments in the power-development field, and in mineral resources survey and production are now yielding results. Beginnings are in production in chemicals and fertilizers, glass, cement, paper, plastics, rubber, engineering, electrical goods, and general light manufacturing (see Fig. 13.6). Small steel plants and other metal smelting and fabricating plants are in operation, but here the dearth of good raw mineral resources still sets down a handicap in the growth of basic industry, and so far Pakistan chiefly depends upon imported mineral ores.

There has been significant development in the field of textiles, and jute, cotton, and woolen manufactures represent Pakistan's best accomplishments to date. Developments in higher-level agricultural processing and food manufacturing have been moving satisfactorily. The growth of light manufacturing has been moving ahead steadily in many different lines.

Government development of industry has been a strong element in the program of industrialization, with much imported capital and technical aid. Planning programs, for a rounded development, were slow to get under way, owing to early political instability, but recent long-term plans promise to round out a fairly effective pattern of growth, as power resources increase, and as domestic skills accumulate. Pakistan's industrial program is still very much in the initial stages, and dissension as to what goes into East or West Pakistan still provides a considerable problem. To date one can state that Karachi and Lahore comprise major manufacturing centers, and that there are two still minor industrial regions, one in East Pakistan and

one in the northwest portion of West Pakistan (see Fig. 13.6).

Pakistan began its independence with only one major port at Karachi in the west and one minor port at Chittagong in the east, and with a very inadequate internal transport network fractured by the partition of India. The development of trade, both external and internal, has remained under handicap, although the patterns are improving as new facilities are installed (see Figs. 13.7 and 13.8). Pakistan will continue for some years to be an importer of manufactured goods and selected raw materials, and an exporter of processed agricultural commodities and a slowly growing volume of specialized agricultural products such as manufactured jute, cottons, and woolens. Raw and manufactured jute will, of course, remain a chief Pakistan export for many years and source of foreign exchange. Unfortunately this source faces strong competition from other cheap fibers around the world. Pakistan, at present, faces a strong imbalance in her import-export trade, as her imports of manufactures and industrial equipment far overrun her earnings in the export trade.

The separation of the two parts of the country by a thousand-mile section of another country (often with such poor relations that even the mails cannot be delivered between countries) poses a real problem in internal trade, for the casual pattern of redistribution of local surpluses and the delivery of products of one sector to the other sector face a costly transport haul. Eventually, it may be possible to shorten this long haul by across-India bonded shipments, but that convenience remains for future development. Internal transport networks both on land and as water-route facilities, in East Pakistan, will be costly to develop in this wet lowland of seasonal floods and changing delta distributaries. West Pakistan may face somewhat cheaper-per mile costs in such matters, but the long-haul element from the coast to the more productive section of the country, in the north, imposes a significant cost factor.

THE PATTERN OF POPULATION

The large share of the Pakistan population has always been rural in distribution, but there are important differences between the two parts of the country. East Pakistan has been very very strongly rural, since the earlier modern urban developments were in the western delta region in what now is India. Politically motivated urbanism is now strong, in administrative, industrial, and economic terms, and newly created cities serving one or more functions are numerous. There were, of course, old cities in East Pakistan as regional-political centers in earlier times, and Dacca was a large city in the seventeenth century, but the rise of British Indian urban trends in western Bengal caused urban decline in the eastern zone. Since about 1900 the regional towns and cities have been growing again, first in political-regional trade terms and, since independence, in broad terms. East Pakistan received relatively few refugees at the time of separation, in 1947, and the rural distribution of population remained fairly stable, though numbers of Hindus tend to shift to West Bengal at times of India-Pakistan short-term crises. Growth in population has been steady but not spectacular in East Pakistan, though some extremely high rural densities are accumulating in local zones. The creation of industrial and port cities will, of course, give East Pakistan rapidly increasing rates of urbanism in the near future, particularly as rural densities reach saturation points. East Pakistan, at independence, contained the larger share of the country's total population, is closer to ecological saturation points, and may face problems of emigration if urban-industrial development cannot absorb rural surpluses in the near future.

West Pakistan has long shown marked contrasts in population density in regional and local terms. Generally speaking the rough hill country is lightly populated, although the northwestern frontier portions have some high local densities in good areas. There are old fortress-trade towns and oasis towns that have varied in size, historically, and in the northwest some of these now are undergoing industrialization on the basis of local power and mineral resources. The lowland zone has always shown the contrasts of heavy population in areas of irrigable land available for agriculture, with trade towns and administrative capitals as localities of high concentrations of population. This apparently was true in ancient India and it continues true in modern time, as Mohenjo-daro and Hyderabad-Sind indicate. Along the Indus River, in the southern sector, there is a scattering of cities, with the large urban pattern of Karachi just west of the Indus mouth. In the Pakistan Punjab, on or near the several tributaries of the Indus, the number of towns and cities has long been high, continuing eastward into what is today the Indian Punjab. West Pakistan suffered a very large exodus of Hindus and Sikhs and a large influx of Moslems from India, at the time of partition, and most of the refugees from India added to the natural trend of urbanism as they settled in towns and cities. The urban pattern of West Pakistan, therefore, is both an older and a stronger trend than that in East Pakistan.

Urbanism, whether in the smaller towns or in the large cities of West Pakistan, has faced serious problems of housing, urban planning, and the creation of the whole range of urban utilities. It has been only in recent years that these problems have been seriously tackled. Karachi and Lahore represent the two really large metropolitan urban entities, but the Rawalpindi-Islamabad complex is rapidly growing into one as Pakistan has created a new political capital at Islamabad. The very rapid growth of industrialization, however, will give impetus to the urban trend, as many old trade centers become industrial cities and as old villages are turned into industrial towns. Karachi, though no longer the political capital, will continue to grow as the country's chief urban-industrial center-port, for its position in respect to foreign trade and the distant productive section of the country almost guarantees its future premier position.

SOCIOPOLITICAL STRUCTURE OF THE BIFURCATED STATE

There are strong inequalities between East and West Pakistan and between portions of West Pakistan, despite the common bond of Islam. Ethnic, linguistic, and cultural differences are strong between East and West, and some strong differences exist between the lowland and the hill country in West Pakistan. Political boundaries in all cases are what might be termed accidents of political history or of crisis. British control of Baluchistan and the Northwest Frontier was a nineteenth century military-political extension of efforts aimed to provide peace to the lowlands of British India, and the inclusion of the western hill country in the state of Pakistan became a political inheritance. The eastern boundary of West Pakistan fell into place in terms of adjudication of the census count of the percentage of Moslems, a matter of religious history. The boundaries of East Pakistan came out of the same kind of religious history. The disputed territories of Kashmir are matters of religious-political history. Although political history is involved in the placement of political boundaries around the state of Pakistan, all those boundaries fronting on India were placed in crisis—boundaries *had* to be drawn in the face of

sociopolitical upheaval, upon any basis that could be found, since the fever of Hindu-Islamic passions complicated the matter of Great Britain's granting of independence to a former colony.

There are two kinds of issues in the structuring of the state of Pakistan: the balancing of East and West, and the internal administrative operation of each part of the country. East Pakistan, with the earlier larger share of the population and a cultural homogeneity of a practical sort (religion had not provoked constant trouble in earlier decades) has regularly felt imposed upon in many ways, as when West Pakistan first tried to establish Urdu as the single national language, ignoring Bengali, and as West Pakistan began the allocation of capital investment funds. Were it not for the fear of absorption by, and submergence into, Hindu India on the parts of both East and West Pakistan, it is doubtful that Islam could permanently serve as the *raison d'etre* that holds the two sectors together, separated as they are in so many ways. The *raison d'etre* for both East and West Pakistan, therefore, is the shared fear of submergence back into India and the shared adherence to Islam as a state religion. Problems of pressures, balancing interests, developmental programs, and future alleviatory programs will remain for the foreseeable future. If these problems can be solved to a degree of satisfaction that exceeds the fears of submergence, the state of Pakistan may continue as two pieces. If they cannot be so solved, then the future of East Pakistan may lie in becoming an independent state on its own bases, with West Pakistan continuing as a unitary region forming a political state.

As has been shown by frequent changes in internal structuring of West Pakistan, there is both cultural and economic differentiation in regional terms and clear disparity in interests. West Pakistan has gone through several restructurings in its administrative pattern in an effort to find a satisfactory system of administering its territory and promoting regional unity and common interest. Recent changes have been made in another effort, and the internal boundaries shown on our map already have been altered and are out of date (see Fig. 13.10). The problem of the internal administrative pattern of West Pakistan is complicated by the matter of balancing political administration between East and West, since the relative homogeneity of East Pakistan has never required its subdivision into formal units. This internal problem, for West Pakistan, will continue to have a bearing on the continuation of Pakistan as a single but bifurcated state.

15

CEYLON: AN INDIAN ISLAND RELATIVE

Ceylon has always been a part of Mother India in the broad sense, but has always been apart from India in the more specific sense. A prominently placed island off the tip of Peninsular India, Ceylon has been among the first to share in human movements in the Indian Ocean, but its physical separation from Peninsular India has always been sufficient that the island could develop its own intrinsic culture, life, and history. Ceylon shared only marginally in the problems that separated Pakistan and India, but received her own independence a few months after that separation, in early 1948. The gradual lessening of ties to Great Britain and with the Commonwealth, has gradually and involuntarily brought Ceylon somewhat closer to India in matters of world relations, but Ceylon still goes her own way.

Physically, Ceylon is a continuation of Peninsular India, and the island displays many of the other environmental characteristics of southern Peninsular India. Historically, Ceylon has shared the life of southern India throughout the centuries, and most inhabitants of Ceylon are "Indians" in the simple sense, though there have been significant differences in the timing at which Indians came to live in Ceylon. With an area of 25,532 square miles, a 1948 population of just under 7,000,000, and a 1969 population of close to 13,000,000, Ceylon is a small sector of the Oriental world, but an interesting and individual portion of that world.

HISTORICAL GROWTH OF A DUAL ECONOMY

The two-part sectoring of Ceylon into a wet zone, in the southwest, and a dry zone, in the east and north, set up conditions making for a dichotomy in the historical life-pattern of the island (see Figs. 7.1-7.8). The first historical effort, perhaps commencing about 500 B.C., focused on the central northern section of the dry zone, in a village-centered rural agricultural economy reputedly patterned after a similar section of northern India. A wet-field rice-growing economy utilized irrigation systems to create an impressive land use pattern in the dry zone, at first leaving most of the rest of the island relatively untouched. This population became, and remained, Buddhist, in the course of time differentiating their culture and language away from the Indian mode into what became Sinhalese. By the early Christian Era many parts of the dry zone had been lightly settled, but the southwest was let alone. During the ninth to thirteenth cen-

340

turies northern Ceylon was under attack by Hindu south Indian Tamil peoples and, during the era, the Sinhalese gradually shifted their focus to the wet zone in the southwest, altering the patterns of their land use technology, abandoning the northern dry zone to the Hindu Tamils. Arab trading voyages touched the coasts of Ceylon during the thirteenth to sixteenth centuries, to be followed by Europeans. By the end of the eighteenth century, when the British took over Ceylon from the Netherlands (which country had previously dispossessed the Portuguese), the central, lower hill country sector of the island, within the wet zone, was the region of strength. Both the hill country and the lowland portions of the wet zone had been maturing agricultural systems, and increasing in population, so that the wet zone was the significant economic region of the island. Hindu Tamil settlement never spread into the interior of the dry zone and, after the shift of the Sinhalese to the southwest, the whole interior dry zone declined into a very sparsely settled region of insignificant economic development.

The British, then, took over an island possessing a thriving Sinhalese peasant-village agricultural economy located in the wet zone lowlands and lower hill country in which wet-field rice, coconut, and tropical fruits and vegetables were the basis of life. There was a thin fringe of settlement around the whole coast engaged in agriculture, fishing, and trading. The interior dry zone was thinly populated, pock-marked with old and largely ruined irrigation systems, and suffering severely from malaria. British interest in the island naturally centered on the thriving southwestern sector, Colombo became the chief British port, and the British turned their attention to the more attractive south-central hill country around Kandy, the then center of Sinhalese political power (see Figs. 12.1 through 13.12).

British colonial administration allowed

Europeans to acquire land and, in the 1830's, coffee growing on large land holdings initiated the beginnings of a new agricultural system, as south Indian labor was brought in to work the new commercial agricultural undertakings. The new plantation development furthered the economic productivity of the wet zone, but there gradually appeared an imbalance in the economy as Sinhalese village agriculture was impaired by the British land system which expanded the plantation economy at the expense of the local village economy. Ceylon increasingly became an importer of rice and other foodstuffs and an exporter of agricultural products not significantly used by the island population. As disease problems affected the coffee plantings in the 1870's, tea plantings replaced them, concentrating on the Kandyan hill country. Expansion in the tea plantations in the previously empty higher hill country above 4,000 feet increased the import of south Indian Tamil labor, which force never produced its own food supply in adequate volume. Rubber plantings, in the 1880's, began to spread around the lower hill country in the central wet zone west of the higher tea plantations, to be accompanied by coconut plantation expansion on well-drained wet zone lowlands.

Although the earlier coffee and tea plantations were almost entirely British owned, as were the first rubber plantations, Sinhalese participation in commercial plantation agriculture has been increasing significantly, and most of the rubber lands and almost all the coconut holdings today are owned by Sinhalese. Smallholder participation in the commercial sector of agriculture has been most marked in coconut and rubber, and many urban professional families and civil servants own small holdings of coconut, rubber, and rice lands in suburban fringes or rural areas, and in some of the minor crops.

Sporadic interest had been shown in the redevelopment of the dry zone by the Dutch and the early British, but it was only in the late nineteenth century that significant rejuvenation of tanks (reservoirs), canal systems, and village lands began to occur as more mature British administration looked beyond the coastal fringes and the wet zone. Increasingly, attention has been turned to the redevelopment of the dry zone, and there have been major efforts in this direction in recent decades, both under British and Ceylon government initiative, and the dry zone now is being resettled.

There is, then, a fairly clear duality to the agricultural economy of Ceylon at the present time, in which the important commercial export crops primarily are grown on plantations of fairly large size, and in which a variably commercialized version of traditional village, peasant agriculture concentrates on rice, finger millet, fruits, and vegetables, distributed all over the island. In that smallholders participate in the commercial export sector, in that in some sections of Ceylon traditional village agriculture now is entirely commercialized, and in that the large monocrop plantations are diversifying, the duality is not fully complete.

Looking specifically at the commercial export sector, tea, rubber, and coconut are the primary crops, arranged in a stepped pattern in the wet zone, with tea occupying the highest lands, and coconut the lower coastal lowlands. These crops provide the largest source of foreign exchange as the big-volume items shipped to world markets, with tea producing slightly over sixty percent of the total. Plantation economy has been on a declining trend which, despite its obvious contribution, appears to have no expansionist possibilities in the sociopolitical milieu of modern Ceylon. Aging plantations of tea and rubber finally are undergoing replanting with fresh and more productive planting stocks. At least the rubber holdings need the infusion of new technical manage-

ment if they are to continue productive. It is not really clear as to the direction plantation economy will go in Ceylon. A few attempts have been made to locate rubber plantings outside the main wet zone, and there are coconut plantations in spots around the coastal fringe. Some modern attempts have been made in diversification.

Minor crops related to the commercial sector of Ceylon agriculture are several in number, some of which are elements in the traditional trade of Ceylon, whereas others are items of the last century only. Cinnamon is one of the traditional crops, and production was stabilized by the Dutch on small plantation holdings in southern Ceylon where it remains today, chiefly controlled by Sinhalese. Citronella, a coarse native grass, produces an oil commercially exploited only in the last century, and its production is in Sinhalese hands on small plantations. Cacao, cardamom, and vine pepper are the only other important items in this group. None of these crops has required much land, has represented a major labor factor, or has been primarily in alien hands, but all of them are elements in the modern commercial phase of Ceylon's agriculture.

In the traditional agriculture rice has always been the dominant crop, grown on wet fields with minor to fairly strong patterns of terracing according to the local relief, since Ceylon always has depended on natural flow patterns in water control. Rice occupies about one-third of all cultivated land. Rice has been grown everywhere but in the higher hill country at some time, but the modern distribution shows little production in a narrow strip of country lying back of the coast, except for the southwest coast. The crop has always been grown on small holdings, about sixty percent of which are privately owned. For the last 150 years domestic production has not met the demand, and in the 1950's rice was the largest single commodity import. The redevelopment of the dry zone and strong government programs of upgrading plant quality and technology lend hope that Ceylon may return toward self-sufficiency in the near future.

Mixed village gardens have always been important in domestic economy, producing vegetables and fruits of a wide variety. In the dry zone villages always occupied positions just below the tanks, so that subsoil water seepage took care of the trees and surface irrigation provided for shrubs and annual plantings. In the wet zone such gardens are found in and around villages without restriction. Traditionally such mixed village gardens were important in local subsistence, but in the modern era many of them have become small holdings producing smaller ranges of products for town and urban markets in a hybridized commercial market gardening.

Shifting cultivation was the third, and complementary, component in traditional economy, being practiced on the nonirrigable lands above the tanks or on the higher lands away from them. Wide ranges of crop plantings normally are common to the *chena* planting, restricted in the dry zone, of course, to annual crops for the most part. In the modern economy shifting cultivation continues in those portions of the island in which open land is available, and frequently the *chena* produces a variety of grains and vegetables for commercial sale, but such commodities as cotton may also be grown. Within the wet zone shifting cultivation has been used also, and here commercial plantings of bananas, papayas, and vegetables today tend to be commercial monocrop patterns.

Depending on the location within the dry zone–wet zone sectoring, much of the modern smallholder agricultural endeavor has become increasingly commercialized in the modern period, represents an investment in a productive holding for the town and urban resident, or is trending to monocrop commercial pattern. Thus, the traditional locally-subsistent element in the economy is breaking down as transportation facilities permit the regional marketing of rural produce to the larger villages, towns, and cities.

The coastline of Ceylon is dotted with villages and old port towns no longer important in the overseas trade since the rise of Colombo. Subsistence fishing by village and some town fishermen-farmers has long been an ecologic specialty of the littoral. However, the social structuring of occupational patterns, in the essentially Indian manner, plus the vegetarian orientation of Buddhism, has made fishing a low occupation, and no culture group in Ceylon has taken advantage of the marine resources off the island. Similarly, almost nothing has been done to utilize the fresh-water tank possibilities of the interior in aquatic-farming. Modern effort to implement fisheries is making some small headway against tradition, but fisheries will probably remain a minor element in Ceylon economy.

The animal husbandry side of the agricultural economy, similarly, suffers from the Buddhist-Hindu traditional bias and, though cattle are used in local transport and for some farm draft power, animal husbandry in any form is now a minor aspect of the economy and will probably remain at a low level of development.

CULTURAL DUALISM

There was, of course, a sparse scattering of peoples of simple culture in Ceylon prior to the arrival of the north Indian groups, and a very few such groups persisted into modern time. The early north Indian immigrants came in sufficient numbers to grow into a large modern population and these, as the Buddhist Sinhalese, consider themselves the primary and native population of the island, today making up its largest component, over sixty percent. The Sinhalese chiefly are wet-zone residents today, and often are differentiated into Low Country Sinhalese (strongly Europeanized in customs and social patterns) and Kandyan Sinhalese (who preserve some of the more complex social structuring of an older period). The protracted attacks of the Hindu south Indian Tamil peoples, with their settlement of the north and northwest coast, introduced an old but divergent element into Ceylon. This group today is known as Ceylon Tamil (sometimes Jaffna Tamil), comprises about eleven percent of the population, and is widely scattered though most have home roots in the far north. The coming of Arab traders to the coasts of Ceylon brought some settlers who became mixed with coastal populations in time. Their descendants, known as the Moors, represent about six percent of the population, are strongly attached to Islam, speak the common language of their local area, and today often are shopkeepers though they are widely spread in all occupational specialties. The Portuguese and Dutch contributed smaller elements to the bloodstream, as did the British, but the descendants of such intermarriages form the small group known as Burghers, are strongly Europeanized, chiefly speak English, and are Christian in religion. The final ethnic element is the Hindu south Indian Tamil labor introduced to the plantations by the British in the nineteenth century, today known as Indian Tamil. This latter group comprises about twelve percent of the population, is chiefly landless agricultural labor or urban professional-shopkeeper-factory worker in occupation.

The cultural traditions, social systems, and customs-complexes of Ceylon are essentially drawn from Mother India over a long era and, therefore, there is considerable complex social stratification in the Ceylon living systems. Although Sinhalese Buddhism, in theory, negates much of caste and its occupational-custom hierarchical implications, in fact Sinhalese society does show a considerable development of such patterns. The very distinctions Sinhalese, Ceylon Tamil, Indian Tamil, Moor, Burgher, and European carry many kinds of implications for social life which carry over into economic and political life.

Modern Ceylon, therefore, has strong regional, ethnic, and cultural differentiation. Within the last century some of these lines have become blurred, but confusion has been compounded. Portuguese missionaries converted both Sinhalese and Ceylon Tamils to the Roman Catholic faith, whereas under the Dutch and the British there has been a significant growth of Protestanism, to the end that about eight or nine percent of the population is Christian, drawn from all the former cultural groups. Kandy remains the home hearth of the more conservative Sinhalese Buddhists, whereas Jaffna serves the Ceylon Tamil. The Low Country Sinhalese, longer exposed to the Europeans and commercial endeavor, tend to be more modernized in many respects, and all urban populations tend toward more education in modern terms. Many coastal towns possess core groups of Moors, though this segment is very widely distributed today. The Sinhalese have trended toward strong political and linguistic nationalism since independence, whereas the noncitizen Indian Tamil population has demanded some political rights and privileges, and the Ceylon Tamils have felt deprived of traditional rights and political privileges. The political orientations of the three large culture groups have been such that political instability, since independence, has replaced the political stability of the colonial era, having strong impingement upon economic conditions, and causing fairly severe problems of both an internal sort and with relations with India. Sinhalese nationalism has gone hard with the small Burgher group and with all those who have been too emphatically "Europeanized."

THE CURRENT SCENE, IN SUMMARY

Ceylon continues to be an agricultural country dependent upon exports of commercial products chiefly grown under an agricultural system basically alien to her cultural tradition. Ceylon is the leading world exporter of tea, though rice production is the primary aim of agriculture. The 13,000 miles of roads provide a fairly good highway network, and the 900 miles of railway form a minimal and skeleton network primarily serving the areas producing export commodities. Ceylon maintains an airline providing both internal and overseas services. All systems focus on Colombo as the chief port, primary center of accumulation of exports and distribution of imports, and communications center. Colombo handles about ninety percent of Ceylon's foreign trade, is the dominant financial and manufacturing center of Ceylon, and is the largest urban entity, with about 800,000 people in the metropolitan area. An old tradition of handicraft manufacturing continues to supply much of the rural and village consumer need, but increasing urbanism and cultural modernization demand a wide range of modern manufactures which have had to be imported. A long-range program for industrialization was adopted in 1959, with widely distributed sources of foreign technical aid, but the program has been behind schedule. Small volumes of steel, cement, paper, refined petroleum, and rubber products are now produced, with many plants under government control. The program does not look to a future in export industry, but it does aim

at the home production of much of the consumer goods volume, and will be concentrated in light manufacturing, agricultural processing, and the food and clothing industries. Colombo and the other cities and towns of the wet zone will be the chief focus of regional development of manufacturing. The Sterling Bloc continues to take about half of Ceylon's exports and to supply much of the import volume, but long-range trade programs are in operation between China, the U.S.S.R., and various eastern European countries, and inadequate capital resources continue to handicap development. It will be quite a few years before Ceylon can provide a reasonable share of her requirement for manufactured goods.

Population growth was fairly steady in earlier periods, but since the end of World War II (as a result of World Health Organization mosquito-control work) the rates of population increase have been very great, and increases threaten to negate patterns of economic development. Programs of redevelopment in the dry zone have so far blunted the distress of over-populated sectors of the wet zone and the Jaffna Peninsula through resettlement programs, but there is only a limited reserve of such usable lands. Urbanism continues to draw population to the cities and towns but delays and conflicts in industrial programs are not satisfactorily absorbing all the in-migrants. The strongly divergent trends of cultural dualism blunt programs of economic development, and pronounced Sinhalese nationalism adds elements of political and economic instability in a situation in which concerted efforts should be made in specific economic development programs to prevent future difficulty.

16

SOUTHEAST ASIA: A CULTURAL SHATTERBELT

Southeast Asia is a relatively new term for a very large territory that, in a sense, belongs to everyone and yet belongs to no one. All kinds of people have traveled the migration routes, or the trade routes through it, and have left members behind. Many kinds of influences have been brought to bear on its parts and have left some imprint, but the region belongs to no one culture group and to no single political state (Fig. 16.1). The sector is difficult to define by any one specific criterion, but there are innumerable lines that can be drawn across it to divide it into pieces. Lines of traditional influences have significance today, but people now are busy at setting up new lines of influence within it. Large numbers of culture groups have moved into the region and have claimed some part of it, but no one has ever brought the whole under one system of control. Overlordships have been claimed in the distant past but rarely exercised in more than token terms. Southeast Asia is coming into the modern world in many ways, but some of the oldest of human traditions linger here. In the sense of physical environment there is much that is alike about the zone, but in the sense of

cultural milieu things are so mixed that no one generalization can apply to the whole. Southeast Asia is a physical region that can be described, but it is a cultural shatterbelt that defies simple generalization.

Such anglicized terms as Further India, Indochina, Little China, Extreme Orient, Greater India, and Indochinese Peninsula have all been used in the inclusive sense with variable definition, but all these refer primarily to the mainland half-world zone. Terms such as Far Eastern Tropics, Malaysia, East Indies, and Island World have also been used in a somewhat inclusive sense, but these refer primarily to the water half-world zone. In the more poetic sense such old terms as the Sanskrit name Suvarna-bhumi (Land of Gold), and the Chinese references to everything in the south as Nan Hai (South Seas) or Nan Yang (Southern Ocean) inferentially included most of both half-worlds. The term Southeast Asia is an old one, but its common use came out of World War II as a residual reference to a territorial zone not elsewhere included. It comprises those lands east of India and south of China, and normally extends through the

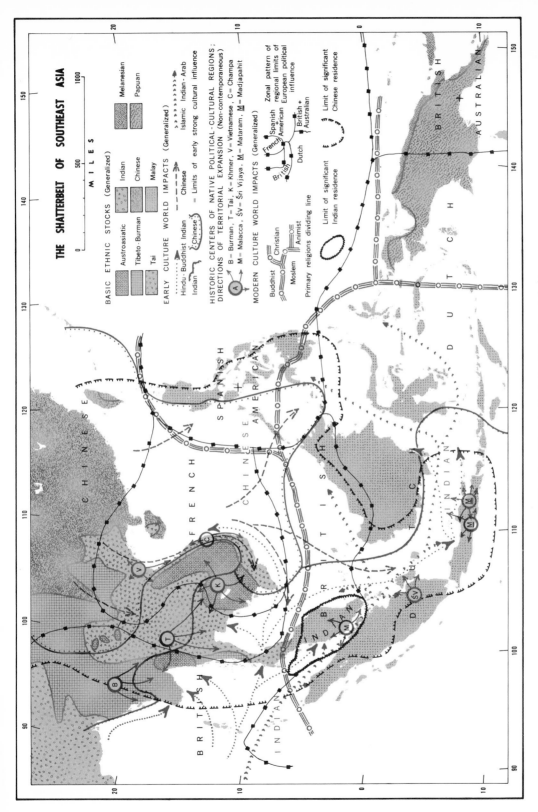

THE SHATTERBELT OF SOUTHEAST ASIA

BASIC ETHNIC STOCKS (Generalized)

- Austroasiatic
- Tibeto-Burman
- Tai
- Indian
- Chinese
- Malay
- Melanesian
- Papuan

EARLY CULTURE WORLD IMPACTS (Generalized)

- Hindu-Buddhist Indian
- Chinese — Limits of early strong cultural influence
- Indian
- Islamic Indian-Arab

HISTORIC CENTERS OF NATIVE POLITICAL-CULTURAL REGIONS;
DIRECTIONS OF TERRITORIAL EXPANSION (Non-contemporaneous)

B = Burman, T = Tai, K = Khmer, V = Vietnamese, C = Champa
M = Malacca, SV = Sri Vijaya, M = Mataram, M = Madjapahit

MODERN CULTURE WORLD IMPACTS (Generalized)

- Buddhist
- Christian
- Moslem
- Animist
- Primary religions dividing line

Zonal pattern of regional limits of European political influence

French — Spanish + American
British — Dutch — British + Australian

Limit of significant Indian residence
Limit of significant Chinese residence

MILES
0   500   1000

FIGURE 16.1. The shatterbelt of Southeast Asia.

former Dutch territories to include the western half, only, of New Guinea, though the eastern half of New Guinea is included on the maps of this volume.

The shatterbelt is no modern phenomenon, for its roots lie far back in the pre-historic settlement sequences through which much of the cultural development of basic resources took place. This is a region of initial plant domestication, of the very early development of the simpler systems of crop growing, and of the invention and development of numerous basic culture complexes. There are many primary human developments whose origins seem related to Southeast Asia but, in an environment in which artifacts disintegrate rapidly and rapid plant growth quickly masks surfaces, the evidence for such origins is hard to come by. Southeast Asia has not been well searched in these matters, the modern superficial simplicity of many cultural elements suggests no great antiquity, and the "authorities" seem loathe to consider seriously possible alternatives to many of the issues of culture origin.

THE NATURE OF
THE SHATTERBELT

Most simply described, the cultural shatterbelt of Southeast Asia is a zone of mixed cultures among which some very early remnants of autocthonous elements have not quite been submerged under historic cultural influences emanating chiefly from India and China, both being overlaid by elements of European culture. It is a region into which steady currents of migration have been moving out of the region we now call China, migration streams that have spread southward along the ridges and down into the valleys to become separated from each other as they penetrated farther southward. Sea-borne influences have reached shores of the region from both India and China, and

have penetrated the island sector to variable distances. Culture groups within the region, historically, have themselves been creative of new complexes and bodies of culture, but they also have adopted in variable degree either Indian or Chinese culture complexes, and in some cases they have adopted culture elements from both sources. Occidental culture complexes variably overlay many "native" patterns. Ethnic separation of once closely related peoples has occurred, but there has been resorption of ethnic elements as intermixtures have occurred. Most of the influences have been eastward or southward, but there have been some reverse currents from what is now Indonesia, back into the mainland and northward into the Philippines. Some peoples traveled far enough to get beyond the reach of Indian and Chinese influence, as into eastern New Guinea, or to escape from Southeast Asia altogether, as out into the Pacific Ocean realm of far islands. Non-Chinese and non-Indian influences have come into Southeast Asia, as brought by the traders from Arabia at an early date, by the Islamic peoples of a later day, by the Japanese as sea traders, and by the peoples of the rest of the world in the post-Columbian era of European colonial empires and patterns of world trade.

Items provided by the environment of Southeast Asia have incited the interest and the cupidity of outsiders, such as the gold, tin, pearls, pepper, nutmeg, false dragon's blood, tree gums, feathers, and fine woods, and innumerable tall stories have been concocted by traders to cover their trails to sources of goods. The routes to and through this far land have been many, and compounded confusion has bewildered those that came to see or to acquire. Southeast Asia is a region of tremendous diversity, and a great deal of confusion still surrounds its consideration by the outsider who seeks for the simple answer.

Southeast Asia is a land of change, and its

historic ups and downs in terms of regional occupance, prosperity, militancy, and successful patterns of life have been numerous. The tropical environment of the lowlands quickly reclaims its own, to the end that human imprints on the landscape often get blotted out under the regenerative growth of heavy forest cover, artifacts decay and disappear, and evidences of cultures become lost. The nineteenth century re-discovery of the great Khmer center of Angkor is a primary illustration, but there are numerous other manifestations of the same kind of happening.

PLURAL ASPECTS OF SOCIETY

Southeast Asia is a plural world in a very real sense in that there is no great portion of the region that does not show mixture in cultural systems. The linguistic map, in its repeated mixture within small areas, is one of the most complex manifestations (see Fig. 1.3). Groups have often impinged upon other groups in the historic processes of moving into or through the region, since the spatial alignment of routes, regions, and travel patterns seldom provided either regional security or relative isolation. As a region of many mountain systems, numerous lowland river valleys, long coastal fringes, and thousands of islands, this great region offered space for many varieties of life, and there are mountain cultures, lowland cultures, land cultures, and water cultures within the region, and almost every sizable sector includes two or more of these divergent elements. One of the threads that runs through the life of all parts of Southeast Asia is the competitive thread of the upland dweller *versus* the lowland dweller; another is the thread of competition between the inlander and the resident of the littoral; and still another thread is that of the land-resident *versus* the boat-resident. These aspects are seen in the conflicts between the hill country

Kachin and the lowland Burmans in early Burma, or between the Annamese of the lowland fringe of Vietnam and the various groups now labeled as "montagnard," between the interests of the sea-empire of Madjapahit as against the land orientation of Mataram, or between the concerns of the fishery-minded "sea-gypsies" that ranged from the Burmese Mergui coast to the Sulu Archipelago of the Philippines and the normal concerns of the land-resident crop-growing peoples.

One can distinguish elements of pluralism in many directions. There is the contrast in religion and associated mores, as between Theravada and Mahayana Buddhism, and between Buddhism, Taoism, Confucian separation of the state and church, Islam, and Christianity. Only in a few places, today, are these patterns not plural, and such issues enter into living customs, occupational ramifications, social structuring, and political systems. There is the pattern of the Thai or Malay crop-growing villager against the shopkeeping commercial interest of the Chinese townsman, a kind of plural competitivism present in every country in Southeast Asia. There is the pattern of the smallholder with the traditional peasant orientation to his home village, and the plantation operator with modern commercial interests in world markets. Along with this pattern of diversity is the associated compound pluralism of the systems of agricultural technology in which, on the one hand, there are the simplest of shifting cultivation technologies linked into traditional social systems depending on the use of magic, favors of the gods, and communal efforts, and in which, on the other hand, there are the most complex of scientific technologies linked to impersonal corporate labor systems dependent on the use of industrial chemistry, power tools, and recruited cash labor. This has been chiefly a rural land with an agrarian orientation motivated by specific, unified socioreligious concerns, but it is facing urban industrialization that is increasingly agnostic, or at least tolerant of multiple social and moral concerns, and that possess little inherent social unity. There have been, and still are, inward looking orientations that seek the exclusion of the larger cultural world, and there are orientations that seek international alignment with the whole world. In this region there are sectors that have often been empty of human occupance, but there are localities that have carried very heavy populations. The region, as a whole, is not now extremely densely populated, but its present rates of increase are much too high.

HISTORIC EFFECTS OF
INDIAN CONTACT

Indian sea traders not only touched the eastern shores of the Indian Ocean but almost certainly traveled the Gulf of Siam and the fringes of the South China Sea. The Malay Peninsula never has been a barrier to an inquisitive people, though crossing it and setting out afresh in other ships doubtless preceded sailing around it. The sailing skills of the Bay of Bengal could sail the Gulf of Siam, for the seasonal winds are much the same, whereas sailing around the tip of the Peninsula involved other problems. Sampling of the coastal fringe by Indian traders went on clear around the coast of Vietnam and as far north as Hainan, and as far east as the east coast of Borneo and the edges of the Lesser Sunda group of islands. And in this sampling, the two delta regions of the Chao Phraya and the Mekong must have been major attractions. Slowly, as in Burma, permanent trade stations grew into small cultural centers jointly inhabited by Indian and local populations.

Introduced by early Indian contacts were trade goods, technologies, crop plants, religious concepts, and the God-King concept of the formation of the religious state. Indian architectural technologies and sculpture systems were introduced along with the form and pattern of the temple and shrine. Little was done in road building, but small streams were canalized, and tanks and reservoirs were introduced into regions lacking water during the dry seasons. The quarrying of laterite as a building stone may have been an Indian introduction. Elements of social structuring and stratification were obviously introduced in varying degrees, the earlier Hindu patterns probably softened somewhat later by the introduction of Buddhism.

HISTORIC LIMITS OF
CHINESE INFLUENCE

Although both Indian and Chinese cultural agents were active in Southeast Asia in the centuries before and after the start of the Christian Era, they never met in head-on competition, nor did they join in struggle over the same regional territory. Chinese influences were often indirect, in that Chinese pressures upon marginal peoples in central to south China caused streams of emigration out of China and southward into Southeast Asia. This cultural pressure began to be exerted prior to the start of the Christian Era, and it has continued right down to the present time.

Direct Chinese influences began to be felt in Tonking about two centuries B.C. and, during the following centuries, Chinese influence grew steadily, penetrating southward along the Annam coast. Architecture, social organization and structure, the patterning of political organization, Confucian concepts of government and administration, organization and structuring of the agricultural economy, and handicraft technologies were among the elements of Chinese influence. In areas in which Chinese influence was not direct, many of the cultural patterns were part Chinese, in that emigrating peoples had adopted certain Chinese practices prior to emigration.

Additionally, the Chinese political state assumed a kind of overlordship over most of mainland Southeast Asia, one that did occasionally reach into the island world. This overlordship was recognized throughout much of Southeast Asia by the numerous "states" through their sending of tribute missions to the Chinese emperor; such missions sometimes were accompanied by requests for assistance in some struggle against some adversary "state." The overlord control by China was not continuous, since it depended upon the strength of political organization in China, but it was expressed repeatedly in sufficient strength to affect political conditions during many periods.

THE HISTORIC CONTESTS FOR REGIONAL CONTROL

In the historic evaluation of regional patterns in Southeast Asia there was no single region around which the whole development took place. Burma was sufficiently separated that it entered only late into the larger game. The Philippines and New Guinea lay too far from the primary scene. Even the Tonking delta, in the early stages, seemed far enough off center that it was not fought over in the earlier stages. It would appear that the zone of competitive struggle involved the lower Mekong Valley, Cambodia, the Lower Chao Phraya Valley, the Gulf of Siam, and the Malay Peninsula zone southward to and including Java and Sumatra. The frequent cross-contact of different trading peoples, perhaps centering on Indian trading stations throughout the area, brought about the first developments. We cannot be sure, so far, about whether or not there may have been several "first developments," such as Cambodia, Java, and Sumatra.

The earliest historiography suggests that, on the mainland, the political and cultural progress of the Cambodian zone was superior to that of any other section of the littoral facing the Gulf of Siam and the southern section of the South China Sea. Trade centers grew into little regional kingdoms controlled chiefly by Indian culture patterns but composed of local populations. As early as the start of the Christian era the first regional "state" appeared in Cambodia, centered west of the present Mekong distributaries and north of the delta itself (Fig. 16.2). The first capital site that can be located lay close to the river somewhat south of the present city of Phnom Penh.

Slowly this "state" expanded northwestward into Cambodia proper, moving its capital and establishing new towns as population grew and more land was brought into productive use. Gradually the culture region included the lowlands lying east of the active Mekong distributary zone and south of the terminal uplands of the Annamite Cordillera, since this region appears to have contained the same native peoples and culture patterns as the section west of the active delta. The chief ports long remained on their original sites, west of the main delta. This "state" early in the Christian era came to be known as Funan, an Indianized culture group possessing a mixture of Hindu and native barbaric elements. Its people seem to have ranged from Negrito and early Indonesian folk, as the base of population structure, to Indian colonists forming the trader-ruler nobility at the top.

Funan spread its influence north toward Korat, west into the Chao Phraya Valley, and south over the South China Sea and the Gulf of Siam, even becoming involved in the affairs of the northeast coast of the Malay Peninsula. It perhaps was more of a maritime culture than a truly land culture, using aquatic resources and sea and river lines of communication rather than land resources and routes. It certainly was not the tightly integrated organism that we define as a political state today, but it did represent the

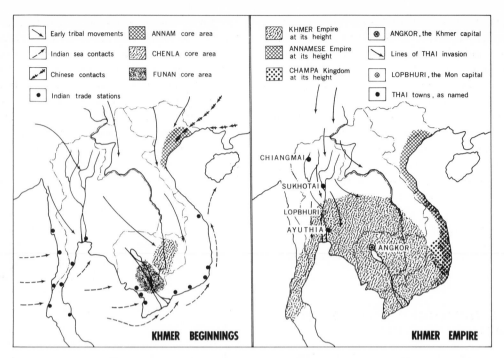

FIGURE 16.2. The Khmer Empire and the advancing Thai peoples.

best integration of region, people, products, and trade in mainland Southeast Asia at the time. The early rise of local piracy in the southern Malay Peninsula, Sumatra, and perhaps Java, interfered with regional organization there and kept Funan an important link in the China-India route, via a series of port way stations in the northern peninsula.

Khmer peoples, on the northern margins of Funan, infiltrating the lowland Chams and gradually becoming Indianized at second hand, grew in regional strength until by the sixth century A.D. their region, known to the Chinese as Chenla, became a rival to Funan. Chenla, a landlocked lowland region of the middle Mekong Valley, shared the common lowland economies and culture patterns except for the sea-trading element. From the sixth to the ninth centuries Funan and Chenla are confused in the Chinese accounts. The historiography is perplexing, since it

lacks a full written record. Capitals frequently shifted, dynastic inheritances intertwined and alternated, domains were divided, grouped, and redivided, Indian influences varied, Hinduism and Buddhism competed and interwove their patterns, peoples migrated, and ancient site after site now is being uncovered which calls for reinterpretation of the patterns. By the eighth century Malaysian dynastic, political, and trade patterns became interwoven into the story as the "state" of Sri-Vijaya took form to dominate the South China Sea and to participate in affairs of the Cambodian lowland.

Fisheries were very important in the domestic economy of all the peoples of the lowland of this whole region. Jungle garden culture, shifting cultivation, product gathering, and hunting also were standard parts of the economies. It is likely that small areas of sedentary rice culture accumulated around the towns and cities and in the most populous areas, but that shifting cultivation was the more common form throughout the general countryside.

The Cambodian culture region grew steadily in strength and population between A.D. 600 and 1225. Its political system matured, and the political state expanded. By the ninth century the capital had been shifted to the northwest side of the Tonle Sap. Lowland Cambodia was the core region, and around it lay local culture groups in many regional patterns with varying degrees of vassaldom tributary to the Khmer rulers. Khmer peoples themselves became settlers in southern Korat, in parts of the Chao Phraya Valley, and along the peninsular east coast. Something of a melting-pot process must have gone on, as Negritos, Chams, Mons, Shans, Malays, Khmers, and even a few Burmans, Indians, Chinese, Arabs, and other racial elements became intermixed in the population of the Khmer state.

Increasingly villages, towns, and cities grew in number, and the agricultural landscape expanded. Canals, tanks, and reservoirs multiplied in number. It has been thought that shifting cultivation always dominated the agriculture of these regions, but it is doubtful that this was so in the core area at least. Many of the larger tanks, reservoirs, and canals seem unrelated to temple and domestic water provision; they must have been designed for rice irrigation here just as they were in India and Ceylon. It is doubtful that the later Khmer population could have supported itself and its works on shifting cultivation alone, for the Cambodian population has been estimated at 4,000,000 in the thirteenth century. Certainly there were large reserve areas in which shifting cultivation did remain the normal system of agricultural land use, and not the whole of the lowland ever was put into permanent

farm. Khmer culture at all times maintained an interest in foreign trade, and Khmer ports were cosmopolitan entrepôts. As economic strength grew, the expenditure of labor resources on religious building grew, as the size, complexity, and magnificence of temple architecture increased.

The Khmer political empire reached its height in the late twelfth and early thirteenth centuries. Its capital was at Angkor, northwest of the Tonle Sap. Although nothing remains of the domestic and commercial building of the city, the very number and size of its religious and politicoceremonial buildings, and its waterworks developments, indicate that it must have been a large city, even by present-day standards. The largest religious building in the world, Angkor Wat, was built here in the twelfth century, and its labor force alone must have been a large one (see photo of Angkor Wat, p. 275). Indian and Khmer temples do not have large interior rooms, for they were not built to shelter congregations indoors, but the very bulk and detail of construction exceeds that of any other religious structure.

At its height the Khmer state came close to controlling all the great lowland region, but the outer parts to the northeast and northwest still lay without the state, and some of the inner areas were not integrated with the Cambodian core region. Korat, the central Mekong Valley, the central and southern Chao Phraya Valley, and the main portion of the peninsula were within the empire, and the Gulf of Siam was a Khmer lake. Through its lack of an effective land transport system, and through its dependence upon local subsistence economy, the Khmer Empire was never more than a loose political structure. And around these far-flung borders the Khmers finally were facing increasing pressures from other maturing culture groups, such as the Vietnamese, the Thais, the Burmese, and the Indonesians who, each in their own area, were integrating region and culture with the result that they possessed considerable combative strength and were themselves expanding regional entities.

Although the lower Chao Phraya Valley went through something of the same process as did Cambodia, the region formed no serious challenge to the Khmers. Indian trader stations developed into little principalities, and these matured into a kingdom, chiefly populated by Mons, long carrying the name Louvo. Lopbhuri in the central Chao Phraya lowland finally became the chief city and political capital. The area never developed the population, economic strength, or political maturity of Cambodia, and the Chao Phraya Valley became a tributary portion of the Khmer state, though its Mon peoples maintained some autonomy and a cultural contact with the Mons resident in the southeastern Burmese lowland. None of the other regional portions of the great lowland region ever early developed regional cohesion of culture or political strength of a sort to threaten Khmer power. It was from the northwest that strong and effective pressures finally accrued, at the hands of the Thais.

It is possible to see, on a broad canvass, that by the thirteenth century the various regions of Southeast Asia were approaching the point of a period of struggle for control of the whole peninsula, which might have resulted in hegemony over the whole of the mainland, if not the island sector. However, during the thirteenth century outside events began to affect the pattern. There is an unaccountable decline in Indian influence and trade contact, China under the Mongols exerted new and strong pressures on Southeast Asia, and the Thai were pushing strongly, injecting a new participant into the older pattern. In the fourteenth century came militant Islam, followed by the Europeans in the sixteenth century. Before the Euro-

peans did establish their colonial patterns, to bring a measure of interregional stability, interregional struggles on the mainland, as between Burma and Thailand, and the impact of the Islamic traders-political princes on the island world, produced such instability in Southeast Asia that almost no one was aware of the rapid decline of the great Khmer state and its final lapsing into an almost forgotten small inland kingdom located in what we know today as Cambodia.

REGIONAL CULTURE SYSTEMS

The historical developments in the several lowland sectors of the whole of Southeast Asia never did result in the hegemony of one culture system exemplified in one political state. It is probable that economic bases never became sufficiently strong, and that transport and military systems never became adequately efficient for such a result. It is possible, however, to suggest that a series of regional focuses slowly became established, each of which varied from others in its local emphasis and each of which varied in being either more Indian and less Chinese, or more Chinese and less Indian. An obvious label can be put on Burma, for example, as an "Indianized" society, and Vietnam can be labeled as "Sinicized." It must be recognized that, in each case, beneath the labeled cultural veneer there is a native ethnic and cultural body of depth and strength.

Without trying to draw specific and sharp lines around these regional centerings it is possible to suggest that there have been several core regions around which historic politicocultural regionalisms ultimately accrued. Upon an incomplete understanding of the full complex history of Southeast Asia, we have suggested that such regional centerings took place in Burma, Thailand, Cambodia, Tonking, the central Vietnam coast, the Malay Peninsula, and Sumatra and Java in what is today Indonesia (see Fig.

16.1). These traditional regional centerings are the primary bases for the modern political states that appear on the map today. In that the process of regional development was incomplete at the time the European came into Southeast Asia to introduce new cultural forces, the political map had not yet reached stability. In that the Philippines had not gone through the complex politico-cultural processes leading to a cultural synthesis, the Spanish took over a region that was easily molded into a quite different pattern. That, within the island world, no really far-reaching development had brought all of the Indies together, the Dutch inherited an amorphous and diverse zone of microsystems. Modern political and regionalizing processes, in the era of European colonialism, have struggled with the issues chiefly in those zones in which problems of regional control and cultural allegiance had never been completely solved in the earlier periods.

MODERN CHINESE AND INDIANS AS AGENTS OF CULTURAL CHANGE

The long-term forces of Chinese and Indian culture have been invoked as playing significant roles in Southeast Asia. Indians came into Southeast Asia before Chinese did, on a more widespread stage, in this historic process, and China's earliest influences were felt more as pressures on peoples in central and south China, causing them to migrate southward. But in the modern era southern Chinese, themselves, have been migrants into every portion of Southeast Asia, though they have not in numbers gone east of the Molucca Islands. Chinese have been more numerous than Indians everywhere, in the modern era, and undoubtedly have played a stronger role in influencing local affairs. This influence has not been overtly political, in major terms, but rather it has been expressed

in commercial and trade terms. Chinese went into the several larger cities, chiefly to set up entrepreneurial activities, from there branching out to small towns and villages where they have been important in the accumulation of export commodities, as agents of importers, and often as agricultural processors. The Chinese often migrated as single men, marrying into the local societies and, thus, creating varying patterns of ethnic intermixture. The Chinese frequently have been restricted by legal restraints or have been the subjects of local violent action in every country. Their "sojourner" characteristic of being short-term residents and going back to China in time has been variable in the different political states, but more recently they have tended to become permanent residents of the country of their choice. More recently, too, southern Chinese women have gone into the various countries, and there are Chinese communities in practically every city of Southeast Asia.

The Indians, on the other hand, have been chiefly active in only a few countries of Southeast Asia in the modern period, chiefly as contract labor on alien-owned plantations. As such, their largest numbers are in Malaysia. There are, of course, Indian commercial agents and shopkeepers in almost every country in Southeast Asia, but their numbers are small outside of Malaysia at the present time. During the nineteenth century, when Burma was linked to India under British rule, there were large numbers of Indians in Burma, where they played the same role that the Chinese played elsewhere. With Burmese independence, however, these numbers have markedly declined.

SUMMARY: THE MODERN SCENE

It sometimes has been said that European colonial controls over Southeast Asia established new and alien patterns of rule, with changed focuses of orientation in new capitals and economic centers, and that independence would make a great deal of difference in the happenings within the whole of Southeast Asia. But it is obvious that, in independence, no striking reversion to "native" orientations has taken place. Political capitals remain where they were, basic geographic orientations continue to exert their long-term locational influences, and the historic focuses of regional development continue as they were. There are two aspects to this matter: First is that a reasonably effective pattern in many areas is older than European influence; secondly, the pressures of colonial economic development are sufficiently strong that they exert a binding influence upon any present political plans.

There is now at work a series of influences that, in directional and orientational terms, are stronger than many of the influences of those same elements in an earlier era. That is, the impact of the railroad line on the location of the center of political power, and on the directional components of economic movement today is greater than the impact of a forest path of an earlier era, and the inertial force of the centering of a national banking system on a given city, today, is greater than was the force of a king's "treasury" in an earlier era. Political capitals, today, cannot casually be moved about at the charismatic whim of a new ruler, nor can the whole of a political state be taken over by another for the same kind of reason as sometimes motivated such operations in the past. Thus, though great diversity, imbalance, and regional contrast still characterize Southeast Asia, and though respective internal patterns will remain in flux for decades to come, the political structure of Southeast Asia may be crystalizing into a mould in which states may retain their present shapes for some time. This is not to say that no change in boundary will take place, or that Malaysia will always include what is now termed East Malaysia and exclude Singapore. It would be imprudent, at this point, to predict the ultimate, precise territorial outlines of what may emerge from the present conflict in Vietnam-Laos-Cambodia, but it is predictable that there will be at least one political state on the territory of the present two units of Vietnam, and it is unlikely that Laos will be divided up into pieces by the surrounding states.

Southeast Asia is basically an agrarian culture zone at present, in continuity with its historic tradition, but there are strong cross currents. Singapore, currently, is committing itself to a capitalistic industrial future which, combined with its entrepot function, will bring it rapidly into possession of many of the elements of world culture and into a cosmopolitan milieu. Burma, on the other hand, has at least temporarily shut out much of the modern world, has turned to a variety of ethnosyncratic socialism which, the Burmese insist, is neither Communism nor tribal communalism, and is only very slowly instituting small programs that can be related to the modern industrial world. If both Singapore and Burma should continue for long periods on their present trend, very strong contrasts in culture patterns will result. Indonesia seems to be moving toward an industrialized future, but with a different mixture of private entreprenurial and state capitalism. The Philippines seem committed to private initiative, industrialization, and participation in the modern world, but the relatively low current level of financial, tax, and political morality endangers the success of this particular national system. Laos is struggling for modern political identity on such basic terms, in its gross mix of tribal cultures, that its future is not clear. Cambodia clings to a traditional domestic system while attempting to operate an international neutrality, but the seeds of modernization are sprouting in many different plots of culture-ground, and Cambodia, in turmoil, is facing change. Thailand clings to the authoritarian individuality that kept it out of the "colonial" world during the last four centuries, but elements of modernization are to be seen rather widely. In the two political units of Vietnam are to be seen the most violent aspects of culture change in political, social, and economic terms. It is difficult to predict the future patterns of directional change in both North Vietnam and South Vietnam during the height of the militant struggle of the last two decades, but it is almost certain that a strong trend to modernization will result in social and economic terms. However, the issues are much more complex than commonly asserted by either the advocates of Communistic or Free World solutions.

In sum, the "trends of the times" in economic, political, and social culture are operating very differently in the several pieces of the shatterbelt. There is much more political nationalism involved, a more narrowly defined variety than has been true in the historic past. Countering such narrowing trends, of course, are such broadening trends as the Mekong Plan which seeks for interregional development, and the several regional politicomilitary groupings as SEATO and ASEAN. Whereas the "trends of the times" involve a common denominator kind of modernization in the hydroelectric project, pressures of modern urbanism, and international air linkage, the several major societies of Southeast Asia are picking and choosing among the trends, with quite unequal kinds of results to date. In each country ethnic and cultural minority elements currently are receiving only grudging admittance into "national" plans for development, and this in itself will contribute to the continuation of shatterbelt characteristics.

17

THE IRRAWADDY VALLEY AND BURMA

THE REGIONAL FRAMEWORK AND ITS EARLY PEOPLES

The political state and culture region known today as Burma lies within the most distinctive physical enviroment in the Orient, because it has but one core area placed within a bounding framework of mountains. This environment is a group of converging, lowland alluvial valleys ending in a broad delta fronting on the Bay of Bengal and surrounded by a series of mountainous uplands lacking good passes. In the north the framework is high and rugged and the valleys are narrow. To the south the mountain frame spreads out widely and the valleys become broader and flatter until they merge with the delta. The mountain frame encloses the delta, leaving open an easy approach only from the Bay of Bengal. This regional environment is one part of the Burmo-Malayan Fan structure described in an earlier chapter (see Figs. 6.7 and 6.8). It is an elongated region in which all essential units have a distributional trend that is chiefly north-south. There are interruptions in landforms, stream patterns, climates, vegetation, soils, and other minor phenomena which prevent pure symmetry in these north-south trends, but none of these destroy the basic alignments.

To early man penetration of this region must have been difficult, but it also brought rewards in the good living to be had in the lowlands. How early man first entered lowland Burma cannot now be stated. In any case the river terraces of the Irrawaddy yield ample evidence of human occupancy at an extremely early date. And whether significant regional specialization developed here in the very early cultures is not yet clear. The whole environment has an extremely wide range of resources and potentialities. Early man in no way exhausted these resources, though he undoubtedly altered ecologic relationships and patterns of plant and animal life in both upland and lowland zones.

Who the inhabitants of Burma were, four to five thousand years ago, is not at all clear. Although there is little evidence of Negrito occupation, southern Burma may well have held such a population at one time. Pre-Mon-Khmer peoples are not well represented. The Mon peoples may have been the first of the alien stocks, drifting into the lowlands of Burma from India. Indonesian peoples are less represented here than in the lands farther to the east. Three thousand years ago there were several different kinds of peoples scattered about the lowlands of Burma, doing a good deal of fishing, growing rice, fruits, and vegetables in jungle gardens, dwelling in villages, and sharing many other culture traits with the rest of southern Asia. They were already accustomed to using boats and aquatic resources, domestic garden crops, and the products of jungle and forest. Whether they were chiefly shifting cultivators or had learned sedentary crop practices is unproved. Since their numbers were not large their total productive ability would not today be impressive. It seems likely, however, that at this date life in the lowland was more bountiful than that in the upland jungles and forests that framed the outlines of the lowland.

As late as four thousand years ago the rich lowland region was a sort of human vacuum. Since that date this lowland zone has been drawing people into it, and supporting their natural increase, until it gradually has accumulated a total population of about 19,000,000 people. In a general way the lowlands have been the final goal of all the varied culture groups that have entered Burma, and the modern Burmese people and Burmese culture have been the final product. The Burmese of today are a lowland people, and their culture is a lowland culture, though the upland frame is home to a wide variety of culture groups with quite different patterns of culture who are politically Burmese in nationality.

Significantly, only two approaches have been commonly used within historical time to get to the heart of Burma, overland from the north along the mountains or the narrow river valleys, and by sea from the south. At few times in Burmese history has a lateral process of movement taken place either into or out of Burma. During World War II much of the drama attached to General Stilwell's famous retreat to India derived from the very fact that his little migration ran counter to the known patterns of historical movement in this part of the world. The one possible

exception to this generalization pertains to the southern extension of the Burmo-Malayan Fan southward in the Malay Peninsula. On this southeastern corner lie the only easy land approaches to the heart of Burma, used occasionally in the past by Khmers, Burmese, and Thais and, during World War II, by the Japanese. A narrow strip of this peninsular zone was included by the British in their sphere of influence in Burma, and this strip has become a part of the modern political state.

The most significant cultural process at work has been the steady drift of peoples out of the north country, from the Tibetan corner of China, southward along the linear patterns of mountains and valleys into the confines of the region that we now call Burma (Fig. 17.1).

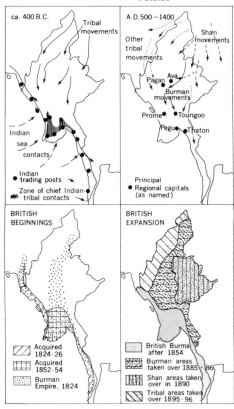

GROWTH OF BURMA

FIGURE 17.1. Growth of Burma.

The final destination for all has been the alluvial lowland, and the pressures of group upon group have been southward and downward pressures. Some of the earliest groups were able to move into a part of the lowland zone and to develop a regional area. Others were able only to secure space on the margins of the lowland, from which individuals were able to infiltrate the lowland area and to become gradually a part of its culture group. Still others, both at early dates and more recently, were unable to secure a foothold in the lowlands, and have had to be content with living in the hill country or mountains of the upland frame.

The above patterns of movement have not been entirely chronologic, so that not all the earliest comers are lowlanders and the latest are mountain peoples, but it is true that some of the last culture groups to arrive have not been able to push into the lowlands. An early group, but not the first, to arrive who spoke a language akin to modern Burmese, were able to find a home in the lowlands. It is this group which has given the basic orientation of language and culture to modern Burma. As the lowland began to accumulate a significant population with patterns of culture distinct unto itself and with a stake in its own wealth and perquisites, it began to resist the raiding of groups from around the upland fringe and the taking over of parts of the lowland by these groups. This resistance slowly grew stronger as lowland political and military institutions developed, so that in later centuries the strength needed to gain a place in the lowland was greater than in earlier periods.

Although few of the southward-migrating peoples now to be identified in modern Burma can date their earliest movements as far back as 2000 B.C., some of these movements must have begun not far from that date. It was a slow drifting, and centuries went by before it began to produce a heavier population in the southern Burmese lowlands. The process surely had been going on before the recorded historic pressures of North China began to be exerted upon southern China and its peoples. We have presumed, therefore, to date the beginnings of this southward drift well back of the conventional historic dates for such migrational movements.

INDIAN TRADERS AND THE EARLY CENTERS IN BURMA

Conventional history suggests that Indian sea travelers began to make colonial and trade contacts at a wide variety of points in southeastern Asia just before the beginning of the Christian era. But Indian traders must have been probing the sea lanes and learning their way across the Bay of Bengal long before this date. Extensive sea travel in the Arabian Sea had begun much earlier, and it is inconceivable that seamen able to navigate the Arabian Sea refrained from similar voyaging in the Bay of Bengal. By at least 400 B.C. there must have been trading posts, with Indian trade agents permanently resident, all along the coasts of Burma and the Malay Peninsula (see Fig. 17.1). Earliest contact probably touched the whole coastal fringe, searching contacts with small yields of gold, precious stones, musk, rare woods, and the other items of interest to Indian traders. By 400 B.C. the choice territory must already have proved to be the delta coasts tapping the lowlands of Burma.

Trading stations set up by a people accustomed to specific social, political, and economic institutions among a people of different institutions led to a contest of strength between both peoples and institutions. Indian culture was quite well developed by this date, whereas the peoples of lower Burma were yet simple in social structure, had only meager economic institutions, and were probably not more than tribal in political system.

It is quite probable that in the quickening political patterns of India of the time, refugees, soldiers of fortune, missionaries, and various other elements of Indian culture traveled ·with the traders to the ends of the Bay of Bengal seaways. In Burma the results of such contacts were small outposts of Indian culture populated by Indians who began to exercise economic, social, religious, and political control over the immediate hinterlands. Interplay between Indian and native peoples gradually led to some absorption of Indian culture traits by native peoples, ranging from religious to agricultural, and stimulated economic production of tradable raw materials and natural resources. Gradually these small trade stations grew into small port towns, the hinterlands expanded, and the culture of the little regions increased in complexity.

It is likely that this was not an entirely peaceful process between Indian and native peoples or between the several Indian centers. Nor was it a process that was rapid in its creation of cities, in its development of regional political institutions, or in the general effect upon the lowlands. In the early periods the native population never became large, its physical capacity in food production was not great, and the numbers of Indians cannot have been large.

By 100 B.C. it would seem that the delta land trade regions stood out as not only the most profitable, but the most populous, the most highly developed in social, economic, and political culture. These several little lowland centers became the nodal points around which the kingdoms of early Burmese history were organized. It is not until about the fifth century A.D. that the regional pattern of affairs comes tentatively into the accounts of the historian. By then there were a number of well-established place names that stood for towns, for petty kingdoms, for peoples, and for cultures. The names we can identify for such patterns are of Indian origin, for the native folk did not write and had little to tell of trade and conquest. Mon, Tailaing, Pyu, Pegu, Thet, Thaton, Prome, and Tenasserim, all are modernized versions of early Indian names applying to such regional units. The names Irrawaddy and Sittang also are of Indian origin. Chinese accounts carry both Chinese and Indian place name reference, further complicating the problem. Only in the ninth century A.D. do specific patterns became recognizable (see Fig. 17.1).

THE INTERNAL CONTEST

From about the fifth century A.D. the central theme of the regional geography of Burma has been the contest over who should control the lowlands. An auxiliary theme has been the contest over who should control what portions of the upland frame and the coastal fringe. To some peoples this latter was a chief objective, but to others it was preliminary to the main theme. Several different culture groups had filtered into the lowland from the north prior to the fifth century, and Indian groups had come by sea from the south. The northern sources had chiefly supplied population, whereas the Indian source had chiefly supplied elements of cultural organization.

Out of the mixing of these two product patterns came the early trading posts and the first regional kingdoms in the southern lowland. As these grew in size, strength, and capacity, the pressures of the hill peoples also grew, and the contest really began. The earliest regional kingdoms were represented by Prome, Pegu, and Thaton, in the areas of most effective Indian influence. These must date from about the late fifth century, and their influence remains dominant until the ninth century. Prome perhaps was the strongest in the earlier centuries, and Thaton in the later period. Their cultural influences probably extended well to the north along the Sittang and Irrawaddy rivers.

During the seventh and eighth centuries pressures greatly increased, and new peoples began to push into the northern and central lowland, to learn how to live in it. Burman peoples came into the central dry zone of Burma by the start of the eighth century probably finding its lighter soils and open plant cover amenable to control. They improved their organizational abilities, took up Buddhism and other new traits, and by the middle of the ninth century founded the new regional kingdom of Pagan in central Burma. By midtenth century they had learned enough to expand their control to a zone some 300 miles north-south by 70–80 miles east-west —the dry heart of lowland Burma. In the mid-eleventh century they added control over much of the southern lowland zone by conquest of Thaton and also spread out along the Arakan coastal fringe. In this expansion process a Burman written language had appeared, regional organizational techniques had improved, irrigation systems had made rice agriculture prosper, and Pagan had become a city. Pagan became the leading kingdom of the lowland, the "defender of the Buddhist faith" in the southern Orient, and its religious capital. An enormous volume of Buddhist religious building in brick probably required deforestation of a wide area for kiln fuel, perhaps contributing to the present arid-land impression of the dry heart of Burma. Burman culture traits spread, Indian and other old culture patterns were modified and adapted, and lowland culture began to shape into a Burman "Burmese" pattern. Education of a sort reached most Burmese youth, chiefly boys, and Burmese society developed a fairly unique pattern not attained either in India or China. A mixed religious and temporal pattern gave its members a general satisfaction seldom achieved elsewhere.

It is likely that control over the northern upland frame by the Tai peoples—then organized into the state of Nanchao in southwestern Yunnan—kept other northern tribal peoples in check and gave the Burmans their opportunity. The dry zone may well not have been usable by earlier peoples. Indian control over the southern zone had died out, and southern kingdoms were under pressures from hill peoples to the east and from piracy by sea, particularly from petty Indian kingdoms on the Arakan coast and from mobile groups along the Tenasserim coast. After the conquest of Thaton, thousands of captives were moved northward into Pagan's home area, to further the blending of lowland cultural and racial stocks.

Nanchao's control of the north finally failed, Chinese pressures increased, the Shan, a branch of the Tai, and other peoples began pushing southward more heavily, and Burman control of the lowlands had not become perfected. In the late thirteenth century Mongol military operations pillaged Pagan and reduced its power, giving the Shan a chance both in the Shan Plateau and in the lowland itself. A Shan lowland kingdom appeared, based at Ava, northeast of Pagan, which pushed many Burmans southward and incorporated others into the Kingdom of Ava. The Shan kingdom was perhaps the strongest single power until about the end of the fourteenth century, but it was a Burmanized society that composed it. The Burmans acted as a buffer, and a kingdom based on Pegu was able to assert itself as a trading state, its port handling a growing trade on the Bay of Bengal which probably serviced most of lowland Burma.

During the fifteenth century the lowland contained three major kingdoms, plus many smaller ones. In the upland frame many tribal peoples held regional control and occasionally were able to organize confederacies strong enough to trouble the lowland kingdoms seriously. Pegu, in the south, was the repository of old Indian culture, and Toungoo was the center of the Burman kingdom, after the Burman shift southward, but its people were no longer a clear tribal strain. Ava was the northerly Shan kingdom, but one learning Burman and Burmanized Indian culture patterns, and itself suffering from infiltration of population from many northern tribal sources.

When occidentals first came to Burma in the sixteenth century, the region was a complex of regional kingdoms and principalities, both in political and cultural terms. A lowland "Burmese" culture was becoming dominant regardless of the exact racial and cultural background of its peoples. The pressures from the upland frame were steady and strong. And from the sixteenth to early nineteenth centuries the whole pattern of regional control was in constant flux, as lowland kingdoms struggled for dominance. In the mideighteenth century Ava's conquest of Pegu thoroughly upset life in the lower delta zone, but the Burmans and Shans were not yet able to settle and develop the delta. Burma was not of prime importance to the occidental traders because of this cultural turbulence.

After the British gained control of trade in the Bay of Bengal they suffered nuisance raids from minor Arakanese and Tenasserim pirates and petty rulers. No lowland ruler of Burma could yet control these outer margins. British conquest of lower Burma and the Arakan and Tenasserim coasts resulted from this cultural turbulence and the raiding of British shipping (see Fig. 17.1). But once in Burma the British themselves had to cope with the old southward and downward pressures and the regional contest for control of the lowland. British colonial government during the nineteenth century was oriented in two directions. First, the administration of the lowland, to permit the development of local and international trade. Second came the adminstrative patterns designed to control the peoples of the upland frame and to stabilize their regional zones of occupation. The British became the second major cultural force to affect lowland Burma from the southern sea approach.

In the hill and mountain country of the upland frame a sorting and mixing process had long been going on. There are perhaps today a dozen different basic culture groups, subdivided into dozens of local groups who have developed both horizontal and vertical stratifications of regional control. Some are mountain peoples living near mountain crests or at other particular altitudes, whereas some occupy a territory and live at all altitudes. The Chin on the west, the Naga and Kachin on the northwest and north, the Shan on the north and northeast, the Karen in the east are the larger and dominant elements. The Palaung, Wa, Kaw, Lisu, and Lahu are lesser groups of the northeast. Most of the upland peoples have resisted Buddhism and remain animists in religion and traditional in social organization.

INDIAN, CHINESE, AND BRITISH OVERLORDS

Burma has often been under the influence or control of some outside power but this has been neither continuous nor competitive. At the time of the early Indian interest in, and colonization of, Burma's southern lowlands and coastal fringes China had not yet spread its control even into Yunnan. Indian influence in Burma never made for close attachment of the area to India in political or economic matters, for neither area had progressed to the point of making this possible. Indian influence in Burma had become unimportant by the time the T'ang Chinese began to assert their overlordship over southeastern Asia in the seventh and eighth centuries. Most of the larger kingdoms of Burma sent tribute missions to the Chinese imperial court in Sung times at least, during the tenth and eleventh centuries, thus acknowledging the suzerainty of China. This may well have been a formality preventive of encroachment until in Mongol times the rebellious independence of the Shans and the Burmans of Pagan resulted in punishing Chinese military invasions. Consequent acknowledgement of subordinate status and occasional tribute missions prevented further too continuous and too active Chinese interest in Burmese affairs. Few Chinese have ever been among the migrants into Burma, and the country today has the smallest Chinese population of any part of southeastern Asia. Chinese culture, directly, has had but little real effect upon Burma or upon any of the Burmese peoples, for most of the peoples of Burma had come out of China to escape Chinese control.

British control over Burma, beginning in the 1820's, evoked no serious protest from China. Early British administration of Burma was partially independent of India, but in 1886 Burma was annexed to India and became a stepchild of the slowly maturing Indian Civil Service. British administrators and the British Colonial Office never seemed to appreciate the cultural separateness of Burma and India. The British in particular, and most occidentals in general, have greatly overstressed the early Indianization of Burmese culture. The British never administered Burma for the Burmese of the lowland or for the people of the upland frame, though there were many individual civil officers who saw beyond the general British program. Out of the annexation of Burma to India, during the late nineteenth and twentieth centuries, Indians gained a protected access to Burma that they had not had since perhaps A.D. 400. Indians became usurious moneylenders, urban shopkeepers, commercial agents, and soldiers in Burma, always protected by British law and civil administration. In 1941 there were nearly 1,000,000 Indians in Burma who were fast gaining an economic stranglehold on southern lowland Burmese economy through their ownership of farmland and their large financial creditor position in respect to the Burmese.

British political overlordship became more far-reaching than had either Indian or Chinese control in earlier centuries. The British brought with them cultural change, political control, and economic exploitation such as the peoples of Burma had never before experienced. As the pattern increased, the animosity and protest grew, though it scarcely was an organized nationalism. Separation of Burma from British India in 1937 was more formal than real, and too few of the mistakes were being corrected when World War II brought the Japanese into Burma. Lowland Burmese welcomed relief from the British, whereas the hill peoples of the upland frame, never much afflicted with the penalties of British rule and emotionally set against the lowland Burmese historically, remained loyal to the British. These two factors both were important items in the progress of the war in Burma. The accumulated animosities of lowland Burmese toward the British and their own regional dominance within Burma led Burma to declare for total independence after World War II.

ECONOMIC BACKGROUND

As the Burmese lowlands grew in population the regional capital towns and cities stand out for their political, historical, and cultural roles. But these urban control points, housing only a minority of the population, cannot describe lowland Burma. The area became a region of agricultural villages surrounded by garden plots and farmlands in which rice agriculture of a fair order of productivity formed the basis of a lowland economy that long has contrasted with the simpler and less productive economy of the upland frame.

The earliest lowland economy that first attracted Indian traders had been a simple one, combining jungle garden cropping with fishing and hunting, and to it the Indians undoubtedly contributed both plants and techniques. Rice, fruits, roots, and rhizome plants were intermixed in use, but the importance of fishing in this southern aquatic zone always was more significant than in the central dry zone or in the upland frame. The wettest parts of the southern delta section, subject to seasonal flood and high water situations, were then unusable for agriculture, since organizational and technological development did not make diking, drainage, and water control possible. This phase of lowland economy was not fully usable in the central dry zone of Burma, where a shortage of water limited garden cropping and where the aquatic aspects of the system could not apply. Occupants of the northern lowland areas and most of the upland frame, at the time of Indian contact with the coastal zone, most probably were shifting cultivators practicing primarily a subsistence economy, based upon gardening, gathering, and hunting.

As simple culture groups came into Burma from the north they continued to practice shifting subsistence economies, gradually changing a few of their crops and some of their specific techniques as they became acquainted with a new economic botany-biology and with new climatic situations. Those peoples who got into the lowland were able gradually to learn a sedentary garden agriculture and many of the other things that went with lowland living. Such later groups as the Burmans and the Shans, upon coming into Burma, were already somewhat advanced in their patterns of economy, and were already familiar with sedentary cultivation and with wet-field rice culture. Their route of ingress lay through country with some open upland sites in which rice growing was possible, namely the Shan Plateau.

Once in the lowlands the Burmans were the first to be able to make real use of the central dry zone of Burma through their knowledge of wet-field rice culture, and perhaps were the first to develop rice culture into a dominant position in the lowland economy. In their dry-zone agriculture the Burmans made auxiliary use of a fairly wide range of crops that were adaptable to local climatic situations. Their development of irrigation facilities in the dry zone was the first big forward step in the intensive exploitation of the lowlands. As they were shoved southward under Mongol-Shan pressures, they carried their intensive system southward into the edges of the wet delta region, and the Shan took over the northern part of the dry zone, in turn to learn how to use this kind of landscape.

The southern wet delta lands presented problems that were slow in solution for a people without highly developed material technologies and without large-scale centralized organization. Earliest use of this area had made more of aquatic resources than of normal land resources. Agriculture remained shifting cultivation in the heavily forested delta zone. Even in late Pegu times this was true, for Pegu was chiefly a trading-fishing economy. Only after the British came in to stabilize political and regional controls, bringing also an advanced technology, have the land use problems of the delta been solved. Only within the last century, therefore, has the large-scale development of the southernmost lowlands occurred.

In the wide range of the upland frame many local situations gradually permitted some sedentary agriculture. Little of this showed up in the western portions, but in the northern hill country and northern humid lowland fringes simple sedentary culture gradually appeared. And in the Shan Plateau's open spots the Shans developed sedentary agricultural villages whereas the rougher uplands remained in the hands of shifting cultivators. The Arakan and Tenasserim coasts remained on a fairly simple level of economy, with jungle gardening, fishing, and mobile trading features characterizing the economy.

The central lowland dry zone of Burma, therefore, accumulated the largest population of any section of pre-British Burma. Pagan, Ava, and Toungoo show cultural remains, indicating a higher population and a generally greater development of the landscape than do those of Pegu, Tenasserim, Arakan, or the northern upland frame. This central reservoir of population had supplied most of the new agricultural settlers that had turned the delta into a great ricefield in the last century. With the success of this recent colonial spread the population of southern Burma expanded greatly, and there came about a shift of economic and political power into the delta region of Burma.

No single land tenure system can be described for pre-British Burma, owing to cultural heterogeneity, nor can there be just one simple description of a social system. And, though the different cultural groups had their own patterns of social stratification, no group in Burma ever developed the highly complex caste patterns of India. From the Burmans came a social democracy and a freedom for women unparalleled in an advanced oriental society. Burman and Shan concepts of law, rather closely related, came to dominate the conduct of lowland affairs. Personal authority within social and economic groups was superior to statutory authority. The village was a social unit, not a territorial one. Civil law developed out of Burman and Shan tribal law, criminal law being the particular code of an individual ruler, subject to alteration under his successor. Even in eighteenth-century times the economy was chiefly a subsistence economy marked by local barter trade, rather than by a money economy measured in currency values. Lowland Burma was in small degree only a part of any oriental interregional trade realm.

The coming of the British caused many changes. The villages became as much territorial administrative units as the British could make them, in civil, criminal, and peace-preservation aspects, introducing problems never previously faced. Education began to lapse as social and religious custom was interfered with. Money trade patterns were introduced, and basic commodities not previously the chief items of trade began to be in demand in large volumes for export. The large-scale colonial settlement of the delta zone required governmental public works and sources of credit to colonists. The rise of the rice-export trade developed in the delta a monocrop money economy in which consumers' goods became import commodities rather than the home handicraft products that they had been. The dry zone and the upland fringe shared in this development to lesser degree than did the delta region. In 1830 the total rice acreage of the delta lands did not exceed 30,000 acres. From a total of perhaps 1.5 million acres of rice land for all of Burma in the early 1850's, the total grew to just over 12,000,000 acres in 1940, about eighty percent of which was in lower Burma.

Although British administration early recognized the need for prevention of moneylender foreclosure of land and the rise of tenancy, it never perfected machinery to accomplish this end, and usurious lending practices took full advantage of the untrained Burmese agriculturist. In the newly settled delta, therefore, the Indian moneylender, after about 1870, began to achieve a significant position as financier of agricultural development. Slowly the control of credit and land accumulated in Indian hands, and tenancy on the rice farms of the delta increased. Indian investment in other parts of Burma remained small, owing to a variety of greater risks involved and to the little new development taking place. Indians came in as laborers but shifted to shopkeeping and money lending as soon as they acquired the means. Between 1926 and 1940 there was almost a doubling in the land held by nonagriculturists, about half of which, some 3,000,000 acres, was owned by Indian moneylenders.

The development of interregional and international transport and trade patterns, under British ownership, altered the whole pattern of Burmese economy. Almost nowhere else in the world was a considerable area so easily exploited as Burma, a linear environment along which a system of water, road, and rail transport could effectively organize trade and control it through a single coastal port. British-built Rangoon quickly became that control port, an overgrown market town, inhabited and run by the British trader, the Indian moneylender, and their Burmese laborers.

World War II severely disorganized Burma and left most nonagricultural facilities inoperative, so that independence came to Burma with the economy at a standstill. Progressive nationalization began with rice lands in the delta in the early 1950's but extended to manufacturing and foreign trading by the early 1960's. Although nationalization was supposed to produce advancing economic development, management has proven unequal to the task, and productivity has gone downhill in almost every respect. Under progressive nationalization the role of Indians steadily declined, and by the late 1960's almost all Indians had left Burma. Foreign economic undertakings were taken over by the mid-1960's and by 1969 Burma was in full control of her declining economy.

AGRICULTURAL BURMA

Burma has often been described as an agricultural country dominated by ricefields (Fig. 17.2). The rice landscape does dominate the delta lands in the modern period, but the varied agricultural economies of the upland frame, and the generalized crop patterns of the central dry zone give considerable variety to the agrarian economy. Rice is the dominant crop everywhere in the country, and sections of the delta lands are almost monocrop in pattern. The expansion of rice lands made Burma the leading exporter of rice during the two decades of the 1920's and 1930's,

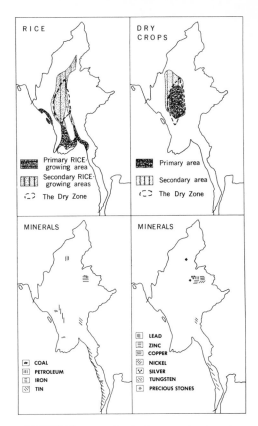

FIGURE 17.2. Agriculture and minerals.

with rice exports of over 7,000,000 tons per year during the late 1930's. By 1940 the total of land in farms had increased to about 22,000,000 acres, of which about 17,000,000 acres were cropped, with about 13,000,000 acres being devoted to rice. Nationalization of land expropriated many landlord holdings, but fragmentation of fields resulted, and the total acreage of rice plantings trended downward during the 1950's and early 1960's. In the pre-war period about 1,500,000 acres in the dry zone had been under irrigation. The low point in agriculture may have been reached about 1965–1967, with under 400,000 tons of rice exported in 1967.

Inadequate data prevents a conclusive presentation of the recent status of agriculture, but it would appear that actual plantings of land to rice in 1968–1969 rose above 12,000,000 acres, land under irrigation rose to a new level of just over 2,000,000 acres in the dry zone, some new rice varieties were expanding in acreage, and the availability of fertilizers was expanding. Poor land management and crop procurement procedures clearly affect the export picture for Burma's agricultural economy, but the population is growing rapidly and Burma may never again be an exporter of huge volumes of rice.

Outside the monocrop delta sector other crops than rice are significant parts of the agricultural economy. Small acreages of fruits, vegetables, sugarcane, sesamum, and cotton have long been complementary crops on the more humid lands toward the head of the delta. It is in the dry zone and its margins, where irrigation is necessary for productive agriculture, that most of the real variety shows up in Burmese agriculture. Sesamum and peanuts for edible oils, both grain and fodder millets, a variety of peas, beans, and related leguminous crops, chili peppers, onion, cotton, and tobacco are the chief crops that compete with, and rotate around, rice in the dry zone. Irrigation facilities do not yet extend to all parts of the dry zone, so that some of the crops competing with rice are dry-land crops, whereas rice here is grown only on irrigated lands. Dry-zone agriculture involves both winter and summer plantings, and much of the Burmese double cropping acreage is in this region.

A wide variety of vegetables are grown in small patches in the general farmland areas, in small areas around villages and towns, and in long strips along river banks. The rivers of Burma all fluctuate markedly in level from wet to dry seasons, and between late October and April the moist alluvial lands exposed by low water are utilized for vegetable culture, particularly in the dry zone. Among the food crops, maize, tomatoes, and varieties of beans occupy the largest areas, but more than forty different vegetable crops are cultivated on these river-bank lands. The largest share of Burma's tobacco is also grown on river-bank lands during the low-water season. Vegetable cultivation in all parts of Burma is chiefly a dry-season occupation, involves considerable regional variety, and almost supplies the total food needs.

Although a large amount of fruit is produced for home use, little of it is on the basis of formal orchards, and little cultivation is practiced. Many of the common fruits, such as the bananas, mangoes, oranges, limes, pomelos, lichis, palms, durians, and jack-fruit, are either native here or have been common to this area for so long that they have become a part of the plant growth around villages and towns, along the roads and trails, and in the jungles of the yet un-cleared lands. Into this same vegetation complex have gone such American fruits as the pineapple, papaya, sapote, and guava. Often it is difficult to determine whether production is from farmed lands or from wild jungle lands. The range and volume of fruits decreases in the dry zone, and in the upper parts of the upland frame.

In most of the rough upland frame shifting cultivation, on a near-subsistence basis, is still the rule for crop production. Normally a mixture of crops is planted together in the small patches and fields, but among some of the hill people certain crops have gained regional preference. In some areas one of the millets is dominant; in others maize, upland rice, buckwheat, or other millets are preferred. Altitude and microclimatic situation, as well as cultural preferences, have entered into this selection. Shan Plateau agriculture is more advanced than that elsewhere in the upland frame. Here wet rice is a staple in the open tracts among the Shans, with shifting cultivation used by other peoples living above them in the rougher areas. The Shans also have developed a specialty agriculture, dealing in commercial crops which are sold in the lowlands. Bread wheat, white potatoes for seed use, garlic, ginger, cigar-wrapper leaf, tung oil, varieties of oranges, tea, and European varieties of vegetables are all produced in various parts of the Shan Plateau.

The Shans also raise large numbers of animals for sale in the lowlands, particularly cattle. Animal diseases in the humid lowlands take a steady toll of most of the domesticated animals, and there is a regular flow of replacement stock from the Shan Plateau to all parts of the lowland Burma. World War II took heavy toll of the animal population, but it is building slowly upward again and, in most cases, the totals are higher now than before the war. The further expansion of Burmese agriculture is related to this in-increase in animal population, since the majority of farms are large enough to require animal power for purposes of cultivation. The total number of work oxen and buffalo now stands close to 2,800,000, a total inadequate to the current need. Although there has been encouragement of mechanized farming in the lower delta, only a small supply of tractors and equipment was imported, no effective replacement program has developed under austere conditions of foreign trade, and the recent trend has been downward.

Burma does not properly participate in the plantation agriculture found elsewhere in southern Asia. There is but a small acreage of coconut plantings, tea production is in the traditional Chinese manner rather than the newer occidental style, and there are no large plantings of sugar, coffee, cacao, or vegetable fibers. The Shan Plateau has a small acreage of tung oil trees, chiefly in large holdings. From near Rangoon southward through Tenasserim there are scattered plantings of rubber. Many of them are in small holdings, but the larger units are in occidental-style plantings. The future of rubber is not great

in Burma, however, owing to the seasonal nature of rainfall, and thus it is unlikely that corporate plantation agriculture will encroach upon Burma.

The occupational censuses of Burma have never listed fishing as an occupational category, but fish supply the second most important source of food, after rice, to the population of the coastal and lowland regions. It is likely that there are in the vicinity of 100,000 people whose basic occupation is fishing, and it is also likely that the part-time fishermen number in the hundreds of thousands. Burma's import of fish products is relatively small, and the local catch is in the vicinity of 85,000,000 pounds per year, with the lower delta region the chief productive area. Rivers, coastal waters, ponds, and other water bodies steadily provide a considerable volume of all sorts of aquatic products, and this traditional economy has not been lost in the elaboration of a dominant rice agriculture.

AUXILIARY PATTERNS OF ECONOMY

The pre-British Burmese carried on a considerable variety of activities other than agriculture and fishing. Mining and lumbering are old occupations. Handicraft manufactures almost sufficed to fill the modest Burmese demand, though these declined under the impact of occidental imports in the nineteenth century. Today it is likely that some seventy-five percent of the population is concerned with agriculture, and that about twenty percent is concerned with industry, trade, transport, mining, and forestry. It is impossible clearly to separate such activities in a country like Burma, where part-time participation in varied activities is normal.

Mining is an old activity. North Burma jade has been mined and sent to China for centuries. The rubies and sapphires of the Shan Plateau were items of barter trade with the earliest Indian traders. Tin has been mined along the Tenasserim coast since the days of those same early Indian traders. Lead, zinc, and silver were mined at Bawdwin, and the petroleum of southern Burma was tapped and locally used long before the European came east. The occidental has found few new minerals in Burma, though he has increased the annual outputs of several. Burma could be a regular contributor of significant amounts of petroleum, lead, zinc, copper, silver, tin, nickel, and tungsten to the markets of the world. World War II destruction of the Bawdwin and Mawchi mines put an end to production. Recently a small start has again been made in mining development (see Fig. 17.2). Hydroelectric resources are large, provided they are developed in such a way as to store the seasonal rainfall of Burma, and there have been some small power projects completed since 1960. As the Indians and Chinese controlled much of the mining in earlier centuries, the British controlled both the mining and the export trade between 1890 and 1940.

Lumbering is not a new-born activity in Burma, but it is not so old as mining. Since about 1800 Burma has been the chief source of teak in the international lumber trade, for teak is one of the strongest and most durable of the world's woods. With the rise of international shipping, in the late seventeenth century, Burmese teak found its chief use in shipbuilding the world over, and its use therein has only recently declined somewhat. Expansion in other uses has maintained the commercial lumbering of teak. Not many other Burmese woods are well known and developed in usage abroad, but there will be such an increase in the future, for the forests of Burma possess many good woods exhausted elsewhere. Burmese forests also could produce rattans, lac, tannins, a variety of resins, gums, and oils of value both in

Burma and abroad. The domestic use of bamboos, construction lumber, tool wood, and firewood amounts to a large annual volume. Firewood and charcoal are the normal Burmese domestic fuels, and a large amount of both is constantly required. Since World War II production of teak and other forest products has trended steadily downward, and it is not clear whether the low point has yet been reached in the forest industries.

With the decline of handicraft manufacturing for home use in Burma, a chronic underemployment of the agricultural population resulted. Modern manufacturing began on a small scale in a fairly wide range, but it absorbed the labor of but a small portion of the population. Burmese have not taken to modern mining, and much of the mine labor was Chinese or Indian. Much of the lumbering labor service is contributed by other than lowland Burmese. The Burmese are mechanically adaptable and make good skilled technicians, but their past opportunities have not been large. Most of the earlier modern enterprises were British or Indian built, owned, and technically staffed. In the past most of the manufactured goods that replaced the handicrafts were imported goods, distributed at the wholesale level by foreign firms, and getting into Burmese hands only at the retail level. A rather normal pattern was developing prior to World War II, in which agricultural processing, the textiles, assembly, light manufacturing involving simple fabrication, and machine shop operations were primary. Petroleum refining, railways industries, dock and shipbuilding, and the electrical industries were foreign owned and managed and often used Indian or Chinese labor. Burma had, prior to World War II, something of a start in modern manufacturing, but this largely was rendered inoperative during the war. Postwar redevelopment had not proceeded very far before restrictive foreign trade controls became operative and before nationalization began. By 1963 nationalization had been almost completed, resulting in the loss of almost all managerial and technical personnel as Europeans and Indians left Burma. Government management corporations were set up to take over and further develop necessary processing and manufacturing operations, but Burmese inexperience in such matters resulted in the steady decline of plants and equipment, declining rice exports permitted few imports of new equipment, and the consumer goods picture trended steadily downward during the 1960's. It is not clear whether the bottom level of production has been reached, as of 1970.

Barter-aid agreements with several foreign countries have resulted in some new and modern installations of several types of manufacturing or processing plants, such as plywood, metals-smelting, teak mill, chemicals, paper, and vegetable oils. The prohibition of private capital investment limits both domestic and foreign development, and government corporations prove slow and inefficient in carrying out effective programs. Barter-aid agreements have not produced comprehensive results, since Burma is reluctant to enter into too-close agreement with any country, and since Burma has only slight means of paying for such developments. Meanwhile, the older group of plants continue to deteriorate through poor operating efficiencies and the inability to secure replacement equipment.

The present transport network of Burma is not comprehensive, and its equipment is small in volume. The first rail line was built in the 1870's, by 1899 it reached from Rangoon to Myitkyina, and gradually increased to a mileage just over 2,500. A present the mileage is just over 2,400, but the serious aspect is that the rolling stock continues to decline in volume and operability (Fig. 17.3). Its pattern taps areas not well serviced by water transport, and the rail system con-

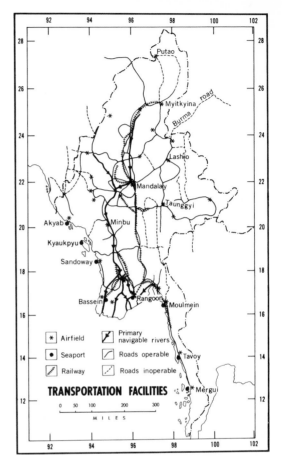

FIGURE 17.3. Burma's transportation facilities.

tinues to carry a very heavy passenger traffic and small volumes of freight. The meter gauge system is operated by the government.

The linear build of the country, traversed by the Irrawaddy, has meant an easy development of water transport. Native traffic in considerable volume has flowed along the Irrawaddy, the Chindwin, and the Sittang for centuries, as well as along the whole coastal fringe. The British started developing steamboat service on the Irrawaddy before road and rail systems were started. River transport provides cheap and effective movement along almost the whole length of Burma, Bhamo being the head of steam navigation, 872 miles from Rangoon. The

Chindwin is usefully navigated for about 400 miles. The volume of water transport throughout the Irrawaddy delta is large. The craft of the nationalized Inland Water Transport Board move well over half a million tons of cargo and nearly 3,000,000 passengers per year along the Irrawaddy and Chindwin. The Sittang is not of much real use for large craft, nor is the Salween, though many native small craft use both rivers.

Cart roads, packtrain trails, and footpaths are old, long traveled, and widely spread in Burma and, in the upland frame, will continue so. The modern road-building program has achieved somewhat over 20,000 miles of vehicular roads, about a third of which are all-weather roads, but only a seventh of the total are fully paved roads (see Fig. 17.3). It is not certain that all roads shown on the accompanying transport map are in regular adequate repair at present. In a linear country, again, this rather small mileage, supplementing the rail and water systems, can serve to a greater degree than might seem the case. In the vicinity of 750,000 animal carts haul an uncounted traffic. Burma has not yet really entered the automobile age, and only some 50,000 motor vehicles are registered. Of these only the trucks and buses really serve a public transport function, and most of the equipment is concentrated around Rangoon. The network of airfields affords rather good basic contact with all parts of the country, and there are many more military fields, but Burma has not been able to support a large plane fleet, and air services are minimal.

With its chief population and economic regions enclosed within the upland frame, it is only natural that Burma's chief trade contact to the outside world has been by sea through the delta zone. Rangoon, well located on that delta and linked to its eastern and western segments by interior canals, roads, and rail lines, has dominated the external trade and passenger traffic of Burma. The shipping has been predominantly British and Indian. Rangoon is the only important port, the center of import and export trade, but the river channel has silted badly, and only small ships may ascend to Rangoon. Lesser coastal ports serve chiefly an interregional role, tying into Rangoon rather than serving as regional centers of external contact.

Rice has been the big export product in point of value within the last century. Second were the petroleum products, followed by teak, lead, tungsten, tin, vegetables, rubber, cotton, and silver, in that order. Indian markets have been the chief goals of Burmese products, followed by British, Ceylon, and Malaysian markets. The position of India as a buyer of rice, teak, petroleum, and vegetables has been a dominant one.

Between 1900 and 1941, cotton and rayon clothing textiles and yarns were the leading imports in point of value. Jute sacking for the grain trade ranked high ever since the grain market reached large proportions. Machinery, iron and steel, vegetable oil products, chemicals, tobacco products, paper and its products, and assorted food products, in that order, have been the other significant imports. India has long been a dominant supplier of the Burmese market, followed by Great Britain. In recent decades Japan and the United States were significant suppliers of Burmese markets, with a wide scattering of minor sources.

Burma's trade balance was distinctly in her own favor for a long period, for her products have found a ready market elsewhere in the world. Indian deficits in rice, timber, and petroleum gave Burma a guaranteed market for those commodities. The rice market, at least, must always be a low-priced one, never producing huge profits to Burmese producers, but it is a steady market. On the basis of the rice and timber trade Burma cannot expect to be able to finance an extremely high level of living, nor can she afford out of such revenues alone to finance modernization and industrialization. Petroleum and other minerals could help, but their reserves are not endless and they are a rather ephemeral resource. Off-setting this favorable balance of trade was the outward flow of profits and invisible items accruing to the British, Indian, and Chinese operators of, and investors in, Burmese economy.

Since independence, however, the trade patterns have altered. Mineral and petroleum exports ceased, and the rice and teak exports trended downward steadily, so that Burma steadily exported less and less. This required stringent reduction in import goods, placing a strong handicap on the import of capital goods. The nationalization of all trade resulted in poor management of commodity flow and capital resources. The scarcity of consumer goods promoted a large black market operation. It is not clear whether the low point in foreign trade was reached in 1968–1969; though the 1969–1970 rice yield may have afforded an increase in the export volume, it is not certain that this took place.

THE IRRAWADDY VALLEY AND THE OTHER BURMAS

Even today, after centuries of centripetal action, the peoples of Burma are not yet one. The process of fusion has worked towards a single cultural whole, but there have been counterinfluences, and one may well wonder whether it will ever completely succeed. Regionalism in modern Burma is strong. In part this is environmental, owing to landforms, climate, and vegetation. In part it is cultural, the peoples of Burma having developed variant cultures en route to their present home areas. The British also contributed to the process.

British administration distinguished a Lower Burma and an Upper Burma, and these terms remain in the literature. The wet delta and the central dry zone do differ, but the terms Upper and Lower Burma refer rather to the historical growth of British rule. They acquired Burma in two basic units, first the coast from Mergui to Akyab, which became Lower Burma; the interior came under control later, and since it was up river, it became Upper Burma. Use of these terms only confuses the regionalisms of Burma.

Currently, the primary sector of lowland Burma, including the Arakan coastal strip and peninsular Tenasserim, is divided into 42 political districts, segregated into 8 divisions. These districts are areas of convenience, based on tradition and on group-culture criteria. Some are old in outline, but others are still shaping up. The 8 divisions are somewhat geographical, made on the basis of historical tradition plus convenience. Divisional limits do not accord with the regional patterns a geographer would draw, using environmental and other criteria. It is common to find that some of the upland frame areas regularly are omitted from statistical summaries, but the omitted areas are not always the same ones. This omission indicates inability of government to manage affairs in the upland frame where villages and farms constantly shift location, and where regionalisms are mobile matters of group culture rather than lines fixed on a map. The areas forming the upland frame of Burma are at present divided into five units, four ethnic autonomous states (Karen, Kayah, Shan, and Kachin), and the special administrative territory in the Chin Hills in the northwest. The Karen state lies east of the delta lowland, Kayah state is located to the north in the area in which Shan and Karen are mixed ethnic elements, Shan state lies in the northeast, and the Kachin state in the far north (Fig. 17.4). This pattern is not yet stable and is subject to change.

In 1826 Burma's population was estimated at 4,000,000. The earliest useful census is that of 1891, incomplete but tabulating a total of 7,722,000. That of 1941, still slightly

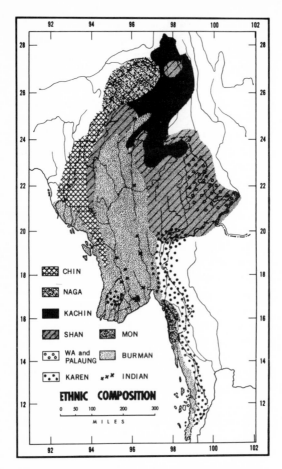

FIGURE 17.4. Ethnic composition of Burma.

rapidly in recent years and in 1969 was estimated at 1,600,000. Mandalay, at 318,000 by a 1969 estimate, and Moulmein, at 157,000 by a similar estimate, are the only other large cities.

Although it is close to impossible to determine accurately the cultural regionalism of Burma today, some idea of its remaining strength can be gained from a linguistic or tribal map, and from data on mother tongues (see Fig. 17.4, and Fig. 17.6). In 1931 some 9,862,000 out of 14,647,000 people claimed Burmese as their mother tongue. A total of 1,341,000 claimed Karen, 1,021,000 listed Thai (meaning the Shans), 1,079,000 gave

incomplete, counted 16,824,000 people. No census has been taken since independence in 1948, but the 1969 population is estimated at about 26,500,000. The heart of the delta and the northern sector of the dry zone are the regional centers of population (Fig. 17.5). Sections of the northern Arakan coast and the northern end of the Tenasserim coast also show population concentrations, but most of the northern lowlands and the uplands show light population patterns.

There are few large cities in Burma, a country primarily of villages and small market towns. Rangoon, in 1947, held about 600,000 people, but it has been growing

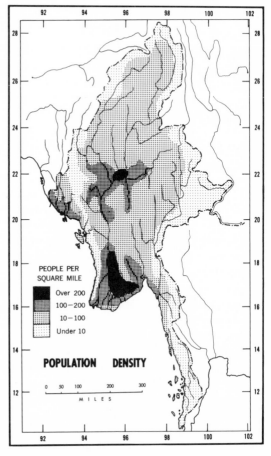

FIGURE 17.5. Population density of Burma.

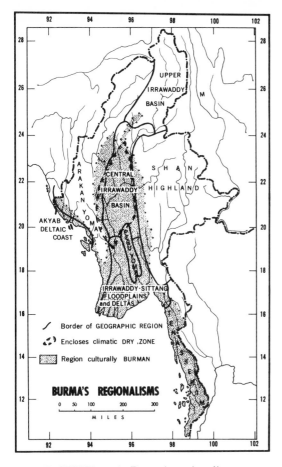

FIGURE 17.6. Burma's regionalisms.

Indian languages, 343,000 listed Kuki-Chin languages, 305,000 gave Mon, 176,000 claimed Palaung, 178,000 listed Chinese, and 153,000 returned Kachin. No later linguistic census date is yet available, but we estimate the tribal peoples at present about as follows: Karens, 2,500,000; Shans, 2,100,000; Kachins, 800,000; Chins, 650,000; Wa-Palaung, 400,000; Nagas, 150,000; and the smaller groups at a total of about 100,000. This would indicate just under 19,500,000 people culturally and linguistically considered Burmese, with some small numbers of Indians and Chinese still remaining in the country. It is noteworthy that Burmese is the only language claimed by the residents of the Arakan or Tenasserim coasts. Many Shans formerly resident in the dry zone also now list Burmese as their mother tongue, as do the descendants of many another group which has gained space in the lowland. Burmese as a language has spread widely, and with it an indeterminant volume of cultural mores. On the other hand, the Karen are gaining political cohesion today and are no longer a shy group retiring before the pressure of others. Much of the political unrest of lowland Burma since World War II results from the fact that the Karen are demanding a share in the affairs of the State. Some of the strongest animosities and pressures within present-day Burma are those of the hill peoples against the lowlanders. Although this is traditional ethnic tribalism, it is now beginning to shape into regional political patterns, and, as the Burmese are achieving a political nationalism for Burma, these minority groups are beginning to develop political nationalisms for their own culture groups. These regional developments are going to increase in the future, as cultural evolution and modernization affects the several culture groups that reside in Burma. This will be unlikely to grow into demands for total independence, but the domestic political map of Burma may well change continuously in the future, as these culture regionalisms further express themselves. The regional boundaries of such units will neither correspond to the so-called geographic regions drawn by the geographer nor to the political divisions drawn up in the past by governmental administrators.

The Irrawaddy Valley, from the delta to Bhamo, is the Burmanized cultural heart of Burma. This is the region with the greatest total population, the potentially most productive agriculture, the greatest advancement in political and economic affairs, and culturally the most sophisticated. It will continue to dominate the affairs of all of Burma.

But the Sittang Valley, and the eastern fringe of the delta, along with some of the eastern hill country, as the home of the Karen, constitutes another and slightly different Burma within the whole. The Shans of the Shan Plateau, heretofore politically fractionated by their strong individualism, may acquire political cohesion on some local regional pattern to change the regional balance of power and culture. Though the Irrawaddy lowland will continue to control the affairs of Burma, there are many smaller regional units that may alter the present life of the whole.

THE FUTURE OF THE BURMESE WAY IN SOCIALISM

In 1970 Burma remains a near-hermit society, struggling with two different kinds of problems with very little assistance, owing largely to her own decision to go it alone in her own way. The throwing off of all foreign ties clearly removed both the British developmental influence and the Indian economic exploitation of local trade and capital resources, but it removed from Burma most of the trained and experienced personnel at a time when Burmese were not equipped to take over economic management, industrial planning, and redevelopment of their economy. The "Burmese Way in Socialism" has remained a somewhat lighthearted and irresponsible philosophy in which plans for the future often were substituted for the hard realities at hand. In the early years of independence many United Nations commissions came and went, leaving mature plans behind for which there were not many chances of practical execution. Somewhat impractical and ineffectual nationalization schemes were put into operation, to be maintained at some partial stage once token steps had been taken. In agriculture this had the drastic effect of steady reduction in the rice exports which could have paid for much of the economic planning, and much the same

result occurred in forest use. Large numbers of plans for projects are shelved pending the day they can be financed but, in recent years, that day has steadily retreated further off into the future.

The second kind of problem has been that of the translating of political philosophy into governmental and administrative reality. There has not been a month since independence during which some rebellious group, clique, or political faction has not raised militant protest in some part of Burma. Part of this has related to cultural separatism between "Burmese" and the ethnic groups of the upland fringe, but part of it, too, has related to the degree to which the term "Socialism" has been interpretable as Marxism–Leninism. Civilian-controlled government has not been able to hold Socialism to something apparently preferred by most of the population, so that military government has operated most of the time since independence.

The years 1965–1968, hopefully, represented the lowest ebb in independent Burma's economic life and, though the current trends are not moving upward in rapid strides, there is hope that Burma has by now gained sufficient experience to better match planning with economic reality in the future. If it proves true that the basic agricultural economy is again in an upward trend, then every small advance can support further developmental growth. At least by 1968 almost all developmental projects had been effected in the lower delta region only, since this was the only area under sufficiently safe military control to permit economic development to be carried forward. There are also faint signs that perhaps Burma's leadership will not continuously prolong the severely closed hermitage that characterized Burma in 1970.

The Burmese landscape is not a heavily worn and sorely depleted resource, for all that it has shown signs of mis-management and short-term unproductivity. Increasing good management can render it highly productive, whatever particular brand of political socialism motivates its leadership, but good management remains the key factor. Burmese management, at this point, is not yet operating at the level at which marked productivity can result, and it will be some years before the level of efficiency reaches that at which marked economic progress can come about.

18

THE EVOLUTION
OF THAILAND

ENVIRONMENTAL REGIONS AND EARLY CULTURE GROUPS

The political region today recognized as Thailand has a complex regional history. Although the Chao Phraya Valley is the heart of modern Thailand, and though the Thais are the dominant culture group, this is a rather recent development. Earlier cultures and political states were arranged on quite different regional lines (see Figs. 16.1 and 16.2). The 300,000 square miles of territory between the Annamite Cordillera and the Dawna Yoma contains three large physical units not well separated from each other. The Chao Phraya lowland, the Korat Platform, and the Cambodian lowland each are large enough to have housed a major cultural development of the past. The problems of organizing all three physical areas were too great for the earlier culture groups, and no one culture ever controlled the whole region. The physical limits separating the three units do not constitute major barriers, and simple contact between units has been well-nigh continuous. But cultural and political beginnings took place on the margins, north or south and, with simple transport technologies, distances and space proved too great for early competing cultures.

Many of the features suggested in the previous chapter hold for this major region. Around the three units the Chao Phraya Valley, the Korat Platform, and the Cambodian lowland, there is a mountain frame. From the north narrow river valleys and tapering hill ranges reach southward into the low country. The basic alignments of physical geography produce a north-south linear pattern, though this is less neat and compact than in Burma. Approaches by land have been via the north, and those by sea have come from the south. Two great extensive alluvial lowlands contrast with the surrounding uplands. The ranges of possibilities for primitive economies were somewhat the same as in Burma. The aquatic habitats, the lowland jungle-forests, and the mountain zones here present much the same conditions for early man as in Burma, though the climatic aridity of the regional rain shadows is here less marked.

Who the first human groups were and where their centers were are even less well understood here than in Burma. There does appear more historic evidence of widespread Negrito occupance, and there are scattered reminders even today. Pre-Mon-Khmer peoples certainly were widely scattered, but their provenance and the duration of their earliest occupance remain speculative. Recent and preliminary archaeologic finds suggest an older history of advanced-level occupance than was formerly accepted. Some Sino-Tibetan stocks must have come in at an early time, proto-Mongoloid to early Mongoloid elements that drifted southward through parts of the region. They are commonly identified as Indonesian peoples. The Chams are one of these stocks, at the dawn of history established in an east-west belt of the country, north of the delta, from the Mekong across the Annamite Cordillera to the sea-coast. There seems reason to distinguish somewhat between Mon and Khmer peoples, but they appear related, and both probably came from the west. The Khmer possibly did not arrive in the Cambodian lowland until after the first Indian contacts with the region. The Mon groups appear to have moved more into Burma and the Chao Phraya lowland, possibly earlier than the Khmer. As Burma was a kind of human vacuum, this region also early invited varied peoples into it, the lowlands being the chief goal sought by most groups. Some southward drift even now is continuing, for such newer elements as the Miao and the Yao are currently on the move southward in the northern mountain zones. Many of the more recent arrivals have had little opportunity to infiltrate the lowlands.

The chief cultural region of the past was based upon the Cambodian lowland, and composed the heart of the great Khmer Empire, of which modern Cambodia is the lineal descendant. The lower Chao Phraya Valley never acquired major status in the early period. The second cultural region became outlined in the northernmost Chao Phraya lowlands at a rather late date by the southward-moving Thais. It is this cultural unit which has expanded into modern Thailand. The Thais came so late as to have been unable to organize the full physical region

before the European also came upon the scene. Internal struggles went on for several centuries to inhibit the Thais. And the French were able to incorporate the Cambodian lowland and the fringe east and north of the Mekong into their nineteenth century colonial empire without effective Thai protest. The French, thus, created a new political boundary across the major physical region where none had existed in the past. Had the Thai cultural and political pattern matured earlier, or had the European come later, the present outlines of political states in this area might well have been different from that found today.

The specific environmental and regional derivation of the Thais is uncertain, for the basic Tai stock originally inhabited much of lowland central and south China just before the Christian era. Out of this Tai stock have come the Shans, Thais, Laos, and other of the present southeastern Asian peoples. When the Thais first came into the orbit of Southeast Asian affairs they were resident in southern and western Yunnan and composed the main populace and rulers of the ill-defined state of Nanchao. Culturally they represent an early and marginal phase of Chinese civilization, but in their Yunnan home they absorbed a degree of Indianization, and were then resident in a tropical upland region. They long constituted a major buffer to Chinese and Tibetan expansion, and they also had to deal with a variety of simpler culture groups moving into and through their area. Over several centuries they developed a skill at using and adapting varied culture traits to their own advantage. They learned city dwelling and wall building, military tactics of varied sorts, regional political administration, settlement infiltration, and the agricultural and economic use of a variety of physical regions. They were able to sustain themselves in Yunnan for a long period but, as southern Sung and Mongol pressures from China grew greater in the late eleventh to thirteenth centuries, they, like other peoples, yielded to those pressures and drifted southward.

Southward infiltration by Thai village farmers had begun pushing down the narrow valleys of northern Thailand as early as the ninth century. Fortified towns followed, with the taking over of the more favorable valley regions, the simpler non-Thai groups being forced into the uplands. The Thais thus came into loose contact with the Khmer realm before the latter had reached its fullest expression. Slowly this contact became closer and more competitive. Tributary vassaldom by Thai frontier regions to the Khmer state existed for a time, and Thais served as mercenaries in Khmer armies in the eleventh and twelfth centuries. Thai settlement infiltration of the lowland was, however, a more solid way of building regional control than was Khmer extension of political power without settlement. The Thai southward drift continued, their lowland population increased, and their lowland competitive strength matured. Local principalities consolidated and, by the thirteenth century, the Chao Phraya Valley Thais were a major threat to the Khmers.

The thirteenth and fourteenth centuries spelled the doom of Khmer control over the great lowland. First to occur was the evacuation of Champa, the southern cordillera, and that part of the lowland east of the Mekong, in the early thirteenth century. Almost contemporary was the loss of most of the peninsular coast and control over the Gulf of Siam. Consequent upon the strong pressures from Mongol China, the Thais and other peoples began moving in force down the valleys of the north country into the upper Mekong, Korat, and the Chao Phraya. First came greater autonomy, under nominal Khmer control, with Sukhotai made the southernmost Thai regional center about 1240 (see Fig. 16.2). Then full Khmer control over the lower Chao Phraya region of

Louvo was lost, as the Thais spread down the valley and into the peninsula. Chiangmai became the chief Thai capital about 1296, still far north but out of Yunnan entirely. The development of a Thai written language, taken from the Khmer, acceptance of Theravada Buddhism from the Mons of Louvo, the intermarriage of ranking Thais with members of high Khmer families, and the wholesale settlement advance by Thai colonists, all typify thirteenth-century aspects of growing Thai strength in the Chao Phraya Valley. An advance capital was set up at Ayuthia about 1350. The Thais became the overlords of the Chao Phraya region, over the old Mon population now intermixed with Khmers, and began organizing the valley into a political state. A century of Thai-Khmer sparring for control of the lowland began, with the Khmer state also having to combat the Chams of Champa, the Vietnamese, and the encroaching tribal peoples of the north. In the northern Mekong Valley, and in Korat, Thai and other peoples lacked the cohesion of those taking over the Chao Phraya Valley, and here many local tribal principalities and temporary confederations developed.

The Thais were neither strong enough nor numerous enough to conquer the whole Khmer Empire in one great sustained campaign. They never became one politically united people. The Chao Phraya Valley Thais chose to try consolidation, studied Khmer culture, and by degrees expanded their own political system of regional control. They increasingly inhibited the operation of the Khmer Empire while strengthening themselves. Thai reduction of the areas from which tributary labor battalions and taxable wealth could be drawn must have played a role in the reduction of the Khmer Empire. Among the other factors that have been given partial credit for the undermining of Khmer power is the spread of Theravada Buddhism. Theravada Buddhism was a simple, ascetic, and rather democratic form of religion emphasizing the individual's responsibility to seek his own salvation and appealing to the lower classes, in contrast to the stratified and hierarchic codes of Sivaism, Brahmanism, and Mahayana Buddhism long in favor among the Khmer rulers. Another factor may have been a series of extensive floods in the early fourteenth century that rendered much of the Cambodian rice land unproductive, consequent upon changes in Mekong delta distributaries, thus undermining the economic support of the Cambodian core. Epidemics of disease, brought in by multitudes of refugees and religious pilgrims, have been given importance in the decline of Khmer power. Gradual soil depletion, under exploitive rice culture using no fertilizing and restorative techniques, has been suggested as of importance also. Lacking Khmer historical documentation of these matters, the several factors must remain unweighed in relative significance, but the cumulative result is quite clear.

The Chao Phraya Valley Thais, with a capital at Ayuthia, gradually developed a political state that included the northern peninsula, the hill country west of the Chao Phraya Valley, the valley lowland itself, the northern mountain and valley area, and Korat. Apparently problems of political and cultural solidification of this region were sufficient so that the Thai rulers sought no permanent conquest of Cambodia. Nor did they successfully include the Thai-occupied upper Mekong region which remained a zone of small regional principalities. Cambodia never threatened resurgence to her former status. In 1432 the Cambodian capital was removed from Angkor to the vicinity of modern Phnom Penh, away from the dangers of Thai attack. The northwest frontier districts of the Cambodian core gradually came under Thai control.

In the Thai dominance over the Khmers many Mon and Khmer culture traits passed to the Thais. In a sense this makes a third cultural orientation of the Thai—Sinicized, Indianized, and Khmerized. Thai rulers tried to become the absolute monarchs that the Khmer kings had been, and made efforts to pattern the social structure of the new Thai state upon that of the Khmers. Thai rulers developed temple and monastery building. The Khmer system of forced-labor battalions of slaves and bonded servants was taken into usage. Administrative structure and patterns of taxation, law, and judicial procedure were copied in part. All these new forms were somewhat alien to the traditional individualities and social freedoms that marked earlier Thai societies and regional groups. The attempted impositions caused inefficiency and organized protest, and they may well account for the slowness of a stable Thai society and political structure to emerge in the modern world.

THE DELINEATION OF MODERN THAILAND

The fifteenth to the nineteenth centuries forms a long period of struggle for unification of the modern political state. Ayuthia remained the chief capital during the early part of the period. Thai ability at political organization of the large area came slowly and with difficulty, for the Thai peoples have been prone to division and individuality rather than to tight cultural cohesion. Both political rivalries for dominance and local sectionalisms were frequent issues in contest. And the growing states of lowland Burma found many reasons for attempting control of the Chao Phraya Valley or the peninsula, so that there were recurrent military invasions. Although each of the several Burmese states could mount a military expedition for invasion, none could ever truly conquer or organize regional control of any part of the peninsula or the Chao Phraya Valley. Punitive expeditions by the Thais, in return, detracted from the main task. These invasions were sufficiently frequent to keep the Thais off balance for several centuries. One such sufficiently destroyed Ayuthia that Bangkok was made the capital in 1768 (see Fig. 4.7, and accompanying text).

Portuguese and Dutch traders first sampled the coasts of the Gulf of Siam and the South China Sea. They made contact both with the declining Khmer center and the new and yet unstable Thai region. Later came both the British and the French, the latter more concerned with the spread of Catholic Christianity than with trade. Neither region, one declining, one yet immature, produced large amounts of those products of chief interest to the European. The Thais adopted Khmer trade administrative controls and government offices, not previously having had much to do with foreign trade, and essayed to deal with European traders as though the Thais were the lords of creation, after the old Khmer system, in which selected patterns of trade were royal monopolies.

The interregional feuding only ceased when the British took over political management of Burma during the nineteenth century. Under British manipulations a western boundary finally crystallized, running through the Dawna Yoma and into the peninsula. Similarly, a southern boundary, far down in the peninsula, finally became adjudicated in such a way that most of the predominantly Malay-populated areas remained in British Malaya, and the rest of the peninsula became part of Thailand.

When the French, in the latter part of the nineteenth century, began carving out their one mainland colonial holding, they commenced in the Mekong Delta. Cambodia came next, though not all the old Khmer core came under French control at one time, since the Thai had dominated its frontier units. French infiltration of the Mekong River region and the advance north along the coastal front were roughly parallel. By 1907

they had maneuvered affairs to the end that all the Cambodian lowland and all the territory east of the Mekong was theirs. The northern ends of the British and French boundaries came together to preclude direct Thailand boundary contact with China.

The Thai were slow to appreciate the realities of the modern world, but they did become wary of all European contacts and entanglements. Often the Thai king chose among the smaller noncompetitive countries, and began playing off the Dutch against the British, against the French during the seventeenth and eighteenth centuries, adding the Americans to the circle in the nineteenth century. This was sufficiently well done so that Thailand came through the period of colonialism without falling prey to any country in the political sense, the only country in Southeast Asia to escape colonial status. But this very escape from colonial status has also left the Thais inexperienced in some of the ways of modern political philosophy and administration. Thai governmental administration of the affairs of society has had less of the modern ways of the world about it than that of most other countries of the Orient, although this has been changing rapidly since the early 1950's.

Although contact with China has been a traditional matter for the peoples of the whole lowland, in which the Chinese adopted the superior role, the Thais have never willingly accepted the role of a tributary vassal people. Ever since the Thai asserted their control over the Chao Phraya Valley they have maintained relations with China, in the form of trade embassies. In 1700 there were only a few thousand Chinese permanently resident in the country. Shortly after 1800 large numbers of Chinese men began to come in, marrying local women and engaging in trade, fisheries, and handicraft manufacture. A few always returned to China after some years in the country, but slowly the total Chinese population has increased. In recent decades

Chinese women have come in with their husbands, causing intermarriages to decline in number. The children of Chinese men and Thai women have usually been brought up within the patterns of Thai culture, and they are considered native citizens before Thai law. The actual number of Chinese citizens resident in Thailand has been reported at 340,000, as a legal statistic, but the total mixed-blood Chinese population exceeds 3,500,000.

This Chinese infiltration may be considered a part of the traditional southward drift of peoples, but in terms of modern political nationalism it has inserted an alien minority into Thailand which is having repercussions in economic and legal matters. For some decades restrictive legislation has narrowed the freedoms of the Chinese and has provoked various forms of opposition. This is not a matter that affects political boundaries, but it may well affect the operation of the Thai state in both the political and economic sense.

The region early recognized as the domain of the Syam, as the Khmer termed the Thais, is thus not a well-defined physical region at all, but is a political region defined by the former competing interests of two occidental powers, Great Britain and France. Thailand is far more a politicohistorical phenomenon than a cultural one, and not entirely one prescribed by physical geography. It is only a part of the great lowland region, and its present boundaries have little or no historical precedent. Thais live outside Thailand, and non-Thais are to be found within it. In the southern peninsular sector are numerous Malays on the Thai side of the border, Karen live all along the western border with Burma, there are small tribal clusters in the far north, and there are Cambodians living in Thailand along the Cambodian border. However, official Thai government policy plays down these issues. This political region is the chief zone in Southeast Asia around which

political boundaries form significant problems in political geography. Since these boundaries of today are recent creations of political manipulation, they are, and will continue to be, fluid items of continued contest. Modern Thailand is only that part of the great lowland, and a share of upland, chiefly settled by infiltrating Thais, which neither British nor French rivalry could further partition without invoking too great protest from the other. Political and cultural nationalism is new to the individualistic Thai peoples, and its rise among them may well provoke further boundary issues. This new nationalism shows up in the very name of the country, for the people of the "land of the Syam" changed their country's name from Siam to Thailand only in 1939. Its meaning, the "land of the free," is largely one of linguistic and political definition.

THE DEVELOPMENT OF AGRICULTURE

Much that was said of Burma in the section on Economic Background applies equally well to Thailand. Substitute Thais for Burmans and Shans, and Chinese for Indians, and the story reads similarly. Details vary slightly, for the dry zone of the Chao Phraya Valley is less pronounced than that of the Irrawaddy, the Korat Platform is not the equivalent of the Shan Plateau, and the culture histories of the two areas are not totally alike. But the Chao Phraya Delta has come into full occupation as recently as has that of the Irrawaddy. Although the British here have had no territorial political control they early secured a leading role in the foreign trade economy. The Thai have long been a people well acquainted with rice growing, and rice was the basic crop of the Khmer state throughout its long period.

And yet not all of Thailand is easily available to productive agriculture. The lower Chao Phraya Valley and its delta form an aquatic region in which the very volume of water makes major diking and canal systems necessary for full cultivation and productive use. In most of the lowlands outside the lower Chao Phraya Valley the seasonality of precipitation and flood runoff has long meant that there has been a scarcity of water for crop irrigation and this problem has been very severe in the Korat Plateau. Even in the Chao Phraya Valley if the summer flood does not develop adequate volume much rice land today goes without water and the crop fails, a happenstance that occurs every few years. The large areas of poor soils containing laterite horizons, and the wide expanses of heavy clays, have meant that soils in much of the country are poor and difficult to work. Many areas of Thailand have old and stable soils, now leached and impoverished; these areas actually would benefit from some erosion that would expose unleached soil materials.

Although rice has long been the basic food crop of the area that we now label Thailand, early agriculture was far more general than it is today, for it was a subsistence agriculture that grew a wide range of crops. Aquatic products such as fish and taro helped broaden the diet and the base of local support. Some of the fruits and vegetables have long been here, if they are not native, whereas others were brought in from Indonesia or India by early trader-colonists.

With maturity of Thai government and the coming of the European diking and drainage systems, canals began to be built in large numbers in the Chao Phraya Valley. With the development of trade in basic consumption products and the decline in native handicrafts, the rice landscape began to expand and Thailand began to be a significant exporter of large volumes of rice after about 1880. This expansion has continued so that much of Thailand today seems to possess a monocrop agriculture (Fig. 18.1). Hundreds of rice varieties are grown, in situations closely adapted to local needs,

ranging from short-season glutinous rices to long-season hard rices, and from varieties adapted to rather dry soils to those termed "floating" rices, adapted to keeping their heads above very deep flooding, though productivity is not always at the highest level. New high-yielding varieties are now being grown, and newer technologies, including better water control and fertilization procedures, are improving the general per-acre yield in many areas today. Actually the height of the dominance of rice in the agricultural scene probably has passed, owing to governmental stimulation of new crop and diversification programs. Much of the wet lowland, however, is not easily put into other crops. The present dominance of rice is statistical, produced by its overwhelming acreage in the wet, lower Chao Phraya Valley. Outside the lower valley rice is the most common food crop, but its comparative position is less obvious. It would seem that almost eighty percent of the crop land is devoted to some kind of rice, and that almost ninety percent of all farms grow some rice, but this may derive from inadequate data on dooryard gardens, areas of shifting cultivation, and the patchy nature of many of the complementary crops grown.

In peninsular Thailand rice lands are scattered in small patches only. Fruits and vegetables together bulk larger than rice in the income pattern. Rubber and coconut here are commercial crops, but they are minor in the subsistence culture of local communities, since both are cash crops shipped outside the region. In the hill country along the western border shifting cultivation, subsistence culture, and a few local specialty crops dominate the economy. In northern Thailand wet rice-fields string out along the valleys and shifting cultivation ranges into the uplands in the hands of various tribal groups. A few specialty crops are also produced here, such as pickled tea for chewing rather than for use as a beverage, tung oil, and certain fruits. Much of the rice grown in the north is

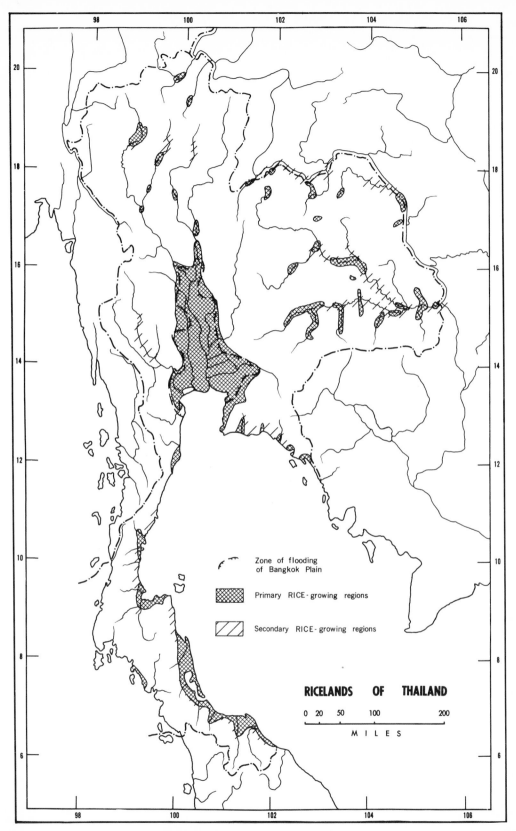

FIGURE 18.1. The ricelands of Thailand.

385

glutinous rice, grown for home consumption, not readily acceptable in export commerce. Throughout Korat permanent rice lands lie along the rivers and around local sources of water, and glutinous rice for home use is more common than the nonglutinous varieties.

Shifting cultivation is practiced on many hillside areas which actually have higher fertility than many of the highly leached lowland areas. Both Thai and tribal peoples practice shifting agriculture as a necessary complement to their permanent farming. There still is reserve land in northern Thailand and in the Korat Plateau, on which extensive pioneer shifting cultivation is practiced as a permanent cropping system or as a prelude to permanent farming.

Everywhere in Thailand fruits and vegetables are grown for local home and market village use. Bananas, jack, breadfruit, papaya, mangoes, rambutan, and citrus are the chief items, but the whole range of tropical fruits is to be found. The commercial trends that have come to affect rice culture do not yet strongly affect these garden and jungle crops, except around the larger cities, for the lack of transportation prevents a commercialization of this type of agriculture. The commercial fruit and vegetable area of western Thonburi, as a modern Bangkok market source, is now notable. There is not much specialization, the more common items being raised all over the country, though peninsular and southeastern Thailand find fruit culture relatively more important than elsewhere. Areas devoted to fruit culture resemble mixed jungle forests rather than orchards because they are a traditional part of the economy. Orchards are not often segregated plantings on fully cleared lands. Fruit and vegetable culture on wet lowlands must use ridges for plantings, with numerous interspersed drainage ditches.

Besides fruits and vegetables some minor crops are of general and local importance. Various of these are increasing steadily in importance as contemporary Thai agriculture is restoring the former pattern of more adequately-based diversity. Tobacco, sugar cane, manioc, legumes, maize, pepper, betel nut, coconuts or sesame for edible oils, rubber, cotton, and such other crops as ramie, sunn hemp, and kenaf are widely scattered in small plantings. Cotton has been a traditional crop in many parts of Thailand, but the other minor fibers remain in small production. Coconut palms formerly were more widely distributed than at present, but diseases and pests have restricted their distribution and their local usages. The palmyra palm, for sugar and leaves, and the areca palm for its nut, are important in many parts of Thailand. Rubber plantings are now scattered in peninsular Thailand, and the commercial aspect of rubber production is now increasing steadily.

Animal husbandry forms a larger segment of Thailand's economy than it does in Burma. Both native cattle and water buffalo are numerous and distributed over the country. The whole of the Chao Phraya Valley does not produce adequate numbers of animals, and in Korat animal husbandry has both a domestic and a commercial aspect on small farms. Korat supplies the rest of the country with its draft animals, and a volume of livestock for export. Chickens are kept in small numbers almost everywhere, and in aquatic situations both Thais and Chinese breed large numbers of ducks. Among the Chinese pigs are common, as they also are in the north country where the Chinese tradition is stronger and the hold of traditional Buddhism is less restrictive. Korat exports live pigs to lower Thailand. In the north country horses are used chiefly as pack animals. Elephants are used in the teak forests, but elsewhere they are chiefly religious and ceremonial animals. Although the Thais widely participate in animal husbandry, they formerly ate little meat, as fish took the place of meat in the Buddhist dietary. This pattern appears to be changing at present toward a larger consumption of meat products. Thailand has had a traditional livestock export, and this continues at present.

The total land in farms appears to be about 26,000,000 acres, of which about 22,000,000 are in regular cultivation, involving about 800,000, or slightly more, acres cropped by shifting cultivation every year. In the 1880's the rice acreage stood at about 2,500,000 acres, as needed to serve the domestic market and a very small export volume. Within the next decade it started increasing, rising to about 4,000,000 acres in 1905, climbed to 14,000,000 by 1950, and in 1970 stood close to 16,000,000 acres. No other single food crop occupies a large acreage, though the total of fruit and vegetable gardens reaches about 1,500,000 acres. The total rubber acreage, both in small holdings and in plantation-size plantings, in peninsular Thailand is just under 1,000,000 acres, about half of which is owned by Chinese in both small and large plantings. Coconuts cover about 250,000 acres, and such crops as maize, sugarcane, pulses, peanuts, and tobacco probably average in the vicinity of 200,000 acres each in most years, with a number of specialty crops using only small acreages. A good share of the rice acreage increase is, of course, in the lower Chao Phraya Valley where near-monocrop landscapes appear, but since almost all farms grow some rice, the increase in rice acreage is not limited to the Bangkok Plain, as is so often stated.

Recent multiple-use water conservation projects are beginning to have significant effects, and these effects will continue in the future to alter aspects of Thai agriculture. Water storage dams for hydroelectric, irrigation, and flood control purposes may well lessen the annual flood in the lower Chao Phraya Valley, increasing the irrigated crop acreages in central and northern Thailand, thus requiring new irrigation projects in southern Thailand formerly dependent upon maximum flooding for productivity. Numerous projects in Korat, linked into the Lower Mekong River Basin Project, will provide both electric power and dry-season irrigation water, slowly changing the picture of regional agriculture there (see Fig. 19.6 for the Korat developments in the western portion of the Mekong Basin project). The long-term implications of these and future projects will be to decrease the seasonal hazard in Thai agricultural economy, aiding patterns of diversification.

As the traditionally agrarian Thai took over the political territory they now hold, the tenure of land posed no strong problem since the conceptual pattern involved the assumption of Thai legal control over the lands of the "state." Population densities were sufficiently low that the traditional concept of individual occupance and cultivation of plots of ground was sufficient guarantee of possession, even to the recognition of possessory rights by such non-Thai ethnic elements as remained within the territory considered as the Thai political state. Customary law recognized the concept of usufructory rights to land actually occupied and cropped, whether sedentary occupance or shifting cultivation was involved. In theory, of course, the overriding concept held that all lands belonged to the king, but that *de facto* occupancy and cultivation by individual families resulted both in the rights of occupancy and the rights of protection by the king from molestation by others and from deprivation from any source. As the Thai population grew larger and the political bounds of the Thai state became more clearly identified, customary law continued in practice, with only minor and local kinds of difficulties normal to rural agrarian societies. At the start of the present century, however, Thai political theory introduced new concepts of control over land, by which legal distinctions were made between occupancy and ownership. Adjustments between customary law and modern legal concepts have been made, and in the current era there is clear distinction between occupance, utilization, and legal ownership.

At present there is confusion in the matter of control over land, since many agrarian families have been in the habit of occupying land cultivated by shifting cultivation, assuming traditional usufructory rights. As the population of Thailand has grown, there have remained fewer and fewer plots of land of the unoccupied sort open to occupance-cultivation by shifting cultivation. The tendency has been to occupy lands, employ shifting cultivation in annual stages until the whole plot is brought under control, and then to become sedentary occupants of all, or part, of the lands initially occupied. The landscape of sedentary occupance has, thus, grown steadily, and the zone of occupance by shifting cultivation has either disappeared entirely (within a well-settled locality) or tended to become a marginal frontier. Since few rural agrarian families have understood the complications of the new land control concepts, which distinguish *de facto* from *de jure* possessory rights, there is coming a growing amount of difficulty in many parts of Thailand concerning rights of legal ownership of land, of disposal of land, and the questions of tenancy. It is customary to say that about ninety percent of Thai families are owners of the lands they cultivate, but this follows the older concepts of customary law. In the fully-occupied portions of Thailand, such as the lower Chao Phraya Valley, there now are arising problems concerning all the aspects of land control. It is a safe current generalization that throughout Thailand farmers are "owners" of the lands they cultivate, and are neither tenants nor deeply in debt, but in the lower Chao Phraya Valley the modern issues are joined, and landlordism, tenancy, debt accumulation, shifting of tenants, and rural dissatisfaction over mat-

ters of land control are accumulating in the wake of commercialized rice, fruit, and vegetable farming, and they are accumulating in those localities in which lands go out of agricultural use into other use categories. This is another area in which the historic circumstance of the noncolonial history of Thailand becomes significant since, in most countries that went through a colonial period, the issues of land systems saw a much earlier readjustment between the body of land law involving customary law and modern juridical law.

SUBORDINATE ELEMENTS OF THE ECONOMY

Thailand long appeared to be one of the least mineralized countries in the world; surveys are not yet complete but it would now appear that Thailand does possess a sufficient range of minerals in adequate volume to support a modest domestic start in many aspects of metals manufacturing. Peninsular Thailand shares in the tin resources of the rest of Southeast Asia, and tin for export has been the most important mineral product in the past. The country produces its own supply of salt for use in the fisheries industry, and for domestic consumption, from evaporated sea water or from springs and wells in Korat. There has long been enough lateritic iron ore to permit handicraft manufacturing of such iron products as the traditional economy demanded in the past, and supplies of a few other common minerals have long been adequate for handicraft manufacturing. Laterite as a building stone exists in quantity, and a few localities have produced precious stones. Future survey may disclose sufficient mineral resources to remove Thailand from her present "have not" position in respect to minerals.

Between sixty-five and seventy-five percent of Thailand still is in some kind of productive forest, dependent on the definition used. The northwest has shared the distribution of teak forests and long has been an exporter of this and a few other varieties of timber, though the large-volume export of teak began only in the late nineteenth century. The best of the teak is now gone, and cultural forestry has not adequately replaced it, so that the contemporary teak export industry is faltering. Lac, rattans, some gums and resins, and a few other forest products are traditional exports which retain a place in foreign trade. Thailand today is one of the sources for wild animals for sale throughout the world. There is a considerable domestic trade in lumber, firewood, and charcoal from the margins of the country into the Chao Phraya Valley. Modern commercial forestry is only beginning to tap the resources of the country other than teak, and Thailand could support a considerable forest industry.

Aquatic resources have been a traditional part of lowland economy in all parts of Thailand. Everywhere in the lowlands some areas are flooded in the high-water season, and these form important fishing waters. About half the farm families engage in some degree of fishing most of the year in order to provide fishery products for their daily dietary. Korat and the upper Mekong Valley have shared in this, and only the hill country of northern and western Thailand does not have local sources of fish and related aquatic foods. The Gulf of Siam and the coastal waters of the peninsula have long been important sources of fishery products, and today these waters play an important role in domestic economy of the country, since fishery products form the second most important article of diet. Marine fisheries actually provide the larger volume of Thai fishery products, the total of which may come to about 300,000 tons per year. A few fish are raised in ponds, but this aspect of fisheries has never been practiced as it might be; it

forms an important aspect of future development.

The waterways of the country have long been the most important routes of traffic flow (Fig. 18.2). The main Chao Phraya Valley was thus oriented toward the Gulf of Siam, but much of Korat was oriented toward the Mekong, away from the Chao Phraya Valley. And the north country, not well served by the Chao Phraya river system, traditionally was connected to Yunnan and the Shan Plateau by overland pack trails. Modern Thailand is a country of numerous cart and pack train trails, and the Korat Plateau is criss-crossed by an old network of cart roads, but the modern development of canals in the Chao Phraya Valley has heightened the problems of road building in the wet lowland. Surfaced highways are now being extended to all parts of the country as trunk-line key roads, and a program of secondary road building is in process, but it will be some years before the secondary network provides effective transport to all rural areas. In 1970 the total of all-weather roads stood close to 7,500 miles, with many projects still under construction. The short rail mileage was built with an eye to tightening the bonds of transport within the country. Although the mileage is only about 2,200, and though the traffic load is not great, the rail system has brought the peninsula, the north country, and Korat into better connection with the Chao Phraya Valley than they have ever experienced before. Although the rail lines cannot serve the whole hinterland of each of these outer regions, they do serve to establish a means of traffic routing which has now re-oriented each of these regions toward the Chao Phraya Valley. The Thai were among the first orientals to take up aviation, and though the number of fields is not large, even now air traffic is significant in volume and also helps orient the Korat region toward the Chao Phraya Valley.

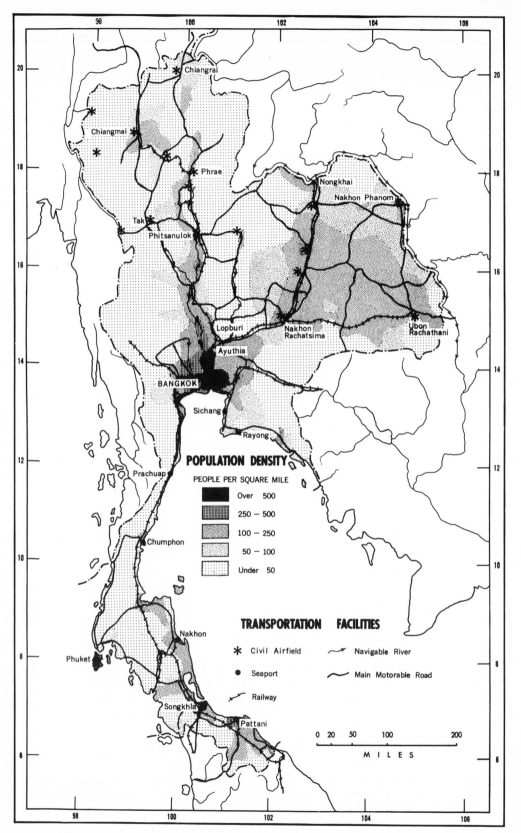

FIGURE 18.2. Transportation facilities and population density in Thailand.

390

In the eighteenth century Thailand's handicraft production was a fairly considerable one, but it had not developed a mature pattern. Gradually imported consumer goods undermined this volume and variety of manufacturing and, as the expansion of rice agriculture in the lower Chao Phraya Valley developed after 1880, the Thais lost more and more of their old technical skills and became more fully agricultural. Chinese and occidental integration of control over the foreign trade of Thailand brought the Chinese into rather complete control of internal trade and occidental firms into control of foreign trade, with the result that most of the manufactured commodities of foreign origin required in Thailand were imported and distributed by aliens. The Chinese are concentrated in Bangkok, but they are scattered throughout the country in the towns and market villages, whereas occidentals have congregated chiefly in Bangkok. Very few branch manufacturing establishments were set up, since Thailand did not become a colonial holding in which governmental regulation could foster such development.

Since the late nineteenth century, governmental awareness of the changing conditions of manufacturing and trade have caused numerous efforts to establish modern factory production in a variety of lines. In recent decades government policy has vacillated between taking over all alien-controlled industries and starting new ventures of a competitive sort. World War II interrupted this program, but it now is in process again. The chief problem has been that Thailand has not yet acquired an adequate volume and range of modern skills in management or technology—there was neither an experienced governmental nor private industrial core of personnel available in Thailand such as developed in India or the Philippines during the period of British or American colonial control. Although Thailand escaped colonial domination Thais acquired little of the training in modern management and commercial-industrial enterprise that a colonial population often learns as it moves toward freedom and economic participation in the modern world.

In very recent decades this inadequacy has been lessening rapidly as Thailand has been placing emphasis upon modernization in economic patterns. Legislation toward nationalization of industry and trade is not being pushed, though the railways, airlines, and broadcasting are government operated, and government projects are being developed in several industrial fields. Rice mills, saw mills, and pottery kilns used to be the most numerous "industrial" concerns, but this no longer is true, as many new types of manufacturing, fabricating, and light industrial establishments and private entrepreneurial undertakings are being organized at the present time. Government factories now produce paper, sugar, cotton and silk textiles, cement, refined petroleum, cigarettes, boats and small ships, canned foods, and a few similar products. A start has been made, but it supplies only a share of the needed consumer goods and very few of the producer goods. Future progress will depend upon a realistic approach to the problems of training of technologists and managers. The situation is complicated by a nationalistic trend in economic policy which is ahead of native developed capacity, and by the intrenched position of the Chinese merchant community in respect to internal trade. Thailand has now begun formal planning for economic development, and is completing its second five year plan, from 1967 through 1971. Currently, of course, with major transportation projects being constructed with aid from the United States, and with wide-ranging economic programs receiving United States financial and technical aid, the currents of economic change in Thailand are moving rapidly. New factories of modern types are being set up rapidly in advance of the normal sequences of the growth of manufacturing. For example, Thailand now produces its own freight and passenger cars for its rail system, eliminating the export drain. The quasi-military nature of United States aid to Thailand, in 1970, obscures the nature of economic development in the country.

Prior to 1850 Thailand did carry on some foreign trade, but it was a relatively unimportant element in the whole of Thailand's economy. Foreign trade normally resulted in a strong favorable balance of trade, since imports were few, and there was export in cane sugar, hides and skins, raw cotton, several kinds of woods, some tin, lac, and rice, in that order of importance. The exports of sugar dropped off after 1880, and the cotton export almost ceased during the 1890's, but the rice trade began to grow slowly and, in the late nineteenth century, the teak trade began to grow significantly. Around 1900 the rice export jumped rather markedly, and rubber began to be an export item by about 1910. During the early part of this century rice, rubber, teak, and tin, in that order of importance, supplied as much as ninety percent of the favorable export balance.

At the present time rice remains Thailand's chief export, the annual volume ranging somewhat above 1,000,000 tons in good growing years, supplying about half the export earnings. Rubber, teak, and tin remain significant exports, and the export volume of maize has been growing steadily. Livestock, hides and skins, lac, gums-resins, tapioca, castor beans, salt, and small volumes of other agricultural products round out the export list. The import trade has grown very rapidly since 1900, and Thailand currently is suffering an unfavorable balance of trade as the consumer trend and the pattern of economic development continue to demand large volumes of import goods of all kinds. Cotton textiles and cotton yarns now lead the import list, but large-volume items are in prepared food products, petroleum, machinery, and industrial equipment, fol-

lowed by a wide range of manufactured items in small annual volumes. With the rise of the export volume of rice Malaysia, Hongkong, and Indonesia have become important customers of Thailand. In the general flow of foreign trade Japan is today the chief trading partner of Thailand, taking exports and supplying Thailand with imports. Important trading also occurs between Great Britain, United States, and India. In recent years Thailand has made a strong effort to broaden the range of her foreign trade partners, and in 1968 a long-term trade compact with Romania was concluded, presaging other agreements with East European countries. The great share of foreign trade is handled through Bangkok and its coastal outport.

THE REGIONALISM OF MODERN THAILAND

Conventionally the country is divided into five regions: the peninsula, the Chao Phraya Valley, southeast Thailand, the northeast or Korat, and the northern hill country. This division omits border areas and is a too simplified set of divisions based primarily on location. Culture history suggests that the present political unit is an artificial one, based more upon political strength than upon distinctive cultural and environmental elements. Thai governmental structure has steadily rearranged its administrative divisions in a search for satisfactory spatial patterns. The late eighteenth-century pattern involved some sixty regional units, and the number has gone both higher and lower. There now are nine major regional districts composed of seventy-one provinces or *changwats*. Thai operation of their geographical territory has not yet found stable regional bases upon which to establish administrative patterns. Actually, sectionalism is more important than regionalism, as people in Korat complain that Bangkok neglects problems in Korat in favor of development in the lower

Chao Phraya plain, and as Islamic Malays in the southern peninsula demand both attention and more local autonomy.

The population map suggests that the central and lower Chao Phraya Valley is the key population region, correlating with the key agricultural region (compare Figs. 18.1 and 18.2). Culturally the Thais have spread their patterns over almost all the lowland. The imposition of the Thai language upon the political state has today made almost all the lowland a Thai region, with the southern peninsula and the hill country margins still speaking variant tongues. In the southernmost peninsular zone are about 750,000 Islamic Malay-speaking people, in the west are Karen, and in the northwest both Shan and Wa-Palaung peoples overlap into Thailand. All through the north country are Yao, Miao, and other peoples who have moved out of China. The Mekong Valley border zone has many small remnant groups, some of whom also are found in the southeastern margin of the country. Near the Cambodian border are many Khmers. The Chinese are chiefly urban and market-town dwellers among the lowland Thai, and Bangkok has 500,000 or more Chinese, depending on the precise definition used. The Chinese are not culturally integrated in their own right, for they speak at least six different dialectic languages, and have important intraminority patterns of cleavage. Currently nationalistic education is attempting to nationalize all parts of the country culturally, aiming chiefly at the urban Chinese of the Chao Phraya Valley and the Islamic Malays of the southern peninsula, but its administration does not yet carry to all parts of the rural back country. Assessing the scene vertically, it appears that Thai culture dominates the lowlands and that, in the hill country margins, there are horizontal layerings of non-Thai peoples, each occupying an altitudinal plane, with the recent Miao immigrants out of China occupying the highest levels in the northernmost portion of the country.

In one sense Thailand is too new a country to show emphatic regionalisms. Clearly the Chao Phraya Valley lowland is developing one pattern, and the peninsular and hill margins show other patterns. Korat is clearly different than the southern peninsular zone, but the bounding lines of regionalisms have not yet become obvious and clearly distinguishable. Modern Thailand does not display the emphatic regionalisms that show so clearly in other parts of the Orient. One notable item is the current contrast between Bangkok as a quite modern city in many respects and the rest of Thailand. In part this is the urban impact of modernization, but its most current aspect relates to the presence of many Americans in the city, with changes being brought to the urban scene.

Except for the peninsula the outlying portions of Thailand are populated beyond capacity for an advancing level of living based upon a simple agricultural economy. These are the regions infiltrated by the peoples out of China, and their continuing long-term tendency is to push toward the Chao Phraya Valley lowland.

The total population of Thailand climbed slowly during the earlier centuries, but since the late seventeenth century it has been rising rapidly. The earliest reliable figure is that of 1854, a total of about 6,000,000. The total had climbed to 14,500,000 in 1937, was estimated at very close to 19,000,000 at the end of 1952, and is estimated at 35,700,000 in 1970. Bangkok-Thonburi, as the one large urban area, held almost ten percent of the total population of the country in 1970 (see Fig. 18.2).

19

CAMBODIA

The homeland of the Khmers is again an independent political state, the modern descendant of the great Khmer Empire of earlier centuries. Cambodia today is a very different political state than its ancestor, for it today is a small state of 70,000 square miles between the territories of Thailand and Vietnam, the two states that caused the final demise of the great empire (see Figs. 16.2 and 19.7). Its 1970 population of about 7,000,000 is probably larger than that of the whole Khmer Empire at its height. Whereas the ancestor state was the dominant power in Southeast Asia in the early thirteenth century, modern Cambodia is subject to many political pressures and has elected to play the role of the small neutralist state whose very survival depends largely on international political agreement and its own neutral position in the militant and turbulent environment in which it now exists. And, whereas the ancestor could draw tribute from a wide zone and many subservient peoples, Cambodia today depends very considerably upon its export of rubber, rice, and maize to bring its people such products from abroad as they can afford. The great empire was a thriving land in which public resources were devoted to the construction of architecturally lavish temples, but Cambodia today is a largely forested and unused land filled with temple ruins. Borrowed funds now are building roads and manufacturing plants

of modern technological variety. The scale of operations in the "outside world" has altered greatly, and modern Cambodia, after a long period of quiescence, is struggling to find its proper place in today's larger world.

The Khmer Empire was at its height in the thirteenth century, at which point politico-economic control stretched far beyond the borders of the core region. Khmer society of that era was marked by adherence of the upper social levels to Mahayana Buddhism, and a strongly stratified culture system was dominated by its leadership's devotion to costly monumental religious architecture, in which the very continuance of the culture system depended significantly upon economic support from the politically tributary regions. By the end of the fourteenth century, the economic and military strength of Khmer society began to decline as a result of political restriction upon all its borders. With the empire reduced to little more than its core region the era of monumental architecture came to an end. During the thirteenth and fourteenth centuries there was a notable shift from Mahayana Buddhism to Theravada Buddhism throughout the core region, and this shift may well help to account for the lessened accent on monumental religious architecture and the abandonment of the old temples. By the end of the fourteenth century the home population remained more or less intact, Khmer culture retained its intrinsic temporal characteristics, and the political state remained functional, although by that date the state clearly was on the defensive in protecting its core region. In none of the many wars with the Vietnamese, Chams, Thais, and island world sea-states during those two centuries did there occur permanent conquest and occupation of the core region. A reduced population, intent on its own local continuance, neither needed nor could maintain the great temples, the extensive water systems, or even all the crop lands that had supported the larger urban populations of the great empire. Angkor was abandoned as a capital in the 1430's, and all future capitals were located at some point near the present Phnom Penh, as various later kings built new "cities" at different points in the local region. The basic Khmer pattern of life, in the fifteenth century, settled down to an austere local regional system in which rice cultivation provided basic support, a fishing economy provided a complement, and there was little extra-regional economic exchange. Although many of its crop lands became overgrown with forest, its innumerable temples and monasteries became deserted and forest grown, and its political and cultural power became diminished, Khmer society did not vanish as is so often inferred in popular writing about Angkor.

Continued harassment by Thai and Vietnamese military expeditions continued during the sixteenth century, involving the weakened Khmer state in costly defensive wars. By the late sixteenth century Cambodia was almost powerless to prevent repeated invasions and exactions, and it is from this period that the true quiescence of Cambodia should probably be dated. Military raids, interference in local affairs, and alternating dominance from both Thailand and Vietnam continued right into the early nineteenth century, by which date Cambodia had lost control over several border provinces. In the early nineteenth century Thailand and Vietnam were intermittently at war about control over Cambodia, and during the 1850's the two countries were sharing this control over Cambodia. Cambodia faced virtual political annihilation by the time the French began seriously building their colonial empire in the mid-nineteenth century. In 1863 a French protectorate was sought as a means of preventing total dismemberment of the now prostrate Cambodian state by Thailand and Vietnam. The French accepted the request for a protectorate, ultimately to interpret that offer to mean much more French control than was assumed by the Cambodian king who sought it, and Cambodia became the second territorial unit in the expansion of the French colonial empire in this part of the world.

If this new political status involved true colonial status, rather than a simple military protectorate, it at least maintained the territorial integrity of the core region of the old Khmer Empire, since France did move against Thailand to force the restoration to Cambodia of the several western border provinces that had been permanently occupied by Thailand, which provinces included Angkor and a valuable rice-producing sector of western Cambodia. The French also maintained the prestige and status of the monarchical institutions of government, by which a Cambodian king continued to be the focus of national and cultural consciousness among the Khmer, and which, until 1970, was a strong element of stability in the resurgence of modern Cambodia as a political state. Other elements in this resurgence contributed by the French were the patterns of relative peace which ensued within Cambodia (despite later local anti-French rebellions), the restructuring and strengthening of the institutions of local government, the abolition of slavery, and the exploratory archeology carried on by French scholars in uncovering, restoring, and interpreting the monumental architectural grandeur and political history of the great age of Khmer culture. Lesser French contributions were the development of a fair network of roads, and the institution of systems of courts and justice in which all members of Khmer society were given much more egalitarian consideration than had ever occurred in the high stratified social structure of the old empire. Phnom Penh was made the new capital in 1867, and in due course the French added the proper political architectural monuments to the city. Unlike Tonking's experience in lower-level participation in colonial "economic exploitation," Cambodia received very little impetus or economic education from French control since France saw very little in Cambodia worth economic development.

French protective control of Cambodian foreign affairs, and the maintenance of a native Cambodian political structure of the state, preserved the territory and the form of the political state of Cambodia, yet did not prevent internal control by the French. Amalgamation of Cambodia into the Indochinese Union in 1887, made possible the peaceful movement of Vietnamese into Cambodia as settlers on the lightly populated landscape, and by the end of World War II nearly 250,000 Vietnamese had taken up farm lands in southeastern Cambodia, and were spreading around the shores of the Tonle Sap. By the date of Cambodian independence, in 1954, this number had risen to over 300,000. French control also permitted the influx of Chinese into Cambodia, and by the date of Cambodian independence there were about 250,000 Chinese resident in the country. The Vietnamese settled on some of the best agricultural lands, were active in the fishing industries, and were numerous in the civil government bureaucracy, and the Chinese were in the process of gathering into their hands control of most of the domestic trade of Cambodia. Cambodia seemed about to lose even ethnic dominance in her own country, and was in danger of losing internal control of her domestic economy, when World War II and its aftermath brought the weakened French to the granting of independence. Cambodian resurgence of Theravada Buddhism, and the popularity of the monarchical institutions of government were the immediate rallying points for the pressures on France for independence. The skilful manipulation in internal domestic politics by aristocratic Cambodian leadership brought complete political independence to Cambodia in 1954. That independence, of course, remains precarious in the Southeast Asia of today, and only time may tell whether the land of the Khmers will have found its place in the modern world.

The Cambodia of today is the primary portion of the core region of the old Khmer Empire, being somewhat reduced on the eastern margin by the exclusion of the upper delta lands of the Mekong River (see Figs. 6.5 and 6.6). In physical form the country is a great shallow saucer with an elongated bottom occupied by the Tonle Sap (Great Lake). The northern and southern margins of the country are hilly to mountainous, the central western margin is a rolling plain providing a drainage divide, and the eastern margin is cut by the Mekong River, so that the saucer drainage system forms a Mekong tributary unit. Within the mountain margins there is a ring of rolling to hilly lands which gently taper off into the central alluvial plain which surrounds the Tonle Sap. Nowhere is the mountain margin severe or impenetrable. The alluvial plain has a very slight gradient toward the Tonle Sap, so that in the summer flood season the lake expands from two to four times its 1,000 square mile dry-season area, as the seasonal Mekong River flood volume backs into the bottom of the saucer, to create a great shallow flood reservoir. A very large share of Cambodia, therefore, forms a watery alluvial plain environment that is amenable to some system of human use, and the Cambodian livelihood structure has long utilized both the aquatic and land elements of this rich region. Today well over half the country is still in some kind of forest, and primary human occupance lies in a ring around the lake and in the eastern zone near the Mekong River flood plains.

ECONOMY

Traditionally the livelihood structure of Cambodia has rested on an agricultural-handicraft economy, complemented by a very small amount of foreign trade since the great era of the past. During the 1930's probably ninety percent of all Cambodians were crop growers or fishermen, often combining the two occupations. By that date the Vietnamese and Chinese already had secured a strong hold on domestic trade and the various professional services. The foreign trade volume was handled by Chinese merchants working through French companies.

Although a basic road system was then operative for communications purposes, and a rail line operated from Phnom Penh into western Cambodia, waterways served the heart of the country in the movement of commodities. There were such agricultural processing facilities as saw mills, rice mills, oil presses, and latex rendering plants, and a few electric plants, but very few other manufacturing facilities were classifiable as industrial plants. There was almost no Cambodian middle class, some of the Vietnamese and Chinese occupying the equivalent stratum of society. A relatively small Cambodian upper class dominated government and participated in some commercial activities. The agricultural pattern was traditional, based primarily on the cultivation of rice by wet fields and by shifting cultivation (Fig. 19.1). Small acreages of fruits, vege-

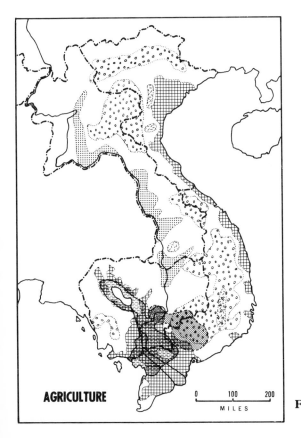

AGRICULTURE

0   100   200
MILES

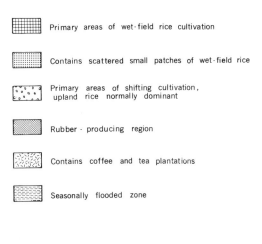

Primary areas of wet-field rice cultivation

Contains scattered small patches of wet-field rice

Primary areas of shifting cultivation, upland rice normally dominant

Rubber - producing region

Contains coffee and tea plantations

Seasonally flooded zone

FIGURE 19.1. Agriculture in Laos, Cambodia, North Vietnam, and South Vietnam.

tables, and complementary crops were grown chiefly in small gardens in a rather wide ranging variety, with maize and various beans being the most frequent complements. In eastern Cambodia small rubber plantations, chiefly owned by French and Chinese, produced an annual volume of a nonfood export commodity. The foreign trade economy rested on the rubber-rice-maize export, complemented by very small volumes of other items, affording a small import of manufactured goods. Cambodia has few known minerals and such resources have not been export commodities here, unlike all other former colonial lands (Fig. 19.2).

Since the end of World War II, markedly stimulated by independence in 1954, Cambodia has been engaged in an active program of modernization and upgrading of her economy, though it is hardly possible to refer to this as the development of any true program of industrialization in so small a country. The road system has been augmented, the rail line connects Phnom Penh both northwestward to Thailand and south to the recently-built port of Sihanoukville (Kompong Som), and air services now provide communication to major portions of the country (Fig. 19.3). Political restrictions have been placed on economic and occupational activities of Vietnamese and Chinese, and the Cambodian government is energetically trying to develop the nonagricultural elements of a rounded economy. Both state-controlled and private developments are being encouraged. Recently established small hydroelectric power systems at regional centers around the upland margins of the country will pro-

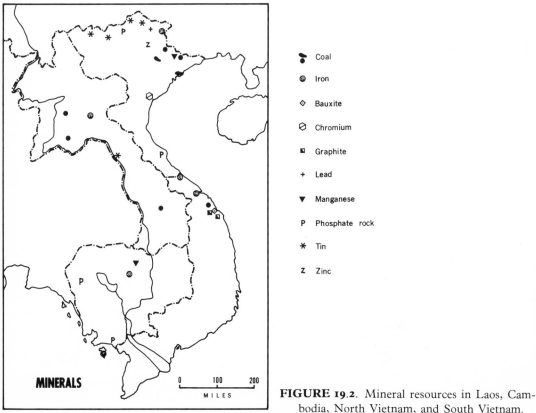

FIGURE 19.2. Mineral resources in Laos, Cambodia, North Vietnam, and South Vietnam.

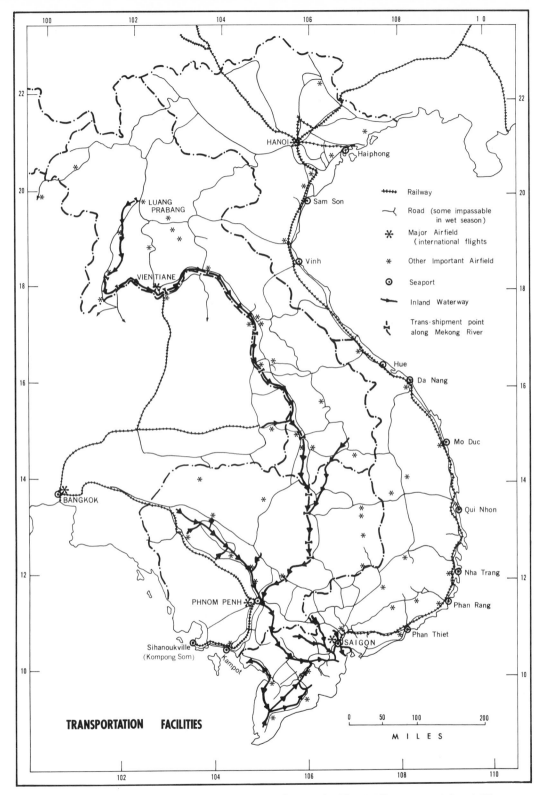

FIGURE 19.3. Transportation facilities in Laos, Cambodia, North Vietnam, and South Vietnam.

vide sufficient power to operate modern industrial factories of a variety providing both semifinished products and consumer goods.

Much of this new development is being located at Sihanoukville (Kompong Som) or at Phnom Penh, but new modern factories are also being located in provincial towns around the country. In Sihanoukville (Kompong Som), in 1970, there were operative a petroleum refinery, a brewery, textile plants, a cement factory, a paper factory, and small shipbuilding facilities, and this core of plants will be added to in future years. Operative or under construction in 1970 in or near Phnom Penh were modern plants producing textiles, paper, plywood, vegetable oils, pumps and other light machinery, glass, and fertilizers. A small steel plant using scrap materials produced wire, nails, and steel for construction purposes. Around Phnom Penh there also are numerous agricultural processing and food preserving plants of many sorts. In various provincial towns textile mills, fertilizer factories, agricultural processing plants, and small machinery works are operative or under construction in 1970. Modern water purification plants are now operative at Sihanoukville (Kompong Som), Phnom Penh, and other provincial towns. Most of this new construction has been and is being carried on through foreign technical programs arranged with a wide distribution of agreements between Cambodia and other governments, to prevent too strong participation by any one country. Cambodia has rejected various aid proposals when strings were attached, and it is clear that the Cambodian government seeks to prevent too great economic penetration by specific countries.

For all that programs of modernization are going on in Cambodia, the economy still rests on its agricultural base. To date only about a half of the arable land is in cultivation, with a total of about 5,000,000 acres in farms. The rice acreage is approaching 3,500,000 acres and yields close to 3,000,000 tons per year in good years, rice being the dominant crop cultivated. The maize acreage is increasing steadily, in 1970 standing at about 600,000 acres, much of the maize crop going into the export trade. The rubber acreage has been expanded over the pre-war pattern, in both plantations and small holdings, reaching close to 125,000 acres in 1969, though much of this was rendered nonproductive during recent warfare. Under government planning there is a beginning in sugarcane on the plantation scale, aimed at domestic self-sufficiency in sugar. A very wide range of other crops in small acreages complements the agricultural economy. Much of this, of course, is in the traditional tropical fruits and vegetables (bananas, citrus, mangoes, coconut, sugar palm, and manioc, taro, cucumbers, various beans, and leafy vegetables), but plantings of tea, coffee, cotton, jute, and ramie are being encouraged as complementary to domestic consumer needs. Pepper production has been largely controlled by Chinese, but its production is being enlarged in area and improved in quality.

Traditionally the Tonle Sap has provided the main complement to Cambodian domestic economy in its fishery. The annual summer flood season involves inland-water spawning of many species of fish, and the Tonle Sap produces one of the highest world fishery yields on a square mile basis. Around its changing shore line are many fishing villages built on piles, inhabited both by Cambodian and Vietnamese, that engage in full-time fishing activities; away from the winter shore fringe are other villages whose inhabitants are summer fishermen. Marine fishing around the southern coast is being expanded markedly in the current era, and the 175,000 tons of fishery products now afford a minor but significant element in the export economy.

The foreign trade pattern of Cambodia

annually sees about 300,000 tons of rice going into the export trade, along with about 14,000 tons of maize, 60,000 tons of rubber, and small volumes of fishery products, pepper, livestock, and forest products. Currently, of course, an unknown volume of rice, maize, and fish disappear into the smuggling trade along the eastern border almost impossible of control. The import trade of Cambodia in recent years has, of course, exceeded the export trade, by value, owing to the large import of capital goods and producer equipment. The current trade pattern finds France in the dominant position in both the import and export trade. Other countries shift rank from year to year, but the leading countries are Hong Kong, Japan, Malaysia, United States, China, and Germany, roughly in that order.

SUMMARY COMMENT

The population of Cambodia had sunk to about one million in the late nineteenth century, at the low point of Cambodian political fortunes. Vietnamese were moving into the country, settling the best lands, and Khmer were moving away from the increasing Vietnamese communities, abandoning them to the immigrants. Chinese were also moving into the country, steadily gaining a stronger control over trade. Some thousands of Thais were resident in the western border zone, and some Khmer lived in the border zones of Thailand, as that border is aligned today. Historic enmity of Khmer against Thai had been the basis of historic aggression on the part of the expanding Thai state, but this enmity ranks below the feeling the Khmer have against the Vietnamese. The southward pressures of the expanding Vietnamese both drove the Khmer out of the delta lands and, under the French permissive colonial control, infiltrated Cambodia in increasing numbers. Although the Khmer felt strongly about French domination, it was the French who

saved them from political annihilation, and Khmer feelings against the French are tempered by this awareness. In the present political pattern about 600,000 Khmer live outside Cambodia, in the southern Mekong Delta and just inside Thailand along the northern and western Cambodian border (Fig. 19.4). Within Cambodia at present, included in its rapidly growing population of about 7,000,000 are about 475,000 Vietnamese, about 350,000 Chinese, about 85,000 tribal peoples, and some 40,000 Thais (Fig. 19.5). About 175,000 of the Vietnamese and 125,000 of the Chinese live in Phnom Penh, making up over half of its estimated population of about 500,000.

There is ample arable land for the expansion of Cambodian agricultural economy for a considerable period of time. Cambodia does not seem to possess much of a mineral resources base, but surveys are incomplete and Cambodia is not yet in a good position to utilize many minerals in internal industry, though the phosphate deposits are the base of domestic fertilizer manufacture. Development of hydroelectric facilities is linked into the program of the Lower Mekong River Basin Project and future availability of water resources will afford considerable power for economic growth (Fig. 19.6). Very little has ever been done with forest resources, but much of the regrown forests, covering lands formerly used at the height of the Khmer Empire, have been despoiled by careless exploitation. In this climatic regime of rapid growth cycles, cultural forestry has some real promise if programs are properly initiated.

There is, therefore, ample ground for the nervous neutralism of the little state of Cambodia. Distrust of the situation in Vietnam was chiefly responsible for the development of Sihanoukville (Kompong Som), on the south coast, since the river port of Phnom Penh is accessible only through South Vietnam. The manipulative actions of scattering economic agreements thinly among many

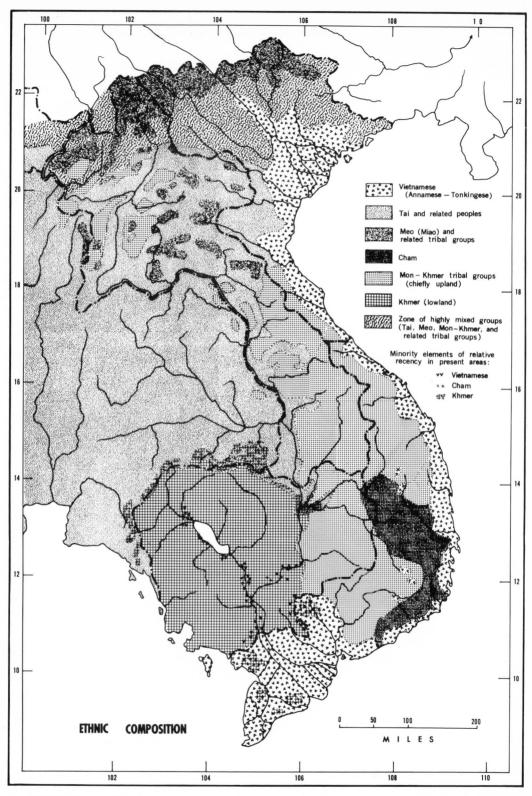

Vietnamese
(Annamese — Tonkingese)

Tai and related peoples

Meo (Miao) and
related tribal groups

Cham

Mon — Khmer tribal groups
(chiefly upland)

Khmer (lowland)

Zone of highly mixed groups
(Tai, Meo, Mon—Khmer, and
related tribal groups)

Minority elements of relative
recency in present areas:

ᵛᵛ Vietnamese

ᵃ ᵃ Cham

Khmer

ETHNIC COMPOSITION

0   50   100   200

M I L E S

FIGURE 19.4. Ethnic composition in Laos, Cambodia, North Vietnam, and South Vietnam.

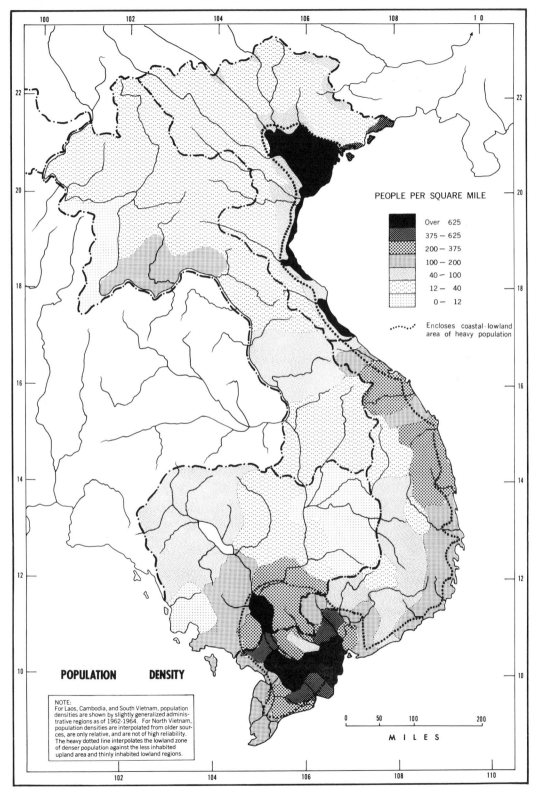

PEOPLE PER SQUARE MILE

- Over 625
- 375 — 625
- 200 — 375
- 100 — 200
- 40 — 100
- 12 — 40
- 0 — 12

.... Encloses coastal-lowland area of heavy population

POPULATION   DENSITY

NOTE:
For Laos, Cambodia, and South Vietnam, population densities are shown by slightly generalized administrative regions as of 1962-1964. For North Vietnam, population densities are interpolated from older sources, are only relative, and are not of high reliability. The heavy dotted line interpolates the lowland zone of denser population against the less inhabited upland area and thinly inhabited lowland regions.

MILES
0   50   100   200

FIGURE 19.5. Population density in Laos, Cambodia, North Vietnam, and South Vietnam.

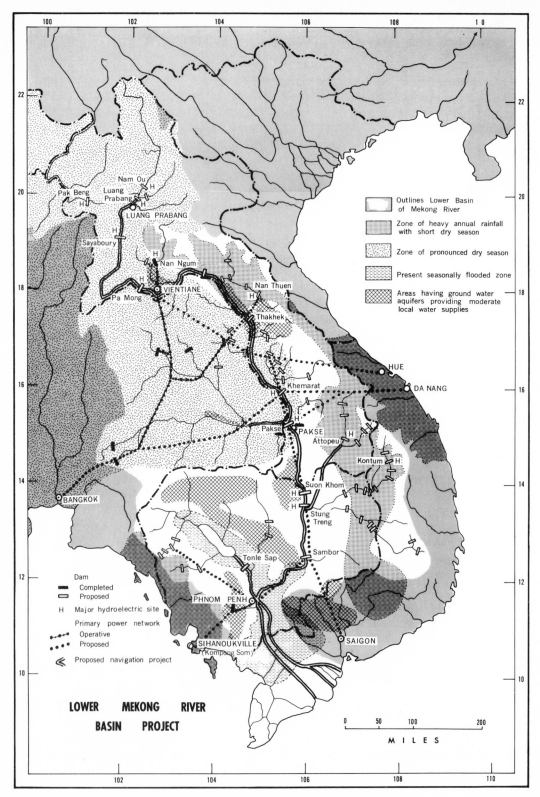

FIGURE 19.6. Lower Mekong River basin project.

404

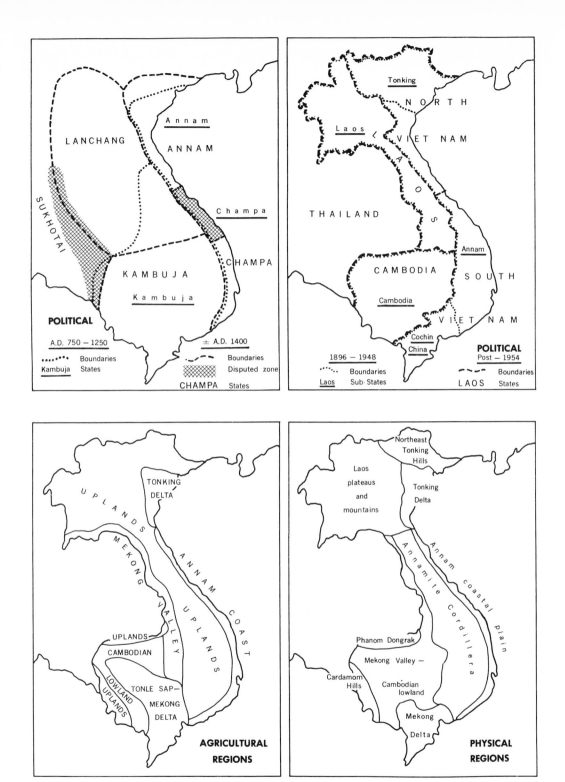

FIGURE 19.7. Regionalisms in Laos, Cambodia, North Vietnam, and South Vietnam.

countries has much the same motivation. Political nationalism shows its pressures in economic terms with regard to internal policies of attempting to bring control of the economy back into Khmer hands, placing restrictions on both the Vietnamese and the Chinese. These restrictions, however, cannot be pressed too heavily at present, since there is the lack of a Khmer middle class and an adequate body of trained and able Khmer personnel does not exist as yet. A large portion of the Cambodian budget has recently been put into education in an attempt to repair this internal imbalance.

Cambodia's future, however, continues to be closely related to the trends of politico-military events in Southeast Asia, but modern, little Cambodia may well attempt neutrality whenever possible. The integral physical linkage of the Cambodian lowlands with the Mekong Valley and the Mekong Delta place Cambodia in such a position that future events in South Vietnam will have a bearing on the future of Cambodia, as demonstrated in 1970 (Fig. 19.7). The shift in leadership of the Cambodian state, in mid-1970, represented an internal effort to maintain the neutralist position, as against alignment with the Communist political system, but whether this will succeed in the long run is an open question, as this volume goes to press. It may well be that the structure of Cambodian society, operative programs of economic development, and the political alignment of the country will continue to depend upon patterns of events affecting the whole major region, just as has happened in past centuries.

20

THE VIETNAM FRINGE

Although the Indochina of the early twentieth century has ceased to exist, it is useful to examine the geographical elements that enabled the French to bring it together in order to orient the discussion for what today are the three states of North Vietnam, South Vietnam, and Laos.

THE LACK OF A NATURAL CORE

The country known in the last century as Indochina was an illustration of the effectiveness of willful political force. It was an artificial combination of regions and cultures brought together by French military and political effort during the latter part of the nineteenth century in a zone straddling areas of Chinese and Indian cultural influence. Indochina of the early 1950's was also an illustration of the futility of political force artificially expended, for it was one country in political and military terms only. In geographic terms Indochina was an assemblage of unlike geographic areas, dissimilar economic entities, and mixed but unequal cultural groups held together by no natural bonds. The physical regions that made up the state are the easternmost parts of mainland Southeast Asia. The Annamite Cordillera occupies the center of the region, and its margins are a varied series of lowlands, coastal plains, deltas, and valley margins. The Cordillera itself is not all true mountain country, for it contains sections of subdued upland and small pieces of plateau. Several lowland areas are good enough to allow a people to develop economic strength and cultural force, but none is so placed as to facilitate the control or the cultural integration of the whole region earlier included in the state of Indochina.

If the limits set by earlier political control are momentarily accepted, but if these areas are examined in their early situations, it is evident that there were several regions attractive to early man. The Tonking Delta in the north was an attractive lowland at a very early date, essentially similar to the tropical lowlands of most of southern Asia. Its moist to aquatic situation was also similar to that of the southern lowlands of China, from which it is not well separated by natural barriers. The old Annam coastal plain is a relatively narrow and irregular strip of lowland leading southward from the Tonking Delta which was an attractive zone because of the possibilities of combining fishing and lowland plant economies. Its linear proportions presented no large resource in any one locality, but its very dimensions meant that many localities within it presented opportunity.

At the southern end of the coastal zone there broadens out the Mekong Delta zone, another useful aquatic lowland. Closely connected with it is the Cambodian lowland, previously discussed. The Mekong Valley is another large area of lowland, arranged in linear pattern, with numerous tributary valleys on the eastern side reaching back into the hill country. Although presenting different local environments from those of the delta or coastal areas there are many good localities, as far north as the sharp bend of the Mekong north of Korat.

The Annamite Cordillera is not one great mountain mass. Its upland areas, both plateau-like and mountainous, are variable and unequal in value. Although much of the more open uplands are today of value in tree-crop plantation agriculture, many areas always have been difficult for man to use. The uplands are generally moist and forested, except for areas of karst development in the north, and they are not so cold as to prohibit many of the more hardy tropical fruits and other useful plants. But the Annamite Cordillera appears long to have been one of the most malarial zones in the whole Orient. It is not the higher uplands that suffer, but the foothill country on both sides. This unhealthiness has kept the peoples of the uplands and lowlands apart historically.

The regions we knew as Indochina until 1954, therefore, present almost the reverse of the situation in Burma—an upland core surrounded by a loosely connected series of good lowland areas. On the one hand, these areas connect with the area of the Chinese world, and, on the other, they form parts of the great region that had early contact with the Indian culture world. This double exposure and the separation of the lowland regions have given to the peoples of Vietnam their diversity. Although the evidence is not yet well assembled, it is clear that man has been here a long time and continuously. Negrito and many other early groups became resident in parts of the lowlands. This region shared in the early southward movements of proto-Mongoloid and Mongoloid peoples, and the continued southward shift of peoples has brought many different groups into the region. The evidence suggests that Vietnam has always contained diverse human groups.

Historically, the Vietnamese (formerly labeled Tonkingese in the north and Annamese in the central coastal zone) first appear as a people resident along the south coast of China and in the Song Hoi delta zone (see Fig. 16.2). Chinese political pressures prior to the start of the Christian Era produced southward migration into the northern end of the coastal plain and also introduced many aspects of Chinese culture. Tributary and colonial relationships, under Chinese overlordship, steadily increased the elements of Sinicization among the Vietnamese. Over the centuries there were varying degrees of Chinese political control, reaching south of the Song Hoi delta, sometimes direct control, sometimes feudal, with varying states of rebellion during short intervals. Mahayana Buddhism, Confucian political philosophy, Chinese legal and administrative institutions, a Chinese-style bureaucracy, and other cultural complexes became adopted and these shaped the evolutionary growth of Vietnamese culture.

Along the coast of Vietnam south of the zone of Chinese influence lay the narrow coastal fringe in which Indian contact was very early, and here events progressed much as in other areas of Indian contact, with trading port centers slowly growing into small regional principalities under Indian leadership. The competitive efforts of the several local areas, and the inability of any one region to achieve superior population, economic strength, and political power, prevented integration of the whole coastal zone into one unified state. The fragmentary history of the Indianized Chams suggests well-nigh continuous rivalry for leadership and constant regional turbulence. The hill country Chams were thinly scattered clear across to the Mekong Valley. The coastal zone was narrow, small in total area, and divided into local regions by projecting spurs of the Cordillera that reached toward the coast. The hill country was irregular in surface and forested, and its economic productivity was low compared with that of the coastal zone (see also Chapter 17, and Figs. 16.1, 16.2, 19.4, and 19.7). Champa achieved temporary unity under occasional dynasties, but the essential limitations of the narrow coastal region prevented its growing steadily in strength, population, and cultural influence. A part of Cham turbulence regularly expressed itself in raids on the Vietnamese peoples to the north and on the Khmer regions to the south and west almost throughout the period of its separate existence.

After the Vietnamese threw off the more direct elements of Chinese political control in the tenth century, there began a steady southward penetration of the coastal plain by the Vietnamese, involving long and often inconclusive struggles with the Chams. By the late eighteenth century the Vietnamese had become the dominant power and their ethnic spread reached into the Mekong Delta. The Vietnamese had strongly benefitted from formal control and organization by the Han dynasty government of China, one of the most effective societal organizing groups of the oriental world. Chinese influence gave them a superior working system and a tight cultural cohesion never achieved by either the Khmers or the Chams. The Vietnamese started from a productive base in the Tonking Delta, and achieved a cultural unity before they began to expand. Choosing to restrict themselves to the healthier coastal lowland, and facing fewer disruptive factors, the Vietnamese retained their cultural cohesion during their long southward expansion.

Relatively independent after the tenth century the Vietnamese were able to overwhelm the Chams and appropriate their territory just at the time the Khmers were suffering their destruction as a powerful people. Thus, the Vietnamese were free to expand into the southern margins of the coastal zone and to begin infiltration of the Mekong Delta

lowland as the Europeans came upon the scene. By this time the Vietnamese held the whole eastern coast, though they by no means populated the area equally from north to south. Concerned less than either the Khmers or the Chams with the building of great religious monuments, they retained considerable of the Chinese pragmatic outlook upon life, while absorbing many of the personal cultural traits of the Chams and the other southern peoples with whom they traded along their long seacoast.

Although it now is popular to treat the Vietnamese superficially as one united people, there are clear differences in regional environmental ecology in their elongated region, there are distinctive differences among the Vietnamese as peoples, and there are different life-styles, so that there is no complete unity between northerners and southerners. The Tonkingese sector of the north has considerable very old intermixture of Chinese ethnic elements and is the most highly influenced by Chinese culture. This ethnic sector corresponds to the Song Hoi delta and its fringes, both north and south. South of about 17° S. latitude, roughly approximating the present boundary between North Vietnam and South Vietnam, environmental ecology, ethnic composition, historic relationships, and cultural complexes become altered. Chinese influence is less deeply ingrained, the Indianized elements from the old state of Champa enter, and the ethnic mix includes the Chams in locally variable and now diluted pattern. The Mekong Delta, again, is different in many respects. This, in the modern sense, is a land of recent settlement in which Vietnamese and Khmer are to be found in rural occupation and village settlements, a land still not fully settled, with towns and the twin cities of Saigon-Cholon holding a large Chinese population not yet significantly intermixed into the Vietnamese bloodstream. The historic back-and-forth patterns of military conflict along the main coast do not permit an easy demarcation of three regional sectors to the whole of the Vietnamese lands, but it is historically evident that the whole of Vietnam cannot be construed as a single specific culture region when it comes to the finer varieties of regional distinction.

THE ASSEMBLING OF FRENCH INDOCHINA

Portuguese and Spanish missionaries visited Vietnam and Cambodia in the sixteenth century, and Portuguese and Dutch traders often touched the coastal ports of both regions in the seventeenth century. The Vietnamese rulers were hard to deal with, the desired products were not in good supply, and in general the Europeans found trade more profitable elsewhere. The French East India Company made late efforts but never achieved much success in attempts to gain a foothold in Vietnam. French missionaries appeared in the seventeenth century in considerable numbers, and their communications with the homeland slightly acquainted France with Vietnam. French missionary participation in Vietnam's internal political struggles in the late eighteenth century restored a southern dynasty to the throne, but it left suspicion of the missionaries and their trader friends.

About the middle of the nineteenth century the French began looking for a route into interior China. First they tried the Mekong Valley, but gave up efforts there when they realized that the valley of the Song Hoi offered the only practical access from the south. As the Vietnamese attempted to prevent missionary-trader-political encroachment by expulsion of the missionaries, the French began using punitive military expeditions to avenge their ill treatment. One event let to another in a somewhat haphazard chain marked by personal decisions of both French and Vietnamese officials. First came French control over the Mekong Delta, then

a protectorate over part of Cambodia, followed by another over the southern portion of Vietnam. Tonking and Laos, in the north, were the last areas to come under French domination in a late nineteenth-century effort to get into western China before the British took over the region. Late maneuvers with Thailand settled western borders and rounded out a half century of imperialistic conquest.

A political state finally had been delimited. At the outset the French had no realization of the physical and cultural complexity of the regions that they were taking over. Finding themselves in control of regions having different culture histories they followed expediency and ended with five different units, in each of which policy and practice differed. These five units, on paper, formed the Indo-Chinese Union, and made up the standard political map of Indochina before World War II. The Mekong Delta, in the 1860's actively undergoing Vietnamese settlement, became Cochin-China, in which the French themselves largely ran things. Cambodia, with its Khmer traditions and a descendant line of royalty, was operated indirectly as a protectorate under guidance. This same pattern was applied to the southern portion of the Vietnamese regions, then designated Annam. Tonking became a partial protectorate, and, centering on the delta of the Song Hoi, this became an important holding. The northern hill country and the Mekong Valley margins on the west, a maze of tribal territories, confederacies, and old principalities, were lumped into the so-called protectorate of Laos, to be administered as casually but as practically as possible.

Although a political state had been delimited and divided into administrative segments, the nineteenth-century French knew too little of their colonial peoples and their ways to govern for the governed. Vacillation at home, governors appointed for short terms, too great use of the military, a tremendous ignorance of oriental ways, and the exploitive urge joined to prevent either a happy or an efficient pattern of colonial rule. The French efforts did much to undermine the traditional close bonds of Vietnamese and Cambodian village culture without replacing them with constructive modern elements. The pattern of divide and rule prevented the formulation of any modern cohesion around the new state that the French created. Indochina remained a somewhat artificial assemblage of regions, peoples, cultures, animosities, and political forms. Belatedly, in opposition to the Communist problem of Indochina since the close of World War II, a start was made in 1948 to repair the damage, but it was an unfair race against time and the growing seeds of destruction. French popular unwillingness to support a wholesale change in colonial policy and an all-out military effort, Vietnamese dislike for the French on any terms, Cambodian distrust of the Vietnamese, and Communist ability to capitalize on political disunity prejudiced the future status of the Associated States of Indochina, the last political combine the French tried to arrange. Intra-group cultural differences among the Vietnamese, and the divergences of political philosophy between north and south have led to bitter dispute in which outside holders of different political philosophy have joined in the regional struggle between north and south. Cambodia remains the unit that it long has been, agitated but attempting to stay neutral. Laos continues as the arbitrary grouping of the rest of French territory involved in both sides of a political struggle for which her peoples have neither vital interest nor controlling influence.

THE TRADITIONAL ECONOMY

The following discussion ignores the current political division of Vietnam into two parts, but discusses variations in terms of geographically significant regionalisms. Much of current crop growing activity in all parts of the country is carried on as described, in technological terms, but the disruption in specific areas caused by military events is ignored.

There has been nationalization of land in North Vietnam and group-working team operation of farm lands, whereas in South Vietnam much of traditional agricultural practice remains operative. In broadly general terms, this discussion remained valid in the early 1960's, but no attempt is made to describe particulars resulting from the disturbed, or constantly changing, conditions as provoked by military operations.

Subsistence economy by hamlet and village groups based upon rice and fish, supplemented by the small use of a wide range of auxiliary crops, was the tradition of almost all the culture groups of Vietnam. Although there have been water shortages in some regions, there are no rain shadows of such magnitude as in Burma to motivate the culture of a wide range of dry-field crops. The contrast in land use between the lowlands and the uplands is at least as striking here as in any other part of the Orient, for most of the population clings to the lowlands, and the agricultural landscape is a decidedly lowland one. Rice dominates rainy season cropping, and most secondary annual crops are grown in the dry season. Receiving its moisture from both monsoon systems, Vietnam exhibits considerable variety in planting and harvesting in different parts of the country. Rice, for example, is being harvested in some region during almost every month of the year. Most of the lowlands have practiced a permanent cropping system, whereas throughout the uplands shifting cultivation is the normal system. Well over half the country has been reduced from its natural forested condition to grasslands or parklands, largely at the hands of the shifting cultivator. Many abandoned tracts in the lower Mekong

Valley reverted to forest after the decline of the Khmer Empire, and are gradually being cleared as the agricultural landscape again expands.

In the Tonking Delta and the northern Vietnam coast the physiologic density of population has long been very high, decreasing southward to the newly settled wet portions of the Mekong Delta. The areal density of the upland territories always has been low, though the physiologic density of many local regions has perhaps been rather high. Parts of the lower Mekong Valley declined in population after the decline of the Khmer Empire, and, though now they are increasing in population, they today carry only a moderate density. In Tonking and northern Vietnam continuous occupation and the full development of the agricultural landscape produced extreme fragmentation of farmlands. In parts of the Tonking Delta, land was divided into as many as 10 to 14 parcels per acre prior to the government's nationalization of land. In these areas of traditional occupation there was only a small amount of tenancy, land was high in price and always in strong demand. The fragmentation of farmland decreases southward along the Vietnam coast. Much of the lower Mekong region was divided into parcels of roughly an acre each, whereas in the more recently settled wet portion of the Mekong Delta there were many large holdings. On these new lands tenancy was reaching serious proportions, and it was common for tenants to remain on a given farm for short periods only. In the Tonking Delta Chinese diking practices have long been followed, and most of the delta was in farmland, but in the Mekong lowlands that have suffered from too much water during a long flood season only modern diking and drainage-canal building has made possible the agricultural occupation of large areas.

In some respects the peoples of Vietnam may be called gardeners rather than technically efficient farmers. The per-acre rice yield for the country as a whole was among the lowest in the Orient, and the relative yields of other crops also were low. Regional differences were apparent in this matter. In Tonking the Chinese practices of using all available fertilizers, including night soil, have long been followed, whereas in the far south practices of soil fertility maintenance are poorly developed. Too few draft animals have been used, and, particularly on the very small holdings, manual labor even now is the chief source of farm power. Until very recently all farmers have used only the simplest of wooden tools. In many areas, and with many crop plants, planting was in garden patches and dooryard plantings. Few of the peoples of Vietnam were highly skilled in the handling of shrub and tree crops.

Rice has been the dominant crop of all parts of Vietnam, and the country rivalled Thailand in having a monocrop economy (see Fig. 19.1). Nearly 13,000,000 out of about 16,000,000 acres of crop land were devoted to rice during the early 1950's whenever peaceful conditions permitted normal agricultural planting. The agricultural activities surrounding rice culture set the seasonal rhythm of life in Vietnam. In the wet lowlands it has been a wet-field crop, though many of the fields have lacked enough water in mid-season. There was some double cropping of rice. On some lands of deepest flooding a tall floating rice was grown, to be followed by minor crops during the dry season. Throughout the uplands rice has been the chief crop of the sedentary and shifting cultivator, but the per acre yield was low. In the last century the acreage of rice was increased markedly, as some of the Mekong Delta lands were diked and drained. The increase in settlement and land use was as marked here as it was in the deltas of the Irrawaddy and the Chao Phraya, with most of the consequent problems of tenancy and shifting of farmers from farm to farm. On these new lands agriculture was distinctly monocrop, and in much of the Mekong Delta rice was the only crop for which there were statistical returns.

All the traditional auxiliary crops of oriental agriculture find their place in some local environment of Vietnam, but government statistical services have been unable to plot their occurrence and distribution properly. The native fruits of the Orient have been traditionally planted in dooryard clumps and small patches throughout the lowlands, but they only selectively reach into the upland. Some of them were regionally centered, following local climatic criteria. The lichi was more frequently grown in the northern lowlands than in the south, whereas the coconut bears fruit only southward of Da Nang on the central Vietnam coast. The durian was restricted to the southern portions of the country. Bananas, citrus fruits, and the jackfruit are among the most tolerant of altitude and location, were the most commonly grown, and, taken together, probably cover several hundred thousands of acres, though no specific data are available.

Sugarcane, taro, yams, beans, pepper, betel, some of the lesser spices, sesame, cotton, mulberries, sugar palms, and a variety of green vegetables, all found a place in the crop patterns of the lowlands, and some of them in the uplands as well. None of the crops was to be found everywhere, but in the older and more stable areas most of them were represented. Mulberries normally were grown on the edge of the lowlands, or on hillocks of well-drained soils. Some of these crops were grown on the river-bank strips of light soils at low-water season. In only a few cases was there adequate production today, for their cultivation has not increased in recent centuries at the same rate as the increase in population. The only items in this group to exceed 100,000 acres per year were the beans and sugarcane, with perhaps 200,000 and 110,000 acres, respectively.

Such American plants as maize, the peanut, tobacco, manioc, white and sweet potatoes, and some of the beans fit well into the traditional subsistence economy. Several had regional specialization, and some were river-bank low-water seasonal crops. Maize was increasing steadily in acreage until it ranked as the second crop in area, covering about 1,300,000 acres per year. As a dry-season crop it was widely grown in the north, following wet rice. The potatoes cover perhaps about 300,000 acres per year, to rank third in area among the food crops.

Animal husbandry was not highly developed. Small native pigs were the most numerous animal, totaling close to 4,000,000. Although they were to be found everywhere, they were important only in those lowland regions of Chinese influence. Cattle of a mixed Zebu-Taurus breed were used sparingly as draft animals where they could be afforded. In the Tonking Delta and the more crowded portions of Annam there is but little room for cattle, and they supplied only a small volume of draft power or meat supply, and in rural areas human energy supplies most of the power. Water buffalo also were sparingly used for the same reasons. The cattle population approached 2,000,000, with water buffalo perhaps numbering 1,400,000. In traditional Vietnamese economy horses were few in total number. In the south they were used chiefly as carriage animals around the towns and cities, and in the northern uplands they were pack animals. The elephant was more an honorific animal than one of husbandry. Fewer than 1,500 elephants were used in economic activities but the military operations may endanger the continuance of the elephant in Vietnam. Other animals such as goats or sheep were few in number, were neither understood nor well cared for, and were not of economic significance. Chickens, ducks, pheasants, and geese were widespread in use, were kept in small numbers for meat and egg purposes, but did not make a large contribution to the food economy of the country.

Fishery products probably supplied the second most important source of food for all but the upland population. Both coastal water fishing and that of the estuarine and inland lowlands is a traditional part of the economy. The Mekong waterways, in flood season, along with smaller streams everywhere, provided a very rich resource tapped by simple methods. Only in restricted inland areas, or along the Vietnam coast, where year-round fishing is possible, were professional fishermen numerous, and most fishing was a seasonal or part-time occupation. The total annual catch probably amounted to some 260,000 tons, but reliable data are scarce. Pond culture was sporadically practiced but was not highly developed. Along with fishery products of the normal sort goes the harvesting of many aquatic plant foods. In season a share of the catch was used fresh, but the more normal methods were to salt, dry, smoke, or process the product into fish pastes.

Outside the areas of intensive lowland agriculture, forest gathering supplied an appreciable annual return. Bamboo for matting, construction, tools, and utensils, and lumber, firewood and charcoal for domestic or handicraft use, gums, resins, turpentine, lac, fruits, and roots, plus a variety of other vegetable products, were among the resources tapped. There was some hunting of game by the upland population. The forests have been stripped of most of their good timber resources and no longer supply the lowland with adequate good lumber. There has been little redevelopment of any of these resources in any part of the country, for the forested areas have not been thought of as areas of potential cultural development of

resources, but chiefly as a natural reserve to be stripped or as a source of arable land when clearing.

FRENCH ELEMENTS IN THE ECONOMY

In a land once lacking effective land transport systems the French built almost 20,000 miles of all-weather highways that traversed most of the major regions of the country, in addition to the many miles of dry-weather highways and the local service roads and trails also laid out (see Fig. 19.3). A railway system of about 1,800 miles once extended from one end of the country to the other along the Vietnam coast, but military operations broke the connection between the north and the south, and render much of the network nonoperative from time to time. The highway system connects both to China and to Cambodia and Laos, and the rail system of North Vietnam connects with Chinese systems, whereas that of South Vietnam is an isolated system. Both roads and railways were built more with political considerations in mind than purely economic utility, but regional interchange of commodities has markedly increased. Harbor and port development and improvements of Mekong River and Tonking Delta navigation allowed the French to develop a variety of international trade, and also to tap the trade of southwestern China. With the diking and draining of heavily flooded lands achieved under the French in the lower Mekong Basin, the expansion of rice agriculture took place, and Vietnam joined Burma and Thailand as the chief sources of export rice. The disruptive situation in Indochina since 1941 has destroyed the normal movement in trade rice, but it may be that neither portion of the region will again be an exporter. The demands of the French home market drew a number of commodities out of Vietnam, so that a share of production developed a cash-crop production pattern. Recently most of the surplus of pepper and corn has moved to the French market.

Considerable French effort was expended in the attempt to develop commercial plantation agriculture. Cotton, mulberries, castor beans, jute, coffee, tea, coconut, sugarcane, lac, ramie, kapok, tung, rice, and rubber, all have been tried within the last 75 years in an effort to match the plantation agriculture of Malaysia, Ceylon, and Indonesia. Only rubber has been at all successful, ranking third in crop acreages with a total of about 325,000 acres before military hostilities threatened severe destruction. Rubber production slowly increased until it more than supplied the French home market, and an increasing volume was going elsewhere abroad. French-owned rice "plantations" were established in the new lands of the Mekong Delta, but in the main these became absentee holdings farmed by native tenants and no longer are true plantations. The first four crops mentioned are no longer grown on plantations at all, having totally failed in the hands of French plantation operators, who frequently came out from France inexperienced in the ways of tropical agriculture but hoping to become wealthy. Coffee, tea, coconut, and sugarcane were grown on a few plantations to the amount of a few thousand acres each, but none became a real success. Lac, ramie, kapok, and tung, all have been tried on small plantations, and the final success or failure cannot yet be determined, but the acreage of none amounts to more than a few hundreds or thousands.

The development of French-owned agricultural enterprise was assisted by land laws very favorable to French citizens, whereas other noncitizens of Vietnam were prevented from acquiring land. Some of these plantation efforts were located in the southern uplands, though most efforts have chosen the better soils of the Mekong Delta margins. The rubber plantations were located in the edge of the uplands, about at the climatic margins for rubber trees. Although inexperience was a cause for the small success of French-operated commercial agriculture, other factors were the failure to adjust homeland import tariffs, the steady attempts to turn Vietnam into a supplier of raw materials for the homeland, and the excessive effort to exploit native labor and land resources.

Late in the nineteenth century industrialization efforts began. Many starts were made in mining, but only that in anthracite coal was really successful (see Fig. 19.2). The coal is well located near the sea just north of the Tonking Delta, and an increasing annual production reached 2,600,000 tons in 1939. Soft coal is found at several points in Tonking, and it was mined in small amounts. Tin, lead, zinc, manganese, chromium, iron, bauxite, graphite, and phosphates complete the list of known mineral resources existing in any quantity, though other minerals had been found in small amounts. Petroleum had not yet been found. The mineral deposits are widely scattered, but the Tonking uplands form the chief mineralized region. Native and Chinese miners have produced small amounts of most products over many centuries, but the modern French record was very irregular, and except for coal production varied greatly from year to year. Although admittedly costly, most mining efforts have failed through bogus stock flotation schemes. In good years perhaps 50,000 native and Chinese miners were employed in the mines, which were almost entirely French owned.

Other forms of industrialization developed slowly, handicapped by the lack of native labor skills and by the French policy of not favoring colonial development of manufactures in competition with home industry. Cement manufacturing was probably the most successful, producing close to 300,000 tons per year, with ample markets in Indochina and the whole of the Orient. Brick and ceramic products were a related type of product which increased in production. Small ships and boats, chemicals, glass, paints, soap, matches, paper, textiles, rubber goods, firecrackers, alcoholic and other beverages, and a few other products were being produced in factories located in Hanoi, Haiphong, Hue, Da Nang, Saigon, and a few other cities and towns. The largest share of industrial output occurred in Tonking. Steam electric power plants were becoming widely scattered, and the larger towns and cities were electrified. The larger factories were French owned, but native participation in ownership and management was increasing.

In agricultural processing the milling of rice, of course, was the leading activity, largely in the hands of Chinese. Milling was widely scattered, but the Cholon section of Saigon did more than any other center, since it was the chief port for export rice. Sugar, tobacco, vegetable oils, rubber, lac, and leather were the chief products processed in native and French-owned plants. The wood industries were scattered and not very significant as industrial performance, since Vietnam no longer possesses woods sufficiently valuable for large-scale production or export. Teak, if it ever was voluminous, is almost entirely lacking in the remaining forests. Bamboo, building lumber, firewood, and charcoal are chiefly products of native handicraft operations, locally produced and distributed. Beyond the labor employed in mining not more than 100,000 laborers were engaged in activities that can properly be labeled industrial.

Although portions of Vietnam actively engaged in international trade at various times in the past, these regions were not very active in trade in the early nineteenth century. Chinese, Indonesians, and others carried on some coasting trade, particularly with Tonking and northern Annam ports, but not many of the natives of these regions were themselves active traders. The Europeans who had begun to participate in the regional and international trade of the Orient in the sixteenth and seventeenth centuries did not have much success in Vietnam. During much of the eighteenth century Tonking and Annam ports were frequently visited by oriental traders, but the Europeans still had little success along this coast.

After the French took over the region they began to develop trade between Vietnam and France, drawing raw materials and agricultural products out and shipping manufactured consumers' goods inward. Slowly this volume of trade increased between Vietnam and France, but the trade with other occidental countries did not grow large. Some of the native products developed production patterns too large for the French homeland market, and restrictive control of trade caused production to decline. The pepper trade is an illustration of this, and production roughly balanced at the figure needed to supply the native and French market. Other products such as coal, cement, and rice found their export markets primarily within the Orient. Gradual liberalization of policy was permitting such a commodity as rubber to achieve its own level of production by competing in foreign markets after supplying the French home need.

The economy of Vietnam was dominated by French financial control, for most of the productive capital operating the economy was French. The Chinese elements and interests corresponded to what often was termed the middle-class portion of a society, though native elements increasingly participated. Through the development of modern trade patterns native farmers were increasingly producing commodities for a commercial market on a money basis. Prior to 1941 rice was the leading export commodity, followed by rubber, maize, coal, fish, tin, pepper, and cement. The import trade found cotton and rayon textile products in the first position, followed by machinery and metal manufacturing, petroleum, processed foods, iron and steel, and sacking fibers. Practically all foreign trade was carried on through the ports of Saigon and Haiphong. Da Nang and Ben Thuy were but minor ports and Hongay was a coal export port only.

VIETNAM TODAY

Indochina was the last and perhaps the least skillful major occidental colonial holding carved out of the Orient. The region now forms one of the last problems for solution in the long history of occidental imperialism in Southeast Asia and, because of its recent complications, it is one of the most difficult to solve. France, between 1860 and 1939, had combined two major ethnic-culture groups and a motley variety of minor groups into one political state administered in five units (see Fig. 19.7). World War II ended French control over the region. In the postwar period France spent both money and manpower in an attempt to salvage the whole of what had been Indochina, replacing the former five states with the three states of Cambodia, Vietnam, and Laos. This separated the Khmer and the Vietnamese, but it left the amorphous zone of tribal cultures divided between Laos and Vietnam, primarily. The boundaries laid out on maps of the region, in modern time, never have fitted the facts of demography, culture systems, or living systems; these boundaries, in themselves have been modern contributions to the complexity of the shatterbelt condition of Southeast Asia.

The Vietnamese and the Khmers are both lowland peoples historically, and their respective regional occupances have included very little of the upland sectors. The Mon and Thai peoples (under various name groupings) have long lived at many different altitudinal levels from the lowlands into the higher mountain country, though their historic trend has been toward the lowlands when that was possible. The minor ethnic elements, both the long-resident and the relatively recent migrants out of China, have lived at varying heights in the uplands, dependent upon what ecological levels and regions were open to them. An historically unhealthy fringe of foothill country has separated the lowland Vietnamese living space from the upland regions occupied by the various minor groups, along the eastern flank of the Annamite Cordillera, but along the western flank of the upland zone the distinctions have been less easy to make, and along this western zone there has been more intermixing of ethnic groups, since the Thai peoples, particularly, were less restrictive in their choices of living space.

It remains true, however, that the present boundaries between political units, as allocated on the map, do not fit the ethnic ecology of the area known in the recent past as Indochina. The 1948 allocation, by France, of three internal states gave the Vietnamese a state area, and it did the same for the Khmer, but the shaping of Laos remained a paper action, in that there was no ethnic unity around which to build a state idea. Each of the state areas involved both territory and ethnic groups foreign to the historic pattern. The Vietnamese state should be only a lowland one, as should the Khmer state; the state of Laos should properly be the northwest sector of territory that has historic continuity as a regional principality. The amorphous upland zone of tribal cultures, in which there are only local ethnic and cultural allegiances, and in which the concepts of citizen, political state, political nationalism, and large-region economic nationalism remain incomprehensible, does not belong in a political state at all. But what to do with it in this era in which political nationalism dominates the thinking? In realistic terms the whole of the amorphous upland zone, including much of the territory now placed politically in Vietnam and in Cambodia, ideally belongs in an international politico-cultural trust territory, wherein its peoples would not be mauled and hauled by the pressures of the current system of nationalisms. It is here that the historic elements of the Southeast Asian shatterbelt continue to pose problems, problems that find no solution in current political or military actions, proposals, or thinking.

Further, it remains true today that, within Vietnam, there never has been such politico-cultural integration as to provide a thoroughly sound basis for one single political nationalism as that concept is held today. There are historic cultural differences from north to south, there are spatial sectionalisms, and there are ecologic-cultural regionalisms within the patterns of what today is insistently termed Vietnamese nationalism by those who argue the contemporary issues of political action. Again, historic elements in the Southeast Asian shatterbelt pose serious problems for the present and the future. The long-operative distinctions between the Sinicized Tonking, in the north, and the less Sinicized and more mixed patterns of the central-southern sectors was ignored in the 1948 creation of a single political state. The 1954 imposition of a formal boundary between a North Vietnam and a South Vietnam, at the 17th parallel, placed a boundary at about as effective a point as human action probably can achieve in our mixed and varied world.

The recognition of larger problems of regional development, as posed by the Lower Mekong River Basin Project, represent the kinds of thinking and formulation of solutions to problems that are needed in the Southeast Asia shatterbelt (see Fig. 19.6). The whole of the zone under consideration badly needs the opportunity for environmental development of physical resources, coupled with the opportunity for cultural development of all of the peoples represented in the larger region. The contest over territory, in terms of what group achieves and exercises power under what political system, remains a feature of military nationalism not far removed from the political concepts that motivated colonial imperialism in the whole of Southeast Asia during the last two centuries.

This is not the place in which to enter the argument as to the right and wrong of the "Vietnam War," and we do not presume to pronounce judgment regarding issues that now involve international pressures and politicoeconomic concepts far removed from the local problem of Vietnamese regionalism and the domination of the long coastal environment by either north or south. Further, there has been, since 1954, so much physical destruction, disruption of normal living systems, and so much change occurring that, coupled with the current inadequacy of reliable data, the present geographic scene almost defies camly-considered assessment. The series of maps presented in the previous chapter have generalized as many significant geographic phenomena as possible (see Figs. 19.1 through 19.7). We conclude this chapter on this presently unhappy region with three short vignettes on the three areas involved.

NORTH VIETNAM

Slightly the smaller of the two portions of the combined area of Vietnam, North Vietnam also retains slightly less than half the total population. Of the estimated 17,000,000 people in North Vietnam, about 14,500,000 are properly Vietnamese, an estimated 2,300,000 are members of tribal ethnic stocks, and about 200,000 are Chinese. In the past there has been considerable intermixture of Chinese and Vietnamese, and there are no significant bars to such intermixture today. A large share of North Vietnam is rough hilly to mountainous country, and the Song Hoi Delta lowland totals under 6,000 square miles as the chief economically productive area, augmented by a small fringing coastal plain on the southern margin. The delta region has carried an extremely high population density, so that it has been a food deficit region in the past century, dependent upon surpluses from southern regions. Most of the farmlands of the delta have been collectivized by Communist government program, but this program has not followed Chinese precedent into commune organization, and not much progress has been made in collectivizing the croplands of the upland tribal peoples. Something over 5,000,000 acres have gone into rice production in recent years and, with good crops in good years, North Vietnam has just fed itself, with the aid of strict food rationing. Maize, sweet potatoes, manioc, sugarcane, and bananas have been the chief complementary food crops employed to balance out the dietary. Small volumes of other tropical fruits and vegetables, and small acreages of other crops round out the agricultural economy.

North Vietnam was the chief area of mineral production under the French, and the chief area of beginning industrialization, there developing a small reservoir of technical skills. The region has recently engaged in a strong program of industrialization, with some foreign technical aid, though military activities have both interrupted production patterns and turned many of them toward military industries. Dispersal of industrial plants for protection from bombing has spread manufacturing industry rather widely into the hinterlands, away from its concentration on Hanoi and Haiphong. Labor shortages, under war conditions, have handicapped both agricultural and industrial production. Given peaceful conditions and properly economic motivation for the development of North Vietnamese economy, the country could achieve an advancing state

of economic development in which planned patterns of organized resource technology could develop high levels of production.

A rather good network of transport lines formerly tied the lowland zone together, with good connections to China, available in recent years for the military transportation of war supplies. The upland interior was not originally provided with more than a skeleton transport network, but Vietnamese road construction has built numerous roads including several probably not shown on Figure 19.3. The port of Haiphong was developed by the French as the primary port for the northern region, and it remains the center of the North Vietnam shipping trade, having never been attacked by air bombing. Hongay, just to the north, served as a coal export port, and minor coastal ports along the southern coast have served the domestic patterns of trade.

The Vietnamese of North Vietnam have been traditional village dwellers, as have most of the upland peoples, and there are on the order of 15,000 villages of varying sizes housing the primary population. Coastal port towns and a few interior market towns have long been present, but urbanism has not been a marked Vietnamese development in the north. Hanoi, of course, is a very old city of long standing, and is the primary urban entity. Its population in recent years, dependent upon the state of air attack and consequent evacuation, has been in the vicinity of 500,000, but under normal peacetime economic development Hanoi would become a very large city. Haiphong, as the primary port city, has been a large city in modern time.

Despite a considerable war-weariness the Vietnamese element of the population of North Vietnam has remained united to a remarkable degree, and there is little doubt concerning the future continuance of a Communist political state of North Vietnam as a small industrialized state employing state controls of resources and production. Mineral resources, an accumulation of political and industrial skills, and strong political cohesion, supported by the traditionally aggressive energy of the northern Vietnamese, almost guarantee that future continuance, with the possibility that political expansion will mark the future. North Vietnam will always live in the shadow of China, as she has done in the past, but China never succeeded in absorbing the Song Hoi Delta region and it is not likely that such will occur.

SOUTH VIETNAM

South Vietnam is slightly the larger of the two geographical halves of the combined area, and it now has somewhat more than half the total population. Of the estimated 18,000,000 people, an estimated 15,400,000 could be classified as Vietnamese, and there are about 1,100,000 Chinese, about 1,000,000 upland tribal peoples, and almost 500,000 Khmer. The Vietnamese of South Vietnam, however, are not nearly so cohesive and integrated an ethnic group as are the North Vietnamese, and there is considerable ethnic variety and mixture and some linguistic variation among them. Both the Khmer and the Chinese are chiefly resident in the Mekong Delta lowlands, but the Khmer are a rural and village dwelling people who keep largely to themselves in the southern sector of the delta. The Chinese are chiefly urban residents, with a concentration in the Cholon section of the Saigon metropolitan area, and are of relatively recent origin in South Vietnam. The Chinese here have not often intermarried into the Vietnamese population, tend to remain Chinese in language and cultural system, and have not become thoroughly integrated into the Vietnamese community as in North Vietnam.

The almost 15,000 square miles of the Mekong Delta form an area not only far larger than the Song Hoi Delta, but an area

more inherently productive in agriculture, with far less population pressure upon it. The Mekong Delta has not yet been fully settled, so that there are large tracts of almost empty country. Under peacetime conditions the Mekong Delta could produce large agricultural surpluses for some decades to come. In addition, there is a somewhat longer and more productive coastal plain than in the north, and there are upland valleys and plateau units in the southern Annamite Cordillera that are more potentially productive than are the highlands of North Vietnam. Much of the increase in the agricultural landscape in the delta region has occurred since the middle of the nineteenth century, accompanied by drainage and flood control projects, though these have not been so well developed as those of the Irrawaddy and Chao Phraya deltas. The rice acreage of South Vietnam had reached a maximum figure of about 6,800,000 before Vietcong guerrilla activities began to lessen the figure by intimidating rural populations and confiscating harvests. Rice has been the dominant crop planted by far, but maize, various beans, peanuts, sugarcane, bananas, and a few other crops have complemented the rice crop. Rubber plantings had come to occupy a considerable area north of Saigon, and there were small tea and coffee plantings in some of the favored plateau areas, but guerrilla activity or outright military warfare has strongly handicapped plantation production of all these crops.

The agricultural economy of South Vietnam has been much more seriously upset by the continuance of military activities of various kinds than has been the case in North Vietnam, since most of the guerrilla action and government counteraction have taken place in South Vietnam. Changing resettlement programs, changing military policy, and the repeated refugeeing of rural populations into towns and cities has lowered the productivity of South Vietnam agricultural economy to the end that the larger towns and cities have not secured adequate food supplies from the rural hinterlands, and have to some extent periodically been dependent upon imported supplies of rice. This is in strong contrast to the earlier situation in which southern South Vietnam was increasingly an exporter of rice and maize.

South Vietnam had undergone very little industrial development beyond the agricultural processing variety, and the latter was significantly controlled by Chinese owners-operators. Although there are some mineral resources in the south, and more may be found through future surveys, South Vietnam would not appear to hold the mineral wealth present in North Vietnam. The Chinese held a control over a significant share of the domestic and foreign trade in the south, and there was relatively less in the way of industrial and management skills available when South Vietnam became an independent political entity. Large amounts of construction by American firms, in support of military operations, are contributing to the accumulation of such skills by South Vietnamese, but there has been little development of productive industrial enterprise of direct utility to the peacetime economy of the country.

The coastal section of South Vietnam, north of the Mekong Delta, had a fairly good transport network prior to 1954, but both the Delta and the uplands had only skeleton elements of transport facilities. The delta sector, of course, had long depended upon water transport along the Mekong River distributaries and through the canal systems. A great deal of road construction which has been effected by American military initiative will be useful in the future. Saigon was developed as the chief trading port for the whole of South Vietnam although there have been a number of smaller ports along the northern coast having much longer historic use. American construction programs have developed numerous port facilities that will remain after war activities have ceased.

In the past the South Vietnamese, the Khmer, and the tribal peoples have all been chiefly village dwellers. Coastal port towns and a few inland market towns have long historic standing along the coastal fringe north of the delta region. Saigon is located on the site of older sea-trading villages but, in effect, the port and the city are modern in development by the French, after 1865. As the premier port of the whole southern sector Saigon has grown rapidly into a large metropolitan urban center, aided significantly by the influx of Chinese. Within the recent past the city has, of course, been the focus for American military support and the refugee center for large numbers of rural people. In 1970, the Saigon metropolitan area held a population of about 1,750,000. Other cities along the coast have grown fairly large in recent years, in part a function of refugeeing and in part a function of American support patterns.

All aspects of life in South Vietnam have been seriously disturbed since 1954. Insurgent politicomilitary action, factional patterns of rivalry that root in sectionalism, and aspects of ethnic separation have combined to keep any national program off balance and have kept portions of the population both wary and nonparticipative. There has been ineffectiveness of national government, even in areas controlled by that government, that has failed to produce the concentrated drive toward specific ends that has shown itself so significant in North Vietnam. Most of this is laid at the door of the South Vietnamese themselves by many observers, and it is quite clear that South Vietnam has lacked the cohesion of the north, but the south has also faced continual interference by northern elements, playing upon the elements of sectionalism, group loyalties, cultural differences, and ethnic separatisms that have long been present in South Vietnam. The past long history of the Vietnamese peoples does not suggest that if northern Vietnamese secured control over the whole country there would be peace, prosperity, and unified patterns of development in the future. As of 1970, it is not at all clear that the peoples of South Vietnam can overcome the present handicaps imposed upon them by their own past, by North Vietnamese interference, and by the pressures of the outside world, so that there is no assurance that a South Vietnam political state will survive the present frustrating currents of divergence.

LAOS

Laos, as a region, is almost half again as large as either North Vietnam or South Vietnam, but it has a very small population widely distributed over its territory. Most estimates place the total population at just under 3,000,000, of which the Lao, closely related to the Thai peoples, comprise about one half. Laos is chiefly mountainous upland, with numerous high valleys and plateau units, but its whole western fringe descends to the valley of the Mekong River in narrow riverine plains. Laos has never been a modern political state in the true sense, but it has been depicted as a political state on international maps. At times in the past there has been a kingdom of Laos, centered in the northwest, shown at its widest possible extent as Lanchang on Figure 19.7. Properly speaking there has been a principality of Laos, a local region dominated by a political elite group of Lao, but this control has never effectively reached out its control, or its support, to the fifty or sixty ethnic communities that are scattered over the rough upland in the small groups and clusters that occupy local ecological niches.

The French created the state of Laos as a last act in the rounding out of their colonial empire. Finding that the Mekong River did not provide a good line of access into western China, the French allowed Laos to languish, supporting its token government structure from revenues derived from other states of the colonial holding. The vagaries of post-World War II French arrangements left Laos an independent political entity on paper, having neither structure nor operating mechanisms of effective sorts, and financially unable to survive. Frequent international dealings have in theory guaranteed Laos as an independent political state, neutral in position, with its political machinery largely supported by American subsidies contributed under one guise or another. Factional rivalries among the Lao political elite have steadily provided political incidents and alternating positions that, were the Vietnam problem not so crucial, would provide good material for comic opera. Communist North Vietnam has intermittently put pressure upon the territory of Laos in one way or another, and American activities have provided relief for some of those pressures, as countermeasures. Laos, as a political state, remains a pawn marginal to, but also critical to, the "Vietnam problem."

According to present knowledge of the region, it is only western Laos that contains areas of significant economic productivity. The population of all parts of Laos is agricultural and handicraft oriented and the system of agriculture is simple, employing chiefly shifting cultivation methods. Portions of Laos figure into the Lower Mekong River Basin Project so that hydroelectric power projects and other elements in modern development do affect parts of Laos at present (see Fig. 19.6). Patterns of international diplomacy help to make Vientiane into a thriving city with a population estimated in 1970 at about 200,000 people, and there are a few other towns of much smaller size. If the international elements were removed, Vientiane would be a small regional market town and the seat of a small regional principality.

In the modern world of political states and political nationalisms Laos cannot be discounted. But Laos, on its own, cannot function as an effective state for a long interval of time so it remains a pawn in various political games. As stated earlier, we believe that Laos belongs in the status of an international trust territory, within which framework cultural development could take place over a period of decades in the creation of some distinctive pattern of internal cohesion and intergroup consciousness. It is doubtful that this will occur and, therefore, it is probable that Laos will continue its paper existence until the outcome of the "Vietnam problem" produces a solution of some sort, and the peoples of Laos will continue to be involved in affairs for which they have neither indigenous interest nor ability to influence decisions.

21

MALAYSIA

THE ENVIRONMENTS AND EARLIEST OCCUPANCE

As a land appendage of Asia the southern, equatorial portion of the Malay Peninsula forms an environment different from any of the other regional units and political states of the Orient. It is not a large region, it is ill arranged as to uplands and lowlands to serve as a core area for the regional development of a culture group, and its lowlands are strung out as coastal plains or as irregular strips of lowland around and between upland masses. Many of the interior lowlands are poorly drained and were earlier rather unhealthy. It is a wet landscape, with many stream channels that carry more water than their length and breadth would suggest, but there is no one great river valley, and no large delta of dominant area and utility. The peninsula's chief historic function has been to serve as a landfall for navigators on the Bay of Bengal and the South China Sea.

West Malaysia is a region naturally covered with heavy forest which repelled early human occupance. At the end of the long peninsula no major modifications of the inland sectors had been produced by waves of shifting cultivators or by immigrant groups of vigorous sedentary farming peoples until the coming of the British plantation farmer of the late nineteenth century. The plant cover repeatedly was able to spread back over the small scars intermittently produced by oc-

cupation of small coastal pockets. Even after a century of modern exploitation of soil and minerals only about a third of the total surface has been laid open to use. The forest only in small degree has been exploited for its own resources, both in the past and today.

Although today interior West Malaysia is still inhabited by perhaps 50,000 refugee jungle peoples of all sorts, comprising several groups of varied ethnic composition, few peoples chose the interior over the coastal fringes and estuarine reaches of the rivers. Although the earliest immigrants certainly were land travelers, they most probably preferred the coastal fringes even then. Among the simpler culture groups, there still were Negrito remnants in the late nineteenth century. There are small groups of mixed peoples, linguistically related to the Mon-Khmer peoples, and a few proto-Malays. The Malays for many centuries have been a people preferring boats, fishing, shore-fringe crop lands, and the riverine and coastal fringes to the interior areas and ways of life. Only in recent centuries have the Malays spread inland, penetrating those river lowlands where they could follow a living pattern related to that of the coastal zone. Sometime before the coming of the European, Sumatran Menangkabaus settled in Negri Sembilan on the west coast, intermarrying with the local Malay population. During the eighteenth century Celebes Bugis, a navigating, piratical people, came into West Malaysia, scattering out along the coastal settlements.

The Mon and Khmer peoples who spread across Burma, Thailand, and Vietnam apparently never moved south into the peninsula. When the first Indians came across the Bay of Bengal their chief zone of contact lay north of Malaysia, in the Kra Isthmus. The shallow sea currents around the peninsula, affected both by the seasonal monsoon winds and by tidal irregularities, plus the vagaries of the monsoon winds themselves, made trader navigation around the peninsula difficult in the centuries before the Christian era. When Indian contact did slowly touch the southern part of the peninsula it remained chiefly interested in ports as landfalls, or was concerned with tin mining. There was some colonial settlement by Indians, but West Malaysia then was lightly populated by mobile peoples and must have presented fewer opportunities than other lands touched by Indian contact. Although small port trading stations developed, with some claim to area control, it is doubtful if large scale regional development by Indian-controlled principalities ever evolved in Malaya.

The daily living pattern of the early Malays or other short-term inhabitants shared in the common tradition of the southern Orient. It revolved around the use of aquatic resources, lowland fruits, and such root crops as the yams and the taros. Rice appears to have been a late introduction. Mobile living patterns related to boats and the coastal waterways, and riverine and coastal habitation in scattered clusters became the tradition among the Malays. Although West Malaysia presented no large rich lowland as did Burma, a small and mobile population possessed an ample set of resources for a simple type of culture. In time Malay culture became somewhat Indianized, for Indian culture elements underlie the Islamic culture patterns of modern Malays.

The west coast of Borneo, of which

Sarawak and Sabah (but not including Brunei) now comprise East Malaysia, undoubtedly shared in some of the early Indian and Chinese contacts, each at different times, though the frequencies were less along the Borneo coast than in the Malay Peninsula. Such contacts may well have tapped the local resources of the littoral and the coastal plain, but the upland interiors were not touched, and then must have carried only a very slight population of early human types. Proto-Malay and Malay peoples also must have ranged the coast, but the firm evidences of such contacts are slight. The Borneo coast lay at the margin of the very early contacts, and it did not then form a significantly attractive zone.

SEA TRADING, PORTS, AND PIRACY

As Indian contact expanded in the whole of Southeast Asia in the early centuries of the Christian era, there gradually appeared two centers of regional focus. Burma, Thailand, and Vietnam have already been dealt with, and the Island World will be discussed in the next chapter. The Malay Peninsula, lying between these two centers, became a site for way stations and landfall ports in the early patterns of sea travel and interregional trade. The local Malays probably participated but little in this trade to begin with, whereas Indians and Arabs were numerous, along with some Mons, Khmers, Sumatrans, and Javanese. There were many river mouths and island-protected harbors on the west coast of the peninsula that served as way stations, as knowledge of navigation developed and sea trade grew more common.

As the evolving political and military strength of the several focal centers developed in Burma, in the Mekong Delta, in Sumatra, and in Java, the Malay Peninsula constituted a no-man's land between these two spheres of influence. Peninsular ports began to be used by the free trader from outside realms and by those in political disfavor in any one region. There gradually evolved the art of piracy, the southern peninsula providing home ports for many of those preying upon trade in these waters. In this some of the Malays may well have joined. Few of these ports ever grew into a regional state, for the patterns of power were personal and subject to constant alteration, based upon through-trade rather than upon local population and resources. For the few ports that did expand into regional states, the sea-trade element remained strong and critical parts of the state structure. Langkasuka, probably located on the east coast in what today would be southern peninsular Thailand, was chiefly a sea-trade state. Kedah, located in what today is northwest Malaysia, probably was a land-based, regional state between the fifth and eleventh centuries, linked with Indonesian Sri Vijaya. Singapura, on the modern island of Singapore, was an important way station-entrepot in the fourteenth century, and in the late fifteenth century Malacca, on the west coast of modern West Malaysia, was perhaps the leading port along the eastern margin of the Indian Ocean, backed by a small land-based state.

As Sumatran and Javanese principalities grew into political states, themselves built partly upon the basis of sea power, each tried to control the peninsula, but the Burmese and Cambodian states rarely could exercise control so far south. The Indonesian state Sri Vijaya exerted some control over the peninsula for several centuries, and Madjapahit for a shorter period exerted some control also. It is obvious that there were many shifting patterns of regional control as ephemeral sea-states rose and fell. Piracy based upon peninsular ports was a strong element in this shifting pattern.

This ephemeral pattern of occupation of peninsular coastal ports was concentrated chiefly on the west coast, largely because of the better weather and navigational conditions. The east coast suffers from high surf, adverse winds, and difficult navigational conditions during the months of the winter monsoon, whereas the west coast is somewhat protected by the reach of Sumatra. Although the little ports were busy trade centers, the ships were small, the cargoes never were large, and the sheer volume of trade was slight as compared with that of today. No extensive port facilities were required, such as are found in modern ports and, therefore, none of the ports ever acquired extensive docks, warehouses, or buildings, and none of the ports ever grew into a large city.

A few products of the Malay Peninsula probably entered the interregional trade of the time. Tin was mined by many different peoples, a little alluvial gold was produced, a few forest products were extracted, but the total demand for these products was not great, and they led to no permanent development of settlements, dependent populations, or cultural landscapes. Today the small scars of tin mining are widely scattered; evidences of buildings are repeatedly unearthed, but the marks in the landscape were slight and easily overgrown by forest.

The west coast of Borneo was a marginal part of this world of sea trade and piracy, shifting allegiances, and changing conditions. Proto-Malay and Malay peoples had been drifting off the mainland and out of Java-Sumatra in small intermittent streams that carried them along the Borneo coast and into the Philippines. For several centuries prior to the coming of the Europeans this had been a more active process, and into portions of the Borneo west coast had come Melanu, Dusun, Kenyah, Kedayan, and Kayan peoples, chiefly occupying the coastal fringe in the north, the area now known as Sabah; in the southern sector, now equated with Sarawak, the Land Dyak and the Sea Dyak (Iban) were the chief components. Although some of these groups remained close to the littoral, others moved slightly inland, to become primarily land-based, village-dwelling shifting cultivators. Malays from the Malay Peninsula joined to some extent in these movements in the fifteenth century, chiefly centering in what today is the small independent state of Brunei, occupying the littoral fringe of a swampy sector of coast.

MOSLEMS, PORTUGUESE, DUTCH, AND BRITISH

The control over the Island World by the east Javanese sea-state of Madjapahit collapsed under the invasions of the Islamic Arabs and Indians in the fourteenth century. There followed a resurgence of autonomy among the ports and small regional entities of Malaysia and Indonesia since, by this time, considerable cultural individuality had developed among the peoples of this region. The Moslems were able to take over political and trade control of port states in piecemeal fashion without an organized military conquest. This Islamic entry was not a politically unified movement but a series of independent ventures by relatively small groups of Indians and Arabs whose chief common attribute was their Islamic religion. Militant effort organized small sultanates around the numerous ports and converted the Malays to Islam. Many little port states were extended into the hinterlands sufficiently to incorporate the Malays into the political and cultural structure of the sultanates.

Although the levying of tribute upon passing ships and a form of piracy again became frequent in these waters in the fifteenth century, some peninsular ports became active way stations in an increasing trade pattern, with ships of almost every oriental country touching some one or more of the ports. The decline of the Khmer state and the immaturity of Thai economy helped to cause the decline of the transpeninsular trade route, so that southern peninsular ports were now on the chief route. The tribute levies and piracy by port sultans did cause many ships to use the route around Sumatra, through the Strait of Sunda, avoiding the Strait of Malacca, but this was a variable detail in the main route.

Islamic initiative expanded trade and travel contact all through the southern Orient and Chinese traders increased in numbers. Malaysia, located on what was now one of the chief trade routes of the world, reached a new peak in its trade activity. Not many of the products passing through its ports were either domestic exports or imports; the trade was in good part transit, and Malaysia was but a landfall en route. Nor were the Malays themselves the chief traders, but the quiet local population that supplied food, water, tools, labor, and services to the passing traders. This very function, of course, stimulated Malays into taking more interest in land and agriculture, and their population began growing rather markedly.

When the Portuguese arrived in Indian ports they soon learned of the importance of Malacca, which then perhaps was the foremost port of Malaysia. Malacca appeared to dominate the trade route, and perhaps the stories led the Portuguese to think of it as a producing area also. If the Portuguese were to monopolize the trade with Europe, control of Malaysian ports was necessary. So, with a few ships and men they were able to take over port after port, and to turn each into a base in much the same way as Moslem traders before them. They did not expand areal control over Malaysia once they found it a nonproductive region. They failed to convert the Moslem Malays to Christianity, and changed little of Malay life. The transit function of ports continued much as before, but with only a new set of traders.

As Malacca passed under Portuguese control in 1511 and new pressures began to develop, Islamic port rulers and sultans began shifting their bases inland, laying claim to areas and territories in more specific terms. The sea-state concept began turning into a land-state concept, and by the end of the eighteenth century the area of present day West Malaysia was claimed by a series of Islamic Malay sultans. There were still conflicts of lineage and territorial control that were to be ironed out by the British at a later date, but Malaysia was now a region of land states with inland state capitals, and growing patterns of land development.

The Dutch attempted to break the Portuguese monopoly, seize what appeared to be the chief ports, control the trade routes, and use the transit ports, but they concerned themselves only casually with Malaysia as a region. British, French, Danish, and Swedish traders appeared, all interested in dominating the Malaysian ports. The arrival of these competitive European traders added diverse elements to the traffic, increased the variety of shipping, added to the competitive struggle for control of ports, and complicated the life of the Malays, but did little to develop Malaysia as a region. Chinese, Indonesians, Indians, Arabs, Japanese, and varieties of Europeans all engaged in a competitive trade contest, with piracy, looting, trickery, naval warfare, and varying group alliances-of-the moment all techniques in the struggle. The Portuguese lost out fairly early, the French, Danes, Swedes, Chinese, and a few others gradually dropped out and avoided Malaysian ports. The Indians, Indonesians, Arabs, Dutch, and British became the chief contestants. Some Islamic port sultans, as native regional rulers of the hinterlands, were able to profit from the contest, but benefits to the Malays as a whole, and Malaysia as a region, were meager. The contest was long and drawn out and it was not until the 1820's that the British finally ousted the Dutch from control of the Malaysian ports. In their post-Napoleonic settlement with the Dutch, the British withdrew any claims to the ports in Indonesia, and the Netherlands gave up claims to ports in Malaysia. But this did not, as yet, mean that Britain had begun to exercise regional control over all of Malaysia—her interest still lay in the ports and their value in trade with the East.

THE GROWTH OF A BRITISH COLONY

The island that we now label Singapore has sheltered waters behind it which served for centuries as a base point for traders and pirates. Stamford Raffles, in the 1820's, dreamed of a great port here, at the very apex of the Malay Peninsula, which could become the primary hub of all eastern trade. Modern Singapore, as city and international port, has grown out of that dream, but in the 1820's it was still only a decadent village port (see Fig. 4.9). The British concentrated on a few spots, such as Singapore, Malacca, Port Dickson, Port Swettenham, and Penang. Singapore soon outdistanced the others, though Penang for some decades remained the base of the British East India Company's administrative operations. Slowly, as settlements grew, and as food and raw-material needs increased, administrative problems led to the extension of police power, treaties with local sultans, and a growing concept of territorial domain. In the latter half of the nineteenth century British investment in tin mining and plantation agriculture began, and the need for territorial administration increased.

Since the frequented ports were on the west coast, economic development began here also, and the growth in territorial administration focused upon the west coast. The chief ports and their immediate hinterlands were grouped into one pattern run by the British Colonial Office as the Straits Settlements, to which for convenience were joined such other stray British holdings as the Cocos-Keeling and Christmas islands south of Sumatra. Nine Malay sultanate states were recognized, and with four of them Britain had treaties which led to a group termed Federated Malay States (Fig. 21.1). The British exercised considerable control over these four states through devious administrative patterns, for these were chiefly the west coast states in which British tin mining and plantation agriculture were carried on. The remaining states were grouped as the Unfederated Malay States in which there was less British control and smaller economic investment. This triple administrative pattern kept Malaysia disunited, kept regional development unequal, and kept it a kind of no-man's land still, for there was no such thing as Malaysian citizenship.

The Islamic Malays, for the most part, during the period of increasing British territorial control and economic development remained a rural, unobtrusive people of agricultural-fishing economy, village dwellers along the coastal fringes, the estuarine lowlands, and at certain inland localities in which they could live their traditional life. Although many came to reside in the ports and cities and to provide domestic services and some labor, they were disinclined to become tin miners, plantation laborers, stevedores, and manual laborers. European comment termed the Malays "lazy, indolent drones," meaning that they were not willing to do the menial work desired of them by the European. Consequently, as tin mining and plantation agriculture began, other labor had to be found, for the British, of course, would only manage and direct. Many Chinese traders had taken early advantage of the peaceful British ports and were willingly enlisted in tin mining, so that there began a steady influx of Chinese laborers. They were less efficient as plantation workers, being disinclined to remain on the job once they had accumulated sufficient resources to set up shopkeeping and trading enterprises. Indian laborers were brought in on term contracts, and proved more satisfactory than the Chinese on the plantations.

As Indians and Chinese came into Malaysia in increasing numbers, and as greater economic development took place, protection of the Malays became necessary. A land policy evolved that prohibited other than Malay ownership of rice land, but permitted the expansion of tin mining and plantation agriculture. Only slowly were Chinese and Indians allowed to own any kind of agricultural land, and there grew up considerable restriction upon both the Chinese and Indians. Both came to Malaysia as temporary residents, the Chinese to go home when they felt rich enough, the Indians normally at the termination of their contracts. Neither Chinese nor Indians participated in government but remained separate cultural groups, and both thought of Malaysia only in terms of economic opportunity. Gradually a few Indians and many Chinese became

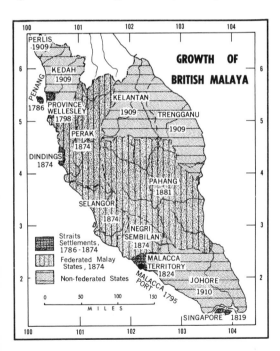

FIGURE 21.1. Growth of British Malaya, 1786–1910.

second- and third-generation residents of Malaysia but retained their cultural ties to their homelands.

The British developed such roads, railroads, ports, and telecommunications as were requisite for economic development. Government effort in geological survey, agriculture, port development, the postal service, and public health was carried out as necessary. Some education of the Malays was slowly provided for, but seldom for the Chinese and Indians, who came to support their own schools, furthering their own cultural traditions. Malaysia became one of the most productive British holdings, but never was administered as one country for its own sake. Gradual changes in government patterns came about, but before World War II no real integration of the threefold administration of Malaysia was achieved. By World War II the 2,500,000 Chinese exceeded the Malay population of 2,100,000, the Indian total stood close to 600,000, the Indonesian population at about 40,000 and the occidental population at about 30,000. Yet there was no integration of peoples, region, and culture, and the British held administrative control with only incomplete participation by the Malays.

Along the coast of Borneo there had been sporadic attempts to find points of trade contact, establish European-controlled ports, and find commodities of trade. Americans and British, in the early nineteenth century vied for concessions and controls and, though personal operations and chartered companies no longer were in favor in England, things ended with a British citizen ruling as the Rajah of Sarawak, after 1841; a chartered company in control of North Borneo, after 1881; and the protected sultanate of Brunei sandwiched between the two. Brunei earlier had laid claim to a large share of northern Borneo and to the Sulu Archipelago, but the Sultan of Brunei ceded away much of the

territory in actions whose validity has recently been questioned. British diplomatic maneuvers protected these British interests to the outbreak of World War II, but only small scale economic development occurred in either section.

THE CREATION OF MODERN MALAYSIA

At the end of World War II it was obvious to Great Britain that an adjustment of political machinery in the Malay Peninsula and western Borneo was required. The Chinese and Indians had been given neither responsibility nor opportunity to consider themselves citizens of Malaysia. The Chinese controlled most of the non-British wealth of the country, and dominated retail domestic trade and much of the foreign trade. They had supported Nationalist China, but after 1949 their allegiance began to waver. And in 1950 many Chinese held the attitude that they would inherit Malaysia when the British lost control of the region in a few short years. The Indians presented no immediate political or economic threat. The Malays had become aware of the Chinese problem and finally were developing a spirit of social and political nationalism.

A Union of Malaya was first tried in 1946, with Singapore, North Borneo, and Sarawak each as a Crown Colony, and Brunei a protected state. The Federation of Malaya plan was put into effect in 1948, and Kuala Lumpur was made the new political capital, but by 1951 there was serious question whether the plan would succeed, since there still were severe restrictions upon both Chinese and Indians. Under the 1948 plan North Borneo and Sarawak remained in the Crown Colony status, and Brunei continued as a protected state.

A Communist rebellion had been declared in 1948, and by 1951 it began to threaten seriously. During 1952–1953 far-reaching changes in procedures concerning citizenship, education, resettlement, and land tenure promised some social integration and for the first time lent hope to the cultural development of one Malaysia, if peace could be restored. Several hundred village and town communities, totalling over a half million people, were moved from their original sites to newly built and militarily protected "new villages," each provided with schools, dispensaries, shopping areas, truck-garden zones, and other local facilities. This was an effort to deny Communist insurgents access to supplies and population. Primarily affected were the Chinese who, in the absence of most civic privileges, showed no patriotic-mindedness toward Malaysia and devoted little of their capital resources to local development. It was the Chinese community that tacitly supported Communist activity. By late 1956 British policy reached the point of preparing for the independence of West Malaysia since the control of Communist activity was gaining headway.

The Federation of Malaya became an independent political state in 1957, technically an elective constitutional monarchy in which a Sultan of one of the states was elected as the supreme head of state for a five-year period. Singapore was included in the Federation, North Borneo and Sarawak each remained a Crown Colony, and Brunei continued as a protected state. The Communist Emergency was declared ended in 1960, and British planning for the long-term structure moved further. In 1963 a new and looser Federation of Malaysia came into being, combining the peninsular and island sectors, But at the last minute Brunei declined to join, and Singapore withdrew in 1965. It is not clear whether political structure has now assumed firm shape for the foreseeable future. In 1970 the Federation of Malaysia included thirteen states in two groupings: West

Malaysia included eleven states in the peninsula, not including Singapore; East Malaysia included the two states of Sabah (renamed from North Borneo) and Sarawak in Borneo, but omitted Brunei. Singapore operated as a self-governing state within the Commonwealth, and Brunei retained its status as a British protectorate.

ETHNIC LIFE AND ECONOMY

Three main sources of support were important in the traditional economy of the Malay; fishing, rice cultivation, and the mixed jungle garden. As the Malay population has markedly increased since the advent of British control, this traditional economy has both continued and expanded in its productivity. The Malay eats a large amount of fish products in many forms, and fishery products are secured from all available waters. Today the Malay provides fish for the Chinese and Indian populations, as well as for himself, so that fishing continues to be an important Malay occupation. The large increase in Malay and alien population has created a large and steady market, and many Malay families derive their chief cash income from fishing. Most of the varied peoples of East Malaysia have been traditional shifting cultivators, providing their own basic food supplies and contributing only very casually to any aspect of commercial economy.

British land policy restricted ownership of developed rice lands to Malays, so that today the Malay is the rice farmer of the country. In East Malaysia there have also been similar restrictions on certain categories of lands, preserving for native ethnic groups the rights of cultivation and usage. The total rice acreage amounts to over 1,000,000 at present. The yield provides just over a third of the total rice consumed in Malaya, but despite this shortage the acreage is only slowly rising. The ricefields provide the one type of open landscape of the country, for trees are not grown along field margins, settlement generally avoids the field areas, and most of the other agriculture of the country involves trees and shrubs (Figs. 21.2 and 21.3).

Aside from rice planting the Malay traditionally was no real farmer in the modern technical sense—his jungle gardens were chaotic plantings of coconut and areca palms, coffee, bananas, durians, jackfruit, rambutans, mangosteens, and a few other fruits, plus tangled patches of taro, yams, manioc, pepper, gourds, sugarcane, onions, and a few other vegetables. This chaotic and tangled planting pattern is hard on the statistician, and it does not make for the ready supplying of town and city markets in large volume. For the rural Malay it was and is sufficient,

and it is also true that jungle gardens of this sort are in far better ecologic balance in this moist and hot climate than are the orderly, weed-free, massed plantings of the occidental. Perhaps some 500,000 acres are devoted to these gardens, aside from the acreage of coconut, rubber, and other commercial crops which now also make up a part of Malay economy.

The rural Malay by preference lives in clusters of homes, each separated and screened by plantings. The larger and more accessible clusters today are more village-like, and many of them have a shop or two. The pile-built house is almost standard, but there are regional patterns of design and decoration. To supplement his living pattern a variety of handicrafts were traditional until occidental machine goods and Chinese artisans came into Malaysia in volume and numbers. Forest products such as rattans, gums, resins, and special woods have always been gathered and sold in small volumes. Gold and tin were mined in small amounts for sale in the past, and some Malay activity in both products remains in the economy today. Cattle, buffalo, fowls, and pigs were kept in small numbers by the Malay, the cattle and buffalo chiefly for ricefield cultivation and local land transport. After becoming a Moslem the Malay largely gave up pig raising. The annual dollar income of the Malay has never been large, but his self-sufficient pattern of living required no large income.

The Malay is not the indolent drone formerly described by so many occidentals, but his pattern of living did not require endless labor. And in the centuries of piracy, despotic local rule by Indian and Moslem rajahs and sultans, and competitive struggle by all manner of aliens, the Malay often found himself heavily taxed on any surplus commercial commodity. There constantly was a deterrent to labor and production beyond that needed for a subsistence economy. And

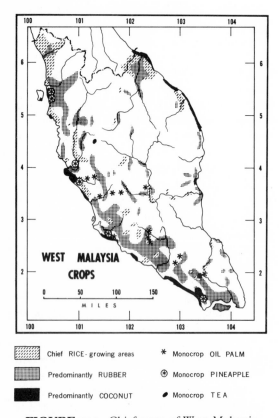

Chief RICE-growing areas   * Monocrop OIL PALM

Predominantly RUBBER   ⊛ Monocrop PINEAPPLE

Predominantly COCONUT   ● Monocrop TEA

FIGURE 21.2. Chief crops of West Malaysia and Singapore.

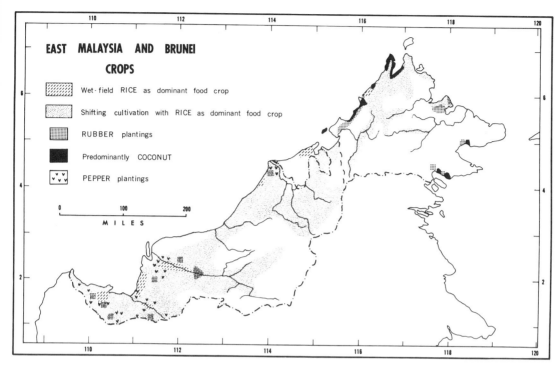

FIGURE 21.3. Chief crops of East Malaysia and Brunei.

in the modern period, when he has faced the competition of the money-zealous Chinese and occidental, he has been at the disadvantage common to every rural people practicing a near-subsistence economy.

Since about 1918 the Malay has taken to planting rubber and coconut in small holdings for commercial production. He has gone into the cities and towns where domestic service, small trading, fishing, and similar occupations were possible, and increasingly the Malay has become a civil servant, policeman, and private entrepreneur. His patterns of living have grown more complex as he has been surrounded by new peoples with new cultures. There are many gradations in living levels, from the rich sultan to the poorest fishing villager, but the majority of the rural Malays live a simple life, on a relatively low annual money income. Under protective British policy the Malays were

not dispossessed of their lands or their traditional occupations, but education and changing opportunities are affecting the way of life of a large share of the Malay population. As industrialization comes to Malaysia, the Malay is taking his place in the modernized urban society, but his background of lesser levels of education and the lack of modern technological skills provides a handicap that remains present, and one that will continue into the future.

The various ethnic elements of Sarawak and Sabah have traditionally followed simple rural livelihood patterns even more than the Malay of West Malaysia. Their opportunities for participation in modernized economy have been less, in the past, and many cling to their traditional systems today.

The Chinese in Malaysia have come from different portions of southern China. They first came as "sojourners" to work in the tin mines and at whatever other occupations where they could make enough money to retire to China. Increasingly, this habituated concept has been dropped, and most Malaysian Chinese now look forward to permanent residence in Malaysia. From the tin mines the Chinese moved into the larger villages, towns, and cities as entrepreneurs, many of them succeeding uncommonly well. In the earlier periods they retained the clan and community groupings of their home districts, and these clustered community characteristics continue to a considerable degree. Chinese are well scattered over West Malaysia at present, but form smaller communities in East Malaysia. Much of modern foreign trade and industrial development finds Chinese active in management and technological operation, for the Chinese have made the most of educational opportunities. In the present era Chinese are to be found in almost every occupational sector of Malaysian life. The Chinese have been the creators of many of the urban living systems in Malaysia, and their town and city architecture, in the past, has been a distinctive feature of Malaysian towns. Building on the ground, in tight-to-compact structures, the Chinese sections of Malaysian towns show features and forms quite different from Malay architecture. Restricted from owning rice lands, Chinese have engaged in other kinds of agricultural activity. Around many towns and cities the Chinese are truck and market garden producers, where their traditional skills have made them proficient, productive, and prosperous. Their combining of poultry and pig keeping, as an integral element in their agricultural system, clearly differentiates Chinese from Malays.

Indians originally came into Malaysia as contract labor on the rubber plantations, and for several decades were inconspicuous members of the population. Frequently, they were short-term residents, but Indians also have turned to permanent residence in Malaysia. In towns and cities former plantation-labor Indians have not added distinctive forms of urban architecture, but they have often gone into characteristic callings, such as dairying, restaurant operation, moneylending, and professional occupations.

Malaysia, even in the rural and small town situation, therefore, has presented a plural pattern of living, of occupation, and of impact on the landscapes of the country. The three-part ethnic structure displays great variety, and has produced a three-part culture system, with different landscape impacts. Increasingly, in the present era, these separate elements are blending and blurring, but many of the characteristic cultural features will persist for a long time into the future.

COMMERCIAL ECONOMY

Tin mining is a key activity in Malaysia's productive economy. Tin is a more valuable product per ton than most of the nonprecious minerals, so that the 40,000–80,000 tons mined annually produce a large financial return. Almost entirely an export product, Malaysian tin is an important item to the foreign trade of the country. Alluvial tin ores are widely scattered around the western foothill margins of West Malaysia where most of the mining has so far been done (Fig. 21.4). Modern alluvial mining techniques severely scar the surface and produce a blighted landscape, so that modern mining is making permanent impressions upon the landscape. In a few cases restorative measures have begun to turn the ex-mining surfaces into crop lands or other useful lands. These measures will be increasingly important in the future. Large-scale mining began during the nineteenth century, and steadily increased in importance until Malaysia became one of the world's chief sources of tin. The ores first were exported to Britain for smelting, but local smelting has

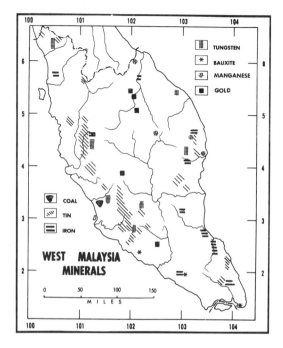

FIGURE 21.4. Mineral producing regions, West Malaysia and Singapore.

increased in importance, and now a share of the tin ores from Burma, Thailand, and Indonesia are also smelted in Malaysian refineries. Earlier mining used simple machinery and much hand labor, which was contributed largely by the Chinese. Increasing mechanization has occurred, though the wartime destruction of equipment brought a temporary resurgence of simpler techniques. In 1969 about 1,100 mines were in operation, with a labor force of about 50,000. Early ownership was entirely British, but Chinese control has been increasing steadily. In 1969 British-owned mines still produced more than half the tin mined. Some of the alluvial ore mines in local areas are close to exhaustion, but there still are fairly large reserves of alluvial ore in West Malaysia. Lode mining in the ore zones around the edges of the granitic uplands will increase in time.

Gradually, other minerals are being produced in West Malaysia. Prior to World War II, soft coal good enough for steam power was mined and used for the railways, tin smelters, generation of electricity, and various other industrial operations. A traditional occupation in central and northern West Malaysia is gold mining, which continues as a small-operator pattern of alluvial mining, though there is now sporadic lode mining. Iron ore, bauxite, manganese, a little tungsten, some ilmenite, and a few other minor minerals are also produced. Iron ore, bauxite, and manganese mining was begun in the years before World War II along the east coast and in southern West Malaysia by Japanese companies operating concessions, and it continues in large volume.

East Malaysia appears to have only poor prospects in mineral development, though mining of antimony, coal, mercury, and bauxite have been carried on in Sarawak in the past (Fig. 21.5). A little gold is still mined and Japanese interests are attempting to develop some new coal mines. Sabah has only mined a little coal, though deposits of a few other minerals are known. Petroleum has been the most valuable item in mineral production, and it may have future prospects. The Miri field in northern Sarawak is about exhausted but the Seria field in Brunei continues productive, and prospecting for other fields continues.

Plantation agriculture has grown to exceed mining in the commercial economy of Malaysia. It began in a small way at Penang in the early nineteenth century when the British East India Company planted pepper, cloves, and nutmeg, hoping to become independent of the Dutch-controlled Moluccas. Depressed markets for pepper and plant diseases which destroyed the cloves and nutmeg trees disposed of the first efforts. But the plantation idea remained; during the nineteenth century there were plantings of sugarcane, coffee, gambier, cacao, tea, pine-

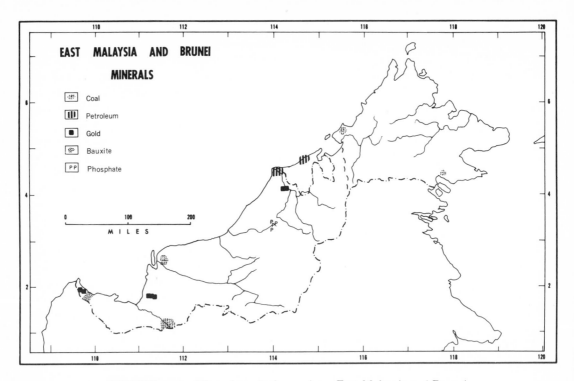

FIGURE 21.5. Mineral producing regions, East Malaysia and Brunei.

apple, and rubber. Sugarcane, tea, and coffee were minor successes for British plantation operators; pineapple succeeded but its cultivation passed into the hands of the Chinese; and cacao and gambier failed as plantation crops. Rubber, of course, succeeded better than all the others and has come to dominate the agriculture of Malaysia. First planted commercially in 1895, the acreage reached 40,000 in 1905, and has continuously expanded until in 1969 the total exceeded 4,800,000.

The first plantings were British, but, once the international rubber boom began, Malays and Chinese began small plantings in patches and small-field totals, and by 1969 the total small holdings stood at about 2,800,000 acres. The roughly 2,000,000 acres of plantation rubber are divided among some 2,300 estates, almost half of which are Chinese in ownership. The European estates contain some of the best varieties of trees. Chinese estates and many of the small holdings until recently were in old trees of poorer varieties, so long tapped that their productivity was declining. Replanting of much of the total rubber acreage has been going on under controlled programs that have gained acceptance by smallholders, finally, and the Malaysian expectation is that natural rubber can continue to compete with synthetic types. Since 1960 total production figures have run over 850,000 tons per year, and rubber is the number-one source of income for Malaysia. Although the plantings are permanent features of the Malaysian landscape, the houses and settlements of workers in the past have been rather shacky and makeshift since there is a tremendous turnover in the working force. West Malaysia long dominated the rubber picture, but the Sabah rubber acreage has been growing steadily, and small plantings have been common in Sarawak for several decades. Recent expansion of the Sarawak plantings with new stock is making rubber the ranking commercial crop there, too.

Coconut is a traditional crop, but in the late nineteenth century a considerable plantation acreage was set out in coconut along the coastal zones of both West and East Malaysia. The total acreage of plantations and small holdings, slightly lower than before World War II, is about 700,000, making coconut rank second among the commercial crops. Only a small share of the production among the local populations is used at home, and coconut for them is a cash crop. A strong program of upgrading plantings has been going on, both to improve yields and the general conditions of production.

Sugarcane, coffee, and tea succeeded as plantation crops but could not compete with rubber, so that the total acreages never grew large. By 1910 sugar ceased to be grown on plantations, and coffee has almost disappeared as a plantation crop, but both are widely spread items in gardens at present. Tea still is cultivated on a few plantations, but the acreage is under 10,000. The oil palm, introduced from West Africa, was set out on plantations after 1917, and now totals about 215,000 acres, with considerable expansion underway. Major plantings of oil palm on estates occur in Sabah, but Sarawak has not yet begun employing this crop plant. Pineapple covers about 25,000 acres of Chinese plantations in southern West Malaysia. Experiments are again being made with cacao, and with abaca, sisal, derris, and a few other plants, with an eye to diversified plantation agriculture. No pronounced efforts have been made with any of the native fruits on plantations.

Cash-crop agriculture among the Chinese shows up in several other forms. The Chinese do most of the market gardening in Malaysia, with small but intensively worked holdings around the cities and towns. Many Chinese, in the past, have grown manioc on rented or squatted lands for a few years in a variant of shifting cultivation. Sugarcane, pineapple, tobacco, peanuts, many of the tropical fruits, and various other minor crops are often grown by Chinese farmers as a part of a commercial agriculture on a small scale. The Chinese also raise pigs, ducks, and chickens, in commercial proportions for the supply of Chinese and occidental urban populations, since these items are not now common and in ample supply among the Malays. Vine pepper is widely grown by Chinese on small plots of land. Pepper is widely scattered over West Malaysia, has seldom been grown in Sabah, but is one of the important export commodities from Sarawak.

Formerly it was common to distinguish local-economy agriculture from commercial-export agriculture, but in recent decades all ethnic groups have taken to production of all types of commercial or export crops and, by 1970, the smallholder contributed the larger share of all Malaysian export crops except the oil palm products. Recent participation of smallholders in replanting projects for rubber and coconut makes it clear that the smallholders of all parts of Malaysia will continue to engage energetically in commercial agricultural operations, and the former distinctions between plantation (estate) production and smallholder production are meaningless so far as the national economy is concerned. Such distinctions are, of course, significant in the appearance of the landscapes of different sectors of the country, for the large holdings create mono-crop landscapes, as opposed to the mixed landscapes of the smallholders.

During the late 1950's the government sponsorship of resettlement projects in different sections of Malaysia has promoted diversified agricultural landscapes. Somewhat formalized village settlements, surrounded by formalized allocations of rubber, rice, coconut, fruit, and vegetable acreages produce both distinctive landscapes and diversified agricultural undertakings. Whether this form of expansion of the agricultural economy is a profitable one cannot be determined as yet, but there are reasonable doubts as to the economic success of such programs.

Forested peninsular Malaya and Borneo traditionally supplied themselves with wood and exported small volumes of exotic products. British nineteenth-century occupance considered the forests something to be cleared for agriculture, and most of the timber supply came to be imported. More recently forest utilization has begun to more than provide for domestic requirements, except for some of the special needs. Forest control and planned production of firewood, construction lumber, and export timber now are turning the forests of Malaysia into an economic asset which undoubtedly can be expanded considerably in the future. About twenty percent of the total national area now has been put into reserved forests, and withdrawn from the reservoir of lands alienable to nonforest uses. As effective surveys continue more such reserves may be established. Working procedures now normally extract merchantable timber before opening up land units for settlement purposes. West Malaysia and Sabah are farther ahead in such procedures than is Sarawak, in which shifting cultivation has worked over much of the earlier forest cover. Internal consumption perhaps uses about two-thirds of the present annual cut of timber, but the export of Malaysian timber, lumber, and wood products is steadily rising and, under controlled patterns, can become a long-term contributor to the domestic and export economy.

No part of Malaysia was a region in which land transport was traditionally important, for this was chiefly a littoral environment in which water traffic was normal to all concerned. The historic pattern did not involve much in the way of port or harbor facilities.

In the nineteenth century, as British economic development began in the modern pattern ports rather logically were the first elements of transport to receive attention. Later the rail system was laid out to connect the tin mines and growing plantations with the ports. Roads first were service lines for the railways, which also was true of telecommunications. All these features became located along the west coast of the peninsula (Fig. 21.6). On Borneo trails led into the interior but anything more than town streets are rather recent in development, except for the short coastal rail line in western Sabah (Fig. 21.7). Slowly all forms of transportation have been expanded into other portions of the country, both in the peninsula and on Borneo, but there still is regional imbalance in the distribution of facilities. Singapore soon outdistanced the other ports of the country, to become the hub of all land and sea transport. Penang and Port Swettenham

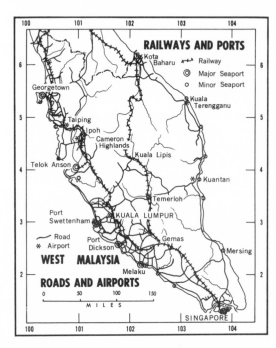

FIGURE 21.6. Transportation facilities, West Malaysia and Singapore.

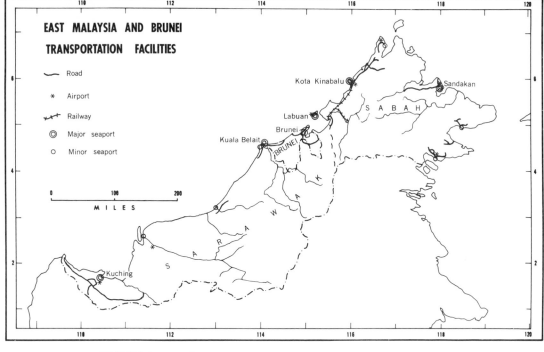

FIGURE 21.7. Transportation facilities, East Malaysia and Brunei.

are other important ports that have risen steadily in ranking use. Present government planning is taking large steps in port development with major development of Port Swettenham in order to lessen dependence on Singapore.

Within West Malaysia, the present network of roads serves the west coastal zone rather effectively, but other portions of the peninsula still possess only a skeleton system. Most of the road system is well-built and well-maintained, and is becoming increasingly heavily used. East Malaysia currently is engaging in major road building programs, but most systems still are local systems reaching inland from the several ports.

TRADE AND INDUSTRY

The nineteenth century economic development of peninsular Malaya began with the primary production of tin as raw ore con-

centrates and with raw agricultural commodities. This led patterns of development into processing activities such as tin smelting and various kinds of agricultural processing. The later development of commercial timbering led into the milling of lumber products. For a considerable period the foreign trade of Malaysia showed the export of tin concentrates, raw rubber, copra, palm kernels, and logs as the primary items of value, and the import list contained a large volume of food products and all the variety of manufactured goods that Malaysian consumers demanded. The position of Singapore, in those earlier trade returns, also involved a large entrepot function, in which import and re-exports rated high by value.

Modern Malaysian economic activity has shown a steady increase in the level of processing, so that smelted tin, processed rubber, and vegetable oils have ranked steadily higher through time. With the recent exclusion of Singapore from the Malaysian trade returns, the entrepot element has dropped off markedly. The annual trade returns, by value, show marked fluctuations, since such commodities as tin, rubber, vegetable oils, and logs-lumber fluctuate rather constantly in world price levels. Imports have shown a steady continuance in rice and other food products, since Malaysia is a food-deficit region, and the range of commodities has altered in favor of capital equipment and producer-machinery, as manufacturing activities in Malaysia gradually increase their production of many of the simpler consumer-goods commodities.

The directional pattern of Malaysian export trade varies rather markedly from period to period, depending upon the regional demand for the primary products tin, rubber, vegetable oils, and timber. In one year China will be a strong buyer of rubber, the Netherlands will be a big buyer of vegetable oils, whereas Great Britain may buy less tin one year than the next. To some extent the import trade volumes fluctuate to adjust to this differential pattern of export movements. In general terms the chief Malaysian trading partners have been Great Britain, the United States, Japan, Canada, U.S.S.R., China, and Australia.

After World War II Malaysia embarked upon a program of industrialization. From the late 1950's, after independence, this program has been increasingly emphasized, and it has aimed at more than domestic sufficiency in manufactures. Rubber manufacturing has steadily increased its volume and its range of products. The food and beverage manufactures have been significant components of recent development. Petroleum refining and simpler aspects of chemicals industries, automobile assembly, aluminum fabrication, and the fabrication of steel products from imported steel shapes have been among the leading aspects of the program so far. A small integrated steel plant is in operation as a start in the supply of raw iron and steel for the domestic economy. Textile manufacturing has a fair degree of development, but this has not been a primary field of Malaysian development. There are a number of establishment beginnings in electronics assembly-fabrication which are suggestive of future developments. Malaysia is beginning to produce small surpluses in a few manufactured items, and these will bulk steadily more important in the export trade.

To date much of the industrial development is concentrated on the mainland near Penang or around Kuala Lumpur-Port Swettenham, but agricultural processing is more widely distributed, and future developments of many of the elements of light manufacturing will be distributed among the other urban areas of the western portion of West Malaysia.

THE POPULATION ISSUE

Malaysia is not overpopulated at the present time, and the problems of population are less those of numbers directly than they are problems of the relative balance of population adhering to ethnic-cultural groupings (Figs. 21.8 and 21.9). In these terms Malaysia is clearly a plural society, made up of Malays, Chinese, Indians-Pakistanis, and several ethnic minorities that relate to, but do not fully merge with, Malays. Lacking a recent census we estimate the Malaysian population at approximately 12,000,000 in 1970, suggestively made up of: Malays, 5,800,000; Chinese, 4,400,000; Indians-Pakistanis, 1,100,000; Sea Dyak, 300,000, other ethnic groups combined, 400,000.

Within the present political construct of the state of Malaysia, therefore, the Malays form the major component and, by including the Dyak and other Malay-related ethnic groups, clearly outnumber the Chinese. When Singapore was included in the Federation, but the Borneo states were not, the

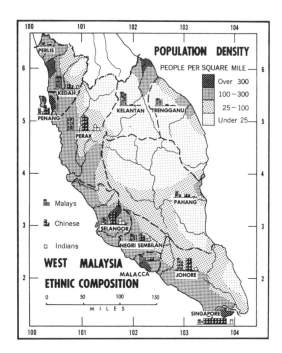

FIGURE 21.8. Population density and ethnic composition, West Malaysia and Singapore. The population map is an estimate of the late 1960's, whereas the ethnic composition is that of 1951.

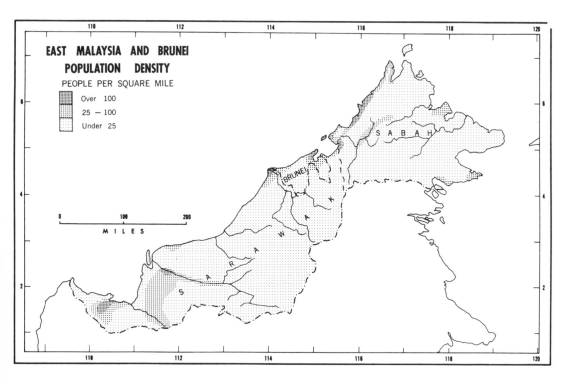

FIGURE 21.9. Population density, East Malaysia and Brunei.

Malays did not form the major component and had no ethnic minorities as politico-cultural allies. The Malays are determined not to lose control of their country to any other ethnic-cultural group-system. The multi-ethnic nature of Malaysian society plus Malay determination to maintain control make goals of "Malaysian nationalism" difficult to attain. Under the earlier British political policy of divide-and-rule, the Chinese had openly anticipated that, with continued immigration of Chinese, they could look forward to the day when Chinese would outnumber the Malays through their combined immigration-birth rate population increases. Recent restrictions on immigration reduce this prospect. All ethnic groups, except some of the small minority components, exhibit high birth rates and high net rates of population increase. Within the present political state the Malays anticipate retaining their position as the dominant ethnic element.

The long-term issue of "control" within the political state may, however, not be a simple matter of population numbers. The Malay birth rates currently are slightly higher than the Chinese birth rates, but so are infant mortality and adult death rates. The rural orientation of the majority of the Malay population, as opposed to the urban orientation of the majority of the Chinese population, makes the matter of control over long-term net population increase a somewhat difficult matter. Government programs in education involve two general mediums at the secondary school level, Malay-medium and English-medium, and at this level there are programs leading to technical-vocational and to liberal arts objectives. The Chinese community privately provides its own Chinese-medium secondary school system. The Chinese are more responsive to educational opportunities than are the Malays, still, and there are larger percentages of Chinese going beyond the primary level of education than is true for the Malays. In

that the Chinese have had very strong representation in the secondary aspects of Malaysian economy in the past, and in that they are more responsive to higher-level educational opportunities, the question of "control" within the state may be temporarily solved by Malay dominance in numbers at present, but merely postponed into the future in terms of economic and technological dominance.

Within West Malaysia, particularly, patterns of urbanism are appearing strong within recent decades, and are affecting all ethnic elements. The earlier dichotomy of Malays as rural, and Chinese as towns dwelling is blurring as population increases and as the nature of the socioeconomic structure changes. It is no longer true that towns are simple market places and cities are religious-administrative capitals. Although Kuala Lumpur as the largest Malaysian city (in 1970 about 400,000) and the political capital has the obvious elements of political-capital symbolism as well as the equally obvious elements of the important marketplace, it is accumulating industrial suburbs in which complex technological skills are increasingly in demand. At the same time Kuala Lumpur is accumulating large numbers of urban residents who do not fit easily into any one of the three primary occupational outlets. Many of these urban residents are absorbed into a services category of occupational activity, but many remain unemployed or underemployed. Although Singapore is not a part of the present Malaysian political state it, too, presents a similar imbalance in socioeconomic structure. Although industrial development in other Malaysian towns and cities is not yet far advanced, the rates of national urbanism threaten to outrun the rates of socioeconomic development within Malaysian life. In that Malaysia, particularly West Malaysia, shows a somewhat higher degree of urbanization than the rest of Southeast Asia, the socioeconomic dilemma is greater here. When these problems are compounded by the ethnic-cultural variety exhibited in Malaysia, they become potential problems affecting the future of the political state and its structure.

SELF-GOVERNING SINGAPORE

Singapore, as the chief port of nineteenth century British Malaya, quickly rose to the position of the largest urban entity in the regional British zone in Southeast Asia. Military and naval bases were established on the island and, later, an air base. The port became a key station in the British Empire's worldwide military, communications, and trade systems. Its entrepot trade function, and its commercial services to western Indonesia, Thailand, and British Malaya were significant elements in its economic development. As such, the city attracted a large immigrant population of Chinese, and Chinese have steadily been the dominant ethnic element on the island and in the city (see Fig. 4.9 and the accompanying text).

After the end of World War II, with the shift in British world policy, as national independence came to both Indonesia and Malaysia, the position and fortunes of Singapore have been changing, but at the same time they have become more precariously balanced. Prosperity of the port and its city has been dependent on regional and world conditions, and the steady decrease of British expenditures on the military-naval-air base, has made this dependence steadily greater. Final withdrawal of British military bases was programmed for 1971; usage may be extended but only on a reduced scale. In the long past the prosperity of any port city in the location of Singapore depended upon good conditions for free trade in the surrounding region, and present prosperity equally reflects that situation.

Singapore was included in the several political formats designed for an independent Malaysia, as previously mentioned. As Malaysian political evolution took more

specifically nationalistic shape, the leadership of Singapore foresaw increasing isolation within a single political structure in which its freedom of trade would suffer increasing restrictions as Malayanization continued. Singapore, therefore, withdrew from the Federation of Malaysia in 1965, and elected to go it alone as a self-governing state within the Commonwealth, a position which would enable enhancement of its port as a center of interregional trade. The population of Singapore, however, had grown too large to subsist upon the fluctuating patterns of trade, alone, since Indonesia was in a pattern of disrupted economic development and the Federation of Malaysia was seeking means of controlling their own foreign trade through Port Swettenham. A program of urban industrialization was therefore embarked upon, somewhat similar to that which has been taking shape in Hong Kong.

The island of Singapore, in political area, comprises 224.5 square miles, and has a population estimated, in 1970, at 2,100,000, of whom at least three-fourths are Chinese. The city of Singapore is located on the southeast sector of the island, but now has spread out widely from the initial core as focussed on the port by Stamford Raffles (see Fig. 4.9). Once the interior of the island was cropped in varying patterns by several different systems, and small areas of rubber plantings still remain, but most of the agricultural production of the island today is devoted to truck garden cropping. Fishing villages, prawn beds, and mangrove swamps once fringed the unused coasts, but these unproductive sections are being turned into industrial sites by massive programs of redevelopment. Urban residential complexes in high-rise multiple-building groupings are being distributed in suburban sections and urban renewal programs are rebuilding the heart of the city.

Government, in Singapore, has taken on a strong socialist trend, perhaps befitting a city-state, in which political controls over labor unionism, urban housing, medical care, the educational system, electric power generation, and industrial development clearly define the directions of future growth and development. Private capital investment from abroad has been sought by which to build the industrial program, with time-limit guarantees on tax and tariff patterns, seeking to capitalize on the large labor force available. The whole development, in 1970, is not yet mature, but the future pattern is indicated. In 1969 the economy of Singapore depended on its traditional entrepot trade for only about one-third of its total income, and manufacturing supplied about one-quarter of that income. The program looks forward to the time when a major share of the total income will be derived from the manufacturing output.

The future of Singapore rests rather clearly on the pattern of world trade and tariff controls, and the prosperity of this great port city may well depend upon the skill of its leadership in maintaining a balance among interregional pressures and in utilizing the skill and energies of its inhabitants.

THE PROTECTED STATE OF BRUNEI

Brunei, today, is a small lowland political state on the west coast of Borneo, set between two larger state-units of the Federation of Malaysia, Sarawak on the south and Sabah on the north. Actually, in detail, Brunei consists of two enclaves totalling 2,226 square miles, separated by the basin of the Limbang River, and is fully surrounded by the political territory of Sarawak. Its 1970 population was estimated at 120,000. Brunei Bay has been the focus of Malay interest along the Borneo coast since about the fifteenth century, and its population is strongly Malay and very heavily Islamic in religion-way of life. At one time the Sultan of Brunei claimed jurisdiction over most of the Borneo west coast, including the Sulu Archipelago. Eighteenth century decline of local political strength, and the limitations on territory resulting from nineteenth century political pressures, reduced Brunei to a small state centered on one port town, with little agricultural base in the hinterland.

Brunei languished in quiet condition until the 1920's, when an oil field was put into production in the southwest corner of the state (see Fig. 21.5). A small amount of agriculture is now carried on in the better-drained portions of the inland area, and there is a little rubber production. Many of the coastal peoples engage in fishing activities. The oil field yields a very large annual income to the state which, in terms of per capita income, makes the population of Brunei seem extremely wealthy. The Sultan of Brunei, however, is a ruler somewhat on the pattern of earlier oriental potentates, and several million dollars were recently spent on a coronation ceremony. In 1970 a deep water port worthy of a large economic hinterland was under construction, as was a jet-class airport. Brunei town has been dressed up in recent years by civic improvements, with a new capitol and an architecturally striking new mosque.

Fear of economic and political restriction, within the Federation of Malaysia, led the Sultan of Brunei to decline to join the new political construct, favoring continuance under the category of British protected state. The markedly reduced military stance of Great Britain in the Far East may pose some political problems, but so long as the oil field continues to produce the economic welfare of the little state will remain fairly secure.

22

THE SEVERAL INDIES AND INDONESIA

The eastern Island World, in the older sense, was a term applied to the realm stretching from the Andaman Islands to Taiwan to the Solomon Islands. The realm is divided among several political states at present. The East Indies refers to the large group of islands between Sumatra and New Hebrides, excluding the Philippines. The Republic of Indonesia includes only those islands, and parts of islands, that belong in one political state. This chapter opens with a discussion that relates to the East Indies, and it will end with brief vignettes on the non-Indonesian portion of the island of New Guinea, and on the Portuguese colony of Timor. The primary coverage will refer to Indonesia as the territory of the modern political state of that name. The applicable frame of reference of any statement will be indicated by the variable use of the terms East Indies, Indonesia, or other specific geographical or political unit. Traditional anglicized names of islands are retained in the general discussion, but Indonesian names are used when the context is appropriate in the contemporary section.

A VARIETY OF ISLANDS AND THEIR FIRST SETTLERS

The ancestors of some of the culture groups now resident in the East Indies doubtless walked overland to the regions they first occupied. When modern man first came to the East Indies the present patterns of land and sea had not yet become established, for glacial ice bound up much of the sea water, and many of the present islands then were the uplands of old Sundaland and its eastern counterpart on the Sahul shelf (see Fig. 6.2). Land connection between Asia and Australia was not complete, but the deep water gaps were narrow and somehow a few culture groups made their way across them. As the last glacial period slackened, rising sea water spread across Sundaland and the Sahul shelf, gradually creating hundreds and then thousands of islands. Sea currents developed in the shallow seas, coral growth spread, the present climatic regions developed, vegetation patterns regionally altered, and faunas developed their modern local regions. The major divisions between the floras and faunas of the Asian mainland and Australia remained effective, along Wallace's and Weber's lines, with man the chief transgressor across the primary environmental boundaries (see Fig. 9.1). The changes in local environments have been considerable, all within the time of occupance of modern man.

As this contemporary environment came into being change in the detailed outlines of islands and interiors continued to take place.

445

Volcanism built up the uplands, created new islands, and blew the tops of volcanoes asunder. Estuarine lowlands became sedimented and shore lines changed, while coral reefs grew and created new islands. Mangrove and other wet-lowland plant associations appeared in new ecologic situations. Early man found some islands easily productive of food and other resources, whereas others were difficult to exploit above the simplest levels. Thus, the contrasts between Java and Borneo, Halmahera and Bali, have been present throughout the occupance of modern man. Java always has been a productive island; Timor has not.

The very wet and heavily forested islands presented difficulties to early man as they do to contemporary man. The rather dry Lesser Sundas also presented handicaps to early culture groups lacking techniques of water control. Java and some of the islands just east of it probably presented a fairly optimum situation to early cultures. Moist enough to provide abundant plant cover and animal life, but too dry to permit dense rainforest, possessing rich volcanic soils and lowlands that were not fringed by deep marsh, Java must have been inviting to early man and provided him a good living. Such regions as the east coast of Sumatra and the south coast of Borneo possessed adequate aquatic resources in their marsh fringes but their forested interiors were handicaps.

This island world offered great variety, but it was a world separated into fragments, and it lacked a core region around which one great pattern of culture could mature into a land-based society. Its separation into pieces early led to great cultural diversity among its parts, but this very separation also stimulated sea traffic which in time bound many of the shores together as opposed to the regional isolation of the interiors of the larger islands.

It is generally held that the Negrito peoples were the earliest groups of modern man to arrive in the East Indies, and their survival in such islands as Timor and New Guinea is a matter of simple survival in regions not heavily subject to the immigration and mixing of later peoples. Early Caucasoid wanderers perhaps were next on the scene, moving through the East Indies and leaving their chief imprint in such groups as the Papuans, who now are generally held to be a mixture of Negrito and Caucasoid. Mixed peoples from mainland southeastern Asia came into the East Indies in gradually moving pulsations, contributing such stocks as the Polynesians who largely moved through and out into the islands of the South Pacific. Early mixed Mongoloids appeared and spread rather widely, themselves mixing into previous groups. Increasingly the later peoples became more and more Mongoloid. As the present pattern of many islands took shape with the final adjustments of sea level, routes of travel shifted to the sea lanes, many islands became by-passed, and quite mixed populations developed along coastal fringes. It is popular to describe crudely concentric arrangement of the racial stocks, the earliest arrivals being in island interiors, and the last comers being the coastal peoples, but there is nothing simple in the regional disposition of the racial stocks, hundreds of languages, and innumerable local culture patterns that have evolved in the East Indies.

No two islands are alike in race, language, or detailed culture patterns. Some small islands became homogeneous in population and culture, whereas other islands, both large and small, came to possess several racial mixtures, many languages, and a variety of local cultures. Later arrivals often penetrated the East Indies less deeply than did earlier peoples. The Malays were among the last comers, themselves mixed but predominantly Mongoloid peoples, who spread as far into the East Indies as the Lesser Sundas in their initial movement. The western East Indies became the home region of the Malays for a considerable period of time. At some early date, however, Javanese, Sumatran, and south Borneo Malays took to the sea lanes in earnest, spreading west to Madagascar, into the Philippines, out into the Melanesian islands of the Pacific, along the China coast, and as far north as southern Japan. Sumatran Malays were late in occupying a part of the west coast of the Malay Peninsula before the arrival of the European. Whereas New Guinea remained predominantly Negrito and Papuan, except for a thin fringe of coastal peoples, Java, Sumatra, and near-by islands became predominantly Malay. The central group of islands became a zone of highly mixed peoples. Here and there individual islands, or island clusters, preserved old stocks in varying numbers.

INDIAN COLONIZATION

The formal historiography of the East Indies suggests that Indian settlers, traders, missionaries, and political rulers were scattered along the coasts of eastern Sumatra, northern Java, and southern Borneo in sufficient numbers by the first century of the Christian era so that one can speak of Indianized principalities and states (Fig. 22.1). All three of the islands mentioned seem to have been roughly parallel in the early development of Indian contacts, but it is apparent that the south coast of Java, the west coast of Sumatra, and the islands off the Sumatran west coast did not share in this early story. The Indian contacts seem derived from the same efforts that led to the growth of trade centers in the Mekong Delta and along the Vietnam coast, this contact spreading out over the South China Sea to the shores of Borneo, Java, and Sumatra during several centuries before the Christian era. A long process of probing and exploring was required to find those areas of sufficient interest. Greater knowledge of sea currents, weather, and sailing possibilities eventually led to the establishment of direct routes from Indian ports to the East Indies, but such direct contact at the start is doubtful.

The evolution of Indianized states in the East Indies proceeded much as in Burma and Cambodia. The peoples to whom the Indians were first attracted were chiefly peoples of the littoral, who lived both from the land and the sea, and who themselves were rather mobile. Trade stations grew into regional centers, local control evolved into political power, and loose communities matured into principalities. These were scattered along the long shore lines of Borneo, north Java, and eastern Sumatra without much competitive overlapping or delimitation of areas of influence. Dependent upon sea travel and sea trade, they became littoral principalities rather than land-based entities, yet they were chiefly concerned with spices, rare woods, forest products, gold, diamonds, and other products of the land surfaces.

Scattered along these coasts must have been many trade stations and local centers of contact. The areas inhabited by Negrito and other peoples of simple culture and low productivity were less attractive to the Indians than were the areas populated by the agricultural-fishing Malays of somewhat higher culture. Local environmental differences also had some influence. With slow growth on land the less productive spots became subordinate to the favored localities as sea travel and sea power matured. The mobility of all the peoples and the shifting fortunes of groups must have led to many local changes of port stations and settlements. The whole region was somewhat similar, geographic knowledge was not yet very complete, and neither Indian nor local historiography can be precise in specific location of the first sea-states. Nevertheless it is clear that Indian colonial effort was concentrated in the western East Indies, and that the first regional sea-states were located in this section of the East Indies.

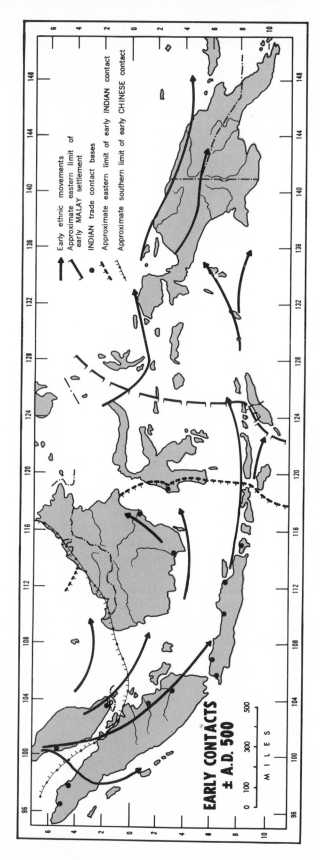

FIGURE 22.1. The early occupance of the East Indies.

Early ethnic movements
Approximate eastern limit of early MALAY settlement
INDIAN trade contact bases
Approximate eastern limit of early INDIAN contact
Approximate southern limit of early CHINESE contact

EARLY CONTACTS ± A.D. 500

MILES
0   100   300   500

In the East Indies, as in Cambodia and Burma, the Indian brought to the area a pattern of culture superior to that of any local population. Not only was some of this culture transmitted to the local population, but the Indians became the merchants, architects, religious leaders, and the political administrators of the little principalities and states that slowly began to appear in the East Indies. Underneath this new Indian veneer of people and culture each local region contained a variety of native populations and native culture patterns. The western East Indies, for all its local variety, possessed a core of similar culture among the Malay peoples, much of which has remained to the present day.

SRI VIJAYA AND OTHER REGIONAL CENTERS

Once the canvass of the East Indies had been made, Indian effort focused upon regional centers. Probably over a dozen chief localities were scattered along the south, west, and southern east coasts of Borneo, the north coast of Java, and the southern east coast of Sumatra. In some of these centers Buddhist missionary influence seems dominant, whereas in others Hindu sects were primary. Trade contacts were extensive, for artifacts from both China and India of the second century A.D. have turned up in Borneo, Java, and Sumatra. Arabs, Chinese, and Indians were the chief traders, but seafarers from all Southeast Asia must have met in the chief ports. The collecting of various spice and perfume products gradually was supplanted by the cultivation of some of the major items. Plants originally domesticated upon the mainland were brought in and gradually became part of the product variety. Rare woods and a few other forest products were collected. Streams in many localities were mined for alluvial gold, and Borneo diamonds and a few other precious stones also were produced in the

same way. The East Indies thus came to be an important part of the oriental trade realm. As Buddhism died out in India Chinese students of Buddhism visited religious centers in Southeast Asia and came to include the Buddhist centers of the East Indies in their travels. Diplomatic missions from several island states visited China, and it is clear that the western East Indies had assumed a considerable status in the world of the East by the fourth century of the Christian era.

In the long run those areas inhabited by cultural advanced peoples, with good and productive local environments, came to be the most powerful and significant. In other less fortunate situations states advanced to a certain level and then retrogressed. Borneo is a region illustrative of this process. Among the first islands to be touched by Indian influences, in the early centuries Borneo possessed several Indianized states, but in the competitive struggle for regional dominance the Bornese states gradually lost out, and Borneo became one of the poorer and less populous regions only periodically exploited for particular resources. This situation has continued throughout the historic period and is true even today.

Java and Sumatra became the chief seats of competing states and regional interests, with a bewildering complexity of alternating rise to power and competitive defeat. The historian is yet unable fully to sort out the precise regional limits and the chronologic pattern of states based upon the Sumatran east coast and on the island of Java. Although the chief states always were those possessed of strong sea power, both commercial and military, the productive land resources of the hinterlands and the socio-political strength of the populations of the states were important factors in this competitive struggle. On Java and Sumatra the productive local environments were those of the rich volcanic uplands, which are located inland away from the coasts. The coastal sea-power pattern was always in conflict with the inland agricultural pattern. On Borneo the paucity of the inland resources kept regional development near the coasts whereas on Java and Sumatra the productive land areas drew peoples inland. On the smaller islands east of Java the conflict between coastal and inland bases of development was less important, since the areas overlapped.

Although several Javanese states seem to have been important throughout the first millennium of the Christian era, the single strongest and largest state was that known as Sri Vijaya, based upon the southern east coast of Sumatra, with its capital near the modern city of Palembang. Sri Vijaya first grew to dominant position in the late seventh century, a combination of land resources, sea power, trade, and Indian political leadership. Its capital occasionally shifted to Java, out of the complex dynastic inheritance relationships, but it always was a Sumatra-based state. At its height it controlled the seaways north to Cambodia, east to the Moluccas, and the whole of the Malay Peninsula, though in the ups and downs of sea power other island and peninsular states and pirate ports were able to compete for trade and political influence. Both close contact and friction with south Indian states were frequent. Sri Vijaya remained chiefly a sea power, never completely able to weld all land regions into one fully functioning political state. It reached its height in the twelfth century, and then faded away under the impact of piracy, regional competition, and the invasion of the Moslems from India.

Java contained several local regional centers in the early centuries. Island dominance at some times lay with one area, at others with another. Occasionally a dynastic family was able to combine most of Java into one state, whereas at other times as many as a half dozen regional entities were able to maintain independence. Religious differences, the overexpenditure of resources upon religious monuments, complex matters of interlocking inheritances by ruling families, and the ever-present issue of competitive sea power were factors in this regional problem. In the thirteenth century the decline of Sri Vijaya made possible the swift rise of the east Javanese sea-state of Madjapahit, whose zone of influence was almost as great as that of Sri Vijaya at its height, though located somewhat farther eastward (Fig. 22.2).

During these many centuries Java was the key economic region of the Indies, for its more satisfactory climate and its rich soils permitted its agricultural productivity to increase to greater extent than that of any other part of the East Indies. Whatever state controlled the seaways, Java was the center of interregional trade, the chief island market for goods coming into the East Indies, and the chief source of manpower and material resources. As piracy affected the outer islands at times when Sumatran or Javanese sea power was ineffective, outer-island productivity was inhibited, whereas Java was much less affected. Thus, the ports of Java, particularly, became the chief centers of trade in this whole island world. Products and traders from all over the Orient came together in the several ports on the north coast, this in itself lending to Java an economic importance lacking in the other regions. The agricultural development, economic productivity, economic wealth, and the population of Java grew steadily greater than those of the other islands, establishing a basic contrast in the regional development of the East Indies long before the Europeans came.

With the exception of a few localities and the steeper uplands Indianized settlements and cultural patterns spread all over the relatively small island of Java, no part of which is many miles from the sea. Such small islands as Madura, Bali, and Lombok were fully brought into this Indianized culture zone, but the interiors of the larger islands were little affected. The uplands of Sumatra

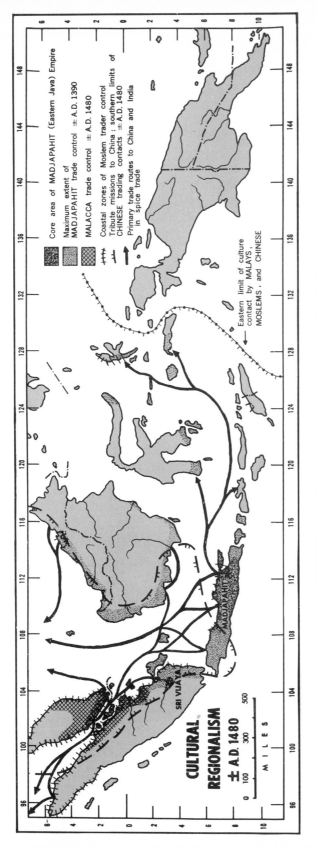

FIGURE 22.2. Early cultural regionalism of the East Indies.

Core area of MADJAPAHIT (Eastern Java) Empire

Maximum extent of
MADJAPAHIT trade control ± A.D. 1390

MALACCA trade control ± A.D. 1480

Coastal zones of Moslem trader control
Tribute missions to China ; southern limits of
CHINESE trading contacts ± A.D. 1480

Primary trade routes to China and India
in spice trade

Eastern limit of culture
contact by MALAYS,
MOSLEMS , and CHINESE

CULTURAL
REGIONALISM
± A.D. 1480

MILES

0   100   300   500

SRI VIJAYA

MADJAPAHIT

451

retained more completely Malay culture groups, and the inland regions of Borneo continued in their simpler ways of life. Such island groups as the Mentawi, off the west coast of Sumatra, largely escaped Indian influence. Although Javanese and other traders certainly traded as far east as Halmahera, the Indianizing of the islands east of Celebes was relatively slight. New Guinea and other islands remained almost completely untouched by Indian influences. Certainly as late as the thirteenth century, when the Islamic invasions began, the peoples of New Guinea and many of the smaller islands off the main seaways continued their Paleolithic or Neolithic ways of life along with the peoples of interior Borneo and even some of the simpler groups on Sumatra. These patterns formed strong contrasts with the cosmopolitan patterns of the coastal ports of Java and eastern Sumatra.

In the early centuries of Indian contact with the East Indies, Indians were the political, social, religious, and economic leaders of port communities and principalities. In time Sumatran and Javanese Malays, by intermarriage and by absorption of Indian culture, came to have a large share in the leadership of society. In the late twelfth and thirteenth centuries Chinese began to become permanently resident in the ports of Sumatra, Java, and Borneo, and by the end of the fourteenth century there were large settlements of Chinese in many ports. Indian influences markedly altered the ways of life in the western East Indies, increasing the contrasts between western and eastern islands already created by the coming of the Malays. Chinese influences, however, were primarily economic, increasingly concerned with the retail distribution of commodities and with the import-export trade of the islands.

Indian influences never penetrated the full depth and breadth of the Malay population and culture. Although the political state and its capital city might be run on Indian lines,

with a close interweaving of religious and political leadership, the rural village communities remained democratic social entities, self-operative, mutually responsible, and Malay in cultural pattern. Acceptance of the shifting controls of political sea-states by local communities preserved local autonomy without risking destructive punitive action. Acceptance of state religious systems, of taxation, and of levies of labor and materials necessarily involved alterations and changes in village cultures, but preserved basic Malay cultural integrity.

THE INFLUX OF MOSLEM CULTURE

Arab traders had operated in Indonesian waters from the earliest centuries of the Christian era. After the rise of Islam the Arabs for some centuries did not mix religion and trade in their contacts with the East Indies. It was only in the late thirteenth century that Islamic missionaries came with the Arab traders. Although the record is not clear there appear to have been both Indians and Arabs from the Hadramaut coast of Arabia among the missionaries of Islam who appeared in Malaya and northern Sumatra. And quickly they learned to mix both politics and trade with their religious efforts. Finding opportunity in the ports of western Malaysia they rapidly spread to the western ports of the East Indies. Their spread was not a solid line of advance but one that skipped about the seaways to such ports as presented opportunities. Islamic contacts touched some of the spice islands in the Halmahera group by 1440, and reached the southern Philippines by 1480, whereas parts of the Borneo coast were not reached until shortly before 1600.

The entry of the Islamic missionary-adventurers came at a time when Sri Vijaya had declined in power, and much of the spread succeeded because of the rapid decline of the sea power of Madjapahit at the end of the fourteenth century. The disappearance of organized political sea power meant that the island world relapsed into an infinite number of small port and village communities, small islands and local regions, all independent, unprotected from the political adventurer, and connected only by the seaways and trade patterns. Here and there a local native regional ruler seized the opportunity to expand his own control, and was able to present some organized strength against the Moslems. But for the most part ports and local communities were wide open for the political opportunist able to capitalize upon the failure of political organization.

The newcomers proved adept at seizing the political leadership of port after port, declaring themselves rajahs and sultans, converting the local populace to a nominal adherence to the Islamic faith, and organizing small regional principalities and states. The interregional trade continued to move, though the importance of individual ports altered under the new controls, and the Chinese role in trade expanded. The traditional antagonism between the Moslems and the Hindus and Buddhists caused the abandonment of the former state religions, the desertion of the great temples, and the superficial eradication of many Indian traits at all levels of society. The lack of unified political organization over the island world caused the rise of piracy which, in many cases, was less true piracy than the competitive attempts of local port sultans to control or profit from the sea trade.

Although not the whole of the population of the western sector of the East Indies had been converted to the Islamic faith when the Portuguese arrived, it is striking how rapidly the Islamic faith spread over the region. Perhaps it was but another expression of the willingness of the Malay to accept certain conditions thrust upon him in order to preserve his basic cultural integrity and the freedom of his village way of life. Under pressure from the Moslems many Indianized Sumatran and Javanese coastal peoples shifted inland on Sumatra, pushed up the rivers into interior Borneo, shifted eastward in the East Indies, and even moved into the southern Philippines.

Certainly in the short space of two centuries the coming of the Moslems superficially altered the Indianized Malay culture of the western zone of the East Indies in a very marked way. The architecturally simple mosque replaced the ornate and costly Indian temple, social customs changed, the petty principality replaced the extensive political state, and economic decentralization followed political decentralization. Islamic influences never completely blanketed the western islands, left large island interiors untouched, and by-passed many small islands. The eastern islands were less attractive to the Moslems, who found simple subsistence economies and simple sociopolitical structures less easy to organize and take over, so that the regional spread of Islamic influences almost paralleled the spread of Indian influences. This new veneer of culture again added to the contrasts between Java and the outer islands, and between the western islands and those east of Halmahera.

THE COMING OF THE EUROPEAN

Rapid as was the spread of the Moslems over the western half of the East Indies, the process of applying a new cultural veneer had not been completed when the European appeared upon the scene to interrupt it and to inject new elements into the picture. In India the Portuguese quickly learned that the real world of spices lay farther eastward. Upon taking the port of Malacca in 1511, the Portuguese felt they had secured an eastern base from which the exploration and exploitation of the East Indies could be carried out. The Portuguese came as exploiters rather than as peaceful traders, and acts of piracy turned all nationalities against them from the start. They pursued with tactless force their ambition to destroy Arab trade in the Indian Ocean and native trade in the South China Sea and the local waters of the East Indies.

Cannon, courage, and greedy ambition gave the Portuguese victory after victory in naval conflict, but the chief centers of the important products so long sought had but recently become converted to Islam. The new Islamic sultans of many of the Banda and Halmahera groups of islands saw profitable trade outlets in the Portuguese traders, but the Portuguese could not be content with normal trade, being bent upon monopolistic control of the world's spice trade. During the period in which they were unsuccessfully struggling with the issues of control of the trade routes and of the producing sources, the appearance of one of Magellan's ships in the Spice Islands (the Moluccas) forced them to even more ruthless action. There ensued a minor Holy War or Crusade, with control of trade the end objective.

Failing to make lasting trade agreements with the sultans, the Portuguese turned to missionary activity but found that they could succeed only with the pagan peoples yet untouched by either Indian or Islamic religions, not many of whom were important spice producers. Animosity to the Portuguese stepped up the Islamic missionary efforts as a countermove, and the religion spread more rapidly than did Christianity in the East Indies in this era. The ruthless greed and tactlessness of the Portuguese foretold the doom of peaceful European contact in the East and also ordained the brevity of Portuguese control of the whole region. In short order the Portuguese became thoroughly disliked throughout the whole of the East,

thus arousing the suspicions of all peoples toward all occidentals.

The Spanish persistence in the Philippines and on the edges of the East Indies, the voyage of the Englishman Francis Drake, crewmen on the ships of other nations and, finally, the appearance of the Dutch at the end of the sixteenth century, all were factors in preventing the monopoly of the Portuguese in the East Indies. But also important was the gradual growth of larger states, alliances, and confederacies among the ports and principalities. Atjeh in north Sumatra, the confederacies of the Sultans of Brunei and Ternate, and the state of Mataram in west Java, all grew large and strong enough to prevent the assumption of political and trade control over territory by the Portuguese. Although they were able to purchase and sell in Europe large volumes of spices, their monopolistic control of a great trade empire remained but a dream.

In spite of the failure of empire the coming of the European introduced new elements into the life of the East Indies in the sixteenth century. The sea power of Java was broken, the spread of the Islamic religion and culture was furthered, a market-Malay language was spread about the ports, new trade patterns developed, important regional patterns of Christianity were implanted, and the political structure of the East Indies was altered. It is remarkable that many of the same small islands that earlier had been bypassed were again left untouched, that the interiors of large islands were but slightly affected, and that the regions and peoples east of Halmahera still continued the same simple patterns that they had followed for many centuries.

In the last years of the sixteenth century Dutch, English, and Spanish trading efforts in the East Indies interfered with the activity of the Portuguese. Not every expedition produced large profits, but the Dutch were encouraged sufficiently to outfit more ships than did the Portuguese and to keep at the venture. The organization of the United East India Company aimed at a Dutch monopoly of the trade with the East Indies. The weaker British traders followed the Dutch into port after port, letting them lead the way and do most of the squabbling. The Dutch learned to be somewhat tactful and careful in their contacts with Indonesians, but there still was trouble. Dutch field leaders planned a great trade empire, and worked toward it, though the home directors never sanctioned the plans. Batavia, on Java, was made the chief Dutch base, and Chinese merchants were invited to settle in the port. This early association of the Dutch and the Chinese really laid the foundations for the success of the Dutch East India Company.

THE DUTCH COLONIAL EMPIRE

The island of Java had declined in economic importance and population in the regional struggles of the various sultans and the Portuguese during the sixteenth century, but Batavia was a well placed base from which to carry on trade. The United East India Company was spread far and wide, from South Africa to Taiwan and Halmahera, and the problems of running a monopoly trade empire became pressing. The Dutch in 1650 controlled the sea lanes of the East Indies from Batavia, largely in the same way that Madjapahit had done at an earlier time from its capital in eastern Java. They governed only Batavia and its immediate environs, relying upon native sultans to govern the various islands, and relying upon treaties with the sultans to maintain trade relations. British, Portuguese, Danish, and a few other traders operated in various ports in the East Indies, conniving with local rulers against the Dutch.

During the latter part of the seventeenth century this uneasy state of affairs produced considerable unrest and military maneuvering. The Dutch East India Company was forced into military operations to control the territories of their trade realm, and by 1700 the Dutch not only controlled trade but had entered into political administration of the chief coastal regions. The Portuguese withdrew to Timor, the Danes were totally ousted, and the British retained only a fortified trading post on the west coast of Sumatra. The Dutch extended their monopoly trade system by which the agents of the Company, the Company itself, the Chinese, and regional rulers all profited handsomely from the production and trade of spices, but by which the rural villager and agricultural producer made but a pittance.

The policy of restriction cut down orchards of spice trees, depopulated some of the spice-producing islands, and reduced many regions to poverty. Piracy and interregional struggles were frequent and serious. Just after 1700 trial efforts at growing coffee on interior uplands of Java succeeded beyond all expectation, for by 1723 the yield amounted to some 12,000,000 pounds of coffee. This foretold a new era in Dutch trade in the East Indies, the dealing with bulk export crops, and coffee became a regular export after this date. But the Company was not yet ready for volume trade, and economic theories of free trade had not yet matured in the Occident. The eighteenth century was one long struggle between the Dutch attempts to restrict trade, make profits, keep the peace, and extend political control over the East Indies, against the Indonesian and non-Dutch efforts to circumvent monopoly, evade Dutch control, secure release from economic exploitation, and preserve the autonomy and freedom of the Malay way of life.

The United East India Company became almost bankrupt trying to manage both government and monopoly trade on a huge scale in the unsettled world of the late eighteenth century, and in 1796 surrendered its charter. The East Indies suddenly became a political colony of the Netherlands, with the home government lacking both a knowledge of the problems of colonial government in the oriental tropics and personnel effectively trained to administer the new colony. Late eighteenth-century Dutch-British world-wide conflict reduced the widespread Dutch trade realm, forcing them out of South Africa, Ceylon, and Malaysia. The latter phase of this struggle saw the British temporarily controlling Java and Sumatra, during Napoleon's occupation of the Netherlands. In the post-Napoleonic settlement a peace treaty finally awarded the Indies to the Dutch and the Malay Peninsula to the British. Upset world conditions for a half century had made profitable trade difficult, and the restrictive patterns and vagaries of Company policy had left the economy of the East Indies in an unproductive state, with the majority of the population living in poverty, but with many native sultans possessing tremendous wealth and power.

As the East Indies became a political colony Java contained the base settlement used in trade and administration. Most of the Dutch populace was gathered in or near Batavia (modern Djakarta), with only small groups at outlying regional control points, particularly along the Sumatran east coast, on the south coast of Borneo, and at scattered points in the Halmahera and Banda Islands. Other nonnatives were similarly scattered, with the most marked accumulations being those of the Chinese around the chief ports and trade centers. West of Halmahera most of the population had become Islamic in religion, except for scattered groups of non-Malay, animistic cultures on bypassed islands or large-island interiors. There was a small regional residue of Indianized peoples on Bali and Lombok, and Christianity had been planted in a number

of small areas. Native sultans held direct political control in many portions of the East Indies, and several tribal confederacies were rather tightly organized culture groups highly resistant to Dutch administration. The Portuguese still controlled part of Timor, and there were significant areas of the western islands in which no regionally organized patterns of Company government or trade contact existed. East of Halmahera was a kind of no-man's land untouched by the cultural and economic currents that had been active in the western East Indies for over 2,000 years. The by-passed islands and large-island interiors of the western zone also shared in this lacuna. Java contained the largest total population, but population densities were in strong contrast at many points throughout the whole of the East Indies.

As Dutch colonial government began, the Indies formed a region of immense contrast in language, law, religion, settlement, agricultural productivity, economic development, and other aspects of cultural development. Java and some nearby islands stood out as a region quite separate from the rest of the western East Indies, and the area east of Halmahera was largely an unknown land. The multiplicity of regional divisions was complex, and no one system could be applied to the whole in any facet of the functioning of government as it operated in the early nineteenth century. The low economic productivity of the whole of the East Indies and the disorganized state of economic affairs involved a large financial burden which the little Netherlands, itself devastated by the Napoleonic wars, was in no position to assume. The East Indies had to be organized in such a way as to become economically productive, and this primary requirement became the chief facet of early Dutch colonial policy. Various reforms and new procedures introduced by the first Dutch colonial government, were hindered by inadequacies, but they were serious efforts in the right directions. As the nineteenth century progressed the Dutch worked hard at the problems of colonial administration, and in the end achieved perhaps the best system of colonial government in Asia of any of the European colonial rulers.

THE INNER, OUTER, AND NON-DUTCH EAST INDIES

Possessing a small country with limited population and home resources, the Dutch were unable to take the whole of the East Indies into their early political and economic program. Late in the nineteenth century the British were able to stake out both political and economic spheres in both northwestern Borneo and southeastern New Guinea in areas yet untouched by the Dutch, and Germany was able to lay claim to north-eastern New Guinea. Portugal clung to, and still holds, a part of Timor. Thus, the East Indies, as a group of over 3,000 islands, came into the twentieth century divided between four European political states. Germany lost her colonial region after World War I when northeastern New Guinea passed into British hands as a League of Nations mandate. Eastern New Guinea and associated smaller islands now have passed under Australian sovereignty or trusteeship. Had other efforts been made by non-Dutch powers in the nineteenth century to attach others of the bypassed islands or regions they, too, might have succeeded and other areas would have passed from Dutch control.

The Dutch colonial empire, as it matured, included parts of almost all of the islands of the East Indies, totaled the largest area, and contained the largest population. Although the Dutch were able to bring to all parts of their empire a certain degree of unity in administrative and cultural patterns, they were unable to develop all of it economically. They had come into an island world with marked economic and cultural contrasts between islands. Their early efforts at trade led to a rehabilitation of Java and Madura, an increase in economic productivity, and marked increase in population. Java and Madura are sometimes termed the Inner Indies or the Inner Islands. The Dutch were not attracted to those islands or areas of low economic productivity and simple culture which were lacking in commodities useful in the Dutch trade in Europe. The long-run efforts of the Dutch, therefore, furthered some of the long-standing differences between the islands. The contrast has long been strongest between Java and the rest of the islands, and in recent times this has been generalized in the term Outer Islands which includes everything in Indonesia beyond Java and Madura. The contrast shows most strongly in population, economic productivity, and in political nationalism, but it runs throughout all matters of culture.

THE BACKGROUND TO CONTEMPORARY ECONOMY

After the Napoleonic struggles in Europe the Dutch were in no position to embark upon a progressive program in the Indies, and some way had to be found to regain prosperity at home and to develop the Indies. There resulted a system of government-controlled agriculture in the East Indies conventionally termed the "culture system." Local government, land control, taxation, crop production, agricultural processing, the export trade, and the import trade in consumer goods were integrated by government regulation in such a way that in Java there began a new era of commercialized agriculture and foreign trade. Monopoly thinking still prevailed but turned from restriction to increased production. Payment in money for crops beyond the tax assessment stimulated production, but the controls turned Java into one great farm estate. Dutch and Chinese managed the processing of exports and the external trade. The profits were great, and the Netherlands rapidly regained its prosperity. That the Javanese population increased, agricultural lands expanded, and a market for foreign goods developed did not lessen the stigma of exploitation and the native dislike for the system. The culture system increased the contrast between Java and the Outer Indies.

Coffee, sugar, and indigo were the chief exports of the East Indies in this period. Subsistence production upon Java increased. The price of spices was declining, and with it the importance of the patterns of trade of the earlier era. During these decades government initiative introduced new crop plants to the East Indies, and, though they did not immediately become productive sources of exports, their spread over Java and the east coast of Sumatra paved the way for later production. Tea, tobacco, manioc, and the oil palm were the most important of the new plants or improved varieties.

After 1850 liberalizing trends in Dutch policy began to make headway and, on private initiative, estates (plantations) were established. The estates increased in number as government policy after 1865 abandoned controlled agriculture. The influx of Dutch settlers began, free trade for all nations was allowed, and participation by native small farmers in commercial production began on their own initiative. The incompleteness of Dutch control in the Outer Indies had prevented development equal to that on Java, but gradually the east coast of Sumatra and a few other regions began to participate in the new trends in agriculture. Tea, sugar, coffee, and tobacco were the first important private estate products. Late in the century cinchona came into production, but this remained a government controlled forest product on Java. As the population of Java and Sumatra increased, with the accent on commercial agriculture, the production of basic

food supplies began to lag. The wet ricefields of Java had been slowly expanding, but insufficiently. Interest in minerals led to some exploration and the development of tin, coal, and a few others, to add variety to the commercial patterns of the East Indies. British activity in Borneo and British and German efforts in eastern New Guinea produced no marked expansion of agriculture or trade until the very end of the century when estate development began on a small scale.

During the present century the early trends were the increase of estate production upon Java and the east coast of Sumatra, with a limited growth of estates on the Dutch Outer Islands, the increase in food imports, and the rise in native commercial agriculture in all parts of the East Indies. Java expanded its production to become the most important producing region. The growth of small farmer and estate agriculture on the Sumatran east coast gave it second rank. On the rest of the Outer Islands productive agricultural areas remained small and scattered. The contrast between Java and the Outer Islands, other than the Sumatran east coast, became greater than it had ever been.

Native land systems involved both the concepts of hereditary land ownership and communal use ownership by shifting cultivation, with many variations in local practice in different parts of the East Indies. The Dutch East India Company sold large tracts of land on Java, regardless of native occupance, and complicated traditional practices. After the abolition of the Company, government policy in the Dutch areas developed in the direction of prevention of alien land ownership, even for the Dutch themselves. But long-term leases for estates were permitted without real limitation, and short-term leases over small holdings accumulated as a means of debt settlement with creditors who often were Chinese. There has not developed in any part of the East Indies a class of large landowners renting to numerous tenants that is characteristic of so much of the rest of the Orient.

THE CONTEMPORARY AGRICULTURAL ECONOMY

It formerly was common to divide Indonesian agricultural economy into the two categories of smallholder and estate on the assumption that the former concerned local subsistence and the latter produced foreign trade products. The entry of the smallholder into cash-crop production in the early twentieth century blurred this distinction. And with Indonesian political independence economic and land policy has trended toward the restriction of estates and the increase in small-holder occupance and production. The rise of the cooperative movement, particularly on Djawa (Java), further blurs the distinctions in production systems. Indonesia has not been able to abolish all estates because of the necessity for maintaining the export sector at maximum possible capacity, for its obvious function of earning foreign exchange funds.

It is possible to divide the agricultural economy into its obvious technological systems (shifting cultivation, sedentary field and dooryard gardening, and plantation agriculture), a pattern that has significance for Indonesian socioeconomic society. In these terms the distinctions between domestic and export sectors become less artificial, but the differences between some of the Inner and Outer Islands clearly show up. Shifting cultivation, termed *ladang* in Indonesia, is the most widespread cropping system (Fig. 22.3). This supports some millions of people in the Outer Islands. Shifting cultivation is a historic and traditional pioneer and simple-culture cropping system utilized by people and culture groups with few technical resources. It employs large areas of land but

crops only a portion in any one year, and is primarily a subsistence economy, producing a small volume of commercial commodities that chiefly are nonfood products or forest extracts. In the western half of Indonesia upland rice is the basic crop of the shifting cultivator, and the taros, yams, sweet potatoes, manioc, bananas, sago, and a few minor items are the local complements. East of Sulawesi-Lombok (Celebes-Lombok), rice drops out as an important crop, and the taros, yams, sago, manioc, and sweet potatoes become more important in the food economy. Shifting cultivation is slowly declining in practice in areas wherein more advanced sedentary occupance and permanent-field systems are gradually expanding in use. On Djawa, formerly, shifting cultivation was often used on those rougher lands not yet terraced or provided with irrigation facilities.

The sedentary field and dooryard gardening system in its modern pattern is the basic system of cropping employed on Djawa, Madura, portions of Sumatera (Sumatra), and some of the Lesser Sunda islands. This system involves the traditional wet-field rice cropping (*sawah*) and the dooryard garden (*pekarangan*), a sedentary village system. Rice is the basic crop plant. Essentially this was a local subsistence-village barter cropping economy in its traditional pattern, and it is what has kept the populations alive in the densely settled portions of Indonesia in the recent decades of war, political disruption, and economic disorganization. The carefully and intensively cropped wet-rice fields have produced large yields per acre, and the intensively cultivated gardens of vegetables and fruit crops situated around the houses and on village outskirts have supplied complements of food, medicinal, and nonfood barter products. It is this kind of agriculturist that has taken to interplanting small holdings of rubber, tea, coffee, and other commercial crops in the

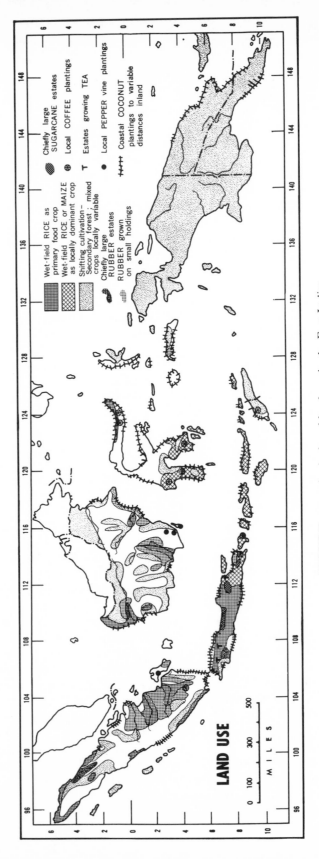

FIGURE 22.3. Agricultural land use in the East Indies.

modern period, augmenting the former subsistence-barter economy by the production of cash crops. Originally chiefly practiced on Djawa, in the classical historical period, the system has been slowly spreading into sections of the Outer Islands as villages and towns have grown, and as regional populations have reached patterns of full occupance of local areas.

In Indonesia, of course, there have been variants of both the shifting cultivation and the sedentary field-dooryard gardening system according to local ecological conditions, the pressures on the land in a local region, and the changing circumstances of economy. In the traditional pattern of lower population densities the village garden was the basic element, but it might have been accompanied by patches of shifting cultivation. On Djawa shifting cultivation has almost disappeared, in the modern era, as the wet-field landscape has slowly expanded through time, and as the permanent-field system has replaced shifting cultivation. As the wet-field landscape expanded, there developed a dry-field pattern of land use (*tegal*), on permanent fields not amenable to irrigation. In the modern period the cultivation of permanent dry fields has increased markedly out of sheer pressure on the land. The planting of commercial tree crops such as rubber, coffee, or coconut by the shifting cultivator in the modern era trends toward the reduction of shifting land use and the increase of the permanent "garden" system. In the modern era there have been plantings of nonfood tree crops or tree crops primarily for their cash-crop utility on lands that might otherwise have gone into wet-field rice cropping. As a result the zones of permanent-field cropping systems no longer supply local populations with adequate volumes of basic food staples. All of these aspects are also to be seen in sections of Sumatera and on Kalimantan (Borneo) and Sulawesi (Celebes). The entry of such new food crops as peanuts, maize, manioc, soybeans, and others into the traditional cropping systems did not alter the basic aspects, but they gave elasticity to the cropping combinations, permitted a closer ecological fit of cropping systems to local soil and climatic regimes, and further intensified the basic elements of the local system. Neither has the entry of such nonfood crops as coffee, rubber, or tea, altered the basic aspects of the economy since they have been integrated into the traditional system of gardening.

The increases in nonfood crops, however, both on Djawa and in the Outer Islands have inhibited the rates of increase in food crop acreage so that the whole of Indonesia must now be judged as a food-deficit region with considerable variation in degree within particular islands or regions. There is no question that population has increased more rapidly than has the pattern of food production. Under fully satisfactory conditions the transport-distributional systems of Indonesia could even out the distribution of both food imports and the variations in local production, but deteriorating conditions since 1940 have brought inefficiency into the distributional patterns, and many areas now suffer chronic undersupply in a way that places local economy on a rather precarious balance not far from the edge of disaster. For example, irregular weather conditions in some of the Lesser Sunda Islands, in the late 1960's, caused less than normal crop yields, bringing local populations to the starvation margin.

Fishponds have become an increasingly important element in the composite local economy of Djawa and in a few other portions of Indonesia by contributing significantly to the local food supply. Both freshwater and saltwater ponds are maintained, and rice-field production of fish is also carried on in localities in which water supply is adequate. Coastal fringes have many part time fishermen. Although not directly part of the agricultural economy, as such, the marine fishery has seen a large increase in small-boat fishing in offshore waters in recent years throughout much of Indonesia. As many as 200,000 small non-powered and small-powered boats have made up the fishing fleet in recent years, and the marine and fresh-water catch has exceeded 800,000 tons.

Rice is, of course, the primary crop throughout Indonesia, and about 18,500,000 acres of land go into rice cropping each year; about 11,000,000 acres are cropped on Djawa-Madura, involving wet-field production, whereas in the Outer islands much of the rice crop is on lands cropped by shifting cultivation. Maize has come to be the second ranking food crop, and is particularly important in the marginally drier sectors from central Djawa through the Lesser Sunda and on southern Sulawesi, normally totalling about 6,500,000 acres. Manioc occupies about 4,000,000 acres in eastern Djawa-Madura and the eastern Outer Islands, and soybeans occupy over 2,000,000 acres, followed by smaller acreages of peanuts, sweet potatoes, yams, and sago, in that order of importance. It is impossible to differentiate the comparative acreage allotments of the village gardens to particular crops, but on the order of 10,000,000 acres of land are devoted to such uses, and the product encompasses a long list of fruits and vegetables, plus the rubber, coconut, coffee and many other tree and shrub plants yielding products for commercial sale or local barter.

Estate, or plantation, agriculture no longer holds the importance it once did in Indonesia, following the expropriation of Dutch-owned estates and the gradual reduction of leases permitted other nationals. During the late 1930's as much as 2,700,000 acres of land were in annual production on about 1,200 plantations, with the larger number and larger acreage located along the east coast of Sumatera, producing about fifteen sig-

nificant commercial crops for the export trade. The total land held by plantation operators was much greater than that cropped each year. Sugar plantations had been the most productive in the earlier period, but rubber plantations increased in acreage and in importance and by 1937 rubber had become the chief plantation product and the chief earner of foreign exchange. In the late 1960's it would appear that the annually cropped plantation acreage had dropped below 1,000,000 acres, that it was chiefly in rubber and palm oil plantings, and chiefly located on Sumatera, although some sugar and tea continue to be plantation products. Plantation production no longer leads smallholder production in any of the commercial export crops. The disorganized condition of Indonesia during the last thirty years has been harder on plantation economy than on smallholder economy, owing to the war, disruption of labor patterns, failure of transport systems, loss of experienced managers and technical experts, breakdown of trading agreements, smuggling operations, and other internal problems.

The animal-raising sector of Indonesian economy has never been of primary importance and is not very important today. About 5,000,000 cattle, 3,000,000 water buffalo, and about 750,000 horses compose the large-animal population, a small figure for so populous a country, both from the standpoint of labor contribution and as food supply. There are perhaps 2,500,000 sheep, 6,000,000 goats, and perhaps 2,500,000 pigs, plus a volume of chickens and other fowl, again an insufficient number to contribute significantly either to the home food supply or to any export component. Djawa-Madura is the area of primary concentration of the animal population, of course, but animal raising is relatively more important in the local economy of Madura-Lesser Sundas than elsewhere. A particular case is the raising of pigs in Hindu Bali, for export to, and consumption in, Chinese Singapore; considered unclean by Moslems, the pig is unimportant in the regions of Indonesia in which the Islamic faith is strong.

The agricultural economy of Indonesia is, in a sense, in a dangerous condition. The production of food is inadequate to the requirements of the population, the pressures on the lands of Djawa, Madura, the Lesser Sundas, Sulawesi, and portions of Sumatera are extremely heavy, and the extensive government paper programs for local and regional development have a way of remaining on paper. Fertilizer supplies remain very inadequate, Djawanese remain reluctant to leave their home villages to pioneer in the Outer Islands, the forest and watershed lands have been cut below the minimal need on Djawa, and the old plantings of rubber, coconut, coffee, and some other items have not been replaced by new and higher-yielding varieties. To date there has not been adequate capital investment in the agricultural sector of the economy, either to keep the land in highly productive state, or to bring technological development to the levels being achieved in other countries. In the areas of heavy pressures on the land, the amount of productive land, despite the careful gardening procedures, is becoming too small for support of the numbers of persons depending on it. On Djawa-Madura, the zone of primary population concentration, the situation is particularly critical, for here conditions are approaching the marginal limit at which added intensive labor no longer produces its keep. There are local regions in the Outer Islands in which this also is true, but in many areas of the Outer Islands there is open land, the pressures are relatively light, and conditions are not in bad straits. One can but wonder how much further the pressures of man on the land can be carried in Djawa-Madura and a few other spots without calam-

ity becoming the norm. The traditional pattern has stood up remarkably well, but how long can it continue to provide for the steadily increasing population?

TRADE AND INDUSTRY

It is notable that the commodities in trade for which the East Indies became most famous in the West no longer are very important, either in agricultural production or in interregional trade. The Moluccas, as the Spice Islands, no longer hold monopolies over cloves, nutmeg, and mace, and recently Indonesia has not produced sufficient cloves for her own domestic use. The peppers, ginger, cassia, and cardamom were not Moluccan monopolies and were widely grown in the East Indies and other parts of Southeast Asia, but the East Indies were among sources of trade volumes of these spices, also, in the early periods. Small volumes of each still move into the export trade but the products are minor trade items today. The production of the several traditional spices today has become distributed around the world's humid tropics and has become a competitive matter in which quality, labor specialization, and international pricing are important, so that Indonesia is not now one of the world's significant producers.

The export products that leave Indonesia today are the commodities of the modern industrial world, and among these rubber, petroleum, and tin are the leaders, followed by coconut products, tea, tobacco, palm kernels and oil, coffee, and sugar. A large number of other products are exported in small annual volumes. Chiefly these leave Indonesia in raw or semi-processed state only, and most are both subject to price competition from other producers and to internal economic disorganization within Indonesia. There has been continuing fluctuation in the importance of the modern export commodities. Sugar, in the 1920's, was the leader and Djawa then was a ranking world producer, but in a recent year or two Indonesia has actually imported sugar, so badly has the disorganization of the industry gone, through confiscation of plantations, government pricing policy, and mechanical deterioration of sugar mills. By the late 1930's rubber production had expanded to a level at which rubber exports became the leading commodity, and rubber has continued to hold this position in Indonesian export economy. Some of the plantations on Sumatera had done some replanting with new high-yielding stocks by the early 1950's, but very few smallholders have replaced their trees. The measure of actual exports, in the vicinity of 700,000 tons per year, has been less a measure of productivity of the rubber plantings of Indonesia than of the relative ability of traders actually to get the product out of the country despite economic and government disorganization. That twenty or more signatures on an export permit have been required is an expression of the inefficient bureaucratic operation of government in recent years. Since much of the rubber has been a product of Sumatera, in good part a plantation product there, local governments have often disregarded national government controls, to "smuggle" shipments out of the country. The export of rubber has fared much better than that of coconut products, which are produced by smallholders in central to eastern Indonesia, thus depending on normally organized trading operations and smooth expediting of transportation by government.

Other elements of the export trade have suffered to one degree or another from disruption, disorganization of transport, conflicting and inhibiting government controls, and taxation. Petroleum, tin, bauxite, nickel, and iron ore mining have all suffered from various patterns of inhibitory controls and disruptions (Fig. 22.4). Conflicts between local governments and the national government over allocation of taxes and the disposition of foreign exchange earned by exports frequently have resulted in regional trading operations labeled "smuggling" by the national government.

The import trade generally has involved varying amounts of foodstuffs, textile yarns or yardage, machinery, transport equipment, and capital goods. Here, too, the inhibitory role of government and bureaucracy has been strong, and that a 1963 shipment of school textbooks still sat in a port warehouse in 1969 because its covering documents had not yet secured the necessary twenty-four bureaucratic signatures suggests the order of inhibition. The previously operating industrial plants, processing plants, primary production machinery, and transport systems gradually deteriorated, between 1940 and 1968, as equipment wore out and could neither be totally replaced nor serviced with spare parts.

In the traditional patterns of trade most of the exchange, of course, was with the Netherlands. In the years since 1946 Japan steadily has increased her trade exchange with Indonesia, now serving as the chief buyer of Indonesian exports and the chief supplier of Indonesian imports. Singapore has held a strong position in Indonesian trade, though this has fluctuated in recent years according to the degree to which national government controls have operated over the Sumatran sector; the "smuggling trade" has often moved through Singapore. The Netherlands and the United States have both been active trade partners with Indonesia, and West Germany, Hong Kong, Australia, and China have been other important trading partners.

Particularly serious in the recent economic decline of Indonesia has been the deterioration of the surface transport system (Fig. 22.5). Shortages of consumer goods and surpluses of raw products occurred within the

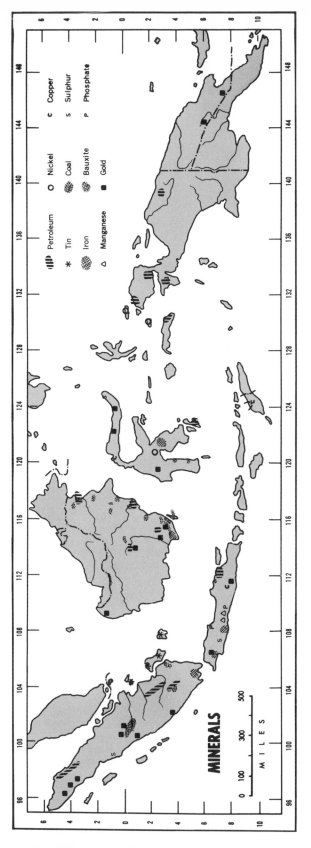

FIGURE 22.4. Mineral producing regions in the East Indies.

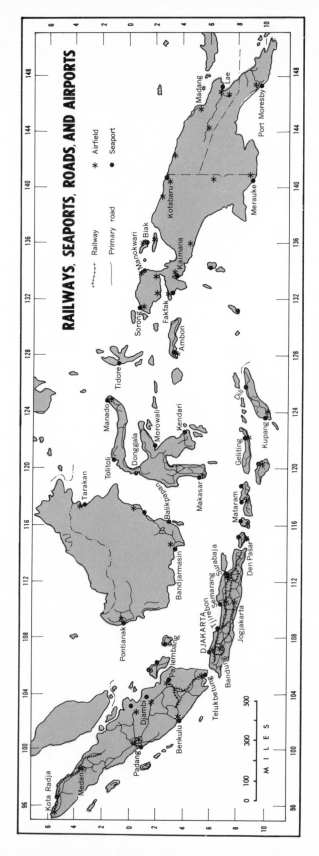

FIGURE 22.5. Transportation facilities in the East Indies.

regional sectors of the island realm, during the early 1960's, and the shipping fleet and port facilities deteriorated to the point that commodity movements sometimes temporarily ceased. Water transport, of course, has played a stronger role in Indonesian economy than in many other countries, but the land transport network on Djawa, Sumatera, and Sulawesi has also declined markedly. In 1969 the total fleet of commercial ships numbered about 225, mostly small coasting vessels, and fairly regular services were possible throughout most of the archipelago, but callings at many small islands were quite irregular, and bureaucratically provoked delays at primary ports often tied up portions of the fleet for too-long intervals. The road network, normally about 30,000 miles in all, in 1969 was less than half operative, but many of the roads in poorest condition were in the Outer Islands. In 1969 Djawa-Madura had about 108,000 operative civilian automobiles and about 42,000 trucks, whereas about 30,000 civilian automobiles and the same number of trucks were operative in the Outer Islands. The maximum rail mileage, in 1938, had stood at about 4,600 but, in the late 1960's, only about 4,000 miles were operable, with the rolling stock rather badly deteriorated.

In an island world such as Indonesia modern air transport presents an effective means of transport integration and the possibility of administrative mobility. Indonesian leadership was quick to realize the potential advantages of air transport in both the international image of modernization and in the internal role of communications connectivity. Garuda, the Indonesian government airline, maintains both international services and an internal network of air fields, to which domestic air services provide connections from Djakarta. Domestic services have varied considerably in frequency, but the distribution of airfields does provide a key to the potential integrative capacity of air transport (see Fig. 22.5).

In 1940 Indonesia was fairly well into a program of beginning industrialization. Agricultural processing, light manufacturing, power development, the textile industries, and such other aspects as cement manufacture, chemicals industries, rubber industries, and paper manufacturing were expanding. Much of this development was concentrated on Djawa and eastern Sumatera, but there were elements of decentralization. Although several five-year plans were structured after 1946, very little real productive development took place during the 1950's and early 1960's, and the actual productivity of many industries continued to deteriorate. By 1968, for example, there was serious imbalance within the cotton textile industries, as the spinning, weaving, dyeing, and finishing establishments were quite out of phase with each other, through breakdowns, lack of spare parts, and the quite inadequate flow of materials through the whole industry.

In the face of the deterioration of its modern industrial establishment, Indonesia has been thrown back on its own domestic resources in good part. This has meant the re-deployment of traditional handicraft manufacturing and partially mechanized establishments, chiefly small in scale of operations and servicing local regions primarily. Perhaps fifteen thousand legitimate "manufacturing establishments" may have been operating in 1968, of which about four-fifths were located on Djawa. Most of these employed well under a hundred employees each, with about a million workers in all. Perhaps almost half the plants were concerned with primary consumer goods such as food and clothing products, with a very wide scattering for the remainder. Beyond this formal designation of the manufacturing establishment, of course, has been the sheer necessity of the revival of rural village household industry, both on Djawa-Madura-eastern Sumatera and in the Outer Islands generally. We cannot supply an effective estimate of the numbers of people involved, but it has been an obvious part of the continuance of living patterns in all parts of Indonesia. From tentative data it would appear that in the Outer Islands, outside eastern Sumatera, most of the manufacturing activities properly must be classified as household industry.

Since the end of Sukarno era, in 1966, there has begun the stabilization of patterns of deterioration and the gradual turnaround of the economy. Controls over national finances and domestic inflation were set in motion, and strong efforts made to restore some degree of government stimulus to the chaotic pattern of interregional and international trade. A new five year economic plan, 1969–1973, with foreign economic aid, set in motion activity to restore the national transport system to some semblance of efficiency, to restore confidence of foreign capital and to begin its developmental inflow, and to begin the restoration of the manufacturing establishment. However, the burden of the past is proving heavier than expected, and progress to 1970 was slow. In 1969 the export trade volume was trending upward and strict import controls were concentrating on the import of productive equipment primarily aimed at reconstruction. It will be some years before the reconstruction program can bring Indonesian economy back to the relative position it occupied before World War II, in terms of the level of living of village populations.

As part of the current program of economic development, there have been made numerous long-term agreements with natural resources corporations around the world, seeking the productive development of supposed, but undeveloped, natural resources. Petroleum exploration off Sumatera, Djawa, and Kalimantan, the development of copper resources in West Irian (west New Guinea), the manufacture of fertilizers from native raw materials on Djawa, and the expansion of paper manufactures in Sumatera, are typical examples. The rather rapid expansion of light manufacturing and manufacturing assembly, in the textile, rubber, and agricultural implements industries form another phase of international corporate development for Indonesia, aimed significantly at the lessening of unemployment.

POPULATION PATTERNS

The island of Djawa has long been the center of economic development and concentration of population within the whole of the East Indies. Since about 1800 Djawa has grown rather rapidly and has regularly been the most heavily populated region. By about 1920 the population imbalance between Djawa and the Outer Islands reached the level at which the Dutch began to attempt the shift of families from Djawa to some one of the Outer Islands. Most of the early programs aimed at settling eastern Sumatera. Djawanese, however, do not seem to take well to such migrational movements and, though there have been projects of population transfer ever since 1920, the efforts have not been very successful. Recently it would appear that a drift of population from the Outer Islands into the cities of Djawa has actually exceeded in numbers the totals of such transfers from Djawa outward.

The total population of Indonesia in 1970 was approximately 117,000,000, and thus fifth in size in the world, next after the United States. Indonesia's population, alone, is greater than the total population of the countries of mainland Southeast Asia heretofore discussed. No recent census data are available to verify the following estimates (Fig. 22.6). Djawa-Madura probably contained about 74,000,000 people on the 51,032 square miles, yielding a crude arithmetic density figure of 1,450 per square mile. About eighty percent of Djawa-Madura is under some form of cultivation at present, a remarkably high figure, but the agricultural density must stand at over 1,800 people per square mile

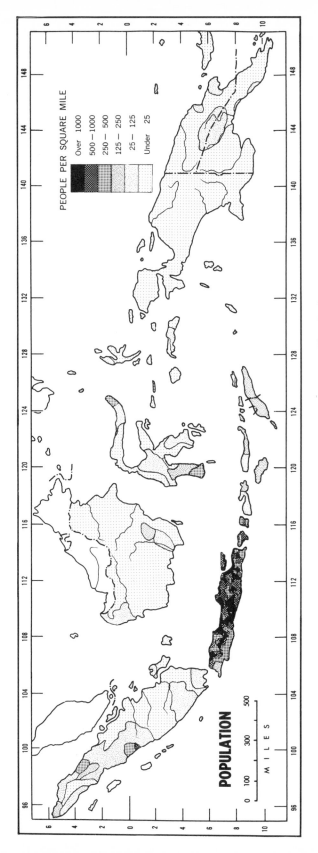

FIGURE 22.6. Population density in the East Indies.

as an average for the whole area, and must certainly exceed that in eastern Djawa-Madura, since western Djawa has always been more lightly populated. Bali, Lombok, and a few other small islands today must have densities that are beginning to approach those for Djawa, but the Outer Islands generally have far lower densities. Eastern Sumatera and some of the highland sectors of the western part of the island now have sizable local populations, and Sumatera now contains about 19,000,000 people. The island of Sulawesi is the third ranking island in population, with about 8,300,000, and the population of Kalimantan (Indonesian Borneo) is probably close to 5,600,000.

Many of the Outer Islands can support far more people than now live upon them. To do so, however, will require the adoption of more advanced systems of land use than shifting cultivation, and the cultural improvement of many of the features of the environment. It will also require a shift in Indonesian economy, lest a series of "little Djawa" concentrations result. The building up of regions of poor soils, the development of water supply in the drier regions, the building of transport systems, and the regional scattering of social, general, and technical education will be required throughout the whole of the Outer Islands. Few of the nonvolcanic islands possess soils rich enough to permit the duplication of Djawanese agricultural productivity, but in the past too little effort and investment has been expended upon the Outer Islands. Current Indonesian programs of cultural improvement and resource development could turn the Outer Islands into productive areas both complementing and supplementing the central core region.

Most of the population of Indonesia is Malay in racial background, though there are many subdivisions with different languages, group customs, and cultural affinities. The second largest single group of peoples is the Chinese, although Indonesian nationalistic restrictions have caused many Chinese to leave Indonesia since 1955. The largest share of the Chinese is urban and commercial, but on Kalimantan and Sumatera they also engage in fishing, and on Bangka and Belitung (Biliton) they engage in mining as laborers. The population of West Irian is not Malay, but chiefly Papuan, forming the one clear ethnic regional minority.

For decades the Dutch worried about the problem of overpopulation on the island of Djawa and tried many methods of moving population to Sumatera and other islands, but emigration from Djawa has not, and will not, alone, solve the problem. Almost the last possible acre of Djawa's crop land has been utilized, and forested surfaces have been too greatly reduced for efficient flood control and water supply. The annual increase continues to be marked; that of Djawa-Madura alone is striking, and Djawa may provide a living laboratory test regarding the possible maximum density of population that a portion of the earth can support. The growth of industrialization will permit further accommodation of some of the population, but within this century the Djawanese way of life must materially change in any event.

The urbanization of Djawa-Madura is, of course, under way at the present time, and the island of Djawa now contains three very large metropolitan areas, and a growing number of cities and towns. The metropolitan area of Djakarta is now well over 3,000,000 in total population, but there is some fluctuation in its total, according to politico-economic circumstances. Surabaja and Bandung are each metropolitan areas of over 1,000,000 each. The cities of Semarang, Surakarta, Malang, and Jogjakarta exceed 500,000 each, and each of the cities of Kediri, Tjirebon, Madiun, Bogor, and Pekalongan probably exceed 200,000, and there may be as many as ten other cities which now approach or exceed 100,000 each in population. Many of the former large rural villages have now grown into small towns.

The Outer Islands are showing increasing patterns of urbanism also but, except for Sumatera, really large cities are few in number and the patterns chiefly are of those of villages turning into towns and small cities, and all of the older towns and cities are growing larger. Palembang, in eastern Sumatera, is probably not far below the 1,000,000 mark, and Medan and Padang are approaching 500,000 each, and there are another four or five cities that exceed 100,000 each. Bandjarmasin, in southern Kalimantan, and Makasar, in southern Sulawesi, are probably above 400,000 each, and Pontianak, in southwestern Kalimantan, probably exceeds 200,000.

Properly speaking, portions of Djawa are undergoing urbanization, but the whole of Indonesia is not yet undergoing really marked urbanization comparable, for example, to the rates occurring in Japan. The economic straits of Indonesia neither facilitate nor permit a high rate of urbanization at present, and the percentage of urbanization stands at about fifteen percent. If the economic development programs of Indonesia in the near future can restore the secondary production patterns, producing a growing rate of industrialization, then the rates of urbanization will markedly increase. Djawa-Madura might then become a region of cities and towns, and incur in-migration in marked terms from the Outer Islands. Economic development programs do include plans for industrial growth in the Outer Islands but, characteristically, such plans center on Djawa-Madura rather than displaying a wide spread over the whole territory.

POLITICAL COHESION

The political map of independent Indonesia has shown several patterns since 1946, and it well may be that it will vary in the future (Fig. 22.7). Historically, what is today Indonesia has never functioned as a single political state. The constraints of distance, numbers of islands, varieties of ecological environments, ethnic subdivisions, and cultural separatisms do not make for easy integration of this island world into one cohesive political state. About three-quarters of the population is at least nominally Islamic in religion, but well under a third of that population, in the late 1960's, could really use the new national language *Bahasa Indonesia,* a modernized and romanized form of the "Market Malay" trader language. Dutch never became widely spoken throughout the island world and, though English is now being widely taught, there is no *lingua franca* for the whole political territory. There are diverse deeply rooted regionalisms and sectionalisms that are inhibitory of the emergence of a strong politicocultural nationalism. In some cases, such as Atjeh in northwest Sumatera, ethnic distinctiveness, common history, a rebellious tendency, and a strong ethnic communalism do not yield easily to a vague and as yet undefined sense of identity in "Indonesianness." Somewhat the same may be said of South Sulawesi, and also of the Ambon island cluster in the eastern zone. In a realm of many islands, island units easily form both regionalisms and sectionalisms. In the face of complaints of political and economic domination from Djakarta the national motto "unity in diversity" has little real meaning so far in modern political terms.

The centering of political power, administration, and bureaucracy on west central Djawa has historic precedent, but the historic tradition points equally to the looseness of political control over outlying island territories, and this is the chief problem in modern political management of a national state. Experience during the 1950's–1960's suggests the readiness of several island or

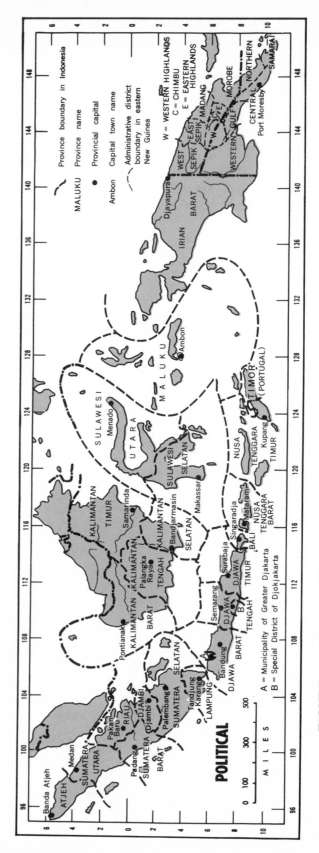

FIGURE 22.7. Present political states: Indonesia, Portuguese Timor, and the Territory of Papua and New Guinea.

regional units to ignore decrees of the national government, to resist acceptance of political management from Djawa, and the tendency to "smuggle" exports outward to finance local patterns of development. The depreciated economic straits of Indonesian national economy do not make for integrative development programs, when most of the foreign exchange earned by the Outer Islands has been spent on rebuilding Djawa, maintaining the livelihood of the Djawanese, or in furtherance of some localized program conceived in Djakarta.

Within Indonesian society there is internal conflict over the issues of little understood socialist versus capitalistic structures for the modern politico-economic state. The political pressures of the movement for independence contained strong trends toward the political left, and Indonesia has an old Communist Party, as such patterns go. Although this trend was checked again, in the late 1960's, the Indonesian Communist Party has shown periodic resurgence, and its influence possibly could again become strong enough to prevail in the face of socioeconomic distress should the present developmental programs not mature effectively. Cutting across the matters of economic orientation is the issue as to whether Indonesia should be organized as an outright Islamic political state. In some islands, regions, and sections both the economic orientation and the religious concern find concurrence, but in others there is complete disparity. The various spatial, political, economic, and religious issues, in this large island world of many sub-cultures do not consolidate readily or satisfactorily into a reasonable number of territorial units that could compose the states, districts, or provinces for either a strongly centralized political state or a more loosely joined federal state, and the present pattern of political districting represents a compromise at best (see Fig. 22.7). The strong anti-Dutch feeling that existed in earlier periods was artificially pre-

served beyond its time of utility, and the feeling is wearing off. There has not yet appeared a clear *raison d'etre* for the Indonesian political state. The center of gravity clearly lies on Djawa, but the traditional cleavage between Djawa and the Outer Islands remains strong and deep. The Outer Islands, among themselves, show no cohesion around a conceptual pattern or political goal other than resistance to Djawa. Were there such elements of cohesion among the Outer Islands the traditional cleavage and modern pressures might well force a division of the state, but in the absence of such possible bases of unity for the Outer Islands it is unlikely that Indonesia will actually soon break apart into a pattern of multiple states. Rather, it is likely that continued friction and the divergence of goals will continue to hinder the emergence of a true politico-cultural nationalism and a truly unitary functioning of the political state, so that further periodic crises will occur, based upon traditional patterns of regional and sectional cleavage.

THE NON-INDONESIAN EAST INDIES

The western sector of the island of Borneo is now a regional unit of the state of Malaysia, and was discussed in the chapter on Malaysia. There remains to be set down commentary on the eastern half of the island of New Guinea, and on the eastern half of the island of Timor (see Figs. 22.1 through 22.7).

Papua and Northeast New Guinea

About 160,000 square miles of the eastern end of the island of New Guinea is excluded from the political state of Indonesia (see particularly Fig. 22.7). This area, with the associated island groups, now commonly referred to as the Territory of Papua and New Guinea, is administered by Australia. It consists of two parts: Territory of Papua, the southeastern part of the island and its associated islands (90,540 square miles, population about 650,000), and the United Nations Trust Territory of New Guinea, the northeastern part of the island and its associated islands (93,000 square miles, population about 1,550,000). The two territories have been administered by Australia as one unit since 1949, though they have separate identity. It is probable that at some date in the near future the whole area will be given self-rule, as a step toward independence.

Dutch claims to New Guinea date back to the seventeenth century, but the Dutch never did more than make marginal contact with the western end of the island, since there seemed to be no significant profit in trade with the island. Dutch territorial claims remained undefined. Early nineteenth century British explorational and missionary efforts in southeastern New Guinea and German trading activity in the island fringes northeast of New Guinea, plus rumors of gold strikes, led to the late nineteenth century political occupance of southeastern New Guinea by the British and the similar occupance of northeast New Guinea and the Bismarck Archipelago by the Germans. A tentative adjustment of claims over New Guinea made in 1884–1885 and concluded in 1895, divided the island between Germany, Great Britain, and the Netherlands, and set up the present political boundaries. The German sector was first operated through a chartered company but the German government assumed administration in 1899, as economic development lagged. Australian occupance of the German territories occurred in 1914, the area became a League of Nations mandate in 1921, and became a United Nations Trust Territory under Australian administration in late 1946. The British zone was first recognized as within the rights of the British East India Company, but then control was placed under Australian administration in 1884, where it has remained. In both the German sector and the British zone there was development of coastal coconut plantations, though German development was principally in the islands off New Guinea, and no significant economic penetration of the interior of the main island occurred.

In ethnic and cultural terms the whole island of New Guinea forms an entity separate from the Malay world to the west, and New Guinea often is categorized as part of Melanesia. The peoples of the coastal fringe may properly be termed Melanesian, but the great bulk of the interior population properly are now termed Papuan, and there is a small population of Negrito scattered over the island interior. New Guinea is a region of intricate subdivision of small ethnic units into 700–800 linguistic groups who chiefly have organized themselves as lineage groups and tribal societies. Chiefly village dwellers who have acutely divided habitable regions into cultural-ecologic niches, the Papuan peoples essentially remained in the Stone Age until almost the onset of World War II, practicing varieties of shifting cultivation and wild resource appropriation, and developing their own autochthonous systems of culture. In some good highland areas their shifting cultivation had developed advanced technological systems supporting 500 people per square mile. In less good regions and in some of the swampy lowland valleys and flood plains population densities were much lighter, and there are some areas that seem not to be occupied at all. The interior has been a region of self-contained and self-supporting living systems, though no total isolation was, of course, possible. Small amounts of simple trade goods from the coast always reached interior points and exotic goods have come out of New Guinea for a long time. In comparative terms, however, interior New Guinea was a world apart from the rapidly changing outside world of the eighteenth and nineteenth centuries, and it has only been since the end of World War II that inter-world contacts have revealed patterns of local development.

Australian initiative had been carrying on exploration in the southeastern half of New Guinea for nearly a half century prior to World War II. The military activities of the war years took Australians to almost all parts of the territory, and at present political administrative controls have been extended almost throughout the combined territory. This, of course, amounts to an entering wedge in altering the whole native structure of life, since tribal wars are lessening, and new tools, new crops, and new elements of culture systems are being introduced. Permanent European settlements, and increasing aspects of occidental-style agricultural undertakings are to be found around the coastal fringes, roads are penetrating the interior steadily, and airfields are becoming more frequent. Port Moresby has now grown from a small port town into a sizable urban entity, with all the benefits of "civilization," including a university, and it may not be long before a Papuan university graduate, a third generation removed from the Stone Age, campaigns for the presidency of the independent twentieth-century political state of Papua–New Guinea. Other towns around the coastal fringe, and frequent anthropologic expeditions into the interior by occidentals, are increasing the exposure of the occidental world to the Papuans, who may make their own adjustment to the outer world.

Timor

The sole remainder from the Portuguese era of exploration and trade in the East Indies is the small holding centered on the eastern half of the island of Timor (see Figs. 22.1 through 22.7). This includes the main eastern sector of the island, a small north-coast, main-island enclave named Ocussi-Ambeno, the small island of Atauro off the

north coast, and the wee islet of Jaco, just off the eastern tip. The total area is approximately 7,383 square miles, and its estimated 1970 population is about 580,000.

In the fifteenth century the island of Timor already was renowned as a source for sandalwood, the Chinese were important in the trade, it was this trade that brought the Portuguese to the island, and the cause that made the island a territory in contention between European powers during the seventeenth to nineteenth centuries. The Timor-Macao-China trade in sandalwood was a strong part of late Portuguese trade in the East. The gradual decline of East Indies sandalwood trade during the late nineteenth century, as other regional sources and near-substitutes were exploited, let the island slip back into a position of unimportance in world affairs.

Timor was long linked with Portuguese India, but from 1864 until 1926 Timor was under Macao in Portuguese political affairs. In 1951 Timor was constituted a Portuguese overseas province, and put under civil administration. There never have been many Europeans in Portuguese Timor, and the Chinese sandalwood trader-community comprised the largest nonnative ethnic element. The island contains a mixed series of ethnic elements in which only local regional differences distinguish the Portuguese sector from the now Indonesian sector. Along the coastal fringe there are strips of coconut, coffee, and rubber plantings which contribute export commodities, and there still is some exploitation of sandalwood. The north coast capital city of Dili, in 1970, held a population of about 55,000, and a small number of other coastal villages has grown into small towns. The interior sector of the island has been very little developed and, to a considerable degree, leads a traditional village agricultural way of life.

Portuguese Timor constitutes an anomaly in the modern world, a holdover from the early era of European exploration and trade monopolies. At present it is administered as an integral home-province of Portugal, but there is uncertainty as to whether such peculiar political constructs can remain. That such a small colonial holding, despite its status on paper, should become an independent political state seems a rather impractical solution. There is little current pressure to absorb the unit into the state of Indonesia, but such a possibility must remain open for the future. No other major political state, save Australia, is apt to enter this political arena, and Portuguese Timor could be taken into Indonesia at any politically advantageous time.

23

THE PHILIPPINES: AN ISLAND BORDERLAND

THE PEOPLING OF A MULTIPLE-ISLAND ENVIRONMENT

With all its 7,083 islands and rocks the Philippines forms one of the most numerous island groups on our globe. Its 37,000,000 people still do not fill it in a manner wholly typical of the Orient. Although many lowland areas seem alike in their surface patterns the archipelago presents a varied group of local environments within a moderate range of physical conditions. A small world of many islands is set on the edge of the Orient, from which it has received most of its people and much of its culture.

All the lowlands are similar to other lowland regions of Southeast Asia in their environmental conditions. The islands belong more to the mainland regions of plants and animals than to the region of the eastern East Indies. Here lowland collecting and fishing economies were at home. Some plants do not reach to northern Luzon, but the basic ones abound everywhere. Many of the islands have hilly to mountainous interiors that call for altered living patterns, and it is only in recent centuries that the

Malay peoples have gone deeply into these hilly interiors.

Once migration of modern man into the Philippines began, it has been fairly continuous, with overlapping effects. The first immigrants probably were land travelers who moved along the land connections with the Island Arcs in the periods during which these were open. They were simple hunters and collectors, and they may have come into the islands about thirty thousand years ago. First came the Negrito and related small peoples. Each new group could find many localities suitable to its particular economy. Following the Negrito were the proto-Malay, who may have used the simplest ideas of crop growing to round out their hunting-collecting economy.

The first Neolithic people came by sea, sometime after the last major breaks in the land bridge routes, and a tentative date is currently placed at about 5000 B.C. As boat-using and fishing peoples who frequented the coastal littoral zones, the Neolithic immigrants were also crop-growing peoples who visualized new criteria for the settlement of coastal landscapes. Whether they came chiefly from the mainland or out of the island world to the south is not clear at present. Earlier concepts described immigration in waves and the earlier patterns as coming from the mainland, but there is doubt as to origins. Slowly drifting patterns in fairly continuous fashion seem more likely, and it also is likely that southern islanders were among the newcomers. If in the earlier periods the several kinds of people occupied given districts with only moderate intermixture, conflicts gradually arose as people with varied cultures began a more active competition for preferred landscapes. The Negritos have left to them few satisfactory landscapes today and, as the islands fill up with people, those few landscapes will be put to other uses.

The Neolithic culture connection between the Philippines and the mainland and island sectors may well have been rather continuous during the primary portion of the Neolithic, bringing selected features of outside culture patterns. As the late Neolithic connection with the mainland lessened, local specialization in weapons, tools, trinkets, and other culture traits became commoner. Some features like the use of jade were abandoned as the mainland contact was altered or broken. In date the Neolithic in the Philippines is tentatively set as covering a period from 5000 B.C. to about A.D. 200. The late Neolithic began about 1000 B.C. The Bronze Age falls across the Neolithic, roughly 800 B.C., and overlaps the Iron Age, which is thought to have begun about 250 B.C. in the islands. There may be some question as to these latter dates, and further research may indicate an earlier date for the beginning of the Bronze Age in the Philippines.

Copper-bronze and gold working techniques came into the islands with the final groups of southern islanders, or perhaps peoples from the Southeast Asian mainland. With them also came irrigated and terraced rice culture, the domestic pig, and several minor items. Since the bringers of these new features were not very numerous their zones of occupance were somewhat restricted. The concept of very careful terracing of ricefields with integrated water supply did not spread beyond northern and central Luzon. In the rugged terrain of Mountain Province are to be found the only Philippine rice terraces executed in the full wet-field manner.

From what is now western Indonesia after about 500 B.C. began the influx of peoples and cultures which finally spread all over the islands. Involved were cultures of late Neolithic through Iron Age, for this stream of people did not cease until the sixteenth century. With them came wooden and bamboo house types, mats and basketry, dress and tattoo patterns, boats and fishing techniques, and a great many domesticated plants and farming customs. After about 500 B.C. came pottery, cotton, and the textile loom, humped cattle, and the water buffalo.* Then also came the knowledge of iron making and its use, trade goods from the Indian Ocean realm, and the sea trading habit. A great many of these traits were really Indian in origin. Many languages spoken in the islands today came with these peoples.

Feeding right into the Indonesian culture streams were the influences of the Indian traders, missionaries, and political organizers. By the first century B.C. their strength was felt over the southern and western Indies, lasting some six or seven centuries. The actual number of Indian colonies located in the islands is not at all clear. The later Indonesians were excellent Indian cultural agents who spread farther than the Indians themselves. Indian influence is shown in language, alphabets, crop plants, old architecture, old religious and art motifs, political and social organization.

*The modern Filipino terms the water buffalo a carabao.

Cutting across the Indonesian-Indian line has been the later influence of the Chinese. After its quiet period in the early Christian era Chinese influence increased in Luzon by the eighth century A.D., and by the fifteenth century the Chinese were influential throughout the islands and were growing steadily stronger as Indian influences died away. Today it is believed that almost 10 percent of the population represent Chinese types assimilated over the last thousand years.

Racial mixing processes have been active for 4,000 years. A Filipino blend has been produced, ultimately and chiefly from Mongoloid racial types. Small additions are the Arab-Persian traces added through early sea traders and later Moslems, with some Japanese, Spanish, and American blood added in the last four and a half centuries. In the multiple-island environment nature seldom repeated her proportions exactly. But the close proximity of islands and the liking for navigation prevented the regional isolation that might be thought possible. During the Neolithic the Philippines formed a major link in the island chain by which mainland culture traits spread throughout the south and western Pacific. Except for the remnant Negrito there are few contrasts in the Philippines of the order of those that mark Indonesia. The Philippine environment is small enough for most incoming peoples and cultural influences to have been able to spread throughout the archipelago. Both the seeming variation and the considerable unity are a partial result of a multiple-island environment in which the same kind of local landscape is repeated over and over again.

MOSLEM AND MORO, SPANISH AND CHRISTIAN

The terminal wave of the stormy eastward flow of Islam reached the southern islands of the Philippine Archipelago about 1480.

Its advocates were Indian and Arab Moslems, both scholars and administrators, successful in spreading their religion and expert at politically organizing small regions into Islamic principalities. In their wake came political chieftains of the little states in western Indonesia, each with a band of followers, in the last Indonesian colonial spread into the Philippines. Within a short period the Islamic faith had encompassed the Sulu chain and had a foothold on both Mindanao and Palawan. This faith changed many aspects of native life, but the most significant changes were social and political. Social and religious organization developed a community of feeling, sympathy, and strength; political organization was expressed in small principalities of a more formal sort than earlier ones.

Many Filipinos are amused at the phrase in occidental history books asserting that Magellan "discovered" the Philippines. In 1521 the islands had long been well known to China, India, and all Southeast Asia, and in several island ports the traders of many lands met regularly. When the Spanish arrived in force in 1565, Islamic chieftains held power in scattered localities as far north as Manila, though the mass conversion of the regional populace to the Islamic faith had taken in only Sulu and parts of Mindanao and Palawan. The Spanish conquest went rapidly except in the far south where the Islamic faith supported its own political and military leadership; there the Spanish never made their conquest truly complete during their whole period of control. Constant Moro raiding and looting, conducted from Sulu, Palawan, and Borneo, caused annual losses along all Mindanao and many Visayan coasts until the middle of the nineteenth century (Moro is the Christian term employed in the Philippines to denote a Moslem).

Spanish rule markedly altered the culture of the Filipinos and, of course, affected a much larger area than had that of the Moslems (Fig. 23.1). In the Spanish system the Catholic priesthood worked hand in hand with temporal power. By 1611 numerous churches had been organized and a share of the population had accepted Christianity. Only in isolated island interiors did there remain non-Christian tribes at the end of Spanish rule. The fairly uniform acceptance of Christianity hastened other changes of a political and economic nature. The Spanish began with the barangay and the datu (the native local political unit and the chief), turning them into the barrio and the teniente, in American terms the ward and the lieu-

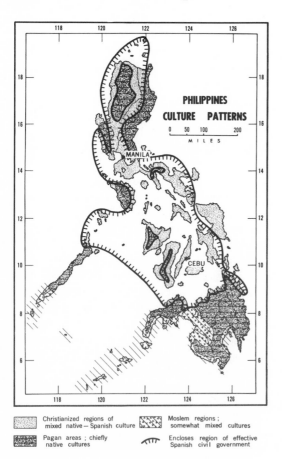

FIGURE 23.1. Philippine culture patterns in late Spanish times.

tenant. Above the barrio they set the pueblo or town system that they had used in the Americas, termed municipio, now renamed the municipality. The barrio and the municipality functioned to bring local affairs under controllable heads, and served as the centers in which fixed residence could be enforced. The centralization of regional government in provinces developed around the granting of encomiendas (rights to tribute or labor from a local populace), given to greedy colonial officers, both political and religious. The establishment of a central government superior to the provinces placed the control of the Philippines in Manila before the end of the sixteenth century.

The introduction of many American crop plants enlarged the cropping combinations of the islands, but Spanish influence did little to improve native agricultural systems. In the nineteenth century the Spanish stimulated the development of a limited commercial agriculture. The reorienting of trade toward Mexico and the attempted operation of the islands as an imperial monopoly altered older trade patterns. The institution of new forms of house building, food habits, forms of dress, social customs, and the Spanish language made over the higher levels of society and the masses to a variable degree. Spanish rule was monopolistic and exploitive. Spaniards almost never engaged in primary production but lived as gentlemen on the fruit of Filipino labor and Chinese trade. Forced labor and tax exactions were heavy at the hands of both the priesthood and the political administrators.

One cannot observe the impressive old churches scattered over the Spanish-controlled parts of the islands without visualizing the heavy hand of the Church. Only in the latter half of the nineteenth century were appreciable improvements made in colonial administration, too slowly and in too little measure. The weight of Spanish rule plus the effect of Moro raids retarded the growth of population until the nineteenth century. From a possible half million in the mid-sixteenth century, population rose to about 1,500,000 by 1800, leaped to about 3,500,000 by 1845, and stood close to 7,000,000 at the end of Spanish rule in 1899.

The Spanish furthered one pattern which now has no easy solution. In the sixteenth century the Chinese already were the leading merchants throughout the islands. Spanish encouragement of Chinese traders increased their numbers, even though periodic oppression temporarily reduced their operations. By the end of the Spanish period the Chinese controlled a good share of the interisland wholesale and retail trade. They were present in every large city and had infiltrated most of the profitable economic enterprises of the islands. They had intermarried among the Filipinos to such an extent that many of the present leaders of the islands are mixed Chinese-Filipinos.

THE COMING OF THE AMERICAN

The Americans came into the islands in 1898 with the avowed mission of improving conditions for the population. American control retained the whole of the Spanish regional administrative machinery, the *barrio*, the *municipio*, the province, and the capital at Manila. American procedure adopted the device of the specially chartered city, from the precedent of Manila. These administrative units grew in number until in 1967 there were almost 30,000 barrios, 1,376 municipalities, and 65 provinces. In 1967 there were 49 chartered cities. The chartered cities are supervised directly by the national government. Among the first acts of American rule were the separation of Church and state and the starting of a public school system. In consequence the Moros have become relatively peaceful members of Filipino society. Their unity of religious feeling, and differences in food and dress, set them off against the Christians, but they are actively a part of the modern Philippines. Under American Protestant missionary competition many recent improvements in the Roman Catholic program have been instituted, particularly in the field of education.

Under American rule changes were made steadily to increase the role of the Filipino in his own affairs. Within the framework of government inherited from the Spanish many American democratic procedures were progressively installed. A limited pattern of free trade, within the tariff wall of the United States, came in 1909. In 1934 Philippine independence was planned for the mid-1940's and granted on July 4, 1946. Unfortunately the Filipinos have also learned many of the American political and social vices that inhibit good government. As American authority relaxed, these vices increased disproportionately in number and volume. The short span of 48 years may have been too short a time in which to learn thoroughly the intricate workings of representative government. And unfortunately American rule did not completely finish many reorganization programs begun with good intention.

By 1970 there were about 8,500,000 children in public and private schools of elementary and secondary level. Faced with some eighty languages and dialects American educators began teaching English, which now is the widely spoken *lingua franca*, even in Moro regions. Pilipino, developed from one of the more widely used native tongues (Tagalog), now has been chosen as the national language. It is taught in public schools along with English but, though the radio and native movies help spread it, years will pass before it will become a truly national language.

The recent influence of the American has increasingly altered the pattern of culture. As one travels over the islands today it is obvious that lipstick, chewing gum, and toothpaste have almost replaced the chewing of betel nut, that soft drinks, and beer are replacing coconut and nipa-palm tuba, that radios, newspapers, and comic books have become extremely popular. The Chinese merchant has been an almost ubiquitous agent by which a standard range of modern occidental consumer goods has been spread throughout the islands. The motor road and the bus, truck, and private car have recently been so widely adopted that motor fuel products now are one of the chief imports. In the homes of better-educated Filipinos one finds a surprising but purposeful reproduction of contemporary American life. Filipinos feel that they have progressed farther than other Far Eastern countries on the road to modern civilization. Though it is expedient on occasions to turn anti-American, most Filipinos look to the United States with affection, respect and, it must be added, economic expectancy. There are some who feel that it was wrong to permit so rapid and full a reproduction of contemporary American culture in a small country which so far has not the economic maturity to support all its cultural aspirations. Through the American implanted educational system, today still somewhat lacking in vocational and mechanical training, the white-collar class has become the admired goal, rather than the mechanical craftsmen and artisans who have been the backbone of American material culture. In this the United States insufficiently countered the demoralizing impact of Spanish rule.

THE PATTERN OF RESIDENCE

In the pre-Spanish period there were several variations in living patterns, owing to racial and cultural differences. Some of the simpler groups were semi-migratory in habit. The practice of shifting cultivation worked against permanently fixed settlements, and the linear coastlines made for random residence at any attractive landing. Fertile local landscapes

brought heavier settlement and groups of villages. Perhaps the Moslems first fortified certain sites and turned them into strategic military and political centers. The Spanish carried the matter further, with formal and fixed sites. The *poblacion*, the central part of the *municipio*, with its church, convent, plaza, garrison barracks, administrative building and headmen's residences, gradually became a small town. The native *barangay*, upon becoming the barrio, often remained straggling and extended, more an administrative unit than a settlement site.

Today one finds homesteads scattered everywhere from the high-tide line to the high mountains. Houses seldom are screened for privacy by special plantings, though they often are partly concealed by a miniature jungle of fruit trees. A barrio often is a long and narrow shoestring alignment of houses along a road or a shore line. As new roads are built people sometimes prefer the convenience of roadside residence to scattered locations in the fields. One often finds the highway between towns almost continuously lined with houses. The poblacion of the municipality today retains its plaza around which are grouped the church, convent, schools, municipal offices, theaters, the municipal market shed, some of the shops, and a few of the houses. Spanish settlement plans, originally rectangular, have not always retained their alignment, as no force has been used in recent decades. New towns in the pioneer regions seldom have a formal plaza and do not show the massive stone churches and other buildings normally built under Spanish rule. Urbanism is a slowly growing part of the residence pattern of the islands, in 1970 slightly under thirty percent of the people living in cities of over 10,000.

Field patterns are of every shape. Where physical conditions permit they often are roughly rectangular. Cane, corn, plantation coconut, plantation abaca, and many rice-fields are fairly rectangular in shape and continuous in planting. Small holdings of most field crops, almost all of the fruit, and many of the vegetables are in very mixed plantings and are irregular in field pattern. The upland farm landscape always is an irregular one containing forest remnants or some of the rank grasses. In only a few places is the surveyor working ahead of the colonial settler, namely in the national land subdivisions. Most farms are delimited and identified by historic usage, customary acceptance, and the payment of municipality taxes. Specific land titles are rather new, and it is customary today in many areas to claim a given tract of land but to crop only a portion thereof, years ahead of the surveyors.

The house on piles, built of bamboo and thatched with various grasses, palm leaves, or mattings, was one of the early importations into the islands. Later crude timber and wooden planks became common for chiefs and wealthier families. There still are a few communal houses and special houses for men and women, but these forms have largely gone from the cultured parts of the islands. Almost basic today in rural areas is the single-family house raised a few feet off the ground on posts of some sort. The house itself may consist of a single squarish room with a steep gabled roof, or it may be as large as a dozen rooms, multiple gabled and formed of a variety of separate rooms and lean-to units. The ground-floor section serves in the place of auxiliary buildings, as pens for animals and fowls, and storage for tools and crops. It often is not walled and seldom is floored. It is characteristic that roofs have a wide overhang and that the sliding windows of larger houses are provided with separate rain-shelter awnings.

Since perhaps 1930 cultural aspiration has been for the wooden house, set on concrete posts, with solid wood floors, a sheet iron roof, a formal entry stairway, electric lights, and a bathroom with running water. Most of the towns have piped water systems and electricity to support these hopes. In simpler economic situations, and in rural surround-

ings, bamboo may replace most of the wood, nipa palm thatch may cover the walls and the roof, and the floor may be of split bamboo. Running water and electric light are rare items in rural localities. Except in northern Luzon, whenever possible there are flowers around the house, in the ground, in pots, or in hanging coconut husks.

There are certain regional differences in house design and in materials, but for the main portion of the islands today the type is fairly standard. Where nipa palm is not available, cogon grass or split bamboo is used. In the higher mountain lands wooden slabs or rough planking are used. In the Batanes group of islands, north of Luzon in the main typhoon track, houses are strongly built of stone, and in the marsh country of parts of Mindanao houseboats form some homes.

Modern urban influences have added to the changes in housing. Reinforced concrete, cement blocks, paint, glass windows, screens, plaster stucco, and garages are combined with the "modern" trend in architecture. This usually omits the posts and an elevated position. Since there is little zoning in practice, the elaborate homes of the wealthy in many communities are flanked by the one-room nipa houses of the poor. These newer features are spreading into the smaller towns and hinterlands, for commonly one may find a Filipino recently back from years in "the States" eager to retain accustomed living habits. Philippine architects are beginning to create their own "styles" in housing and commercial buildings, and the newer urban developments clearly show this influence.

PHILIPPINE AGRICULTURE TODAY

The Philippines is primarily agricultural but does not feed itself. This became true in late Spanish times, and, despite efforts at correction, it remains true today. Changes in dietary habits are involved in this food deficit. After running a rice deficit for years, production in 1970 provided a small surplus, but the increasing demand for wheat products, for meats, and for midlatitude fruits and vegetables involve demands that domestic agriculture cannot meet. American commercial stimulation of agriculture for export was not accompanied by enough teaching in scientific agriculture to replace the former simple crop growing. Agriculture today, therefore, is not as highly productive as it needs to be both to feed a rapidly growing population and to provide commercial exports with which to finance the higher standards of living made appealing by the cultural progress of the islands (Fig. 23.2). Free entry into the United States, after 1909, gave export agriculture both a good market and a kind of guarantee. The share of land devoted to export crops is about twenty percent. This would be satisfactory if the per-acre food crop yields were high, but they are among the lower yields for the world as a whole.

Farming Conditions

Farm equipment ranges from the simple digging stick to power machinery, and farming practices are a curious blend of science, easy-going tropical habits, and folk lore. Draft power is quite inadequate. Fertilization, crop rotation, and conservation practices are not yet generally practiced by the average small farmer. But mechanization and improved farming have a greater potential in the islands than in many other parts of the Orient, provided that the right kind of government program carries it out.

Until about 1915 in no part of the islands was there a severe pressure of men upon the land. This has since developed in parts of Luzon and in the Visayas, particularly on Cebu, Bohol, and a few of the small islands. There still is land for a larger population, but the need is for efficient use of present farm lands; this need will grow steadily stronger as the good lands are taken into

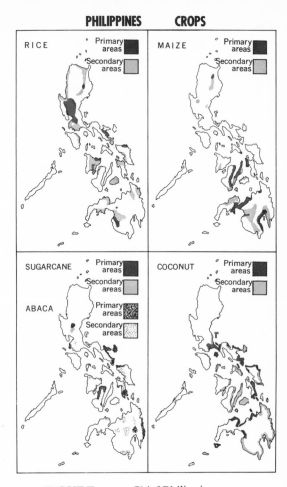

FIGURE 23.2. Chief Philippine crops.

farms. The very lack of intensive farming is responsible for a share of the low yields. Ricefields often are not level, so that the water must stand in pockets. Often what water there is is derived from immediate rainfall only. For years writers on the islands have commented on the need for irrigation. In north Luzon where the famous rice terraces of Mountain Province have been built over the centuries the chief engineering operation is the elaborate provision of water for each field. These fields total only some 70,000 acres, and include land planted to crops other than rice. In addition to the terraced lands there are many steep-slope fields cropped by shifting cultivation operated by the farmers who work the terraces, and on these steep slopes the practices are as wasteful as those of the terraces are saving.

The Filipinos developed their rice culture in the cheapest way possible, without always providing a water supply and without care for the soil. In recent years much of the expansion of the rice acreage has been on lands not provided with any irrigation facilities, and the rice acreage has grown faster than has the provision of irrigation supplies. Animal power is used when available, but its inadequacy requires a large volume of human labor per volume of crop. As farmland has increased in amount, without concurrent provision of water, the cost of irrigation engineering needed has cumulatively grown until today the problem is a formidable obstacle in improving agriculture, both to private farmers and to the government.

With rice the primary crop the future provision of water and the level terracing of small fields along the lines of the Chinese or Japanese system of intensive, man-powered farming is one avenue to greater crop yields. Enlargement of fields, mechanization of farm work, and the application of modern science in agriculture are another. The two routes to increased production are not fully compatible and cannot both be applied to the same fields. The islands still have a chance to use either or both on selected tracts of land. Several forces are at work, and it is difficult to predict the direction of change. Although shifting cultivation is now prohibited by law, it continues on a rather large scale on the mountain hinterlands. Mechanization sometimes fails through improper training and equipment not suited to the task. Successful experimenters in mechanization are copied by their neighbors, but the Filipino farmer is as hard to change as those elsewhere.

A little over one-fourth the total area of the islands is actually taken up by about 2,300,000 farms (Fig. 23.3). Of this area of some 22,000,000 acres about 18,000,000 are cultivated every year, the balance either lying idle or being utilized as pastures, wood lots, or noncrop areas. By double cropping, the total land cropped each year is raised to about 20,000,000 acres. Approximately fifty percent of the farmers are tenants, the proportion ranging downward from a maximum of about three-fourths in central Luzon. Recent land laws have improved the legal position of the tenant, but the actual position of the back-country tenant has changed but little, and actually effective tenancy reform is one of the most needed improvements in

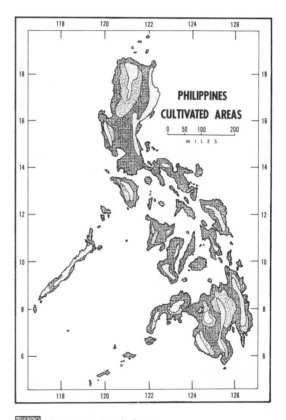

Predominantly land in farms

Partially claimed ; areas undergoing settlement

Upland regions of forest and scattered farms ; chiefly shifting cultivation

FIGURE 23.3. Cultivated areas of the Philippines.

agriculture. There are very strong contrasts among land operators, from the small tenant who cannot secure even rented land sufficient to grow his own basic rice supply to very large farms running to thousands of acres. The latter chiefly date from the Spanish period, but American-introduced land laws, aimed at the prevention of large holdings, contained loopholes used by the wealthy families to accumulate large farms.

The Crop Pattern

The outstanding crop is rice, of which there are hundreds of varieties (see Fig. 23.2). About 8,500,000 acres annually are planted in rice, meaning slightly over forty percent of the total cropped land. About half the total agricultural labor is concerned with rice. Over 2,500,000 acres of upland rice, grown on plowed and hand-dug or cleared but unworked slopes and dependent upon rain alone, consists mostly of quick-growing 3-to-5-month varieties with light per-acre yields. Over 2,500,000 acres of rice are grown on plowed lowland fields that depend upon rain water impounded within their borders. These varieties require a growing season of 5 to 7 months, yield moderately but seldom are double cropped. About 3,500,000 acres of irrigated long-season rice are grown every year, including a considerable second crop, with high yields. Some rice is grown in every province, and about half of all the farms grow some rice, but there is an uneven balance of sufficiency. Central Luzon is the chief surplus region, but metropolitan Manila more than absorbs this surplus.

Maize totals about 5,000,000 acres, about twenty-five percent of the cropped area, and uses about twenty percent of the agricultural labor volume. About twenty-five percent of the population lives chiefly on maize the year around. Cropping practices vary markedly, from one to four crops per year on the same land. Most varieties are rather poor producers. Losses by corn borers often are heavy, and their seasonal life-cycle often controls the planting of maize. Some maize is grown all over the islands, but the coral limestone portions of the Visayan Islands unsuited to rice are the chief growing center (see Fig. 23.2). The lands of Mindanao to which Visayan colonists have gone are put into maize, rather than rice, out of cultural preference. The Cagayan Valley, in northeast Luzon, is an important cash-crop maize-growing region, shipping its surplus to the Visayan region.

Sweet potatoes and bananas are of about equal importance as supporting food crops, the former occupying about 750,000 acres of land, and the latter about 450,000 acres. Rarely is either crop grown on wide acreage, but in garden patches around the farmsteads in many varieties. Each is grown almost everywhere in the islands, though the northern Luzon hill country has extensive areas of sweet potatoes and few of bananas. Manioc (for cassava) and mongo (mung bean) are other minor crops, usually occupying about 200,000 and 125,000 acres, respectively. Manioc is but little grown in northern Luzon. Sweet potatoes and manioc, with such other minor root crops as taro and several kinds of yams, vary considerably in cultivated area from year to year, depending upon food scarcity and the success of the major food crops. In bad years root crop plantings increase greatly, to be fed to the pigs when better human food can be had.

There are over a dozen minor food crops, roots, vegetables, and fruits that are scattered over the islands or concentrated in particular localities possessing attractive local environments. Such vegetables as tomatoes, green beans, eggplant, and the bitter cucumbers, along with peanuts and such fruits as the mango, papaya, lanzone, jackfruit, breadfruit, orange, coffee, and cacao are widely scattered and well liked, though almost nowhere are they grown in organized plantings of any size. Except for peanuts, tomatoes, and mangos, a few plants of each of the others share the junglelike planting around many farm homes. Pineapple, a minor crop in acreage, is a significant export product grown in Mindanao on three American-operated plantations, but it is grown elsewhere in small home plantings only. The total acreage of these crops amounts to close to 1,000,000 acres per year.

Sugar has been the chief commercial export crop in past years when free access to the United States markets was assured. Under the quota system adopted during the mid-1930's, the destruction of mills during World War II, and the gradual increase of United States tariff barriers, Philippine sugarcane planting faced an uncertain future, but the United States embargo on Cuban sugar gave the Philippine sugar industry a new lease on continued production. Something over a half million acres normally go into commercial cane, grown both on big plantations and on small holdings, and sugarcane is widely grown on small farms to be chewed as a snack food. The islands of Negros, central Luzon, eastern Panay, and northern Cebu are the sugarcane centers, where refiners operate "sugar centrals" to crush cane and produce raw and white sugar (see Fig. 23.2). Widely distributed over the islands are small plantings of cane used to produce the older style domestic brown sugar in small crushing and boiling plants. Domestic consumption takes about twelve to fifteen percent of the crop.

Coconut is coming to be the chief export product of the islands, despite the rather low quality of coconut products turned out, and is promoted by the steady planting of new lands both by the small planter and the plantation owner. There are now about close to 200,000,000 trees planted, almost 150,000,000 of which are of bearing age. Supposedly preferring lowland sites and sandy to loamy soils near the seacoast, coconuts today are doing well under a variety of other conditions. Commercial plantings reach from central Luzon southward, southern Luzon being the most densely planted region (see Fig. 23.2). The northern part of Luzon and the interiors of the larger islands contain no commercial plantings, but a few trees around homesteads are common, up to altitudes of about 2,000 feet. Most coconut products, fresh coconut, copra, desiccated coconut, coconut oil, and tuba (a fermented alcoholic drink made from juice extracted from the growing tip of the tree) are produced by the small landholder. He is individualistic in habits and slow to adopt progressive techniques. Less than two percent of the yield is used domestically. Coconut lands often are planted to other crops when the trees are young. It is hard to tabulate the acreage devoted to coconut, but the figure is probably not far from 3,000,000 acres, about fifteen percent of the cropped area. In addition to typhoons, which seriously damage coconut trees, there has been severe infestation by a virus disease which gradually kills the tree, and the disease is thought to be spreading.

Abaca is the third ranking agricultural export, covering about 400,000 acres. The southern end of Luzon, Samar, and Leyte, and eastern Mindanao are the chief producing districts, though the Visayan Islands generally produce some abaca. Southeastern Mindanao, before 1941, had developed as an area of Japanese-operated plantations, producing the majority of the export. Post-war land-holding readjustments eliminated the Japanese and greatly increased the role of the small planter who grows abaca as a cash crop along with corn, bananas, and vegetables as food crops. This tended to production irregularities of some importance. As southern Luzon, Samar, and Leyte suffer occasional typhoons, very hard on the banana-like plant producing the fiber, the future of the export industry is not entirely an assured and happy one. Severe infestations of disease have been hard to control in the Philippines, since small farmers often resist efforts aimed at control. In recent years abaca has also suffered from competition from synthetic rope and string materials, and the abaca industry is going through a marked decline.

Tobacco, a major export crop during late Spanish times, was operated as a government monopoly on large land holdings. In the American period the crop first increased and then gradually declined, being largely Spanish controlled. Between 1930 and the late 1950's tobacco occupied about 150,000 acres of land, used less than two percent of the agricultural labor, and accounted for about two percent of the exports. War-time destruction was hard on the organized tobacco industry, and imports of American tobaccos in the prosperous postwar era made development difficult. In the late 1950's government policy brought in new plant varieties and began restricting imports, strongly stimulating the domestic tobacco-growing industry, so that the total acreage had climbed above 300,000 for the country as a whole by 1970. Northern Luzon, particularly northwest Luzon and the Cagayan Valley, is the chief producing area, with Cebu also important, but small garden plantings are found almost all over the islands.

There are a number of minor export crops, such as maguey (producing a type of sisal fiber), derris root for insect killers, rubber, and bananas. Rubber, so important in Malaysia and Indonesia, has been only a minor item in Mindanao until rather recently. The rising importance of automotive transport and economic nationalism have combined to make domestic production valuable, and rubber is now being grown on numerous small plantations on the Zamboanga Peninsula of Mindanao Island and on Basilan Island just to the south. A new export crop is now appearing in production, as two of the large banana companies have established plantings in southern Mindanao for export purposes.

The ten major Philippine crops, ranked by area of land, are: rice, corn, coconut, sweet potatoes, sugarcane, bananas, abaca, tobacco, manioc, and the mango. By value of product the first ten are: rice, coconut, sugarcane, corn, tobacco, abaca, bananas, sweet potatoes, coffee, and pineapple.

The animal population of the islands is considerably less than needed, whether for draft power or for food purposes, though totals had been climbing steadily until excessive World War II slaughtering set the islands back a good many years. In rank, hogs, carabao, cattle, goats, horses, and sheep, and chickens, ducks, and pigeons are the most numerous among the animal and fowl groups. Of pork, beef, and carabao the average urban Filipino consumes a total of about 40 pounds per year, which is far less than the American average, but well above that of the Orient as a whole. Fish form a very significant part of the island diet, and the annual consumption per person runs above 50 pounds, though unevenly divided between coastal and interior consumers. The average Filipino prefers a basic menu of rice and fish in three daily meals, supplemented by varying amounts of bread, meat, vegetables, and fruit. The fish volume is made up of commercially caught sea fish, locally caught fish from the sea, rivers, lakes, and rice-fields, fish culturally raised in ponds, and a significant import volume. The annual catch in 1968 approximated 850,000 tons, against a consumer demand for about 1,300,000 tons. The fish-pond harvest is substantially increasing as coastal mangrove swamps are diked and turned into ponds for the raising of one particular fish, the bangos.

About twenty-five percent of the islands' area now is in farmlands. Almost twenty percent of the total area now is in open grass and parklands, largely the effect of shifting cultivation and annual burning. Commercial forests are estimated to cover some thirty-five percent of the area, and noncommercial forests, being second growth and worked-over lands, about ten percent. Swamp and marsh-lands cover about two percent. The annual growth rate is thought to be over 3,000,000,000 board feet per year, whereas present commercial timber cutting has barely reached 1,000,000,000 board feet annually. Besides commercial timber production, how-ever, is an unknown but serious drain upon forest lands by the continued illegal practice of shifting cultivation, and by the un-controlled permanent removal of forests by colonial settlers.

Most of the commercial timber is secured from some sixty species entering the market under about twenty different names. The chief commercial lumbering islands at pres-ent are Mindanao, Negros, and Mindoro, though lumber is widely produced by small operators. The Philippines already enjoys an export market in lumber, rattan, and minor forest products. This market, if properly developed, can increase and, if the forests are properly handled, timber export could be-come a permanent and valuable aspect of Philippine economy.

TRANSPORTATION AND TRADE

In 1949 the Philippines still had not re-covered its pre-war status as regards roads, railroads, the communications system, and domestic and foreign trade patterns. Recov-ery was largely being financed by American rehabilitation grants, which poured large sums of money into the islands. These funds upset the normal trend of domestic affairs and promoted a prosperity unlike that in any other country that suffered damage during World War II. The large demand in world markets for edible oils, sugar, and fibers pro-moted high prices, and the Filipino national income moved steadily upward. This income, plus the obvious need for reconstruction materials, produced a great upsurge in the import of manufactured goods and perma-nently altered the pattern of consumer

demand over what it had been prior to World War II.

The Philippine highway system reached about 18,000 miles of national and provincial paved and all-weather roads by 1952, when the primary reconstruction program had been completed. Palawan and Mindoro were then most notably lacking in roads, but Mindanao had only a skeleton system, and many of the larger islands lacked secondary roads. Since 1952 the road system has been expanded to over 35,000 miles, providing far better basic access to inland localities (Fig. 23.4). The total number of motor vehicles now exceeds 300,000, of which a significant

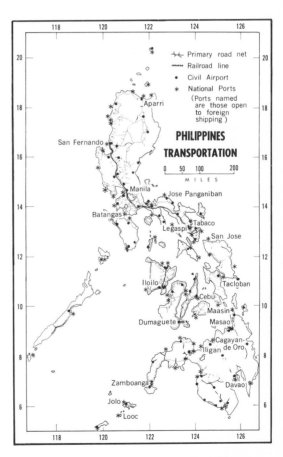

FIGURE 23.4. Transportation facilities in the Philippines.

number are trucks, buses, and taxis providing public transport facilities. Bus lines operate large fleets over the primary road system.

There were, in 1941, some 850 miles of railway on the three islands of Luzon, Panay, and Cebu. Portions of the Luzon system were not replaced after World War II, and the short line on Cebu was abandoned. In a multiple-island environment railways are less serviceable than other forms of transport, and it is not likely that the Philippine rail mileage will ever become large. The rail lines suffer from competition from water transport and from parallel bus and truck transport. However, the present short systems totalling 700 miles hauled 11,000,000 passengers in 1968, plus almost a million tons of freight. A long desired extension of the Luzon line to the northeastern Cagayan Valley is again under active planning, and this could prove useful to a region whose water transport outlet is disturbed by typhoon weather much of the year.

During the early-to-middle Spanish period Chinese watercraft handled most of the traditional trade with China and served the wholesale inter-island trade within the Philippines, with primary contacts in the Manila-northwest Luzon, Panay-Negros-Cebu, and Sulu sectors. Spanish ships handled a more selective traffic to Mexico-Spain. After about 1835 European ships began operating in the foreign trade patterns, with British interests foremost, though much of the trade remained designated as Chinese, since it was directed to Chinese ports, from which European goods came and to which Philippine exports were shipped. A Spanish inter-island fleet gradually developed in the late nineteenth century, and by 1900 the basic pattern of inter-island routes had been worked out. Manila became the chief foreign trade center and base-point of inter-island routes, with Cebu a secondary node. At present the inter-island fleet is made up of several thousand vessels operating at different levels, and

Manila and Cebu are the chief ports. A primary fleet operates scheduled runs to about 40 ports outside of Manila. A secondary fleet, much larger in numbers but smaller in ship-size, operates on irregular schedules to several hundred local ports. Special-purpose ships operate throughout the islands on more restricted patterns. Small craft, powered and nonpowered, are operated as needed at the local levels. A group of well-distributed ports is open to international shipping, in which Philippines-based ships operate along with those of other nations (see Fig. 23.4).

In the Philippines, as in Indonesia, air transportation finds very great advantages in linking the archipelago together. Air services now connect every large island and almost every large city to Manila in a matter of hours. Manila is the primary base of the pattern of air services, with the Cebu (Mactan) airport serving as a secondary base for southern island air routes (see Fig. 23.4).

In domestic trade there is an interesting dual pattern. Many American and Filipino, and some British, and other European manufacturers, importers, and exporters have headquarters in Manila and selected towns appropriate to their lines. The American and Filipino firms handle the largest share of the major wholesale trading at the international level. The Chinese commercial investment is greater than the American investment, though on a quite different plane. The Chinese form a powerful group of domestic wholesalers, retailers, and middlemen handling a large share of the domestic trade beyond the primary wholesaling ports. It is difficult to distinguish the strictly Chinese share in this from the Filipino share, since the ethnic mixtures of Chinese and Filipinos during the late eighteenth and nineteenth centuries have blurred the community lines. The domestic trade involves moving manufactured goods from Manila throughout the islands, and the moving of rice, corn, and the export crops from the rural countryside to the major urban consumption areas and major ports on the several larger islands.

In the field of foreign trade the islands have made steady growth. In 1855 the total foreign trade amounted to about $5,000,000, with exports slightly larger than imports. By 1899 this total had climbed to some $34,000,000, amounting to about $5.00 per capita, with imports slightly larger than exports. In 1941 the figure stood at almost $300,000,000, with exports a little larger than imports, and the per capita figure at about $17.00. In the late 1960's the total trade regularly exceeded one billion dollars per year and the per capita trade exceeded $30.00. During most years of American control the islands had a favorable balance of trade. The American share in the total trade in 1899 was very small; that of Spain was very small by 1941. In 1941 the United States supplied some eighty-seven percent of the imports and took about sixty percent of the exports. The value of the 1947 trade, somewhat inflated by high prices, jumped to some $775,000,000, with imports about twice the exports, amounting to a per capita figure of $40.00. A considerable share of the imports naturally represented reconstruction materials, but too much was spent on expendable consumer goods. The bulk of the trade fell to the United States.

By the 1947 trade returns some 41 countries each did more than $1,000,000 total business with the islands. The leaders were: United States in a position by herself, followed by Canada, France, China, Great Britain, Denmark, Italy, Belgium, and Indonesia, in that order. In the commodity pattern of exports sugar led in the pre-war years, but coconut products, taken altogether, held first place in 1947. Gold, from mines all over the islands, ranked second or third, with abaca fourth to form a first group of really important exports. In a second category, in order, were tobacco products,

embroideries, timber and rattans, iron ores and the ferro-alloy minerals, and canned pineapple. Mine products were then rather new in the export pattern. Mining was largely American engineered and at least partly American controlled.

Among the imports cotton goods ranked first in 1947. Iron and steel, petroleum products, tobaccos, paper and its products, grain and their preparations (mostly whole rice and wheat flour), rayons and other synthetic fabrics, automobiles and tires, meats and dairy products, and chemicals, cosmetics and drugs completed the list of major commodities. The import of tobaccos exceeded the export, a post-war development. The importance of iron and steel and petroleum among the imports reflected the inability of the islands to produce its own metal products and the lack of adequate native petroleum supplies. Since the islands do not grow wheat on an economic basis, but Filipinos increasingly have demanded breadstuffs and macaronis, the permanent import of wheat is likely. The full import lists were comprehensive in range, reflecting the industrial immaturity of the islands.

Examining the patterns of foreign trade in recent years, several features stand out rather clearly. Most notable is the steadily lower position of the United States in respect to total Philippine foreign trade. As late as 1947 nearly eighty percent of all trade was with the United States, whereas in the late 1960's the total had dropped close to forty percent. Japan has become an extremely important market and supplier, but the European countries and Canada have also risen in rank. Notable also has been the steady increase in the export of manufactures and the increase in the import of raw products and producer goods, signifying a steady change in the internal economic structure of the Philippines. The import of transport equipment and petroleum fuels has risen markedly. Finally, and somewhat discouraging to anyone interested in the true facts of trade movement, is the steady drum-beat of reports about falsification of trade returns, corruption within the Customs services, and the increase in outright smuggling. This has reached the level at which the whole statistical computation of Philippine trade must be questioned. There can be no argument as to the increases in total trade, both import and export, but there is question concerning the specific data published concerning its nature, direction, and commodity composition. The published returns of trade in the late 1960's indicate a widening unfavorable trade balance, and there is no question that Philippine government bank monetary control indicates problems in the balance of payments for the country. It is impossible to determine, however, how much of the problem derives from illegitimate operations.

In formal terms, conventionally stated, the ranking export commodities in the late 1960's were coconut products, sugar, timber products (logs, plywood, lumber), copper concentrates, abaca, base metals (iron and chromium ores), tobacco products, and food manufactures (canned pineapple and other fruits). The ranking import commodities were: transport equipment, petroleum, fabricating machinery, steel manufactures, wheat (and wheat products), raw cottons, chemicals, and textile manufactures. The ranking of both sets of commodity categories is probably approximately correct, but the precise figures are probably inadequate.

A final note may be added concerning the patterns of trade. As of 1974 the Philippines, technically, should lose its favored position in respect to trade with the United States, a result of political agreements reached in the years after World War II. Filipinos, on the one hand, remain critical of the former American economic domination provided by the early twentieth century trade rules but, on the other hand, continue to want favored access to the American market for their exports. The future development of Philippine trade patterns, to some extent, depends on whether some late modifications may take place with respect to the 1974 tariff parity agreements. The Philippines clearly is broadening the range of its trade and changing the nature of that trade, but the future of the range and nature remain subject to further political agreements.

THE GROWTH OF INDUSTRY

A variety of traditional skills still are practiced all over the islands. Basketry, several types of matting, hats, varied textiles, wooden clog-shoes, fish nets, ropes and twines, native boats and carts, metal tools and utensils, and varied ornamental and decorative items are among the commoner products. Certain regional specialties distinctly stand out, such as the brass products of Moro Cotabato and Lanao provinces, the abaca textiles of the non-Christian hill peoples of Mindanao, the cotton textiles of the Luzon Ilocanos, the wood carving of Luzon's Mountain Province, and the shell products of Sulu and Palawan. In the older household there was little formal furniture and fittings, and the Filipino was used to living and working with the simplest of materials. In general, however, there seems to be less regional specialization and rather a smaller volume of handicrafts surviving in the Philippines than in other parts of the Orient. Over a half million people are engaged full time in the making of handicraft products, with many more part-time performers. Many aspects of the traditional handicrafts have been decreasing during the American period under the impact of Chinese-merchandised, occidental-made machine goods. The chief sources of these modern goods recently have shifted from the United States to Hong Kong, Taiwan, Japan, and Korea.

Processing of the current chief crop exports has been carried on since Spanish times. The Chinese started exporting abaca and refining sugar, and they perhaps also processed some coconut products. Tobacco is a Spanish commercial product. Sugar processing still is done in two ways, the small and crude old "muscovado mill" making brown sugar and the modern corporation factory "sugar central" making raw and refined sugar for home use and export. Coconuts are processed by farmers, small concerns, and corporation factories. Most of the coconut oil and desiccated coconut are factory produced, but most of the copra and tuba are the work of small farmers using virtually handicraft techniques. Periodic shifts in the export of coconut products from oil to copra and back again are dependent upon world prices and tariffs. The tobacco industry is divided between the small home operator and the companies making cigarettes and cigars for domestic consumption and for export. Abaca gradually was becoming mechanized before the war, but the elimination of the Japanese plantations increased the share of hand operations in fiber production.

Much of the handicraft output of the Philippines has been fabricated from plant products. Handicraft metallurgy has a long history in the islands, but it has had a minor role. The mineral resources were more than adequate. Viewed from the standpoint of modern industry, the mining of metals and other ores in quantity is rather new to the Philippines, for the Spanish never found conditions in the islands such as they found in the New World. Gold mining has been the most productive of the modern developments, but it has declined in recent years under advancing cost patterns. Only small amounts of conventional types of iron ore are found to be present, the region has little good coal for industrial purposes, no productive petroleum fields have been found so far, and the general minerals base is not really adequate for a program of industrialization (Fig. 23.5).

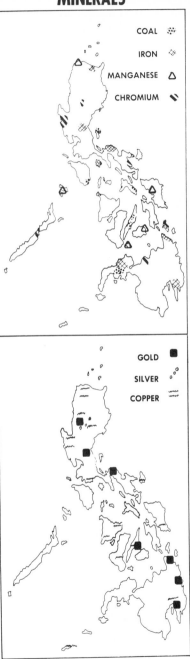

FIGURE 23.5. Mineralized regions of the Philippines.

In the Philippines, however, prevailing opinion strongly favors industrialization as an avenue of future economic development, despite the lack of capital resources and accumulated technological experience. To hasten this aspect of the islands' economy government corporations with long-range plans had begun operation in widely separated lines before World War II. Fresh and canned fish, rice and corn milling, coconut and abaca products, cotton textiles, shoe manufacture, cement production, fertilizer minerals, metals production, and hydroelectric power were some of the lines under production and planned for development for government concerns. Government corporations were engaged in rail, bus, and air transport. Well-planned and administered leadership of this sort could stimulate island industrialization, but the Philippine record was not particularly good. It was expected that private industry would follow gradually and eventually replace the function of government in part of the industrial program. The industrialization of the islands has not yet gone far by the late 1960's, but plans are being implemented to further elevate the Filipino's level of living, to restore the normal balance of trade, and to increase the productive capacity of export products against the day when complete tariff separation from the United States makes world competition necessary.

To date progress has been made, and the share of the national income derived from manufacturing is climbing steadily, but the patterns suggest those of early development only, and the maturity that is sought remains still to be achieved. Capital resources for basic programs have not been forthcoming, and private investors chiefly have sought the aspects of manufacturing in which low rates of capitalization yield high profit returns. The chief developments so far have been in expansion of processing of agricultural export commodities and in the processing of timber products and mineral ores. More of the coconut product now goes abroad as oil or dessicated coconut, canned and manufactured food products are now being exported, timber products are being exported as plywoods, veneers, and sawed lumber, and mineral ores are being enriched into higher-level concentrates.

There are, however, indicative signs of growth in a number of directions. Cement production has risen well above the domestic need, raw cotton and raw wheat imports are replacing the imports of textiles and flour, and producer machinery is replacing the import of finished manufactured goods. The first integrated steel enterprise is operating at Iligan, in northern Mindanao, thereby reducing a great part of the need for imported sheet steel and steel shapes, and a second integrated plant is under construction. These two establishments would give the islands a finished steel volume of over 500,000 tons per year. Electric power production in central Luzon is rapidly expanding, making possible the development of further industrialization in that region.

Until the early 1960's most of the manufacturing activity in the islands was concentrated in central-southern Luzon, in the Manila hinterland, and much of the further development will take place in this region. The city of Iligan, in northern Mindanao, based upon good hydroelectric power, is a rapidly expanding industrial city, and much of the near-term future development will take place around this city, since both power and steel products will be available. The various milling operations, processing agricultural and timber product exports are, of course, widely scattered over the country, though northern Mindanao, Negros and Panay islands, northern Cebu, and central Luzon are locations of many.

There are some signs that more effective growth of industry may be coming, and that the Philippines is close to a takeoff point in an economic spiral, but the general financial difficulties of island economy could provide some hindrance. There still are lacking many of the technical skills in both industrial processes and management that are needed, but it is clear that the process of industrialization has set in for the Philippines and, if other kinds of problems can be held in check, the process will continue at an increasing rate of development.

POPULATION GROWTH AND FUTURE PROSPECTS

Between 1900 and the end of American control of the Philippines in 1946 the Philippine population grew from about 7,000,000 to about 18,000,000. The 1970 population stood at approximately 37,000,000 (Fig. 23.6). In 1900 most of the area of the Philippines was in heavy forest, and farm land was to be had for the taking. In 1970 there still is reserve land left for those who will venture to the regions and localities where land remains open, but the cream has been skimmed, and the good reserves will not remain open much longer. Too many areas within the Philippines already have too-high local densities of population consisting of rural peasantry carrying on an out-of-date pattern of life. Currently the population is increasing at one of the world's high rates, at well over three percent per year, and the future projections look ominous for a society that still is basically agricultural. Principally a Roman Catholic country with no present incentives toward population restraint, the Philippines is a generally healthy environment in which the death rate still is declining as a young population increases its birth rate.

Urbanization is moving at about the rate of industrialization at the present time, but the urbanization rate may well just be beginning to pick up. An agricultural revolution is needed in several different ways:

Technologically with regard to production systems; in terms of land tenure systems and modernization of rural family social relationships; and in size and nature of farm operations in economic terms. The building of a sound future economy on the slim basis of current agricultural productivity is a precarious operation, and continuing financial crises clearly indicate this.

During the late 1940's and early 1950's rural agrarian unrest provoked a serious pattern of internal dissension in the Philippines. Its pressing margins were placated by the provision of farm land to a share of the unhappy rural tenancy, coupled with a strong expression of militant force. During the late 1960's the same sort of problem has been increasingly coming to the fore, but this time the easy allocation of land will be less simple. And, during the late 1960's, many of the long-term ills of the government system began to exhibit disquieting signs. Inefficiency, corruption, and disregard for the national good in many places, was being matched by the wilful abuse of the legal codes by many private citizens who had the means by which to effect such abuses. The executive branch of government, since 1946, never has been able to enforce the broad pattern of law, and has often been at the mercy of the rich landed families who dominantly control political life in the Philippines. There is no question that, for the highest levels of Philippine society, national economic development is proceeding at a fairly rapid and satisfactory pace, since the processes of industrialization and international trade increase opportunities for those who can share in them. But at the lowest levels of Philippine society there is, at present, no real economic or social progress being made, for the small rural peasant farmer has no means of sharing in the present patterns of national economic development. In between these two levels an ever increasing population is building up, a young

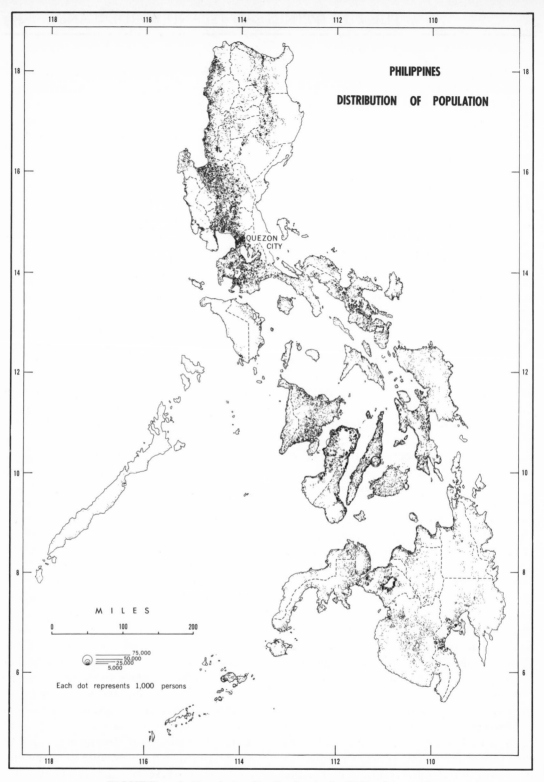

FIGURE 23.6. Population distribution in the Philippines, 1960.

population caught on the horns of dilemma. Educated chiefly in the liberal arts, law, and medicine, coming from all economic and social levels, finding inadequate economic opportunity, and finding no effective voice in government because of increasingly corrupt election practices, a large body of young Filipinos feels shut out of current aspects of life and livelihood. Can government be made to operate with sufficient efficiency at all levels that the Philippines can mature into the productive agricultural-industrial society which is its potential, or will pressures and abuses endanger the future for the island nation that is part of Asia, on the one hand, and part of the occidental world, on the other? These lines are not written to suggest that the sun is about to set on an independent and operating society or to imply that a cataclysm is impending, but the patterns of development, in the late 1960's, suggest that there are several zones of danger and several kinds of problems that may well provoke an era of serious difficulty for the Philippines unless patterns of change strongly come into operation. The checking of the rates of population growth, the onset of an agricultural revolution, the functional maturing of industrialization, cessation of patterns of abuse of economic and political privilege by the ruling classes, and the re-establishment of a governmental system involving efficient operation are the primary elements of the problem zone. There may be a few years, still, in which the problems can be resolved.

24

THE CHINESE WORLD DURING FIFTY CENTURIES

Although the popular notion has been widely current that China has existed without change for the last four thousand years this could hardly be more inaccurate. The Chinese probably are justified in claiming the oldest continuous living civilization, but this is precisely owing to constant and steady culture change within certain limits rather than to no change at all. Scholarly opinion itself regarding the age of Chinese culture has gone through a full cycle of change in the last century, so that occidental literature today displays a wide variety of opinion on the question. Early in the nineteenth century the West accepted Chinese folk chronology, which began seriously with the "Yellow Emperor" about 2700 B.C. Somewhat after 1900 historians became critical and would accept only dates proved by documentary evidence, reducing Chinese folk chronology by about 2000 years. Archaeologists have uncovered an impressive array of evidence pointing to a very old and long-continued occupation of China by the Mongoloid races, an occupation reaching clear back toward Peking Man himself, perhaps 500,000 years

ago. Whereas the literal dates of the serious folk chronology have not yet been replaced, it now is evident that the nuclear body of Chinese culture must have been forming at a period at least as early as 2700 B.C. That formation certainly was conditioned, initially, by the environment in which it developed, but the Chinese eventually constructed a culture complex which became independent of a specific landscape and particular environmental complex and one which has retained its traditional features in several different landscapes and different environments. It is the purpose of this chapter to inquire into this long process. First it is necessary to examine briefly the nature of the primary or hearth environment, along with other landscapes of early China.

THE QUALITIES OF THE ENVIRONMENT

The physical landscape of China today is rather different from that existing six or seven thousand years ago. The beautiful mosaic patterns of terraced fields did not

498

exist, the thousand of miles of dikes had not been built, forests of several kinds covered much more of the country than is true today, and soil erosion had not dug its destructive fingers into many parts of China to lessen the value of the land to a farming people. It seems a fair statement that no other landscape in the world has had such a percentage of its surface made over by man, purposefully or because of him. As previously described, the landscape of China is a checkerboard pattern of mountain strips and lowland plains and basins. The lowlands are scattered widely, and the dissected hill and mountain landscapes comprise by far the greater portion of the area of China. In soils, vegetation, and climate there is a tremendous variety from northern Manchuria to Hainan Island. After several thousand years of living in parts of the landscape the landscape today shows that the Chinese have made the most of its variety while at the same time planting certain common cultural traits everywhere. However, it certainly must have been possible, let us say, at 2700 B.C., to pick out several clear types of local environments, separated not by linear boundaries but merging through transition zones. This environmental complex is not able to support the present enormous population of China, although it was more than adequate for any demands upon it in earlier periods.

The area that was covered by loess and alluvial deposits, the Loess Highlands and the North China Plain, certainly must have comprised a unique region of North China. It probably was an open landscape without a heavy or difficult vegetation cover, with soils that were easily worked by simple means and that were rich enough to yield good returns under casual treatment. The hard-rock highlands projecting above the loess and alluvial cover probably never lost all their soils or forest covers. The soft loess lands certainly were without widespread surface water supplies, but the scattered highlands, and their margins, must have had better water supplies all during the loessial period. The main streams throughout the area must have carried a seasonably variable volume of water. Climatically this whole region had a long, cold winter with much dust and wind, and a medium-length hot summer with low, variable precipitation. The precipitation total may have been a little greater than at present. If its winter dust, low temperatures, and its precarious summer precipitation make it seem less attractive today than our modern conception of a Garden of Eden, it did have the very real advantages of rich soil, rock, wood, and water all relatively near at hand everywhere, with a wide variety of wild grains, fruits, and animals to choose from. Early man asked less of his environment that we do today. All these resources were present in an area of North China large enough to permit a scattering of several local centers or groups of tribes who did not, in the beginning, have to fight for possession of a single small prize area. The corridor along the northern footslope of the Tibetan Plateau afforded a passable connection to all of central Asia and constituted, from the very beginning, an important feature of the North China environment.

It is hard to suggest the regional limits of the open loess and alluvial landscape. To the northwest, however, it must have faded off into the more arid and monotonous landscapes of the Mongolian Plateau country. Here the shallow, open basins, with seasonal flood lakes or dry sandy and salty floors, alternated with the grass-covered aprons, basin margins, and rocky drainage divides. The better-situated spots were usable grasslands; the poorer localities were barren rock flats or desert strips from which the loess had been removed. No sharp line separated these two landscape types, but rather a broad and gradual transition. The structural elements of the Chinese checkerboard do not accord with the distribution of precipitation in this part of China. The lines of the Yin Shan and the Ala Shan lie well out in the grasslands and in no sense formed a significant environmental boundary. Farther and farther out in the grasslands the volume of easily exploited environmental resources became more and more limited, and this open grassland presented a poorer environment than that of the loess and alluvial landscape nearer the coast.

Southward from loessland there was a sharper change of another variety. Particularly in the west of China the high Tsinling Shan system sets a barrier across the land. The north and south sides of the Tsinling present one of the strongest and sharpest zones of contrast in all China. Eastward as the Tsinling Shan steadily lowers and becomes less formidable the contrast becomes less sharp and more of a transition, but the facts of contrast have been there at all times. South of the Tsinling the landscape was a subtropical environment, moist and rainy much of the year, with an all-year growing season, and with vegetation in the form of forests covering all except the floodplains. Bamboo, the citrus fruits, palms and a host of other trees, shrubs, and flowering plants were present. The water buffalo, rhinoceros, elephants, monkeys, and other tropical birds and animals replaced the fauna of North China. Here, less effort was needed to secure a fair existence in a mild environment, but the very lack of a natural nucleus probably prevented human concentration upon a particular region.

Other minor contrasts might be mentioned. The littoral of the coastal fringe from southern Korea around to the southern coast of Chekiang, Shantung and Liaotung excepted, presented a marshy, muddy fringe of saline soils, high water table, and tall grass and reeds that was less usable than the higher, drier parts of the alluvial fill. A part of the Yangtze floodplain undoubtedly shared this same water-logged nature. Even today the Chinese only partially have mastered the appropriate uses for this kind of landscape, and in the earlier periods it was not a sought-after section of China. Similarly, northward into Manchuria where neither loess nor alluvial fill provided soft and easily tilled land, the shorter growing season, the colder snowy winter, and the heavier forest cover combined to frame an environment that has attracted the Chinese only within the present century.

THE PEOPLES AND CULTURES OF FOLK HISTORY

The discovery of Peking Man and his contemporaries seems to indicate that perhaps the same types of people have lived in China throughout much of human history, but it proves nothing with regard to the origin of the body of culture now labeled Chinese. And the continued presence in this part of eastern Asia of related physical types does not preclude repeated migration and countermigration across, into, and out of the separate local environments within the major region. It is quite impossible today to place the specific regional home of the Mongoloid races and, similarly, it is almost impossible to place the exact region in which the Chinese type of Mongoloid man first developed. From numerous bits of evidence much of Chinese folk history appears truly to point to migrations within eastern Asia and to long-continued residence in North China.

With respect to material culture, the earliest folk history indicated interest in problems of water control, in flood, drought, and irrigation. It related the beginnings of crop growing mainly concerned with the evolution of cultivation and crop handling. However, this folk history suggested that animals had a place in folk economy, and that there also was a place for fishing operations. It was concerned with several rather unique items, among them being silk and jade. It showed an awareness that in other geographical regions there were other ways of supporting existence. Metals and the fabrication of various implements are parts of the pattern but do not dominate it.

Beyond the material aspects of culture in this Chinese folk history the manner of dealing with human relationships was somewhat different from that of other folk histories. Calculations regarding the seasonal and calendar cycles became tied up with divination of floods, droughts, and other supernatural troubles, and rites propitiating the gods became interwined with ceremonies honoring the ancestors. There accumulated a mass of folk culture rather unlike that accumulating in other parts of Eurasia, and with it came a peculiar awareness of the differences between this culture and those about it.

The specific statements of Chinese folk history are as impossible of application in a literal sense as the doings of the divine beings of Greek mythology or the accounts of the earlier eras among the American Sioux. But since 1930 a critical pursuit of archeology and history has gradually pieced together a long and complicated story that promises to outdo the folk history not only in complication but in duration of time and sheer variety of performance. Only a start has been made in unraveling the Stone Age geography of China, and no critical judgment so far can be set upon the period. Chinese culture seems to be not as old as that of India and the Near East. Many of the fundamental inventions came in from the Indian-Near Eastern realm, but numerous features were acquired from southeastern Asia. It may well be that agriculture itself, as a technique, came from some other part of Asia, transmitted along the central Asian corridor. But under these additions is a basic body of Chinese culture, formulated in an early North China hearth,

that even today is fundamental to an understanding of China.

THE PRIMARY CULTURE OF THE NORTH CHINA HEARTH

Good soils, water, wood, stone, and domesticable plants and animals in abundance all lay close at hand in the landscape of the Chinese culture hearth in the Huang River Basin. There certainly were variations in the region, and numerous local, superior sites were separated from each other in space and situation. The total area of such landscapes is in the vicinity of 300,000 square miles (Fig. 24.1). After the close of the glacial era, as loess deposition and alluvial sedimentation slowed down, this region would seem to have been the most attractive part of eastern Asia to groups of people just learning to handle the simplest problems of rudimentary crop production and animal husbandary, settlement formation, and societal organization. And if it was a superior environment it also was a malleable one which could reasonably be changed and shaped to fit the early group decisions and organizational politics of the peoples who permanently occupied it. This simple flexibility was, so to speak, an essential virtue of a hearth environment for any culture group just entering its formative stage and not yet crystallized into specific modes of operating a landscape or an economy.

Although this open landscape covered a large territory it graded off into other kinds of landscapes in all directions. Along these marginal transitions, in the earliest eras, there was no conclusive environmental stimulus in one direction only. It is only in more recent periods of culture history that we can begin, even, to draw sharp boundary zones between distinctive landscapes, after a long process of selective human use and development has accented certain features of the environment. Once development started, the pertinent natural resources gave the primitive

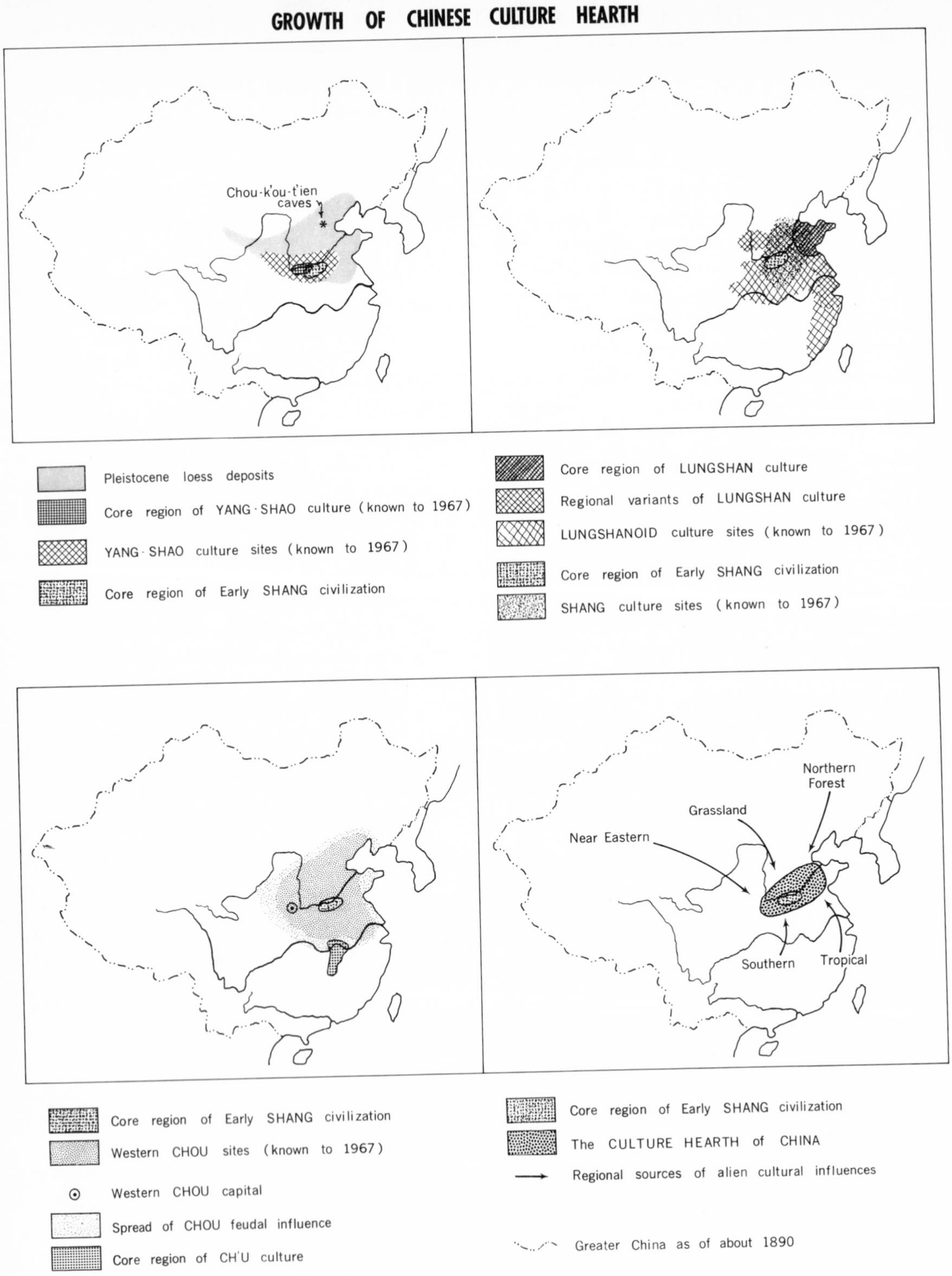
GROWTH OF CHINESE CULTURE HEARTH
Chou-k'ou-t'ien caves
Pleistocene loess deposits
Core region of YANG-SHAO culture (known to 1967)
YANG-SHAO culture sites (known to 1967)
Core region of Early SHANG civilization
Core region of LUNGSHAN culture
Regional variants of LUNGSHAN culture
LUNGSHANOID culture sites (known to 1967)
Core region of Early SHANG civilization
SHANG culture sites (known to 1967)
Core region of Early SHANG civilization
Western CHOU sites (known to 1967)
Western CHOU capital
Spread of CHOU feudal influence
Core region of CH'U culture
Northern Forest
Grassland
Near Eastern
Southern
Tropical
Core region of Early SHANG civilization
The CULTURE HEARTH of CHINA
Regional sources of alien cultural influences
Greater China as of about 1890

FIGURE 24.1. Evolution of the culture hearth of China.

economy an advantage over that of surrounding territories. Every forward step slowly increased that advantage to make this an outstanding region. Even under primitive conditions its population density must have exceeded that of neighboring regions, a fact which further favored the hearth area. In this central North China hearth there was organized a pattern of domestication that drew upon many native wild plants, such fruits as the apricot, peach, plum, persimmon, and pear, such plants as several millets and buckwheat, and that early adapted plants and animals from other domestication centers. In addition there were forest-borne nuts and many wild animals available for the hunting. The irregular rainfall and the presence of streams in the alluvial lands fostered an awareness and a promotion of primitive irrigation once crop production was understood. Already the initial step had been taken in setting up an intensive cropping system. The differences between portions of the hearth were slight and unimportant compared to the larger contrasts between the hearth and the grasslands or the subtropical southern forest.

Conventional history suggests that the Chinese began as sedentary agriculturists of a high order of technological skills. This is directly counter to what we know of evolutionary processes in respect to crop growing. It is most likely that rudimentary cropping systems and the elements of shifting cultivation were employed in the earliest period of the formation of the culture hearth, complemented by collecting, animal hunting, and fishing. That residence systems were sedentary in basic terms was no bar to the employment of shifting cultivation by relatively small populations in territories of ample size. It may well be that elementary irrigation practices were learned or developed in this zone of hazardous summer rainfall possessing streams flowing out of mountain

blocks, as suggested by the folk history. Such practices would have been helpful in the maturing of a simple agricultural system in terms of developing its permanent-field cultivation systems in stream valley lowlands. The combining of sedentary cropping systems with shifting cultivation in areas away from stream channels is historically very old in other parts of Asia. Still lacking animal draft power and the plow tools, all such early cropping systems were essentially gardening systems dependent upon the input of human labor. It is in the development of human-labor gardening systems that the intensive elements of Chinese cropping practices must first have evolved, since these are the primary hallmarks of all later Chinese agricultural practices.

Material culture was not only the product of the hearth. Inevitably certain culture traits were fostered in this homeland unlike those developed in outside, unlike environments. As the hearth developed there followed the universal tendency to look down upon those who did not practice the same customs. Gradually and somewhat unconsciously the hearth population came to think of themselves as "we, the cultured" and of all peoples of the transitions, margins, and lands beyond as uncultered barbarians. This is a common human tendency, but Chinese culture eventually developed this feeling into a very strong self-centeredness.

THE CULTURES OF THE BARBARIAN FRINGE

The self-centeredness of the North China hearth has a very real basis. On the Mongolian grasslands the mature pastoral economy that, later, characterized Genghis Khan's time had not yet evolved. The economic opportunities of the grasslands in the third millennium before Christ cannot have been great, even though repeated overgrazing had not yet worn them down. Then its contrast to the loesslands was less than it now is, but its resources permitted no great development without an integrated social organization. The simple pastoral economy of the northwestern grassland transition was in contrast to the crop-growing gardening economy of the North China hearth. The precarious environment constantly produced human surpluses which flowed toward the hearth in a steady movement that is one of the most marked features of the history of eastern Asia. The process, certainly at work by the end of the Neolithic period, has operated throughout recorded Chinese history.

Northeastward short summers and cold winters combined with an irregular forest cover in pointing inhabitants toward some variety of hunting-fishing-gathering-pastoral economy. The Korean section and the southern, unforested, portion of the Manchurian lowland eventually became a Chinese colonial fringe, but in the earliest periods no regional economy here could compare with the pattern of the open lands farther south.

Southward in the Yangtze Valley a watery lowland landscape made reeds, boats, stilt houses, and aquatic food of greater human significance than in North China. Here human inventiveness was being exercised upon the innumerable potentialities of such plants as the bamboo. A marginal sprinkling of Negrito peoples in the coastal lowlands of South China, and a backwash of proto-Malay seafaring folk along the whole South China littoral, gave the coastal fringe a marked racial variety and pointed up the use of tropical items in the environment. South China was a big country, with much local variety, a hilly landscape with many local basins and a long and irregular coastline. There were many variations in its earliest sprinkling of population. A number of locally favored regions became minor culture centers. Most of them used the common mate-rials of the subtropical environment, but there was no outstanding hearth, and none that rivaled the North China hearth.

THE FEUDAL ERA AND ITS FRUITS

The dawn of Chinese written history found a pastoral people making the final move into the settled hearth area. The Chou were a simple people who had lived in the northwestern transition zone long enough to add the crop-growing systems and the economic methods of the hearth to their own pastoral economy. Political and administrative organization had not then progressed far, but it was a military conquest by a semibarbarian group so closely related in racial origin that no clear distinctions can be made. The conquest was followed by the parceling out of fiefs and the setting up of an essentially feudal society. The conventional date for the Chou conquest usually is given as 1122 B.C., a date still subject to upward or downward revision.

The first few generations of Chou feudal lords rapidly picked up skill in handling the culture and the peoples of the hearth, becoming completely immersed therein. This was a period during which the techniques of intensive irrigation agriculture were being more fully elaborated in the hearth area. Village settlement and the walled city as a primary center of culture, wealth, and administrative power probably owe their final systemic development to this period. The local region, centered around a city, became the focal unit for group organization and operation in crop growing, flood control, irrigation, and public works, and from this time forward it formed the primary territorial unit in Chinese administrative operations. Iron first came into China during middle to late Chou times. The introduction of sufficient iron to allow use as tools came a little later, perhaps 700–400 B.C., but it marked a primary step forward in Chinese economy.

The several local centers of the hearth filled out, and a period of internal competition began. No longer were favored sites sheltered one from another, scattered throughout an extensive landscape. Centrally located feudatories, hemmed in on all sides by increasing pressures, sometimes were swallowed up in the conflicts. The marginal peoples, on the other hand, suffered attacks by the barbarian peoples knocking at the door of the hearth, seeking entry. The feudal period did much to heighten the contrast between the hearth and the outer barbarian lands. As a result there was a never-ending series of rival groups edging closer to the hearth to carry on the regional struggle for power within the hearth itself. Most pressures came from the north and northwest, but not exclusively. The late feudal era was marked by political arrangements which remind one of the League of Nations of the 1920's, and by an era in which protective wall building became a habit and the basis was laid for the final project of the Great Wall of China (Fig. 24.2). Political historians consider the feudal era to end in the late third century B.C., but the last several centuries of the era developed an intensity of cultural activity that makes closer scrutiny necessary.

THE FORMATIVE ERA AND THE BIRTH OF "CHINA"

The sixth century before Christ was a period of intense political and social activity in North China, as it was in India and in the Near East. The struggles of the feudal era were becoming acute, and there was a great restlessness among mankind. This was a time when men were searching for a progressive, practical plan for the operation of feudal society when that society in the North China hearth was nearing the stormy end of an era. Confucius was born about the middle of the sixth century in what now is western Shantung, a member of an aristocratic family

of one of the smaller feudal states. He was a scholarly leader in the search, formulating an ethical, moral code of human conduct based upon his editorial synthesis of the past history of Chinese hearth society. Undoubtedly he arranged a "lawyer's brief" to fit his beliefs and edited the chronicles of the past with a liberal hand to provide precedents for his case. Although that editing has confused historians no end, it did provide in shortened form a code of conduct and a concept of ideas that slowly became the central hallmark of Chinese culture.

Other scholars formulated bodies of philosophy, religion, and ethics during the period which took other directions than the political-social-economy of Confucius, though they all contributed to the culture complex. Many contemporary and later disciples and students of Confucius became government bureaucrats and practicing politicians, all eager to try out their ideas of political economy in the complex political geography of the day. Many of them drifted from feudal state to feudal state, searching for the right combination of situations and opportunities. The more these practicing politicians applied themselves, the more acute grew the struggle, with marginal members constantly less honorable in their adherence to the "civilized" codes of conduct in war, politics, and economics. The advantage lay with these marginal peoples, semibarbarian still, constantly pushed by other peoples behind them. The fact that they were ignorant of many of the somewhat artificial ethical codes of the hearth made some of them welcome ambitious itinerant scholar-politicians who could be useful in the struggle for power. By the latter part of the third century B.C. the contest had ended in the conquest of the hearth by a semibarbarian people from the northwest who, in a generation, instituted political and economic changes of a kind and degree that permanently ended the feudal era and carried the formal culture of the

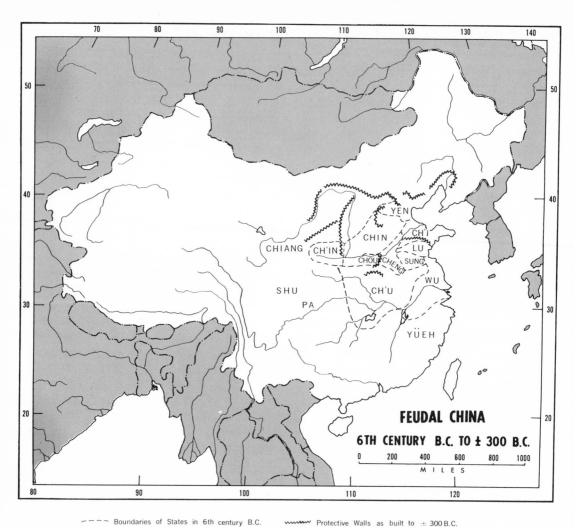

FEUDAL CHINA

6TH CENTURY B.C. TO ± 300 B.C.

- - - - Boundaries of States in 6th century B.C.   ᴡᴡᴡᴡ Protective Walls as built to ± 300 B.C.

FIGURE 24.2. Feudal China, 6th century B.C. to ± 300 B.C.

hearth far outside its standard bounds. Much of the basic content of the hearth culture had spread much earlier.

The political-military process should not obscure other developments that were equally significant. The influx of new blood was sizable, and the population of the hearth was growing. The exchange of material goods increased between the barbarian south, the forested north, the pastoral northwest and the hearth. Contact along the central Asian corridor and the southern littoral brought new ideas, new crops, and new tools into China (see Fig. 24.1, lower right). Many of these things cannot be very closely dated as yet, but it must have been very early in the feudal era that wheat became the staple north China food grain, and wet-field rice spread northward and across into central Asia as a random, minor crop. During the later feudal era a new and formalized style of writing was developed; the system of private land ownership began to replace the serf, fief, and feudal lord, the growing skill in water control and the oxdrawn plow improved agricultural productivity. Then followed changes in the tax system, the growth of handicraft manufactures, the development of trade, and the appearance of a merchant class. The chopsticks so diagnostic of Chinese culture became common at this time. All these and many more new features attest to the fact that the hearth area had matured. The hearth was not the center of a political empire. It had become the key region, economically and politically, of a North China that stretched from the grasslands deep into the subtropical south. At this point one might venture, at last, to talk about a "China," and a "Chinese culture" in distinction to the less-developed, barbarian cultures round about, and opposed to the earlier feudal culture of the hearth area itself.

THE HAN EMPIRE AND IMPERIALISM

The date usually given for the political conquest of the hearth area by the semibarbarian State of Ch'in is 221 B.C. The new empire lasted only through the life of creator Ch'in Shih Huang Ti, until about 209 B.C. (Fig. 24.3, upper left). However, the forward steps that had been taken were permanent ones, and shortly a native of what today is northern Kiangsu had gathered the reins of power and established the Han dynasty, that was to administer China for some four centuries, 207 B.C. to A.D. 220 (see Fig. 24.3, upper right). The early years of the new dynasty were a period in which changes initiated in the previous century were put into effect with greater thoroughness, and were given wider regional application. This meant, in the broadest sense, a spread of "Chinese

culture" outward over much of what today constitutes modern China. It was carried out by military conquest and political expansion of the simplest imperialistic type. Toward the north and west countermeasures were taken by the new Chinese state against the continuous encroachment of the pastoral nomads. These measures eventually led Chinese imperialism along the central Asian corridor into what today is Sinkiang. Contact with Rome along the overland trade route followed. Similarly imperialism touched southern Manchuria and northern Korea. Southward it bypassed some of the hilly negative blocks of central and southern China to encompass the basins scattered over the whole country, reaching into the lowlands of Tonking in North Vietnam. In the terms of political geography it was the dynamic drive produced by the unified force of the then most significant geographic region of eastern Asia. And it was expressed at a time when no other people had mastered the use of any landscape region short of India and Persia.

The key economic region of eastern Asia became the political center of the new empire, and the capital was located at Ch'angan (see Fig. 24.3, upper right). As such it gathered the ambitious personalities from all over China. The hearth region began, in a simple way, to derive some economic profit from the empire. It drew tribute missions and students of society from outside what today is China proper. And with them came strange goods to widen the material economy of the heart of China and strange ideas to expand Chinese culture itself. By the end of the Han many a barbarian trait had quietly slipped into Chinese culture to become so deeply embedded as to seem to later generations that it always had been there.

The process of cultural growth and expansion served to increase the strength of Chinese culture and to crystallize its struc-

CHINESE   EMPIRES

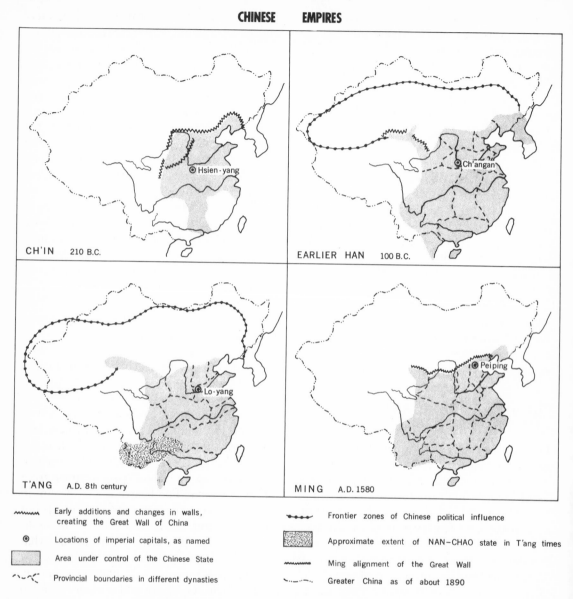

FIGURE 24.3. The regional patterns of Chinese empires.

ture. During Han times the scholar-bureaucrats cemented their gains tightly into the fabric of Chinese life. Although the scholar not holding any political office often served as the cultural conscience of China to protest the action of the scholar-practical-politician in office, the combined results of their activity was to raise Confucianism to the status of an official state cult. The scholar-bureaucrats, as a group, became an integral part of the Chinese administrative system of government. That a system of political economy thus succeeded in becoming a state cult, while, in other societies, organized religions became state cults, is a fundamental distinguishing characteristic of early Chinese culture.

THE ECONOMIC PHILOSOPHY OF HAN SOCIETY

The Chinese culture hearth had developed as an intensive agrarian society operated by villages administered by regional city centers. Only a simple range of implements, tools, and mechanical agents were available. Self-sufficiency was not complete, but only a relatively small volume of trade was needed and commercialism was a minor aspect of hearth culture. The end of feudalism required time; practical methods of land ownership and the adjustment and shifting of taxation from crops to land and to the individual owners could not be devised overnight. Chinese hearth society had not developed a large slave labor force as did Greece and Rome, but corvee labor was exacted by the state to accomplish its public works projects. Convicts and " political criminals" also were used on public works. The last century of feudal time and the whole of Han times were a period in which the economic principles of operating an agrarian society were strongly debated. A few revolutionary reformers were rejected, and Chinese economy remained true to its older patterns. Confucian scholars divided into schools of thought over taxation principles, land tenure, the place of trade and handicrafts, and the admissible degree of state participation in agriculture and handicrafts. Some of the discussions read almost word for word like recent debates about the economic philosophy of American society.

In spite of the best intentions of government a landlord class arose, along with a a segment of the population who became landless tenants. Similarly, a small though prosperous merchant class developed and maintained itself. The scholar-bureaucrats did very well by themselves economically. Han times were a period of settling into accepted molds and patterns of conduct, and of rejecting patterns that involved too great change from the past. Various ills of the state were adjusted, or corrected, or manipulated as they arose. There had been no real precedents to go on, though all adherents to a cause drew such justifications from the Confucian classics as could be found. Although there unquestionably were maladjustments in the patterns of society that crystallized by the end of the Han, the system worked reasonably well for all concerned. Successful molds had been poured for a regionally self-contained agrarian society that operated intensively with a minimum of equipment and a minimum of commerce and handicraft industry.

Modern comparative study of mechanized American agriculture proves that intensive oriental agriculture produces somewhat more actual food per acre than does the American system. However, the man-days of labor involved are far greater in oriental agriculture and the present volume of food production per capita in the Orient is far below that of contemporary United States. However, during Han times it was significant that the intensive system was an improvement over any other economy then operative in eastern Asia and led to a dominance by the Chinese hearth area. The spread of this intensive system was a part of the spread of Chinese culture. It was supervised by a centrally pyramided but very loosely articulated professional bureaucracy with a definite stake in the over-all success of the system. The system involved drawing enough food, manpower, and materials from the empire at large by imperial authority to properly maintain the hearth's political power, to maintain the military power to defend the empire from aggression, and to keep the system in operation.

Although draft animal power and plow

tools, by Han time, had been added to the North China farm tool assemblage as a technological development, they did not become universal elements in the agricultural system, and they did not dominate it. Draft animals, plows and other farm tools, along with carts and sleds, remained complementary accessories on the dry-field farm landscapes of North China, used when they were appropriate or when they could be afforded by peasant farmers. In the wet-field landscapes of central and south China the water buffalo replaced the cattle, horses, and donkeys of northern China, and specially adapted wet-field tools came into use but, again, these remained accessories to the operation of the wet-field cropping systems. The Chinese agricultural system of Han times was best described as a semipowered intensive gardening system, rather than as an extensive plow agricultural system.

SETTLEMENT MORPHOLOGY

From incomplete study of the subject it would appear that at a very early time the inhabitants of the culture hearth came to prefer two definite settlement forms, the compact village and the centrally located city. Dwelling in fixed settlements had developed into one of the fundamental features distinguishing Chinese culture, as opposed to the mobile residential systems of the pastoral or forest hunting peoples of the northwest and north, and as opposed to the sometimes shifting hamlet residential systems of some of the simpler forest dwelling shifting cultivator societies of parts of southern China.

The Chinese village is always a compact affair, though it may have various shapes. Houses are built tightly against one another, and there seldom are spacious yards and gardens as in the American small town or hamlet. The most common shape is the shoestring village, a double row of houses along a single street. The site often is a dike top or a stream terrace or bench. Sometimes among the larger trade villages is found the rough grid pattern with one or two streets dominating, and now and then irregular and odd-shaped villages occur. The village varies in size from perhaps a dozen buildings to a thousand houses, with about a hundred houses seeming to be a fair average. Common to all Chinese villages are tea shops, restaurants, inns, and a temple-shrine, plus the itinerant goods peddler. Only large villages have grain, cloth, metal, furniture, and other shops. Almost all shops double as private homes, and there seldom is zoning of functions in a village. In north China villages normally are walled, but elsewhere in China it is uncommon to find many walled villages.

The Chinese city is a settlement synonymous with the management of the affairs of society. Size or volume of commerce and trade are not at all the criteria for a city, though most cities are local trade centers. This means that a city is the center of political, economic, and cultural power in its regional landscape. The city is the location of the skilled handicrafts, the religious center of the district, the residence of landlord families, of scholars, and of political officials. Since early times the city has been walled, and today the common word for city is the word for wall, the wall being the personification of those features that distinguish the city from the village or the simple, overgrown mart of trade. Several types of cities are common to China, according to their rank and standing in the management of affairs. Lowest in rank is the frontier march site city, in the past a special rank of frontier outpost. Such a city often was but a walled village, crudely built and possessing little wealth or culture. The average county seat, which in modern China is scattered every 15 to 30 miles apart all over China, had something of a grid pattern to its layout. This might range from two simple cross streets with alleys and lanes to a regular multiple grid with rectangular blocks. The wall often was irregular in outline, conforming to the site, and of such size as the local economy could afford. Such cities generally show a zoning of economic functions, and frequently have one or more suburbs lying outside the walls. Today, in population they range from perhaps 5,000 to 200,000 people. District and provincial cities usually were laid out on larger, more formal lines involving true grid patterns, large walls, numerous gates, and considerable formal public architecture. After 1911 some cities tore down their walls, and turned the space into circular streets. Many also have gone through modernization programs of street widening and installation of water, telephones, and electricity.

In architectural features Chinese settlements show an amazing diversity while at the same time exhibiting a striking superficial similarity. Adobe brick is the commonest building material all over China, but many regional special forms are found. Roofs normally are of gray tile or of straw thatch. North China seldom spruces up its buildings, but west and south China frequently uses whitewash and decorative designs. Domestic architecture in China always has been plain and simple, but public architecture has had a flair for the ornate, elaborate, and highly decorated. The curved roof popularly associated with China is a feature chiefly of public building that has been developed in recent centuries, though some homes of the wealthy families also show it. Out of the culture hearth of North China came the basic features of Chinese building, which have spread wherever the Chinese have gone. These features are the rectangular room unit with few doors and windows. The roof is normally supported on a skeleton of wooden poles independent of the walls which normally are panels filling in the spaces. The room unit can be multiplied any number of times, arranged in L, U, or closed square

shapes, the whole set upon a terrace foundation to get it above ground level. In compact settlements various modifications of the rectangular room are found. Most Chinese building is single storied in villages and single or double storied in cities. Only special public buildings and monuments normally reach more than two stories, so that the average traditional Chinese settlement shows a flat skyline unlike that of the large occidental city. In their spread over China, however, the Chinese have taken on many extraneous building materials and housetypes, which actually provide, today, a widely varied architecture. The flat mud-roofed houses of the northwest of China, for example, contrast with the steel and concrete skyscraper of the port cities of the China coast.

THE EXPANDING COLONIAL FRONTIER

Following upon the Han military conquest of the neighboring regions was the process of implanting Chinese culture in the conquered areas. The devices that had accompanied the transformation of feudal China into imperial China worked with considerable satisfaction. The *hsien*, or county, the *chun*, or military corps area, and the *chou*, or political district, were the principal administrative regional units that were set up over the new territory. Each was subject to change according to conditions of the specific region. The *chun* was at first less a region of so many square miles than a route between the hearth and some outlying district. Eventually the *sheng*, or province, matured out of a variety of major political regions of control. Along with the regional devices went the walled city as the functional heart of each new region incorporated into the political administration. The walled city became an advance outpost in an alien landscape and culture. The walled city offered security in times of stress, but infiltration of the countryside was carried out in peaceful periods. The village became the normal rural unit in advance of the city, but not everywhere was it used. In Szechwan Chinese penetration had actually preceded the end of feudal times, and, here with the walled city as a primary protective control, settlement spread out first over the Chengtu Plain and then the rest of the Szechwan Basin in the form of scattered homesteads.

It is possible to see, in the evolving morphology of the Chinese settlement system, an interesting structural alignment that has been described by modern urban geographers. As the Chinese settlement frontier expanded, a "mother" village grew and later hived off secondary villages. Often the primary village became a fortified post (either a *chun* or a *chou*) and then slowly evolved into a regional administrative center. Once the military danger was past, the settlement was made the seat (*hsien* city) for a civil government county or district (*hsien*). This city funtioned as a central place. Since transport and communications were simple in technology, counties (*hsien*) could not be too large in area, and the county seats came to be closely spaced. The county, with its city as the seat of government and as the center of functional operations, was a cell-like unit. The first such arrangement of space and functional arrangements dates prior to the beginning of the Christian era, but the system was effective and was implemented, so that the "cells" multiplied until modern China has over 2,100 such units. Unlike counties in the United States, the boundaries of the *hsien* were repeatedly altered to accord with changing transport, economic, and political conditions. Below the county level smaller spatial units gradually evolved, arranged in sub-cellular structure. Above the county level, largely for political administrative purposes, nineteenth century China was organized into three levels in multi-cellular pattern, with the province representing the most significant, but not the uppermost, spatial unit.

Where there were barbarian peoples occupying the areas of colonization they were dealt with in various ways. In some areas forced transplantation was used, whereas in others continued residence eventually produced assimilation into the Chinese blood and culture complex. Some of the barbarian groups kept shifting southward ahead of Chinese colonization, themselves pushing still others in a slow drift southward into southeastern Asia. Regardless of what precise method of disposal was used, the Chinese were dominant in culture, administrative control, and numbers. Commencing with the best local centers and those most easily built into bases of operation, the slow process of Chinese colonization of the southland began to fill in the regions bypassed in the earlier military conquest. It was to be a long process, and one not yet complete at the present time. In Fukien the remainders of alien peoples and cultures today are but vestigial remnants. Hainan Island, Kueichou, and Yunnan, on the other hand, are regions in which the Chinese no more than equal the so-called "non-Chinese" at the present time, and in Kwangsi the Chuang still outnumber the Han Chinese. The latter have pushed modern "barbarians" off the best lands, monopolized the political, economic, and social administration of the territory, and extended their lines of influence completely throughout the region. The "non-Chinese" have given the Chinese many things and have absorbed much of Chinese culture, but many such groups persistently cling to language, dress, ceremonial customs, and other marks of their own cultures. Along the Tibetan frontier the Chinese colonization stalled somewhat against the rough and rugged landscape not easily amenable to sedentary, agricultural settlement, and there are blocks of territory occupied by "barbarian" peoples over whom the Chinese have only recently gained full control.

On the north and west Chinese culture found landscapes not so amenable to the techniques of colonization used in the south. The Chinese have repeatedly pushed out into Inner Mongolia, away from the old hearth and into the grasslands. In wet cycles and periods of strong Chinese power they have advanced their lines, only to blow away in the "dust bowl" episodes of dry cycles, and to shrink back under nomad raids in periods of inadequate Chinese strength. Along the central Asian corridor the standard Chinese technique of making Chinese of all other peoples did not work well either, since the Chinese themselves were always a minimal element in the population totals. Repeated efforts in Sinkiang over the centuries achieved only bitterness, unrest, and internal distress, as alien cultures have held strong against Chinese political and military pressure. Northward into Manchuria the Chinese, in this century, have swarmed in such numbers as to sweep all before them in the southern and central lowlands. The northern fringe and the hill strips on either border are not yet colonized. Although their political control has been, until very recently, shaky, Manchuria is Chinese in blood, culture, and economics. The process of Chinese colonization and frontier expansion is not complete on any modern frontier of China, and there is no indication that activity has ceased. In the remaining bypassed zones in southwest and west China the process will go on to the inevitable end that eventually all people and all culture will be Chinese. Of course, there will be regional variations and specializations. The question of Chinese expansion on external frontiers will be considered later.

CHINESE ACCULTURATION THROUGH EXPANSION

The earliest expansion out of the hearth found the Chinese firmly convinced that they were superior to any and all barbarian folk of the marginal landscapes. This self-centeredness did not prevent Chinese assimilation of many barbarian customs, in a rather selective manner. Pastoral folk assimilated into Chinese culture brought relatively little; they never did motivate the Chinese to take up the use of dairy products. South of the Tsinling the process was relatively more complete but still selective. Bamboo, rice, and the water buffalo were not integral elements of the original ancient hearth culture, but they are intrinsic parts of modern China wherever climatically practical. The elephant, however, was apparently not liked by the Chinese as a domestic animal, though as an art form it is very common in many parts of China. These are but random examples of the process.

Chinese who went beyond their own borders, as the pilgrims to India, as the traders to the Indies, or as the diplomatic emissaries to tributary kingly courts, brought many things back to China not only of religion and the world of ideas but also of art, architecture, plants, tools, and methods of artisanry. Tribute missions to the Chinese court always brought the special products of their own home environments. The Chinese have taken these things into their culture and transformed them variably to their own ends. Not a century was without some new features; scarcely a generation did not witness the gradual increase in the ideas and the materials that made up Chinese culture. Naturally there were peak periods and low periods in this acquisitional process. The several centuries of the Han, the time of Sui and T'ang, the Mongol Yuan dynasty, the early Ch'ing dynasty, and the last century have been, possibly, the peak eras of cultural expansion.

But in all this contact the Chinese never have lost control over the process of acculturation. Although the process seems largely to have been an unconscious one, strong reaction has always set in against any feature that threatened the fundamental balance of Chinese culture. Never was the firm stable nucleus of the classical China of the North China culture hearth ever basically altered.

Even the impact of the modern world has not succeeded in changing this balance, so far, though more will be said of this subject later.

THE CHANGING PULSE OF CHINESE HISTORY

Chinese scholars sometimes assert that there is a repeating cycle of rise and fall in Chinese history, though there is little agreement upon critical dates and cycle lengths. Regardless of the possibility of determining repetitive cycles as such, there certainly has been the repetition of a process and a comparable sequence of events. Once the Han dynasty had spread to its widest limits it began a slow decline under the endlessly increasing problems of empire, the decreasing efficiency of political administration, and the lessening prosperity of its populace. The rise and fall of the Han empire completed a sequence of Chinese cultural operations. The Han fell, in the last analysis, because the operating machinery of society became hopelessly cluttered and inefficient. Government slowly piled an overwhelming burden of taxes, vested interests, special privileges, and procedures which had outlived their need upon the populace, whereas it grew less and less able to mobilize its strength to hold off the semibarbarian tribes pressing inward toward the hearth area. There followed a period in which these semibarbarian groups struggled with each other and with the peoples of north China for the mastery of the north, while the Chinese and non-Chinese in the southern parts of the empire struggled for autonomy or hegemony. Several centuries passed during which a variety of short-term alignments prevailed, but eventually the Sui achieved a near-hegemony over all China, but then diverted their attention toward Korea. Out of this divergence the T'ang dynasty (A.D. 618–907) came to the top as a Chinese dynasty, aggressive, virile, dynamic, leading the energetic Chinese realm to new accom-

plishments (see Fig. 24.3, lower left). The pattern of gradual decline under the weight of too much government and too great increase in the social and economic diseases of society, repeated itself in the later decades of T'ang. Next came the Sung, after a shorter interval of chaos, with its dynastic period (979–1278) repeating the story of a fresh start, a prosperous peak, and a declining segment of unrest, dissension and invasion. By the Sung dynasty, however, the Yangtze Valley had been developed significantly as an economic region, playing a vital part in empire affairs. When the pastoral invasions pressed too hard upon the north in the 1120's, the Sung were able to roll with the punch, withdrawing their capital to Nanking and continuing to operate a reduced Chinese state for another century and a half before finally falling to the Mongols. During that period a number of peoples fought for control of the northern marches and for the old Chinese hearth in the north of China.

Mongol control of China (A.D. 1279–1368) presented another, if slightly varied, cyclic act in the long historical pageant. Mongol rule was unique in that for the first time a people had cemented most of the power of the pastoral realm into a single political-military machine to batter down Chinese opposition and take over all China. A further distinctive feature was that the Mongols ruled, not with the self-centeredness of Chinese culture, but with an open-door policy that used Turks, Moslems, Italians like Marco Polo, and many others, in one great machine. More than any other Asian people until the modern era the Mongols had a concept of a kind of pan-Asia, controlled from their pastoral heartland, with interchangeable officials and ideas, a great political and military empire that enveloped many cultures but elevated no one creed or society to a position of dominance. This was a peak period of Chinese culture change, and it also was a period that spread knowledge of the East into the West.

Although the Mongol political concept was a vast one the machinery of operating it was unequal to the task. Accumulating unrest in China brought mobilized opposition in the Yangtze Valley which finally grew great enough to retake the hearth area in the north and give the Ming dynasty control of China proper (1368–1644). Although the capital was shifted northward again to Peking, the Yangtze Valley was a much more vital part of the Ming empire than it had been during the Han (see Fig. 24.3, lower right). Ming control never reached so far into central Asia as had Han power, but political overlordship was expressed much further southward, so that the Vietnamese, the Khmer, the growing Thai and Burmese cultures, and even the Indies, acknowledged the political hegemony of China. The decline of the Ming and the ascendance of the Manchus again repeats a very familiar theme, with its own special embroidery upon the patterns of history. Manchu China was a prosperous climax era of Chinese society, but the same accumulation of cultural rubbish finally weighed China down and gave voice and volume to a protesting people, to end Manchu imperial rule in 1911.

CHINA OF THE MANCHUS

The Manchus did not come into China the crude barbarians that history sometimes pictures them. They had spent a period upon the northeastern borders learning to use the tools of Chinese administration, and trying to devise some social techniques that would enable them to control a sedentary China while retaining their own pastoral mobility. These techniques worked well enough so that by 1900 Manchus still were a distinct nucleus in many a large Chinese city. However, racial independence and social separation were not sufficient to guarantee permanent dynamic leadership in a society that, at its height, was perhaps the most prosperous and complex society in the world, so that the Manchu rulers of China declined along with the society they headed.

The China of the seventeenth and eighteenth centuries was a mature and full-flowering plant in the oriental garden. Every rise and fall of a dynasty had enlarged the roots that fed the Manchu plant. Every era of peace, prosperity, and trade, every era of imperial expansion, every era of invasion and foreign control, every Chinese who ventured abroad, every stranger newly come to China, brought something that enlarged Chinese culture. A steady stream of new crops, new tools, new techniques, new ideas, and new blood had been added to the variety of material culture and to the depth of social culture. And with every passing century there had been an increase in the cultivated land, in the mileage of roads and canals, in the length and strength of the river dikes, and in the manpower available to intensively operate the Chinese economic system. China of the Manchus was a richer, stronger, more cultured, and more sophisticated society than any that had gone before.

There still was the perennial barbarian fringe upon the north and northwest, but the pastoral peoples now were knocking less strongly at the gates. Troubles in the southern imperial domains, beyond China proper, called for occasional expeditions, reprimands, and mediatory gestures. The trade and tribute that came from the South Seas, however, offset trouble from that quarter.

In organizational form Manchu China was genetically the same China that had flowered first in the Han Empire. The same Confucian bureaucracy administered the broad lands of the empire, using the Confucian codes and the classics, and the same machinery of government that had worked so well for the Han. This not only was a peak era for the mass of Chinese, but it was also a peak era for the Confucian Way. And in the pride and satisfaction of the Manchu rulers, the

Chinese Confucian bureaucrats, and the Chinese peasantry there lay the old self-centered concept of China as the center of a cultural world, surrounded in all directions only by barbarians of lesser standing. These included the first Europeans who came to China by sea in the sixteenth century from a distant corner of the barbarian world scarcely mentioned in Chinese accounts.

Europe of the sixteenth and seventeenth centuries was just struggling out of the pinched and bare patterns of the Dark Ages. The geographical discoveries were on, but the economic fruits of empire had not yet fattened the lean societies of Europe. As much as Europeans were impressed by the spotty brilliance of India and the Indies, it was China that created the strongest impression. Undoubtedly China of the Manchus was the most prosperous society on the face of the earth at the time. It had greater and more universal prosperity, a greater volume of material goods, and a better standard of living than had India or Europe. Perhaps one must partially excuse the early, wealth-hungry European visitors for forgetting what little cultivated manners they possessed when face to face with the peaceful plenty of China.

THE OLD CHINA TRADE

The contact of European explorers-traders-pirates and sophisticated Chinese represented the greatest conflict of rival self-centeredness that occurred during the great discoveries. In the presence of the prosperity of Manchu China the Europeans were most eager for trade on any terms. The Chinese South Sea traders then were keen merchants, and the Chinese market was a large one for buyer and seller alike.

The first European purchases were made with cash payments of silver dollars from Spain, Mexico, and Portugal. Trade was administratively centered on Canton by the Chinese because this was the chief port to which foreign sea-going traders had come throughout Chinese history. The newcomers had little to offer so that there was not much interest in trade with Europeans. Arabs, Indians, Malays, and others had long carried on trade that took no special government machinery to administer; this new trade, therefore, evoked no new Chinese ministry or bureau to handle it.

The earliest period of trade was one in which the European sampled the wares of China and sought for something abroad that could evoke Chinese interest in order to lessen the cash outlay. Of interest to Europe were tea, silks, lacquers, porcelain, carved wood, and a wide variety of art goods.

The volume of trade gradually settled around tea and silk, which also spread out beyond the specified port of Canton to the whole of the south China coast. In return the Europeans found that a variety of items somehow attracted Chinese buyers. Furs for clothing in the north China winter, ginseng for medicine, opium as a luxury product for a prosperous society with a leaning toward some exotic outlet. The best products were the cotton textiles of India and a wide variety of luxury goods from the South Seas. It was not long before the British were ruthlessly pushing the opium trade because of its tremendous profits, Britain later going so far, in the 1840's, as to fight a war with China to force China to buy more of a vicious drug that the Chinese were already regretting that they had started using.

The European traders found that China had many a natural monopoly whereas Europe, by 1800, had no satisfactory line of goods to exchange with China. Gradually this led to efforts to break Chinese control over trade in such things as tea and silk. Later on other commodities came in for monopoly breaking also. Eventually a degree of success was attained, and India gradually became the tea-producing country wherein

British capital not only profited from the trade but also from the initial production. Japan was encouraged as a silk producer and eventually took most of China's market. Other minor commodities have gone through somewhat the same cyclic patterns of trade, in that Europe pressed China to trade in a commodity but eventually moved the trade elsewhere. The normal European statement of this change concerns the fact that the Chinese refused to produce in sufficient volume in standardized units, sizes, or qualities. The facts were that the Chinese had never had a large trade in any of the products that Europe wanted in large volume, had an economic system which did not make for large production of such goods, were attracted by nothing the European brought in exchange, and saw no great reason for changing the long-accepted patterns of Chinese society. China could not see ahead to what was coming, but no more could Europe foretell the effects of clumsy dealings and avaricious pursuit of trade.

The Portuguese were the first to reach Canton. Not long behind them were the Dutch. The British were the first to intensively cultivate the China trade and to work it in conjunction with their trade in India. Gradually the British and Yankee colonists forged ahead in trade relations with China, France, Holland, and Portugal being minor participants. Colonial American trade was largely carried on by New England's seaport towns, carrying furs, ginseng, and a few odd products to China. The Indian textile trade largely was in the hands of the British East India Company, to whom also goes the black score of the opium trade.

EUROPEAN SPHERES OF INFLUENCE

The Portuguese came first to Canton in the decade between 1510 and 1520. They secured a permanent establishment at Macao in 1557, but no other permanent footing in China was secured by any European until well into the nineteenth century. Until perhaps 1700 the volume of trade remained small and its problems no more than minor vexations to Chinese bureaucracy. As the volume of trade began to grow in the early eighteenth century it coincided with the most vigorous period of Manchu rule, when an expanding economy in China could easily absorb the shock of a new orientation, or turn it to an advantage. European economic pressure upon China did not become significant until after 1800. The first civil unrest, expressive of an ailing society, had shown itself just before the death of the great Emperor Chien Lung in 1799. None of his successors more than fractionally measured up to the ability of Chien Lung, one of the most able men of his time. Three factors, therefore, coincided to contribute progressively to the social, economic, and political ailments that caused China to be characterized as the "Sick Man of the Orient" during the early twentieth century. These were: Increasingly heavy economic and political pressure by Europe, the general economic and social decline of Chinese society toward the end of an era, and the steady weakening of what had been a dynamic Manchu leadership.

The Chinese failure to diagnose the increasing European pressure (exerted from the sea rather than from the pastoral northwest) as something totally unprecedented in Chinese history gave them no start in making those changes that were needed. At a time when the whole of the Occident was rapidly gathering energy through a creative period of invention, productive manufacturing, and exploitation of the world's economic resources, China had become frozen in the molds of Confucian bureaucracy, self-centeredness, and passive unresponsiveness. Chinese and Manchu officials made more bad moves than good within a series of set patterns that led only to greater involvement in, rather than to any solution of, the problem. And the aggressive West, with a taste of colonial imperialism, became steadily more rapacious. The Chinese realm was too big a series of geographic regions to be taken over by any one European power. The situation turned into a political-economic race for spheres of influence among Britain, France, Germany, Russia, and Japan. A series of political treaties were exacted from China, under various kinds of military pressure, giving European powers special concessions of an economic and political nature, usually accompanied by the lease of small areas of

land in port cities along the coast of China and the Yangtze River. The first such "treaty port" arrangement occurred in 1842; the last such exaction was in 1898 (Fig. 24.4). Just before the close of the nineteenth century the drive of imperialism became more frantic. France held economic claim to most of southwest China, Britain to the Yangtze Valley, Germany wanted Shantung, Japan had Korea, and Russia was interested in Manchuria. The United States had no regional unit in mind, but held the newly acquired Philippine Islands. And in a spell of self-interested altruism the United States

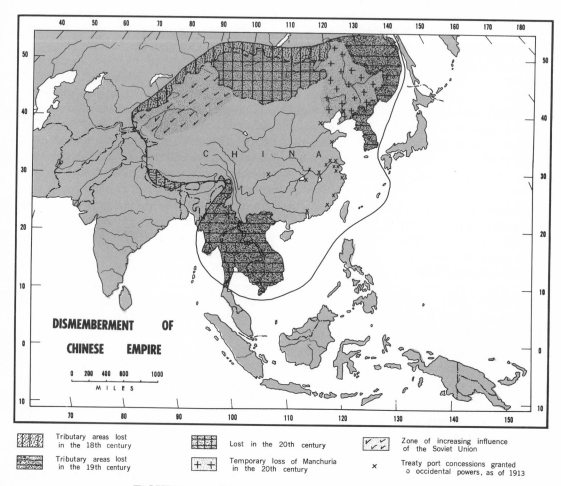

	Tributary areas lost in the 18th century		Lost in the 20th century		Zone of increasing influence of the Soviet Union
	Tributary areas lost in the 19th century		Temporary loss of Manchuria in the 20th century	×	Treaty port concessions granted
				o	occidental powers, as of 1913

FIGURE 24.4. Dismemberment of the Chinese Empire.

set forward the open-door doctrine, which proposed an end to regional, political imperialism in China. Its real effect, however, was to sanction economic imperialism for everyone, since the treaty ports and treaties giving the European special rights were not canceled. The Chinese of the last generation felt as seriously about these unequal treaties as American colonials ever felt about "taxation without representation" at the hands of Britain.

Not only did the Occident carry economic and political imperialism throughout China but also at least once inhibited the normal processes by which Chinese society, in the past, threw off a decadent dynasty. What is known to historians as the Taip'ing Rebellion (1851–1865) swept out of Kwangtung and forged a long black trail of destruction, possibly taking more than 20,000,000 lives, before it ebbed out in the Yangtze Valley. It is just possible that, had the Europeans not given financial and material aid, the rebellion might have succeeded. It is equally possible that the violent unrest that has marked the twentieth century would have begun at a time before the final acts of imperialism had been committed and that Chinese society would have shaped its reorganization into the modern world far differently from the present pattern.

As the years of the twentieth century passed, the obvious occidental imperialism has slackened. More subtle and pernicious undercurrents in the form of financial loans, and large-scale commercial dealings protected by unequal treaties, continued. And with the slackening of occidental imperialism there arose Japanese imperialism, a century late in the race, even more seriously to plague Chinese society. Commencing with the seizure of the southern Ryukyu Islands in the 1870's and reaching its disastrous climax in the eight years of the Sino-Japanese War (1937–1945), the Japanese effort exceeded any of the illustrative examples set by the Occident. There are those who hold that the economic imperialism of the outside world was rapidly beating China down to the role of an economic slave producing volumes of low-cost raw materials at the price of a steadily lowered Chinese level of living. In the eighteenth century China possibly had the highest level of living in the world, whereas in the early 1930's China was a rival for the questionable rank of one of the lowest levels of living in the world. The self-centeredness and crystallized rigidity of Chinese bureaucracy both refused and were unable to change, but the Occident carried exploitation to completely unjustified extremes in fattening its own economy.

THE CHINESE WAY IN REVOLUTION

Throughout the long period in which Chinese culture has been subject to the impact of outside elements there has been a rather standard form of reaction. The Chinese always have been fully committed to the process of peaceful change by slow gradual election, with a Confucian maxim for justification. To the sudden major shift, the change imposed from without, the change that would create a break with the past, the change decided by a few key officials, the mass of Chinese have always been unalterably opposed. In other words, steady change that is held to a rate and an amount that does not threaten the continuity and the major tenets of Chinese life is acceptable; change that threatens the continued existence of established Chinese society finds a weight of objection that usually is passive but that can break into sudden and violent storm upon occasion. During the major span of Chinese history the Confucian bureaucracy was in charge, and anything that threatened to change the essential system of society enlisted the opposition of those in charge. It is worth noting here that the change of a dynasty did not involve the change of the system, but merely of the reigning family.

At times the scholar class unquestionably fattened upon the toil of the masses, but over the long period of Chinese history the scholar class served as the cultural conscience of China, maintaining society on the path laid down in the Confucian classics, battling all divergent trends that threatened the Chinese state, serving as the repository of the permanent values of Chinese culture in a changing world. Made up of human beings drawn from all walks of life and all parts of China, there was a perennial air of democracy about the scholar class that was much more apparent than real, for only sufficient peasantry were admitted to the chosen calling to maintain the ranks of the scholar class. For 2,000 years this cultural conscience changed with the passing centuries yet remained constant to the goals of Confucianism to provide the thread of continuity in Chinese civilization. Within the last century has come the severest test of all, and it now often seems that the old scholar bureaucracy totally collapsed under the impact of the West. In fact this is not so, and a new scholar bureaucracy is in the forming, though both groups are buffeted by the turbulence of changes taking place in Chinese culture today, and the new group has not yet synthesized a centralized body of culture to serve as the ideal and standard of society.

The Chinese have been stubbornly individualistic in their acceptance of change and their opposition to new culture traits. Always there have been reformers, experimenters, true revolutionaries, and men ahead of or behind their times. However, an unproved new cultural device has never been accepted quickly without trial. Objection to change sometimes has seemed the dominant motif of Chinese culture, but this, also, is much more apparent than real. Objection may be individual, by family, by village, by local region, or by major geographic region.

Chinese culture never has been uniform throughout the whole country, a fact that never has bothered the Chinese, but one that often has caused foreign observers to reach simple generalizations falling far short of the truth.

The Chinese essentially are a practical people, even though the logic of their reasoning follows paths unfamiliar to the occidental. Sometimes their acceptance, rejection, or discard of culture traits seems odd to the occidental but is soundly based in their own psychological background. Selectivity in these respects ranges from matters of individual food and dress to regional adoption of a political creed, or general acceptance of electric light by the country at large. The process of nation-wide adoption of particular segments of culture, therefore, is an extremely complicated affair. It sometimes involves a long period of years before the protest dies down around a particular instance, like the railroad. Or it may involve civil uprisings that eventually lead to armed conflict, like the political manipulation that has grown into Chinese Communism. Variation of the procedure is unlimited, but there is one certain feature in all cases, which is that the Chinese people eventually decide for themselves regardless of the dictates or the lobbying of special interests, groups, parties, or regions. It may take even as long as a century for the process of acceptance or rejection to work itself out. Chinese history is full of these periods of readjustment, periods that impress the reader of history as being full of chaos, anarchy, and disorganized political institutions. The last century constitutes such a period, during which the cultural choices thrust upon the Chinese populace have been greater than at any time in the past.

One other certainty in the Chinese process of change, whether it be in religion, dress, or political machinery, is that no new culture trait, however simple, has come into the

Chinese realm and long remained unchanged by Chinese group personality. In the spread of Buddhism from India to China, with its sculpture, its architecture, and its metaphysics, the end product differed greatly from the original. In accepting the growing and smoking of tobacco the Chinese devised instruments and techniques quite unlike those of the bringers of the plant and the habit of smoking. In the progressive spread of Democracy and Communism in China from their respective homes, the future ultimate blend of both into a peculiar system of Sino-socialistic-democratism would no doubt equally astonish Washington and Jefferson, and Marx and Lenin. It took Buddhism several centuries to flower anew in China after its spread from India. So too, then, one should expect neither a full repetition of American Democracy nor Russian Communism in China in the long run. Although this progressive change is true of all cultural diffusion, it particularly needs to be emphasized for the China which suffers so much from conventional overgeneralization.

The Chinese definitely recognize that the Occident has some culture traits and some techniques of using a landscape that are superior to those of the Orient. There is a very positive appetite in China for much of the material equipment of the West, varying from preventive medicine and diet-balancing vitamins to radios, automobile passenger buses, and hydroelectric projects. These material advantages notwithstanding, the present-day Chinese, as a nation, retain their self-centeredness to the point that they reject occidental materialistic and scientific philosophy as epitomized in "pure science" and "untouched by human hands" and do not accept the latter concept as a mark of engineering efficiency. In the apparent chaos that marks modern China there is at work the essentially Chinese spirit of individual rationalization and group compromise in regard to how much of the West can safely be accepted by the East without endangering the soul of Chinese culture. The Chinese way in these things is to tolerate enormous tribulation for this generation, and the next if need be, in order that future generations may live within a pattern of culture first crystallized into the Confucian code 2,500 years ago. The Chinese today are weary of the struggle to rationalize the East and the West, but until some kind of common denominator finds general acceptance the struggle will continue. As a well-educated Chinese said shortly after the termination of Sino-Japanese hostilities in 1945: "If we do not find peace in my lifetime, we will in that of my grandson."

25

MODERN CHINA
IN TRANSFORMATION

THE AGRICULTURE OF CHINA

The basic elements of the agricultural system of modern China are essentially those developed in the ancient Chinese culture hearth of the loesslands. This is in spite of all the new crops, the new tools, and the new climatic regions to which the Chinese have gone. Intensive hand labor with a minimum of mechanical power, closely integrated crop succession, and large yield per acre are as descriptive of Chinese vegetable gardening or rice culture in Yunnan today as of the agriculture of southern Shensi or Shantung in the sixth century B.C. The taro and rice of the southern regions called for wet fields and terracing, and these are common in central to south China today. American potatoes, maize, peanuts, and tobacco have greatly altered the map of cultivated lands since the Columbian discoveries by extending the agricultural area to upland regions. The export of tea, silk, soybeans, and tung oil to foreign markets seriously upset the balance of agriculture. Communist government has abolished private landownership in favor of state ownership. But these are not changes in the system itself. The small size of the truck gardens and fields and the intensity of cultivation apply to any of the fifty centuries during which the Chinese have farmed northern China. In point of fact, the intensification of Chinese agriculture has grown greater during the last two centuries than ever before. This is a detailed sharpening of the system caused by the desperate struggle to keep ahead in the feeding of a hungry but growing population that has not been really well fed since the end of the eighteenth century.

The Land Problem

By the close of the feudal era communal and feudal land holdings slowly gave way to privately owned land. In the abolition of the feudal system there can have been no even division of land among the population and many families must have managed to secure or retain title to various choice farmlands. Since agriculture already had been placed above trade and manufacture as occupational callings, land already was the chief depository of any surplus wealth, individuals and families adding to their holdings whenever opportunity presented itself. Out of the emphasis upon agriculture the Chinese had, by the beginning of the Christian era, much experience with the problems of land taxation, deeds and titles, sale and exchange, accumulation of land in the hands of the wealthy families, and the inevitable formation of a landless class of farmers who became hired hands and tenant farmers on the lands of the city-dwelling absentee landlords. At times monasteries and temples or guilds and speculative associations secured control over large land holdings, but these nonpersonalized owners never have seriously threatened the personal ownership of China's land. Individual family or clan holdings sometimes have reached huge proportions, but these are special forms of Chinese personal ownership not often found in the Occident. Most of the usable land of China became private, personal property as colonization spread out of the hearth, and the ownership of the farmlands of China has consistently remained in private hands.

Over the centuries land has changed hands continuously. Always families economically on the way up have been anxious to invest their savings, and families suffering ill fortune, for one reason or another, have been forced to sell off their lands. During waning periods in Chinese history, when the burden of inefficient government was great, the peasantry lost much of its land to the large landlord families. The return of peace, and steady colonial expansion over China, added to the total land volume. Resettling of unclaimed lands, building of dike systems, cultivation of new alluvial delta lands, lands cleared and newly terraced for cultivation, lands made cultivable by new crops, all have been means of increasing the volume. The peasantry thus continuously acquired new lands. The pattern of Confucian society made it possible for certain peasants continuously to rise into the class of landlords and scholar-bureaucrats, while others again sank back into the tenant farmer group. The Chinese family and clan systems were important agents in this process.

At the beginning of the Manchu dynasty, in the seventeenth century, conditions were favorable to the acquisition of land by the peasantry. All the above-named factors were operative, plus the fact that the government generally gave a tax-free period to anyone claiming new lands. However, by the middle of the nineteenth century the dynastic downward swing of Chinese history plus the force of occidental economic exploitation began causing a serious deterioration of land ownership. By the outbreak of the Sino-Japanese War in 1937, conditions sank to a level seldom reached previously, and made it almost impossible for an agricultural society to participate in an enlarged world of foreign trade, industry, and expanded material culture. It is a commonly accepted statement that for all China, in 1945, perhaps sixty percent of all Chinese farmers were tenants of some kind, and that well over half of them were deeply in debt. This is more serious in agricultural China than is a similar figure of tenancy in industrial United States. The situation generally was held to be worse in the outh of China than in the north, with Manchuria the best off of any section. In southwest China most good land was in the hands of Chinese landlords, with peasant Chinese as tenants and non-Chinese tribespeople often forced onto the barren hill lands or into the position of tenants.

Average land holdings varied considerably, but figures running from 1 to 10 acres per farm family could be found in many parts of the country, with an over-all average perhaps below 3 acres per farm family. There were many millions of landless families, many millions of owner-tenants, a section of the peasantry owning adequate land, and some hundreds of thousands of families that owned large amounts of land. Some estimates indicate that five percent of the population owned fifty percent of the cultivated land, whereas seventy percent of the farming population owned but twenty percent. This was one prominent factor in the internal trouble in China, usually designated the Kuomintang-Communist dispute of the period between 1925 and 1949. Inadequate and non-realistic government land reform policy by the Kuomintang was countered by over-emphasis on agrarian reform by the Communists, but this strong focus on land problems remained a vital part of any debate over which path China should follow.

One feature that was true in 1930 but that probably was absent in earlier China was the fragmentation of land in small patches. The Chinese inheritance system permitted division of a father's land among his sons though many families and clans held certain lands in undivided form. As the present dense population of China has built up, the constant division process made for smaller and smaller holdings. Not only were the holdings small in total, but they were made up of as many as ten or a dozen plots of ground, scattered over a distance of several miles. Whereas all agrarian reform urged the reshuffling of land to give farmers unified holdings, the peasantry objected, fearing another fleecing in the process. This fragmentation and division of an absolute maximum of 290,000,000 acres of farmland among possibly more than 400,000,000 farm people out of the total Chinese population of about 500,000,000 in 1930 indicates that, there was one unsolvable problem in China —there was not enough land to go round. When the formative period in Chinese culture elevated land into the position of the primary economic good, there was more than enough for all. But the very fecundity of the Chinese soil has produced so huge a human crop that China now is facing a situation in which there will never again be land enough to satisfy the classic Confucian value. This must be taken into account in any study of Chinese agriculture, for it is one factor that accounts for much of the social and political unrest of the past century.

Frequent reference has been made by travelers, economists, and critics in recent decades to the fact that the Chinese waste land in several ways. Such items as the burial custom of placing coffins in the fields received caustic comment, along with the neglect of river bottom or delta lands that could be cultivated, and quite arable land left in simple waste. It is only in the non-rice-growing parts of China that coffins are placed in the fields, and any close observer could have perceived the speed with which local erosion, decomposition, and the seasonal plowing returned this land to crop use. Locally grave mounds did reduce the crop lands, and the absence of country-wide flood control planning also prevented use of some river bottom land in a number of places. Civil unrest, punishing taxation, and economic dislocation caused the noncropping of some land every year. Soil erosion, over the last 3,000 years had made its inroads upon many parts of China before terracing had put many areas into shape for permanent farming, though the cultivating of marginal hill lands in the last two centuries has also caused serious soil erosion. These and other factors did reduce the net total of land cropped in any one decade, but the Chinese compare favorably with any other society in the best use of their land. The addition of every single foot of cultivable land in China would still leave the volume too slight to suffice both to feed China and to provide every family with a sound investment in the classical tradition.

Pre-Columbian Crop Patterns

The mainstays of Chinese agriculture are rice and wheat. Both were introduced before the colonial spread of the Chinese out of the culture hearth over China, and both became integral parts of food-crop patterns. Wheat came into China via the Kansu corridor from the west, and became the staple crop in southern Manchuria, northern Korea, and north China. Rice, the domestication of which may have taken place in a region that included south China, very early became the staple crop of central and south China and of the Pacific littoral clear around to the east coast of Korea and southern Japan. The Yangtze River Basin became the meeting ground of the two crops, resulting in a seasonal division of the land, wheat being a winter crop and rice a summer crop.

For each of the two basic crops, rice and wheat, there were complementary crops, some indigenous and some imported from neighboring regions in early periods. The second, fourth, seventh, and thirteenth centuries were notable periods in which numbers of crop-plant additions occurred, but this undoubtedly was a steady process. Such items as cotton, kaoliang (a sorghum), peas, and some of the beans, melons, and many of the garden vegetables, came from southwestern or central Asia, via the Kansu corridor. Taro, some of the spices, bananas, sugarcane, and some of the tropical fruits came from southeastern Asia or India. North China agriculture had as its native complementary crop complex some of the soybeans, several millets, a variety of vegetables and fruits, hemp, and silk. South China's native complementary patterns included the bamboos, citrus fruits, other soybeans, a variety of vegetables, tea, and tung oil. During the historic period there slowly developed many regional patterns of crop dependence based upon local soil and climatic conditions, smoothness of land surface, water and flood conditions, and the ease of handling native plant cover. Native and imported crops shared in this regional development. The evolution of the wet field for rice led to terracing for better water control and to the extension of crop land into the lower hill country.

The record of ecological fitting of crops to particular localities is a complicated one involving many factors. In some cases it seems to have occurred very early, whereas in other situations the integration of basic and complementary crops came rather late. The introduction of wheat into the Yangtze Valley is an example. Wheat became a part of the regular sequence of crops grown in rotational pattern in Szechwan at a very early date by some of the earliest migrants out of the culture hearth area, but only entered the cropping sequence in parts of Kiangsu and Anhwei during the fourth century A.D. as diking and drainage works relieved the flooded-soil conditions of the lowland plains. Wheat growing underwent a second spatial enlargement at a later date with further development of regional drainage systems. In some areas the modern balance between wheat and rice only came into regular cropping patterns in the eighteenth century. The spread of sorghum, despite its earlier introduction into China, came only in the thirteenth century, and the agency of its spread is not clearly known. There are clear records of imperial decrees, governor's admonitions, and local officials' pushing particular crops. In part the ecological process was a matter of population pressure and the demands for larger food supplies; in particular regions where in early periods land was plentiful and demands were light, single croppings per season were sufficient, but in later periods during which land scarcity began to appear, integrative cropping combinations were undertaken to secure larger returns from given farmlands. New varieties of old crops sometimes produced better, or fitted better into a summer-winter rotational sequence of multiple cropping of the same land. All such ecological fittings were part of the process of the spread of the Chinese intensive garden cultivation system over the whole of China. Although the generalizations can be stated, as above, the regional details of the cropping ecology have only been hinted at in writing on China, and much remains to be explained regarding the southward spread of the Chinese agricultural system.

Earliest China possessed only a moderate range of crops, north and south. The steady accretion of new plants broadened the base considerably. However, it appears that China lacked complementary crop plants that would make easy the exploitation of her rough hill lands. The main grain crops, rice, wheat, barley, millet, and kaoliang were all crops of smooth, plowed fields. The peas and beans, and a few oil seeds were not easily grown on the rough, hilly, poorer lands. The garden vegetables needed good soils and close handling. Although there were fruits available, fruit culture on a large scale never seemed to appeal to the Chinese. Pastureland and animal culture was not an important part of the agricultural system, north or south. A fairly considerable proportion of the normally arable land of China, therefore, was not well suited to any of the crops that had been brought into China prior to the Columbian discoveries. These marginal lands, then, never could be put into really developed food crop production. Perhaps this was one of the limiting factors that long held down the population to a figure which left considerable elbow space for all. In this early agriculture of China one final fact should be noted. Although some tea exporting to Tibet and Central Asia is rather old, the product of China's farms traditionally was consumed at home, there being practically no international trade in food products. There was, however, a significant drainage of surpluses from all over China into the key economic area of North China as a part of imperial tribute.

Modern Agricultural Factors

Few of the crops introduced since the Columbian discoveries has seriously or permanently displaced a previous crop. However, opium seriously upset the productive balance of agriculture over almost all of China during a 40-year period extending from perhaps 1880 to 1920. The opium poppy began to be grown before 1880 but reached its major proportions during the last two decades of the nineteenth century. It displaced food crops primarily, reducing the food volume at a time when the population was growing rapidly, and causing a hike in the land-tax structure consequent upon the very large returns from opium compared to food crops. Opium poppies continued to be grown after 1920 but on a reduced scale, and gradually its production tapered off over most of China proper. The cessation of poppy cultivation often caused a period of land abandonment until the land-tax structure again was lowered to fit the productive income pattern.

Maize, the sweet potato, the white potato, the peanut, tobacco, and such minor items as the tomato, pineapple, grape vine, and some vegetables, all fitted into segments of the agricultural complex in such a way as to round it out, broaden it, and increase the productive yield without the serious displacement of any previous crop. Thus, the white potato became either a truck garden crop around the cities inhabited by the white man, and was consumed by him, or a crop of the back-country rough-hill or marginal lands suitable to no native crop. In the twentieth-century spread of Chinese settlement into Manchuria the white potato came into its own as a basic crop in the short-season northern sectors, where it replaced the grain crops. Maize filled in many local areas and was grown as a hill land crop. Gradually maize came to compete directly with some of the poorer, older crops on poor soils, rough lands, and other local handicaps for the older crops, and, since the early nineteenth century, has been increasing its acreage steadily. The sweet potato spread rapidly and in many areas became a staple crop on the hill crests above the terraced rice lands. Particularly in rolling, hilly Szechwan the sweet potato found a ready welcome, becoming the basic crop of the poorer peasant farmer. The peanut supplied a more productive and plentiful cooking oil than any plant previously cultivated. The cumulative effect of these modern introductions, since the late sixteenth century, has been to increase tremendously the food supply available from lands that were not very productive previously, giving one more stimulus to population growth.

Commercial production of various crops for modern international trade did not alter the major regional balance of Chinese agriculture, though it upset the productive economy within many individual regions. Thus, the export of tea, silk, egg products, pig bristles, goat skins, soybeans, cotton, sesame, tung oil, grass cloth, and lac affected the economy of one or more regions. The effects have been separately expressed during the period of modern foreign trade. At first the trade in each grew slowly, then boomed, and finally collapsed in a number of cases. Such economic reactions have not been permanent, but each has contributed to the economic problems of modern China.

In spite of all the varied introductions Chinese agriculture has a very high dependence upon grains, particularly upon rice and wheat. Its per capita meat consumption is very low and the pressure of men upon land is such that modern China cannot afford food for many animals. Fruits, nuts, fish, and fowl likewise play a small part in the diet of most Chinese. Nutritional levels under a high-grain diet are today less high in China than in many other parts of the world. This is in part a question of sheer pressure of population and inadequate supply.

With all the positive and negative factors, Chinese agriculture has faced a crisis situation in this century. The occidental agricultural missionary, the university research station, and the provincial experiment station did a great deal to stimulate the productive-ness of modern Chinese agriculture. In spite of Chinese skill in maintaining soil fertility, many sections of China today seriously need fertilizers, particularly organic ones. And despite the large amount of diking and water control work done prior to 1930, there remained a significant amount still to be done. Despite the new developments, improvements, and refinements applied to the modern Chinese landscape, it remains true that China cannot feed and clothe herself in any but the most successful crop year at the present time. This condition first began to appear about 1875 and, despite Communist claims, it remains true today. It appears that the intensive gardening system of crop production that first gave the culture hearth of China its advantage some 4,500 years ago had come to the end of the line by the twentieth century, and that it had brought the large Chinese population up against a dilemma for which there was no solution short of a first order revolution in the very nature of agriculture, the reduction of the Chinese population, or the development of an industrial export economy that could support the purchase of foodstuffs and clothing textiles from abroad. There were many Chinese, in the 1930's, who were well convinced of the seriousness of this dilemma, but there was wide difference of opinion as to how China should attempt to work out the solution to the problem.

Regional Crop Patterns

The most significant regional line of demarcation in the agricultural picture of China is the Tsinling Shan, which roughly corresponds to the northward limits of rice, water chestnut, taro, canals, flooded-field patterns, bamboo, citrus fruits, the palms, tea, and a number of minor crops or agricultural practices (see Figs. 6.9 and 6.10, pp. 130-131). In broad terms one can describe North China as the wheat-millet-barley-white potato zone, plus midlatitude fruits and vegetables. South China, then, is the rice-sweet potato-tea zone, plus tropical fruits and vegetables (Figs. 25.1 through 25.3, and Table 6). Such crops as maize, soybeans, kaoliang, broad beans, some of the peas, and tobacco are to be found in both regions. Brief generalization about Chinese agriculture is difficult, for Chinese farmers, after centuries of trial and error, have worked out rather complex cropping systems based upon many local factors. Changing conditions of transport, plant breeding, and marketing economics affect these patterns, but less rapidly than in our own country. Central China, particularly Szechwan, has the most complex crop pattern of any part of China, growing a larger number of the common crops than any other agricultural region. Manchuria, the northwest spring wheat region, and the southern rice double-crop region have simpler crop patterns than the blended agriculture of central China.

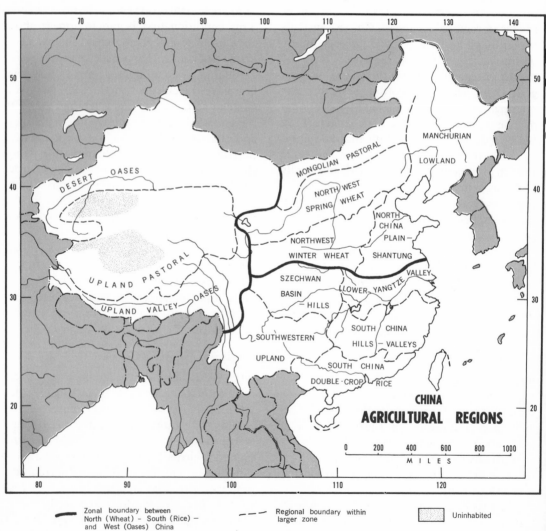

FIGURE 25.1. Agricultural regions of China.

TABLE 6
China's Crop Patterns by Agricultural Regions

Region	Primary Crop	Millet	Kaoliang	Wheat, spring	Wheat, winter	Barley, spring	Barley, winter	Broad beans, winter	Soybeans	Peas	Maize	White Potatoes	Sweet Potatoes	Peanuts	Rape	Sesame	Sugarcane	Bamboo	Citrus fruit	Persimmons	Pears	Stone fruit	Melons	Tea	Tobacco	Cotton	Mulberry	Silk	Pig bristles	Goatskins	Eggs*	Tung oil	Common Animals (Listed in order of importance)	Growing Season (in days)
Manchurian Lowland	Soy beans, Kaoliang	×	×	×		×			×		×																						Cattle	150–170
Northwest Spring Wheat†	Millet	×	×	×		×						×											×										Cattle, sheep, horses, camels	175–200
Northwest Winter Wheat	Winter wheat	×	×	×	×	×	×	×	×	×	×	×				×				×		×	×			×							Cattle, donkeys, sheep, horses	200–225
North China Plain-Shantung	Winter wheat, Kaoliang	×	×	×	×	×	×	×	×	×	×	×	×	×	×	×				×	×	×	×		×	×					×		Cattle, donkeys, horses, mules, fowl	190–240
Lower Yangtze Valley	Rice						×	×	×		×	×	×	×	×			×	×	×	×	×	×				×	×	×	×	×		Water buffalo, cattle, swine, fowl	260–300
Szechwan Basin-Hills	Rice		×		×		×	×			×	×	×	×	×		×	×	×	×	×	×	×					×	×	×		×	Cattle, swine, water buffalo, goats	330–360
South China Hills-Valleys	Rice								×				×	×	×		×	×	×					×	×			×	×	×	×	×	Cattle, water buffalo, swine, fowl	300–330
South China Double-Crop Rice‡	Rice								×				×	×	×		×		×					×	×		×	×	×	×	×	×	Water buffalo, cattle, swine	340–365
Southwestern Upland	Rice				×						×		×		×				×					×	×		×	×	×	×		×	Water buffalo, cattle, horses, swine, goats	340–365

*Refers to important commercial production only.

†Oats, buckwheat, wool and pastureland are significant in this one area alone.

‡A number of subtropical fruits are significant in this one area alone.

529

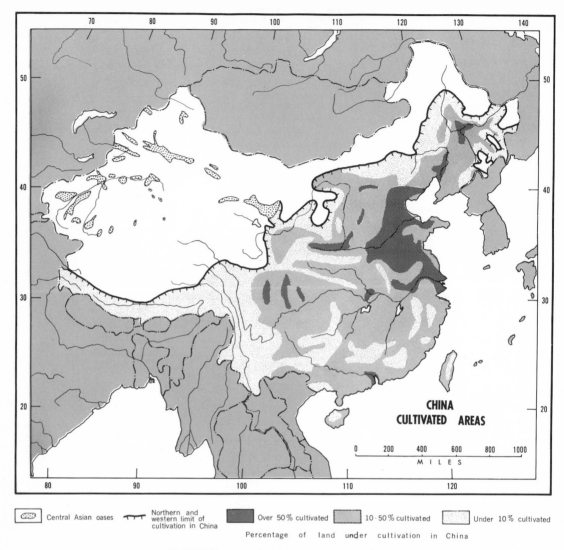

FIGURE 25.2. Cultivation of land in China.

Northward from the Tsinling Shan double cropping becomes more and more unusual until in northwest China and Manchuria it is rarely practiced. The Yangtze Valley has about half its land double cropped, combining southern summer and northern winter crops. Perhaps three fourths the land of southeastern China is double cropped, two crops of rice and minor subtropical products being grown in the extra-long growing season but with few northern-type winter crops. About half the crop land of China is irrigated, most of this being in rice, of course, with a minor amount of irrigation agriculture throughout the north until one reaches the dry Kansu corridor zone of oasis culture. Over a fourth of the cultivated land of China is in small, terraced fields, and much of the total field surface has been so rearranged as to represent a man-made landscape. There is

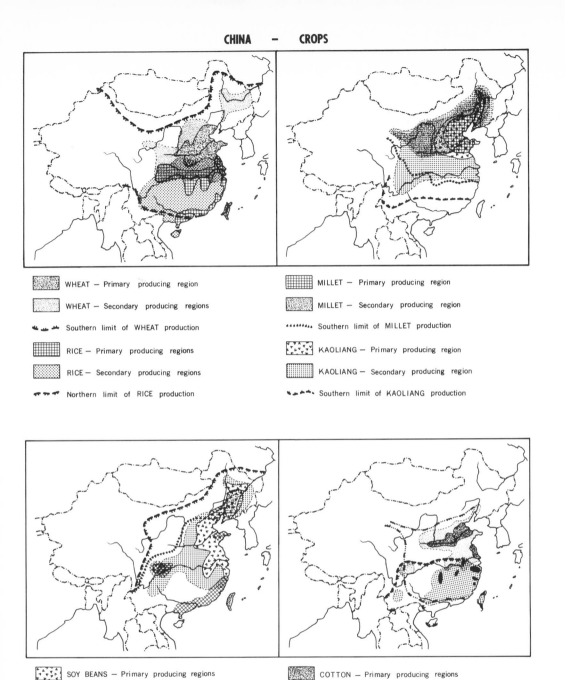

WHEAT — Primary producing region

WHEAT — Secondary producing regions

Southern limit of WHEAT production

RICE — Primary producing regions

RICE — Secondary producing regions

Northern limit of RICE production

MILLET — Primary producing region

MILLET — Secondary producing region

Southern limit of MILLET production

KAOLIANG — Primary producing region

KAOLIANG — Secondary producing region

Southern limit of KAOLIANG production

SOY BEANS — Primary producing regions

SOY BEANS — Secondary producing regions

Arid-cold limit to production of SOY BEANS

WHITE POTATOES — Primary producing region

SWEET POTATOES — Primary producing regions

Arid-cold limit to production of SWEET POTATOES

COTTON — Primary producing regions

COTTON — Secondary producing regions

Encloses zone of scattered plantings of COTTON

TEA — Primary producing regions

TEA — Secondary producing regions

Encloses zone of scattered plantings of TEA

FIGURE 25.3. Principal crops of China.

531

almost no square mile of China that does not show the cumulative hand of man. Almost all rice land is terraced, of course, but terraces of a sort are found throughout the Loess Highlands and in various other parts of the country.

The northwest and southwest of China are the only regions that have not significantly shared in the agricultural export trade. Northwest China has a very strong dependence upon spring wheat, with a rather small crop range. Southwest China is isolated and also has the most dense packing of population per square mile of cultivated land of any part of China. Despite the stake in international trade Chinese agriculture still is mainly a local consumption affair. Transport mechanisms are inadequate and per ton-mile costs are high, so that very few common products will support a long haul. Agriculture is the chief source of income for perhaps three fourths of the Chinese today, and, since there are many factors limiting the over-all efficiency and success of agriculture, Chinese economy as a whole suffers.

Although the North China culture hearth developed its dietary economy around wheat, the millets, and barley as the grain staples, rice has become the most widely preferred grain staple of modern China. Under the present pressures on crop land the total agricultural landscape of about 290,000,000 acres, through double cropping, is planted to about 375,000,000 acres of crops in most years. Of this latter total the estimated annual acreage plantings are: Rice, 80,000,000; wheat, 60,000,000; maize, 33,000,000; soybeans, 32,000,000; millets, 24,000,000; potatoes, white and sweet, 26,000,000; kaoliang, 18,000,000; barley, 10,000,000; miscellaneous grains and pulses, 38,000,000; miscellaneous edible oil producers, 14,000,000 (see Fig. 25.3). The crop landscape is larger today than it has ever been, of course, and the index of double cropping is greater. About A.D. 1400 an estimate places the crop

landscape at approximately 60,000,000 acres, for a population of 65,000,000; wheat was then a much higher-ranking crop in the acreage totals than it is today, there was much less double cropping, and crop combinations were small ones. Cotton was a rather new crop in 1400, grown chiefly in the northwest of China, although the plant and the fiber had come into China much earlier. Communist policy has markedly increased the cotton acreage in recent years, to reduce the textile import, and the crop recently has averaged about 14,000,000 acres per year (see Fig. 25.3). It is notable that Communist policy, in order to get the maximum return from agriculture, has increased the traditional emphasis upon the grain crops.

The position of fruits and vegetables in the agricultural economy is considerable, but there never have been any data on acreage or production. Chiefly fruit trees are planted as extras, along field boundaries, and at odd points about the homestead, though orchards of solid plantings of particular fruits are present all over China. Vegetables chiefly are an urban-fringe market garden product, in volume, with relatively small acreages kept in production as much of the year as the local growing season will allow. In recent years, of course, the private plot allowed by government is chiefly a vegetable plot of quick-growing plants and, presumably, vegetable growing is a more widely distributed matter than formerly.

Livestock never have figured extremely importantly in Chinese domestic economy since the very earliest focusing of effort on crop production, though they have always been present. Although there evolved a tabu on the use of milk products, and though pasture land has never been significant in Chinese land use, no tabus ever evolved on the eating of meat products, in the primary sense. Pigs have long been the most numerous animal, and every rural family has aimed at raising them. Horses, mules, and donkeys are chiefly animals of North China and the dry interior, though small horses are common in Kueichou and Yunnan. Cattle in the north, and water buffalo in the south, supply a source of draft power and meat although they have never been numerous enough for either purpose, with a present-day total averaging about 76,000,000 animals in all. Sheep and goats, for wool, mohair, and meat have been increased in number somewhat, under Communist policy, and may total not far from 90,000,000. In recent years the pig population has grown markedly, and recent estimates suggest a total of about 150,000,000, perhaps double that of the pre-Communist period. The pig, kept around the homestead and fed on scraps, plant wastes, sweet potato tops, and allowed to scavenge, provides both meat and valuable manure for the private garden plot, and is a readily sold cash product. Communist China has been a steady exporter of pork products in recent years, and the pig fits both the rural and the national economy. Most rural homesteads have chickens, ducks, or geese in small numbers.

The Communist Impact on Agriculture

Superficial consideration suggests that the Communist government collectivization of land has produced a major impact on Chinese agriculture, but this is not strictly true. It is true, of course, that the collectivization program has drastically altered a basic tenet in Chinese classical economic theory, that the Communist program has greatly altered the livelihood structure of the Chinese rural agrarian population, and that the government taxation system has drastically altered the post-harvest disposition of crop commodities. The agricultural system remains basically what it was, a semimechanized intensive gardening system, one which primarily depends upon simple tools and large expenditures of human labor. The organization of the rural populace into mutual aid teams, collectives, and communes, in theory, serves the better to marshall the labor force for the intensive effort more efficiently than did the former system, one which always found a portion of the labor force underemployed. If the rural labor force can be kept on the job, it should be possible to get more work out of that labor force, thereby increasing the intensity of the gardening system, and its productivity.

In Chinese classical economic theory, the primary economic "good" was land, and every family aspired to own as much land as possible. In that no person now may "own" land, no landlord class, presumably, can again appear; that the whole of the rural populace has been reduced to a landless class of agricultural laborers without prospect for the future does both alter Chinese economic theory and alter the basic livelihood structure of rural society. It does appear that Communist leadership recognized the difficulties of absolute enforcement of the principle of state control of all farm land, by the practical device of allowing individuals and families the "right" to garden a small plot for individual gain, but the administration of this device has been subject to periodic tightening of control and increasing restriction. Government appears to relax the rule when unrest develops strongly in the rural hinterland, tightening the controls again when that seems possible, at all times restricting the exercise of the right to the minimal amount. The collection of agricultural taxes in kind has eliminated the former patterns of crop disposition in the post-harvest period thereby, in turn, eliminating the squeeze on the tenant farmer group that had to sell crops at low harvest-time prices. This has been replaced by a tax system in which the assessment is made on annual quotas set in pre-planting periods rather than on actual harvests. Whatever its relative justice, the system has markedly altered an aspect of rural livelihood structure.

Under good management with a willing peasantry, the present collectivized land control system probably does get more out of the land than did the former system. It is possible to put a higher share of arable land under crop than formerly, by a small margin. In that the labor force can be put either to renovative or to developmental projects for the improvement of crop land, a good many restorative measures have been taken in areas suffering from soil erosion, inadequate drainage, or inadequate irrigation water supply. The planting of improved varieties can be enforced more fully, as can the applications of fertilizers and pest controls. All these measures are aspects of further intensification of agriculture, through the greater application of human labor. The efficacy of the measures, of course, depends on the willingness of the peasantry to cooperate by expending the added labor, something that has not always been the case. Good management and a willing peasantry may work together in a given year, but Communist government has no way of avoiding the factor that always has been important in Chinese agriculture—the climatic hazard and the bad year. Press releases normally blame poor crop years on the bad annual weather sequence, but credit results in good years to Communist organizational procedures. Since collectivization of agriculture was completed in 1956 there have been five rather bad years, four average years, and four quite good years, about average conditions for China.

Mechanization of Chinese agriculture is being pushed as rapidly as practical under the circumstances in those areas in which it is possible by nature of the spatial extent of field patterns; in the intricately terraced small-field landscapes only specialized types of mechanization will ever be possible. Mechanization has been carried further in Manchuria and on the North China Plain than elsewhere (see Fig. 10.6, p. 253), which is only partially complete as to the most recent distribution of mechanized state farms). Considerations in the issue of mechanization involve the potential disposition of the labor force that could be freed from farm labor; it is clear that the industrial plant of China is not yet able to absorb the large amount of unskilled labor that could be freed by more rapid mechanization.

Comparative notes on yields from collectivized fields and from private garden plots makes it clear that the rural peasantry still is of a mind to work harder and more efficiently on the private plots than on the collective fields. It is also clear that those private plots have made the difference between survival and widespread famine during several intervals in which government pressure became excessive, centralized planning went astray, natural climatic disaster struck, or social disorganization was produced by some extraneous government program.

Through the system of agricultural taxation in kind the government rationing system has been able to achieve a more effective distribution than formerly obtained of such foodstuffs as are permitted general consumption. The system has facilitated the export of chosen volumes of particular commodities as are decided by planning policy, and this has been a regular element in agricultural administration which has put rather heavy pressure on agriculture. The domestic rationing system is relatively efficient, per the differential policy adopted (by which selected segments of the urban work force, ranking government functionaries, and other elite can be rewarded with enlarged rations), so that even in a lean year the actual per capita distribution of food and other absolute necessities can be sufficient for biological survival for all those members of society whose behavior has been sufficiently good that they were not confined to a hard-labor camp. In part this has been achieved by the import of both rice and wheat, in order to maintain adequate reserve foodstocks against bad crop years, and it is probable that the reserve stocks have stood at higher levels since 1952 than they have for decades.

China has embarked upon a comprehensive and far-reaching program of industrialization (a necessity foreseen by all varieties of political opinion) and, of necessity, is extracting the capital resources by which to finance the program from the already heavily burdened agricultural sector of the total economy. This has meant under-investment in the agricultural system while laying the foundation for industrialization. This, in turn, has meant driving the rural populace as hard as it can be driven, austerity in consumer living, and the retention of the old agricultural system while manipulating its labor input and its product output so as to both feed the total labor force and extract the maximum capital resource from agriculture for investment in industrialization.

By open admission of Communist leadership the Chinese agricultural system has not been basically altered. The transformation of the system is, thus, estimated as taking a good many years. What leadership has tried to bring about is the maximum possible productivity of the already intensive gardening system of the past, on a national scale, on the premise that it is the only thing that can be done until the industrialization of China reaches the point at which it may take the pressure off the agricultural system. This is a very different proposition from the campaign slogan of "lower rural taxes and turn the land back to the farmers" by which Communism came to power in China.

FORESTS AND THE TIMBER PROBLEM

Was all of China ever covered by forest? This remains an unsolved problem. It seems most probable that the zones of active loess deposit, and stream erosion, flooding, and sedimentation in north China and the lower Yangtze Valley were never fully covered with forest in the ordinary sense. Most of the Tibetan highlands lie above the timber line. Inner Mongolia is too dry for natural forest and so is all of central Asia except for high mountain zones. It would also seem that there was open parkland within a good share of western and southern Manchuria. Probably the mountain projections above the loess maintained their forest cover, within the Loess Highlands zone, including the Shantung upland. Most of central and much of southern China are natural forest areas, though bamboo and subtropical grasses prevented the tree cover from reaching completeness in particular ecologic niches. It is likely that bamboo, the grasses, shrubs, and some scrubby plants have increased in area within historic time, since their rates of reproduction under tolerance are greater than that of forest.

Undoubtedly the Chinese have deforested large areas, not once but several times, though there have been some areas that never have been reforested. The Shantung upland, for example, possessed a good forest cover in the early centuries of the Christian era, but has shown progressive degrading of plant cover ever since. In periods during which the economic pressures of men upon land for food, lumber, and fuel were less than those today the Chinese successfully practiced reforestation in several different portions of China proper. Numerous replantings within recent decades have suffered at the hands of needy but irresponsible fuel gatherers. For the rural poor peasantry the fuel problem has been an oppressive one in modern time in all of North China.

Today most of China's good timber is gone though there remain a few forested patches in isolated locations. The northern Manchurian forests are being mined at present in face of the urgent need, as are forests in other sections of China. Elsewhere timber is almost a farm crop that is regularly cut too young. China today is a timber importer on a steadily increasing scale without hope of reducing the import volume. Possibly three-fourths of China proper would be forest covered if man let nature take its course, but in modern China that is literally impossible.

Shelterbelt plantings have been notable in recent years, with a good measure of success in regions in which the climatic regime affords sufficient moisture in the long term. Shelter belts were planted too far out into the dry margins in some cases, and these did not survive. Some of these shelterbelts will succeed sufficiently well to provide some timber supply in the future, but they do not answer the present need for wood.

It can be asserted that the future problem of wood products for China will be a severe one since usage currently exceeds reproduction in all areas despite considerable reforestation now going on. The demand for wood products does not decline with maturing industrialization, and currently China is operating on a deficit principle in this respect, postponing the accounting of the problem into the future.

FISHERIES

In the traditional dietary of the middle and upper classes of all Chinese except those in the far western inland areas every well-ordered evening meal included fish in some form. The list of aquatic products consumed by the Chinese is smaller than the Japanese list, but considerably greater than that used by occidentals. The primary fishing waters are from Hangchou Bay southward to Hainan Island, but Chinese boats range the whole of the China coast, a distance well over 3,000 miles. Over 100,000 boats, some of which are motorized, are engaged in full-time fisheries work, and the total of professional fishermen including fresh-water fishermen is above a million. Few large, powered, long distance trawlers are used by the Chinese. The sea fisheries bring in the widest range of fish, shrimp, oysters, and edible seaweed. Canton, Ningpo, Shanghai, and Lüta are the leading fishing ports, from which fresh fish are sold to the immediate urban markets and salted fish shipped to wider, inland markets. Almost every port along the China coast has its fishing fleet of boats built and decorated by special local designs, though the fleets of the flat, alluvial north China coast are small and unimportant, since there are few ports along this coast.

Fresh-water fisheries are significant in the Yangtze Valley and southeast China, but they are less important than the sea fisheries. Relatively few professional fishermen work the inland waters, but many members of farm families casually engage in fishing during slack seasons and free hours. In the rice lands of east and south China there are perhaps a half million acres of reservoirs and ponds in which pond fish culture is carried on. Particularly in Kwangtung such fish culture makes an important contribution to farm incomes. It is difficult to assess the contribution of fish to the Chinese food supply, either quantitatively or dietetically. The annual catch is estimated at about 1,500,000 tons from all sources, and there is some import of fish products, but it seems probable that the consumer market would take several times this volume if the products were readily available.

TRANSPORT AND COMMUNICATIONS

The enormous contrasts in communications existent throughout the world today are occidental creations of the last century and a half. In the China and the Occident of 1800 transport and communications had not greatly changed for many centuries. Only the Roman Empire had had a system of courier routes and roads that were the equal of the Chinese system. Since the Chinese never made exceptional use of wheeled vehicles roadbuilders could use steps in constructing their routes through hilly and mountain landscapes. All main routes were paved with stone slabs to a width of several feet, and many secondary paths had single slab centers. Pack animals and the human carrier were the basic elements in transport, both of passengers and of cargo. In southwest China as late as 1930, it required some 60-days' travel to go from Chungking to Kunming, via Kweiyang, by native means over native roads. In 1939 the senior author made that trip in three days by car over gravel-surfaced highways. On United States standard roads two easy days would have sufficed. In 1930 in many parts of China the human carrier still handled almost everything that was moved, and over most of the country the human carrier, the sedan chair, the pack animal, the wheelbarrow, or the two-wheeled oxcart were the prevailing transport mechanisms. Per ton-mile costs were high, transport time was great, and the very roads and equipment limited the volume and type of materials that could be moved. In those portions of China in which human porterage was primary, a porter could carry wheat only two days before the transport charge equaled the value of the load, thus limiting the distribution of local surpluses. Such introductions as the pony taxi and the rubber-tired two-wheeled cart pulled by two to eight men were costly and slight improvements in the face of tremendous need. Transportation problems still plague modern China in most areas.

In central and south China natural waterways and canals play a role of enormous importance. The barbarian Wu tribes, resident in the Yangtze Delta, developed the first sections of what came to be the Grand Canal. Various additions were made until a single waterway was developed from south of the Yangtze to the Yellow River in the sixth century. The Grand Canal has attracted much attention, though it was but one of a number of important waterways. The total of navigable waterways, river and canal, is estimated as high as 40,000 miles (Fig. 25.4). The development of modern transport in China reflects both the conservatism of a people in accepting new devices and the severe exploitation by the Occident. At first contact with the European the Chinese sea-going junk was a better vessel than any possessed by Europe, but the native sailing vessels of the Chinese today are little better than they were in the sixteenth century. Only slowly did the Chinese take to steam and steel, but by 1937 they had built a large fleet of steam launches, tugs, and small steamers. A fair coastwise shipping fleet had been purchased from abroad but it suffered severe foreign competition under unequal controls. British, Japanese, French, and American shipping concerns handled most of China's foreign trade, most of her coastwise trade, and much of her shipping on navigable rivers. Post-war nationalizing of China's shipping waters and the destruction of most of the former operating fleets left China in a desperate fix. This will take time to correct, and perhaps for a generation China will have inadequate water transport. The replacement of coasting vessels is progressing slowly, and a beginning is being made in the sea-going fleet. The inland waterway fleet of junks, barges, and tugboats is in fairly good shape.

The first railways were built by occidental concerns on concession from the Chinese government. There followed a mad scramble which left China short of railroads, but with loans to be repaid. Including Manchuria the railways operating in 1937 totaled just short of 10,000 miles. World War II saw many lines ruined and new ones poorly built in the emergency. In 1952, using Nationalist Government surveys, and doing some new

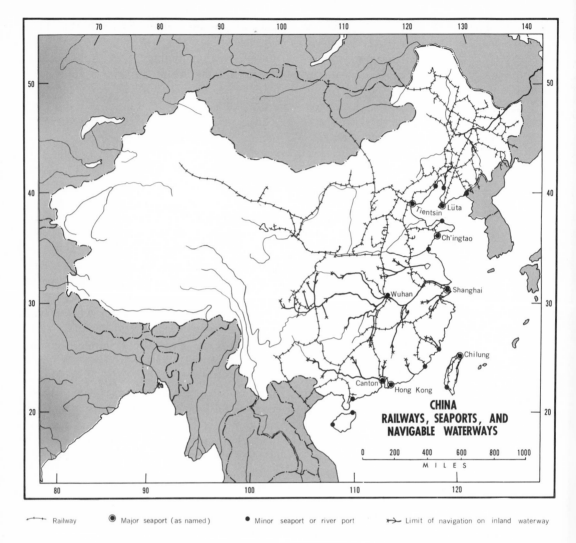

FIGURE 25.4. Railways, seaports, and navigable waterways in China.

construction, the Communists had about 17,000 miles of railway operating. For the time being the rail mileage has stabilized at just over 20,000 miles of track, a fair share of which is double-tracked. Eventually China will need perhaps 60,000 miles of railways covering the country in a well-planned network, so that the task has only begun.

There was less foreign exploitation in the building of modern highways. The old stone steproads, the narrow winding paths of South

China, and the rut-ridden earth roads of the northwest were unfit for modern wheeled vehicles. China is having to revise a whole land transport system that has served for many centuries. It is both costly and slow going. World War II greatly spurred the building of strategic roads to open up western China, but the campaign will be long, for China's highways at present are but a fraction of those needed. Before World War II, the total road mileage was about 70,000 miles of all qualities of modern roads, and automobiles and trucks numbered only about 50,000. In the late 1960's the road mileage stood at just over 300,000 miles of all types of roads, but perhaps half this total was of lightly built roads open only to light traffic (Fig. 25.5). The modern roads, though sometimes longer than the native routes, are on better gradients and afford easier travel so that there is much profitable use of the new roads other than by automotive traffic. China now is building some of her own automotive equipment, chiefly trucks adapted to local conditions. Gradually the truck and bus fleet will be built up, but there still is strong reliance on the bicycle.

In aviation the revolution has had to be even more sudden than in roads, even though Szechwan was familiar with the airplane before the railway and the automobile came. It is likely that aviation will develop faster and to a greater extent than was true with rail and roadways, since the urgency of the times is greater and China must skip some stages in transport development. World War II left China with a large number of

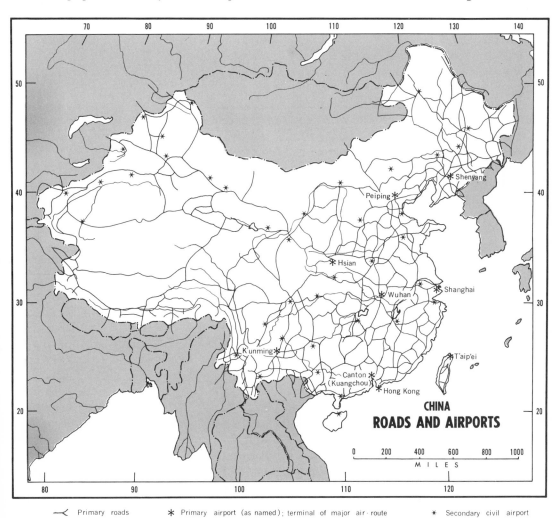

Primary roads   * Primary airport (as named); terminal of major air·route   * Secondary civil airport

FIGURE 25.5. Roads and civil airports of China.

airfields, many of which have been turned to civil transport use. Russian planes provide an effective passenger and freight movement, and the volume certainly will grow in the future.

Today one can pass quickly from one extreme to another, for China is only beginning to develop her modern transport equipment. In Shanghai, alongside a riverside street, one can see the modern ocean freighter, the steam tug pulling a long line of barges, the stubby local passenger boat, the sea-going junk, the inland water junk, the one-man water taxi boat, and the raft of bamboo poles floating downstream to the lumber yard. And along the street will pass the private limousine, the scurrying taxicab, the trackless trolley, the motor truck, the coolie-pulled cart, the bicycle, the ricksha, and the human carrier. Close to Shanghai one can pass into the native scene where the small rowboat, the inland junk, the ricksha, the water-buffalo pack animal, and the human carrier still control the movement of goods and people.

MINERAL WEALTH

The Chinese appear to have learned the use of metals from their western neighbors, but they were among the first to burn rocks out of the earth known as coal, for heating purposes. Once learned, this knowledge was used in the making of some of the world's finest bronze art goods and in the making of iron agricultural implements. Even gunpowder was developed and used in firecrackers and in the defensive forerunners of the rifle and trench mortar, but elaborate inventive effort in the use of metals was not continued because of the early decisions that agriculture was the preferred calling for civilized man and that minerals should only be used to assist man to the necessary minimum. The Occident did the first surveying of China's mineral resources in

modern terms, in the late nineteenth century, and the early stories were phenomenal. During the 1920's–1930's the trend of opinion was that China really did not have the quantity, range, and quality of minerals to permit major industrialization. To some degree this was based on beliefs that iron ore, petroleum, copper, and bauxite were either almost lacking in modern industrial quantities, or were very low in grade. It now turns out that the mineral surveys were very rough and incomplete. Recent Chinese surveys have found large amounts of iron ore and copper in qualities adequate to modern industrial processing. There is plenty of bauxite for the day when industrialization matures to the level of using aluminum. The Geological Survey of China was founded only in 1916, and knowledge of the mineral wealth is even now only reasonably approximate. Certain minerals have been mined and exported for decades and represented one source of foreign exchange. In this list were tungsten and antimony, over which China held a monopoly until 1940. China was a small but significant contributor to the world supply of tin and has exported salt to Japan. Reserves of tungsten, antimony, and tin are ample for a reasonable future, whereas salt primarily is produced by the solar evaporation of sea water and is a limitless resource.

The chief mineral resource is coal, in which China ranks at least fourth in the world list, with about 240 billion tons in proven reserves, and a possible total much larger than this (Fig. 25.6). The best coal is concentrated chiefly in Shansi and Shensi, which is hardly the best location, but reserves sufficient for several decades at the very least are found in every province. The annual mine total ran about 30,000,000 tons per year prior to 1945, about half of which normally was used in industry; since 1960 the annual total has always exceeded 200,-000,000 tons per year. With this large coal supply goes sufficient iron-ore reserve of good

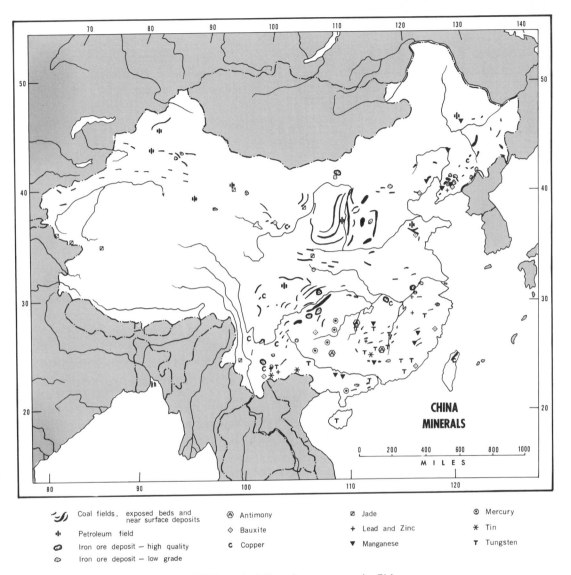

FIGURE 25.6. Mineral occurrences in China.

quality to satisfy industrial needs for a long period, fairly widely distributed. Manchuria has the best combination of the two minerals. Much of the coal throughout the country is satisfactory for coking, but the best iron ore is somewhat limited in volume and most of it needs blending for the best results. In the third primary mineral resource of the modern world, petroleum, China

appears to have found widely distributed amounts in small volumes, though the surveys still are quite incomplete. Some of the petroleum is poorly located, in central Asia. In the alternative power source, China has a reasonably large water-power potential, but it is of such a nature as to be rather costly to develop, in which field China is only getting a start. Several small projects have been completed recently, and more are under construction at present.

The balance of the mineral prospect is reasonable. Such ferro-alloys as chromium, nickel, molybdenum, cobalt, and vanadium appear to be lacking, though a modest amount of manganese is present to go with the tungsten and antimony. Lead, zinc, sulphur, mercury, and gold exist in significant amounts, but silver and a number of minor minerals appear to be present in inadequate amounts only. Of the light metals the actual volume and value of magnesium ores must await further geological field work, but they appear significant, and there is ample bauxite for China's needs. Copper deposits reported so far are not of huge volume, but are well within the range of industrial technology.

In summary, it would appear that China has the largest volume of mineral resources of any country of the East. This resource is quite ample for such industrialization as China is able to mount in the near future. It may be that in the final geological canvass of the remaining back country sufficient resources will be found to permit industrialization to go to whatever lengths the Chinese wish to take it.

INDUSTRIALIZATION

In early Chinese society a preventive restriction to the growth of industry was repeatedly applied. Such restrictions were meant to insure that neither trade nor manufacturing dominated the agricultural society. Within its limited sphere, however, handicraft industry was permitted to develop to its fullest. Historically this meant that each local region had to be self-sufficient. With an approximately similar major culture pattern extending over the country there resulted a widespread duplication of handicraft industry for the production of tools, utensils, weapons, clothing, and art goods. But with varied climate, agriculture, local resources, and local cultures, there resulted endless variety in the products of a handicraft society. Over the centuries there were ups and downs in the patterns of manufacturing, as well as regional shifts in the centers of production. Government from time to time felt called upon to take over, regulate, stimulate, or restrict the production and distribution of goods. And certainly there was progress in the use of metals, woods, stone, textiles, lacquer, and ivory, so that the handicraft industry of the early Manchu dynasty was a richer, fuller one than had been that of the Han. Thus it was that early modern Europe was so greatly impressed with the products of China at a time when Europe's industrial revolution was only beginning to produce results.

However, by the third quarter of the nineteenth century European products began increasingly to flow into China as European industrial production grew. Occidental concessions extracted from China in mining, trade, industry, and settlement gave foreign-owned enterprise a foothold. Foreign control over Chinese import tariffs, special concessions to foreign-owned factories, and the manning of these factories by cheap Chinese labor produced a flow of goods within China that successfully competed with the products of any early Chinese-owned factories. This foreign activity gave considerable training to Chinese labor in modern industrial skills and, in fact, formed the only such training ground that existed. In the long run, the native handicrafts themselves have suffered tremendously, the Chinese found themselves outdistanced, and Chinese per-capita production of material goods during the 1930's was probably less than at any time since the establishment of the Manchu reign.

Between 1912 and 1937, however, in the cities along the coastal seaboard, a very considerable start was made in almost every type of industrial enterprise, and the pace was picking up. Chinese capital, organizational know-how, and labor skills were accumulating around every large city and slowly moving back into the hinterland. Had the Sino-Japanese War not intervened, Chinese industry would have made significant strides forward during the last two decades. This very fact undoubtedly was one of the causes for the decision of the Japanese to strike in 1937—it could not be put off much longer. Chinese industry was set far back, through destruction and dislocation, and in 1945 faced a slow recovery complicated by serious internal dissension.

Patterns of industrialization differ and programs for future industrialization also differ. In modern China the first efforts combined private industry and state ownership. Increasingly the state participated in all types of industry. Most Nationalist official government statements, between 1927 and 1949, variably followed the plans of Dr. Sun Yat-sen, made during the early 1920's. The groups composing and supporting the National Government aimed at something part way between the free economy of the United States and the state-operated economy of the U.S.S.R., seeking to industrialize China to the fullest at the earliest opportunity. These groups also spoke to the need for agrarian reform, but it was implicit in their planning that agrarian reform could not be financed at the same time as the program of industrialization, and that agrarian welfare must take second place to the broad program of urban industrialization. This program envisioned the export of minerals and agricultural products as providing the foreign exchange to finance industrialization, and foreign capital was expected to participate in such programs. An opposition view held to the classical Chinese position that as an agrarian society China should have only such industry as was imperative, and that this must be introduced only at such a rate that it would not disrupt

Chinese society. The view of the Communist Party in China openly spoke to the aim of creating a Communist state, urged agrarian reform in explicit terms, and spoke vaguely of the economic reconstruction of China. To Communist planners that reconstruction clearly included industrialization, but public propaganda rested squarely upon the matter of agrarian reform. It now is a matter of historical record that Mao Tze-tung understood the basis for political support in agrarian China better than did Chiang Kai-shek, so that the Communist Party came to power on the strength of its promise of agrarian reform. The peasantry of China could understand that promise. Once in power, of course, the Communist Party maneuvered the nationalization of land, and set the captive agrarian labor force to work at increased intensity in agricultural production to supply the capital for industrialization, using many of the plans of Sun Yat-sen, plans of the Nationalist Government, and newly developed plans made possible by urgent mineral resources surveys.

The industrial program of China took into account the off center pattern of earlier developments and the inadequacy of the transport network, going back to an old economic principle that regional units of China should be as self-sufficient as possible. China was divided into a series of economic regions and work commenced to create major industrial centers in each (Fig. 25.7). Previous patterns of development could not be ignored, so that coastal cities and the former Japanese industrial cities in Manchuria were made the lead centers, both for actual production and for the training of a skilled labor force. The most important industrial region is that of Shenyang(Mukden)–Fushun–Anshan, followed by the Hangchou–Shanghai–Nanking area, both being centers of pre-Communist development. Ranking third is the Tientsin–T'angshan–Peiping region, actually one of the earliest

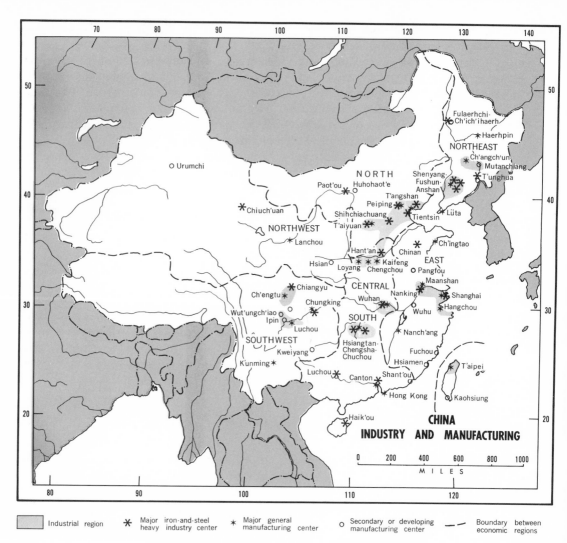

FIGURE 25.7. Industry and manufacturing in China.

areas of modern manufacturing. South and west of Tientsin many old handicraft manufacturing cities have been turned into modern industrial cities, as the region has expanded. Wuhan, in central China, had developed a substantial industrial labor force in the prewar period, but has been turned into the fourth ranking industrial region.

Although a number of other cities had small concentrations of manufacturing, and small totals of skilled labor in the prewar era,

their elevation into higher status has been relatively recent, and they have developed little maturity. Each major industrial center is planned to have iron and steel manufacturing facilities as the base pattern with secondary forms of manufacturing and by-product integration as rapidly as possible. Each such planned industrial region has both coal and iron ores within local transport range, to support the basic heavy industries. Labor forces can be moved about as needed in the evolutionary development of particular industries, having received the technical training at some existing plant in another region. The nature of secondary industries, industrial plants using by-products as raw materials, and complementary manufacturing patterns depends considerably upon the general availability of raw materials other than coal and iron ore. Thus, the southern Canton area shows less manufacturing in heavy machinery, mining equipment, and railway materials than Wuhan, in central China, and aims more at the manufacture of consumer products that can be exported to foreign markets through Hong Kong. Paot'ou, on the upper Yellow River, is a new basic heavy industry city that by the late 1960's still had not gone far beyond its initial development of iron and steel manufacturing, since in earlier years this city had been a caravan terminal for the overland central Asian trade. Most of its industrial work force was trained in Manchuria and transferred to the new city to begin operations in the new plants. In coming years secondary and complementary manufacturing will develop, by plan, around Paot'ou, to round out the industrial program. Lanchou, in the northwest at the inner end of the Kansu Corridor, is developing into a scientific research city carrying on petroleum refining, instrument manufacture, light machinery manufacture, and general consumer goods manufacturing without having iron and steel as its basic support.

Chinese industrial development shows considerable ecologic fitting to the patterns of population and to the distribution of resources. In that wide distribution of resources permits the scattering of basic manufacturing industries, China will be spared the economic differential that has always accompanied manufacturing in the United States with its "slightly higher west of the Rockies" small print disclaimer of consumer bargains. In that the population of China is most heavily concentrated in the eastern portion of the country, it is natural that the largest number of developed industrial regions, and planned major heavy industry centers should be in the east. Shenyang, Shanghai, Tientsin, and Wuhan will continue to be very strong regional centers of all kinds of manufacturing in the future. The pre-World War II industrial labor force probably did not exceed 2,500,000 in all. The war years scattered that labor force widely over China. Mobility of industrial labor remains a planned element in contemporary industry and in future development, entirely possible in such a political structure as that of China. The industrial labor force, in the late 1960's, had grown to a figure of over 60,000,000, and the training programs are continuing. By and large the industrial labor force is a young one, chronologically, with a strong concentration in the 25–40 age bracket.

FOREIGN AND DOMESTIC TRADE

Trade, like industry in the classic concept, was an occupation to be held to the minimum consistent with the satisfactory operation of an agricultural society. Contact with the far ends of the earth naturally involved contributions of products from the outer areas to the Chinese capital, since all outer territories were considered tributary thereto. These shipments took the form of tribute sent by periodic political missions, with return gifts made by the Chinese court. On the side there usually was considerable barter and exchange of products by all such missions, to make life interesting. With the barbarian tribes immediately surrounding China there usually was some informal trade arranged for by the Chinese, not so much to make a profit as to secure a distribution of Chinese goods among the border peoples and perhaps limit the threats of invasion. The earlier organization of the Chinese government reveals no provision for trade administration, and there was no office corresponding to the United States cabinet position of the Secretary of Commerce. This provision never was made and, in the end, the occidental traders were forced to make their own arrangements, which eventually grew into the present Customs Bureau, and the Postal Administration. This is an oversimplified statement, but it indicates the directional orientation of historic Chinese thinking about foreign trade. But despite all restrictions trade and the traders flourished, for the Chinese love of bargaining and the acquisitive instincts are strong.

Domestic Trade

Exchange ranged from local community barter to secular interregional trade and to tax-in-kind tribute grain shipments. The self-sufficient local handicraft economy involved constant community barter and exchange on a small but active scale. This statement can only be a crude generalization. The traditional imperial road system did not facilitate overland transport of goods, so that local self-sufficiency, within *hsien* (county) limits often held true, and transport costs on such short hauls were not exorbitant. For areas possessing water transport facilities much longer hauls were within cost limits. Cities drew grain from their hinterlands, but one limit on the size of older cities was the availability of low-cost grains and other staple food items. The tribute grain shipments to provincial capitals and to the imperial capital did not face transport-cost limits as did secular trade commodities. Special commodities in food, jewelry, clothing, art goods, medicines, and charms circulated all over China to be purchased regularly by the upper classes and upon festival occasions by the lower classes. Besides the regular shops of the large village, town, or city, the agencies that handled internal trade were the guild, the periodic fair, the middleman, and the itinerant peddler. Trade guilds

in effect took the place of the American Chamber of Commerce, Better Business Bureau, Growers' Association, and Interstate Commerce Commission. Guild houses served as clearing houses on financial settlements, warehouses, offices, and hotels for traveling members, and as forwarding agents and commission houses for merchants operating from a distance. The middleman performed much as does the American commission agent. These two agencies handled what might be termed the wholesale trade, as well as some of the retail business. The village fair was seasonal or periodic, depending upon the region, and most effectively functioned among communities too small for permanent shops or guild branches. The itinerant peddler is found all over China, in city and rural countryside, each with his distinctive sound identification, handling retail trade of the smallest caliber and including every kind of product. Although the modern bank, corporation, and department store have cut into the upper segment of urban domestic trade, the above pattern still operates everywhere in China today. Once modern transport systems became established, the traditional local self-sufficiency element began to break down, and secular trade goods began moving in much larger volumes to distant markets against a new pattern of cost-distance limits. Communist economic controls have introduced a whole new system of equating exchanges above the private level, new transport facilities were made available, the programs of industrialization at forced draft got under way, and new concepts of mobility for both persons and goods were introduced. A certain element of regional self-sufficiency, then, remains.

Foreign Trade

The first century of Chinese trade with Europe saw China gradually accustom herself to selling the European such natural monopoly products as tea, silk, and art goods. More recently exports have included minerals and nonmonopoly agricultural products. That there have been a succession of new export items has been China's good fortune. As previously suggested, these monopolies have been broken, one by one, followed by declining trade in each. Although there has been an increase in total exports over the decades it has not been adequate for China's needs, since, for the most part, it has been made up of cheap agricultural produce and raw minerals. On the other hand, the imports into China steadily increased, once the Chinese acquired a taste for machine-made, occidental products. The import total has risen more rapidly than the export total, giving an increasing divergence in the trade balance. The war years, 1937–1945, naturally reduced all exports and imports of civilian goods and caused a huge increase in military imports, to further worsen the trade balance and require heavy borrowing abroad.

In the early post-war period the Nationalist Government encouraged homeward remittances from overseas-Chinese, and restricted import of luxury goods by foreign firms which were being sold to the rich to be used for speculation in an inflationary market. Other measures also conserved the limited sources of foreign exchange for investment in the program of industrialization by which Nationalist China sought to achieve her own program of modernization. When Communist control replaced Nationalist control in China, and international cold-war politics replaced earlier patterns, China was temporarily restrained from trading with some sectors of the West and had temporarily to develop more trade with the U.S.S.R. As the Russian trade lessened, China developed trade relations with eastern Europe and began barter trade agreements with numerous other countries. If the restraint becomes long-time full embargo, China's foreign trade

patterns will become peculiar ones, but, if relaxation of restraint occurs, a marked development of trade will be resumed, its nature dependent upon political factors and open markets. The present trends are toward relaxation, but no clear pattern has yet emerged.

The Chinese provided the West with a market for a period of time, and it is one that the West now misses. If it is restored in our lifetime, it is one that will have to be judiciously cultivated with careful long-range planning on all sides, and with a careful program by the West. The Chinese now have a consumer interest in almost all the material goods of the West, but, in order to buy them, China must export. Until Chinese modernization has developed some momentum, there will be only a limited range of products available for export.

Chinese trade has moved through many ports, but a few stand out in dominant position. Shanghai has frequently handled nearly 50 percent of all foreign trade, Lüta is the chief Manchurian port, Tientsin and Ch'ingtao serve North China, and Canton handles the major share of South China trade. Hong Kong serves as a forward export point for a considerable share of the export of consumer goods, and as a center handling imports from countries that do not do much direct trade with China.

The commodities of export in the past were, in order, and subject to some yearly variation: soybeans and products, tung oil, silk, egg products, tea, raw cotton, coal, pig bristles, hides and skins, tin, wool and camel's hair, tungsten, and antimony ores. Recently in addition to the above items, cement, cotton textiles, art goods, pork products, and even rice have been exports. Excepting Hong Kong, which has been a special kind of center for Chinese trade, the direction of this trade in recent years has been toward Japan, Southeast Asia, Great Britain,

West Germany, and France, roughly in that order. Many hoped that Nationalist Government post-war China would be able to take over the Japanese export trade to southern and eastern Asia, and undoubtedly Communist leaders would like trade with that part of the world to grow as China becomes able to provide the economic grades of products acceptable to that market.

Chinese imports since 1930 have been scattered over the whole range of world trade products, after a long period of importation of consumer goods. Despite Communist tactics and foreign embargoes China will continue to require petroleum, unfabricated metals, foods, rubber, fibers, timber, and such manufactured articles as finished machinery, tools, and industrial equipment. China has purchased whole manufacturing plants in the chemical and fertilizer fields. In more recent years there have been large fertilizer imports. In the direction of purchasing Southeast Asia could stand high, supplying rice and other foods, petroleum, ores, rubber and fibers, and the balance of her imports will come from that part of the world which best cooperates with China's needs. It was to be expected that Japan would continue to play a large role in both the import and export trade of China, since both China and Japan would have to buy cheaply whenever possible, if they are to buy at all. Chinese foreign trade, since 1949, has been markedly affected by political issues, and there have been ups and downs in annual trade volumes with particular countries, according to the level of political accord. In 1968–1969, the Chinese trade volume with little Albania, a political ally, was almost twice that with huge U.S.S.R., with whom China then had poor political relations. There also is an arbitrariness about Chinese foreign trade patterns, reflecting both central planning and political policy; wheat imports were stopped in 1956, but

commenced again in 1960, continuing for different years with different countries. In 1967–1968 China exported rice to pay for fertilizers from Japan despite a none-too-good crop year.

MODERNIZATION PROCESSES

The last century has thrown Chinese society into the greatest cultural turmoil since the formation of the empire over 2,000 years ago. Earlier it was suggested that the joint self-centeredness of the Chinese and the occidental provoked a considerable cultural clash. China had met and weathered clashes of culture before the European came. However, with a base beyond the seas and never-ending streams of people who never settled permanently in China as had previous invaders, a surplus of military power, and cultures that were both complex and dynamic, it was inevitable that Chinese Confucian culture should begin to give way. Involved was an about-face from the old frontier entrance in northwest China to a front door upon the Pacific Ocean, symbolic of the full shift in culture. The effects of the impact of the West are everywhere visible in the landscape of China today and in the social and political turmoil of her people. It is clear that the effects have not been equally distributed over China, and that some parts of the country have progressed further in the adjustment of cultures than others. Among many of the coastal urban Chinese something of occidental culture has penetrated deeply, though among others it is but a thin veneer which cracks occasionally to expose the traditional core within. Most rural populations cling to the traditional patterns and there is a reservoir of population yet almost untouched by any visible part of the West. Regionally it appears that the coastal fringe of China has changed most and the Tibetan border least, but the situation is less simple than that. The urban seaports are perhaps the centers of radiation of non-Chinese culture, both material and social. The inland city felt the effects before the coastal village, the banker and merchant before the peasant farmer.

The modern Christian missionary was a tremendous factor in the modernization of China. The movement commenced with straight evangelism; as it grew its effects multiplied. The agricultural, medical, and educational efforts of many mission groups were often begun in order to get clients to whom to preach, but these efforts spread far and wide beyond their original aims. Most agricultural research in China originated in mission work. Similarly, modern Chinese medicine and education arose out of Christian mission programs. And out of the need for hospitals and schools came mission architecture and Chinese contractors, with distinctive effects upon Chinese architecture. The foreign slick paper and pen and ink spread far outside the schoolroom through graduated class members. The need to print evangelical literature produced modern print shops, which finally helped lead to the Chinese newspaper and periodical press. There are endless illustrations of the ramifications of the process.

Another potent agent of modernism was the occidental businessman who used a variety of innocent tricks to induce the purchase of his wares. Bobby pins, cigarettes, or tinned cherries, for example, could in the 1930's be purchased far beyond the limits of European residence and the advertising poster. The appetite for new material goods mushroomed in the last generation, but the process is really only in the beginning.

Not least among the agents of change have been the Chinese who went abroad. The letters home and the remittances of money came first, and then the family members returned with their new traits picked up abroad. Many South China villages and towns clearly show the imprint of money and ideas gained in Indonesia, Malaysia, or the United States.

Change has not been in material terms alone. The mission school book often inculcated a strong brand of patriotism for China along with something that the teacher called democracy but the student failed to understand perfectly. In time there came a wholesale selling of this particular feature, but with it were unequal treaties, the treaty ports, and pinching economic exploitation. There came opium with its deadening effect upon morals, health, and family welfare. There came ideas about labor rights and eventually a labor movement. During the 1920's there was a potent vaccination of Communism into China from the U.S.S.R. which "took" more effectively than did the democratic inoculations of the Christian missionary.

All this change began slowly and worked in small but widening circles. With each decade the volume of new material confronting the Chinese increased. Radio, the airplane, and the atomic bomb came in closer sequence than many of the earlier products. Since 1949 industrialization, something never permitted in traditional China, has begun. Vaccination upon inoculation, and dose after dose, raised a severe fever in the patient. The individualism of the Chinese has seldom permitted sudden country-wide decisions by a few people as was the case in Japan. Not until masses of the Chinese have experienced much of the modern world can there be a satisfactory decision as to what course China will take. The fever still rages but must be allowed to slacken at its own pace. Despite the denunciations of the United States, the West, and any society that displeases China's political leaders, China is adopting a great deal of the newer cultural developments of the West about as rapidly as they accrue. The tremendous amount of culture conflict within China today will require a further period of time to resolve. At first glance Communist control of China seems dictatorial action by a few people. The Chinese have often accepted programs put forward by a small group of leaders, but in the end either have rejected those leaders and their program, or have modified the program in the course of time.

IS THERE A POPULATION LIMIT?

China is the most populous country in the world though the exact figure can neither be stated nor agreed upon. For the purposes of this book the population of greater China is taken as 730,000,000, as of 1969 (Fig. 25.8). Expressed in simple average for all of China, the figure of about 200 per square mile is not impressive. Stated as population per square mile of cultivated land the total is about 1,600. Another type of comparison, used by several writers on China, is illuminating. If a line were drawn from southernmost Yunnan to northernmost Manchuria, some 2,500,000 square miles of territory would lie to the west, along with about 35,000,000 people, whereas on the east there would be about 1,750,000 square miles and almost 700,000,-000 people. Expressed in averages, the eastern section would have about 400 people per square mile of territory, but the agricultural density would not change appreciably. This emphasizes the fact that both the cultivated land and the people of China are placed east of this imaginary line. With a landscape as described in an earlier chapter, that part of the Chinese checkerboard west of the line, and the central Asian lands, is made up of the higher blocks, the rugged parts of mountain massifs, and the high filled basins. All the larger, useful lowland basins lie east of the line, including most of the Szechwan Basin.

The annual rate of increase in population

seems rather high, if current estimates are at all reliable. The total volume of increase for present-day China is among the highest in the world, with a recent annual excess of births over deaths of perhaps 15,000,000 a year. It raises the question as to how much longer it can possibly continue. Useful data are scant throughout all of historic time and always have been made unreliable by the Chinese peasantry's fear that truth telling to inquirers can only end in heavier tax burdens. Interpretation of Chinese history would suggest that the hearth area became a population center with several accompanying minor concentrations, and that China has not really been filled up until rather recently. Over the centuries ascribed totals are: 5,000,000 in 1600 B.C.; 35,000,000 in the first century A.D.; 45,000,000 in the early eighth century; 60,000,000 in 1400 A.D.; 180,000,000 in 1750; 295,000,000 in 1800; 400,000,000 in 1900; and 730,000,000 in 1969.

These figures indicate that China has long been among the world's more populous regions, but they indicate too that the modern totals show a tremendous increase over earlier ones, and that several stimulating factors have been at work within the last century or two. China shares this recent increase with the rest of the world. The effect of American crop plants and large-volume foreign trade has been mentioned. A potent factor has been modern curative and preventive medicine as brought to China by the Christian medical missionary and spread into wide Chinese acceptance. This has reduced the impact of endemic and epidemic diseases. Another factor of unanswerable but significant results is the discouragement of infanticide, a custom today relatively unpracticed. Modern transportation, and flood and famine relief projects, have reduced perennial limitations. Civil wars probably are less effective checks today than formerly. Until China filled up and put to use most of

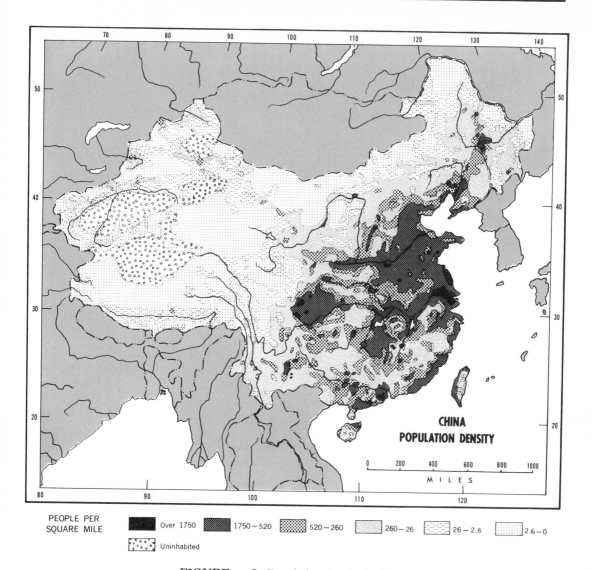

PEOPLE PER SQUARE MILE — Over 1750 — 1750–520 — 520–260 — 260–26 — 26–2.6 — 2.6–0 — Uninhabited

FIGURE 25.8. Population density in China.

her cultivated land, increases in population usually made for a higher level of living, since they were accompanied by new bases of material culture. As suggested earlier, there are those that feel that China has been suffering a decreasing level of living, becoming a marginal-existence producer of low-cost agricultural export products only. The stimulating factors of the last two centuries may have run their courses without any effective new bases of support coming into operation.

The growth process still sweeps forward, however, and it raises the question as to whether China has outgrown her natural environment. Self-sufficient agriculture and widespread handicraft production were the historic sources of income. Industrialization has been held to be the answer to this kind of problem, and it has worked so far. China is now undergoing industrialization, and if the program matures rapidly enough, it may relieve the pressure as well as raise the level of living. But for how long at present growth rates? China is in a dilemma and is debating a program to follow in the future. Unless agreement upon the aims and plans of Chinese society can allow effective mobilization, it is conceivable that the consequent unrest could unleash "the Four Horsemen" to start a real balancing operation. In Communist economic theory, production rates are raised as needed to meet increasing population and consumer demands. The theory suggests no maximum limit on growth patterns. In 1956 measures were taken to limit the birth rate, but they ran into political trouble and the public campaign was shelved. More recently efforts at control over population increase have taken forms which do not clash with Communist economic theory such as urging the postponement of marriage, having fewer children simply because smaller families are happier families, and similar kinds of arguments. Quietly progressing, without public fanfare, are various other measures aimed at population limitation, but their actual effectiveness cannot be measured on the short term.

THE REGIONALISM OF MODERN CHINA

It is customary for the rest of the world to speak of the Chinese and China as though everyone were alike and the country one homogeneous geographic region. An effort has been made to show how the several densely populated lowland basins are set apart by strips of negative mountain highland, how soil and climate divide China, and how culture history has added to the variations (Fig. 25.9). There is something in Chinese culture that tended to negate the harmful impact of these natural regional divisions upon society. Perhaps part of it

lies in the common written language that transcended all the bounds of spoken languages. Perhaps it is summed up in the Chinese proverb, "Within the four seas all men are brothers," applying to the Chinese realm only. It is worth noting that the large subcontinent of China historically has possessed far more unity than the smaller subcontinent called Europe. The temporary disunity of modern China often blinds the occidental to this regional unity that is a part of the cultural continuity of China.

The motives for regionalism in China are soundly based on the natural environment and have been historically developed over the centuries. The earliest distinctions between occupants of the culture hearth and the barbarians were matters both of material and social culture, growing slowly into regionalisms. The process of spreading over China, imposing Chinese culture, and absorbing the crops and customs of the conquered non-Chinese seriously mixed up the simple early distinctions that divided the cultured from the barbarian. Despite this intermixing, regional distinctions are quite clear to the Chinese themselves.

The proverb "In Szechwan the dogs bark when the sun shines" is matched by the name of Yunnan province, "South of the Clouds," both rather limited but effective characterizations. Shansi province for good reason is the recognized butt of the Chinese "Scotch" joke. Tientsin wheat noodles and Canton white rice are two major poles in a complicated pattern of regional dietary distinctions. "The south is sweet, the north is salt; the east is sour, and the west is hot," referring to the four respective predominant food flavorings of sugar, salt, vinegar, and chili pepper has no basis in climate, soil, crop patterns, or ethnic mix, but it remains very real. Fukien faces the sea, and its separate river valleys are subregions of a physical and cultural province that turns its back on China and is the most sea-conscious

CHINA'S   REGIONALISMS

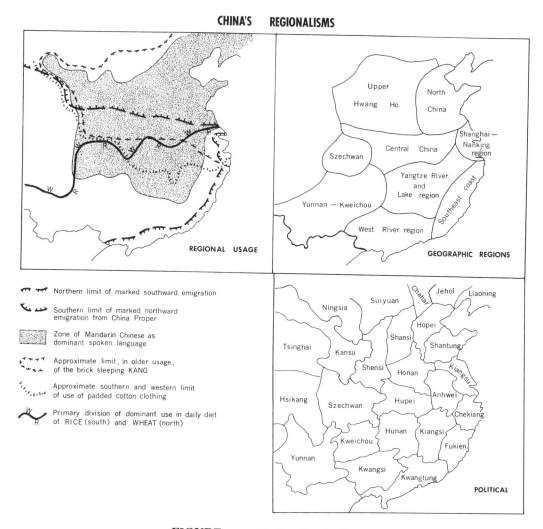

FIGURE 25.9. Regionalism in China.

of any section of the country. What seems significant here is that, although the Chinese even appear to foster certain of their regionalisms, in some way they never let them get out of hand to become separating factors, as happened in Europe. Modern Chinese regionalisms resemble the friendly, good-natured sectionalism of California, Texas, and Brooklyn.

The political divisions of early China repeatedly shifted about but gradually settled into a system of fairly fixed regions that has

been stable for centuries in some parts of China and is still being formulated in others (Fig. 25.10; compare Figs. 25.9 and 25.10 with 24.3). Under early Manchu rule China was divided into fewer provinces than at present. In part the provincial boundaries were arbitrary lines drawn for administrative convenience across a section of landscape that possessed few good natural boundaries. Others are the crystallized acceptance of environmental lines that appealed to the common people who made up and administered

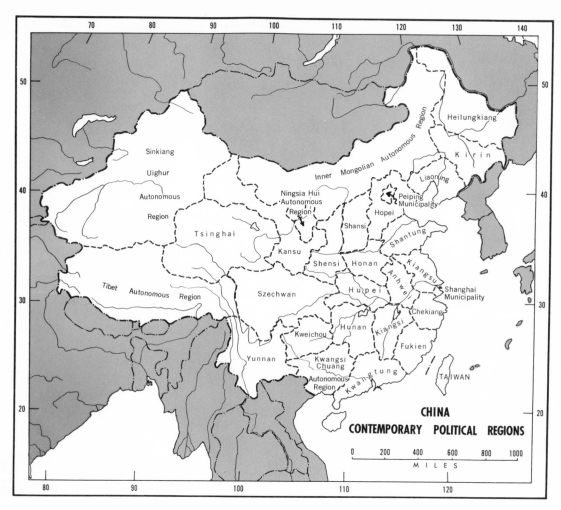

FIGURE 25.10. Contemporary political regions of China.

China. As such they usually are drawn through the negative zones surrounding the several positive nuclei. As Manchu China grew more populous, boundaries in the marginal parts of the empire were formally delimited. In the central portion of the empire, often termed China Proper, the lines are significant of many things, but in Outer China they are still ephemeral and subject to change. The compounding of human events has been too fluctuating in a landscape in many places lacking sharp natural divisions to allow closely drawn lines that stay put.

The temporary Communist organization of a new province in the North China Plain reflected a population pressure and local administrative problems of modern development; the arrangement did not solve the problem, and boundaries reverted to their former positions as the best practical solution.

Modern China is a complex group of cultures, regions, physical zones, and psychological concepts. Within the old China proper one could do worse than to accept the old administrative boundaries employed by the last Chinese Imperial Government (as given on Fig. 25.9). Accenting the subjective re-action of human events to the physical land-scape, the provincial boundaries serve reason-ably well and accord with statistical sum-maries. Most of these lines mean more than do the boundaries of Nebraska, Wyoming, Colorado, and Kansas. The so-called geo-graphical region, setting more emphasis upon crops, climate, vegetation, and land-forms, produces a map with some agreement with, and some divergence from, the political region. Other selective criteria can be used to draw still different maps.

TAIWAN

In the elaborate fictional parlance of the United Nations Taiwan has no individual identity, mainland China is outside the pale, and Taiwan is the Republic of China. Taiwan is a thriving island entity of not quite 14,000 square miles in area lying 100 miles off the Asian mainland, with an early-1970 popula-tion of about 14,400,000. Technically, the territory presently under the jurisdiction of the government of Taiwan, the Republic of China, includes 99 islands in all; Taiwan Island itself; the 13 marginal islets im-mediately off the Taiwan shores comprising 31 square miles; the Penghu Islands, or Pes-cadores, involving 64 islands and islets comprising 50 square miles lying thirty-odd miles off the west coast of Taiwan; the 12 islands normally given the single name Quemoy, lying off the harbor of Hsiamen (Amoy) on the southern Fukien coast of mainland China, with a total of 60 square miles; and the 9 islands normally given the single name Matsu, lying off the harbor of Fuchou on the central Fukien coast of main-land China, with a total of about 20 square miles.

Taiwan Island is a bastion on the series of island arcs that fringe the Asian mainland, but the island itself is a great tilted, unstable, fault-block standing on the edge of the continental shelf. Broadly speaking the island can be divided into two sections, a complex eastern unit of folded, faulted mountain ranges of old hard rock with enclosed struc-tural valleys and a precipitous volcanic mountain range fronting on the Pacific Ocean to the east; and a low and sloping foothill-coastal plain unit on the west, with steep-gradient streams draining the moun-tains across the flat, alluvial coastal plain. In detail the eastern unit may be divided into several physiographic sections; similarly the western unit may be subdivided into several sections, for the foothills are not continuous and there are valley units that stand apart and, in the north, the coastal plain is dis-continuous. Very roughly, the island has a radial drainage pattern, though the longest streams drain to the north, west, and south. The main mountain mass has many peaks over 10,000 feet altitude, a cover of glacial debris masks the western flanks, and the soils of much of the western coastal plain contain water worn cobbles. The foothill and coastal plain unit of the island encompasses about a third of the total area. Climatically, Taiwan is best described as humid subtropical; the lowlands have a warm, year-long growing season, but the higher parts of the island reach into microthermal winter conditions. Originally Taiwan probably possessed a sub-tropical broadleaf forest cover, but most of that is gone today from the lowland areas and the lower hill ranges. Some coal, copper, sulphur, gold, and a little petroleum com-prise the mineral resources of the island, and the hydroelectric potential is relatively large.

Taiwan still possesses small and remnant groups of Indonesian peoples who comprised the very early migrants along the island arcs. These chiefly occupy the mountain upland today. Chinese off the Asian mainland have been active immigrants into Taiwan since the fifteenth century. During the mid-seventeenth century large numbers of ref-ugees migrated to Taiwan to escape the

Manchu takeover of mainland China, but the mainland government extended its reach to Taiwan late in the seventeenth century to include all the islands within the Chinese state. Intermittently migrants from the mainland continued to come to Taiwan, chiefly from the Fukien coastal zone during the eighteenth and early nineteenth centuries. European contacts with Taiwan were intermittent and in conflict, after the Portuguese arrival in the late sixteenth century (the name Formosa is from the Portuguese name for the island) with Portuguese, Spanish, and Dutch the contestants, until the Manchus incorporated the island into their mainland empire in the 1680's. Taiwan remained a marginal sector during Manchu time, with little direct attention, though colonists received the same treatment here as on the mainland when taking up new land for agricultural development. Most of the immigrants from the mainland came from different parts of the Fukien coast, some from the Kwangtung coast, and a minority from elsewhere in China. Normally they settled in localities already having people from similar homelands, so that by the late nineteenth century the island possessed a wide variety of cultural regionalisms correlating with those of the mainland coastal zone. There were at least seven different spoken languages employed. Agricultural occupance was scattered along the western coastal plain, with the largest concentration in the southern sector. The chief crop was rice, complemented by sugarcane and tea, all of which were produced in surplus amounts, yielding sizable exports to the mainland.

Japan took control of Formosa in 1895, after the first Sino-Japanese War, and proceeded to develop its agricultural resources rapidly. Considerable economic development had taken place in the last decade of Chinese control, as the island had been made a separate province and provided with an able governor. Japanese economic development concentrated first on facilitating the expansion of rice and sugarcane, whose export went to Japan. Irrigation facilities on the coastal plain made possible the extension of wet-field rice production, road development facilitated transport, and hydroelectric power generation provided processing plants with energy. Japanese development was aimed at permanent control of Taiwan, and at the Japanization of the population. An educational system involved teaching Japanese in the schools and Japanese became the *lingua franca* of the island.

In the 1930's the increase in hydroelectric power made possible the beginning industrialization of the island, involving the reduction of aluminum ores, refining of some of the ferroalloys, some iron and steel manufacturing, the refining of copper, and beginnings in the chemical industries. These developments were complementary to Japanese home industry, utilizing the island's power resources and cheap labor supplies.

Taiwan and the Penghu Islands were returned to China in 1945 at the end of World War II. Upon Communist supremacy on the mainland, an estimated 2,000,000 refugees migrated to Taiwan in 1949 and the early 1950's, reminiscent of the movement in the seventeenth century, but drawn from a wider range of provincial origins. The government of Nationalist China migrated *en masse*, setting up a government-in-exile on Taiwan, using precedent of European patterns from early World War II. The United States has both defended Taiwan from potential mainland attack since 1950, and has poured large sums of money into Taiwan to facilitate economic development. American aid has not been purely financial, for large efforts have gone into stimulating social and economic agrarian reform, the expansion of public health facilities, the expansion of educational facilities, and the further development of transportation and communications.

In the fourteenth century the population of Taiwan may have been in the vicinity of 250,000. By 1905, the date of the first Japanese census, the population stood at just under 3,000,000. In 1945 the population stood close to 6,500,000, but by 1956 the population had risen close to 9,500,000, after the repatriation of 350,000 Japanese and a large influx of military and civilian emigrants from the mainland. The early population distribution patterns were chiefly rural village concentrations, and urban places remained chief market centers and coastal ports. Under Japanese controls urban development began to produce larger towns and cities. Since 1945 the patterns of urbanism have increased rather markedly, and Taiwan is about to go through a strong trend in urbanization. In 1956 there were six cities of over 100,000 each; in 1969 there were eleven such cities and the Taipei metropolitan area included over 1,700,000. The population is essentially a young one, and formal population control mechanisms now are part of the public health program since the population still is growing at well over two percent per year.

Taiwan, despite its simple arithmetic density of over a thousand people per square mile, now has only a small majority of its labor force involved in agricultural production, and Taiwanese agriculture is an intensive semimechanized gardening system with a highly integrated cropping system that comes close to two crops per year as a general average. There are about 1,000,000 farms, comprising about 2,200,000 acres, planted to about 4,100,000 acres of crop each year, with some lands producing three crops per year. The use of small-powered tractors, tillers, threshers, and other forms of mechanical equipment is becoming a significant productive element in the agricultural economy. Rice is the chief crop, planted on about 2,000,000 acres per year. Sweet potatoes are planted on about 600,000 acres per year, sugarcane, vegetables, and peanuts are each planted on about 250,000 acres per year, tea occupies only about 100,000 acres as a perennial crop, and over a dozen other crops fill out the primary agricultural pattern. Sugar, tea, bananas, citrus, and pineapple are large-acreage export crops, but some of the small-acreage crops, such as mushrooms and asparagus, now are also important export products. A considerable share of the minor crops, in acreage, involves crops with a high economic yield per acre. The land being put into agriculture is still rising in total, but the reserve land now available is chiefly marginal land, and the agricultural economy of Taiwan cannot expand much further; instead any added development will need to be in increased intensification or into high-yield crops using small amounts of land. Although Taiwan still is exporting some sugar and rice, the total food import (chiefly wheat and soybean products) now averages about fifteen percent of the total food production so that, in net terms, the island no longer is feeding itself. As agriculture intensifies further in high-yield crop specialties the basic food import will trend upward.

There has been a very marked expansion of two other aspects of Taiwan's economic development. Fishing has long been an occupation along the west coast, using small boats for in-shore fishing, or raising fish in ponds. Recent development has greatly added to the commercial fishing fleet, as well as to the pond-raising of fishery products, so that the 1969 catch was about 475,000 tons, about fifteen percent of which came from pond-raising activity. This increase about doubles the return of a decade ago. The other line of development is in wood products. The camphor extract from wild forest trees was one thing Taiwan was noted for a century ago, and it still continues as a minor economic element. Although various special woods have long been extracted from the Taiwan forests for export purposes, very little commercial lumbering took place on the island until very recently. Selective logging and the careful handling of the timber cut finds an annual product plus significant imports going into plywood and other refined wood products, with a manufactured export volume now occurring every year.

There are about 11,000 miles of highway on Taiwan, and some 950 miles of rail line, with a part of the west-coast main line double tracked. Extensive bus services carry a huge passenger traffic and the rail lines serve large volumes of passengers and haul large amounts of freight. Numerous airfields provide internal transport connections, and Taiwan maintains an international airline providing external connections.

Since 1953, in addition to the large amount of United States aid given Taiwan, about $425,600,000 has been invested in Taiwan's economic development by overseas Chinese and foreign investors from the United States, Japan, Canada, France, West Germany, and Australia. Much of the aid money and most of the above sum have gone into the development of industrial enterprises, the largest lines of which have been electronics and the chemicals industries, with a wide scattering in general manufacturing. The industrial development of Taiwan shows a very wide range at the present time, from the basic iron and steel industries through machinery manufacture, textiles, electronics, fertilizers, chemicals, electric appliances, and wood products. A significant share of many of the products are now being consumed in Taiwan itself, and such items as refrigerators and washing machines have become common necessities rather than luxury items. The chief exports in 1968 were textiles, electrical manufactures, and manufactured wood products, and the manufactured export volume was almost double the value of all agricultural exports.

Most political reference to Taiwan concerns the issues of continued independence and further relations to Mainland China.

There are, however, some internal issues, in that many of the Chinese resident on Taiwan prior to 1949 feel rather strongly that the 1949 refugee elements from the mainland have forcibly taken over control of the island, have dominated its patterns of development, and have unilaterally dictated its cultural orientation. This may pass in a generation, or the attitudes may continue to be divisive elements in internal politics. Whatever the future political fortunes of Taiwan may be, the quiet little island of former centuries has turned into a populous and busy island in the present century with a high level of living, a comparatively high per capita annual income, and plans for an active industrial future, closely connected to the trade and tourist routes of the whole world.

HONG KONG AND MACAO

In 1945 there were two small territories left that had not reverted to China: Hong Kong and Macao. These remain under British and Portuguese governance, respectively, and it appears convenient to China to allow them both to continue under alien rule. Hong Kong appears to thrive under its somewhat uncertain status despite the expiration of the lease on the New Territories in 1997. Although the New Territories have been primarily agricultural in the past, the expansion of the new manufacturing districts has been largely in that sector, and urban patterns are spreading inland behind Kowloon. We have included Hong Kong in the discussion of metropolitan cities, earlier, and no added comment is here called for (see Fig. 4.10 and accompanying text, pp. 96–98).

Macao remains an Overseas Province of Portugal, a rather densely inhabited urban entity of six square miles and about 300,000 inhabitants. Long a quiet and leisurely backwater, Macao now is following the lead of Hong Kong, with a growing industrial program aimed at modern economic development.

26

KOREA, THE LAND BETWEEN

A PENINSULA OF HILLS

Korea presents one of the hilliest landscapes in the world. Few landforms are outstanding since only one volcanic mountain, Paektu-san, with its white rock crest resembling perennial snow, reaches 9,000 feet in height far to the north on the Manchurian border. Only some thirty-six peaks exceed 7,000 feet, most of which are in northern Korea. The highland spinal cord runs southward from Paektu-san along the east coast, with ridges tapering off to the west and south to fill the whole peninsula. The uplands reach into southern Korea, which has some crests higher than 6,000 feet. Almost every lowland plain is so small that hills are a part of the landscape. Small patches of lowland are scattered around the coastal fringe, the largest occurring on the west coast.

The higher north country is a cold, rocky, and rather grim region, surfaced with volcanic lavas, covered with coniferous forests, and deeply notched by river gorges and canyons. The narrow east coast is but a slim shelf set between the mountains and the sea. Most Korean rivers are short, drain south and westward, and empty into deep estuaries that would form many good harbors were it not for the high tidal ranges. Locally west-coast tides exceed 30 feet, whereas those of the east coast seldom exceed 3 feet. All along the west and south coast are hundreds of islands, which nearly double the length of the long coastline. The south-facing valleys and coastal plains of southernmost Korea are the mildest and most hospitable part of the country.

The hilly and divided Korean landscape contains some very beautiful and picturesque scenery, but it presents a rather formidable environment to the 42,000,000 Koreans. The East Manchurian Highlands set a barrier between the peninsula and the Asian mainland which is increased by the canyon of the Yalu River. One might look to this peninsular environment for a story of continued isolation such as Korea tried to maintain during the seventeenth and nineteenth centuries. However, the peninsula stands between the northern mainland of China and the Japanese Island Arcs. As the land between two regions of active cultural development, Korea has been subject to the expanding energies of both.

On the one hand, Korea was the land link in the long-continued contacts of China and Japan, but, on the other, the Koreans have been mauled in the struggles for control of the peninsula (Fig. 26.1). Throughout this hilly country inviting spots have always attracted man. None is very large, nor has Korea possessed extremely high value in soils, useful plants, or climatic assets. Not an outstanding assemblage of local regions, Korea nevertheless has been made into a productive territory by the diligent efforts of its peoples.

THE PEOPLE OF KOREA

It is hard to distinguish the diverse human elements that have combined to produce the modern Koreans. Far from being a single racial type, the Koreans are a heterogeneous people. Into their racial history has gone a little of almost every known east Asian group, plus a number of unknown components. Within the historic period the additions have been Chinese, Mongol, and Tungus-speaking peoples as well as Japanese blends. The Japanese blends are a complex factor, however, for a rather important element in Japanese racial development itself has been the Korean one. Korea always has been a connecting link between the mainland and the island world. Refugee colonists, invading conquerors, temporary residents, and passers-through have left their mark upon the present inhabitants of Korea.

This process began when man first started to migrate about eastern Asia and has continued to the present time. Despite the constant mixture, one can distinguish between northern and southern Koreans. In general, northwestern Koreans possess more Chinese and Tungus elements than do other sections, and southern Koreans possess more Japanese elements. Several different language groupings were once present but were never mutually unintelligible. Basically there is just one language in Korea today though there are several different dialectic versions, the result of long-term regionalism. These simple differences were lessened in the past, however, by a rather closely unified group psychology, surrounded by a culture that has borrowed much on all sides but somehow managed to develop an extremely distinctive individuality of its own.

THE ROAD TO JAPAN

The Koreans take real pride in the age of their own culture, but there is little that is purely Korean about the earliest culture history of this region. It shared the ideas and traits of all early eastern Asia and gave many of them a local twist. At the end of the Manchurian littoral extension of North China, northwestern Korea became a marginal part of that pattern at an early date. But northern Korea adjoined the forested and mountainous East Manchurian Highlands, and so shared in a second pattern of culture. The southern coast, however, had affiliations with the Island Arcs and the separate growth of a third culture. There was no great distance between the margins of these zones of influence. Although it is difficult to date, this linking must have occurred in informal and unplanned ways long before the beginning of the Christian era. The first known and conscious contact of China with Japan occurred through Korea just before the start of the Christian era.

Chinese movement toward Korea was an intermittent process. As feudal strife in classical China sharpened toward the final struggle and organization of the empire in the third century B.C., dissident elements sought refuge in the surrounding regions. The Korean Peninsula was one of these, and numerous Chinese refugees scattered into vacant localities or were given sanctuary by resident tribal peoples. Within a century this leavening effect began to show in a quickening and development within the peninsula itself. Formal Chinese contact came first in northwest Korea in the late second century B.C. as the Chinese Han empire expanded eastward along the Manchurian littoral. Several frontier districts were set up taking in the

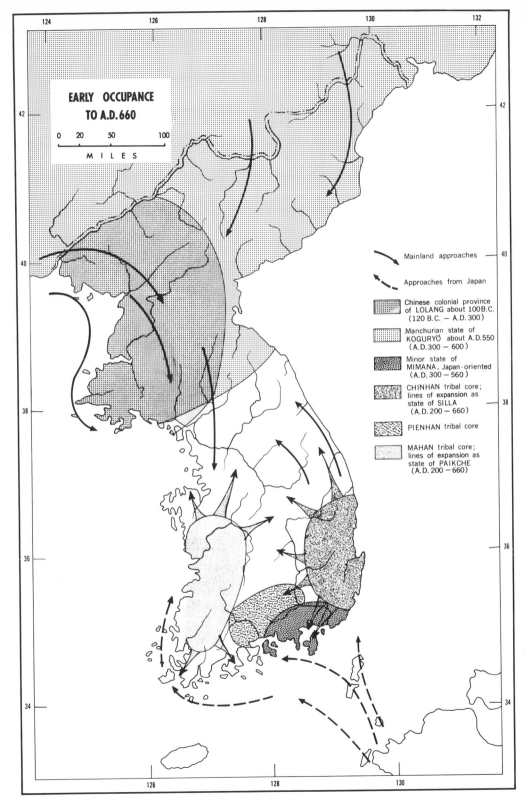

FIGURE 26.1. Early occupance of Korea, to A.D. 660.

561

northwestern half of Korea. As Chinese home strength waxed and waned, so did her influence in and upon Korea. Before the Mongol conquest of Korea, Chinese control never was exerted over the whole peninsula. Only the Mongols tried to go beyond Korea into the Island Arcs. The attention of the Ming Chinese was little drawn to Korea, and Manchu China was satisfied with a tributary Korea. Throughout the historic period the Chinese showed a tolerant and scholarly interest in both Korea and Japan, China playing the role of tutor and donor. Chinese culture actually was enriched by a number of items both from Korea and from Japan.

Conscious Japanese contact with Korea began in the first century B.C., but a link with Chinese culture beyond soon became the chief interest. In the early period contact was by land along the southern and western Korean lowland and through the Manchurian littoral. Later contact was by coastal waters when the Korean principalities became too unruly. Military action became a standard part of the Japanese program to maintain and enlarge the link with China. Japanese attempts to control south Korean principalities seemed less a matter of imperialist expansion than a matter of keeping open the route to China. Japanese headquarters in Korea served as route stations and forwarding offices in this process of culture contact, in which the Japanese definitely were the active agents. Koreans often were intermediary tutors, themselves going in large numbers to Japan. In historical retrospect Koreans usually considered China the benefactor and Japan the interloper, while strongly resisting the efforts of either to control their peninsular regions.

EARLY KOREAN REGIONALISM

The Korea that before 1945 appeared one national unit, divided into thirteen administrative provinces, is a result of a long process of accretion. Earliest Korea seemed to be a land of innumerable tribal groups, each occupying a small, separated lowland, or upland tract in the hilly landscape. Chinese and Japanese influence now hindered one group, now favored another. To skip the earlier outlaw regions, the first regional entity to appear in the Korean Peninsula was the Early Han dynasty border region of Lo-lang, which took in much of the country south of the Yalu River (see Fig. 26.1). South of this lay a march zone serving as a refuge to outlaw Chinese, into which the native tribes began to push from the south.

North of the Yalu lay mountain country in which a northern forest people who had taken up Chinese agriculture and absorbed some Chinese culture organized a petty kingdom that began expanding southward at about the end of the first century B.C. By the early fourth century A.D., the little kingdom had expanded to include southeastern Manchuria, and had taken over the Chinese border region of Lo-lang and the northern section of the march country. China never again directly colonized, controlled, or regularly governed any portion of Korea. The marches became a zone of contest for nearly two centuries between the Sinicized forest-mountain peoples of Koguryö and the growing political groups of southern Korea for nearly two centuries.

At some very early date southern Korea had been occupied by groups of mixed tribal peoples, the Han, customarily divided into three, Chin Han, Pien Han, and Ma Han. The largest elements in these groups now are thought to be derived from Tungusic ethnic stocks of northern interior Asia, but there must have been some southern Asian elements among the tribes since wet-field rice culture gradually became a widespread cropping procedure. The Chin Han occupied the lower east coast, the eastern hill country, and the hill margins of southernmost Korea. They perhaps were the most advanced in culture levels, having a socially stratified population which lived in walled villages, carried on cropping, mined iron ore, and fabricated iron products. By the customary dating for the introduction of iron-working into eastern Asia this would place the arrival of at least the iron-working immigrant elements among the Chin Han as later than the sixth century B.C. The Pien Han tribes held the coastal low country and islands of southernmost Korea. Seemingly least affected by Chinese culture, they were village dwelling, crop-growing, and fishing peoples, had affinities for some of the southern Japanese tribal groups, and probably included some ethnic elements from southern Asia. The Ma Han tribes occupied the southwestern portion of the peninsula, were the most fractionated into divergent tribal elements, were village dwelling and crop-growing, fishing peoples. It is likely that among the Ma Han groups there were also southern Asian elements.

The customary dates for the formal organization of "states" for the Han tribes range from 57 B.C. for the Chin Han initiation of the state of Silla, to 18 B.C. for the Ma Han organization of Paikche, and A.D. 42 for Mimana, the Pien Han state. It is not at all clear whether these first "states" comprised the whole of each set of ethnic stocks, whether leading military tribes forced the pace, nor yet what the initial spatial patterns were. Mimana often came under Japanese influence in the effort of the Japanese to open a route to China, along which a slow filtering of Chinese culture traits was moving. Paikche received intermittent assistance from the Japanese in the struggle against Silla and Koguryŏ, since this also furthered Japanese interests in the route to China. The Silla-Japanese contact seems to have been chiefly one of Japanese pirate raids along the east coast of Korea. Buddhism was introduced into Paikche in the late fourth century A.D. from southern China and it gradually spread among the ethnic elements of all parts of southern Korea. Chinese influences continued to diffuse southward, and political organizational elements were notable in this spread. During the sixth century A.D. Silla effected a strong military-political structuring and began expanding her territorial controls at the expense of both Mimana and Paikche, expanding northward at the same time. As Paikche regressively lost strength and territory, many leaders, artisans, and farmers migrated to Japan, both adding to the Japanese ethnic mix and taking cultural skills with them.

UNITY, HERMITAGE, AND CONQUEST

By the start of the eighth century A.D., Silla had become dominant over the whole of the Korean Peninsula except for a central northern mountain tract, and Mimana, Paikche, and Koguryŏ disappeared as separate political states. Japan, having found a direct sea route to China, caused less trouble for Korea. A period of spatial organization followed, during which some elements of the Chinese political institutional system were installed, along with some elements of Chinese economic systems modeled to some degree after the pattern of T'ang China. The aristocratic rulers of Silla also furthered Mahayana Buddhism, and Buddhist monasteries, temples, and shrines were built all over Korea. The Chinese written language became widely used, but gradually a phonetic code was developed for indicating the pronunciation of Chinese characters, since the Korean spoken language, polysyllabic and very different from Chinese, was ill-adapted to the Chinese written language. As a vassal state of T'ang China, Korea flourished during the T'ang era, but conditions deteriorated in parallel with the dynastic decline of T'ang China in the late ninth century.

The Koryo dynasty re-established Korean

political power in the early middle ninth century, employing a more complete Chinese political system down to the county level of administrative districts, and employing the Chinese civil service system of developing the government bureaucracy. However, a formalized class structure separated the aristocracy from the common rural Korean peasantry. The political history of Korea for several centuries suggests dynastic feuding, political trouble from Manchurian pastoral tribal kingdoms, difficulty from Japanese coastal pirates, and later domination by the Mongols ruling China. The aristocratic political classes taxed the rural peasantry rather heavily, forcing some of the population into virtual serfdom, there were continuing peasant uprisings, the Buddhist monasteries put heavy pressure on the rural agrarian populace, and there was repeated looting and devastation of some local regions by Mongol armies trying to invade Japan. Nevertheless, there was a steady expansion of the agrarian landscape, a steady growth in population, and an increasing development of the internal economy as the simple agricultural system matured into a highly productive and rather intensive gardening system complemented by the use of oxen and plow tool technologies. Between the ninth and fifteenth centuries Korean culture synthesized many aspects of the borrowed Chinese culture complexes and increasingly made them over into a Korean subsystem of culture. The debt to Chinese origins is clearly visible, but in many respects Korean traits, complexes, and systems, by the fifteenth century, showed their divergence from the Chinese models.

Another dynastic shift occurred in Korea, correlating with the fall of the Mongols in China. A new Korean dynastic rulership began by accepting tributary relationship to the Chinese Ming dynasty state. Complete land reform measures wiped out the debts of the past, a new capital city was founded as the forerunner of modern Seoul, a new

Korean written language system was introduced, based on phonetic principles adaptable to spoken Korean, the Buddhist monasteries were reduced in political and economic power, the civil bureaucracy was restructured to a degree, and the basic outlines of the present political districts matured. There still was a strong class structuring maintained and, in some respects, the rural peasantry was tightly bound to the land. During the late fifteenth century population pressures in the south began to be fairly strong, though northern Korea remained relatively lightly populated, and government enforced resettlement programs moved many families northward.

In the late sixteenth century Korea suffered a severe invasion from Japan, though this was really aimed at China. The military operations, tactics, strategy, and destructive patterns were paralleled in the early 1950's by the American-Chinese fighting in central Korea. As the Manchus took over China, Korea suffered somewhat from its support of the Ming dynasty of China, but accepted tributary status to the new Chinese state. Having suffered depredations from both China and Japan, however, Korea began to seek isolation from the outside world. Korean ports were virtually closed to Japanese traders, the Yalu River country became a march zone against China, and Korea sought to live the life of a hermit society. The rural peasants at first continued to live their agrarian rural life, but the upper structures of Korean society deteriorated in several respects, so that Korea did not profit from her period of isolation. The whole economy suffered as an inefficient governmental system only increased the levels of taxation resting on the peasantry without providing any compensatory services. Although Christianity began to spread its influence in Korea, in the late eighteenth century, it had to do so by underground efforts, and Korea did not receive the stimulation toward culture change that was noticeable in China in the same period. The new American crops did not get disseminated in Korea, the educational and social changes brought by the missionary movement could not be put into play and, in the late nineteenth century, Korea was actually in poorer economic shape and more retrogressive in cultural orientation than was China where the seeds of change were already beginning to grow.

The breakdown of this self-isolation of "The Hermit Kingdom" resulted from the inability of China to hold off the Occident, and from the sudden expansionism created in Japan by the West. Japan actually was the first country to breach Korean refusal to deal with the world, in 1875. A series of commercial and diplomatic maneuvers between Korea, China, and various foreign powers soon stripped Korea of her position as a tributary to China. But before any occidental country could take advantage of this independence, Japan suddenly, in 1895, turned Korea into a part of the new and growing Japanese Empire, as a result of a war with China. This time a united Korea became wholly Japanese, in contrast to the earlier puny Japanese efforts to control the overland route to China. Although it is customary to cite 1910 as the date of Japanese annexation of Korea, this was a last political flourish, as the exploitation of Korea actually began shortly after 1895. The domination of Korea soon became complete, under Japanese control, and for the first time in Korean history an outside power ruled the whole peninsula. Increasingly efficient exploitation put an increasingly heavy burden on the Koreans, and they were turned into second-rate citizens of the Empire, laboring for the advancement of Japan. Economic development of Korea did take place, of course, but not for the interests of Koreans. Japanese control of Korea ended with the close of World War II, to be followed by a splitting of the peninsula into two states, one democratic and the other Communist, in 1945; the present actual dividing line dates from 1953.

MODERN KOREAN ECONOMY

This section will discuss the modernizing of the general economy of Korea. A short section will follow on each of the present two Korean states. The general use of the terms northern and southern is merely geographical, but occasionally the two political states will be distinguished as North Korea or South Korea.

In 1876, when Korean isolation was forcibly ended, the Korean population stood at about 10,500,000. It was essentially a peasant agrarian society, carrying on handicraft manufacturing, internal trade through barter and market fairs, and carrying on some fishing as an economic complement. Chiefly the Koreans were village dwellers, with a much heavier density in the southwest than in the northeast and northern upland. There were administrative cities, in the Chinese tradition, and the upper classes were largely urban. Seoul was a city of about 150,000, and there were a half dozen other cities of population in the range of 50,000, plus a good many small cities of about 15,000. Mineral exploitation was in keeping with handicraft economy. A very limited amount of trade goods got out of Korea, and a very few imports came in. Only few Koreans lived outside Korea. As an agrarian society carrying on an intensive garden-cropping pattern, much of the valley and lower hill country landscapes in western and southern Korea were already in terraced wet-field rice cropping. Wheat, millets, barley and a few other hardy grains were the mainstays of the higher uplands and northern Korea.

In 1945 just over 3,000,000 farm families cultivated about 11,300,000 acres of farmland, divided into millions of tiny plots. Systems of land inheritance and control had become rather complex during a long history and the fragmentation of fields had reached considerable proportions. In the central and southern lowlands agriculture was a stable matter, involving wet fields and water control. In the northern hill country the practices of dry-field cropping and a great deal of transient cropping locally designated "fire-field" cropping (owing to its consistent practice of burning off fallowed grass, brush, and tree-grown lands) are common. This was squatter shifting cultivation carried out by poor families on lands that could be cropped only for one, two, or three seasons before a shift must be made to other fallow lands. Nearly a half million acres were annually cropped in this way, the total having actually increased under Japanese control. In Korean agriculture a variable amount of double cropping is employed and an index figure of 1.3 is often used; it is frequent in the warmer south but less common in the cooler north country. The 463-mile length of Korea is increased in climatic contrast by the altitudes of the northern hill and mountain country, and there are many agricultural differences between north and south. These involve crops, farming techniques, tools, animals, and food consumption (Fig. 26.2).

Expressed most simply the farms of Korea average between 2 and 4 acres. In fact, however, the most common size of farm is between 0.8 and 2.5 acres, broken into disconnected plots. A small landlord class of Koreans owns a goodly share of the total farmland. Tenancy is most common in southern Korea and, before 1950, was least common in the north. In southern Korea, where Japanese inroads upon land ownership were most pronounced, the proportion of landless farmers had reached about seventy-five percent by the end of World War II. Well over half of the total farm families then were landless. When owners who also rented a little land were included, the proportion of tenancy for all Korea

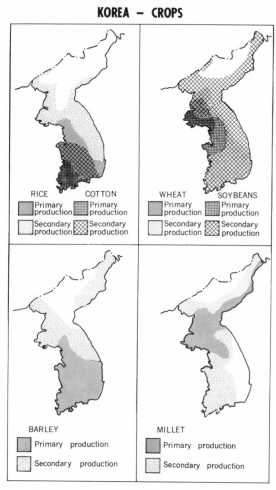

FIGURE 26.2. Chief agricultural crops in Korea.

reached a figure of about eighty percent, one of the highest in the world. Agrarian reform measures introduced after 1945 by American occupational forces expropriated nearly 700,000 acres of Japanese-owned lands in South Korea and sold them to almost 600,000 tenant families on a long-term payment basis. Subsequent land reform measures have moved more slowly. In North Korea all large farms were expropriated and cultivation rights turned over to tenant farmers on a purchase plus "contribution" basis. As the population has grown the size of farms and the per capita acreage steadily has decreased.

In southern Korea there is little reserve land available, particularly little that is suitable to rice culture. In the hilly and more northerly areas there still is some reserve land amenable to dry-field culture. That 42,000,000 people should try to live on the produce of no more than 13,000,000 acres of land, is but the bare statement of a hard fact. About twenty-four percent of Korea may be considered arable land by inclusion of some newly terraced lands formerly not cropped. The crowding of refugee North Koreans into the southern half of the country has greatly aggravated this condition.

The crop patterns of Korea long have been dominated by rice. This single crop, grown on summer-flooded fields, normally totals somewhat over 6,000,000 acres per year, about 4,000,000 of which is in South Korea. Barley, the next ranking crop, totaled more than 3,000,000 acres per year. Barley chiefly is a winter crop, grown on rice, bean, and cotton lands. Cotton is an important crop, now grown on perhaps 400,000 acres per year. Ramie and other industrial fibers, tobacco, some of the less hardy fruits such as persimmons, grapes, peaches, and plums, and a wide variety of vegetable and root crops complement the crop patterns of southern Korea. Owing to Japanese pressure to increase rice production prior to 1945, however, these crops now occupy smaller acreages than in the traditional pattern.

Toward the northern border wet-field agriculture becomes increasingly less important. Rice gives way to several kinds of millet, the dominant crop which covers over 2,000,000 acres. Here double cropping is less often found because agriculture operates primarily on a single summer cycle. A variety of beans, maize, buckwheat, sorghums, oats, and white potatoes are the auxiliary crops. Only the hardiest of fruits can be grown and the range of vegetables decreases.

A certain range of crops is sufficiently tolerant, or climatic tolerance has been bred into local varieties so that they can be grown almost all over Korea. The soybean is the chief of these, forming one of the ranking crops in all parts of Korea, and formerly totaling about 2,000,000 acres. The mulberry tree, for silkworm feeding, is another which is evenly distributed, to total perhaps 150,000 acres. Hemp, peas, radishes for home use, and sesame for cooking oil are widely distributed crops of small acreage for each. Wheat, a major crop, totaling some 800,000 acres, chiefly in central Korea, is unimportant either in the far north or far south. Apples and pears, the chief commercial fruits, are centered along the lowlands and hill country of the western half of Korea.

Animals play a relatively small role in Korean agriculture. About 3,000,000 lightweight cattle provide but a small amount of draft labor, little meat, and almost no dairy products, the latter being in rural disfavor. Small dairy herds are now to be found around some cities. A few thousand sheep, goats, and horses are insignificant. Pasture lands and forage crops do not figure in Korean agriculture. About 2,000,000 pigs are kept in the village and, like the cattle, add to the food supply only in a minor way. An estimated 20,000,000 fowls of all types provide a few eggs and some meat in relation to the total food supply.

The strong hand of the Japanese can be seen in the changing crop patterns and food habits between 1900 and 1945. The rice acreage increased but, despite the large increase in population, Korean rice consumption had decreased to a low figure in 1945. Marked increases had taken place in the production of millet, barley, maize, buckwheat, and potatoes. A large import of Manchurian millet had developed. Millet, barley, maize, buckwheat, and potatoes formed an ever larger share of the Korean food supply, all cheaper products eaten from necessity. Some shifts in this dietary pattern have taken place in recent years, but in view of the pressure on the land, a large share of the poorer population has not been able to go back to a basic rice dietary. The increases in cotton, tobacco, wheat, and commercial fruits were at Japanese urging and were turned to Japanese profit. Japanese development of irrigation facilities and the reclamation of tidal lands in southern Korea were motivated by the desire for an increased rice export. Little effort was expended by the Japanese to increase the total of dry fields on a permanent basis. There can be no question but that in a single generation the Japanese forced the people of Korea to accept a markedly lower level of living.

Attempts to increase food production to meet the needs of a swelling post World War II population have met with some success, and Korea is almost self-sufficient in basic agricultural needs. The fishery catch has returned to normal, fisheries ranking second to agriculture in Korean domestic economy, and the total catch may run to about 1,000,000 tons per year. North Korea has imported some wheat in each of recent years, suggesting that grain outputs are on

KOREA – MINERALS

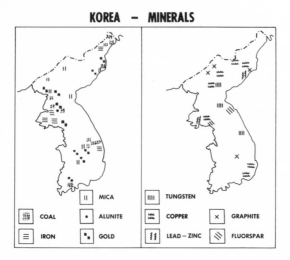

FIGURE 26.3. Mineral occurrences in Korea.

the inadequate side, but this may only partially offset the arbitrary export of rice to countries with whom North Korea wishes to develop trade exchanges.

For a small region Korea has a large amount of mineral resources, which are distributed widely over the country (Fig. 26.3). Koreans themselves have made some use of their resources in the past in the development of handicraft manufacturing. The development of modern mining began under American engineers during the late nineteenth century, but the exploitation of minerals chiefly was by the Japanese, who utilized them in Japanese industry rather than for the domestic development of Korea.

Of the primary industrial minerals coal and iron are widely scattered and voluminous in total reserve, but petroleum is lacking. The coal is chiefly anthracite, and some of the iron ores are relatively low grade. The hydroelectric potential of Korea is very large, and the Japanese developed a widely distributed system of hydroelectric power plants.

Of the ferro-alloys tungsten is present in important amounts, and there are small resources of manganese, molybdenum, and nickel. Korea is an important producer of low-grade graphite for the world market. Lead and zinc are rather widely distributed over the country. Gold has been one of the most valuable of the auxiliary Korean minerals, scattered all over the country. There are deposits of alunite, an aluminum ore that cannot economically be utilized at present, though the Japanese did make aluminum from it during World War II. Copper is scattered as a mineral secondary to zinc, lead, and gold in a number of areas. There are small resources of a few lesser minerals.

For a unified territory able to utilize its own mineral resource this list is fairly large for the modern world. However, most production, heretofore, went to Japanese industrial development and did Korea but little good. More recently a political line across Korea and disruptive conditions both inhibit mineral production and make problems of local occurrence far more significant than these would be in a peaceful and united country. In general one can say that most of the minerals are widely scattered, both north and south of the 38th parallel.

Unfortunately, some of the best coal and iron resources lie in northern Korea, along with more than half of the hydroelectric resources. Some of the other mineral resources also have been chiefly produced in northern Korea. This has meant that the current economy of South Korea is restricted in its power and mineral volume.

In the Korea of the old order, roads and the system of communications strongly resembled those of China. Stone-paved step roads traced their routes across the landscape, regardless of landforms, and were traveled chiefly by human carriers, pack animals, and a few riding horses. An elaborate country-wide system of signal fires implemented government couriers. Considerable coastwise water traffic probably handled most of the long-distance movement of commodities. The Japanese proceeded to install all the modern forms of transport and communications during their period of control. They developed a railway network and turned many of the step roads into vehicular highways. A telegraph system was developed, telephones became common around urban centers, and radio communications systems were developed. A government postal system was organized, ports were built, and coastwise shipping improved. A considerable network of air fields was developed after 1930 (Fig. 26.4). Although these facilities do not compare with those of the Occident and were relatively smaller developments than those of Japan, they gave Korea a better set of modern services than were available in China at the same time.

Statistical tabulations of industrial produc-tion and of foreign trade during the period of Japanese control indicate that a considerable volume of manufacturing had been developed before 1945, and that Korean trade had risen to large proportions. The range of manufacturing was considerable, and some of the activities were in advanced and highly technical lines. Heavy industry and the chemicals accounted for a very significant share of the total production. The number of concerns increased markedly, and the value of the total output was progressively enlarged. Household handicraft industry was encouraged and somewhat expanded. Trade patterns showed a large volume of export products in both raw materials and manufactured goods, and a large import trade in semiprocessed and manufactured goods, in fuel supplies, and in consumers goods. Korea, as a Japanese colony, seemed to be developing along the lines of industrial capitalism.

Close examination of the situation, however, as indicated in several recent studies of Korea, indicates that the transport map and the statistical records give a quite false impression regarding the economic development of Korea under the Japanese. By far the greater proportion of all these developments was carried out, not for the essential good of the Koreans, but for the strengthening of Japanese economy. In many lines of industrial production, Korea was not independent and self-contained, but interlinked with operations in Japan. It is perfectly true that on Korean soil the Japanese were effecting an industrial revolution, but it was not of, or for, Korea, and it had little constructive impact on Korean domestic economy.

Korean industry was manufacturing close to raw materials, but it was an integral part of Japanese economy. This was unlike British-developed manufacturing in India, which in part was designed to produce goods for the Indian market. In Korea banking, the financial system, economic regulations of

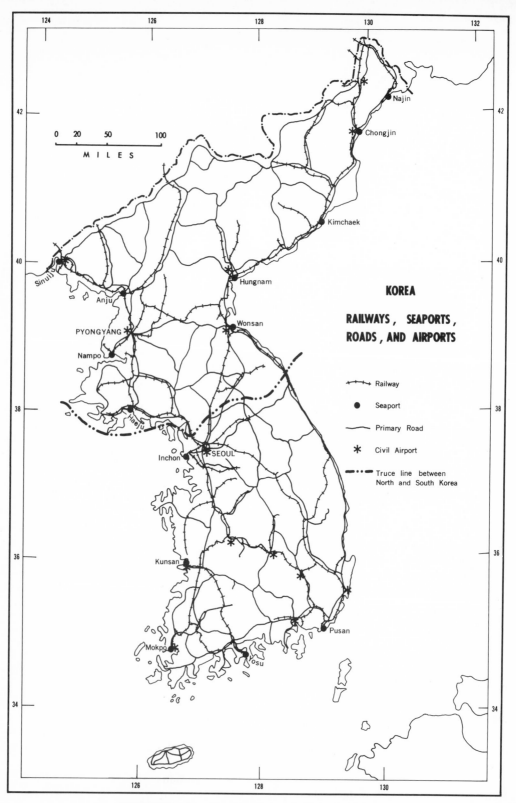

FIGURE 26.4. Transportation facilities in Korea.

570

government, controlled patterns of trade with Japan, all were arranged to benefit the economy of Japan. Increasingly after 1930 Korean industry was military industry aimed at increasing the military striking power of Japan. Transportation and communications were aids in this process. Their further utility lay in the better draining of Korean minerals, fishery products, rice, wheat, soybeans, and other agricultural supplies out of Korea for the benefit of Japan. Korean trade during the late 1930's was almost exclusively with Japan. Korean participation in this whole development was limited to agricultural production, mineral production, and to un-skilled and semiskilled labor in Japanese manufacturing plants. Only occasionally were Koreans permitted to acquire modern tech-nical skills and to participate in the owner-ship of manufacturing enterprise. Korean participation in government was either at the clerical level or at the median level of col-laborationist activity of a few Korean land-lords and merchants. This all amounted to a more efficient economic exploitation of a colonial holding than that carried out by any occidental colonial ruler. Koreans became a kind of "lesser Japanese" working for the advancement of Japan.

Although the record would suggest that Korean economy developed broadly under the Japanese, that manufacturing and secon-dary economic activities rose in productive value, and that agriculture and other primary activity production declined in relative im-portance, this was largely a statistical illusion so far as the Koreans were concerned. Domestic economy remained unchanged in its patterns: a force of over 800,000 Japanese operated a secondary economy on Korean soil drawing its strength from, but also keeping it divorced from, domestic economy. The great majority of Koreans remained agricultural, and after 1930 the Japanese restrained the use of raw materials in domestic handicraft manufacturing. As a result, Koreans were forced to become even more dependent upon agriculture. But as larger and larger supplies of agricultural products were squeezed out of Korea by the Japanese, the Korean dietary position declined along with the economic position of Korean farmers who increasingly had to sell their products at prices fixed by their overlords.

After 1945 much of Korean industry was dismantled and stripped of its productive capacity by Russian and American military teams. Much of Korean industry was of no purpose in a peacetime, post-war Korea. The sharp drawing of a line across Korea resulted in the separation of many elements in Korean economy. The northern and southern portions of the country were com-plementary parts of a whole, and the effect of drawing a line at the 38th parallel was to make the economic operation of either half extremely difficult. Russian refusal to permit the regional interchange of raw materials, power, food supplies, and other items were continuing elements of a process rendering Korean life difficult. The steady stream of emigrants out of northern Korea increasingly compounded the problems of southern Korea from all points of view.

The events after June, 1950, only furthered the long process of disturbing Korean life and economy. Although many efforts and much money have been put into increasing productivity of southern Korea, much of it has a wartime pattern, and the draining of economic resources continues. Regardless of what detailed pattern of settling the issues of control in Korea finally results, the balance sheet of over a half century of ex-ploitation, war, and regional disruption can show only a net loss for the Koreans.

POPULATION AND REGIONALISM

Although the Koreans have a diverse racial background, by the present century they had become one people, with one language, one culture, and with few basic regionalisms or

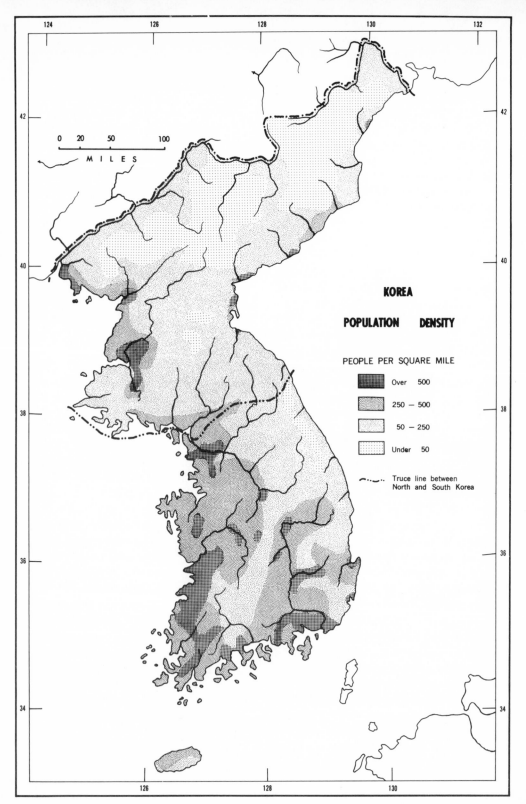

FIGURE 26.5. Population density in Korea.

cultural variations such as those compounded in Indonesia or Vietnam. As a village-dwelling people they have had few really large cities, but there have long been many port and market towns of some size, and the capital city has been a large city for some centuries. An early eighteenth-century population figure of slightly less than 7,000,000 seems fairly accurate. The first real census of population was that of 1925, after Japanese exploitation had begun, but also after some Japanese public health measures had been introduced. The 1925 total was 19,522,-000. The 1944 census totaled some 25,900,-000.

Both of these censuses failed to include those Koreans who had left the country, a figure which steadily had increased since just before 1900. As economic and political exploitation had increased, large numbers of Koreans had moved into Manchuria, some of whom moved on into Siberia after the Japanese took over Manchuria in 1931. Large numbers of Koreans went also to Japan as industrial labor, a few to China, and a very few scattered elsewhere in the world. This emigration was chiefly of rural Koreans, and it replaced the more normal modern growth of urbanism. After 1945, Japanese were sent back to Japan, and most of the Korean population abroad returned to Korea. The 1970 estimate of the total Korean population suggests a total very close to a total in excess of 42,000,000, of which 11,500,000 were in North Korea and 30,600,-000 were in South Korea (Fig. 26.5).

The marked increase in population is recent, and most of the population is a young rural population. This means that the future increases will be rapid, and that the population will continue its present rate of increase for some years, unless the current disruptive conditions continue both severe enough and long enough to materially affect population structure and its rates of growth.

In 1944 the present area of South Korea, somewhat less than half the total territory, contained slightly under 16,000,000 people of the total of just under 26,000,000. The 1955 estimate of the total population of Korea suggests a total very close to 31,000,000, though no precise data were available. This calculation is rendered difficult by continued emigration out of North Korea, much of which cannot be tabulated. If the estimate for all of Korea is at all accurate, it would appear that North Korea was losing population by emigration, but that South Korea was rapidly increasing. The latter increase was compounded of three elements: the natural increase, the post-war repatriation of Koreans abroad, and the steady influx of emigrants from the north.

In South Korea there has been a marked increase in urbanization since 1920, promoted by the lack of space in the rural countryside, and by the congregation of refugees in urban areas. Seoul and Pusan have grown markedly in their total populations, the former being close to 5,000,000 in 1970, and the latter being about 1,500,000. Other large cities are Taegu, 850,000; Inchon, 550,000; Kwangju, 425,000; Taejon, 325,000; and Chonju, 225,000. Many other small cities now are growing and will soon join the large-city class.

North Korea has also gone through urbanization, though to a lesser degree. In 1970 the estimates suggest: Pyongyang, 650,000; Hungnam, 250,000; Chongjin and Kaesong, each 200,000, Sinuiju, 175,000, and Wonsan, 150,000. Several other cities were approaching 100,000 each.

Before 1945 the chief regionalisms of the country were those arising out of the natural environment. In an agricultural society, uniform in its major cultural patterns and living in an environment of marked physiographic and climatic variety, these regionalisms become chiefly matters either of environment or of population distribution, agriculture, diet, and detailed patterns of living. Southern Korea has a heavier population pattern, more cultivable lowlands, a more widespread rice landscape, and auxiliary agriculture containing a wide variety of crops applicable to a milder climatic regime. Northern Korea is a rougher, upland landscape, chiefly of dry fields, fewer and more hardy crops, shifting "fire-field" agriculture, and lesser and scattered population patterns (Fig. 26.6).

The insertion of such items as the 38th parallel and markedly different kinds of political systems into the issue of regionalisms may have a long-run future effect. Although the 38th parallel was but a line on a map, and has been shifted to accord with an actual truce line, and although it corresponds to nothing in the physical environment, its cumulative effects over the years can be significant. Not only political systems but also education, psychological reactions, and social change are involved. The northern part of Korea has been subject to greater disruption than has southern Korea since 1950. If some kind of settlement is reached that could permit a united Korea before too long an interval passes, these new factors of regionalism may not become too deeply established. Since they run counter to the cultural currents of the Korean people, the temporary effects could be erased through a unified program of cultural action. However, if the separation of north and south goes on long enough for one or more generations of people to reach maturity with different political and social orientations, a pattern of cultural regionalism could be developed that might long stand against the trends toward unity. There is the danger, therefore, that the opposing cultural programs of Communism and Democracy may produce a lasting impression upon the Korean people and their culture.

KOREA'S REGIONALISMS

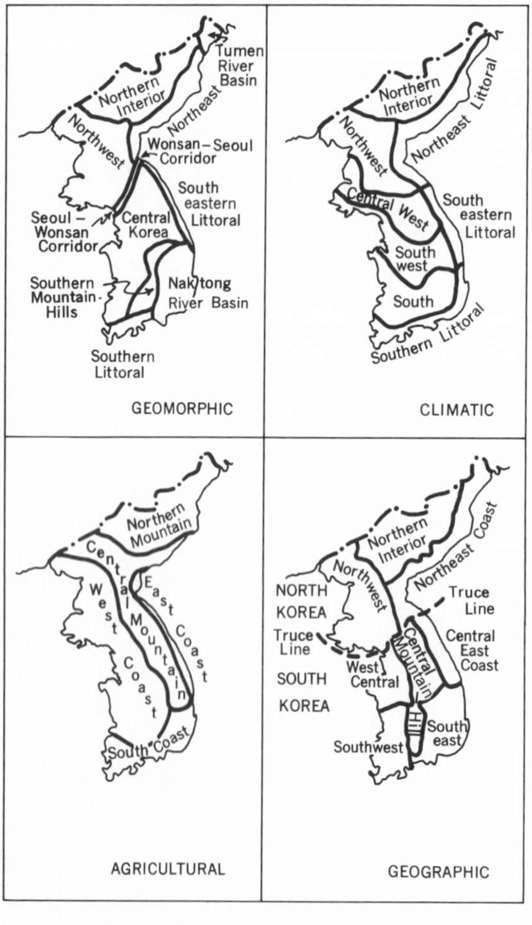

FIGURE 26.6. Regional patterns in Korea.

NORTH KOREA

North Korea is the rugged large half of the Korean Peninsula. It covers an area of 46,540 square miles, but has a minority of the population, 11,500,000. Much of the interior is rough upland, and the total agricultural land is under 6,000,000 acres, most of which can be cropped but once per year. North Korea was not a zone of marked tenancy at the end of World War II but, under Communist control, went through the normal Communist "land reform" program by which all land holdings over 2.5 acres were first given to landless peasants, and then the whole agricultural landscape was put through the cooperative phase and finally amalgamated into about 4,000 state controlled communes, with the rural agrarian element turned into an agricultural labor force. There has been a steady program of trying to raise the cropped area to 7,000,000 acres, but, since the program still is a current one, it apparently has not been achieved. Considerable mechanically powered equipment was in use in the late 1960's on the collective farms. One recent development was the planting of fairly large acreages of hardy fruit and nut trees, with more such plantings to be done.

The main leadership of North Korea is comprised of Koreans who were resident in some part of the U.S.S.R. prior to World War II, and who have been thoroughly indoctrinated in the Communist program. There have been some purges and North Korea is governed under rather tight controls by a relatively small but strong leadership group.

Having a large share of the mineral resources, much of the pre-war Japanese hydro- and thermo-electric power installations, and many of the industrial plants, the North Korean economy quickly became involved in mining and manufacturing, and agriculture is carried on chiefly as a basis for feeding the home population. Of a labor force of slightly over 2,000,000 just over half are involved in some mining or manufacturing enterprise, with about twelve percent directly engaged in primary production in agriculture. Iron ores, other ores, crude pig iron, non-ferrous metals, some machinery, cement, some timber products, and fishery products have been among the North Korean exports during the 1960's. Imports have involved electrical machinery, cotton and woolen textiles, transport equipment, small volumes of wheat products and other food supplies, finished chemicals, and pharmaceuticals. There is some textile manufacturing, but since textiles are a relatively large import the domestic production does not clothe the population. Other lines of manufacturing aim at the production of home consumption goods of various types, and apparently adequate commercial fertilizers are manufactured to supply the domestic needs. The great bulk of North Korean trade is carried on with the U.S.S.R. and China, but most of the other Communist-bloc countries are represented. Only Japan, Hong Kong, and France, among the non-Communist countries, carried on any significant trade with North Korea during the early and mid-1960's, but in the late 1960's North Korea was attempting to make trade agreements with several south Asian countries. Total foreign trade during the late 1960's seemed to average about $450,000,000 per year.

Some 2,600,000 young people were reported attending schools, with a compulsory nine-year polytechnic curriculum in effect. Beyond the basic compulsory curriculum a considerable population of young people were attending the 98 advanced technical colleges and universities.

The tenor of North Korean public commentary normally refers to great steps forward, the improving level of living, the increases in industrial output, and the technological accomplishments, but it also contains frequent references to the need for austerity, continued patience, extreme care in not wasting resources, natural calamities having prevented goals being reached, and the urgent need for all labor forces to work a full work day. The frequency of the latter kinds of comments would suggest that the upward progress in the level of living is not entirely satisfying, and the extension of the 1960–1967 Seven Year Plan to 1970 would suggest that rates of economic development had fallen short of the goal.

SOUTH KOREA

South Korea is the smaller half of the peninsula, and the milder climatic half with a less rugged physical landscape, 38,012 square miles, but it has to bear the pressure of a much larger population that, in 1970, was estimated at 30,600,000. Much of the eastern sector of the country is hilly upland to mountainous, but the coastal plains of the southwest are wider and larger in extent than those of North Korea. The total arable land may be in the vicinity of 7,000,000 acres and about a third of the total may be cropped a second time each year by integrated cropping combinations. There is further intensification of agricultural production, making for increased productivity, but recent advances have been countered by seasonal droughts which have reduced crop yields in the southwest, so that average net productivity has not increased recently. The cattle and pig populations have been slaughtered down to the danger point, in terms of maintaining the productive animal populations, and South Korean agriculture is showing the strains of over-demands being made of it.

In the division of the country South Korea inherited a lesser amount of mineral resources and less than half the developed power resources, but once new developments were put into production, South Korean industrialization was not retarded. Hydroelectric power resources have expanded only slowly in South Korea, whereas coal mining has expanded markedly. In the late 1960's coal supplied about two-thirds of the energy produced. Although the percentage of the work force employed in agriculture is dropping, in 1970 just over half the labor force still was engaged in primary agricultural production. The labor force in 1970 totaled about 10,800,000, and about 1,500,000 of the total were employed in industrial production. Automobile assembly operations have been the brightest of the recent additions, but iron and steel, petrochemicals, basic chemicals, commercial fertilizers, cement, glass products, textiles, footwear, rubber manufactures, paper products, electrical machinery,

manufactured wood products, tinned foods, and beverages are among the progressing lines of development. United States financial aids have been significant in getting South Korean industrialization under way, but in the late 1960's South Korean industrial development was reaching a point of financing some of its own expansion, and was anticipating the final termination of economic aid in 1971. Much of the industrial output has been aimed at the foreign trade market so far, and only a lesser portion of modern production goes into consumer goods for home use. Of the production lines, finished textiles and wood products have been the large items in the export list. A wide range of other goods in small volumes go into the export trade.

On the import side South Korea has bought large amounts of raw cotton and synthetic fibers, petroleum, logs, wheat, and fertilizers. It is probably to be expected that food products will gradually range higher in the import trade as the increasing population puts further pressure on the land, but that fertilizers will drop as home production supplies the domestic need. The United States ranks first in both the import and export trade of South Korea, followed closely by Japan, with other important countries being West Germany, Hong Kong, Taiwan, France, Canada, and Sweden. Two countries from whom South Korea imports significantly, but does not export to, are Malaysia and the Philippines—log and rubber purchases from Malaysia and log purchases from the Philippines.

In 1969 about 6,800,000 young people were in elementary and secondary education, a somewhat lower proportion than in the case of North Korea, but a somewhat higher percentage of South Korean young people were involved in advanced educational training.

South Korea, in starting out its independent career in 1946, was somewhat handicapped by the free-wheeling patterns of democracy in which conflict between hundreds of political parties, programs, directional urgings, and aspirations rather blunted early patterns of progress. In continued development there has not been the tightly disciplined control of social, economic, and political patterns as has evidently been the case in North Korea. North Korea, which feels more strongly the need for future re-unification, has consistently put both political and military pressure on South Korea. The large population of the south, swollen by dependent refugees from the north and most of the labor force returned from Japan at the end of World War II, severely strains the resources of South Korea. There is hope, however, that despite the severe crowding and the lack of economic opportunity for a significant share of the present population, the economic spiral has turned upward for South Korea, and the coming decade will see a considerable share of economic progress. South Korea has aspirations toward reunification, too, but wants such to be on a basis of voluntary free union rather than on terms forced by the present leadership of Communist North Korea. Re-unification of Korea in the near future is most uncertain.

27

JAPAN: A MODERNIZED ISLAND WORLD

A SERIES OF ISLAND ENVIRONMENTS

The Japanese islands lie toward the northern end of the long line of Island Arcs that rim the eastern margins of the Asian continent. They form a relatively small environment situated between the largest land mass and the largest ocean. The lands of Japan are mostly uplands, the tops of steep and rugged mountains projecting above the present sea level. In earlier human time the level of the ocean was slightly lower, and Japan then was a larger region of land grouped into a small number of islands fringed by considerable areas of relatively broad and open lowlands. These lowlands are covered today by the Inland Sea and the coastal shelf toward Korea and China. The rise of the ocean level in post-glacial times has subdivided Japan into about 3,000 islands, and deprived modern man of a significant area of lowland. Today one tends to think of Japan as a very small country made up of steep surfaces, but it really is small only in terms of the amount of its arable land in relation to its large population. The earliest Japan known to man was neither so small in actual area, nor was it small relative to need and population. The smallness is clearly relative even today, for Japan stretches some 1,200 miles from northeast to southwest.

The Japanese islands form a mosaic of small individual units, blocks, peninsulas, and islands, broken by fault and fracture lines, grouped into a number of major units, and littered with the products of volcanism. There are a number of structural depressions between these major units, and one of the largest of them is occupied by the Inland Sea, in itself a very real part of the Japanese environment. Maximum altitudes reach 12,000 feet, and the steep uplands dominate this environment. In many places steep rocky coasts drop directly into the sea. Scattered around the fringes of islands and between some of the less deep structural depressions are small lowland patches, alluvial areas filled with coarse to fine sediments, which provide agricultural surfaces. Many coastal sections show uplifted marine terraces and benches, for some of the areas of Japan have been above sea level only in Recent geologic time. These additional relatively smooth and open areas have been put to agricultural use, though many of them are of comparatively low value. Much of the volcanism has produced acid materials which weather into poor soils, though volcanism has provided many beautiful and scenic landforms.

The south-facing portions of southwestern Japan possess mild climatic regimes and some subtropical plants, whereas the north coast,

578

the southern uplands, and all northern Japan is cold and snowy in the winter and possesses mixed and coniferous forests. These conditions are amenable to occupance and use by modern man, but for early man they presented a somewhat difficult set of conditions. Natural food supplies were not abundant for a population of limited technology, and living conditions were on the rigorous side. The best regions were the coastal fringes in which early man could combine the use of land and aquatic resources, but the range of possibilities was far less in the Japanese environment than in the more varied regions of southeastern Asia.

The Japanese environment is one not bountifully provided with those natural complements of soils, plant resources, animal life, and other features which made for easy productivity of material goods for early man. The aquatic resources around these island shores are rich, but they were less available to early man than to modern man. By dint of hard work through a long span of time the Japanese have made their environment a productive one, but many of these advances had to await the introduction of techniques developed in other parts of the world, and then carefully be fitted to the local scene. The historic pattern of the introduction of developed techniques into Japan has led to the false conclusion that the Japanese have been only an imitative people, whereas in the perfection and fitting of techniques to their environment the Japanese have displayed almost as much originality as did the Chinese, who also copied and adapted many alien features of culture.

Earliest man may well have been able to walk overland from the mainland to the lowland fringes of southwestern Japan (Fig. 27.1). The Ainu aboriginal population, proto-Caucasoid in origin, established themselves in such numbers that they have steadily contributed to the racial composition of the modern Japanese. Man moved upward onto the present alluvial lands and the lower up-

land fringes as the post-glacial patterns of islands and coastal outlines developed. Neolithic man came into the islands by sea both from the north and the west, bringing different elements of culture and probably representing different and mixed racial strains. The northerners brought useful elements of fishing economies, but they did not add greatly to the population as such. The main line of immigration lay through Korea, and the chief elements were proto-Mongoloid and Mongoloid in origin, to set the racial basis for modern Japan.

Out of the south, probably South China, moving along the coastal fringes came some southern peoples after the present lines of land and sea had developed. In popular thinking this stream of peoples bulks high in contributing to the Japanese population, but it is doubtful that this is so. These southern peoples undoubtedly did bring many culture traits into Japan related to the use of the sea and the subtropical elements of the environment.

Since most of these migrants came into southwestern Japan, bringing higher culture traits, it is logical that this was the early center of Japan. In a rigorous environment not bountifully providing for early man, the coastal lowlands of the southwestern portion were both the most livable and the most productive. Here the mixing of the early racial stocks and patterns of culture took place, and here also began that conversion of alien traits into traits distinctively Japanese.

THE SOUTHERN CULTURE HEARTH

The southern part of Japan was not only a more productive environment but also in closer contact with that part of mainland Asia in which Chinese culture was expanding and maturing during the late feudal era. Refugees from China, during the final bitter struggles of feudalism and the appearance of

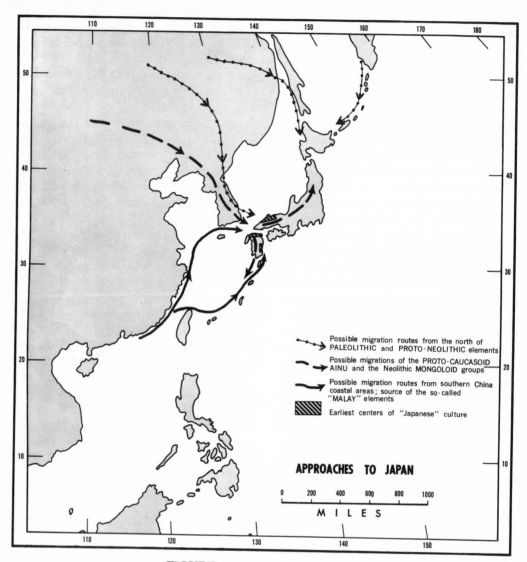

FIGURE 27.1. Approaches to Japan

the Han state, carried Chinese culture into Korea and brought it into range of southern Japan whose peoples were themselves in contact with Korea. These contacts can be traced to at least the third century B.C., and they gradually raised the culture level of southern Japan out of the Stone Age, though central and northern Japan lagged behind. The peoples of southern Japan were grouped in matriarchal tribal and clan patterns, each occupying small coastal sections. A competitive situation developed among these local groups, with the Yamato of Kyushu gaining the ascendancy and moving their headquarters to the eastern end of the Inland Sea by about A.D. 300. There was a general eastward movement of tribes and clans, including immigration from Korea and perhaps from the China coast.

Although the precise racial and cultural

origins are not clear, rice culture, horses, cattle, the pig, and the dog appeared in southern Japan during these centuries. The horse came with the cavalry-warrior complex and was taken up by clan leaders and tribal chiefs as a means of solidifying their regional and group controls. Rice culture brought with it other crops, agricultural practices, and domestic use techniques. Metallurgy, domestic architecture, village settlement, and social patterns, all filtered in slowly. Many of these items came from China but not all from the North China culture hearth, some coming undoubtedly from the Yangtze Delta and coastal country, and others from Manchuria and Mongolia. A few features may have come from South China, from the same centers that had spread many culture traits southward into southeastern Asia, but it is doubtful if much of Japanese direct cultural origins lie as far afield as southeastern Asia.

Kyushu, Shikoku, and the portion of Honshu fronting on the Inland Sea were the regions in which both human and culture migrations occurred. Water movement and fishing economies remained strong, mixing peoples and the details of culture. Replacement of primitive practices occurred, and new ideas were blended into old ones. Population grew, and the most of the lowland alluvial tracts were settled. This whole process of development was restricted to southern Japan, and gradually there came to be marked differences between this southern region and the areas north of the Inland Sea. In the north country the Ainu and possibly other Stone Age peoples were thinly scattered and culturally undeveloped. As time passed the contrast became greater and as the southern peoples more and more fully occupied their lowlands, local pressures for space began to develop. Slowly the southern peoples began moving into the edges of their own upland regions and also pushing northward along the lowland fringes of Honshu. This southern section, therefore, as the culturally advanced region, became the source for the colonizing of the rest of the Japanese islands and the local source of the cultural patterns that gradually have grown into modern Japanese civilization. There are several different interpretations of the history of the culture hearth involving different dates, chief sites, and ruling lines, derived from separate clan-group oral histories all of which were recorded at much later dates. Our presentation, in Figure 27.2, is just one of the possible developments prior to the Nara Period.

THE CHINESE CULTURAL IMPRINT

Japanese culture possesses many similarities to the culture of China, some of which trace back to introductions before the Christian era. And during the early centuries of the Christian era, when the southern peoples were making their first real advances in civilization, many Chinese traits were taken up in an unconscious pattern of acceptance. This hit-and-miss learning process went on until the late sixth century. By then Japanese leaders appreciated the value of Chinese culture, appeared to realize that their knowledge was incomplete, and they set out to broaden their contacts and patterns of learning. Early in the seventh century Japanese leaders dispatched commissions to the Chinese court that compare with the modern system of organized dispatch of students abroad to centers of learning. The best educated young Japanese were selected to study all possible aspects of Chinese culture. Some remained in China for many years and upon their return to Japan became leaders in a program of "modernization," as it were, that spread elements of Chinese culture throughout southern Japan. All manner of subjects were studied, from Buddhist theology to city planning, from painting to manufacturing. This constituted an enormous program of cultural borrowing, but the learning can

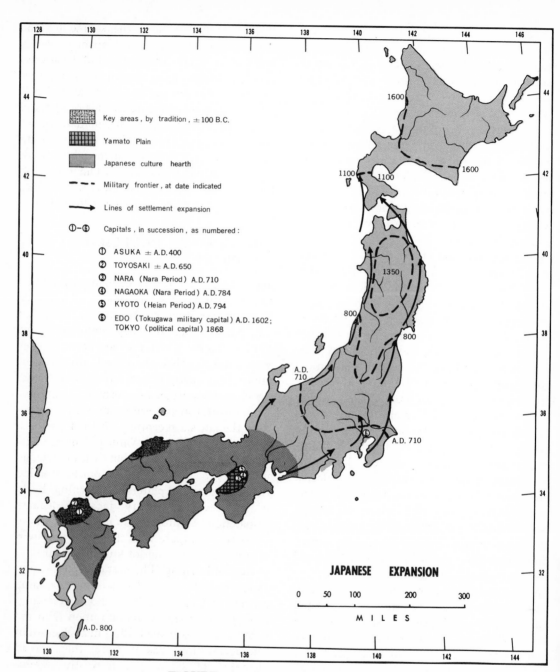

Key areas, by tradition, ±100 B.C.

Yamato Plain

Japanese culture hearth

Military frontier, at date indicated

Lines of settlement expansion

①-⑥   Capitals, in succession, as numbered:

① ASUKA ± A.D.400
② TOYOSAKI ± A.D.650
③ NARA (Nara Period) A.D.710
④ NAGAOKA (Nara Period) A.D.784
⑤ KYOTO (Heian Period) A.D.794
⑥ EDO (Tokugawa military capital) A.D.1602;
TOKYO (political capital) 1868

JAPANESE   EXPANSION

0   50   100   200   300

MILES

FIGURE 27.2. Japanese internal expansion.

hardly be called mere copying, for it had to be integrated into a whole and blended with the elements of native existing culture. And the very organized manner of approaching the problem was far in advance of any process of cultural development in vogue elsewhere.

The whole program perhaps evolved because China had just begun to blossom again into one of its high periods of development. The Sui had begun to organize North China into one state, and the T'ang were just completing the task of making China the greatest political and cultural empire in the world at that time. The Japanese thus were able to study China during one of its best periods when Chinese culture perhaps stood foremost among the world's cultures. But another significant element was the fact that administrative power in Japan was, in the sixth century A.D., sufficiently centralized in the hands of a small group of leaders for a major program of action to be decided upon and carried into effect without a long period of debate or struggle. It is important to note this early illustration of the far-reaching results of the decisions of a small number of Japanese leaders at a particular point of time because it is a phenomenon that has occurred repeatedly throughout Japanese culture history.

The first cultural missions to China were so successful that they were repeated rather continuously for over two centuries. By the middle of the ninth century official sponsorship for study of China came to an end, though privately the process continued for almost two centuries longer in lesser degree. By the latter part of the ninth century the T'ang were declining in China, and perhaps there was less to learn that could be of use to the leaders of Japan. This long period of study made the leaders of Japan familiar with the workings of Chinese civilization and spread Chinese culture traits throughout those parts of Japan inhabited by the peoples spreading out of the southern hearth region.

The impact of Chinese culture showed up in many ways. In the early eighth century the Japanese set out to build an imperial capital city of Nara, off the Inland Sea, which they modeled upon the great T'ang capital of Ch'ang-an (see Fig. 27.2). Grid-plan streets were laid out, buildings were built in the Chinese style, functional zoning was applied, and the city had come to stay. The matriarchal society of early Japan finally disappeared in favor of the patriarchal system of China, and the social status of women became permanently altered. The tribal and clan leaders saw utility in the nationalized political system in China, topped by an emperor, and so they installed it and in so doing rewrote Japanese history to give the system an ancient status. But the leaders of Japan could not bring themselves to install the full pattern of Chinese education, the examination, and the civil service, which would have meant throwing open to all Japanese the opportunities for political power. Thus, they kept alive the clan system which facilitated the preservation of real power in the hands of hereditary leaders. Similarly they reorganized the land system and systems of taxation, but in the end let the land system degenerate while keeping the tax system. The net result was more effective consolidation of power in the hands of the few.

Japanese religion grew into a mixture of Buddhism and native animism, but the study of Chinese Buddhism was serious and it became an important element drawn from China. Chinese art, handicraft manufacturing, and agriculture were studied and adapted so far as practical and possible. In such areas there was less danger to real power in the hands of leaders if a full application of Chinese practices took place. A far-reaching item that was taken from China was the written language, but the results have been less than satisfactory. At the time of earliest contact with Chinese culture no system of writing was known in Japan, but the spoken languages were polysyllabic. Chinese is a monosyllabic language easily written by single ideographs or characters. The first writing employed in Japan was Chinese, written by people brought from Korea. These immigrant scholars became the first recorders of Japanese historiography, the first scribes, and bookkeepers. Slowly the Japanese learned this complex system of writing, and it gradually became the written language of Japan. The grafting of a monosyllabic writing onto a polysyllabic speech resulted in a cumbersome system that never has been outgrown.

Although the adapting of only a few features of Chinese culture has been discussed, it must be obvious that the process involved selective adaption rather than indiscriminate imitation. A close study of Japanese culture in this period suggests that a clear imprint of Chinese culture was spread throughout much of Japan with the result that Japanese culture is modeled upon that of China. But it is equally discernible that slavish copying was never permitted in many lines and that the leaders of Japan were extremely skillful in checking those trends which would have truly converted Japan into a little China in all respects. Chiefly the checks were applied at those points which preserved in the hands of the old line of Japanese leaders the power, wealth, and control of Japan.

SYNTHESIS AND OUTGROWING THE HEARTH

As the knowledge of Chinese culture began to pile up in Japan there arose the increasing problem of how to integrate the new elements into Japanese life. The earlier solutions were to adapt it wholesale, but slowly Japanese became sufficiently skillful to be able to discriminate between the really useful and the merely innovative Chinese traits. Not only was this process operative among the political leaders of Japan who dropped features they did not like, but it gradually became applied throughout the whole range of Japanese life. In the mild climate of southern Japan the domestic architecture of North China was hardly necessary, and its strictly utilitarian features were too subdued to appeal to the Japanese. Slowly there evolved several distinctive Japanese housetypes, variably using movable panel walls, designed to let in light and sun, clean floors and mats, and a minimum of furniture reminiscent of southeastern Asia. Taken from Chinese patterns, Japanese housing still resembles its origins in many respects, but it is distinctively different.

Japanese agriculture basically resembles that of China, but it has developed its own distinctive methods, tools, and customs. The early arts of Japan closely resemble those of China, but gradually subtle distinctions have evolved that often are hard for the occidental to recognize. This holds true in painting, sculpture, literature, drama, and the whole range of decorative and utilitarian arts. It holds true for many of the social customs such as the ceremonial greeting, for dietary habits such as the use of tea as a national drink, for the patterns of clothing, and many other elements of culture. In all these things the Japanese have slowly modified the basic elements into something peculiarly Japanese.

The process of converting Chinese cultural examples into Japanese customs and material developments was not done rapidly. The earliest elements in this adaptation of Chinese culture came early during the period when the Japanese were still consciously studying Chinese affairs. The most distinctive transformations, of course, came in the centuries after the Japanese had stopped observing China, and were independently living their own lives. The culture historian is apt to classify the centuries between about A.D. 900 and A.D. 1400 as the most important era of activity in the field of cultural transformation. The political historian is apt to divide the time span between about A.D. 800 and A.D. 1550 into two eras in which he first distinguishes the attempt to install a system of political nationalism and, second, the development of feudalism in Japan after about A.D. 1000.

In the sixth century A.D. the Japanese already were pushing northward beyond the Inland Sea and into the edges of the hill country of central Japan (see Fig. 27.2). As their culture developed more and more, and their population increased, the contrasts between the southern peoples and the aboriginal population of the north and the hill country heightened. There began a process of expansion northward out of the hearth that can be likened to the expansion of the seaboard American colonies westward across the United States although it was a slower process, and it involved different kinds of issues. The Japanese had to fight their way northward against a stubborn resistance on the part of the hunter-collector aboriginals who did not want to see their hunting ranges turned into farmlands. There developed a professional soldiery on the frontier who resembled the American "Indian fighter," settlers often found their advance locations raided, and forts and a frontier force of farmer-soldiery were employed. Some Japanese left the settled areas for various reasons and took up residence among the Ainu, often inciting them to resistance. By the end of the eighth century the lowlands well north of modern Tokyo had been cleared of Ainu, and considerable settlement by southerners had taken place. During the eighth and ninth centuries the Japanese pushed steadily northward, slowly learning the military techniques required to conquer the Ainu. By the end of the ninth century the strength of the Ainu had been broken, though groups remained in the uplands to bother the Japanese for another century or more. Some intermarriage steadily introduced Ainu blood and physical types into the Japanese people.

The Ainu had been a hunting and collecting people who lived along the shores of the islands and used the lowland interior regions that provided fish, game, and some plant resources. In the north they found little of value in the mountain country, and increasingly found their range of support reduced as the southerners conquered the coasts and lowlands. Ainu had also inhabited the shores of Hokkaido for a long period, and some of them retreated to Hokkaido when dispos-

sessed on Honshu. In Hokkaido, however, the upland country was largely barren of resources useful to hunters and collectors, and the Ainu stuck to the coastal fringes and some of the more open lowland areas. In taking over Ainu territory the southerners found little developed land upon which to base their own occupation. They faced a forested environment with a cooler climate having few directly useful land resources to begin with. Their occupation of the north country, therefore, was a slow matter of clearing forests, developing fields on rough surfaces, changing their crops, and finding short-season varieties of crop plants that would mature in the cooler, shorter growing seasons.

Throughout northern Honshu, therefore, settlement and resource development was slow. Many Japanese settlements came to depend more upon fishing than upon agriculture. In many respects the southern people moving northward did not basically alter their southern patterns of culture. House-types, clothing, food patterns, customs, and habits remained much the same. The northern, colder parts of Honshu were slow to fill up with settlers, many of whom found this northern country unattractive in comparison to the milder portions of southern Japan. It was almost A.D. 1400 before most of the easily settled land of northern Honshu was occupied by initial patterns of settlement.

FEUDAL PATTERNS AND THE ECONOMY

It was noted previously that the leaders of Japan carefully rejected those elements of Chinese culture that would have endangered their positions of control over Japan. They were even anxious that the utilitarian arts be learned well, that agriculture develop, that settlement of all of Japan through northern Honshu be possible, but they were also anxious that the early patterns of social stratification remain strong, and that there remain a sharp line of demarcation between the mass of the population and the small group of leaders, rulers, holders of wealth, and large owners of land. There slowly developed, therefore, a complex set of multiple rules and standards which reminds one of the patterns of feudal Europe in which the commoner lived by one pattern and knighthood and the nobility lived by another. Out of this feudal development Japan has emerged with a set of social patterns second only to India in stereotyped inequality between the bottom and the top of the scale.

Since the leaders of Japan never really installed the Chinese centralized system of political administration, and since they let clan leaders gain control of large areas of land all over Japan which became tax-free estates, the clan leaders attained the real control of Japan. When it suited the most powerful clan, the emperor and national authority was invoked, but provincial administration never grew in strength and the emperor remained a figurehead for centuries. This situation inevitably led to competitive struggle between the leading clans, with the most powerful actually holding the balance of power throughout Japan. In the early periods this placed the center of power in southern Japan, but since the Japanese were expanding northward, the center of power gradually shifted eastward and northward also. These struggles for power also developed a professional soldiery, some of whom were concerned with the northern frontier problem, with others concerned only in the interclan struggles. The power of the Buddhist church alternately grew and receded, often becoming an important element in the feudal struggle as monasteries and church leaders sought themselves to gain commanding position.

After the Ainu frontier was pushed into northern Honshu the slow shift of the center of population, of agricultural productivity, and of general economic wealth finally made it possible for the regional rulers based upon the Kanto Plain around modern Tokyo to assume the lead in the regional struggle (see Fig. 27.2). Tokyo was developed into a city, connected by roads with the rest of Japan, and made the *de facto* capital of Japan. This occurred in the early seventeenth century, and by ingenious devices the Tokugawa clan became the real rulers of Japan. Tokyo soon became a large city, reaching a total of over 1,000,000 by 1800 (see Fig. 4.6, and the accompanying text).

After the frontier problem ceased to be important the professional soldier turned his attention to the regional and clan struggles, particularly during the feudal era. Considerable destruction of property and loss of life occasionally followed the more bitter struggles for power. The professional soldiery gradually became the *samurai* class, entrenched in social and legal position, and entrenched economically with a considerable annual income derived from taxation of the peasantry. Out of this pattern comes the modern Japanese tradition of the soldier, the semi-religious cults, and the other military elements that were so successfully exploited by the leaders of Japan within the last century. In the late sixteenth century this military tradition took the form of the first Japanese attempt to conquer the known world, which then meant Korea and China, and a decade of fighting in Korea followed. The effort failed because of the inability of the home base to maintain and supply a large army at a distance, and because the leaders involved could not then command the resources of all of Japan. The effort was a factor in the last major shift of regional power to central Japan.

Throughout the feudal era Japan remained primarily an agricultural country, dependent upon an intensive small-farmer economy which paid taxes in kind to support the upper classes. Handicraft manufacturing developed a fairly broad base, regionally concentrated in southern Japan and following slowly upon the eastward and northward shift of population. Northern Honshu, until the late nineteenth century, remained an underdeveloped region dependent chiefly upon agriculture, fishing, and forestry. Road systems were laid out sufficiently to connect all parts of Japan together, but these were chiefly of use in administration and local movement. Fishing grew steadily in importance in Japanese economy, developing skills and familiarity, but it still was chiefly a subsistence matter in which only coastal and shore waters were exploited.

From prehistoric times the southern peoples had maintained sea contact with Korea. And during the period of studying Chinese culture the Japanese traveled around the coast of Korea at first, and later directly across the Yellow Sea to the China coast. Water transport along the coast in Japan, within the Inland Sea, and to the north country, is of long standing. From about 1200 to 1620 Japanese traders engaged in a considerable sea traffic, consisting both of legitimate trade and of piracy. In this period Japanese merchants and traders established connections with and had trader colonies in the Philippines, Malaysia, Thailand, Vietnam, the China coast, Taiwan, and Korea. Some of their ships steadily ranged into the South China Sea, and a Japanese pirate looted an English ship off Singapore in 1604. It was in the latter part of this era of sea trade that the Japanese made their first contact with the Occident, that the occidental traders found their way to Japan, and that a few products and ideas of the West got into Japan.

The luxurious living patterns and fighting of clan leaders that went on over the centuries consumed a goodly share of the surplus of the country, but did not really destroy the productive economic base. The population grew rather steadily until, by about 1600, it probably stood a bit over 18,000,000. The

agricultural area had steadily developed and, except for some of the northern Honshu marginal and upland areas recently brought into use, had developed close to its maximum. Manufacturing, fishing, and trade were productive phases of the Japanese economy. Japan had reached a mature plane of economic development of the pre-industrial variety.

Throughout the whole feudal era the peasantry of Japan had protested their treatment, sometimes with local effect but never with the success that attended Chinese rebellion during the decline of a dynasty, so that by 1600 there were many stresses that had developed in Japanese society. The leaders of Japan saw in the arrival of the occidental a possible threat to their continued control of the country. Christianity was a threat, for its acceptance carried with it allegiance to a God who lay beyond the sea outside Japan. Although tobacco and firearms were willingly accepted from the European, the Tokugawa clan, just coming to power at the start of the seventeenth century, decided that continued contact with foreign elements might overbalance an already touchy and unstable set of affairs in Japan. For the third time, therefore, the leaders of Japan rather abruptly made a decision for all Japan that changed the whole pattern of events. They decided to close Japan to the outside world, both in respect to outsiders coming into, and Japanese venturing out of, Japan. Within a few years, in a series of edicts all backed up by severe penalties, and successful in result, the Tokugawa closed the ports of Japan to occidental and Asian traders, expelled the troublesome Spanish and Portuguese, stopped the conversion of Japanese to Christianity, stopped Japanese going abroad, limited the size of ships that could be built in Japanese yards, and sealed Japan up in an unprecedented kind of hermit-like existence. The Tokugawa also took many internal measures to weaken the strength of other clan leaders. They forced the permanent residence of hostages in Tokyo, allowed internal land transport routes to deteriorate, rearranged fiefs and land grants, and reduced the power of regional subordinate rulers.

These measures were all carefully planned and rather well executed. They succeeded in stabilizing the economy of Japan, and in stabilizing the patterns of regional control in such a way that Tokyo became the real seat of power in Japan, and the Tokugawa clan became the real rulers of the country. This procedure had other results. It kept occidentals out of Japan, except for the one small Dutch trading center which served as a listening post. Thus Japan escaped the fate of colonial status, so distasteful to the Orient. But in so doing Japan also lost touch with the rest of the world and with the progress of world events, for the knowledge gained through the slight contact with the one Dutch post was, on the whole, inconsequential and of little value to the Japanese leaders and the Japanese population alike.

The long period of hermitage did accomplish solidification of Japanese culture. The control of the Tokugawa clan was sufficiently tight so that no large scale internal changes or developments took place in Japanese culture. But the period of self-containment did serve to make the Japanese self-dependent in economic matters, and it tended to stabilize the population of Japan at a figure between 25,000,000 and 30,000,000. When population was growing rapidly in most other parts of the world, this is a rather remarkable demographic event in world history. And it served also to put the finishing touches upon Japanese culture, developing many kinds of things into even more distinctive patterns. By the middle of the nineteenth century, when Japan opened up to the rest of the world again, Japanese culture had become a rather specific pattern of its own. One could easily see the Chinese influences in things Japanese, but the detail of the pattern was clearly different from that of Korea and China, more clearly so than at any previous time in Japanese history.

EMERGENCE AND MODERNIZATION

The Tokugawa clan still ruled Japan in the 1850's when Commodore Perry sailed into Tokyo Bay and called upon the Japanese to end their two and a half centuries of hermitage. Repeated overtures to this end had been declined earlier, and Japanese administration had been extended to Hokkaido early in the nineteenth century to prevent Russian encroachment. The American overture was more than a casual invitation, however, for it was made through a show of military force which was not lost upon either the Tokugawa or other leading clans. The Tokugawa still held firm control internally but they were quick to realize that Japan could not stand up to outside forces that could muster many large guns in the big steam naval vessels such as those in the fleet. Within a few years they had signed trade treaties with several occidental countries, and had taken the first steps to modernize their own military establishment. This was the fourth time that a small group had changed the whole course of Japanese history.

The changes could not be undone, and they were the undoing of the Tokugawa and of the older order of feudalism in Japan. The emperor and some of the other clans that ruled Japan under Tokugawa control had not had the foreign fleet in their own home ports and were inclined to a decision to expel the foreigners. A few "incidents" soon convinced other leading clans of the futility of resistance to the outside world. The Satsuma clan of western Japan turned to developing a modern navy, and the Choshu clan began the building of a modern army. General opposition to the long rule of the Tokugawa took the form of restoring the emperor to a kind of power that the imperial family had not exercised for centuries, swept the Tokugawa from internal control, and started Japan on a course of modernization that both startled and impressed the whole world in the 75 years between 1866 and 1941. The Tokugawa had committed Japan to this program without the original support of the country, but other clans took over the lead, carried on the program, and managed to retain control of Japan until the end of World War II. Japan entered upon this new era in sound economic, social, and political circumstances, for there had been no time for a long series of disastrous internal wars to dissipate either population or resources.

A first step in modernization was the abolition of landed feudalism and the outmoded administration of government. Direct rule by the emperor and a bureaucracy, the abolition of feudal fiefs (for a reasonable price in government bonds), the establishment of new political administrative regions, and the pensioning off of the old regional rulers and the parasitic soldier group were the first steps in internal organization. This process, of course, gave to the ruling classes privileged opportunities for those members discerning enough to take them. Some old clans rose to new political power, and others acquired new economic strength, but it is notable that in general the control of Japan continued in the hands of the same groups that had run Japan for many centuries.

Although the Tokugawa had actually sent a few observers abroad before the opening of the country, Japanese culture was sadly out of date compared to the foreign trade, industrial, military culture of the West. Realizing this the new leaders of Japan fell back upon a useful precedent, that of sending students abroad to study the superior cultures. Since many of these new leaders were derived from the old military clans and the professional soldiery, their first concern was the building of a strong military force which could deter the colonial imperialism of the Occident. Appreciating also that such a force could now be built only upon the basis of an industrial technology, they undertook a thorough-going industrialization. So for nearly 50 years the Japanese government sent commissions, study groups, observers, and students all over the world to study the material economy of the West in a determined effort to bring Japan up to date as quickly as as possible. German military and medical science, French and German law, British ship building, and the railroad, manufacturing techniques, and the business methods of the United States were all carefully studied. Observers all over the world studied the patterns of trade, colonial imperialism, the development of agriculture, mining, transportation, and architecture. Educational systems and political institutions were examined.

The Japanese government took the lead in these matters, paying for the studies and then subsidizing the developments in Japan. The first railway was built between Tokyo and Yokohama in 1872, and by the end of the century hundreds of power plants and factories were operating. The operation of concerns was turned over to private companies formed by the leading clans, so that not only did Japan industrialize rapidly, but also the control of the modern aspects of the economy remained in the hands of the old leading elements. It is a commonplace to say that in a nonindustrial country the evolution of manufacturing begins slowly and somewhat on a hit-and-miss basis. Not so in Japan, for by 1900 most of the kinds of things being done abroad were also being done in Japan. As new industrial developments occurred abroad, Japanese continued to study them and to adapt them at home.

In the first few decades of modernization industrial skills were not sufficient to keep pace with developments of the economy, operating efficiency was rather low, and the occidental rather easily came to the conclusion that the Japanese were not creative but only imitative. To put the question of copying in proper balance it should be sufficient to remind an American that as late as the end of World War II the United States was still following the lead of Germany in many matters of industrial evolution. The amazing thing is that Japan went at modernization in a wholesale manner, in the way in which she had studied Chinese culture centuries earlier, and in a way seldom attempted by any other society. This was long-range planning well before five-year plans became the vogue. The process of synthesis always follows slowly after the process of learning about new culture traits, and Japan even today has hardly had the time to synthesize the whole of the mechanical economy of the industrial West.

It is notable that, whereas almost everything industrial was accepted, the leaders of Japan chose carefully in the fields of social, political, and cultural institutions. They did not disseminate many of the cultural ideas of the more democratic countries of the Occident but showed a preference for many of the elements of such authoritarian societies as Germany. A great many aspects of Japanese society went untouched by the hand of modernization, and a rural, agricultural Japan which neither participated in, nor received benefit from, the process of modernization continued to exist. At the same time the rural farm youth became easy subjects to indoctrinate with the military tradition, the divinity of the emperor, the acceptance of the new order, the need for colonial expansion, and the continued leadership of the upper classes.

THE PATTERNS OF MODERN ECONOMY

The Japanese economy of today is compounded out of agriculture, fishing, transportation, manufacturing, and international trade. Between 1875 and 1945 Japan utilized colonial imperialism also but, having lost World War II, Japan now has no colonial holdings. Of all the countries of the Orient Japanese economy at present most closely resembles the economies thought to be characteristic of the Occident. This is what the leaders of the late nineteenth century wanted, and they reproduced much of the bad along with the good. But, since this modernization was grafted upon an oriental base already mature in most of its features, the resulting blend is neither typically occidental nor oriental.

The settlement patterns of Japan were well fixed, and the agriculture of Japan was thoroughly matured when modernization came, so that few striking changes were introduced into the agricultural economy. Some new crops, a few tools and practices, some processing methods, commercial fertilizers, and an increased productivity resulted, particularly in the northern island of Hokkaido, but agriculture and its population remained essentially that of the older Japan until the end of World War II. In the several parts of the colonial empire changes in agriculture were introduced in contrast to the static situation in Japan proper. Some mechanization occurred in parts of Manchuria, and the plantation system appeared in Taiwan.

The Japanese have been fishing around their coasts for centuries. After the restrictions of the Tokugawa were lifted, the fisheries of modern Japan benefited tremendously by being able to sail out of sight of land again, and from the introduction of the larger, powered boat, the new types of nets used with trawlers, the canning of fishery products, the advanced ship-cannery techniques, and the expenditure of financial resources upon the fishing industry. Japan has advanced to the rank of one of the world's chief fishing countries, developing techniques and practices in advance of the rest of the world. These developments have resulted both in an increased home use of fishery products as food and in the production of a significant item in international trade.

The rapid development of industrial power of both thermal and hydroelectric variety, the wholesale establishment of industrial plants in a wide range of production, and the acquiring of advanced technical skills have produced a large amount of corporate urban manufacturing in Japan. This was designed to give Japan both military strength and a productive export economy. In the process both mining and forestry have been modernized. Corporate urban manufacturing has not replaced the older community workshop manufacturing entirely, but rather has blended with it to supplement and extend its range. An early concentration upon producer goods for domestic use and consumer goods for the export trade meant that Japanese retail consumers were not greatly benefited.

Railroads, urban and lowland highways, ports, ocean shipping, airfields and the airplane, telegraph, telephone, and radio communications have all been significant elements of the modernization of Japanese transportation and communications. These elements have been part of a complex system, so that Japan ranks among the leaders of the modern world in most of these matters, while at the same time retaining, in the upland and rural areas, many of the features and means typical of the older Orient.

As the modernization of Japan took place the scarcity of many raw materials became evident. To aid the acquisition of these needs the Japanese became active in international trade. The foreign trade of Japan more closely resembles that of Great Britain than that of any other oriental country.

As Japan became increasingly modernized, and as its population grew, the limitations and shortages of the home environment became more and more obvious. A colonial imperialism designed to supply such shortages as they appeared was developed from the first. The first step was the taking over of the Ryukyu Islands in the 1870's, followed by the militant acquisition of Korea and Taiwan in the 1890's. Then followed the stemming of Russian strength in the Far East in the first decade of this century. Thus, Japan acquired the Kurile Islands, the southern half of Sakhalin, and control over valuable fishing waters. Japan also gained the opportunity for economic exploitation of Manchuria, though political title remained in the hands of China. Attempts in China during and after World War I were not very successful, but a mandate was secured over the Marianas, and the Marshall and Caroline Islands. Political control over Manchuria in 1931 was the next step implementing economic control. The attack upon China in 1937 was one of a series that followed upon control of Manchuria and the spread of influence into Inner Mongolia, but other than simple issues of markets and raw materials had now begun to enter. The Japanese phase of World War II came as a logical development of colonial imperialism, but it, too, involved factors other than those of raw materials. Historians may argue the issue of how many people were involved in deciding to attack the United States in December, 1941, but we would note in passing that this was another authoritarian leadership act typical of past Japanese decision-making.

Modern Japan is a unique blending of oriental and occidental cultures in all their forms. The American dime stores full of handicraft goods marked "made in Japan" prior to 1941, the Japanese freighter in almost every port of the world, the cultured pearl, Tokyo University, the Japanese Army, Mitsui as a supercorporation, the American-type farmstead of Hokkaido, and the religious shrine-summer resort-tourist center, all were expressions of the modernizing process. Japan, as the loser in World War II, in 1945 was given an ultimatum to further reorganize this blend into something more suitable to the rest of the world. Now hedged about with international limitations, and forced to live upon her home political area, Japan is attempting the balance of a process that involves many serious questions. Having grown so greatly in population during the first phase of the process can she now continue to feed herself? Can she arrange peaceful patterns of industry and trade so as to fill the shortages and lift her standard of living sufficiently to remain at internal peace? Can she find that blend of East and West needed for peaceful existence on the international plane? Can she modernize her social and economic institutions in compliance with demand without losing her own soul? It is obvious now that the past modernization of Japan was of a special sort only, advanced yet incomplete. The finishing of this program will require a considerable span of time.

CONTEMPORARY AGRICULTURE

Japanese agricultural economy was not much affected by the beginnings of the program of industrialization and foreign trade, but as the population began to grow, agricultural output did not proportionately increase, so that a food deficit appeared which grew steadily larger. As industrial cities grew in size and food demand, the internal trade in both food products and other outputs of agriculture shifted their directional flows somewhat, commercializing of crop dispositions took place, and surplus labor was drawn out of the rural hinterlands into the industrializing cities, but Japan gradually began to import food supplies to satisfy the deficit as the Japanese population grew steadily in the late nineteenth and early twentieth centuries. The agricultural labor force remained relatively stable, technologies did not change much, and the output of Japanese agriculture went up only slowly during the period.

There was a net gain in the total cultivated land by the addition of some new lands in Hokkaido, northern Honshu, and in some of the hill country sectors of central Honshu and Kyushu and, of course, there was a decline in the percentage of population directly concerned with agriculture since the labor force held stable and the total population of Japan grew markedly. By about 1960 it might be said that the agricultural landscape had reached a pattern of spatial stability in that there was very little possible addition to be made to the cultivable landscape. Japan normally loses some arable land every year, through earthquakes, floods, and losses to urban-industrial expansion, but this is compensated by reclamation of earlier losses, reclamation of tidal flats, and small increases in terracing of hill lands.

After World War II there were changes in land ownership enforced by military occupation in that the larger holdings were broken up and sold to tenant operators. This temporarily increased the number of farm families, and the total number of farms by the Japanese definition (any homestead plot over one-fourth acre having any planted food crop, or having a cow, or a pig, or chickens), but the present trend is again moving to consolidate small "farms," and the number of farm operators is dropping.

After World War II elements of mechanization began to enter agricultural technology, as small electric motors were put to work pumping water on the rice landscape, as miniaturization of power tools, finally, produced something applicable to the small farm of terraced fields. Rototillers, small hand tractors, small threshing machines, power-cutters for harvesting, and other types of small-powered equipment now are spreading through Japanese agricultural technology. This, in turn, permits a withdrawal of some of the human labor force formerly doing the work, though it increases farming capital costs. In 1969 the agricultural labor force had dropped to under 9,000,000, and it is possible that it will continue to drop slowly in the near future span of years.

Since the early 1950's, there has been further development of agricultural productivity in Japanese agriculture. Such factors as plant breeding, elimination of poor-yielding varieties and crops, an increase in the double cropping index, consolidation of holdings for improved operational efficiency, the heavier usage of fertilizers, perfection of scientific planting practices, and improved controls over plant diseases and pests have increased the output of agriculture while the labor force has decreased and the net acreage cropped has grown only slightly. Whereas, in the late 1930's Japanese agriculture provided no more than three-fourths the food demand of the home population, and used almost half the total labor force, in the late 1960's domestic production was far closer to the demand pattern, and employed directly less than one-tenth the total labor force. It is not likely that Japanese agriculture can improve this ratio very much, since such improvements cannot continue to be made in the same proportionate pattern in the future.

There are distinct regional differences in Japanese agriculture, many of them related to the environmental situation of Japan, though it is not easy to map a clear set of regional patterns. Southern Japanese agricultural landscapes reach well into the hill country to fairly high altitudes, but the profile of maximum altitudinal cultivation drops steadily from southern to northern Honshu, and in northernmost Honshu and Hokkaido the hill country is not much used, owing to the progressive shortening of the growing season in the northern sectors. Holdings are larger in Hokkaido than in central Honshu, but the areas of smallest holdings are around the Inland Sea. Much more of southern Japan is terraced than is true in northern Honshu and Hokkaido, and terracing is done

on steeper slopes in southern Honshu and on Shikoku than elsewhere in Japan. Part-time farmers are numerous from central Honshu southward, particularly on the west coast of Honshu, whereas they are very few in Hokkaido. The labor force makes up a larger proportion of the total population in northernmost Honshu and southernmost Kyushu than elsewhere. The crop patterns show clear regionalisms, in that many crops cannot be cultivated either at high altitudes or in northern portions of the country. However, almost all crops may be cultivated in the higher hill country on Kyushu, but their northern limits are confined to lowland situations (Figs. 27.3 and 27.4). Citrus can be grown to a little north of Tokyo on the lowlands. Only the hardier crops may be grown in Hokkaido, so that the actual productivity and the appearance of the landscapes of Kyushu and Hokkaido are rather different.

The total agricultural landscape of Japan amounts to about 15,000,000 acres, just over sixteen percent of the total area, with only a slight possibility of increasing that total. The practice of double cropping for all Japan produces an annual cropped acreage of about 20,000,000 acres. Much of this double cropping amounts to growing hardy annual winter crops on lands devoted to rice during the main summer growing season.

Rice, by tradition, preference, and landscape engineering of the water-fed terraced field, has long been the dominant crop, and rice has spread northward into Hokkaido to the end that it is the dominant crop even there. In the late 1960's rice occupied almost 8,000,000 acres of land all over Japan, every year. Other grain cereals total about a third of the cropped land, with wheat being the most important single crop, totaling about 1,600,000 acres, and the others being several kinds of millets and barleys, along with oats and maize. Sweet and white potatoes, and a variety of peas and beans fill out the range of major food crops, with sweet potatoes yield-

JAPAN — CROPS

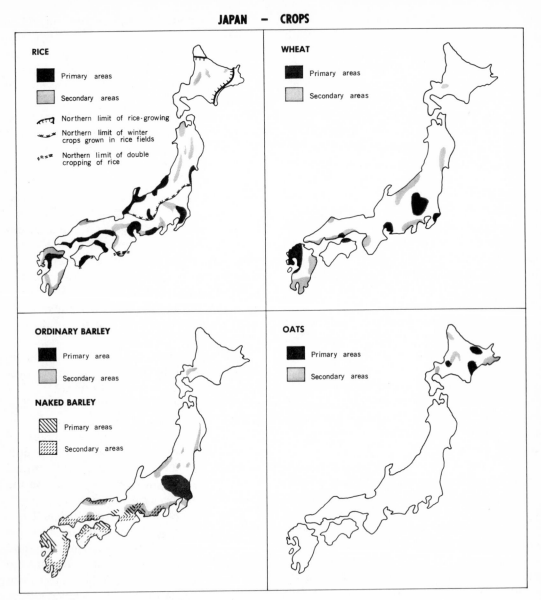

FIGURE 27.3. Primary grain-cereal crops of Japan.

ing the largest caloric volume of food after rice.

About 1,300,000 acres of green vegetables are grown every year, in wide variety, these being a repetitive short-term crop occupying a small share of the total land. The fruit acreage of Japan has increased rather strongly since the 1930's, and now amounts to about 600,000 acres, still notably less significant than in other parts of the Orient. Fiber crops occupy less than 100,000 acres, with other miscellaneous industrial crops about doubling this figure. Green-manure crops cover over 1,000,000 acres and form an integral

JAPAN – CROPS

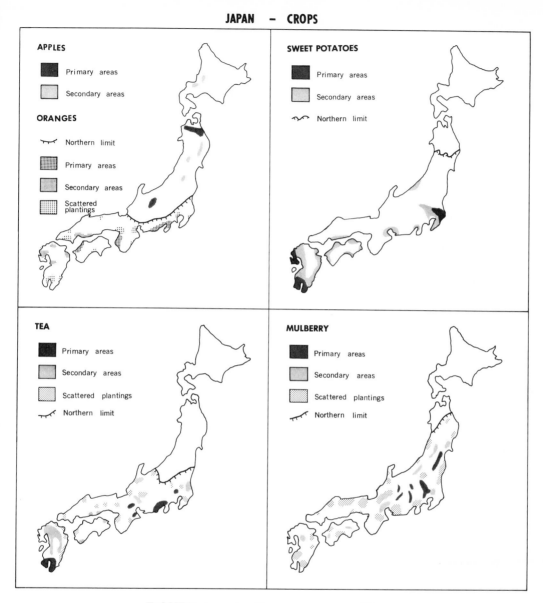

FIGURE 27.4. Auxiliary crop patterns of Japan.

part of cropping practice. Tea now covers only some 120,000 acres, grown on perhaps 30,000 farms only. Silk mulberry trees occupy no more than 450,000 acres, against the total of about 1,700,000 acres in 1930. Silk production has decreased notably since the start of World War II; it may never recover its former importance. The total number of farm cattle in the late 1960's was declining slightly, numbering about 2,000,-000. Horses, chiefly used in southern Kyushu and Hokkaido as draft animals, now number under 600,000, and are declining in number as small tractors increase. Urban-fringe dairy cattle, on the other hand, are steadily increasing in number, and they now exceed 2,500,000. There are close to 600,000 sheep. Chickens total some 140,000,000.

The dominance of rice in the agricultural scene suggests that as the southern peoples spread northward over Japan they carried southern land-use patterns with them, despite the climatic hazards faced in the more northern areas. Slowly short-season rice varieties, terracing, careful water control, and other cropping practices spread with them. Almost all rice grown is of the wet-field variety, upland rice everywhere being a minor item. Rice is chiefly a crop of the alluvial lowlands, but in many areas of lesser slope the terracing has reached well into the uplands.

Many of the upland fields of Japan today are only crudely terraced or leveled, and they lack water control facilities. Dry-field crops thus are significant items in the total agriculture. Although the crop list is a large one, and though rice does not dominate the agriculture of Japan as fully as that of modern Thailand, Japanese agriculture remains essentially that of the Orient, intensive gardening with a very high per acre yield. The addition of the powered equipment has increased the efficiency and brought Japanese agriculture to a very high level. Increasing efficiency can be achieved still, but the agricultural revolution so long needed is underway now, and extremely large gains in the future are less probable. The complete modernization of Japanese agriculture will take time, more capital input, and further changes in operational practice. A visitor is duly impressed by the facts that in Japan today there is very little wastage of lowland arable lands, and that on the existing farms there is no small patch of ground wasted. It is also impressive that in the industrial expansion of Japan a minimum of farmland was diverted from agricultural productivity, in contrast to the situation in parts of the United States where urban land developments of the last century have often driven the farmer off the very best crop lands. Nevertheless, a large area of uplands is still unused, and it does not seem true that there is no opportunity for the expansion of Japanese agriculture.

The physiologic and agricultural population densities of Japan are among the highest in the world. The regional crowding of farmers and farmland is strongest, of course, in Kyushu, Shikoku, and parts of southern Honshu, and obviously least in Hokkaido, which is the least agriculturally productive portion of Japan. Most of the farms are very small, the country-wide average being a little over two acres. The Japanese farm often is fragmented in location and is divided into wet and dry plots, so that an individual farm often consists of from two to ten individual field plots in several locations. There has been some readjustment of the traditional irregularity of fields in flat lowlands to improve workability, irrigation, and drainage, and to achieve consolidation of plots into larger units for increased operational efficiency.

FISHERIES

The Japanese have long shared the common oriental liking for fish and other aquatic food products. Japanese fishing techniques include most of those common throughout the Orient. Fishing of the shore waters of the Inland Sea was one of the basic elements of economy by the beginning of the Christian era. As the Japanese spread northward along the coasts of Honshu, fishing villages were among the early settlements. During the centuries prior to the closing of Japan by the Tokugawa, fishermen ranged over much of the Yellow Sea, the Sea of Japan, and the offshore waters around Japan itself. During the Tokugawa period only the immediate shore waters were fished, but by this time the Japanese had learned to use many aquatic foods, in a range of variety well beyond that common in the Occident. The rise of population in the last century, and the modern techniques learned abroad, have led to a remarkable development of the fishery industry in modern Japan, with the result that the Japanese eat more fish per capita, harvest a larger range of fishery products, and export more fish than does any other country.

Fresh-water inland sources of fish are not very important in Japan. The pond raising of fish dates only from the nineteenth century, and the culture pearl industry from 1915. The Japanese fishery industry, therefore, is essentially a marine fishery, although the pond fishery is expanding. Japan lies close to the zone of mixture of northern and southern ocean currents, and is surrounded by waters rich in aquatic life. Although the number of fish species is less than that found in southern waters, the Japanese have developed their modern fisheries to a greater extent than those of any other oriental country. The use of simple power boats has been an integral part of this modern development, along with the application of line and trawl techniques. After 1920 the Japanese in the fishing industry developed, to a greater degree than found elsewhere, the floating fish cannery and the mother ship serviced by many small power boats. Japanese concerns have engaged in fishing along the whole coast of Asia, as far south as Singapore and Indonesia, and as far north as the Bering Sea and the Gulf of Alaska. Although this extensive distribution of fishing sometimes was handmaiden to military intelligence, it was a profitable economic venture in its own right.

Many of the fishermen of Japan are farmers who engage in seasonal or part-time fishing, using small sail boats and working the shore waters within a radius of a few miles only. This variety of fishing has produced the largest share of the total catch, and has in good part supplied the domestic supply of fish, seaweeds, shell fish, and miscellaneous aquatic foods. This is the traditional fishery pattern, which ranges from following the ebb tide as a beachcomber to the small boats that dot the shore waters and fill the harbors. The offshore fisheries are chiefly those developed by organized groups and corporate concerns, fishing with modern equipment. Most of this catch is canned and is a contribution to the export trade. Since early in the present century the Japanese export of fishery products has been a major item in foreign trade. This trade was carefully built up, and led to the shipping of herring to Great Britain and tuna to the United States.

The productivity of the offshore Japanese fisheries in part depended upon the spread of political power with the growth of empire. Japan now finds her fishing area restricted. She is prohibited from ranging widely in the Pacific, and no longer can she fish Russian Arctic waters. This will restrict the volume of the catch and will reduce the export trade quota, but fisheries will continue to be important in the over-all Japanese economy. It is likely that the immediate shore waters and the off-shore regions open to Japan will be fished intensively in the future, as population rises and the pressure upon food supply increases. In the late 1960's about 600,000 fishermen in some 215,000 boats, working out of 2,000 fishing ports, were again operating, with a total catch that was averaging over 7,000,000 tons. The demand for fishery products was running ahead of the catch.

FORESTRY

In rough and chiefly mountainous Japan a larger share of the landscape has remained in wild and semiwild plant growth than is true in many other heavily populated regions. About half of the total area of Japan is in productive "forest" growth of some sort, though some of this represents modern purposeful reforestation, with government control over about one-third of all forest lands. Japanese forest lands range from the subtropical into the boreal zones, from the southwest to the north, and from the lowlands into the mountains. Much of southern Honshu, Shikoku, and Kyushu has been contaminated by replacement species in recent centuries, so that the subtropical forest area does not now produce much valuable timber. Much of the temperate forest has also been cut at some time in the past, and reforestation has chiefly replaced the original cover by coniferous species. The northern boreal forests are chiefly coniferous forests. Saw timber can be harvested from perhaps a quarter of the total forest land, but pulpwood and fuel wood are extractable from most of the rest of the area.

The Japanese have always built in wood, and have used wood or charcoal for domestic purposes, and both of these drains on the forest resource continue today, despite the increasing use of new kinds of building materials and the increasing use of electricity for domestic purposes. The annual cut from the forests, for all purposes, continues to exceed the annual growth pattern, in most sections of Japan. Recent restrictions on cutting mean a larger wood products deficit, and Japanese imports of wood products have been increasing rather rapidly since about 1950. In the late 1960's Japan imported about one-third of her total consumption of wood products.

COMMUNICATIONS AND TRANSPORT

The earliest Japan we know of was essentially a region using for transportation the waterways of the many bays and the Inland Sea of the southern parts of the country. The northern folk used a network of mountain paths and trails. The Japanese learned to build the stone-paved step roads used by the Chinese in hilly landscapes, and adopted the shoulder pole and the sedan chair for primary use on these roads. They also took over the ox sled, the wheelbarrow, and the two-wheeled ox cart for use on locally smooth surfaces. They learned the better building of boats from the Koreans and possibly the Chinese. From the continent the horse was adopted by the Japanese leaders as an element in military tactical transport for their own better control of the peasantry, only in the relatively modern era becoming a draft animal on the farm in Hokkaido and in southern Kyushu.

Slowly the Japanese adapted these mechanisms of transport to their own home environment. Small boats and ships and also the detailed patterns and uses of land transport were altered to fit the local situation. The coasts of Japan were dotted with harbor and port facilities, and the network of "roads" gradually spread thickly over southern Japan, and formed a fairly close network in the north. The trunk roads of this old system were important elements in the system of political control of Japan. Before the coming of the occidental, however, the Chinese and Korean origins of the Japanese transport system remained very clear. In the program of modernization of the last century the Japanese effectively revolutionized most of their systems of transport and communications (Figs. 27.5 and 27.6).

They soon began building both naval and merchant shipping and, within recent decades, the Japanese sea transport equipment, naval, mercantile offshore, and coastal, has ranked high among the world's fleets. Port and harbor development has accompanied the growth of boats and ships. The opportunities offered by World War I were capitalized upon effectively when other shipping was scarce, and the Japanese mercantile fleet has been among the world's large fleets since that time. Modern Japan, turning out some of the most modern types of equipment

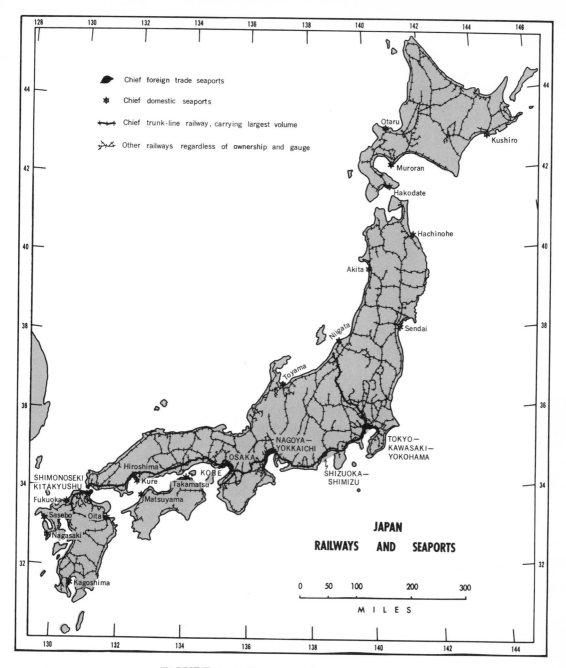

FIGURE 27.5. Railways and seaports of Japan.

such as the gigantic tankers, is also a leader in the shipbuilding industries. Most every significant world port is familiar with the Japanese freighter, and this commercial fleet has facilitated the growth not only of Japanese world trade but also of the world's general ocean trade.

On land the Japanese launched into a

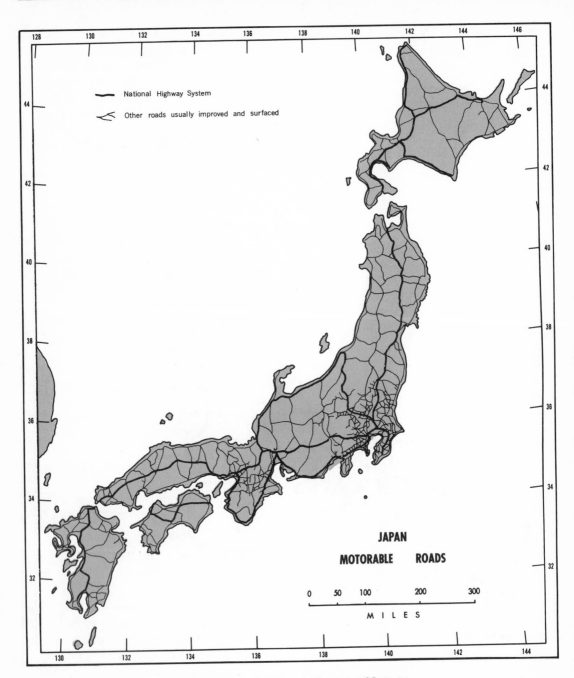

FIGURE 27.6. Motorable roads of Japan.

program of railroad building that has given it the most effective rail system of any part of the Orient (see Fig. 26.5). Since Japan is a small country, elongated and divided into many islands, it has no region that is far from the sea, and so the actual mileage of rail lines and roads required was far less than that needed by China or India. Sheer mileage is here of less significance than utility and efficiency. Rail lines are of several sorts, ranging from the long-distance railway carrying freight and passenger trains, through the rapid interurban transit lines around large cities, to the urban street-car systems and subways found in several cities. The rail system totals just over 29,000 miles. In recent development of high-speed trains (see p. 267), Japan has shown the best results of any country to the late 1960's. The Japanese railways are of meter gauge for economy of building in a mountainous country, and their rolling stock is light weight. The main rail system is government owned and operated, but there are numerous private short feeder lines. Compared to Great Britain the rail system is neither as dense a network nor as efficient a system, but it carries a tremendous passenger traffic and a respectable freight volume. Many of the key rail lines follow the old trunk roads of earlier periods, serving political ends as well as economic ones.

Roads in Japan have never been fully modernized, since they were not very important in political control of the country. Only a small mileage of modern motor roads had been built by the 1960's, and these roads were less effective in modern transport than were the rail lines. The total road mileage was about 38,000 (see Fig. 27.6). A network of narrow roads of relatively steep gradient in the mountainous terrain has resulted, many of them but little wider than the old step roads. Roads are chiefly of local utility in the rural regions of Japan and were not key items in the industrial modernization of the country. Around the large cities fairly adequate road systems were laid out to facilitate industrial development. Many of the roads on the alluvial lowlands are narrow and elevated above the ricefields. Most road traffic is local in character, and involves carts, wagons, bicycles, and foot traffic. Interlocking with these roads is the old network of local paths, trails, and step roads that long has serviced the villages and hamlets of rural Japan. Even

though the road system is less well developed than the rail system, the road map indicates that Japan is fairly well connected by roads open to modern vehicular traffic, though few of these roads could carry the types and volumes of traffic that roll over many American highways. In 1970 there were nearly 10,000,000 automobiles, trucks, and buses on the roads, but until very recently these have been chiefly urban-suburban in usage. This is a result of the recent rise of Japan as an automotive manufacturer. Cross-country bus lines and long-distance motor transport services in Japan are relatively unimportant, trains here chiefly providing for passenger traffic. In 1970 Japan appears to be on the verge of making a modern commitment to the automobile and an enlarged public road system, though urban smog problems from automotive sources open a question of how far the trend may go. Cross-country expressways are under construction, and the utility of automotive transport now appeals to Japanese in both urban and rural areas.

Air transport was relatively slow to develop in modern Japan which, itself, does not greatly need air services. It was only with the political and economic development of the colonial empire that air services began to be developed. The decade of the 1930's showed a striking expansion of civil air services. Aviation became chiefly a military function with the growing imperialism of Japan in recent decades. There is a good network of airfields throughout Japan which can serve whatever ends the Japanese wish. It is chiefly in international air traffic that Japan is active today, and Japan Air Lines circles the globe along with the other big flag carriers.

Telecommunications were of interest to the leaders of Japan in the furtherance of modernization, and Japan today has a widely distributed set of telegraph, telephone, and radio facilities. The rural population has not made much personal use of modern communications systems, but these systems are a significant element in the governmental, industrial, and urban development of modern Japan. Japanese developments in this field were greater than those of other parts of the Orient to the end of World War II.

THE GROWTH OF MODERN INDUSTRY

Prior to World War II Japan was the best example of an industrial country outside the Occident. Other portions of the world today are rapidly undergoing industrialization, and Japan now is going through a period of evolutionary maturity in her industrial patterns. The present is a period of transition, but Japanese industrial growth and development could, in the coming two decades, match any pattern of the Occident.

In the 1860's there was a considerable volume and variety of manufacturing in Japan, modeled upon the handicraft patterns of Korea and China. Household industry of a primary sort was very widely spread, and less widespread, simple powered and community workshop patterns were highly developed. Japanese artisans were skilled in the textile manufactures, in bamboo and wood, porcelains, lacquer, and in many of the metals. There were few large urban centers of manufacturing, and there was but a small volume of power available other than human energy, the auxiliary power being chiefly derived from water wheels. Charcoal was the primary source of fuel and energy. Japanese leaders quickly realized that these facilities, skills, and products were inadequate in the modern world.

As previously suggested an interlocking pattern of government and private initiative sponsored the modernizing of manufacturing in Japan. A determination that Japan would not become a colonial holding of some occidental power predisposed part of the program. The refusal to utilize foreign capital concentrated control and ownership in the hands of a few leading combines, but also meant that only as capital resources accumulated could the program increase its own rate of development. The periods between 1890 and 1900, 1913 and 1920, and 1930 and 1941 were important periods for the growth of industry.

An early concentration upon light manufacturing and the textile industries was rather natural, since it could call upon many old skills at least partially usable in the new patterns. Most of the rural population of Japan was too poor to buy the industrial output, and the need for additional income led to a development of the export trade, which could help pay for the needed imports of raw materials. Gradually developments in the chemical industries, the iron and steel industries, and in general metals manufacturing began to rise. There was an early concentration upon hydroelectric development to provide an adequate power supply, but there has been a steady increase in power development throughout the whole period since the 1890's.

Cheap labor and the fairly close integration of community workshop manufacturing of many individual parts in small shops associated with the larger factories permitted Japan to undersell many occidental firms in supplying consumer goods to the world. Lower operating efficiency often was compensated by multiple shift operation of factories at a time when the "swing" and "graveyard" shifts had not yet become common in the Occident. Although the Japanese home market consumed but a small share of the industrial output, rural Japan contributed to the growth of industrialization through bearing a much heavier share of the national tax burden than did the commercial and manufacturing sectors of Japanese society.

About 1930 it was commonly stated that Japanese industry was concentrated upon the textile and light manufacturing fields but had not yet made great headway in heavy industry. Of this the Japanese were well aware, and after 1930 a noticeable shift in the industrial program took place. Consumer goods, textiles, and light manufacturing were steadily reduced in emphasis as a concentration began upon the heavier variety of manufacturing. Increasing efficiency and greatly increased labor skills made possible this sort of shift, but the increasing capital resources of Japan were also significant.

In the early stages of the growth of manufacturing the regional development was most marked in and around the large cities from Tokyo southward along the Inland Sea. Here were concentrated the larger share of the artisan skills and the older patterns of manufacturing. As hydroelectric and thermal power development made power available in many parts of Japan there was a gradual regional diffusion of manufacturing. As the development of mining and the growth of the iron and steel industries took place, some activity began to show up all over Japan. With the maturing of secondary manufacturing, using by-products, related skills, and new materials, there developed an industrial region stretching from Tokyo to the northern part of Kyushu, with nodal concentrations in and around the large cities. Smaller regional industrial locations developed in northern Honshu and southwestern Hokkaido. There began a drift of population from rural Japan to the industrial region and the large cities of Japan.

Early in the program it became obvious that Japan proper did not possess all the mineral resources necessary to a great industrial growth, either in volume or in variety. More and more the colonial empire was called upon to furnish raw materials, and gradually there developed a pattern of decentralization of manufacturing at various points throughout the empire. Korea, Manchuria, and Taiwan all shared in the growth of Japanese manufacturing, and both their raw materials and their manufactured goods were

integrated into the industrial operations of Japan proper.

The most significant Japanese mineral resource is coal, but it lacks the range of quality needed in a strong industrial economy, being poor in coking coals (Fig. 27.7). Kyushu and Hokkaido possess the largest reserves. The volume is adequate to a small industrial use for a long period, but in the projected use pattern of the late 1960's the coal supply will be exhausted in a century. Korea and Manchuria formerly supplied the necessary coals for blending with Japanese coal in industrial processes.

The petroleum resources of Japan are small, and the annual production has never been large. Northwestern Honshu and Hokkaido are the regions of Japan proper that possess petroleum, though Japan formerly drew an annual production from Sakhalin.

Compensating for this shortness of industrial fuel supply, Japan now has many hydroelectric plants, most of which are small in capacity but effective in providing a widely distributed power supply. Over 1,500 hydro plants had a maximum output close to 17,000,000 kilowatts in 1968, but not all plants can operate at the maximum rating since there is a strong seasonality to water flow in many parts of Japan. There are over 400 thermal power stations and one atomic station, and the maximum capacity of these stations slightly exceeds 28,000,000 kilowatts.

Iron ores are widely scattered over Japan, but they normally are mixed ores of variable quality occurring in small volume, rather difficult and expensive to mine and to smelt. These were adequate to a handicraft economy, but not to an advanced industrial economy.

The emphasis upon electrification led to the development of copper mining and, for a peacetime economy, domestic sources are adequate. Ores are widely scattered over Japan. Military industry during the period 1933–1945 required more copper than pro-

JAPAN – MINERALS

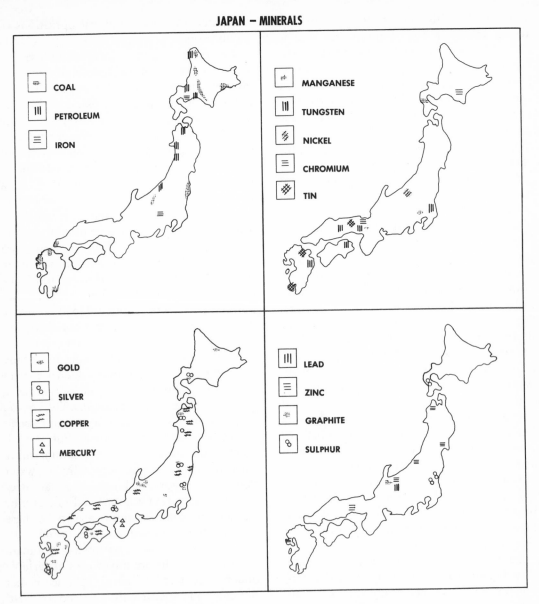

FIGURE 27.7. Mineral occurrences in Japan.

vided by domestic sources, and a greatly increased manufacturing pattern again has made Japan clearly dependent upon outside sources. Some of the copper ores contain sufficient amounts of gold and silver for normal Japanese use. Sulphur is a mineral present beyond normal Japanese needs, but for most of the rest of the auxiliary industrial minerals Japan has but partial supplies, and does not have tremendous reserves. Dependent upon the scale of industrial use Japan needs small to large volumes of many of the ferro-alloys, lead, tin, zinc, graphite, refractories, and phosphates. Bauxite is entirely lacking in Japan.

In summary Japan is not rich in minerals.

Only sulphur is truly surplus to an industrial economy. Coal, gold, copper, and chromium are sufficient for a modest industrial program, but not for a large one. The shortages of iron ore, petroleum, the ferro-alloys, bauxite, and several auxiliary minerals are serious. The large agricultural need for phosphates makes the shortage in this mineral acute. So long as Japan possessed a colonial empire many of these home shortages could be bridged, but the present Japanese industrial economy is handicapped. How greatly it is handicapped depends upon what level of operation can be achieved. On the present patterns of industrial production Japanese merchants are widely seeking mining concessions and purchase agreements in many parts of the world, and the expectation is toward still larger demands for raw materials.

As industrial development matured, government maintained a strong directive influence upon its course, but actual ownership increasingly trended into the hands of a small number of supercorporations, owned by the big families, known as the *zaibatsu*. The older and more important of these, Mitsui, Mitsubishi, Sumitomo, Yasuda, and Fuji controlled literally hundreds of industrial, mining, and trading concerns, interwoven in very complex patterns. With the development of the colonial empire a few lesser combines grew, and there were many small manufactuting concerns not directly owned by, but tributary to, the large concerns. Much of the remaining community workshop manufacturing was independent but also at the mercy of government control. During the 1930's there was considerable consolidation and streamlining of industrial ownership, and government again began to participate. With the end of World War II there was attempted, at the behest of occupation forces, the complete dissolution of the great holding companies. By 1948 this process has been fairly well completed, resulting in lessened industrial productivity.

A notable part of the maturity of Japanese industrial society is the degree to which her manufactured products are now finding markets inside the country. Electric and gasoline powered equipment on the farms, and television sets, refrigerators, washing machines, and many of the other "export items" are now to be found in both urban and rural homes in ratios quite comparable to those of countries of western Europe, countries which used to be held up in comparison against Japan.

Examining particular aspects of Japanese industrialization since 1951 yields interesting diagnostic percentages and rankings. Close on fifty-five percent of the Japanese now live in cities of over 20,000. Manufacturing now utilizes over thirty percent of the labor force, and the services category percentage has risen to over forty percent. Japan has had the highest economic growth rate of any of the industrial countries since 1960. She leads the world in shipbuilding, photographic instruments, and the manufacture of transistor radios. She has the second largest shipping fleet, behind only Liberia. In 1969 about three-fourths of Japanese steel production was done in basic oxygen furnaces, compared to about forty-three percent for the United States. Japan has the second largest telephone system in the world, and the waiting list is longer than that of any other country. Japan now is second only to the United States in such varied lines as electrical machinery manufacture, textile manufacture and the production of synthetic fibers. Japan ranks third in the production of cement, plastics, and steel, and she recently became the third ranking automotive producer (cars, trucks, and buses). The Japanese gross national product recently ranked fourth among the world's nations, and the per capita income has passed that of several European countries. Japan is among the world leaders in providing economic aid to developing countries. There now are more than 20,000,000 private individuals in Japan who own stocks in enterprises organized as public corporations. Over eighty percent of all Japanese industrial plant managers are college graduates, and Japan is the second ranking user of computers.

For all that the broad industrial patterns of Japan resemble those of other mature industrial societies, the structure of industry is still rather different reflecting the old characteristics of handicraft manufacturing. A very large share of manufacturing and trade is controlled by about fifteen large combines, derived ultimately from the old *zaibatsu* cartels that were supposedly dissolved just after World War II; there are a number of new economic combines that have been formed and that have grown large so that the original half dozen no longer controls industry completely. At the other end of the scale are the small establishments representing the older pre-industrial handicraft manufacturing system but now participating in aspects of modern industry. A rather large share of the work force is employed by these small entrepreneurs, who handle the organization and management of economic enterprises, but who ration out raw materials to numbers of individuals for fabrication. The dualism is more complex than the subcontracting that is present in the American manufacturing system since the scale of operations is often such that fabrication of parts or elements takes place in individual homes. Of the roughly 500,000 "manufacturing establishments" operative in the late 1960's, well over 400,000 employed very small numbers of workers each and had few plant establishment or maintenance costs. There are some tens of thousands of establishments in a middle range that operate plants and employ moderate numbers of people. These establishments represent the sub-contractor element in the American scene. There are approximately 450 large corporations operating numerous plants and employing large numbers of workers, and it is these plants which carry on the heavy basic manufacturing. Many of the small estab-

lishments have interlocking working agreements with larger companies in a complex system that feeds component elements into the assembly or fabrication process toward the production of finished goods. Once industrialization reaches a certain scale these very small establishments, theoretically, should disappear and their employees should participate in modernized industry, but in Japan this has not so far occurred. It may be expected that there will be a decline in the future in this small scale operational sector, but the sector may well continue permanently as a reflection of the Japanese socioeconomic system in the larger sense. It is notable that over thirty-five percent of the industrial work force is employed on a life-time basis, and that among most of the large firms almost the whole work force is so employed.

The spatial distribution of contemporary manufacturing follows the patterns previously established during the late nineteenth century. Thus, the largest part of the industrial activity takes place in the urban-industrial zone reaching from the Tokyo locality southwestward to northern Kyushu, with extreme concentrations at four nodal centers, Tokyo, Nagoya, Kobe-Osaka, and Kitakyushu (Fig. 27.8). At present the margins of the Inland Sea form an almost continuous series of manufacturing towns and cities. There are secondary manufacturing districts, now steadily growing larger, on both coasts of central-northern Honshu, and a growing secondary manufacturing district is located in southwest Hokkaido. The Tokyo region is the primary concentration of almost every kind of manufacturing operation, and it produces in the vicinity of thirty percent of the total industrial output. Although the Tokyo nodal region does not dominate every one, it is represented in the production of each of the twenty-odd categories of manufacturing employed in the Japanese classification of industrial operations. Both the Nagoya and Kobe-Osaka nodal regions are similarly represented,

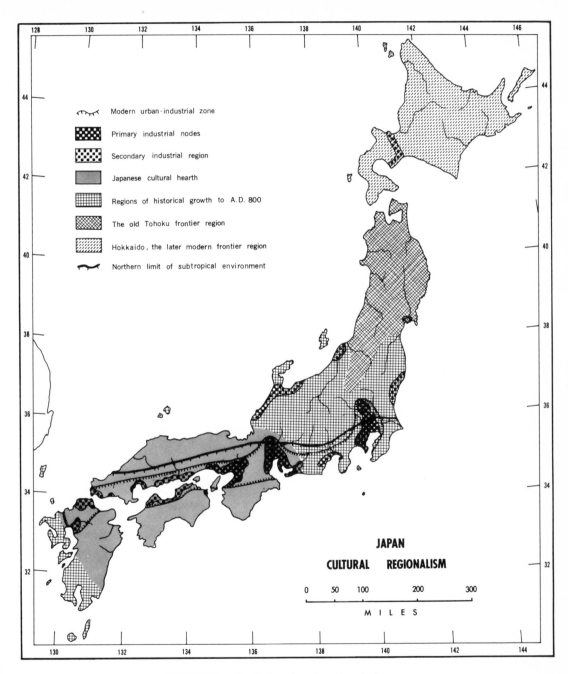

FIGURE 27.8. Cultural regionalism in Japan.

though a little less strongly in some lines. The Kitakyushu nodal region is the least mature of the four, and is not represented in every line; Kitakyushu is strongest in iron and steel, chemical fertilizers, and pulp-paper products.

The secondary districts have strengths in particular aspects, and do not participate in every line of activity, but in no case does a secondary district rival the three primary nodal regions of Tokyo, Nagoya, Kobe-Osaka. The southwestern Hokkaido district, for example, produces iron and steel, builds ships, processes food products, and manufactures a wide range of paper products, and the central west coast of Honshu produces iron and steel, railway equipment, general machinery, chemical fertilizers, pottery products, and has its greatest strength in the textile industries. Many changes are currently taking place, however, as the present industrial growth rate is such that new plants are being established in the various secondary districts every year.

In summary, since 1951 Japanese industrialization has matured, and Japan now ranks as one of the leading industrial countries of the world. Japanese factories produce the full range of manufactures turned out elsewhere although Japan was only getting back into airplane manufacturing in the late 1960's. Engineering technology has matured and is beginning to strike out on its own. Skilled labor shortages exist in Japan today at the highest levels of technology, but probably at no greater rate than among other mature industrial societies. The Japanese dual industrial structure provides a reservoir of skills from among the small establishments that can be absorbed gradually into the work force of the larger manufacturers as needed. The Japanese government and the banking system of Japan still are closely interlocked with the industrial program of private concerns in such a way that the overall industrialization can remain current with developments in other industrial societies. Japanese contacts throughout the world, in trade and natural resources development, are sufficiently widespread to assure Japan a continuing flow of raw materials and contacts with markets. Internal Japanese consumer habits are changing with the rising levels of living, and the internal market today forms a significant element in the whole of industrialization. The national concern for further development of an industrial society is such that this seems assured. Finally, it may be remarked that the scale of performance in making inventions has been less important in Japan that the matter of accepting the inventions of others and finding technological zones overlooked by others in which these adapted inventions may be put to work profitably. In this, the Japanese have had singular success in recent decades. Providing future international political relations remain satisfactory, further expansion and technological advancement of Japanese industry appear probable.

THE GROWTH OF TRADE

During the long period of Tokugawa control of Japan there had been very little foreign trade, and even domestic trade was restricted to little more than local trade. With the opening of Japan to the world, there began a tremendous change in patterns of productivity, with a consequent large-scale development of trade, both domestic and foreign. From the very start the leaders of Japan attempted to arrange a favorable pattern, by which she exported chiefly manufactured and processed commodities and imported raw materials. This was not always entirely possible, of course, but in the long run it is true that Japan never descended to the role of supplier of raw materials that was characteristic of so many of the other oriental countries.

During the early decades, after the 1860's, Japanese exports consisted of such items as raw silk and tea, both of which were really processed commodities, silk textiles, porcelains, lacquerware, and the other manufacturing products of community workshop industry. Quite early there began the import of minerals, raw cotton and other fibers, food grains, and lumber. As industrial production began to rise there appeared in the export list cotton textiles, cement, glass, chemicals, varied consumer products, and simpler items of machinery. Accompanying this export trade, other raw products such as rubber and sheet and shaped metal products to be further processed began to flow into Japan. Gradually a wide range of exports began to flow out of Japan, and the import volume continued to expand and to rise.

From the start oriental sources of raw materials were important, and oriental markets for manufactured goods ranked high on the list. The United States for a long period ranked high also, both as a source of imports and as a market for the products of industry and agriculture. The United States steadily consumed the largest share of Japanese silk and tea, Japan replacing China as a supplier on both counts. As Japanese shipping increased in volume raw materials were drawn from all over the world, and exports flowed to all parts of the world. The United States, China, India, and the Indies have been the biggest single source of raw materials and markets for export goods. Japan successfully competed with Great Britain, the United States, Germany, and France in oriental markets for her export products, lower quality and cheaper prices being relied upon to appeal to the larger bulk of the population having a low purchasing power. In the American market Japan concentrated for several decades on low-priced products which could undersell the increasingly costly domestic manufactures of the United States. The dime-store trade was a significant share of this market for manufactured goods, and Japanese manufacturers were skillful in meeting the commodity pattern.

Within Japan, as mineral and forest products from many local regions began to be needed in the growing industrial centers, an important coastwise shipping trade developed which handled the bulk of internal commodity movements. Japan has nearly 4,000 ports and landing points usable in domestic trade. Railway traffic in coal, wood products, rice, and a few other commodities has been significant, but is less important than water traffic. Despite the wide range of domestic consumer goods, however, a strong growth of internal trade never occurred and domestic trade is restricted to local products.

In recent decades Japan has added new raw material imports such as petroleum, bauxite, copper, lead, zinc, tin, and iron ore to its earlier list as the shift in industrial emphasis has taken place. A serious decline in the export of raw silk was temporarily damaging, with long-range reactions in land use, as noted earlier. After 1937 the Japanese export trade began to decline in range and volume of commodities, and the import trade changed its character markedly in order to provide strategic war materials. The colonial empire supplied a considerable share of the imports of food products and raw materials, taking a share of the exports as well. And during the war years Japan drew a wide range of commodities from the occupied areas in an exchange which could hardly be called trade.

With the tightening of economic bonds after 1937, government restriction of production, local trade, and consumption patterns altered the range and variety of domestic trade. Adoption of controlled patterns of food collection after harvests from rural Japan distorted these domestic trade patterns.

The end of World War II brought trade to a standstill both in domestic and foreign markets, political controls over Japanese economic activity, trade, and fishing restricted her actions, and most of the commercial shipping fleet no longer existed. The prohibition on certain types of manufacturing had repercussions on the import trade. As Japanese economic reconstruction took place a large food import became mandatory since the revolution in Japanese agriculture had not yet begun.

In more recent years Japanese foreign trade has boomed in terms of its range and total, but some notable shifts have taken place in the commodity patterns. As change has taken place in Japanese agriculture the rice imports have gone down. No longer is finished complex machinery a leading import. Instead, the raw materials bulk larger now: iron ores and scrap steel, crude petroleum, wood products, nonferrous metals, and chemical agents. There still is a large total import of food products but in new ranges, wheat instead of rice, with greater present amounts of meats and dairy produce. In exports finished machinery now leads the list, followed by refined and shaped metals, iron and steel in shapes and formed aspects, chemicals, automotive equipment, radio equipment, optical instruments, and manufactured food products. Fishery products, formerly high on the list still are among the exports in the same general volume, but they no longer rank as high as formerly. On both the import and export lists the commodity patterns run the full range of the world's goods.

The largest amount of Japanese foreign trade with a single country still flows to and from the United States, normally comprising about one-third of all Japanese trade. Another third is with Asian countries, but here there are variations, in that large imports of petroleum come from both Saudi Arabia and Iran, but only a modest volume flows the other direction in the export trade, whereas Japan supplies a large volume of exports to Thailand but imports only modest volumes from Thailand. However, it is notable that the whole world has become a Japanese market for manufactured goods and a supplier of raw materials and specialty manufactures.

Today, no one country can either provide the market for manufactures, or make available the wide range and volume of raw materials needed in Japan. Since 1960 the total trade of Japan has jumped upward, the balance varying from favorable to unfavorable in different years. The 1969 total trade amounted to some U. S. $31,000,000,000, with a slightly favorable balance.

POPULATION AND REGIONALISM

Japan has been a well-populated country for many centuries, and a very heavily populated country for several centuries, but within the last century Japan has come to be one of the most densely populated countries of the earth (Fig. 27.9). With its 102,000,000 people in 1970, the arithmetic density is almost 720 per square mile, including the top of Mount Fuji. In terms of agricultural density the figure now exceeds 4,300 per square mile, with some of the food supply coming from fishery products, and complemented by an imported food supply of perhaps ten percent. Both the above are artificial figures, of course, for the mass of the Japanese population now resides on a very small area of land within this fairly small country. Traditionally, a few Japanese lived by dispersed settlement, though most lived in clustered villages. Market towns are quite old, and there have been a few cities for some centuries. In the modern sense, however, there were only five large cities in Japan in the 1860's when Japan shifted her cultural focus. The cities were Tokyo, Osaka, Kyoto, Nagoya, and Kanazawa, and their total population was in the vicinity of 1,300,000. There were, in addition, about a hundred towns of 10,000 or more each. Over eighty percent of the Japanese would then have been described as rural, nonurban in residential pattern.

In the late 1960's the properly urban share of the population is not far from fifty-five percent. This is an interpolated figure since

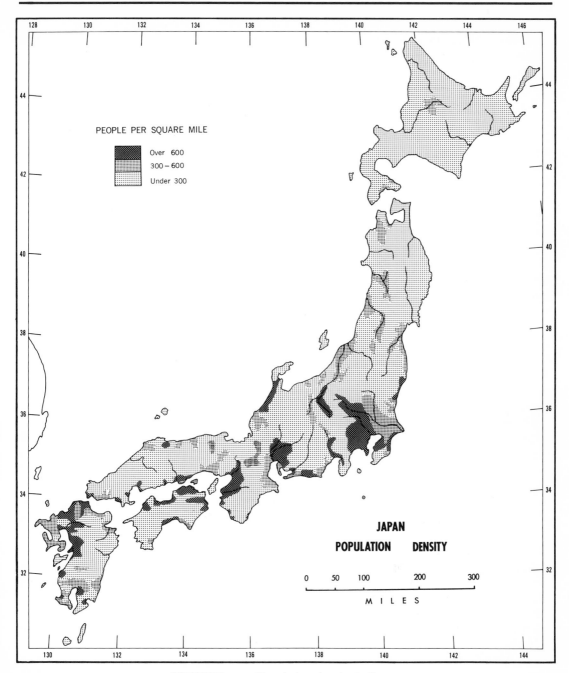

FIGURE 27.9. Population density in Japan.

many of the urban administrative districts include rural populations within their limits. It is clear that urbanization has been going on for the last century, but there has been a marked increase in the rate of urbanization since the early 1950's. This increased urbanization is related to two economic factors—the mechanization of the Japanese farm and the inability of the small farm to support the rural population on the level of living it now is demanding and the rapid increase in industrialization of the Japanese economy in which there has been an increasing shortage of labor.

It is clear that the rural landscape cannot support, in modern socioeconomic terms, the large population that was formerly content with its traditional village pattern of livelihood. For all the improvement in Japanese agriculture in the last twenty years, the costs have been significant, and the small Japanese farms simply will not provide for a large population at a high level of living. Japanese industry has been drawing off the surplus rural population during most of the last century, into its urban zonal pattern, chiefly concentrated in cities from Tokyo southwestward to northern Kyushu (see Fig. 27.8). The present rural-to-urban migration stream is an accented long-term movement. At the present time Japanese industry is able to support the large urban population on a level of living that produces satisfaction. All portions of Japan are currently facing migration into the industrial regions, and all rural sectors of Japan currently are losing population. The cityward movement is chiefly localized; that is, the migration path is chiefly to the nearest city, even in Hokkaido. The location of Tokyo, however, means that the Tokyo metropolitan area is drawing the largest in-migration streams, and Tokyo is growing more rapidly at present than any other metropolitan region (see Fig. 4.6 and accompanying text). Hokkaido is the region undergoing the least rapid rate of urbanization at present.

Factors of significance in the modern growth of the Japanese population are the birth and death rates, the rate of infant mortality, and the changing life span of the Japanese. The birth rate stood at about 32/1000 in 1900, reached its peak of 35/1000 in 1920, and has been declining since then,

to an all-time low of 13.7/1000 in 1967. The 1968-1969 rates were slightly higher, on the short term. The death rate stood at about 20/1000 in 1900, reached a figure of about 25/1000 in 1920, and has declined ever since, to a low of about 6.8/1000 in 1969. Infant mortality was about 155/1000 in 1900, but has steadily decreased to the current stable figure of close to 15/1000. Life expectancy (somewhat higher for females than for males) was about 43 years in 1900, but now is just over 70 years. There are close to 7,000,000 Japanese over age 65 at the present time, and the figure will slowly trend upward.

Another factor in the present and future growth rate of the population is the attitude toward population control. During the late 1950's Japanese leadership became concerned over the still-strong growth rate, and took steps to make possible the limitation of population. Legalized abortion and other measures of control effectively produced annual declines in the birth rate to the low annual rate reached in 1967. It now is clear that Japan can control her rate of population growth for, in 1968, three-fourths of all children were born to mothers in their 20's, with the older group of women (still within the child-bearing age group) having significantly fewer children. Recently questions are being asked as to whether, with the stable low death rate and infant mortality rate, a birth rate of under 17/1000 may not cause serious problems in the age structure of the Japanese population, leading to shortages in the labor force, and to serious socioeconomic implications.

The age structure of the Japanese population is now showing the impact of the declining rate of population growth. In 1968 the rate of high school completions began to drop, with fewer additions to the labor force than in earlier periods. The age structure already has shifted from the normal pyramid pattern, showing a distinct bulge, in 1970, in the age group of the late 20's-early 30's, with a smaller component of very young people. This is of concern to industry, of course, now faced with a high growth rate, labor shortages, and an interest in an expanding labor force, but in terms of population policy for a nation the ability to hold its growth rate within broadly defined limits has long-term significance. One current projection foresees a population of 120,000,000 in 1985, but only 140,000,000 in the year 2025. National policy, of course, can change direction.

For a nation with a rather homogeneous population Japan still presents a rather wide range of regional differences of many separate kinds (see Fig. 27.9) Such elements as language, race, religion, and cultural affinities are less significant in creating regionalisms in Japan than in most oriental countries since there is rather strong homogeneity. The regionalisms of Japan relate more to the environmental characteristics and to cultural history. The Inland Sea and its margins as the land of cherry blossoms, silk kimonos, openable houses, and traditional history is the old, slightly nostalgic heart of Japan. Tokyo, today the political and economic heart of Japan, is the ranking center of modern industrial Japan, a new internationalized facade constructed within the last century, contrasting dramatically with the traditional rural village of the hinterland. The northwestern Honshu coast, with its several feet of snow on many days each winter, is not the Japan so often described. Hokkaido is still a frontier of settlement, with its larger fields, its un-Japanese rural farmsteads, its slight urbanization, and its short-summer agricultural landscapes. The Japanese Alps, with their winter trainloads of skiers from Tokyo, represent a region quite different from the traditional hot-spring village resort tucked into a mountain valley in the foothills of the subtropical Japan of bamboo groves and luxuriant gardens. Japan often has been painted as the clean, polished, and neatly

sculptured landscape of clear mountain streams and brilliant vistas, but these pictures form a stark contrast to the smoke-begrimed and smog-ridden vistas of Osaka-Kobe, the heart of the heavy industrial belt of modern Japan. Possibly the regional contrasts within Japan today are sharper than they have ever been because they reflect the mixing of two cultural worlds.

THE RYUKYU ISLANDS

One of the great Pacific island arcs extends from southern Japan to Taiwan. This arc, the Ryukyu Islands (Liuchiu, Loochoo), contains 143 islands and islets totalling 1,291 square miles, and a population of about 950,000 in the late 1960's, with about 760,000 of the total resident on the one large island, Okinawa. The island chain is normally considered to be made up of three parts: the Amami group of 70 small islands in the north nearest Japan; the Okinawa group in the center; and the Sakishima group in the south nearest Taiwan. Less than half of the islands are permanently inhabited since many of the small islands and islets are little more than coral reefs. The larger islands are volcanic in nature, with some sedimentary rocks included, and are large enough to provide arable land, water supplies, and ports or landing points. In 1952 the 70 islands of the Amami group were returned to the control of Japan, the other 73 islands remaining under United States military control. Okinawa is the largest of the islands, 485 square miles of itself, and 510 square miles with its associated islands.

The Ryukyu Islands have long been inhabited, and it is certain that they were occupied in the Neolithic Age. The earlier population seems to have been a mixture of Ainu and other early peoples who moved along the Asian coast and through the island arcs. There must have been some contacts with both China and Japan, if not by purposeful intent then certainly by ships blown off course by typhoon winds that so often sweep these waters. Although both the Japanese and the Chinese knew of the islands by the seventh century A.D., neither nation exerted either influence or pressure on the Ryukyuans. A native sociopolitical system evolved that reflected knowledge of both Japanese and Chinese systems' distinctions between the upper and lower classes. The Ryukyuan structure was made up of a ruling leadership and a class of common agricultural-fishing peoples. Okinawa was large enough that regional rivalry for political control developed among several factional units of the aristocracy. By the fourteenth century one faction of Ryukyuan leadership, located on central Okinawa at the traditional capital of Shuri, accepted a tributary relationship to the Chinese emperor which initiated a period of trading contact in which a considerable amount of Chinese culture rubbed off on the Okinawans. Okinawan sea trading, however, touched at many of the ports of the Asian mainland from Korea to Vietnam, and included Japan on the north and Indonesia on the south, also affecting Ryukyuan culture systems. In the fifteenth century Okinawa came under one political control, with Shuri the capital and the lower west coast port of Naha the chief center of trade. Japanese influence had been growing in the northern islands, however, and in the early seventeenth century Japanese invading forces asserted authority over the northern and central Ryukyu Islands, even though the Okinawans continued to express their tributary relationship to China. For over 200 years the Okinawans lived a dual system, tributary to both China and Japan, isolated from both, but free of neither.

In the late nineteenth century, as European contacts in the East exerted stronger political pressures, Japan moved to "protect" the Ryukyu Islands, the Ryukyuan king "abdicated" and Japan assumed administrative control over the whole of the Ryukyu Islands. In 1879 the Ryukyu Islands became a prefecture of Japan. A period of assimilation followed, as Japanese systems were installed on Okinawa and the other islands, Okinawans left the island to work in various parts of the growing Japanese empire, and the islands were increasingly tied to Japan.

The end of World War II brought a renewal of an old situation, a relationship to Japan but a control by the United States, similar to the earlier pattern of tributary allegiance to China but with control in the hands of Japan. American military installations on Okinawa, particularly, and the consequent economic and cultural influences on the Okinawans, have both disrupted their older patterns of life and implanted large elements of culture change. The return to Japanese administration, in 1952, of the Amami group of islands clearly indicated the eventual intentions of American policy and, in the late 1960's, Japan began to agitate for the return of the rest of the island chain. Restoration of the balance of the Ryukyus to Japan is tentatively scheduled for 1972. Ryukyuans, themselves, are pawns in a larger game of political strategy. This has often been, in world history, the fate of an offshore, outlying region which is too small and under-strengthed to maintain its own position.

Of the 73 islands remaining under American control in 1970, only 47 are permanently inhabited. The traditional economy was badly upset by the military invasion of Okinawas during World War II. In the post-war era an artificial economy has developed, significantly affected by the American military presence. In domestic terms three-fourths of the Okinawan population are small-holding sugarcane growers, farming poor soils and operating under small profit margins. There is some pineapple production, and sugar refining and pineapple canning are the chief domestic manufacturing activities, with the products going to Japan. Sweet potatoes, rice, tea, and tobacco are the chief home-used products of agriculture, though cattle raising is beginning to be significant on some of the lesser islands, and though fishing is an important element in the economy, with some export to Japan. In the 1960's the whole of the Ryukyu Islands comprised a food deficit area, though the American military presence makes evaluation difficult. There are some traditional handicraft manufactures, chiefly small operations. Modern industry represented by cement manufacturing, and servicing operations to the American military installations are indicative of change, but what directions such economic developments may take after a return of the islands to Japanese administration is not at all clear.

Urbanization of Okinawa is marked in the contemporary situation, but how much of this is owing to American military presence is uncertain. Five of the seven Ryukyuan cities are on Okinawa. Naha had a population of about 275,000 in 1969, but the other cities are each much smaller. Without a very strong Japanese program of economic development in the post-American period, after 1972, it seems likely that the Ryukyu Islands will again find themselves isolated and left to their own alternatives, an over-populated region suffering from international politics.

PART III

FOR USE IN REFERENCE

STATISTICAL ABSTRACT

Estimates of Populations, Densities, and Mortality Rates, as of 1970

COUNTRY	Area in sq. mi.	Pop. in '000's	Capital City	Capital Pop. in '000's	Arith. Density per sq. mi.	Agricul. Density per sq. mi.	Birth Rate Per 1000	Death Rate Per 1000	Life Expec. in years
PAKISTAN	365,529	110,000	Islamabad	*	301	940	52	19	53
INDIA	1,269,640	515,000	New Delhi	3,100	406	965	40	16	52
CEYLON	25,532	13,000	Colombo	800	514	1980	32	8	62
NEPAL	54,362	10,400	Katmandu	200	191	1600	41	21	39
BHUTAN	19,305	750	Thimpu	11	39	*	*	*	*
SIKKIM	2,744	185	Gangtok	17	65	*	*	*	*
KASHMIR	82,258	3,800	†	†	46	*	*	*	*
MALDIVES	115	110	Male	12	956	†	50.3	23	*
BURMA	261,789	26,500	Rangoon	1,600	101	1600	48	28	46
THAILAND	200,148	35,700	Bangkok	1,750	178	1038	36.4	7.1	55
CAMBODIA	69,898	7,000	Phnom Penh	530	100	897	41	20	46
LAOS	91,429	2,900	Vientiane	200	31	*	47	23	52
NORTH VIETNAM	63,360	17,000	Hanoi	500	268	*	*	*	*
SOUTH VIETNAM	66,263	18,000	Saigon	1,750	271	1175	37	16	38
MALAYSIA	128,430	12,000	Kuala Lumpur	400	93	†	56	7.2	60
SINGAPORE	224.5	2,100	Singapore	1,800	931	†	27	5.6	62
INDONESIA	735,268	117,000	Djakarta	3,300	160	1670	43	21	45
PORTUGUESE TIMOR	7,383	580	Dili	55	78	*	*	*	*
PAPUA—NEW GUINEA	183,540	2,200	Port Moresby	55	*	*	*	*	*
BRUNEI	2,226	120	Brunei Town	30	54	†	39.3	6.8	*
PHILIPPINES	115,826	37,000	Quezon City	510	319	1185	50	13.5	59
CHINA	3,690,546	730,000	Peiping	7,350	197	1612	34	11	*
TAIWAN	13,885	14,400	Taipei	1,700	1074	2630	29	7.1	61
HONG KONG	365.5	4,000	Victoria	700	1093	†	21.1	4.1	*
NORTH KOREA	46,540	11,500	Pyongyang	650	247	1064	42	12.8	*
SOUTH KOREA	38,012	30,600	Seoul	4,000	805	2885	38	12	58
JAPAN	142,767	102,000	Tokyo	11,800	720	4300	17.6	6.8	71

Source: United Nations Publications.

* = Data not available. † = Not properly applicable.

TABLE B

Estimates of Significant Agricultural Crop Acreages and Animal Populations as of 1968–1970

Acreages and numbers of animals are in millions or tenths of millions.
★ Significant crop grown or animal kept, but data too scanty for effective estimate.
+ Occasionally grown as a minor crop, or present as a minor animal, but essentially unimportant.
− Crop cannot be grown in practical terms, owing to climatic limits.
A blank square indicates lack of record of presence in normal reference sources.

CROP	PAKISTAN	INDIA	CEYLON	BURMA	THAILAND	CAMBODIA	SOUTH VIETNAM	MALAYSIA	INDONESIA	PHILIPPINES	CHINA	TAIWAN	SOUTH KOREA	JAPAN
RICE	30	90	1.1	13	16	3.5	7	1.4	18.5	8.5	80	2	4	7.9
WHEAT	12	33	−	+	+	−	−	−	−	+	60	+	.4	1.6
MAIZE	1.3	15	−	.1	.2	.6	.1	+	6.5	5	32	+	+	+
BARLEY	1.0	10	−	+	+			−	−	−	10	+	2.2	2
SORGHUMS	2.0	30	★	+	+				+	+	18	+	★	+
MILLETS	2.0	45	★	.6	+				+	+	24	+	.5	+
OATS	+	+	−	−	−	−	−	−	−	−	5	−	+	.2
SWEET POTATO	+	+	+	+	+	+	+	+	1	.7	19	.6	.2	.8
WHITE POTATO	+	+	+	+	+	+	+	+	+	+	7	+	.1	.5
SOY BEANS	★	★		+	+	+	+	+	2.5	+	33	.1	.7	+
OTHER BEANS (1)	1.1	30	+	.3	.4	.2	+		★	.2	10	.1	.2	1.6
RAPE-MUSTARD	1.2	10	+	+	+	+	+				7	+	+	.6
SESAMUM (2)	★	8	+	1.6	.3	★	.1	+	★		4	.2	+	+
PEANUTS	★	16	+	1.2	.2	+	+	+	.9	+	7	.2	+	.6
COCONUT	1	1.8	1.1	.4	.3	★	★	.7	★	3.5	.1	+	−	−
SUGARCANE	1.3	6	+	+	.3	★	.1	+	★	.7	.7	.2	−	−
FODDER CROPS	3	11	+	+	+	+	+	+	+	+	.2	+	+	.3
TEA	.1	.8	.6	.2			★	−	★	.1	2.1	.1	−	.1
COFFEE	+	.2	+	+	+	+	+	+	+	.1	+	+	−	−

622

TOBACCO	.2	.7	+	.1	.1	+	+	+	.4	.1	.1	+	.3	1.5	.2
RUBBER	1.1	.1	.8	.2	.2	1	4.8	.1	.1	.2	.2	.7	+	—	—
JUTE	1.5	1.5	+	+	—	—	—	—	—	+	+	1.5	.3	—	—
ABACA		+	*	—	+	+	+	+	+	—	+	—	.4	—	—
COTTON	3.5	19	*	.4	.1	+	+	+	+	.1	.4	14	+	.4	.4
OIL PALM	+	+	*	*	*	+	.2	—	—	—	—	—	+	—	—
CITRUS	*	*	*	*	*	+	+	+	*	*	+	*	+	+	.3
BANANAS	*	*	*	*	*	+	*	*	*	*	.4	*	.4	.1	—
MANGO	.5	1.5	*	*	*	+	+	+	+	*	*	*	.1	—	—
MANIOC	+	+	.2	+	+	+	*	+	4	+	.2	+	.2	+	+
TARO	+	+	+	+	+	+	+	+	*	+	*	*	*	+	—
CATTLE	25	175	2	4	6	1	*	.3	.3	5	1.3	62	.3	.7	4.5
WATER BUFFALO	3	50	.8	1	7	.4	*	.3	.3	3	3.5	14	.3	—	.8
SHEEP	.7	30	+	+	+	+	+	+	+	2.5	+	30	+	+	.8
GOATS	12	30	*	.2	+	+	+	.2	.2	6	+	60	+	+	+
HORSES (3)	.5	2	+	+	.2	+	+	+	+	.7	.3	7	+	+	.6
PIGS	+	+	*	.4	4.0	.5	*	.5	.5	2.5	6.2	150	4	.7	5.5

(1) Including various pulses.
(2) Includes various oil seeds for India and Pakistan.
(3) For China includes donkeys and mules.
Source: United Nations Publications

TABLE C
Selected Social Indicators

Source years indicated by the number in parenthesis, thus:
(1) 1964 or 1965; (2) 1966; (3) 1967; (4) 1968.
* = No data available.

COUNTRY	Population per doctor	Elementary School Enrollment '000's	Secondary School Enrollment '000's	Daily Newspapers/ Circulation (circ. = '000's)	Cinemas/Seats (seats = 000's)	Radio Receivers '000's	Television Receivers '000's
PAKISTAN	3,000 (2)	6,814 (2)	2,525 (2)	95/1,839 (1)	325/162 (1)	1,014 (2)	20 (2)
INDIA	4,800 (2)	61,000 (1)	15,050 (1)	49/6,253 (2)	3,843/3,200 (1)	7,500 (3)	6 (3)
CEYLON	5,280 (1)	1,781 (1)	823 (1)	16/491 (1)	156/103 (2)	552 (4)	*
NEPAL	41,000 (2)	386 (2)	60 (2)	12/28 (1)	*	*	*
BURMA	10,000 (2)	1,887 (1)	503 (1)	27/231 (2)	452/365 (1)	367 (2)	*
THAILAND	6,830 (4)	4,168 (1)	366 (1)	*	373/124 (1)	2,765 (2)	210 (2)
CAMBODIA	15,000 (4)	1,000 (4)	119 (4)	18/69 (2)	53/*	990 (1)	7 (1)
LAOS	20,000 (1)	161 (1)	6 (1)	4/10 (1)	115/7.6 (1)	50 (1)	*
SOUTH VIETNAM	13,560 (2)	1,661 (1)	381 (1)	43/750 (2)	*	1,300 (2)	130 (4)
MALAYSIA (WEST)	6,000 (1)	1,415 (2)	355 (1)	60/620 (2)	381/337 (1)	500 (3)	67 (2)
SINGAPORE	1,800 (4)	373 (2)	133 (2)	*	70/50 (1)	389 (1)	98 (3)
INDONESIA	22,000 (3)	11,483 (3)	76 (3)	85/709 (3)	*	1,250 (2)	46 (2)
BRUNEI	4,000 (1)	24 (2)	5.5 (2)	1/8 (3)	7/5.5 (3)	12 (3)	*
PHILIPPINES	1,330 (1)	5,578 (1)	1,037 (1)	23/906 (1)	951/1,225 (1)	1,225 (1)	210 (3)
CHINA	*	90,000 (1)	9,900 (1)	392/12,000 (1)	*	8,000 (1)	100 (1)
TAIWAN	1,420 (3)	2,383 (4)	664 (1)	32/906 (4)	734/626 (4)	1,468 (4)	500 (4)
SOUTH KOREA	2,700 (1)	5,405 (2)	1,369 (2)	41/1,490 (1)	701/415 (1)	2,632 (2)	177 (4)
JAPAN	900 (1)	9,776 (1)	11,025 (1)	174/45,978 (2)	4,649/2,300 (1)	24,878 (2)	19,000 (2)

Sources: United Nations Publications; *Far Eastern Economic Review Yearbook, 1970.*

TABLE D
Selected Economic Indicators

Source years indicated by the number in parenthesis, thus: (1) 1966; (2) 1967; (3) 1968; (4) 1969.

COUNTRY	Merchant Fleet '000's Tons	Motor Vehicles '000's	Electric Energy Capacity '000 KW	Industrial Index 1963 = 100	Agricultural Index 1952–56 = 100	Imports US $ in Millions	Exports US $ in Millions	Total Foreign Tourists '000's
PAKISTAN	600 (3)	218 (1)	1,175 (1)	129 (1)	128 (1)	1,045 (2)	571 (2)	90 (3)
INDIA	2,000 (3)	1,298 (3)	9,745 (1)	169** (4)	123 (1)	2,880 (2)	1,728 (2)	180 (3)
CEYLON	n.a.	119 (1)	220 (1)	115 (1)	118 (1)	360 (2)	348 (2)	19 (1)
BURMA	75 (4)	50 (1)	191 (1)	n.a.	117 (1)	157 (1)	193 (2)	2 (3)
THAILAND	n.a.	148 (1)	559 (1)	n.a.	191 (1)	1,060 (2)	680 (2)	342 (4)
CAMBODIA	n.a.	30 (1)	33 (1)	n.a.	n.a.	96 (2)	83 (2)	54 (4)
SOUTH VIETNAM	n.a.	75 (1)	439 (1)	149 (1)	n.a.	538 (2)	n.a.	n.a.
MALAYSIA	n.a.	547 (3)	2,640 (2)	n.a.	159 (1)	1,122 (2)	1,252 (2)	46 (1)
SINGAPORE	82 (4)	142 (1)	464 (1)	n.a.	n.a.	1,440 (2)	1,140 (2)	290 (3)
INDONESIA	1,030 (3)	272* (1)	586 (1)	n.a.	119 (1)	573 (1)	679 (1)	80 (3)
BRUNEI	n.a.	7 (1)	24 (1)	n.a.	n.a.	43 (2)	82 (2)	n.a.
PHILIPPINES	720 (2)	508 (3)	1,222 (1)	121 (1)	151 (1)	1,054 (2)	812 (2)	116 (4)
CHINA	805 (3)	n.a.	n.a.	n.a.	n.a.	1,421 (2)	1,558 (2)	n.a.
TAIWAN	1,000 (4)	40 (1)	1,574 (1)	170 (1)	166 (1)	1,204 (2)	1,110 (2)	414 (4)
HONG KONG	796 (2)	80 (1)	894 (1)	n.a.	n.a.	1,814 (2)	1,524 (2)	618 (3)
SOUTH KOREA	306 (2)	49 (1)	947 (1)	152 (1)	184 (1)	996 (2)	320 (2)	90 (4)
JAPAN	22,000 (4)	8,100 (1)	44,991 (1)	215**(4)	137 (1)	11,674 (2)	11,442 (2)	608 (4)

n.a. = not available.

* = includes military vehicles.

** = 1960 = 100.

Sources: United Nations Publications; *Far Eastern Economic Review Yearbook, 1970.*

625

BIBLIOGRAPHICAL SUGGESTIONS

COMMENTARY OF WARNING

The total bibliography concerning Monsoon Asia has reached enormous proportions, and it is impossible for any one volume to present more than a bare selection of that total. The following bibliographical suggestions are restricted to books except for a very few longer journal papers. Every regional specialist will bewail the omission of items that are critical to some phase of understanding, but such should be able to supply their own additions. Older and sometimes classical studies have been omitted except for a very few items, and our listings chiefly comprise materials published since the end of World War II. The more recent volumes themselves present bibliographies by which selected topics may be pursued. The listing has been separated by chapters for the easier selection of items of interest. By the restriction to books, such a separation discloses the lack of book-length treatment of many subjects for several different portions of the Orient. In such cases, reference will need to be made to the literature listed under the regional subject headings. No mimeographed or other limited-circulation materials have been included, and the list is by intent almost entirely restricted to materials in the English language.

BIBLIOGRAPHIES

Australian National University, *An Ethnographic Bibliography of New Guinea*, Australian National University Press, Canberra, 1968, three volumes.

Baqai, I. H., *Books on Asia*, Indian Council of World Affairs, New Delhi, 1947.

Barquissau, R. (Ed.), *L'Asie française et ses écrivains*, Vigneau, Paris, 1947.

Berton, P. A., *Manchuria: An Annotated Bibliography*, Library of Congress, Washington, D.C., 1951.

Brown, J. M., and H. C. Parish, *Thailand Bibliography*, University of Florida Library, Gainesville, 1958.

Bureau of the Census, *The Population and Manpower of China: An Annotated Bibliography*, International Population Statistics Reports, Government Printing Office, Washington, D.C., 1958.

Cheeseman, H. R., *Bibliography of Malaya*, Longmans Green, London, 1959.

Goonetileke, H. A. I., *A Bibliography of Ceylon*, Inter Documentation Company AG, Zug, Switzerland, 1970, two volumes.

Herman, Theodore, *The Geography of China, A Selected and Annotated Bibliography*, State Education Department, Albany, New York, 1967.

Hobbs, C., *Southeast Asia, 1935–1945, A Selected List of Reference Books*, Library of Congress, Washington, D.C., 1946.

Indochina, A Bibliography of the Land and the People, Library of Congress, Washington, D.C., 1950.

Jones, H. B., and R. L. Winkler, *Korea, An Annotated Bibliography of Publications in Western Languages*, Library of Congress, Washington, D.C., 1950.

Maretzki, T. W., and H. T. Fischer, *Bibliography of Indonesian Peoples and Cultures*, HRAF Press, New Haven, 1955, 2 volumes, as revision of Kennedy bibliography.

Pelzer, K. J., *Selected Bibliography on the Geography of Southeast Asia*, Part III, Malaya, HRAF Press, New Haven, 1956.

Rahman, Mushtaqur, *Bibliography of Pakistan Geography, 1947–1967,* University of Karachi, Karachi, Pakistan, 1968.

Sorich, R., *Contemporary China: A Bibliography of Reports on China Published by the United States Joint Publications Research Service,* American Council of Learned Societies—Social Science Research Council, New York, 1961.

Trager, F. N. (Ed.), *Annotated Bibliography of Burma,* HRAF Press, New Haven, 1956.

Ware, E. W., *Bibliography on Ceylon,* University of Miami Press, Coral Gables, Florida, 1962.

Yuan, T. L., *China in Western Literature,* Far Eastern Publication, Yale University, New Haven, 1958.

Yuan, T. L., *Economic and Social Development of Modern China; A Bibliographic Guide,* HRAF Press, New Haven, 1956.

The Journal of Asian Studies publishes an annual supplement devoted entirely to bibliography, and forms the best single source for periodical and book-length materials available; *Current Geographical Publications,* published by the American Geographical Society, provides reference to new materials in geography.

MATERIALS OF GENERAL REFERENCE

Cressey, G. B., *Asia's Lands and Peoples,* McGraw-Hill Book Company, New York, 3rd edit., 1963.

Dobby, E. H. G., *Monsoon Asia,* University of London Press, London, 1961.

East, W. G., and O. H. K. Spate, *The Changing Map of Asia, A Political Geography,* Dutton, New York, 1950.

Far Eastern Economic Review, 1970 Yearbook, Far Eastern Economic Review, Hong Kong, 1970.

Freeman, O. W. (Ed.), *Geography of the Pacific,* John Wiley & Sons, 1951.

Ginsburg, Norton (Ed.), *The Pattern of Asia,* Prentice-Hall, Inc., Englewood Cliffs, New Jersey, 1958.

Peterson, A. D. C., *The Far East, A Social Geography,* Duckworth, London, 1949.

Robinson, Harry, *Monsoon Asia,* Frederick A. Praeger, New York, rev. edit., 1967.

Stamp, L. D., *Asia, A Regional and Economic Geography,* Methuen & Co., London, 12th edit., 1966.

Thompson, Warren S., *Population and Progress in the Far East,* University of Chicago Press, Chicago, 1959.

Wint, Guy (Ed.), *Asia Handbook,* Penguin Books, Harmondsworth, England, 1969.

Chapter 1: ON PEOPLES

Bell, C., *The People of Tibet,* Clarendon Press, Oxford, 1928.

Chang, S. D., "The Distribution and Occupation of Overseas Chinese," *Geographical Review,* Vol. 58 (1968), pp. 89–107.

Doumes, J., *Les Populations Montagnardes du Sud-Indochinois,* Derain, Lyons, 1950.

Harrisson, Tom (Ed.), *The Peoples of Sarawak,* Sarawak Museum, Kuching, Sarawak, 1959.

Howells, W. W. (Ed.), *Early Man in the Far East,* American Association of Physical Anthropologists, Philadelphia, 1949.

Izikowitz, K. G., *Lamet, Hill Peasants of French Indochina,* Etnologiska Studier, Vol. 17 (1951).

Komatsu, I., *The Japanese People: Origins of the People and the Language,* Kokusai Bunka Shinkokai, Tokyo, 1962.

Majumdar, D. N., *Races and Cultures of India,* Asia Publishing House, Bombay, 1958.

Mamoria, C. B., *Tribal Demography in India,* Kitab Mahal, Allahabad, India, 1958.

Movius, H. L., Jr., "Early Man and Pleistocene Stratigraphy in Southern and Eastern Asia," *Papers of the Peabody Museum Harvard University,* Vol. 19 (1944). (1944).

Movius, H. L., Jr., "The Lower Paleolithic Cultures of Southern and Eastern Asia," *Transactions of the American Philosophical Society,* Vol. 38 (1949), part 4.

Purcell, V., *The Chinese in Southeast Asia,* Oxford University Press, London, 1951.

Seidenfaden, E., *The Thai Peoples,* Siam Society, Bangkok, 1958.

Unger, L., "The Chinese in Southeast Asia," *Geographical Review,* Vol. 34 (1944), pp. 196–217.

Wijesekera, N. D., *The People of Ceylon,* Gunasena, Colombo, 1950.

Zelinsky, W., "The Indochinese Peninsula, A Demographic Anomaly," *Far Eastern Quarterly,* Vol. 9 (1950), pp. 115–145.

Chapter 2: ON HISTORICAL CONTACT AND MODERNIZATION

Beckmann, G. N., *The Modernization of China and Japan,* Harper & Row, New York, 1962.

Brown, L. R., *Seeds of Change: The Green Revolution and Developments in the 1970's,* Praeger, New York, 1970.

Cameron, M. E., *China, Japan, and the Powers,* Ronald Press, New York, 1952.

Coedes, G., *The Indianized States of Southeast Asia* (Edited by W. F. Vella), East-West Center Press, Honolulu, 3rd edit., 1968.

Eldridge, F. B., *The Background of Eastern Seapower,* Georgian House, Melbourne, 1945.

Emerson, R., L. A. Mills, and V. Thompson, *Government and Nationalism in Southeast Asia*, Institute of Pacific Relations, New York, 1942.

Fairbank, J. K., Edwin C. Reischauer, and Albert M. Craig, *East Asia, The Modern Transformation*, Houghton Mifflin Company, Boston, 1965.

Friis, H. R., *The Pacific Basin, A History of Its Geographical Exploration*, American Geographical Society, New York, 1967.

Hall, D. G. E., *A History of South-east Asia*, St. Martins Press, New York, 3rd edit., 1968.

Hubbard, G. E., *Eastern Industrialization and its Effect on the West*, Oxford University Press, London, 1938.

Hughes, E. R., *The Invasion of China by the Western World*, Macmillan, New York, 1938.

Huzayyin, S. A., *Arabia and the Far East, Their Commercial and Cultural Relations in Graeco-Roman and Irano-Arabian Times*, Royal Society of Geography, Cairo, 1942.

Jacobs, Norman, *The Origin of Modern Capitalism and Eastern Asia*, Hong Kong University Press, Hong Kong, 1958.

Latourette, Kenneth Scott, *A Short History of the Far East*, The Macmillan Company, New York, 1964, 4th edit.

Majumdar, R. C., *Hindu Colonies in the Far East*, General Printers, Calcutta, 1944.

Murphey, Rhoads, "Traditionalism and Colonialism: Changing Urban Roles in Asia," *Journal of Asian Studies*, Vol. 29 (1969), pp. 67–84.

Pratt, J. T., *The Expansion of Europe into the Far East*, Sylvan Press, London, 1947.

Quaritch Wales, H. G., *The Making of Greater India, a Study in Southeast Asian Culture Change*, Bernard Quaritch, London, 1951.

Reischauer, Edwin O., and John K. Fairbank, *East Asia, the Great Tradition*, Houghton Mifflin Company, Boston, 1960.

Romein, Jan, *The Asian Century, a History of Modern Nationalism in Asia*, University of California Press, Berkeley and Los Angeles, 1962.

Rowbotham, A. H., *Missionary and Mandarin: The Jesuits at the Court of China*, University of California Press, Berkeley and Los Angeles, 1942.

Sansom, G. B., *The Western World and Japan, A Study in the Interaction of European and Asiatic Cultures*, Knopf, New York, 1950.

Sastri, K. A. N., *South Indian Influences in the Far East*, Hind Kitabs, Bombay, 1949.

Simkin, C. G. F., *The Traditional Trade of Asia*, Oxford University Press, London, 1968.

Spear, P., *India, Pakistan, and the West*, Oxford University Press, New York, 1949.

Villiers, A., *Monsoon Seas*, McGraw-Hill Book Company, New York, 1952.

Webber, C., J. M. van der Kroef, and C. Du Bois, "Culture Contact and Culture Change in Southeast Asia, a Symposium," *Far Eastern Quarterly*, Vol. 11 (1951), pp. 3–34.

Chapter 3: ON RELIGION, LAW, AND SOCIAL STRUCTURE

Archer, J. C., *The Sikhs*, Princeton University Press, Princeton, 1946.

Ball, W. M., *Nationalism and Communism in East Asia*, Melbourne University Press, Melbourne, 1952.

Bouquet, A. C., *Hinduism*, Longmans Green, New York, 1950.

Ch'en, Kenneth K. S., *Buddhism, the Light of Asia*, Barron's, Woodbury, New York, 1968.

Cragg, K., *The House of Islam*, Dickenson Publishing Co., Belmont, Calif., 1969.

Fey, John T. (Ed.), *Studies in the Law of the Far East and Southeast Asia*, The Washington Foreign Law Society, Washington, D.C., 1956.

Geertz, Clifford, *The Religion of Java*, Free Press of Glencoe-Collier Macmillan, New York, 1960.

Holtom, D. C., *The National Faith of Japan*, Kegan Paul, Trench & Trubner, London, 1938.

Hooker, M. B., "The Relationship Between Chinese Law and Common Law in Malaysia, Singapore, and Hong Kong," *Journal of Asian Studies*, Vol. 28 (1969), pp. 723–742.

Jacoby, E. H., *Agrarian Unrest in Southeast Asia*, Columbia University Press, New York, 1949.

Jurji, E. J. (Ed.), *The Great Religions of the Modern World*, Princeton University Press, Princeton, 1946.

Landon, K. P., *Southeast Asia, Crossroads of Religion*, University of Chicago Press, Chicago, 1949.

Lasswell, H. D., et al, "Religion and Modernization in the Far East: A Symposium," *Far Eastern Quarterly*, Vol. 12 (1953), pp. 123–202.

Lin, M. S., *Men and Ideas, an Informal History of Chinese Political Thought*, John Day, New York, 1942.

Needham, J., "Human Laws and Laws of Nature in China and the West," *Journal of the History of Ideas*, Vol. 12 (1951), 194–230.

Northrop, F. S., *The Meeting of East and West*, Macmillan Company, New York, 1946.

Parrinder, E. G., *An Introduction to Asian Religions*, S.P.C.K., London, 1957.

Quaritch Wales, H. G., *Ancient Southeast Asian Warfare*, Bernard Quaritch, London, 1952.

Quaritch Wales, H. G., *Prehistory and Religion in Southeast Asia*, Bernard Quaritch, London, 1957.

Rankin, G. C., *Background to the Indian Law*, Cambridge University Press, Cambridge, 1946.

Soothill, W. E., *The Hall of Light, A Study of Early Chinese Kingship*, Butterworth, London, 1951.

Thompson, L. G., *Chinese Religion: An Introduction*, Dickenson Publishing Company, Belmont, California, 1969.

von der Mehden, Fred R., *Religion and Nationalism in Southeast Asia: Burma, Indonesia, The Philippines*, University of Wisconsin Press, Madison, 1963.

Yang, C. K., *Religion in Chinese Society*, University of California Press, Berkeley and Los Angeles, 1967.

Zinkin, T., *Caste Today*, Oxford University Press, Calcutta, 1962.

Chapter 4: ON SETTLEMENTS AND ARCHITECTURE

Boyd, A. C., *Chinese Architecture and Town Planning, 1500 B.C.–A.D. 1911*, University of Chicago Press, Chicago, 1962.

Brown, P., *Indian Architecture, Islamic Period*, Taraporevala, Bombay, 1942.

Brown, P., and H. C. Brookfield, "Chimbu Settlements and Residence: A Study of Patterns, Trends and Idiosyncracy," *Pacific Viewpoint*, Vol. 8 (1967), pp. 119–151.

Chang, S. D., "Some Aspects of the Urban Geography of the Chinese Hsien Capital," *Annals*, Association of American Geographers, Vol. 51 (1961), pp. 23–45.

Chang, S. D., "The Historical Trend of Chinese Urbanization," *Annals*, Association of American Geographers, Vol. 53 (1963), pp. 109–43.

Davis, S. G., *Hongkong in its Geographic Setting*, Collins, London, 1949.

Griffiths, P. J., *Better Towns, A Study of Urban Reconstruction in India*, Kitabistan, Allahabad, 1945.

Izikowitz, K. G., "The Community House of the Lamet," *Ethnos*, Vol. 8 (1943), pp. 10–60.

Loeb, E. M., and J. O. M. Broek, "Social Organization and the Long House in Southeast Asia," *American Anthropologist*, 49 (1947), 414–425.

McGee, T. G., *The Southeast Asian City, A Social Geography of the Primate Cities of Southeast Asia*, Frederick Praeger, New York, 1967.

Murphey, R., "New Capitals of Asia," *Economic Development and Cultural Change*, Vol. 5 (1957), pp. 216–243.

Murphey, R., *Shanghai, Key to Modern China*, Harvard University Press, Cambridge, 1953.

Nishi, M., "Regional Variations in Japanese Farmhouses," *Annals*, Association of American Geographers, Vol. 57 (1967), pp. 238–266.

Pithawalla, M. B., "Settlements in the Lower Indus Basin," *Journal of the Madras Geographical Society*, Vol. 13 (1938), pp. 323–357.

Spate, O. H. K., "The Burmese Village," *Geographical Review*, Vol. 35 (1945), pp. 523–543.

Spate, O. H. K., "Five Cities of the Gangetic Plain, A Cross Section of Indian Culture History," *Geographical Review*, Vol. 40 (1950), pp. 260–278.

Spate, O. H. K., and L. W. Trueblood, "Rangoon; A Study in Urban Geography," *Geographical Review*, Vol. 32 (1942), pp. 56–73.

Spencer, J. E., "The Houses of the Chinese," *Geographical Review*, Vol. 37 (1947), pp. 254–273.

Trewartha, G. T., "Chinese Cities, Numbers and Distribution," *Annals*, Association of American Geographers, Vol. 41 (1951), pp. 331–347.

Trewartha, G. T., "Chinese Cities; Origins and Functions," *Annals*, Association of American Geographers, Vol. 42 (1952), pp. 69–93.

Yang, M. C., *A Chinese Village, Taitou, Shantung Province*, Columbia University Press, New York, 1945.

Chapter 5: ON MEDICAL GEOGRAPHY

Balfour, M. C., *Public Health and Demography in the Far East*, Rockefeller Foundation, New York, 1950.

Bates, M., *The Natural History of Mosquitoes*, Macmillan Company, New York, 1949.

Covell, G., "Notes on the Distribution, Breeding Places, Adult Habits, and Relation of Malaria to the Anopheline Mosquitoes of India and the Far East," *Journal of the Malaria Institute of India*, Vol. 5 (1944), pp. 399–434.

Feng, L. C., "The Anopheline Mosquitoes and the Epidemiology of Malaria in China," *Chinese Medical Journal*, Vol. 51 (1937), pp. 1005–1020.

Fonaroff, L. S., and A. Fonaroff, "The Cultural Environment of Medical Geography in Rural Hindu India," *Pacific Viewpoint*, Vol. 7 (1966), pp. 67–84.

Fredericksen, H., "Economic and Demographic Consequences of Malaria Control in Ceylon," *Indian Journal of Malariology*, Vol. 16 (1962), pp. 379–391.

Gill, C. A., "The Influence of Malaria on Natality with Special Reference to Ceylon," *Journal of the Malaria Institute of India*, Vol. 3 (1940), pp. 201–252.

Learmonth, A. T. A., *Health in the Indian Sub-Continent, 1955–1965*, Department of Geography, Australian National University, Canberra, 1965.

Learmouth, A. T. A., "Medical Geography in Indo-Pakistan: A Study of Twenty Years' Data for the Former British India," *Indian Geographical Journal*, Vol. 33 (1958), pp. 1–59.

May, Jacques M., *The Ecology of Malnutrition in the Far and Near East*, Hafner Publishing Co., New York, 1961.

Simmons, J. S., et al, *Global Epidemiology*, Lippincott, Philadelphia, 1944.

Snapper, I., *Chinese Lessons to Western Medicine*, Interscience Publishers, New York, 1941.

Chapter 6: ON THE PHYSICAL LANDSCAPES

Ahmad, E., "Geographic Regions of Peninsular India, "*Journal of Ranchi University*, Vol. 1 (1962), pp. 1–29.

Bemmelen, R. W. van, *The Geology of Indonesia*, Government Printing Office, The Hague, 1949, 2 vols.

Gansser, A., *Geology of the Himalayas*, John Wiley & Sons, New York, 1964.

Huang, T. K., "On the Major Tectonic Forms of China," *Geological Memoir, Geological Survey of China*, Series A, No. 20, 1945.

Institute of Geography, U.S.S.R. Academy of Sciences, *The Physical Geography of China*, Frederick Praeger, New York, 1969, two volumes.

Krishnan, M. S., *The Geology of India and Burma*, Higginbothams, Madras, 1960, 4th edit.

Lee, J. S., *The Geology of China*, Murby, London, 1939.

Misch, P., "Remarks on the Tectonic History of Yunnan, with Special Reference to its Relations to the Young Type of Orogenic Deformation," *Bulletin of the Geological Society of China*, Vol. 25 (1945), pp. 47–155.

Takai, F., T. Matsumoto, and R. Toyiama (Eds.), *Geology of Japan*, University of California Press, Berkeley and Los Angeles, 1963.

Wadia, D. N., *Geology of India*, Macmillan, London, 3rd edit., 1961.

Wager, L. R., "The Arun River Drainage Pattern and the Rise of the Himalayas," *Geographical Journal*, Vol. 89 (1937), pp. 229–250.

Chapter 7: ON CLIMATE

Chang, Jen-hu, "The Indian Summer Monsoon," *Geographical Review*, Vol. 57 (1967), pp. 373–396.

Manalo, E. B., "The Distribution of Rainfall in the Philippines," *Philippine Geographical Journal*, Vol. 4 (1956), pp. 104–167.

Pedelaborde, Pierre, *The Monsoon*, Methuen & Co., London, 1963.

Sawyer, J. S., "The Structure of the Intertropical Front over NW India during the Monsoon," *Quarterly Journal of the Royal Meteorological Society*, Vol. 73 (1947), pp. 346–370.

Sternstein, L., *The Rainfall of Thailand*, Indiana University Foundation, Bloomington, 1962.

Tu, C. W., and S. S. Hwang, "The Advance and Retreat of the Summer Monsoon in China," *Bulletin of the American Meteorological Society*, Vol. 26 (1945), pp. 9–22.

Watts, I. E. M., *Equatorial Weather, with Particular Reference to Southeast Asia*, University of London Press, London, 1955.

Chapter 8: ON MINERAL RESOURCES

Braake, A. L. Ter, *Mining in the Netherlands East Indies*, Institute of Pacific Relations, New York, 1944.

Brown, G. F., et al, *Geologic Reconnaissance of the Mineral Deposits of Thailand*, U.S. Geological Survey Bulletin 894, Washington, D.C., 1951.

Brown, J. C., and A. K. Dey, *India's Mineral Wealth*, Oxford University Press, Calcutta, 3rd edit., 1955.

Chhibber, H. L., *Mineral Resources of Burma*, Macmillan, London, 1934.

Clegg, E. L. G., *The Mineral Resources of Burma*, Times of India Press, Bombay, 1944.

Fermor, L. L., "Mineral Resources of Malaya," *Bulletin of the Imperial Institute*, 1940.

Mineral Resources of China, Bureau of Mines, Washington, D.C., 1948.

Mining Industry in the Philippines, Bureau of Mines, Manila, 1947.

Van Royen, W., and O. Bowles, *The Mineral Resources of the World*, Prentice-Hall, Inc., New York, 1952.

Wang, K. P., "Mineral Resources of China with Special Reference to the Nonferrous Metals," *Geographical Review*, Vol. 34 (1944), pp. 621–635.

Chapter 9: ON BIOGEOGRAPHY

Carter, T. D., J. E. Hill, and G. H. Tate, *Mammals of the Pacific World*, Macmillan Company, New York, 1945.

Hornell, J., *Fishing in Many Waters*, Cambridge University Press, Cambridge, 1950.

Khin, U., *Fisheries of Burma*, Government Printer, Rangoon, 1948.

Osborn, F., *The Pacific World*, Norton, New York, 1944.

Raven, H. C., "Wallace's Line and the Distribution of Indo-Australian Mammals," *Bulletin, American Museum of Natural History*, Vol. 48 (1935), pp. 179–293.

Scrivenor, J. B. (Ed.), "A Discussion on the Biogeographic Division of the Indo-Australian Archipelago," *Proceedings of the Linnean Society of London*, Vol. 154 (1941), pp. 120–165.

Simoons, Frederick J., *A Ceremonial Ox of India, The Mithan in Nature, Culture, and History*, The University of Wisconsin Press, Madison, 1968.

Smith, H. M., *The Fresh Water Fishes of Siam, or Thailand*, United States National Museum, Bulletin 188, 1945.

Tate, G. H. H., *Mammals of Eastern Asia*, Macmillan Company, New York, 1947.

Chapter 10: ON SOILS, FORESTS, AGRICULTURAL PRACTICES

Asian Development Bank, *Asian Agricultural Survey*, University of Washington Press, Seattle, 1969.

Bardhan, P. K., "Chinese and Indian Agriculture: A Broad Comparison of Recent Policy and Performance," *Journal of Asian Studies*, Vol. 29 (1970), pp. 515–538.

Barrera, A., *Handbook of Soil Surveys for the Philippines*, Bureau of Soils, Manila, 1961.

Bohlin, B., *A Contribution to our Knowledge of the Distribution of Vegetation in Inner Mongolia, Kansu, and Chinghai*, Sino-Swedish Expedition, Publication 33, Stockholm, 1949.

Burkill, I. H., *A Dictionary of the Economic Products of the Malay Peninsula*, Crown Agents for the Colonies, London, 1935, 2 vols.

Champion, H. G., *A Preliminary Survey of Forest Types of India and Burma*, Indian Forest Records, New Delhi, 1936.

Chang, C. W., et al, *Rural Asia Marches Forward: Focus on Agricultural and Rural Development*, University of the Philippines, College of Agriculture Textbook Board, Los Baños, Philippines, 1969.

Dudal, R., and F. R. Moorman, "Major Soils of Southeast Asia," *The Journal of Tropical Geography*, Vol. 18 (1964), pp. 54–80.

Gangolly, S. R., et al. *The Mango*, Indian Council of Agricultural Research, New Delhi, 1957.

Klein, Sidney, *The Pattern of Land Tenure Reform in East Asia after World War II*, Bookman Associates, New York, 1958.

Kowai, N. E., "Shifting Cultivation, Fire, and Pine Forest in the Cordillera Central, Luzon, Philippines," *Ecological Monographs*, Vol. 36 (1966), pp. 389–419.

Lam, H. J., "Notes on the Historical Phytogeography of Celebes," *Blumea*, Vol. 5 (1942), pp. 600–640.

Learmonth, A. T. A., *The Vegetation of the Indian Sub-Continent*, Department of Geography, Australian National University, Canberra, 1964.

Merrill, E. D., *Plant Life of the Pacific World*, Macmillan Company, New York, 1945.

Mohr, E. C. J., and F. A. Van Baren, *Tropical Soils*, Van Hoeve, The Hague, 1959.

Naik, K. C., *South Indian Fruits and Their Culture*, Varadachary, Madras, 1947.

Puri, G. S., *Indian Forest Ecology*, Oxford Book Company, New Delhi, 1960, 2 vols.

Richardson, S. D., *Forestry in Communist China*, The Johns Hopkins Press, Baltimore, 1966.

Shand, R. T. (Ed.), *Agricultural Development in Asia*, University of California Press, Berkeley and Los Angeles, 1969.

Spencer, J. E., *Shifting Cultivation in Southeastern Asia*, University of California Publications in Geography, Vol. 19, 1966.

Steenis, C. G. G. J. van, "On the Origin of the Malaysian Mountain Flora," *Bulletin Jardin Botan. Buitenzorg*, Serie 3, Vol. 13 (1934), pp. 135–262, 289–417.

Thorp, J., *Geography of the Soils of China*, National Geological Survey, Nanking, 1936.

VanderMeer, C., "Changing Water Control in a Taiwanese Rice-Field Irrigation System," *Annals*, Association of American Geographers, Vol. 58 (1968), pp. 720–747.

Van Royen, W., *The Agricultural Resources of the World*, Prentice-Hall, Inc., New York, 1954.

Walker, E. H., "The Plants of China and Their Usefulness to Man," *Annual Report, Smithsonian Institution for 1943*, Publication 3741 (1944), pp. 325–361.

Wang, C. W., *The Forests of China*, Maria Moors Cabot Foundation, Harvard University, Cambridge, 1961.

Wickizer, V. C., and M. K. Bennett, *The Rice Economy of Monsoon Asia*, Food Research Institute, Stanford University, Stanford, California, 1941.

Chapter 11: ON GENERAL REGIONS

Bacon, E., "A Preliminary Attempt to Determine the Culture Areas of Asia," *Southwestern Journal of Anthropology*, Vol. 2 (1946), pp. 117–132.

Bacon, E., "Problems Related to Delimiting the Culture Areas of Asia," *American Antiquity*, Vol. 18 (1953), pp. 17–23.

Broek, J. O. M., "Diversity and Unity in Southeast Asia," *Geographical Review*, Vol. 34 (1944), pp. 175–195.

Naroll, R. S., "A Draft Map of the Culture Areas of Asia," *Southwestern Journal of Anthropology*, Vol. 6 (1950), pp. 183–187.

Chapter 12: ON EARLY INDIA

Allchin, B., and R., *The Birth of Indian Civilization, India and Pakistan Before 500 B.C.*, Penguin Books, Baltimore, 1968.

Bose, A., *Social and Rural Economy of Northern India, Cir. 600 B.C.–200 A.D.*, Mukhopadhyay, Calcutta, 1961.

Brown, D. M., *The White Umbrella, Indian Political Thought from Manu to Gandhi*, University of California Press, Berkeley and Los Angeles, 1953.

Brown, W. N. (Ed.), *India, Pakistan, and Ceylon*, Cornell University Press, Ithaca, 1951.

Chatterjee, S. P., *Bengal in Maps*, Orient Longmans, Calcutta, 1949.

Dani, A. H., *Prehistory and Protohistory of Eastern India*, Mukhopadhyay, Calcutta, 1960.

Davies, C. C., *An Historical Atlas of the Indian Peninsula*, Oxford University Press, Calcutta, 1942.

Frykenberg, R. E. (Ed.), *Land Control and Social Structure in Indian History,* University of Wisconsin Press, Madison, 1969.

Gordon, D. H., *The Pre-Historic Background of Indian Culture*, Tripathi, Bombay, 1958.

Hourani, G. F., *Arab Seafaring in the Indian Ocean in Ancient and Early Medieval Times*, Princeton University Press, Princeton, 1951.

Mahalingam, T. V., *Economic Life in the Vijayanagar Empire*, University of Madras Press, Madras, 1951.

Majumdar, R. C., and A. D. Pusalker, *The History and Culture of the Indian People*, George Allen & Unwin, London, 12 volumes 1951–

Mazumdar, B. P., *Socio-Economic History of Northern India, 1030–1194 A.D.*, Mukhopadhyay, Calcutta, 1960.

Piggott, S., *Prehistoric India, to 1000 B.C.*, Penguin Books, Harmondsworth, England, 1950.

Saletore, R. N., *Life in the Gupta Age*, Popular Book Depot, Bombay, 1943.

Singh, S. D., *Ancient Indian Warfare, with Special Reference to the Vedic Period*, E. J. Brill, Leiden, 1965.

Terra, H. de, and T. T. Paterson, "Studies on the Ice Age of India and Associated Human Cultures," *Carnegie Institution, Publication No. 493*, Washington, D.C., 1939.

Toussaint, A., *History of the Indian Ocean*, University of Chicago Press, Chicago, 1966.

Toy, S., *The Strongholds of India*, William Heinemann, London, 1957.

Trotter, H., *Manual of Indian Forest Utilization*, Oxford University Press, London, 1940.

Wheeler, Mortimer, *Early India and Pakistan, to Ashoka*, Frederick Praeger, New York, rev. edit., 1968.

Wheeler, Mortimer, *The Indus Civilization*, Cambridge University Press, Cambridge, 1960, issued as a supplementary volume to the Cambridge History of India.

Chapter 13: ON MODERN INDIA

Ahmed, Z., *Dusk and Dawn in an Indian Village*, Frederick Praeger, New York, 1965.

Berreman, G. D., *Hindus of the Himalayas*, University of California Press, Berkeley and Los Angeles, 1963.

Bhattacharyya, S. N., *Fisheries in Indian Economy*, Metropolitan Book Co., Delhi, 1966.

Bondurant, J., *Regionalism Versus Provincialism: A Study in Problems of Indian National Unity*, University of California Press, Berkeley and Los Angeles, 1958.

Brush, J. E., "The Spatial Patterns of Population in Indian Cities," *Geographical Review*, Vol. 58 (1968), pp. 362–391.

Chandrasekar, S., *India's Population; Fact and Policy*, John Day, New York, 1946.

Chaudhuri, M. R., *Indian Industries, Development and Location*, Oxford & IBH Publishing Co., Calcutta, 1966, 3rd edit.

Davis, K., *The Population of India and Pakistan*, Princeton University Press, Princeton, 1951.

Dayal, Edison, "The Changing Patterns of India's International Trade," *Economic Geography*, Vol. 44 (1968), pp. 240–269.

Dube, S. C., *India's Changing Villages*, Cornell University Press, Ithaca, 1958.

Etienne, G., *Studies in Indian Agriculture, The Art of the Possible*, University of California Press, Berkeley and Los Angeles, 1968.

Frykenberg, R. E. (Ed.), *Land Control and Social Structure in Indian History*, University of Wisconsin Press, Madison, 1969.

Hagen, T., *Nepal: The Kingdom in the Himalayas*, Kummerley & Frey, Berne, 1961.

Hart, H. C., *New India's Rivers*, Orient Longmans, Calcutta, 1956.

Karan, P. P., and W. M. Jenkins, *Nepal: A Cultural and Physical Geography*, University of Kentucky Press, Lexington, 1960.

Karan, P. P., and W. M. Jenkins, *The Himalayan Kingdoms: Bhutan, Sikkim and Nepal*, D. Van Nostrand, Princeton, New Jersey, 1963.

Karve, D. D., *The New Brahmans, Five Maharastrian Families*, University of California Press, Berkeley and Los Angeles, 1963.

Malenbaum, W., *Prospects for Indian Development*, Allen & Unwin, London, 1962.

Mayer, A. C., *Land and Society in Malabar*, Oxford University Press, London, 1951.

Mayer, A., et al, *Pilot Project, India, The Story of Rural Development at Etawah, Uttar Pradesh*, University of California Press, Berkeley and Los Angeles, 1958.

Michel, A. A., *The Indus Rivers, A Study of the Effects of Partition*, Yale University Press, New Haven, 1967.

Nath, V., "The Growth of Indian Agriculture: A Regional Analysis, *Geographical Review,* Vol. 59 (1969), pp. 348–372.

Owen, Wilfred, *Distance and Development: Transport and Communications in India*, Brookings Institution, Washington, D.C., 1968.

Randhawa, M. S., et al, *Farmers of India*, Indian Council of Agricultural Research, New Delhi, 1959–1961, 2 volumes, so far, covering southern and northwestern India.

Rao, B. R., *Surveys of Indian Industries,* Oxford University Press, Calcutta, 1957–1958, 2 vols.

Remy, *Goa, Rome of the Orient*, Arthur Barker, London, 1957.

Singer, Milton and Bernard S. Cohn (Eds.), *Structure and Change in Indian Society*, Aldine Publishing Company, Chicago, 1968.

Spate, O. H. K., and A. T. A. Learmonth, *India and Pakistan, A General and Regional Geography*, Methuen & Co., London, 1967, 3rd edit.

Turner, Roy (Ed.), *India's Urban Future*, University of California Press, Berkeley and Los Angeles, 1962.

Vakil, C. N., *Economic Consequences of Divided India, A Study of the Economy of India and Pakistan*, Vora & Co., Bombay, 1950.

Chapter 14: ON PAKISTAN

Ahmad, K. S., *A Geography of Pakistan*, Oxford University Press, Karachi, 1964.

Ahmad, M. R., *Pakistan, An Economic Proposition*, Kitabistan, Allahabad, India, 1948.

Ahmad, N., *An Economic Geography of East Pakistan*, Oxford University Press, London, 2nd edit., 1968.

Ahmad, N., *The Basis of Pakistan*, Thacker & Spink, Calcutta, 1947.

Andrus, J. R., and A. F. Mohammed, *The Economy of Pakistan*, Stanford University Press, Stanford, Calif., 1958.

Callard, K., *Pakistan, A Political Study*, Macmillan Company, New York, 1957.

Campbell, R. D., *Pakistan: Emerging Democracy*, D. Van Nostrand Company, Princeton, New Jersey, 1963.

Davis, K., *The Population of India and Pakistan*, Princeton University Press, Princeton, 1951.

Ghosh, B. B., *Indian Economics and Pakistani Economics*, Mukkerjee, Calcutta, 1949.

Ikram, S. M., *Muslim Civilization in India*, Columbia University Press, New York, 1964.

Maron, S., et al, *Pakistan: Society and Culture*, HRAF Press, New Haven, 1957.

Michel, A. A., *The Indus Rivers, A Study of the Effects of Partition*, Yale University Press, New Haven, 1967.

Qureshi, M. L. (Ed.), *Population Growth and Economic Development With Special Reference to Pakistan*, Institute of Development Economics, Karachi, 1960.

Spate, O. H. K., "The Partition of India and the Prospects of Pakistan," *Geographical Review*, Vol. 38 (1948), pp. 5–29.

Spate, O. H. K., and A. T. A. Learmonth, *India and Pakistan, A General and Regional Geography*, Methuen & Co., London, 1967, 3rd edit.

Tayyeb, A., *Pakistan, A Political Geography*, Oxford University Press, London, 1966.

Vakil, C. N., *Economic Consequences of Divided India, A Study of the Economy of India and Pakistan*, Vora & Co., Bombay, 1950.

Wheeler, R. E. M., *Five Thousand Years of Pakistan*, Johnson, London, 1950.

Chapter 15: ON CEYLON

Cook, E. K., *Ceylon, Its Geography, Its Resources, and Its People,* Macmillan, London, 1951.

Das Gupta, B. B., *A Short Economic Survey of Ceylon,* Associated Newspapers, Colombo, 1949.

Farmer, B. H., "Ceylon," Chapter 26 in Spate, O. H. K., and A. T. A. Learmonth, *India and Pakistan, A General and Regional Geography*, Methuen & Co., London, 3rd edit., 1967.

Farmer, B. H., *Ceylon: A Divided Nation*, Oxford University Press, London, 1963.

Farmer, B. H., *Pioneer Peasant Colonization in Ceylon, A Study in Asian Agrarian Problems*, Oxford University Press, London, 1957.

Geiger, W., *Culture of Ceylon in Medieval Times*, Harrassowitz, Wiesbaden, 1960.

Jennings, W. I., *The Economy of Ceylon*, Oxford University Press, Madras, 2nd edit., 1951.

Knox, Robert, "An Historical Relation of Ceylon," *The Ceylon Historical Journal,* Vol. 6 (1956–1957), reprinted as a single publication, Colombo, 1958.

Pieris, R., *Sinhalese Social Organization—The Kandyan Period*, Ceylon University Press, Colombo, 1956.

Ryan, B., et al, *Sinhalese Village*, University of Miami Press, Coral Gables, Florida, 1958.

Wijesekera, N. D., *The People of Ceylon*, Gunasena, Colombo, 1950.

Wikkramatileke, R., *Southeast Ceylon: Trends and Problems in Agricultural Settlement*, Department of Geography, University of Chicago, Chicago, 1963.

Wriggins, W. H., *Ceylon: Dilemmas of a New Nation*, Princeton University Press, Princeton, 1960.

Chapter 16: ON SOUTHEAST ASIA, GENERALLY

Bastin, J., and H. J. Benda, *A History of Modern Southeast Asia: Colonialism, Nationalism, and Decolonization*, Prentice-Hall, Englewood Cliffs, New Jersey, 1968.

Bekker, C., J. M. van der Kroef, and C. Du Bois, "Culture Contact and Culture Change in Southeast Asia, a Symposium," *Far Eastern Quarterly*, Vol. 11 (1951), pp. 3–34.

Buchanan, Keith, *The Southeast Asian World, An Introductory Essay*, G. Bell & Sons, London, 1967.

Butwell, Richard, *Southeast Asia Today—and Tomorrow, Problems of Political Development*, Praeger Publishers, New York, 1969, rev. edit.

Cady, John F., *Thailand, Burma, Laos, Cambodia*, Prentice-Hall, Englewood Cliffs, New Jersey, 1966.

Coedes, G., *The Making of South East Asia*, University of California Press, Berkeley and Los Angeles, 1966.

Cowan, C. D., *The Economic Development of Southeast Asia*, Frederick A. Praeger, New York, 1964.

Dobby, E. H. G., *Southeast Asia*, University of London Press, London, 1964, 8th edit.

Fisher, Charles A., *South-East Asia, A Social, Economic and Political Geography*, Methuen, London, rev. edit., 1966.

Fryer, Donald W., *Emerging Southeast Asia, A Study in Growth and Stagnation*, McGraw-Hill, New York, 1970.

Golay, F. H., Ralph Anspach, M. Ruth Pfanner, and Eliezer B. Ayal, *Underdevelopment and Economic Nationalism in Southeast Asia*, Cornell University Press, Ithaca, 1969.

Hall, D. G. E., et al, *Atlas of Southeast Asia*, Macmillan, London, 1964.

Hunter, Guy, *South-East Asia—Race, Culture and Nation*, Oxford University Press, London, 1966.

Le Bar, Frank M., Gerald C. Hickey, and John K. Musgrave, *Ethnic Groups of Mainland Southeast Asia*, HRAF Press, New Haven, 1964.

Morgan, T., and N. Spoelstra (Eds.), *Economic Interdependence in Southeast Asia*, University of Wisconsin Press, Madison, 1969.

Robequain, C., *Malaya, Indonesia, Borneo, and The Philippines*, Longmans Green, London, 1954.

Schaaf, C. Hart, and Russell H. Fifield, *The Lower Mekong, Challenge to Cooperation in Southeast Asia*, D. Van Nostrand Company, Princeton, 1963.

Tilman, Robert O. (Ed.), *Man, State, and Society in Contemporary Southeast Asia*, Praeger Publishers, New York, 1969.

Vandenbosch, Amry and Richard Butwell, *The Changing Face of Southeast Asia*, University of Kentucky Press, Lexington, 1966.

Wyatt, W., *Southward from China, A Survey of Southeast Asia Since 1945*, Hodder and Stoughton, London, 1952.

Chapter 17: ON BURMA

Andrus, J. R., *Burmese Economic Life*, Stanford University Press, Stanford, California, 1947.

Cady, J. F., *A History of Modern Burma*, Cornell University Press, Ithaca, 1958.

Cheng, S. H., *The Rice Industry of Burma, 1852–1940*, University of Malaya Press, Kuala Lumpur, 1968.

Christian, J. L., *Modern Burma, A Survey of Political and Economic Development*, University of California Press, Berkeley and Los Angeles, 1942.

Furnivall, J. S., *Colonial Policy and Practice, A Comparative Study of Burma and the Netherlands Indies*, Cambridge University Press, Cambridge, 1948.

Hall, D. G. E., *Europe and Burma*, Oxford University Press, London, 1945.

Harvey, G. E., *British Rule in Burma, 1824–1942*, Faber & Faber, London, 1946.

Khaing, M. M., *Burmese Family*, Indiana University Press, Bloomington, 1962.

Koop, J. C., *The Eurasian Population of Burma*, Yale University, Southeast Asia Studies, New Haven, 1960.

Nash, Manning, *The Golden Road to Modernity, Village Life in Contemporary Burma*, John Wiley & Sons, New York, 1965.

Tinker, H., *The Union of Burma, A Study of the First Years of Independence*, Oxford University Press, London, 1961, 3rd edit.

Trager, F. H., *Burma, From Kingdom To Republic*, Frederick Praeger, New York, 1966.

Chapter 18: ON THAILAND AND THE EARLY KHMER EMPIRE

Blanchard, W., et al, *Thailand, Its People, Its Society, Its Culture*, HRAF Press, New Haven, 1958.

Briggs, L. P., *The Ancient Khmer Empire*, American Philosophical Society, Philadelphia, 1951.

Busch, Noel F., *Thailand, An Introduction to Modern Siam*, D. Van Nostrand Company, Princeton, 1959.

de Young, John E., *Village Life in Modern Thailand*, University of California Press, Berkeley and Los Angeles, 1955.

Fraser, T. M., Jr., *Fishermen of South Thailand*, Holt, Rinehart and Winston, New York, 1966.

Ingram, J. C., *Economic Change in Thailand Since 1850*, Stanford University Press, Stanford, California, 1955.

International Bank for Reconstruction and Development, *A Public Development Program for Thailand*, The Johns Hopkins Press, Baltimore, 1959.

Kingshill, K., *Ku Daeng—The Red Tomb, A Village Study in Northern Thailand*, Bangkok Christian College, Bangkok, 1965, rev. edit.

Majumdar, R. C., *Kambuja-Desa, or an Ancient Hindu Colony in Cambodia*, University of Madras Press, Madras, 1944.

Moerman, M., *Agricultural Change and Peasant Choice in a Thai Village*, University of California Press, Berkeley and Los Angeles, 1968.

Pendleton, R. L., *Thailand, Aspects of Landscape and Life*, Duell, Sloan, and Pearce, New York, 1963.

Phillips, H., *Thai Peasant Personality*, University of California Press, Berkeley and Los Angeles, 1965.

Pym, Christopher, *The Ancient Civilization of Angkor*, New American Library, Mentor book, New York, 1966.

Seidenfaden, E., *The Thai Peoples*, Siam Society, Bangkok, 1958.

Skinner, G. W., *Leadership and Power in the Chinese Community of Thailand*, Cornell University Press, Ithaca, 1958.

Srisavandi, B. C., *The Hill Tribes of Siam*, Khun Arun, Bangkok, 1963.

Young, Gordon, *The Hill Tribes of Northern Thailand*, Siam Society, Bangkok, 1962.

Chapter 19: ON MODERN CAMBODIA

Birnbaum, M., *Angkor and the Mandarin Road*, Vantage Press, New York, 1952.

Delvert, Jean, *Le Paysan Cambodgien*, Mouton, The Hague, 1961.

Herz, Martin F., *A Short History of Cambodia, From the Days of Angkor to the Present*, Frederick Praeger, New York, 1958.

Steinberg, D. J., et al, *Cambodia, Its People, Its Society, Its Culture*, HRAF Press, New Haven, 1957.

Willmott, W. E., *The Chinese in Cambodia*, University of British Columbia, Vancouver, 1967.

Chapter 20: ON MODERN VIETNAM AND LAOS

Bertrand, G., *The Jungle People, Men, Beasts and Legends of the Moi Country*, Robert Hale, London, 1959.

Buttinger, Joseph, *The Smaller Dragon, A Political History of Vietnam*, Frederick A. Praeger, New York, 1958.

Fisher, Charles A., "The Vietnamese Problem in its Geographical Context," Geographical Journal, Vol. 131 (1965), pp. 502–515.

Halpern, Joel M., *Government, Politics, and Social Structure in Laos*, Southeast Asia Studies, Monograph Series, No. 4, Yale University, New Haven, 1964.

Halpern, Joel M., *Economy and Society of Laos*, Southeast Asia Studies, Monograph Series, No. 5, Yale University, New Haven, 1964.

Hammer, E., *Vietnam, Yesterday and Today*, Holt, Rinehart and Winston, New York, 1966.

Hendry, J. E., *The Small World of Khanh Hau*, Aldine, Chicago, 1964.

Hickey, G. C., *Village in Vietnam*, Yale University Press, New Haven, 1964.

Honey, P. J. (Ed.), *North Vietnam Today, Profile of a Communist Satellite*, Frederick A. Praeger, New York, 1962.

Le Bar, F. M., and A. Suddard (Eds.), *Laos, Its People, Its Society, Its Culture*, HRAF Press, New Haven, 1960.

Meeker, O., *The Little World of Laos*, Charles Scribner's Sons, New York, 1959.

Robequain, C., *Economic Development of French Indo-China*, Oxford University Press, London, 1964.

Chapter 21: ON MALAYSIA, INCLUDING MALAYSIAN BORNEO

Alisjahbana, S. E. et al (Eds.), *The Cultural Problems of Malaysia in the Context of Southeast Asia*, Malaysian Society of Orientalists, Kuala Lumpur, 1968.

Chai, H. C., *The Development of British Malaya, 1896–1909*, Oxford University Press, Kuala Lumpur, 1964.

Cowan, C. D., *Nineteenth-Century Malaya, The Origins of British Political Control*, Oxford University Press, London, 1961.

Dobby, E. H. G., "Padi Landscapes of Malaya," *The Journal of Tropical Geography*, Vol. 10 (1957), pp. 1–143.

Firth, Raymond, *Malay Fishermen, Their Peasant Economy*, Archon Books, Hamden, Conn., 1966, 2nd edit.

Fraser, Thomas M., Jr., *Rusembilan: A Malay Fishing Village in Southern Thailand*, Cornell University Press, Ithaca, 1960.

Ginsburg, N. (Ed.), *North Borneo, Brunei, Sarawak (British Borneo)*, HRAF Press, New Haven, 1956.

Ginsburg, N., and C. F. Roberts, Jr., *Malaya*, University of Washington Press, Seattle, 1958.

Gullick, J. M., *Malaysia*, Praeger, New York, 1969.

Hodder, B. W., *Man in Malaya*, University of London Press, London, 1959.

International Bank for Reconstruction, *The Economic Development of Malaya*, Government Printer, Singapore, 1955.

Jackson, James C., *Planters and Speculators, Chinese and European Agricultural Enterprise in Malaya, 1786–1921*, University of Malaya Press, Singapore, 1968.

Jackson, James C., *Sarawak, A Geographical Survey of a Developing State*, University of London Press, London, 1968.

Lee, Y. L., *North Borneo (Sabah), A Study in Settlement Geography*, Eastern Universities Press, Singapore, 1965.

Mills, L. A., *Malaya: A Political and Economic Appraisal*, University of Minnesota Press, Minneapolis, 1958.

Neville, Warwick, "Singapore: Ethnic Diversity and its Implications," *Annals*, Association of American Geographers, Vol. 56 (1966), pp. 236–263.

Newell, W. H., *Treacherous River, A Study of Rural Chinese in North Malaya*, University of Malaya Press, Kuala Lumpur, 1962.

Ooi, J. B., *Land, People, and Economy in Malaya*, Longmans, Green, London, 1963.

Purcell, V., *The Chinese in Malaya*, Oxford University Press, London, 1948.

Ryan, N. J., *The Making of Modern Malaysia*, Oxford University Press, Kuala Lumpur, 1967.

Sandhu, K. S., *Indians in Malaya (1786–1957)*, The University Press, Cambridge, England, 1969.

Sandin, B., *The Sea Dyaks of Borneo Before White Rajah Rule*, Macmillan, London, 1967.

Silcock, T. H., and E. K. Fisk (Eds.), *The Political Economy of an Independent Malaya*, University of California Press, Berkeley and Los Angeles, 1963.

Stone, H., *From Malacca to Malaysia*, George Harrap & Co., London, 1966.

Swift, M. G., *Malay Peasant Society in Jelebu*, The Athlone Press, University of London, 1965.

Tregonning, K. G., *A History of Modern Sabah, 1881–1963*, University of Malaya Press, Singapore, 1965.

Wang, G. W. (Ed.), *Malaysia, A Survey*, Pall Mall Press, London, 1964.

Wheatley, Paul, *The Golden Khersonese, Studies in the Historical Geography of the Malay Peninsula Before A.D. 1500*, University of Malaya Press, Kuala Lumpur, 1961.

Wheelright, E. L., *Industrialization in Malaysia*, Melbourne University Press, Melbourne, 1965.

Wikkramatileke, R., "State Aided Rural Land Colonization in Malaya: An Appraisal of the F.L.D.A. Program," *Annals*, Association of American Geographers, Vol. 55 (1965), pp. 377–403.

Winstedt, R., *The Malays, A Cultural History*, Philosophical Library, New York, 1950.

Chapter 22: ON INDONESIA AND EASTERN NEW GUINEA

Bastin, J., *Essays on Indonesia and Malayan History*, Eastern Universities Press, Singapore, 1961.

Belshaw, C. S., *The Great Village, The Economic and Social Welfare of Hanuabada, an Urban Community in Papua*, Routledge & Kegan Paul, London, 1957.

Benda, H. J., *The Crescent and the Rising Sun, Indonesian Islam under the Japanese Occupation, 1942–1945*, Van Hoeve, The Hague, 1958.

Berndt, R. M., *Excess and Restraint, Social Control Among a New Guinea Mountain Peoples*, University of Chicago Press, Chicago, 1962.

Bowman, R. G., "Prospects for Settlement in Northeastern New Guinea," State University of Iowa, *Studies in Natural History*, 19 (1948).

Brookfield, H. C., and P. Brown, *Struggle for Land; Agriculture and Group Territories Among the Chimbu of the New Guinea Highlands*, Oxford University Press, Melbourne, 1963.

Daniel, H., *Islands of the East Indies*, Putnam, New York, 1944.

Dekker, N. A. D., *Tanah Air Kita, a Book on the Country and People of Indonesia*, Van Hoeve, The Hague, 1951, 2nd edit.

Furnivall, J. S., *Colonial Policy and Practice, A Comparative Study of Burma and the Netherlands Indies*, Cambridge University Press, Cambridge, 1948.

Geertz, C., *Agricultural Involution, The Processes of Ecological Change in Indonesia*, University of California Press, Berkeley and Los Angeles, 1963.

Geertz, C., *Peddlers and Princes, Social Change and Economic Modernization in Two Indonesian Towns*, University of Chicago Press, Chicago, 1963.

Glamann, K., *Dutch Asiatic Trade, 1620–1740*, Nijhoff, The Hague, 1958.

Held, G. J., *The Papuas of Waropen*, Nijhoff, The Hague, 1957.

Higgins, B., and J. Higgins, *Indonesia, The Crisis of the Millstones*, D. Van Nostrand Company, Princeton, New Jersey, 1963.

Hogbin, I., and P. Lawrence, *Studies in New Guinea Land Tenure*, Sydney University Press, Sydney, Australia, 1967.

Kahin, G. McT., *Nationalism and Revolution in Indonesia*, Cornell University Press, Ithaca, 1952.

Lett, L., *Papua: Its People and Its Promise*, Cheshire, Melbourne, 1944.

Loeb, E. M., and R. Heine-Geldern, *Sumatra, Its History and People*, University of Vienna, Vienna, 1935.

Mair, L. P., *Australia in New Guinea*, Christophers, London, 1948.

Mattiessen, P., *Under the Mountain Wall, A Chronicle of Two Seasons in the Stone Age*, Viking Press, New York, 1962.

McVey, R. T. (Ed.), *Indonesia*, HRAF Press, New Haven, 1963.

Meilink-Roelofsz, M. A. P., *Asian Trade and European Influence, In the Indonesian Archipelago Between 1500 and about 1630*, Nijhoff, The Hague, 1962.

Metcalf, J. E., *The Agricultural Economy of Indonesia*, Department of Agriculture, Washington, D.C., 1952.

Pelzer, Karl J., *Pioneer Settlement in the Asiatic Tropics*, American Geographical Society, New York, 1945.

Ormeling, F. J., *The Timor Problem, A Geographical Interpretation of An Underdeveloped Island*, Nijhoff, The Hague, 1956.

Reed, S. W., *The Making of Modern New Guinea*, American Philosophical Society, Philadelphia, 1943.

Salisbury, R. F., *From Stone to Steel, Economic Consequence of a Technological Change in New Guinea*, Melbourne University Press, Melbourne, 1962.

Spate, O. H. K., "Changing Native Agriculture in New Guinea," *Geographical Review*, Vol. 43 (1953), pp. 151–172.

Taylor, N., *Cinchona in Java*, Greenberg, New York, 1945.

Ter Haar, B., *Adat Law in Indonesia*, Institute of Pacific Relations, New York, 1948.

Vandenbosch, A., *The Dutch East Indies, Its Government, Problems, and Politics*, University of California Press, Berkeley and Los Angeles, 1942.

van Leur, J. C., *Indonesian Trade and Society, Essays in Asian Social and Economic History*, Van Hoeve, The Hague, 1955.

Van Niel, R., *The Emergence of the Modern Indonesian Elite*, Van Hoeve, The Hague, 1960.

Vlekke, B. H. M., *Nusantara, A History of Indonesia*, Van Hoeve, The Hague, 1959, rev. edit.

Wertheim, W. F., *Indonesian Society in Transition*, Van Hoeve, The Hague, 1956.

Wertheim, W. F. (Ed.), *The Indonesian Town*, Van Hoeve, The Hague, 1958.

White, O., *Parliament of a Thousand Tribes, A Study of New Guinea*, Heinemann, London, 1965.

Willmott, D. E., *The Chinese of Semarang, A Changing Minority Community in Indonesia*, Cornell University Press, Ithaca, 1960.

Wolf, C. Jr., *The Indonesian Story, the Birth, Growth, and Structure of the Indonesian Republic*, John Day, New York, 1948.

Wolters, O. W., *Early Indonesia Commerce, A Study of the Origins of Srivijaya*, Cornell University Press, Ithaca, 1967.

Chapter 23: ON THE PHILIPPINES

Agpalo, R. E., *The Political Process and the Nationalization of Retail Trade in the Philippines*, University of the Philippines, Quezon City, 1962.

Alip, E. M., *Philippine History*, Alip & Brion, Manila, 1948.

Carroll, J. J., *The Filipino Manufacturing Entrepreneur: Agent and Product of Change*, Cornell University Press, Ithaca, 1965.

Corpuz, O. D., *The Philippines*, Prentice-Hall, Englewood Cliffs, New Jersey, 1965.

Darrah, L. B. and F. A. Tiongson, *Agricultural Marketing in the Philippines*, University of the Philippines College of Agriculture, College, Philippines, 1969.

Dozier, E. P., *Mountain Arbiters, The Changing Life of a Philippine Hill People*, University of Arizona Press, Tucson, 1966.

Farwell, G., *Mask of Asia, The Philippines Today*, Frederick Praeger, New York, 1966.

Felix, A., Jr., *The Chinese in the Philippines, 1570–1770*, Solidaridad Publishing House, Manila, 1966.

Golay, Frank H., *The Philippines: Public Policy and National Economic Development*, Cornell University Press, Ithaca, 1961.

Guthrie, G. M., et al, *The Psychology of Modernization in the Rural Philippines*, Ateneo de Manila University Press, Quezon City, Philippines, 1970.

Hartendorp, A. V. H., *History of Industry and Trade in the Philippines*, American Chamber of Commerce, Manila, 1958 and 1961, two volumes.

Hayden, J. R., *The Philippines, A Study in National Development*, Macmillan, New York, 1955.

Hollnsteiner, M. R., *The Dynamics of Power in a Philippine Municipality*, University of the Philippines, Quezon City, 1963.

Huke, R. E. (Ed.), *Shadows on the Land: An Economic Geography of the Philippines*, Bookmark, Manila, 1963.

Keesing, F. M., *The Ethnohistory of Northern Luzon*, Stanford University Press, Stanford, Calif., 1962.

Nelson, R., *The Philippines*, Walker & Co., New York, 1968.

Pelzer, Karl J., *Pioneer Settlement in the Asiatic Tropics*, American Geographical Society, New York, 1945.

Phelan, J. L., *The Hispanization of the Philippines: Spanish Aims and Filipino Responses, 1565–1700*, University of Wisconsin Press, Madison, 1959.

Ravenholt, A., *The Philippines, A Young Republic on the Move*, D. Van Nostrand Company, Princeton, New Jersey, 1962.

Scott, W. H., *On the Cordillera, A Look at the Peoples and Cultures of Mountain Province*, MCS Enterprises, Manila, 1966.

Sicat, G. P. (Ed.), *The Philippine Economy in the 1960's*, University of the Philippines, Quezon City, 1964.

Smith, R. A., *Philippine Freedom, 1946–1958*, Columbia University Press, New York, 1958.

Starner, F. L., *Magsaysay and the Philippine Peasantry*, University of California Press, Berkeley and Los Angeles, 1961.

Takahashi, A., *Land and Peasants in Central Luzon*, Institute of Developing Economics, Tokyo, 1969.

Tantuico, F. S., Jr., *Leyte, The Historic Islands*, Leyte Publishing Corpn, Manila, 1964.

Taylor, G. E., *The Philippines and the United States, Problems of Partnership*, Frederick A. Praeger, New York, 1964.

Wernstedt, Frederick L. and J. E. Spencer, *Philippine Island World, A Physical, Cultural, and Regional Geography*, University of California Press, Berkeley and Los Angeles, 1967.

Wickberg, E., *The Chinese in Philippine Life, 1850–1898*, Yale University Press, New Haven, 1965.

Zaide, G. F., *Philippine Political and Cultural History*, Philippine Education Company, Manila, 1957.

Zamora, M. D. (Ed.), *Studies in Philippine Anthropology (in Honor of H. Otley Beyer)*, Alemar-Phoenix, Manila, 1967.

Chapters 24 and 25: ON GREATER CHINA

Beckmann, G. M., *The Modernization of China and Japan*, Harper & Row, New York, 1962.

Buchanan, Keith, *The Transformation of the Chinese Earth*, Praeger, New York, 1970.

Buck, J. L., *Land Utilization in China*, University of Chicago Press, Chicago, 1937, 3 vols.

Buck, J. L., O. L. Dawson, and Y. L. Wu, *Food and Agriculture in Communist China*, Frederick Praeger, New York, 1966.

Burki, S. J., *A Study of Chinese Communes, 1965*, East Asian Research Center, Harvard University, Cambridge, 1969.

Callis, H. G., *China, Confucian and Communist*, Henry Holt & Co., New York, 1959.

Carrasco, Pedro, *Land and Polity in Tibet*, University of Washington, Seattle, 1959.

Chang, C. L., *The Income of the Chinese Gentry*, University of Washington Press, Seattle, 1962.

Chang, J. K., *Industrial Development in Pre-Communist China*, Aldine Publishing Company, Chicago, 1969.

Chang, K. C., *The Archaeology of Ancient China*, Yale University Press, New Haven, 1968, rev. edit.

Chang, K. N., *China's Struggle for Railroad Development*, John Day, New York, 1943.

Chao, K., *The Construction Industry in Communist China*, Aldine Publishing Company, Chicago, 1968.

Chao, K. C., *Agrarian Policies of the Chinese Communist Party, 1921–1959*, Asia Publishing House, New York, 1960.

Chen, Nai-ruenn, *Chinese Economic Statistics, A Handbook for Mainland China*, Aldine Publishing Company, Chicago, 1967.

Cheng, C. Y., *Communist China's Economy, 1949–1962*, Seton Hall University Press, South Orange, New Jersey, 1963.

Cheng, T. K., *Archaeology in China*, Heffer & Sons, Cambridge, England, 3 vols., 1959–1963, with Supplement to Vol. 1, 1966.

Chi, C. T., *Key Economic Areas in Chinese History as Revealed in the Development of Public Works for Water Control*, Allen & Unwin, London, 1936.

Ch'ien, T. S., *The Government and Politics of China*, Harvard University Press, Cambridge, 1950.

Ch'ü, T. T., *Law and Society in Traditional China*, Mouton & Co., The Hague, 1961.

Ch'ü, T. T., *Local Government in China under the Ch'ing*, Harvard University Press, Cambridge, 1962.

Cottrell, L., *The Tiger of Ch'in, The Dramatic Emergence of China as a Nation*, Holt, Rinehart and Winston, New York, 1962.

Cressey, G. B., *Land of the 500 Million, A Geography of China*, McGraw-Hill Book Company, 1955.

Dawson, Owen L., *Communist China's Agriculture*, Praeger, New York, 1970.

Eberhard, W., *a History of China*, University of California Press, Berkeley and Los Angeles, 1964, rev. edit.

Eberhard, W., *Conquerors and Rulers, Social Forces in Medieval China*, Brill, Leiden, 1952.

Eberhard, W., *The Local Cultures of South and East Asia*, E. J. Brill, Leiden, 1968.

Eichhorn, Werner, *Chinese Civilization, An Introduction*, Frederick Praeger, New York, 1969.

Ekvall, Robert B., *Religious Observances in Tibet: Patterns and Functions*, University of Chicago Press, Chicago, 1964.

Fairbank, J. K., A. Eckstein, and L. S. Yang, "Economic Change in Early Modern China: An Analytic Framework," *Economic Development and Cultural Change*, Vol. 9 (1960), pp. 1–26.

Feuerwerker, A., *China's Early Industrialization, Sheng Hsuan-Huai (1844–1916) and Mandarin Enterprise*, Harvard University Press, Cambridge, 1958.

Fitzgerald, C. P., *China, A Short Cultural History*, Cresset Press, London, 1950.

Freedman, M., *Lineage Organization in Southeastern China*, University of London, The Athlone Press, London, 1965, rev. edit.

Gernet, J., *Daily Life in China on the Eve of the Mongol Invasion*, The Macmillan Company, New York, 1962.

Gernet, J., *Ancient China, from the Beginnings to the Empire*, University of California Press, Berkeley and Los Angeles, 1968.

Goodrich, L. C., *A Short History of the Chinese People*, Harper & Bros, New York, 1959, 3rd edit.

Gould, S. H. (Ed.), *Sciences in Communist China*, American Association for the Advancement of Science, Washington, D.C., 1961, a symposium held in 1960.

Hermann, A., *An Historical Atlas of China*, Aldine Publishing Company, Chicago, 1966 (new edition edited by Norton Ginsburg).

Hinton, William, *Fanshen, A Documentary of Revolution in a Chinese Village*, Monthly Review Press, New York, 1966.

Ho, C. S., and C. N. Lee, *Economic Minerals of Taiwan*, Geological Survey of Taiwan, Taipei, Taiwan, 1963.

Ho, P. T., *The Ladder of Success in Imperial China, Aspects of Social Mobility, 1368–1911*, Columbia University Press, New York, 1962.

Ho, Ping-ti, "The Loess and the Origin of Chinese Agriculture," *American Historical Review*, Vol. 75 (1969), pp. 1–36.

Ho, Ping-ti, and Tang Tsou, *China in Crisis, China's Heritage and the Communist Political System*, University of Chicago Press, Chicago, 1968, 2 vols.

Hou, C. M., *Foreign Investment and Economic Development in China, 1840–1937*, Harvard University Press, Cambridge, 1965.

Hsiao, K. C., *Rural China, Imperial Control in the Nineteenth Century*, University of Washington Press, Seattle, 1960.

Hsieh, C. M., *Taiwan—Ilha Formosa, a Geography in Perspective*, Butterworths, Washington, D.C., 1964.

Hsu, Mei-ling, "Taiwan Population Distribution," (Map Supplement), *Annals*, Association of American Geographers, Vol. 59 (1969), pp. 611–612.

Jen, Y. T., *A Concise Geography of China*, Foreign Language Press, Peking, 1964.

King, F. H. H., *A Concise Economic History of Modern China, (1840–1961)*, Praeger-Pall Mall, New York, 1968.

Lang, O., *Chinese Family and Society*, Yale University Press, New Haven, 1946.

Lattimore, O., *Inner Asian Frontiers in History*, American Geographical Society, New York, 1940.

Lattimore, O., *Studies in Frontier History, Collected Papers, 1928–1958*, Oxford University Press, London, 1962.

Levy, M. J., Jr., *The Family Revolution in Modern China*, Harvard University Press, Cambridge, 1949.

Ling, N. M., *Tibetan Sourcebook*, Union Research Institute, Hong Kong, 1964.

Liu, T. C., and K. C. Yeh, *The Economy of the Chinese Mainland: National Income and Economic Development, 1933–1959*, Princeton University Press, Princeton, 1965.

Michael, F., *The Origin of Manchu Rule in China*, The Johns Hopkins Press, Baltimore, 1942.

Needham, J., *The Development of Iron and Steel Technology in China*, The Newcomen Society, London, 1958.

Needham, J., *Science and Civilization in China*, Cambridge University Press, Cambridge, to be 7 volumes, 1954 and later years.

Perkins, Dwight H., *Agricultural Development in China, 1368–1968*, Aldine Publishing Company, Chicago, 1969.

Phillips, E. C., *The Mongols*, Frederick Praeger, New York, 1969.

Potter, Jack M., *Capitalism and the Chinese Peasant: Social and Economic Change in a Hong Kong Village*, University of California Press, Berkeley and Los Angeles, 1968.

Purcell, V., *China*, Ernest Benn, London, 1962.

Quaritch Wales, H. G., *The Indianization of China, and of South-East Asia*, Bernard Quaritch, London, 1967.

Richardson, H. E., *A Short History of Tibet*, Dutton, New York, 1962.

Riggs, F. W., *Formosa Under Chinese Nationalist Rule*, Macmillan, New York, 1952.

Schafer, E. H., *The Vermilion Bird, T'ang Images of the South*, University of California Press, Berkeley and Los Angeles, 1967.

Schurmann, Franz, *Ideology and Organization in Communist China*, University of California Press, Berkeley and Los Angeles, 1968, rev. edit.

Shabad, Theodore, *China's Changing Map, A Political and Economic Geography of the Chinese People's Republic*, Frederick Praeger, New York, 1956.

Shen, T. H., *Agricultural Development on Taiwan Since World War II*, Cornell University Press, Ithaca, 1964.

Shen, T. H., *Agricultural Resources of China*, Cornell University Press, Ithaca, 1951.

Siren, O., *Gardens of China*, Ronald Press, New York, 1951.

Skinner, G. W., "Marketing and Social Structure in Rural China," *Journal of Asian Studies*, Vol. 24 (1964–1965), pp. 3–44, 195–228, 363–400.

Sun, J. C., *The Economic Development of Manchuria in the First Half of the Twentieth Century*, Harvard University Press, Cambridge, 1969.

Sung, Y. H., *T'ien-Kung K'ai-Wu; Chinese Technology in the Seventeenth Century*, Pennsylvania State University Press, University Park, Penna., 1966.

Szczepanik, E. F. (Ed.), *Economic and Social Problems of the Far East*, Hong Kong, 1962.

Tang, P. S. H., *Communist China Today*, Research Institute on the Sino-Soviet Bloc, Washington, D.C., 1961.

Tregear, T. R., *A Geography of China*, University of London Press, London, 1965.

Tsang, C. S., *Society, Schools, and Progress in China*, Pergamon Press, London, 1968.

Tuan, Yi-fu, *China*, Longman Group Ltd., London, and Aldine Publishing Company, Chicago, 1969.

Walker, K. R., *Planning in Chinese Agriculture, Socialisation and the Private Sector, 1956–1962*, Aldine Publishing Company, Chicago, 1965.

Watson, Francis, *The Frontiers of China*, Frederick Praeger, New York, 1966.

Wheatley, Paul, "Geographical Notes on Some Commodities Involved in Sung Maritime Trade," *Journal of the Malayan Branch of the Royal Asiatic Society*, Vol. 32, Part 2, 1959.

Wiens, Herold J., *China's March Toward the Tropics*, The Shoestring Press, Hamden, Conn., 1954.

Wiens, H. J., "Cultivation Development and Expansion in China's Colonial Realm in Central Asia," *Journal of Asian Studies*, Vol. 26 (1966), pp. 67–88.

Wu, Y. L., *Economic Development and the Use of Energy Resources in Communist China*, Frederick Praeger, New York, 1963.

Wu, Y. L., et al, *The Spatial Economy of Communist China, A Study on Industrial Location and Transportation*, Frederick Praeger, New York, 1967.

Yang, C. K., *Chinese Communist Society, The Family and the Village*, The M.I.T. Press, Cambridge, Mass., 1965, paperback edition combining two volumes separately published in 1959.

Yang, C. K., *Religion in Chinese Society*, University of California Press, Berkeley and Los Angeles, 1967.

Yao, S. Y., "The Geographical Distribution of Floods and Droughts in Chinese History," *Far Eastern Quarterly*, Vol. 2 (1954), pp. 357–378.

Chapter 26: ON KOREA IN GENERAL

Chung, K. C., *Korea Tomorrow, Land of the Morning Calm*, Macmillan Company, New York, 1956.

Clark, A. D. and D. C. Clark, *Seoul, Past and Present*, Hollym Co., Seoul, 1969.

Grajdanzev, A. J., *Modern Korea*, John Day, New York, 1944.

Ha, Tae-hung, *Guide to Korean Culture*, Yonsae University Press, Seoul, 1968.

Mattusch, K. R. (Ed.), *Industrial Structure of Korea*, Economic Research Center of Korea, Seoul, 1962–1963, 2 vols.

McCune, G. M., *Korea Today*, Harvard University Press, Cambridge, 1950.

McCune, Shannon, *Korea's Heritage, A Regional and Social Geography*, Charles Tuttle, Rutland, Vermont, 1956.

McCune, Shannon, *Korea, Land of Broken Calm*, D. Van Nostrand Company, Princeton, New Jersey, 1966.

Nelson, M. F., *Korea and the Old Orders in Eastern Asia*, Louisiana State University Press, Baton Rouge, 1945.

Oh, C. K., *Handbook of Korea*, Pageant Press, New York, 1958.

Osgood, C., *The Koreans and Their Culture*, Ronald Press, New York, 1951.

Chapter 27: ON JAPAN

Allen, G. C., *A Short Economic History of Modern Japan*, Allen & Unwin, London, 1946.

Anesaki, M., *History of Japanese Religion, With Special Reference to the Social and Moral Life of the Nation*, Charles Tuttle, Rutland Vermont, 1963 reprint of original edition.

Beardsley, R. K., J. W. Hall, and R. E. Ward, *Village Japan*, University of Chicago Press, Chicago, 1959.

Beckmann, G. M., *The Modernization of China and Japan*, Harper & Row, New York, 1962.

Befu, H., and C. S. Chard, "Preceramic Cultures in Japan," *American Anthropologist*, Vol. 62 (1960), pp. 815–849.

Benedict, R., *The Chrysanthemum and the Sword; Patterns of Japanese Culture*, Houghton Mifflin, Boston, 1946.

Broadbridge, Seymour, *Industrial Dualism in Japan*, Aldine Publishing Company, Chicago, 1966.

Chambliss, W. J., *Chiaraijima Village, Land Tenure, Taxation, and Local Trade, 1818–1884*, University of Arizona Press, Tucson, 1965.

Cohen, J. B., *Economic Problems of Free Japan*, Center for International Studies, Princeton, 1952.

Cohen, J. B., *Japan's Economy in War and Reconstruction*, University of Minnesota Press, Minneapolis, 1949.

Dempster, Prue, *Japan Advances, A Geographical Study*, Methuen & Co., London, 1967.

Dore, R. P., *City Life in Japan, A Study of a Tokyo Ward*, University of California Press, Berkeley and Los Angeles, 1958.

Fukutake, T., *Japanese Rural Society*, Oxford University Press, London, 1967.

Glacken, Clarence J., *The Great Loochoo: A Study of Okinawan Village Life*, University of California Press, Berkeley and Los Angeles, 1955.

Goodman, G. K., *The Dutch Impact on Japan, 1640–1853*, E. J. Brill, Leiden, 1967.

Hall, Robert B., Jr., *Japan: Industrial Power of Asia*, D. Van Nostrand Company, Princeton, New Jersey, 1963.

Harrison, J. A., *Japan's Northern Frontier*, University of Florida Press, Gainesville, 1953.

Isida, Ryuziro, *Geography of Japan*, Kokusai Bunka Shinkokai, Tokyo, 1961.

James, D. H., *The Rise and Fall of the Japanese Empire*, Macmillan, New York, 1951.

Jones, F. C., *Hokkaido, Its Present State of Development and Future Prospects*, Oxford University Press, London, 1958.

Keene, Donald, *The Japanese Discovery of Europe, 1720–1830*, Stanford University Press, Stanford, California, 1969.

Kerr, George H., *Okinawa, The History of an Island People*, Charles E. Tuttle, Rutland, Vermont, 1958.

Kidder, J. E., Jr., *Japan Before Buddhism*, Frederick Praeger, New York, 1959.

Kuwahara, M. (Ed.), *Economic Approaches to Japanese Agriculture*, Fuji Publishing Co., Tokyo, 1969.

Lockwood, W. W., *The Economic Development of Japan: Growth and Structural Change, 1868–1938*, Princeton University Press, Princeton, 1954.

Lockwood, W. W. (Ed.), *The State and Economic Enterprise in Japan*, Princeton University Press, Princeton, 1965.

Nakamura, J. I., *Agricultural Production and Economic Development of Japan, 1873–1922*, Princeton University Press, Princeton, 1966.

Norman, E. H., *Japan's Emergence as a Modern State*, Institute of Pacific Relations, New York, 1940.

Ohkawa, K., Johnston, B., and H. Kaneda (Eds.), *Agriculture and Economic Growth: Japan's Experience*, Princeton University Press and University of Tokyo Press, Princeton and Tokyo, 1970.

Sansom, G., *A History of Japan, to 1867*, Stanford University Press, Stanford, California, 1958–1963, 3 vols.

Schumpeter, E. B., et al, *The Industrialization of Japan and Manchukuo, 1930–1940*, Macmillan, New York, 1940.

Seki, K., *The Cotton Industry of Japan*, Japan Society for the Promotion of Science, Tokyo, 1956.

Sheldon, C. D., *The Rise of the Merchant Class in Tokugawa Japan, 1600–1868*, J. J. Augustin, Locust Valley, New York, 1958.

Smith, T. C., *The Agrarian Origins of Modern Japan*, Stanford University Press, Stanford, California, 1959.

Stewart, J. R., *Japan's Textile Industry*, Institute of Pacific Relations, New York, 1949.

Stone, P. B., *Japan Surges Ahead, The Story of an Economic Miracle*, Frederick A. Praeger, New York, 1969.

Taeuber, I. B., *The Population of Japan*, Princeton University Press, Princeton, 1958.

Tobata, Seiichi, *An Introduction of Agriculture of Japan*, Maruzen Co., Tokyo, 1958.

Trewartha, Glenn T., *Japan, a Geography*, The University of Wisconsin Press, Madison, 1965.

Wilkinson, Thomas O., *The Urbanization of Japanese Labor, 1868–1955*, University of Massachusetts Press, Amherst, 1965.

Yanaga, C., *Japan Since Perry*, McGraw-Hill Book Company, New York, 1949.

Yazaki, T., *The Japanese City, A Sociological Analysis*, Japan Publications Trading Co., Tokyo, 1963.

INDEX